"I myself once began with a clean slate, not knowing much at all about Christianity. It was the beginning of a long life of continuous exploration. I have written this book in the hope that it will help some reader follow the same path. He will not regret it."

—Bo Giertz

To Live
with
Christ

DEVOTIONS BY

Bo Giertz

TRANSLATED BY BROR ERICKSON

WITH RICHARD WOOD

CONCORDIA PUBLISHING HOUSE • SAINT LOUIS

Manufactured in the United States of America

Library of Congress Cataloging-in-Publication Data

Giertz, Bo, 1905-1998
  [Att leva med Kristus. English]
  To live with Christ : devotions / by Bo Giertz ; translated by Richard Wood.
    p. cm.
  ISBN 978-0-7586-1382-0
  1. Church year meditations. 2. Devotional calendars. I. Title.
    BV30.G5413 2008
    2428.3--dc22
                                          2007012703

4   5   6   7   8   9   10   11   12   13   29   28   27   26   25   24   23   22   21   20

FOREWORD

I first became acquainted with Bo Harald Giertz through his novel, *The Hammer of God*. It was assigned reading in Dr. Trygve Skarsten's church history class at the Lutheran Theological Seminary (now Trinity Lutheran Seminary) in Columbus, Ohio. As a first year seminarian in the fall of 1975, I came to appreciate *The Hammer of God* as a reminder that God's truth would endure and therefore His Church would survive trendy theology despite the theologians. Moreover it was my introduction to a genuinely Lutheran pastoral theology. I will be forever grateful to Dr. Skarsten for requiring us to read *The Hammer of God*. Serving in campus ministry at Valparasio University and the University of Minnesota, I used *The Hammer of God* with students while discovering additional riches in *The Message of the Church for Times of Crisis, Liturgy and Spiritual Awakening,* and *Preaching from the Whole Bible* by Giertz. Following the example of my old teacher, Trygve Skarsten, I now assign *The Hammer of God* as required reading for my first-year field education students here at Concordia Theological Seminary.

Bo Harald Giertz (1905–1998) journeyed from atheism to become the bishop of Gothenburg in the Lutheran Church of Sweden. His earthly pilgrimage spanned nearly all of the twentieth century. Well-known for a sturdy confessional Lutheranism wedded to a warm piety born of confidence in the Gospel, Bo Giertz was a genuine bishop. He was theologically tough without becoming brittle. He knew how to contend for the faith without slipping into contentiousness. Convinced as he was that God's Word forbids the ordination of women to the pastoral office, Bishop Bo Giertz stood steadfast in opposition to this novelty and suffered scorn for his unyielding stance.

Even as he witnessed his beloved Church of Sweden crumble in doctrinal decadence, Bishop Giertz remained a faithful churchman. Trusting in the promise that the Word of the Lord would not return empty (Isaiah 55:11), Bishop Giertz continued to speak and write. North American Lutherans know him best as the author of *The Hammer of God,* a novel that so winsomely demonstrates what Luther and Walther called the proper distinction of the Law and Gospel. The novelist/bishop demonstrates how the Gospel finally does predominate over rationalism, pietism, and liberalism. Readers of this book will witness that same evangelical clarity in these devotions, as they breathe the lively certainty the Gospel of the crucified and risen Lord will triumph over doubt and decay.

Certainty characterizes Bo Giertz's witness to the Gospel of Jesus Christ. This certainty is not naïve optimism but the confidence in our Lord that enlivens Giertz to say with Dr. Luther, "This is most certainly true." A dozen years before his death, Bishop Giertz penned a little piece entitled "My Last Will and Testament" in which he noted "It is not without sadness that we look back on those happy years. In my dark moments I wonder if ever a church, which has been given such a rich inheritance, has been so careless about it. My old eyes have had time to see so much of what in the long run means sickness unto death for the Church. I mean the doubt that we possess a revelation, a truth—to say with the Scriptures—'which was once for all delivered to the saints'

(Jude 1:3). The truth that Christ is the Savior; that He is the way, the truth, and the life; that there is no other way to the Father; that Christ with His Spirit led the apostles into all truth, and given the Church a foundation, which can never be changed. Heaven and earth will pass away. Everything else is submitted to the law of change, but His Word will remain—and it is for us to hold on to that steadfast to the end. This faith is on a collision course with some of the pet dogmas of our time: the belief that everything is relative, that everything is continually changing, which at the same time means progress, even in new concepts of faith and altered codes of morality."[1] As a watchman on the walls of Zion, Bishop Giertz called a sleepy church to wake up to the inroads of unbelief. Like John the Baptist, he would preach repentance and faith, God's judgment and Christ's comfort. Bo Giertz knew that spiritual fads and theological trends come and go but the Word alone remains.

The daily devotions contained in *To Live with Christ* move according to cadence of the Church Year for it was by that calendar that Giertz lived and prayed. He was at home in the liturgy even as he sought to shepherd his people to find in the services of God's house a place of refreshment and strength. These devotions are thoroughly biblical and consistently centered in Christ's atonement. We are deeply indebted to the translator for enabling Bishop Bo Giertz to speak to yet another generation the words of Jesus, words that are spirit and life, to the end that many might believe that He is the Christ and live within the fellowship of His Church.

John T. Pless, Assistant Professor of Pastoral Theology
Concordia Theological Seminary, Fort Wayne, Indiana
Saint Michael and All Angels 2003

---

1. "My Last Will and Testament," Lutheran Forum, Winter 1998, 13.

TRANSLATOR'S PREFACE

Bo Giertz (1905–1998) was a talented and gifted writer. As an author he was something akin to the North Star in the Church of Sweden. He served as a compass for many faithful Lutherans in Sweden throughout a dark century of liberal theology that set upon his homeland like an ugly sunset before a great storm. The century saw very few stars shining in the northern skies to shed the Gospel's light on the issues at hand. Through this dark century, in which biblical truth had not been so overshadowed since the medieval papacy, Bo Giertz remained true to the biblical faith and the Lutheran Confessions. His writings served as a vehicle bringing the Gospel to the people. The poetical quality of his prose always spoke truth in love. His explanations of doctrinal controversies were intimate in a way that never let the truth compromise love nor love compromise the truth. It was for his unique abilities in writing that he was selected to be Bishop of Gothenburg in the middle of the last century.

Becoming bishop was quite a development in the life of Bo Giertz, considering he was an atheist in his youth. But it was an even more important development for the Church of Sweden, whose confessional witness had been eroding for quite some time. Giertz, who was a parish pastor before becoming bishop, knew firsthand how much the confessions meant for the practice of a pastor. (The relationship between the confessions and pastoral practice has never been shown more clearly than in his novel, *The Hammer of God*.) It was for this reason that he stood firm on the historic confessions of the Church as bishop. He understood the importance of the Bible and the confessions for the so called "modern man," who supposedly had no room for religion in the twentieth century, because he knew the warmth and comfort only the Gospel can give after suffering in the coldness of the "modern world" that offers no hope.

The idea of translating this book came up first at the suggestion of Pastor Eric Andrae at a meeting of Ssalt and the Society of St. Eric at Ft. Wayne Seminary during Symposia in January of 2002. Hearing of its existence, I immediately ordered the book, although I had little intention of translating it. I merely wanted something that would offer a form of daily practice for my Swedish skills. It wasn't until I began reading these devotions that I felt compelled to translate them because of their immense value for the Church. Bo Giertz was able to take a very difficult passage of Scripture and, in explaining it, teach the principles of biblical interpretation, church history, and doctrine. But the most awe-inspiring aspects of these devotions are the prayers that accompany them.

The prayers that Bo Giertz wrote in these devotions are powerful, Christ-centered prayers that not only ask for the help of Christ in the daily life of a Christian, but teach the Christian to believe in and depend on Christ alone. Christ was also the source of strength, patience, and fortitude for Bo Giertz's own confessional stance, the only source of strength, patience, and fortitude there is for a Christian.

Translating is an art that is learned over time with much practice. I can only hope the reader finds the translation to be half as enjoyable as the work of translating it was. That said, translation is inherently inaccurate. This translation is no exception. Where it is inaccurate, I accept full responsibility and ask for charity. Some of my friends have been charitable enough to read and check sections of the translation beforehand, and to them I am grateful.

I would like to thank Tom Shumaker for teaching me Swedish in the first place. Birgitta, Bo Giertz's daughter, deserves special thanks for her willingness to have this book translated and published. I would like to thank the members of the Society of St. Eric and Ssalt for their help and encouragement throughout the project. I would also like to thank the members of my vicarage congregation, Immanuel Lutheran Church in Parkers Prairie, Minnesota, for their encouragement and support as I worked on this, pulling late hours in the office they provided for me. But most of all I would like to thank my wife, Christa, who spent many a cold winter's night taking care of our newborn son, John, alone, as I burned the midnight oil in my office. Her patience has not gone unnoticed, and if not for her support, this project never would have been completed.

Bror Erickson
Fort Wayne, Indiana
Pentecost
Anno Domini 2003

TRANSLATOR'S PREFACE

People seeking help and guidance in the Christian faith are offered this devotional book, which could also be considered a textbook of faith. Each daily reading begins with a Bible passage *that must be read*, as the text that follows is an explanation of the passage. After the explanatory text, the devotion ends with a prayer, under the assumption that you may add your own prayers. The Bible verses follow the Church Year, but are also chosen to give the reader a fairly coherent education in Christianity.

There are specific sections in the back of the book for Mid Summer Day, St. Michael and All Angels, and All Saints' Day, as well as Thanksgiving Sunday and the Sunday after All Saints' Day with devotions for the following weeks. However, for the week after St. Michael and All Angels, you will have to read the devotions that follow the Sunday after Trinity the year it was replaced by Michael. Explanations are given in the text when necessary.

Richard Wood
Frölunda Sweden

INTRODUCTION

The following instructions should be read before you begin reading this book.

My wish is that this book will help people who are confronted with the not-too-unusual question of what they should do to know more about Christianity. They want more knowledge, help in prayer and in understanding the Bible, and structure in their devotional lives. They're willing to set aside at least fifteen minutes every day for this, but don't know where to start.

This book provides a devotional reading followed by a prayer for every day. They're especially written to follow the Church Year. They should be helpful in preparing you for the Sunday worship service. At the same time, they try to provide an understandable description of the most important aspects of Christianity. When you have finished this book, ... you also will have completed a short doctrinal study.

Bible readings are selected in such a way that during the course of one year, you will read through some of the Bible's most important parts. The daily devotional readings are, as a rule, connected to that day's Bible passage and give, at least to some extent, a further explanation of it. In addition, if you want a guide for Bible reading that is short yet still contains explanations of the passages and explains passages that are especially difficult to understand, you can use Hedegård's *New*

Testament in Contemporary Language[2] for the readings from the New Testament.

I assume that those who use this book will have their own prayer concerns and will accordingly add other prayers for their work, family, and possibly some standard morning and afternoon prayers, the Lord's Prayer, as well as blessings or other prayers over and above those proposed here. Therefore, the final amen has been left off of the proposed prayers.

It's a good idea to have a Church Year calendar on hand, if you're not sure which Sunday comes next. It's possible to get off track if you only continue the readings from day to day. In the text there are instructions at appropriate places to help you follow the Church Year.

The four common prayer days are omitted.[3] For several reasons it would probably be best, during those weeks, to read the devotions for that Sunday (with the following weekdays), that in that particular year is replaced with a prayer day. The subject for the different prayer days is nevertheless found in other contexts of the devotions.

The different parts of this book are connected. They are not, individually, an entity by themselves. It can very well be that you will have questions the text does not answer immediately. The answer will come later in the following texts—if the author was aware of the questions in the first place. That's the way Christianity works: Everything is connected and gradually becomes clearer. The more you read, learn, and experience, the clearer these wonderful doctrines and their immense profoundness will become to you. And so I wish the reader well. I myself once began with a clean slate, not knowing much at all about Christianity. It was the beginning of a

2. This has not been translated.
3. The four common prayer days are special days in the church of Sweden not represented elsewhere in Christendom.

long life of continuous exploration. I have written this book in the hope that it will help some reader follow the same path. He will not regret it.

FIRST SUNDAY IN ADVENT

Matthew 21:1–9

"Hosanna to the Son of David! Blessed is He who comes in the name of the Lord!" Matthew 21:9

Jubilation erupted as Jesus rode toward the city along the Old Pilgrims Road over the Mount of Olives. It was spring. The sun was shining, and little red flowers peeked out from between stones. The air was full of singing birds and expectation. Shouts of "Hosanna" resounded so that the echo rolled along the Kidron Valley and reverberated off the temple walls on the other side. It was something of a folk festival as well as a political demonstration. But above all it was a yearning and a hope that sought out fellowship with God. The people cried out their distress and confessed their faith. Hosanna is a prayer. It means: Help us, Lord. Save us. Intervene and rescue us. The basis for these cries was all the knowledge they had about God the Almighty, who had done remarkable things for their ancestors. God had helped them so many times before. Hosanna was almost a cry of jubilation, with some of the resonance from Psalm 22:4: "In You our fathers trusted; they trusted, and You delivered them."

Isn't it things like this that made the first Sunday in Advent such a great day in our church? There is something in the psalms and their texts that allows us to become affected by the joyful cry of hosanna descending from the Mount of Olives. This is the church's New Year's Day. Someone is coming to us, a merciful King with the promise of yet another year of grace.

A year of grace? Wishes like those can be just as unfulfilled as conventional New Year's Day wishes normally are. Everything continues as it did before. Nothing happens, except that I have lived one more year and have one less year left when the next new year comes along.

And yet it was sincerely meant, this year of grace. He meant it, and maybe I also mean it in the depths of my heart. In truth, we are never the same again: When one year has passed, it has done something to us. We have either come closer or farther away. Faith has either grown or withered.

A year of grace? This year I won't only wish for it and hope that it comes by itself. I will pray for it. I will open myself up for it. I will attempt to follow Him so I don't miss anything He has to give.

So here I stand, Lord, among all the people who sing and rejoice when You pass by. And now, Lord, I don't want to just stand aside and look on. I want to come along so I may see and hear. I know You will come and enter the city, and go up to the temple. You come to speak to us. I want to stand there and listen. I know that strange things happened, terrible things, important and critical things happened there in Jerusalem. I want to see it with my own eyes. So I pray to You, that this Church Year will be a year with You, full of what You have to give, full of the word that comes from Your lips, and full of Your own presence. Lord, help. Lord, may all go well. Hosanna in the highest.

MONDAY AFTER THE FIRST SUNDAY IN ADVENT

Isaiah 40:1–11

"Blessed is the King who comes in the name of the Lord!"
Luke 19:38

When we follow Jesus as He enters Jerusalem, when we listen to the chatter and voices surrounding Him and see what happens, we understand that what is happening now must be a continuation of things that previously happened in this nation's history. Previous events must have been significant to what is happening now. It is written about Jesus that He came when the time was fulfilled (Galatians 4:4). God had been preparing His work for more than a thousand years before He intervened like He did when He sent His Son into the world. That's why the people could understand—and we can understand—what God's purpose was. There's a purpose for everything that happened to Jesus when He entered Jerusalem.

There was profound significance in calling Him the Son of David. They knew He was from a royal family, one of the many descendants of David, but He wasn't just anyone who had a claim to the throne. This wasn't a political matter, in any case, not for those who understood the Scriptures. The Messiah was to be born from David's lineage. He was to come as a Savior, not only for Israel, but for the whole world. When the people called out, "Blessed is the coming kingdom of our father David!" (Mark 11:10) it might have been similar to a slogan heard in a demonstration for some of them, a political demand, or a hope for rebellion against the Romans. However, the disciples knew God had something else in mind. They cried, "Peace in heaven and glory in the highest" (Luke 19:38)!

A few days later Jesus Himself would explain to a perplexed Pontius Pilate what all this had to do with His kingdom. His kingdom was not of this world. Were it of this world, then His servants would be fighting with weapons in hand. But He forbade them to do that. Yet, He was the King of a kingdom—the kingdom of truth. This is the reason His kingdom and His realm concern us as much today as it concerned the people then. "Everyone who is of the truth listens to My voice" (John 18:37). This has always been and always will be true. We can do as Pontius Pilate did: avoid the matter with a skeptical shrug and counter with the question What is truth? This question isn't meant to be answered, but is an excuse not to be concerned with such things. But we can also say, as the devout in Israel said, "Lead me in Your truth and teach me, for You are the God of my salvation" (Psalm 25:5).

So then, Lord Jesus, You are a king. Your ancestors ruled in David's city over this small nation that Your Father chose in order that I also learn to know Him and His salvation. The prophet was talking about You when he said, "Of the increase of His government and of peace there will be no end, on the throne of David and over His kingdom, to establish it and to uphold it with justice and with righteousness from this time forth and forevermore" (Isaiah 9:7). You prepared a place for me in Your kingdom. You Yourself have baptized me and given me citizenship. I praise You because You came, because You established the kingdom that shall never end—and because You also did this for my sake.

TUESDAY AFTER
THE FIRST SUNDAY
IN ADVENT
Isaiah 40:12–21

Behold, your King is coming to you. Zechariah 9:9

When God created us, He gave us something the animals didn't receive: the ability to feel His presence, experience His reality, and talk with Him. You don't need to be a Christian to know that God is here. He is everywhere in His creation. You can encounter Him in a hundred different places: in nature, in the sunset and in a storm, in a birch forest and in a snowfall, in art and music, in your own heart, in the demand for honor and justice, in the work for the oppressed, and in the love for your children. Therefore, the word *God* is in every language. Even if it's only a feeling, there is something that can be known about God and His nature. There is something that fascinates us and draws us to Him. There is, at the same time, something that is so exalted, so holy, so pure, and so demanding that it intimidates us. God is not to be toyed with, and yet we are drawn to Him as children to their father.

We can only talk in pictures about God, the infinitely exalted. When the prophet says God "has measured the waters in the hollow of His hand and marked off the heavens with a span, enclosed the dust of the earth in a measure and weighed the mountains in scales and the hills in a balance" (Isaiah 40:12), he is only using pictures, but pictures that give a correct conception about the infinitude of God and His overwhelming power.

But now a strange thing occurs. This God, who is so infinitely exalted above everything and who lives in a ray of light no one can approach, has come to us. The greatest, the most meaningful and decisive thing that has happened on earth is that God has descended to us and become one of us. This is what the disciples gradually began to understand as they walked with Jesus. Even others understood that God visited His people. They knew that the prophet's word was being fulfilled: "Behold, your King is coming to you" (Zechariah 9:9). But the disciples knew that another Prophet's word was being fulfilled here too. This is what Jesus Himself taught them patiently and gently: "Whoever has seen Me has seen the Father" (John 14:9). This isn't a doctrine that has to be believed in order to follow Jesus, but it's a truth you discover and learn to believe in when you follow Him.

Lord, I ask You for only one thing: that You help me to see and understand. You came to us from Your Father because You wanted to help us. I know I need this help, and You know it even more. Therefore I pray that You let me see and hear what I most need to see and hear. I don't want to decide by myself. I pray only for Your guidance. I don't want to be wiser than You. Let me hear only what You want to say and nothing else. I know that You govern in the kingdom of truth, that You have truth, that You are truth. Let me see the truth. Praise be to You, who has come with truth.

WEDNESDAY AFTER THE FIRST SUNDAY IN ADVENT

Isaiah 40:22–30

Behold, your King is coming to you . . . humble and mounted on a donkey, on a colt, the foal of a donkey. Zechariah 9:9

You could've expected God to come to us in power and glory. All we can imagine about Him tells us that He is infinite, overwhelming, and beyond words. Millions of light-years mean less to Him than a centimeter for us. Nebulae and the Milky Way are like specks of dust that dance in the sun for Him. He upholds everything with His almighty power. He knows everything, even the invisible electrons that revolve in their orbit. What about us? "When I look at Your heavens, the work of Your fingers, the moon and the stars, which You have set in place, what is man that You are mindful of him?" (Psalm 8:3–4) "Who brings princes to nothing, and makes the rulers of the earth as emptiness" (Isaiah 40:23).

But when God descended to earth, He allowed Himself to be born in a manger. When He entered Jerusalem, the symbol of His everlasting realm, He rode in not upon a warhorse but upon a little donkey. He did not wear a purple mantle, but was clothed in the people's cheap homespun clothing. He first received the king's red mantle a few days later in ridicule, and then it was only a soldier's tattered cape. There was no sign of the power that no one could defy, nothing of the all-powerful sovereignty over His creation. To many, it was proof that He could not be God. To others, this was the deepest revelation of God's nature: an almighty power that at the same time is a boundless love so great it allows Him to be trampled upon and sacrificed to save the children He loves.

Lord, this is going to take me a long time to fathom.
I understand that I cannot imagine it. I must be
allowed to see it. If this is true, then only You can
convince me of it. You have come into our world
in this way. It was Your plan and Your purpose.
You knew what needed to be done, and You did it.
I can never comprehend this completely. Therefore,
I want to listen and see now. Only You can help me
comprehend it. Now I wait for Your light and truth.
Let them come even to me, for Your mercy's sake.

THURSDAY AFTER THE FIRST SUNDAY IN ADVENT
Isaiah 42:1–12

A bruised reed He will not break, and a faintly burning wick
He will not quench. Isaiah 42:3

These words are among many in the Old Testament that
speak about Christ. Words like these don't always reveal who
they are speaking about. They speak in pictures, mysterious allusions and hidden-behind words that hint at a deeper
meaning. In their entirety, however, they were clear enough
to give Israel the assurance that Someone was coming; a
Messiah who would reestablish this fallen world and save the
human race. These words first became fully understandable
when Jesus came. The Scriptures were fulfilled. What was
promised was completed. With amazed eyes the disciples

saw that there was profound significance even in insignificant verses that they had never reflected over.

This verse was one that characterized Jesus. It explained why He was so different. People expected the Messiah to appear in power. He was expected to pass judgment on God's behalf. Ordinary people hoped for a devastating reckoning with the Romans. Others expected judgment over all the sinners in Israel. John the Baptist had also warned about the approaching judgment of wrath. But Jesus appeared as a friend to the publicans and sinners. With infinite mercy, He took care of those whom everyone else had given up as lost. The disciples understood that this was a part of the very essence of His nature—something God desired.

This thing about not crushing what is broken pertains not only to individuals who are lost and unsuccessful; it pertains to all of humanity and creation. All of it is a broken reed. All of it is ruined, torn asunder, and no longer functions as it should. No one can ever comprehend what happens in the world without listening to what Jesus has to say about evil. He doesn't talk about *evil*. He talks about the evil one. There's a particular force that desires evil. It isn't a question of an imperfection in creation. It's a matter of insurrection. Among all the beings to whom God gave an autonomous life, a personal consciousness, and an independent will that they would rejoice in their existence and take part in God's own fortuity, one of them turned against Him. This one tried to become like God and make his own decisions. He tried to do something other than God's will, which by definition is something evil. Since that time, God's glorious creation has been tattered. The one Jesus calls the man slaughterer, the enemy, Satan, has left traces of himself everywhere.

But God will not crush the broken reed. He has not rejected His work. He wants to repair the damage.

How?

Jesus wants to tell us about this. This is the work He came to carry out.

Lord, I don't know why, but so often I believe that You come with only demands. I have often been scared of You. You know, Lord, how hard it can be to live. So much has to be done. It's so hard to go on. And on top of everything else, one has to be a Christian. That's just another thing a person ought to do. Why do I feel like this, Lord? You're the One who gives. Help me to receive. Help me not to just ask what I have to do and what will become of me. Help me first to see who You are, what You have done, and what You have to offer. Bless my Advent and my Christmas and the whole Church Year, and fill it with Your gifts.

FRIDAY AFTER THE FIRST SUNDAY IN ADVENT
Isaiah 43:1–13

I have called you by name, you are Mine. Isaiah 43:1

The Old Testament is as much about us as it is about Christ. When the promises were fulfilled and the purpose God had for Israel's long history was completed, Christ came to establish a new Israel that includes all people. What God had previously done throughout the centuries was done with consideration for the times of fulfillment. So when Paul spoke about what was written regarding the children of Israel in the desert, he could say with certainty that it was written for our sake, it was recorded for our learning.

As a result, Christians repeatedly come across Bible verses they can apply to themselves as if they came directly to them from God Himself. Today's verse is one of them. God has called me by name. I am His. Just as God once called Israel and chose them as His people, and just as every Israelite, through circumcision, received an external confirmation of God's call, so God has called me in Baptism. God had a purpose when He lit the fire in my life. Earthly parents want their children to have someone to care for and love. There's no big difference with God. He wants us to share in His joy, the joy of existence. And I am one of those He wanted to give this joy to. He could have made me into a butterfly or an earthworm or some other living thing, but He has given me more than temporal life. He has given me the right to be His child and take part in His life that can never end.

But this means that I must be born into this world with all the risks that entails. God realizes the risks. He hasn't left me alone to handle them myself. He came at the very beginning of my life, before I even knew about it. He said: "Fear not, for I have redeemed you; I have called you by name, you are Mine" (Isaiah 43:1). He said it by an action so clearly and so unmistakable that it is recorded in one of the biggest books in the parish office.[4] And behind all the exterior—which shouldn't be taken lightly—He stood by Himself, the Invisible One, the One who commanded all of this and who once became visible Himself and lived among us as one of us. It is, of course, by Jesus' command that I was baptized. It was He who said, "You are mine; now I have called you just as I

---

4. Translator's note: In Sweden, the church was responsible for census recording, and therefore kept records of births, deaths, marriages, and Baptisms.

once called Peter, James, and John. Fear not. Whatever you then must go through, I will be with you."

If You say so, Lord Jesus, then it is so. Then it is not I who tried to choose to follow You, but You who chose me; it is Your desire. It is not my decision, undertaking, conclusion, or choice that it depends on. You are behind all of it. Is this why my thoughts have not been able to let go of You? Is this why You've always returned? Is it for this reason there is desire and yearning in my heart? Lord, I am glad that it is so. And now I ask only that You complete Your work in me and let it become as You have wanted it to be from the very beginning.

SATURDAY AFTER THE FIRST SUNDAY IN ADVENT
Isaiah 43:21–28

Therefore do not pronounce judgment before the time, before the Lord comes, who will bring to light the things now hidden in darkness and will disclose the purposes of the heart. Then each one will receive his commendation from God. 1 Corinthians 4:5

The Lord is coming. *Advent*, as we know, means arrival— the Lord's arrival. We think both about how He once came to earth and how He will come again. One day the Lord will come for the last time, and that day is not infinitely far off. God has a purpose with this series of events. Although we like to think the future has no end, Christ teaches us something completely different. God can't repair the fundamental fault in His creation without recreating the whole world. And He will do it. He won't wait millions of years. Time is short. In that sense, we always live in Advent. The final act of Christ remains. We are now in a period of transition, a temporary state, waiting in expectation for that decisive moment. We live in a fallen world. Here in time, there are no definite solutions. But we live with the hope and promise of God's final solution to all the world's problems.

There is so much we can't understand. We are quick to judge, as if we know what goes on in the hearts of men, but God withholds judgment for Himself. He persuades and modifies. He can postpone intervention for so long that we become impatient. He can let His judgment strike individuals as well as nations, but we can never believe that we understand everything God does. We can only wait and see.

We learn to understand God's manner of working best through His own Word. The Bible is basically history, specifically the history of salvation. It is a description of how God links the fate of the world directly to the goal He has set for history. We hear how He chose and reared Israel. We see how He dealt with sinful men throughout time, men who were full of pettiness and passion and capable of the worst transgressions. This is also true for many of those who were God's instruments. "Your first father sinned, and your mediators transgressed against Me" (Isaiah 43:27). Occasionally, it looked like God had forsaken His people, but He was going about His work the whole time. He still does, even today. We're moving toward the journey's end when the Lord will come to make everything new.

Come, Lord Jesus. Thy kingdom come. Lord, I have prayed these words so many times, but I hardly understood what I was praying for. I have prayed that You would come with Your help and be near me. I wanted You to help me understand, to love, and to do the right thing. But that You would come in this manner—in Your glory—and terminate all our plans and the whole world, draw the line, sum up everything, and bring everything into the light. How many of us are prepared for that? There are so many who do not seek You, Lord. Many of them are people I love very much. You know this, Lord. Is this why You wait? Lord, help us to use this time correctly. Lord, help me to remember every morning that this is the season of Advent and that I have received another day to live before You come.

SECOND SUNDAY IN ADVENT
Luke 21:25–36

Heaven and earth will pass away, but My words will not pass away. Luke 21:33

This is the exact opposite of what people usually think. The everlastingness of matter has been one of this century's favorite dogmas (although it is now a little antiquated). People normally think that heaven and earth will exist no matter what happens. However, they, too, shall pass away, Christ says. Just as God Himself once said, "Let there be!" and everything came to be by His command and according to His will, there also will come a day when God will say there's no more time. People don't regard it as remarkable that God, in the beginning, created heaven and earth. As a matter of fact, the creation isn't any more remarkable—while a tremendous miracle—than God's revelation that He will create a new heaven and a new earth at the end of time.

Nothing in this world is eternal, with one exception: "My words will not pass away." There is one thing we encounter in this life we can deal with and attain that is eternal and will always exist: It's Christ's Word.

Christ calls Himself "the Word." He is the Word that was already there at the very beginning when the world was created. He is "the Word became flesh and dwelt among us" (John 1:14). He had something from God in Himself that can never be destroyed: "The eternal life, which was with the Father and was made manifest to us" (1 John 1:2). We acquire this life from Him through His Word. "The words that I have spoken to you are spirit and life" (John 6:63). Therefore the Word extends itself into this life and allows us here, where everything is gradually decaying, to encounter something that will remain throughout time. To come in contact with the Word and receive what it has to give means that here in this world, we receive a piece of the world to come. It's this world to come that Jesus calls the kingdom of God. He speaks to us about this when He says the kingdom of God is near, repent and believe in the Gospel.

Dear Father in heaven, You are the origin of every-thing I see around me. You hold it in Your hand, and it exists only as long as You want. However, You have planted eternity in my heart. I have

*received something that only You possess. You
have embraced me and enveloped me with something that can never pass away. I thank You
because I have Your Word, because You allowed
it to take hold of me, and because I can hold on
to it. Never allow me to let go of it. May it hold
me firmly, even if I should want to break free. I
know that Your Word lasts forever, and I thank
You for that.*

MONDAY AFTER THE SECOND SUNDAY IN ADVENT
Isaiah 44:1–18

"I am the LORD's . . . the LORD's." Isaiah 44:5

That's how life really is, the prophet says. When God has poured out His Spirit, when everything is as it should be, this will be our greatest joy: that God exists, and that we belong to Him, live in His presence, and take part in His joy.

But it's not like that now. In this fallen and irreparable world, people tend to take one of two equally erroneous positions in their behavior toward God.

The first one is to make our own god. The prophet gives us a drastic and mocking description of this. A man forges and carves, chops down the trees, and cuts up the wood. He uses part of it as fuel, and he makes the rest of it into a god. Part of the wood ends up in the fire. And before the rest of it, he falls down on his knees and says, "Deliver me." We must remember that during the prophet's lifetime, this was accepted behavior for the cultured and powerful in the world. It was what everyone did—everyone except for one reluctant race of people on the edge of ruin who persisted in believing that their invisible God was Lord of the whole world.

The other attitude is probably the most common one in our day. It is portrayed by the prophet Isaiah when he describes the proud of Babylon. There was a particular mentality in this presumptuous city: the coddled and extravagant. They appeared so confident and secure. It can be expressed in the words: "I am, and there is no one besides me" (Isaiah 47:8). It can also be expressed as "No one sees me" (Isaiah 47:10). This is one of the signs of unbelief throughout time: the certainty of being alone, of being in possession of your own life, a life that received its breath by accident only to be snuffed out for all eternity in a world without meaning, with no binding standards or goals.

Sometimes we find ourselves between these two viewpoints. We might not believe in God, but we still have a foggy suspicion that there is a power that steers the world. The prophet Isaiah describes how the Babylonians measured the heavens and looked at the stars and at every new moon would attempt to predict their fate (47:13). In our day, we read our horoscope half jokingly and yet with a dark fear of unknown powers—a last, crude, distorted reminder of the correct perception that we are not alone.

The truth is that we don't exist by chance. At the essence of our lives and also of the whole universe, there is a good will. We need not grope around in the darkness and attempt to create for ourselves a picture of this strange power that upholds everything. God has revealed Himself. He comes to us. We hear His voice. There's a very good reason for God creating us.

My God and Father, I thank You because I can call You Father. I thank You because I can talk with You. I thank You because I know You are not just a power that rules over everything or hides Your purposes and intentions from us. You share Your life and Your joy, the joy of existence, and the infinite wealth in Your kingdom. And since I belong to You and am a part of Your work, I pray that You let these words remain written on my mind and on my hands: "The Lord's own." I pray to You for thoughts like this, for desires like this, and for deeds like this so my whole life and character witness to how good it is to belong to You. Praise be to Your name that I have the opportunity to do it.

TUESDAY AFTER THE SECOND SUNDAY IN ADVENT
Isaiah 45:15–25

"To Me every knee shall bow." Isaiah 45:23

When Israel received that promise long ago, even the most devout had a hard time believing it would be fulfilled. This promise was given at a time when Israel was as powerless and their entire existence was as threatened as any nation could be. Yet this remnant of a nation continued to embrace faith in the Lord of hosts. The idea that this faith would someday become a world religion must have appeared to all realistic men as preposterous fantasy.

Well over half a millennium later, Paul quoted this same passage when he wrote his letter to the Philippians. He wrote that God had exalted Jesus, whom men crucified, in order that at the very mention of His name, every knee would bow and every tongue confess that He is Lord (see Philippians 2:9–10). That kind of faith might have appeared to be equally preposterous, but when God gave His promise, He said, "From My mouth has gone out in righteousness a word that shall not return" (Isaiah 45:23). It turned out He is the only Savior, that everything is in His hands, and that it is folly to try to live as if He didn't exist. This doesn't mean that we admit that God was right through a majority vote. As long as people have the right to make free choices, not every one will rally around Him. On the contrary, the longer the world remains, the fewer the confessors will be. As humanity approaches the end of time, the Church will be a persecuted minority. Christ has made this clear to us. And yet God is still right. When He is finished with this world, when there is nothing left to gain from further delay or a lengthened period of mercy, then God's kingdom will come in all its clarity, overwhelmingly, "in His power."

Christ invited mankind to this kingdom. Every new Advent means that the invitation goes out to us once again. The kingdom of God is near. A greeting comes directly to us from our God, He who said to Israel: "I did not speak in secret, in a land of darkness; I did not say to the offspring of Jacob, 'Seek Me in vain' " (Isaiah 45:19). God really doesn't want us to live in darkness. It was never His intention for us to get by with the small crumbs of religion we could scrape together from our own thoughts, from glimpses of His glory in creation, by feeling a breath of His holiness in our heart, or by worshiping in nature and staying with our conscience.

It was never God's intention that these rays of hope would be enough for us. They tell us that God exists. They encourage us to seek Him. And He promises us that the search will not be in vain.

Lord, You alone awakened my longing for You. I never would have sought You out if You had not sought me. I never would have thought about You if I had not first been in Your thoughts. I know You are an unfathomable God, but You are also our Lord Jesus Christ's God and Father. It is Your glory that radiates from the face of Jesus. I know that my eyes cannot endure the sight of Your light, and yet You have let it come down here to earth, so mild and soft that I can see it. I know You are like a consuming fire, and yet the glow of Your zeal becomes like the warmth of a father's embrace when You come to me in the Savior. Teach me to know You better and better and to love You more and more. You have given me my life, and it's in Your power at this moment. Help me always say, truthfully and sincerely, that You are my life.

WEDNESDAY AFTER THE SECOND SUNDAY IN ADVENT

Isaiah 49:1–13

"I will make you as a light for the nations, that My salvation may reach to the end of the earth." Isaiah 49:6

A person is never finished with God's Word after reading it once. There is much more to it than anyone can see at just a glance. When God spoke to Israel, 25 or 30 centuries ago, He also had the coming millennium in mind. He wove a picture of Christ not only into the prophecies, but also into the stories about Israel's kings and high priests. He wove a picture of the new Israel, Christ's Church, into the stories of Israel's people. He spoke to them and to us and to everyone in times to come. Therefore, there is often a double meaning in these words. What is said about Israel—God's chosen people who would convey His message of salvation to the whole world—tells us something about Jesus Christ too. It's also a message about and for His Church (the passage about salvation that we just read, for example).

God's salvation is something that has happened here on earth. It's not just an eternal truth or a spiritual power that has always existed and will always be true. Sin, misfortune, and the fall were real occurrences, things that happened and that still happen. They have their place in history. And they can be rectified only by another equally essential occurrence that also has its place in history. This is why God has intervened and worked among us. The history of salvation is a part of world history. It's this history that Scripture imparts to us. It's a history about real occurrences, real people who followed God's command, acts that were done in His name, words spoken on His behalf. That's the reason we can hear how

He miraculously saved Joseph and kept his brothers alive, how God called Abraham from his country to be the father of a new nation, how Moses led God's persecuted people out of Egypt and to the Promised Land. We follow the long and often bloody history of Israel's struggle for its existence and for its faith. It's not a story about morality or ethics, and we seldom meet any role models. But it's a story about how God's forgiveness could come into a world that didn't deserve it and didn't really want it. It's a story about God's light that shines in great darkness.

We often take for granted that God has to save the world by giving us righteous moral instructions and seeing to it that we live by them. But God says: "I, I am He who blots out your transgressions for My own sake" (Isaiah 43:25). This is the reason He sent Christ to us, not just as a great teacher and example, but as our Redeemer and Savior.

Lord, I cannot comprehend how You put up with all of us. You see the immense course the world is taking and its multitudes of people. And yet, You care so much for each and every one of us, as if You had no one else to think about. You know me better than I know myself. And all the great things You have done in the past, all Your wonderful deeds the Scriptures witness about, You've also done for my sake. Help me to see and know deep within my heart that all this is for me. Help me see Abraham as my father, a father for all believers, who walked in Your path so You could create a nation on earth that knows You. You have included me with these people. Your salvation stretches to the ends of the earth, and I have been able to hear about it for as long as I can remember. I pray to You for the grace

to be a good child for Your people and a righteous
servant of Your holy will. For Jesus' sake.

THURSDAY AFTER THE SECOND SUNDAY IN ADVENT
Isaiah 50:1–10

"Why, when I came, was there no man; why, when I called, was there no one to answer?" Isaiah 50:2

The world had turned away from God, but God had not turned away from the world. He hasn't issued a certificate of divorce, the prophet says in Isaiah 50. He hasn't broken off relations with the world and left it to its fate. On the contrary, He has intervened over and over again to save what could be salvaged. He has spoken through His prophets. And finally He Himself came down to us.

And the result?

God says it Himself through the prophet Hosea: "The more they were called, the more they went away; ... they did not know that I healed them" (Hosea 11:2–3).

Sometimes God intervenes so obviously that we cannot avoid seeing it. It leaves its mark on all the generations to come. Christmas is an example. It is a celebration that leaves its mark upon all of society. We, however, have a remarkable capacity of avoiding an encounter with God. The holiday we celebrate to remember that God has come to us can be an excuse and a means of moving even farther away from Him. Advent reminds us that the Lord is near, that time is short, yet people make it a time of worry and haste. They bury themselves in their work more than in any other season. They want to increase sales or to be finished with all the practical details. Jesus said of the people in Lot's time that they ate and drank, they bought and sold, until everything suddenly ended for all of them. And Jesus says that's exactly what will happen on the day and time the Son of Man is revealed (see Luke 17:22–33). That's exactly what happens before our eyes. People buy and sell—that's their Advent. They eat and drink—that's their Christmas. And all this because Christ has come and shall come!

In today's Bible reading from Isaiah, we read what usually happens to God's messengers. The prophet's words fit Jesus remarkably well. It's one of the many places in the Old Testament where we see a picture of Jesus. He received "the tongue of the learned" (Isaiah 50:4). He could comfort the weary with His words, and He did not shrink away when God spoke. Therefore, He offered His back to those who beat Him and His cheeks to those who jerked on His beard. He didn't cover His face from their blows and spit.

There's a price to pay when you believe in God. Maybe that's why people shy away. They instinctively sense that there is something entering their world that can rock their boats. As long as they can keep God at a distance, they think they can make their own decisions. They believe that is ultimate happiness. The password of disbelief is "I and nothing else; no one sees me."

Lord, I so gladly want to be one of those who won't avoid You when You come. But You know how much there is inside me that would prefer to avoid You. You know how I want to avoid the tasks You give me. You know how lethargic I can be when

*You give me an occasion to hear Your Word. You
know how unwilling I can be when I have a chance
to do something for a difficult or miserable person.
You know how cowardly I can be when I have a
chance to witness about You. And yet, Lord, You
know also that I do not wish to be without You.
Therefore I pray to You that You take me in Your
hand and that You mold something from my coarse
and filthy clay that can be used in Your service.*

FRIDAY AFTER THE SECOND SUNDAY IN ADVENT
Isaiah 51:1–8

"For the heavens will vanish like smoke, the earth will wear
out like a garment, . . . but My salvation will be forever."
Isaiah 51:6

Once again, we read about the world's last Advent when
Christ will come again, not riding upon a donkey but in all
His power and glory. The Bible speaks mainly in pictures
about this day. Pictures can't be read exactly like descriptions
in an encyclopedia. They actually say and do much more.
They get our imaginations and emotions working. They
allow us to visualize things words can hardly express. A child
can understand them just as well as a scholar. And we're
never done examining them. We have all seen a cloud of
smoke vanish into nothing. We have seen worn-out clothes
thrown away. That's what will happen to the earth someday,

the earth we now trample beneath our feet and the whole universe that surrounds us. A new creation is coming, but God will take everything that can be salvaged from the old destroyed creation and incorporate it in the new. This is the reason Christ comes to us now. The new creation begins with Him. The fact that He has come with His salvation means that right now, here among us, something can happen that can transform us into new creatures. We won't be totally transformed, but there will be something in us that belongs to God's new world. It's that salvation that "lasts forever."

"Fear not the reproach of man," the prophet says (Isaiah 51:7). People usually protect themselves against God's salvation with pretentious contempt. People laughed at Noah when he built the ark. In Sodom, no one thought the status quo could change, except for Lot. Men are sure of themselves, but God's children are safe, however. That's something completely different.

Lord, security exists only in You. I so readily trust in everything else and take it for granted that my life is dependent on things I can put my hands on. I like to trust in myself, thinking I can get by with what I can do and what I have. And yet everything is dependent upon You. I thank You for the new day You have given me today. I thank You that my body and brain work, that my heart beats, and for all the mysterious functions of my body I cannot control or understand. I know You are in command of all this. But most of all, I thank You because You hold Your hand over the whole world and guide everything toward the goal You have set. It's assuring to know that everything is in Your hands, everything I can do nothing about.

It's enough for me to know that You have a plan
and a purpose for my life and my days. Your will
be done, on earth as it is in heaven.

SATURDAY AFTER SECOND SUNDAY IN ADVENT
Isaiah 52:1–12

How beautiful upon the mountains are the feet of him who
brings good news, who publishes peace, who brings good
news of happiness, who publishes salvation, who says to
Zion, "Your God reigns." Isaiah 52:7

There are those who turn a deaf ear to God when He
speaks, but there are also those who lift their heads and listen. There's something inside them that shivers with joy and
expectation. They feel just like Isaiah described it in the verse
above.

Here we have another example of how profound the biblical word is. Who brings good news? Who comes over the
mountains? Maybe at one time it was the prophet. Hundreds
of years later, when the Scriptures were translated into Greek,
someone chose a word that literally means, "the one who
comes with the Gospel." That's how we got the word *Gospel*.
The disciples knew what this joyful message meant. They
experienced the "beautiful . . . feet of him who brings good
news" when Jesus came to them from the mountains. They
knew the great joy of finding the precious pearl and the treasure in the field. They saw how Zacchaeus hurried down from
the tree and received the Master with joy. They were with

Him when the publican, Levi, prepared a feast in his house.

There's not only a natural opposition to God's message, there is also a spontaneous joy over it. What is it that determines if one or the other will be victorious in a person's heart? It's something we can't explain. Jesus spoke about this many times. When He sows His Word, some of it falls upon the path, some upon the stony ground, still more amongst the thorns—but some also falls on fertile ground (see Matthew 13:1–9). He said that when the Light came into the world, there were those who loved the darkness more than the Light because their deeds were evil. But there were also those who came to the Light because it would reveal that their deeds were done for God (see John 3:16–21). People have had to deal with God every day of their lives, even if they haven't heard about Christ. Small, crucial moments are always occurring when we admit that God is right or deceive ourselves over what we know is true and right. This is what makes it spontaneously joyful or spontaneously aversive when Christ comes.

Lord, You know that both of these sides are inside of me. There is cowardice and laziness that prefers to be left alone and evade. But You see, Lord, I still know that You are right. I am glad I have been able to hear the echo of Your steps. I understand that there is a purpose to this existence. This is what You proclaim when You come with Your Good News. Now I know, Lord, how lovely the feet of Him who brings Good News can be. They are the footsteps of a Messenger from heaven, footsteps which still touch upon this earth, footsteps that I can hear myself. And they come with a good message, a message from Your Father,

*from God Himself—the message that at the very
essence of existence is a Father's heart and pure
mercy. Blessed are You because You came with
this message.*

THIRD SUNDAY IN ADVENT
Matthew 11:2–10

"Are You the One who is to come, or shall we look for
another?" Matthew 11:3

How strange that John the Baptist could ask a question
like that. In his preaching, he said that He who was greater
than himself would come after him (see Matthew 3:11).
And he was right. Even while in prison, where he was now,
rumors about the works of Jesus reached him. Why then did
John have to ask? Did he doubt?

It's possible that he doubted. He had said that the Messiah
would pass judgment and have a pitchfork in His hand so He
could carefully clean His barn. He would burn the chaff in
a fire (see Matthew 3:12). Yet nothing of this judgment was
apparent.

Here we learn what it's like to have questions and doubt.
Jesus often appears to be so entirely different from what we
expect. You might ask yourself: If something is possible, is
it true? Then you should do what the Baptist did and go
directly to Jesus with your question. John relied on the fact
that Jesus really came from God. He would tell the truth.
There was no need to be frightened of asking Him. It's okay
to express doubt.

John got his answer. John's disciples needed only to tell

him what they heard and saw. Faith begins when one sees and hears what Jesus does. The greatest and most remarkable thing that happened here was that the Good News was preached to the poor.

When the disciples were sent on their way, Jesus began to speak about John the Baptist, giving him the best report a man can get: he was the greatest of God's witnesses prior to Jesus. It's probably good for us to hear that even a witness like this can wonder, doubt, and question, and this doesn't stop him from being God's chosen witness.

Everything that was previously written was done so for our instruction. We hear this in Sunday's epistle (Romans 15:4–13). Naturally, it's about God's Word. God has allowed it to become the way it is because He has something to tell us in exactly those words. That's how Jesus read His Bible. That's how the apostles understood it, and that's the way we also can read it. Therefore, this report about John's doubt is a word of comfort and help to us. John, the forerunner who prepared the way, also prepares the way for us today. This is why Jesus meets us now in Advent.

I thank You, Lord, because You are the One who was supposed to come. And I thank You because I may come to You, even if I am uncertain about it. Give me so much trust in You that I dare to come to You with everything and to speak to You about everything. Once, You sent John the Baptist with Your Word so he would prepare the way for You. Do that this Advent also. Eliminate all the obstacles that stand in the way. Bridge all the voids that separate us from You. Help us here in the congregation to receive You with open hearts.

Grant us a blessed Church Year full of joy that You are with us, and full of the great joy that comes from serving You.

MONDAY AFTER THE THIRD SUNDAY IN ADVENT
Isaiah 55:1–13

And we have something more sure, the prophetic word, to which you will do well to pay attention as to a lamp shining in a dark place, until the day dawns and the morning star rises in your hearts. 2 Peter 1:19

We have been occupied with the prophetic word for the entire season of Advent, just like our reading from the end of Isaiah. We have seen that God sent this word not only to Israel, but to us as well. And when God sends out His Word, it is to do something in the world. It's like rain and snow, as is the analogy in Isaiah 55:10. It waters the ground and makes it fertile and bounteous. There is a living power in the Word that comes from God's lips. It's like water for the thirsty or bread for the hungry. It grants life that needs to be nourished daily. Who can drink enough water to quench his thirst or eat enough food to be full for a month? Faith isn't an idea. It's a way of life, and this life can be sustained only by the power of God's Spirit. And God sends His Spirit with the Word. Therefore He says, "Hear, that your soul may live" (Isaiah 55:3).

The Word isn't something you can just put aside and pick up again only when you think you need more of it. The Word is like an order in the military, a prescription from the hospital, or an invitation to a celebration. It is relevant now. It is for this reason the Word says, "Seek the LORD while He may be found" (Isaiah 55:6). You might think it's all right to seek Him next year, but we don't live in a constant state. What's possible today might not be possible in another year.

If we don't respect the Word, won't it be rendered ineffective? Won't it be a futile effort to read it? No. Refusing the Word is also an action. It's impossible to do without becoming harder and more inaccessible—perhaps without even noticing it. Therefore the Word is always in action, causing faith or defiance, grace or judgment. We either come closer to God or further away. No one is ever left unaffected.

I pray to You, Lord, that Your Word may always work in my life the way You intend it to work. I pray to You that it may work here in our world, here in the congregation and in our church body, in our people and in our land, as You want it to. None of us can receive it, Lord, if You don't help us. Do not let us ever rest in peace and tranquility if we try to close our hearts to it. Allow us no peace before we have peace with You. Don't get tired of us. We haven't earned it, but don't take Your hand away from us. Help all those who preach Your Word. Let it ring out as powerful, commanding, and intimate as it is. Help us to hear so our souls may live.

TUESDAY AFTER THE THIRD SUNDAY IN ADVENT

Isaiah 58:1–10

Cry aloud; do not hold back; lift up your voice like a trumpet; declare to My people their transgression, to the house of Jacob their sins. Isaiah 58:1

This Bible passage is inscribed on countless Swedish pulpits from the time the Swedes call "The great empire."[5] It says something very important about the prophetic Word. God even rebukes His own people. They have a responsibility to Him as God's people. It's an infinitely immense privilege to belong to God, but it doesn't mean guaranteed forgiveness and it doesn't give us a solid claim to shelter under God's particular protective care.

Israel heard these words from the prophets. The Jews heard them from John the Baptist. John came and inspired great excitement. For centuries no one had heard any prophet, but now here one stood, and he came with the unprecedented news that the time was fulfilled and God's kingdom was near. Now, God would intervene, as He had promised the patriarchs. But no one should believe that everything was all right simply because one was a child of Abraham. John gave very specific advice to everyone regarding their situation in life and their particular temptations and possibilities. His advice could very well apply to everyday situations, like

---

5. This refers to the time during and after the Reformation when Sweden became a great power in and around the Baltic. At their zenith, they conquered Finland, the Baltic States, Poland, huge areas of Russia, and a good portion of Germany. At this time, they saved Lutheranism from the invading Catholics during the Thirty Years' War. During this war, the German Catholics instructed their children to pray saying, "Bet, kinder, bet, für morgen kom der Schwede." That is, "Pray, child, pray, for tomorrow comes the Swede," referring to the Lion of the North, Gustav Vasa.

simply showing mercy and righteousness (we might call it human kindness and social responsibility). For instance, if you have two suits of clothes, you should share one of them with someone who has none. If you have more food than you need, you should share it. The publicans (who collected taxes on commission) should avoid lining their pockets. The soldiers should be satisfied with their pay and not extort money. The message we read in today's Bible reading is also God's Word to us today.

During the Middle Ages, Advent was a time of fasting. One abstained from something to prepare himself to receive the Lord Christ. It is no longer the custom to fast in this manner, but we all have reason to ask ourselves: From what does He want me to abstain for the sake of righteousness and to show compassion toward others? Giving at Christmas can be a way to abstain from something in order to make someone else happy. But often we do it in such a way that we are painfully reminded of Jesus' words, "If you greet only your brothers, what more are you doing than others? Do not even the Gentiles do the same" (Matthew 5:47)? And "If you do good to those who do good to you, what benefit is that to you? For even sinners do the same. And if you lend to those from whom you expect to receive, what credit is that to you? Even sinners lend to sinners, to get back the same amount" (Luke 6:32–34). Showing happiness for Christ by giving presents is a good Christian custom, but a Christian also asks his Lord how He wants us to give those presents.

Lord, I thank You for all I have received. I know it comes from You. I know I am merely a steward. Everything is Yours, although You have laid it in my hands, so help me to use it properly. What I may use for myself, I will receive from Your hand so I can use it with joy, thankfulness, and good conscience. And

Lord, what You want to make others happy with, I will place in Your hands. Help me see clearly and behave properly and be blessed enough that I may be Your servant in this way also.

WEDNESDAY AFTER THE THIRD SUNDAY IN ADVENT
Isaiah 60:1–11

The word of God came to John the son of Zechariah in the wilderness. And he went into all the region around the Jordan, proclaiming a baptism of repentance for the forgiveness of sins. Luke 3:2–3

Luke tells us that this occurred in the fifteenth year of Caesar Tiberius's rule, when Pontius Pilate was the Roman governor in Judea, and Herod, Philip, and Lysanias were tetrarchs (tributary officials) over his territory. So this happened in the midst of everyday life, as history was being made. Officials, scribes, and high priests came and went. People cultivated their land and business was as usual. Then God's Word came to John and he became John the Baptist, the greatest among the prophets. It was long thought that the time of the prophets had past. But suddenly this great penitential preacher appeared and rumors spread throughout the land: " 'A great prophet has arisen among us!' and 'God has visited His people' " (Luke 7:16)!

His message was not new. What he said was just this: What the Lord has proclaimed for a long time will finally happen. Now the great Light will ascend over Israel, a Light that will become a light for all people (see John 1:6–10).

How could John know this? And how could he be right? Unbelievers might try to explain things like this as coincidental. For the believer, it is clear that God really was at work here. He who had sent one prophet after another to say something to the world that appeared altogether preposterous had now intervened and showed that it wasn't mere fantasy. This small miraculous nation that the Egyptians, Babylonians, and Greeks could not successfully annihilate—although many of them had tried with the help of great and powerful military resources—had truly been chosen by God to play a part that would be essential for all of mankind. Politically and culturally, materially and economically, Israel was confusingly similar to its neighbors. That's been clearly shown by archeological excavations. When it came to construction and pottery, everyday life, and the art of war, they lived precisely the same as the other people on the small coastal strip between Africa and Asia. Yet the Israelites knew they had been separated and called by God. One prophet after another had confirmed it. They pointed to the great day when God would send a Prophet greater than Moses, a righteous King, a Prince of peace, a Branch from the stump of Jesse. In the time of Caesar Tiberius, the skeptics could calmly demonstrate that all this was pious fantasy. The Romans governed in Judea, and the surrounding provinces were governed by the half-heathen children of Herod or other foreigners. The prophets' families had become extinct, and it was clear that they were wrong. People could pretentiously smile and devote their time to more useful things until the day John appeared and said that now it would happen. And it happened.

Lord Jesus, I thank You because You link the history of the nations together and because this world, where so much evil occurs, still lies in Your hands.

I thank You for Your great plan of salvation that You have completed. I thank You because You have everything in Your hands even today. You came, Lord Christ, when the time was fulfilled. And I know You will come again when the time is ripe. We see that darkness overtakes the earth and shrouds the people. You say that in this darkness a great light shall rise up. Help us all to see it. Let the light be so clear that even our blind eyes have to see it. Allow the nations, ours too, to walk in Your light. For Your name's sake.

THURSDAY AFTER THE THIRD SUNDAY IN ADVENT
Isaiah 60:18–61:4

For no prophecy was ever produced by the will of man, but men spoke from God as they were carried along by the Holy Spirit. 2 Peter 1:21

"The Spirit of the Lord is upon me . . ." (Luke 4:18).

This was the passage from the Scriptures on which Jesus preached the only time He preached in His home town, Nazareth. He stepped forward to preach. Someone gave Him the scroll that contained the book of Isaiah. He rolled it out and found today's reading. It wasn't an accident. Jesus was able to say, "Today this Scripture has been fulfilled in your hearing" (Luke 4:21). Maybe the prophet Isaiah at that time was talking about himself and the commission he received. But no prophecy has ever emerged by the will of man. It was God, together with His Spirit, who moved the prophet to speak. There is a deeper meaning to this passage than the prophet and his contemporaries could have realized. The day of fulfillment would come when it would be revealed to whom the passage really alluded and how unexpectedly wonderful was the reality it spoke about.

That's the way it is with the prophetic Word. Peter says here that prophecy never had its origin in the will of man. Just as God gave it form and shape, it is also God who interprets it. He shows that interpretation in the events of history, in what He allows to happen, when the Word is carried out and fulfilled. Jesus Himself is the great fulfillment. "For all the promises of God find their Yes in Him. That is why it is through Him that we utter our Amen to God" (2 Corinthians 1:20). But God's Word is fulfilled in another way too. Since it speaks to all people and to all times, it perpetually finds situations where its meaning is directed to specific individuals and becomes a message from God to them in their particular circumstances. The Holy Spirit interprets the Word. He opens our eyes and makes us exceptionally wise. He can convince us and make us feel ashamed. He can fill us with a comfort and a joy that is out of this world.

Lord, open my eyes and my heart so I receive Your Word. I don't want to hear anything but Your voice. Take all my thoughts from me, everything that is mere human thought or personal opinion. Give me Your Holy Spirit's help so I hear what You want to say. Help everyone You've chosen to be servants of the Word. Give them the gift to understand and the gift of explanation. Bless everything that will be

*said now during Christmas. You know who will
hear it. You know what we need to hear most. Let
us hear the Word. And let us understand that You
are the one speaking.*

FRIDAY AFTER
THE THIRD SUNDAY
IN ADVENT
Isaiah 11:1–10

There shall come forth a shoot from the stump of Jesse, and
a branch from his roots shall bear fruit. Isaiah 11:1

This prophecy inspired the Christmas hymn, "Lo, How
a Rose E'er Blooming." Isaiah—which in Greek means
Jesse—was David's father. A branch from this root means
a descendant of David's. And the stump refers to the overthrown kingdom.

Some 2,700 years have now passed since the prophet
spoke these words. At that time, David's direct descendants
still had been ascending to the throne in Jerusalem in direct
succession, but then their kingdom was overthrown and their
successors lived as poor insignificant individuals. Jesus really
emerged, "like a root out of dry ground" (Isaiah 53:2).

We have seen only half of this prophecy's fulfillment.
God had caused the Branch from David's root to grow. The
Spirit of the Lord rested upon Him with wisdom, understanding, power, and knowledge that no other man has ever
possessed. He came with a judgment that affected people

much more profoundly than human eyes can see. He could say: "You have heard that it was said to those of old, . . . but I say to you . . ." (Matthew 5:21–22). His words penetrated as only God's Word does, so that selfishness was unveiled and the conceited stood in shame. But there was something else about His judgment. The word for *to judge* in Hebrew also means to govern, to lead, to restore, and to help. The Branch from Jesse's root would "with righteousness . . . judge the poor" (Isaiah 11:4). The profound meaning behind this verse was revealed when Jesus walked among sinners. His judgment became what Paul calls a righteous judgment. He, who alone was righteous, gave and shared His life, His peace, and His position as a child of God.

This half of the prophecy has been fulfilled, but the second half remains. It refers to a paradise: a world where there is no evil, a world where we don't persecute one another, where there is nothing to fear, where nothing kills and nothing dies. It's a creation without the fall into sin, a world like this one was when it was first formed by the Creator's hand, "And God saw that it was good" (Genesis 1:10).

Christ will also fulfill this half of the prophecy. We can say with the prophet, "For still the vision awaits its appointed time; it hastens to the end—it will not lie. If it seems slow, wait for it; it will surely come; it will not delay" (Habakkuk 2:3).

I thank You with my whole heart, Lord Jesus, that I may experience this Advent. I thank You for Your arrival. I thank You because You came to our world and became our Brother. What would I have known about God if You had not let me see Him? I thank You that You now make Your entrance and come every day. I thank You because

You come to seek and save those who are lost. I
thank You because You will come once again in
the future on Your glorious day. You will make all
things new and put an end to all evil and create
new heavens and a new earth, where the righteous
will live. Blessed are You who came in the name
of the Lord.

SATURDAY AFTER THE THIRD SUNDAY IN ADVENT
Zechariah 9:8–12

The Lord is at hand. Philippians 4:5

Tomorrow is the fourth and last Sunday in Advent.
Christmas is knocking at the door. The deeper meaning is:
Christ stands at the door and knocks. We begin to understand
that when we listen to the prophetic message, as we have for
the last three weeks. What God has done in the past concerns
us also. It isn't just something that has happened. It's something that is continuously happening. Jesus still walks on the
earth and travels throughout our country. He does it in the
words that describe His arrival two thousand years ago. The
Gospel is the image in which Christ is visible. The Word has
become the feet of the One who brings Good News, the feet
that carry Him over the mountains. It isn't just a story from
ancient history that we learn at an early age and remember
as we get older. It's current history, something that happens
to us. It's a course of events occurring in the here and now.

Christ really does come to us now, while we celebrate His birthday and Christmas.

The Lord is near! The children are counting the days to Christmas. We are also children. But the great Christmas Eve we look forward to is the wonderful day when Christ comes—not concealed in His Word, but manifested in His glory. Maybe we will see that day while we are still here, with the eyes that see the Christmas tree and lights in church on Christmas morning. Maybe we will see it when we wake from death's sleep. We look forward to it. The future is always uncertain. We do not know what will come, but we know who will come. The Lord is near! Behold, your King comes to you. Righteous and victorious is He.

My Lord and my King, I pray that You make Your entrance as King into my heart also. There is a throne in my heart that is Yours. I'm afraid that my old Adam has often been seated there. I've made my own decisions and wanted to live my own life. But now I pray that You take the place You alone should have, You who are my Creator and Savior. You have come into this evil world because You want to save and liberate us. You shed Your blood that we may live. I read in Your Word: for the sake of the blood of Your testament we, who were captives, can now be released out of this hole that lacks living water. If we're prisoners, at least we're prisoners who have hope! So liberate me, Lord, first from all my guilt and then from everything that wants to hold me back and drag me away from You. Finally, take me from this old world into Your new world where all the struggling is over and only Your will is done.

FOURTH SUNDAY
IN ADVENT
John 1:19–28

Among you stands One you do not know. John 1:26

An envoy of distinguished people, priests, and Levites, had come to John the Baptist from Jerusalem. They had traveled down through the hill country and the blistering heat of the Jordan valley. Now they approached him with an important question: Who are you? The question wasn't asked disrespectfully. The prophetic power in John the Baptist's word was unmistakable.

John began by putting an end to the rumor that had been circulating. No—he was not the Messiah.

Then who was he? Elijah possibly? It was written in the Scripture—in the very last verses of our Old Testament—that God would send the Prophet Elijah before the great day of the Lord.

Again John denied it. Strangely enough, Jesus would later say that John really was the promised Elijah. Obviously, John didn't think that highly of himself, but Jesus knew he was the voice of the one who called in the wilderness, the voice Isaiah had spoken about. It was enough for John merely to be a voice calling out in God's service. He knew he had been sent before Someone else and that everything depended upon the One who was already there. He stood among men, although they did not know Him. John told them this also.

These words are applicable today. The Lord is near, He is among us. But do we know Him—this Jesus, whose birth we now celebrate? For many He is still unknown. Perhaps they have heard of Him or even learned quite a bit about Him, but people so often have humanly distorted pictures and thoughts;

maybe of a "sweet Jesus," a sentimental, weak, and romantic dreamer. It may also be a picture of a surreal miracle worker, a wizard of sorts, or maybe a pale figure of our imagination. All this is the result of disconnected recollections, faded pictures in the mind with transient extensions and third- and fourth-hand thoughts.

The next day John would have the opportunity to say: Behold, there He is. "Behold, the Lamb of God, who takes away the sin of the world" (John 1:29)! The result was that the first disciples began to follow Jesus. That's what John wanted. Everything depended on this fact: that people would learn to know Jesus as He really was.

This is what we do now when we follow Jesus from His birth to His ascension during this part of the Church Year. Many who have are able to say with Job, "I had heard of You by the hearing of the ear, but now my eye sees You" (Job 42:5).

Lord, I pray to You for a real Christmas, a good Christmas, as only You can give. Everything we prepare for now is only a reminder of the most unprecedented event in the world. All gifts should remind us that we received You as a gift from God. And all joy should be joy that we live in a world where You also lived, under a heaven You opened for us. Lord, let Your peace protect our hearts amidst all the haste and busyness of this season. Lord, let Your presence fill the hours of the days, everything we do and everything that makes us happy. And help those who don't know You to also see a ray of Your light and know how good it is that we have You among us.

MONDAY AFTER THE FOURTH SUNDAY IN ADVENT
Luke 1:1–25

The time is fulfilled. Mark 1:15

Jesus said this when He appeared before the people with God's Gospel. Paul sums up what happened the first Christmas in these words: "But when the fullness of time had come, God sent forth His Son" (Galatians 4:4). The preparations were complete. They had taken a long time. Now God at last accomplished what He had planned the whole time.

Luke begins his Gospel by describing this fullness of time. It was the final days before the first Christmas in world history. The preparations had been made. Israel had survived every storm. The people were certain that the God who had chosen them was the Lord of the whole world. There were Jews all over the Roman Empire, which encompassed most of the then-known world. They had obtained a certain amount of attention, something like reluctant respect, for their belief in God. Some considered them fanatics; others were drawn to their church services and wanted to hear more about this holy and invisible God, who was completely different from the variegated and deficient Roman gods whose statues filled the Roman temples.

Many in Israel took God's Word seriously. Zechariah and his wife were among them, as were those who belonged to "the silent in the land," the ones who waited for the consolation of Israel. They were very conscious of the fact that God had the right to make the demands He did. Even if they were among the ones who were considered above punishment and who carefully tried to fulfill all the Law's demands and regulations, they were also deeply conscious of the fact that no one could stand before the Lord, who sees into our heart and knows all our desires and thoughts. Therefore, they also took great care regarding temple service. All the different types of sacrifice were decreed by God. They could thank God with them. They could also acknowledge that they had broken God's commandments and deserved to suffer His punishment, although now instead they were allowed to carry out a sacrifice of propitiation that was firmly grounded in the Law of Moses. Many thought that all this was a useless custom or possibly a sort of business transaction with God. But for many others it was a deeply personal confession of sin and of the heart's need for forgiveness. The groundwork was prepared. It only had to be gone over one last time. This was the task John was called to do. The priest Zechariah was allowed to know that now, in his old age, he would receive a son who would prepare the way of the Lord.

How could Luke know all this? We read his own explanation: "Just as those who from the beginning were eyewitnesses and ministers of the word have delivered them to us, it seemed good to me also, having followed all things closely for some time past, to write an orderly account for you" (Luke 1:2–3). Since he spoke of many remarkable things that never happen in our everyday life, some thought that he—like Matthew—was spinning a yarn. The Greek world had many different stories about sons of gods. Many of the Greek Christians would have considered it logical to try to explain Christ's gloriousness in this way. However, these parts of the Gospels have an altogether distinctly Hebraic background. This is obvious both in the language used and the ideas expressed. These ideas must have been recorded very early, while there were still Jewish Christian parishes in Palestine. Here—maybe while Mary still lived or among people who knew her and Jesus' brothers—Luke gathered this information and recorded it for us. This happened because God wanted us to know it.

Lord, I thank You because I have been able to know that even Zechariah doubted the message he received from You. I, too, would have doubted it. I know well enough that You are capable of anything, yet it is hard to believe that something so incredibly different than I am accustomed to seeing happen would be possible. But everything depends on You. You, of course, are the One who controls the laws of nature. How then can I believe that they control You? For Thine is the kingdom and the power. Praise be to Your name because You used Your powers to let Your Son enter this world and become man for our sake.

TUESDAY AFTER THE FOURTH SUNDAY IN ADVENT
Luke 1:26–45

But when the fullness of time had come, God sent forth His Son, born of woman, born under the law. Galatians 4:4

"For nothing will be impossible with God," the angel said to Mary (Luke 1:37). Even Mary hesitated. That isn't so strange. What was going to happen now was something that had never happened before and would never happen again.

When the time was fulfilled and God intervened in our world, He did it in a manner that was altogether extraordinary, entirely and completely unique. You can't argue against what is recorded about the birth of Jesus by saying: Things like that don't happen; we have never seen anything like that before. This is precisely what the Gospels say. Things like that would never have happened otherwise. It happened only once, when God sent His Son and let Him be born of a woman.

When you read the first two chapters of Luke, you can't avoid thinking that Luke must have heard this from Mary herself, or at least from someone who was very close to her. Everything is told just as Mary must have experienced it. The events in Nazareth, her long journey to Judea to see Elizabeth, the trip to Bethlehem and the census, and her baby son's presentation in the temple are recorded just as they must have been seen through Mary's eyes. It all becomes alive and particularly moving when it is read against this background.

Lord Jesus, I thank You because this picture of Your mother has also been preserved in the Gospel. You were born of a woman as all others are. You had a mother that gave birth to You. Lord, it is so far beyond my understanding, this miracle that You, who are God and Lord of all heavens, once rested in Mary's arms as a helpless little child. You received the care her hands could offer. You needed it then. You, who take care of us all, the Shepherd and Caretaker of our souls, You Yourself were swaddled as a child. You did all this so You could come into our world and become one of us. You, the Lord of all things, were subjected to the law established for our sake. You took upon Yourself everything we had to bear. I praise and thank You, Mary's Son. You, who were born of a woman and subjected to the law for our sake.

WEDNESDAY AFTER THE FOURTH SUNDAY IN ADVENT
Luke 1:46–56

Blessed is she who believed. Luke 1:45

Mary is an example of a person of faith for us. She is given a place in the Christmas Gospel and by every Christmas crib. She herself could say: "From now on all generations will call me blessed" (Luke 1:48). Yet too much has been made of these words in many areas of Christianity and Mary has become an intercessor, a helper in all trouble, and a mediator of God's grace. All this honor is due to her Son. We should not take that from Him. But we can consider Mary blessed because she believed.

It could not have been easy for her to believe that it would happen like the angel of the Lord told her. It wasn't believable because it was contrary to the laws of nature. It wasn't believable because she was just a poor woman in Galilee. People must have thought that if God were ever to enter the world, there are so many other homes and so many other environments that would have been more worthy and would have given the Savior a better start in His life on earth.

Mary must have pondered these things. You can read a portion of the answer she received in her prayers in the Magnificat that is part of today's text. God has a way of turning our expectations upside down. He can reject what looks powerful and influential in our eyes and in the world, and He can choose and use what appears to be nothing. He has a different standard of measurement than politicians and economists, and a different standard of measurement than the champions of piety and zealous role models. There is an insignificance, an impoverishment, a yearning emptiness, that feels worthless but has true faith. To believe is always a need for God, confidence in His mercy and power, a conviction that He knows and wants what is best for us. Faith makes us open and receptive. This is how men of faith become instruments of God. True greatness exists in those who expect great things of God and allow Him to do great things with them.

Lord, dear heavenly Father, when I look upon the great things You have made, things that go far beyond anything I can fathom, I can only praise Your name. I praise You because You sent Your Son into the world; because You let Him come here in the way You did. I praise You for the awesome miracle that You let Him become man, that You let the fullness of Your whole kingdom live in the body of a mere man. And I thank You for the very greatest of all miracles: that You have let all the blessedness and all the life that came to the world with Him come closer to us so it also lives in our hearts and in our lives.

THURSDAY AFTER THE FOURTH SUNDAY IN ADVENT
Matthew 1:18–25

"Behold, the virgin shall conceive and bear a son, and they shall call His name Immanuel." Matthew 1:23

From Luke we learn about the events surrounding the birth of Jesus the way Mary must have experienced them.

From Matthew we encounter the same events the way they likely appeared to Joseph. Matthew doesn't hide any of the shock that Joseph must have experienced when his betrothed was found pregnant. Betrothal in Israel was as binding as marriage. It could be terminated in the same way. Joseph had the right to serve his betrothed divorce papers. He could have made the matter public, running the risk that Mary might have been punished as an adulteress. If worse came to worst, an adulteress could be stoned to death. But Joseph was an upright man and didn't want to cause a scandal, so he considered finding a way to arrange the divorce in secret. Then he received a revelation in a dream. God can make use of dreams, but this doesn't mean that all dreams have a revelation. On the contrary: the Scriptures say that dreams can be deceitful. Sometimes, though, God uses dreams to reach us, and that is what happened to Joseph.

Joseph took Mary and her child home with him. Therefore, the child, according to Jewish law and justice, became Joseph's heir and descendant. The boy Jesus then belonged to the house and line of David.

Matthew reminds us that Isaiah had prophesied about a virgin who would be with child and bear a Son. The Boy would be called Immanuel. In Matthew we can see how Jesus and His contemporaries read the Bible—and how we should read it. There is a bigger picture that affects the individual words. Often they are written in such a way that they have a deliberate double meaning. The names *Jesus* and *Immanuel* mean the same thing, just as so many Jewish names have shared meanings. There is often a confession, a prayer, or an expectation in the name given to a child. In the name *Jesus*, there is an attribute, a prophecy about this child's mission: "For He will save His people from their sins" (Matthew 1:21). Immanuel has the same significance; it says that God is with us. The word has often been misused. It has been given the meaning "God agrees with us," that He stands by our side when we engage in conflicts or even in war. But it has a much deeper meaning here. God should really be against us for the way we've behaved, broken His Commandments, gone against His will, and destroyed His creation. He has every reason to be against us and to let us bear the consequences of our fall. But He is on our side. He made our loss His loss. He descended to us to live with us, to suffer with us, and to share all the consequences of our evil actions with us. All this has happened through Mary's Son. This is why He received the name Jesus, the Savior.

My Lord and Savior, You who are Immanuel, God's outstretched hand, a helper in distress whom none of us deserve. I have been opposed to You so many times. There is something in my heart that will not stop opposing You. There is something inside me that wants to resist doing Your will. You know best Yourself, Lord, how often I have done, acted, spoken, and thought contrary to what I should have. And yet You are not against me. You have come here and stood by my side. Not to bolster my ego but to save my lost cause and make it possible for me to follow You to Your Father. You, Lord, know best how little my promises can be relied on, but You see that I love You. You know You are my joy, my comfort, and my wonderful consolation. I thank You because You came into the world and because You have come to stand here by us and be with us.

FRIDAY AFTER THE FOURTH SUNDAY IN ADVENT
John 1:1–18

The Word became flesh and dwelt among us. John 1:14

"In the beginning was the Word." John began his Gospel with these words. He purposely began the same way the Old Testament begins: "In the beginning, God created the heavens and the earth" (Genesis 1:1).

John says to us that Jesus already existed at that time. He is eternal like His Father. Through Him, everything has come into existence. When He came into the world on Christmas Eve, He came to His own, to the world He Himself created. I, too, belong to this world. Even I have been made by the Savior's hand. Nothing has come into being without Him. He has a purpose for my life.

But why does John call Him the Word? An entire book could be written about this. There is a similarity between Christ and the Word. God's Word isn't just "empty words;" it is not the mere names for things. It's a creative Word, full of God's own power, of His Spirit and life. When it emanates from God, God is a part of it. Therefore, the Word can give everything God can give. It's the same way with Christ. All that God is and has, wills and does, lives in Christ. The creed says He is "the only-begotten Son of God, begotten of His Father before all worlds, God of God, Light of Light, very God of very God, begotten, not made, being of one substance with the Father" (*LSB*, Divine Service, Setting Two).

We need to keep this in mind to get an idea of what is implied by "the Word became flesh and dwelt among us." Here flesh means whatever is created, whatever consists of molecules and atoms, the same kind of molecules and atoms that are found in the air and the water, stone, and clay. The term for the Word becoming flesh in academic language is incarnation. The Creator became a part of His creation. The Lord of the whole world made His dwelling in a man's body. God's Son became a human child — so we could become God's children. Through this great miracle an even greater miracle has become possible: God can dwell in our hearts with His eternal life.

Lord Jesus, I pray to You now for a great miracle: That You be born in my heart also and make Yourself at home with everything You've brought with You from Your Father. Lord, it is the greatest and most incomprehensible of all miracles that You, with Your glory and Your love, with Your purity and Your zeal, would be able to live in me, a sinner. Lord I am not worthy. You know this better than I do myself. But You became a man just so this very thing would happen. So I pray to You: let it happen. Do this miracle for me, for Your name's sake, because You are the Savior that You are.

SATURDAY AFTER THE FOURTH SUNDAY IN ADVENT
Luke 2:22–32

I see Him, but not now; I behold Him, but not near: a star shall come out of Jacob, and a scepter shall rise out of Israel. Numbers 24:17

The Bible reading from Luke today is also the reading for Candlemas Day (February 2), but it is included here for the sake of continuity. Without it, the texts about Jesus' childhood are hardly understandable. It gives us a picture of the people who waited for Jesus. They waited "for the consolation of Israel" (Luke 2:25). They were often poor, like Joseph and Mary. They knew the Law and the prophets well. They knew what God had done, and they knew what God would do. God had, of course, spoken in the distant past. Almost a thousand years before, when Israel was still on its way to Canaan, one man named Balaam had been hired by King Balak to curse Israel. But God overpowered him, and to the king's great displeasure, Balaam had to bless those whom he was paid to curse. And when he blessed them, he, as a prophet, saw the future and spoke glorious words about what he saw coming—not then however, and not in the near future. He saw a Star coming from out of Jacob and a Scepter rising out of Israel. Many after him saw the same thing. The pious in Israel knew it would happen. He would come from David's descendants, and He would be born in Bethlehem. Old Simeon had been promised that he would not die before he saw the Lord's anointed. *Messiah* means exactly "the anointed." Kings and prophets used oil in the inauguration of their offices. The Messiah would be greater than all the prophets and kings. He would be anointed with God's own Spirit.

Maybe now we can understand the words Jesus spoke to His disciples and to us: "For I tell you that many prophets and kings desired to see what you see, and did not see it, and to hear what you hear, and did not hear it" (Luke 10:24).

I can never thank You enough, Lord, for my being able to see and hear this. You have allowed me to celebrate Christmas again. I would never have been able to do it, if You hadn't fulfilled Your promise when the time was right. Now I will no longer belong to those who see with seeing eyes but still don't understand. I pray to You for open eyes to see only what You wish to reveal and receive only what You wish to give. I will not be unthankful. Only You can teach me to be thankful from the heart. Stretch out Your hand, Lord, and make Your mark upon my forehead so I never forget You and never waiver from what You've allowed my eyes to see, and my ears to hear.

SUNDAY AFTER CHRISTMAS
Luke 2:33–40

Please note: This Sunday can sometimes be replaced by either Christmas Day or Boxing Day, and if so, there are separate devotions for these days at the end of the book. During the coming weekdays or by next Sunday, New Year's Day will have occurred, which also has its own devotion. You should read all other devotions on their respective weekdays. There is also a separate devotion for the first day of Epiphany, which ought to be mentioned here, since the day could fall already on Saturday of this week.

"Behold, this child is appointed for the fall and rising of many in Israel, and for a sign that is opposed." Luke 2:34

Simeon blessed them, but what a strange blessing! There will be struggling around her Son, and a sword would even pierce Mary's soul.

That's the kind of strange blessing that comes through Jesus. He will be the dividing factor. He stands there like a rock, forcing the river to divide. The coming of Jesus is not pleasant assurance that everything will be fine. It's a cry that says God's kingdom is near! Now is the day of salvation! Help is here, the only salvation that makes it possible for all to be saved from wickedness.

Many thoughts of the heart are revealed here. The appeased, the contented, and the self-righteous are offended; He's a stumbling block for them. But the poor, the hungry, the unfortunate, the exposed, and the destitute come with amazement and thankfulness that this is possible. They see an unfathomable gift is offered to them here.

Anna, Phanuel's daughter, of the tribe of Asher, also came. She was a prophetess, one of the devout adherents to the Old Covenant who had insight into the ways of God, who understood the signs of the times and could interpret what happened. She also spoke of a peculiar blessing. She embodied it. She was one of the world's most fortunate people, which was really unbelievable. She married in her youth, like most in Israel at that time, then was widowed after seven years. After that, she voluntarily lived her long life as a widow. She lived in the temple. She literally lived there, probably in some little closet she was allowed to have to herself. She had few needs. She fasted for long periods of time. She lived only to be near God in His temple. This, too, can be a mission in life: to witness to the joy of believing in God and knowing you are His, a treasure that makes it possible to exist with nothing else and not miss it. She belonged to those who were still waiting, and yet she was so joyful that she was radiant. And we? We who are living in the fulfillment of time? What she saw a glimpse of in her 84 years has filled our life since childhood. How much happier, then, should we be? And how much have we already learned from those who were happy to wait because it was God they waited for?

Many thoughts of the heart will be revealed through
You, Lord. What is it that will be revealed in my

heart when I stand before You? I am beginning to at least imagine it. First, there are several things that have little to do with You but have been very important to me. They have filled my days and my heart. Many of those things have been bitter and painful. I don't like them. Yet I cling tightly to them. I have no power over them. I think about them when I am awake, and they keep me from sleeping. There is only one thing that could have power over them and that is You, Lord. When You come into my heart, when I know that You are in my presence, when I think about You and speak with You, then everything else has to get out of the way. Therefore, I pray that You come. You know how helpless I am otherwise. I ask You for the blessing of Your presence. I ask You for the fortune and joy to be Yours.

MONDAY AFTER THE SUNDAY IN CHRISTMAS
Matthew 2:13–23

"Out of Egypt I called My Son." Matthew 2:15

As always, the evil one tried to thwart God's plans. He tried to remove Jesus from the world again. Herod, the dictator with his suspicious nature and hunger for power, was a willing instrument. It suited his interests. The newborn King of the Jews should die.

But God saw through Herod's plans. Joseph gathered his young family and fled in the middle of the night to Egypt in order to save the baby's life. Jesus was a refugee.

So Herod died, and finally the day came when Joseph could return. But not to his family in Bethlehem; there the son of the tyrant would've been less than six miles away. Joseph chose to go back to Nazareth, despite the fact that he was a foreigner there, too, and the town had a bad reputation.

Matthew knew his Old Testament. He read it in the same way Jesus and all the devout people of that day did. What once happened to God's people would happen again and lead them forward. God had at one time led Israel out of Egypt. Egypt was the land of bondage, but it was also the richest and most powerful land, the land of bodily comforts, the land that was full of wisdom, of fortune tellers and secret arts, of temples and remarkable creations from highly developed techniques. In all we call civilization, Egypt excelled over Israel by leaps and bounds. But God chose what was small in this world and let the strong be put to shame. When He led Israel out of Egypt, He knew that the Word He had given His people was more than anything the world could offer. And just as He, during the time of Moses, had triumphed over all of Egypt's wisdom and all of Pharaoh's military power, He showed again, when He brought His Son out of Egypt, that His weakness was stronger than men's strength—as Paul said in 1 Corinthians 1:25. He showed that He had called His people, His Son, and His Church out of the spiritual Egypt, out of the security of creature comforts, away from the wisdom that demands guarantees for everything. His kingdom is not of this world. That's why it can't be conquered.

When God makes His plans work, He can afford to squander. The children in Bethlehem died so Jesus could live. The Church has always recognized them as the first martyrs. That means that those who gave their lives for Jesus also received life—eternal life. God can give a hundredfold again in His kingdom. He can dry the tears that desperate and tormented human beings shed in this world. This is precisely what He will do when He opens the kingdom's gates for us, where there will be no more worries or complaints or persecution.

It's so wonderful, Lord, that You were also a refugee as a child, who in the last hour was saved from a great massacre in the city where You were born. You have been a peer and a brother to all the world's poor refugees. I know that You understand them and Your heart goes out to them. You Yourself were one of them. And You are with them even today. Let our hearts also go out to them and to all the others who suffer because of human cruelty. Give us companions in this work who have both understanding and compassion, and give us all a great willingness to do what we can, faithfully and with perseverance, as long as there are those whom You desire to reach with Your help.

TUESDAY AFTER THE SUNDAY IN CHRISTMAS
Hebrews 1:1–14

He is the radiance of the glory of God and the exact imprint of His nature. Hebrews 1:3

We don't know who wrote Hebrews. Some suggest it was Paul, but that's highly unlikely. Luther guessed it was the devout and learned Apollos, who was mentioned in Acts. In any event, whoever is speaking here is someone who was close to the apostles and understood them. Here we can see how someone during the generation after the death of Jesus began to get a perspective of everything that had happened since He came into the world.

First we read that God had, in the past, spoken through the prophets many times and in many ways. Now, however, He spoke in an entirely new way: He spoke through His Son. This has a very unique status in the universe. Jesus is the reflection of God's glory and the image of His being. God's glory is the unspeakable, unattainable light-penetrating radiance and joyfulness in God's nature that our eyes cannot see without becoming blind. However, Christ is a reflection of God's nature. We can see the Father in Him. We can see His salvation, like old Simeon did.

Once again we read that Christ is not created. The angels are created. We should not picture the heavens as empty. God is not just a supreme idea. He's a living being and loves to surround Himself with life, to fill it with fortune and joy. Beyond our world there is another. Jesus speaks about it often. There are living beings that exist in the presence of God. They sing and rejoice.

But Christ is something else. He is eternal like His Father. He is outside of time. Time belongs to creation. The world has a beginning, when the years began to roll on, but God is above all that. We live here as prisoners in time. Time slips inevitably away from us and inevitably consumes the number of days we've been apportioned. We aren't the only ones who grow old, the world also grows old. It will also wear out. But Christ is always the same; His years will know no end. In God's world, we are above the passage of time. There, we never have to remember anything with a sigh because it is hopelessly past and can't be changed. There, existence is always filled with new meaning. To exist is always a joy. This is what is called eternal life, and this is what Christ has come to give us.

Lord Jesus, You will remain when everything else passes away. You also rule over time. You created it. You are not bound by it. You stretch out Your hands and reach from the world's beginning to its end. You have the same power over what has been as You have over what will come. They're both that close to You. In Your kingdom no one counts the days. No one needs to hold on to happiness. I can't fathom it, and yet You want even me to experience it. You Yourself have stepped into time in order that I would be able to step into eternity. It's more than anything I could thank You for, and yet it's only a small part of everything You have done for me. Praise be to Your name in everlasting eternity.

WEDNESDAY AFTER THE SUNDAY IN CHRISTMAS
Hebrews 2:1–18

He is not ashamed to call them brothers. Hebrews 2:11

We may have difficulties calling some people "brothers" or "sisters." We may do it with our lips, but our heart is hard, both emotionally and intellectually. There are people who are so completely different. They can have so many bad habits, such a lack of hygiene, such a lack of the simplest concepts of justice that it can seem impossible to have anything truly in common with them. Yet the difference between them and us is nothing compared to the difference between us and God. Nevertheless, Scripture says about Christ and man: "He is not ashamed to call them brothers."

We have become so accustomed to this fantastic thought, we have heard so many times that Jesus loves us (such as in today's reading from Hebrews), that we don't really comprehend the implications. The first Christians did, however. When Christ came to us as our Brother, it meant He would suffer death. We were so different and so far away that the abyss could not be bridged with anything less than Christ's death. He partook "in flesh and blood" (Hebrews 2:14) so He, who was God, would be able to suffer and die. It was really the only way that "He might destroy the one who has the power of death, that is, the devil" (Hebrews 2:14). Here we encounter the dismal fact that we come across with every step of Jesus' life. There is a power that destroys God's creation. It's a real power. It must be brought to its knees. We can't handle it alone. Christ became one of us in order to help us. He suffered, and He was tempted. He met the other power to "deliver all those who through fear of death were subject to lifelong slavery" (Hebrews 2:15).

Many try to escape this bondage by simply not thinking about death. They stick their head in the sand. There are those who have never seen a dead person. But nothing can change the fact that our lives become shorter every day. Death is the only certain thing in our future. For every year that goes by, more and more sand falls through the hourglass, and there is no way of knowing how much is left. Death holds us fast within its grip. There is no opportunity for escape.

But the seriousness of death's power is something no one can imagine. What's crucial is that there is Someone who has power over death. Just as there is a good will behind life, there is an evil will behind death.

It's good for us that we have Christ!

Lord Jesus Christ, You became man so You could be my brother. You let Yourself die so I could also be a child of Your Father. You intervened in this evil world and were plagued by temptations and death just like us so we would be able to be free from all that plagues us now. I ask You to help me not to be afraid, as I no longer need to fear. Help me not to cling to what must be left behind and will not prevail anyway. Lord, I thank You because I no longer need to worry about the death that waits for me because I know that I have a Father in heaven who waits for me, and that You will take me by the hand and lead me to Him. What else do I need as time goes by, when I know I have You? You remain and Your years have no end.

THURSDAY AFTER THE SUNDAY IN CHRISTMAS
Hebrews 3:1–19

Today, if you hear His voice, do not harden your hearts.
Hebrews 3:7

You can harden your heart, the author of Hebrews says.

He must have seen frightening examples of that kind of hardening. He comes back to this several times and emphasizes that it can go on for so long that you will no longer be able to return and receive forgiveness. God comes to meet us. He longs after His children. He sends invitations to us and prays we will feel welcomed at His house. He never did it so consciously and with so much affection as when He sent His Son into the world. It's not easy to say no to Him, but it's possible. There is something called "an evil unbelieving heart" (Hebrews 3:12). Even if you've been able to see and experience all God has to give in the way of forgiveness and mercy, you can still tear yourself away and "fall away from the living God" (Hebrews 3:12). But this doesn't happen unless you harden your heart. You can make your heart so hard that it is frozen solid. Then you have become hardened and nothing more can help you. Hebrews says about men like these that it's impossible to come back to repentance. Jesus warned people like this about the sin against the Holy Spirit. They were people who had been allowed to see all of His good deeds. They couldn't deny His miracles, but they said: "He is possessed by Beelzebul" (Mark 3:22).

This was very clear to the original Christians. God had done His best. After sacrificing His own Son, He could do no more. If they still didn't want to receive, it was hopeless. We find that there was an example of this in old Israel too. The generation that was brought out of Egypt and saw God's enormous deeds but still fell to temptation in the desert was not allowed into the Promised Land. The reason was obvious—they were unable to enter because of unbelief: "In spite of this word you did not believe the LORD your God" (Deuteronomy 1:32). It's the same way with us. If we can't enter heaven, it's because of our unbelief. There isn't any great sin that can't be forgiven. Jesus made it possible. But no one enters without forgiveness.

Help us, Lord, never to harden our hearts when You
speak. If we try, let Your voice speak even louder.
Let there be a fire therein that burns us. Give us
no peace and no tranquility. Let us know that we
are wandering in the dark and soon will no longer
be with You. Have mercy on us all, on our parish,
and on our people. You have every reason to be
tired of us. You Yourself have said that You will
chop down a tree that does not bear fruit. But You
have also prayed often for the tree that bears no
fruit. Therefore, we ask You for another year and
for the understanding to cherish it. For that, we
need Your grace and Your help, Lord. Give it to us
for Your mercy's sake.

FRIDAY AFTER THE SUNDAY IN CHRISTMAS
Luke 3:1–9

A baptism of repentance for the forgiveness of sins. Luke 3:3

John the Baptist's preaching had aroused an enormous
sensation. People flocked from all around to hear the new
prophet, the first to set foot in Israel for centuries. Many
believed he was the Messiah, but he denied it. He was only a
forerunner, a path maker. After him One would come who
was stronger: the Messiah Himself. God's kingdom was near.

This is what caused all the commotion. The Messiah
would, of course, restore David's fallen house. For many Jews
it was evident that this would involve a political revolution

and a national rebirth. Israel had lost its independence. They lived in an occupied country. The Messiah would free His people and drive the oppressors from the land.

John worked hard to correct these thoughts. Belonging to God's people did not result in political privileges. It wasn't enough to be a child of Abraham. Belonging to God's people meant being God's servant. Therefore, there would be a settling of accounts and an inquisition. The ax was put to the root of the tree.

This is why John baptized. His Baptism was a Baptism of repentance for the forgiveness of sins. It meant acknowledging that they belonged to a sinful and fallen people, that they had broken the covenant with God, and that they repented, acknowledged their sin, and prayed for the forgiveness of sins. That was the forgiveness they hoped for when the Messiah came to save His people.

All baptism is not alike. The Baptism Jesus instituted, the Baptism we received, is different from John's Baptism. If we were to look for something in our life that reminds us of John's Baptism, the closest would be the confession of sins before Communion. But there is still a big difference: John and those who gathered around him waited for the Messiah. We know He has come. He is among us.

Lord, You can raise up the children of Abraham from dead stones. You had mercy on us, who weren't Your people, and allowed us to share in the Gospel too. You also stretched out Your hand to me and included me in Your people, although I did not have the right to belong to them. You have awakened my dead heart to life so I can believe in You. You have made me a child of Abraham so I can know that I am included in Your good thoughts and Your saving work. Maintain this faith in my *heart, and let me live with You and for You all the days of my life.*

SATURDAY AFTER THE SUNDAY IN CHRISTMAS
Luke 3:10–20

He who is mightier than I is coming, the strap of whose sandals I am not worthy to untie. He will baptize you with the Holy Spirit and with fire. Luke 3:16

John made a distinction between his Baptism and the Baptism the Messiah would bring with Him. "I baptize you with water, but . . ." there is a better Baptism, a Baptism in the Holy Spirit and fire. A Baptism that is entirely God's work.

John's Baptism was something people performed in repentance and obedience to show that they submitted to God's judgment and sought His salvation. John's Baptism was an act of obedience. Those who were shaken and saw the light through John's preaching of repentance all asked themselves: What should we do?

For our salvation's sake, we can and should hear what God says and listen to His voice. We can speak to Him in prayer. The Bible, the divine service, and daily devotion all belong to the life of a Christian. We can also do our best to practice putting into action what we hear. This is what John told people to do when they asked him for advice.

What is most important, however, is something we cannot do. We can't achieve faith and new life. God must create that.

Lord Jesus, I pray to You with all my heart for two things: that You help me do what I can do and that You do to me what only You can do. Make me faithful in the little that I am able to do. Make me faithful in Your Word and persistent in prayer. Remind me when I am negligent. Help me to gladly do the work that You give me the opportunity to do. And then, dear Lord, do everything I can't do and can't achieve. Ignite faith in my heart and keep it alive. Renew my desire. Open my eyes. Let my barren fig tree bloom and bear fruit. All to Your glory.

SUNDAY AFTER NEW YEAR'S DAY
Matthew 3:13–17

It is fitting for us to fulfill all righteousness. Matthew 3:15

Jesus came from Galilee to be baptized by John in the Jordan River. John refused for a good reason: his Baptism was one of betterment for the forgiveness of sins, a Baptism for sinners who hoped for their Savior. It was fitting for everyone except Jesus.

But Jesus insisted that He be baptized too. All righteousness would be fulfilled.

What did He mean by this?

Here we come to the central aspect of Christ's work, something we see again and again in the New Testament. He would not only be a teacher or an example. He would also be a Savior and a Redeemer, who completed everything His brothers neglected and violated, and who took all their guilt upon Himself and finally suffered and died in their place. He would fulfill all righteousness and show that God's Law is really valid. Yet at the same time He would make it possible for all those who had broken the Law to be liberated from all their guilt.

That's why Jesus also wanted to be baptized. It meant He identified Himself with guilt-ridden humanity. He didn't put Himself above us, although He could have. On the contrary, He subjected Himself to judgment. He took part in penance and made our burdens and guilt His own.

That's how Jesus was baptized. His Baptism was different. It wasn't only a Baptism by John and it wasn't quite the same Baptism that He Himself instituted. It was a Baptism of consecration into His work of salvation. At the same time, a voice from heaven proclaimed that He was God's beloved Son. The Spirit descended upon Him—not because He didn't possess the Spirit before this, but to show that He was the Messiah, to show that He was anointed by the Holy Spirit. Jesus was consecrated into the work that would now follow. This Baptism also consecrated Him into a different baptism, one He would later endure: the baptism of death, the agonizing and sufferable baptism into death. This was all a part of His work of salvation. He was now dedicated to this work.

I thank You, my Lord and Savior because You were like us in this way. You alone had the right to say You were without guilt and did not deserve to suffer anything. Yet You did not separate Yourself from us. Instead, You became our brother and shared everything with us. So I pray now that I may share everything with You. I want to share in all the good You have done and in all the disgrace

*and burdens You want me to bear during my time
on earth—if it now must be so and if it can be of
use to someone or be to the glory of Your name.
I surrender myself into Your hands and pray only
for this: that I may be with You, belong to You,
and serve You.*

MONDAY AFTER THE SUNDAY IN THE NEW YEAR
John 1:29–42

"Behold, the Lamb of God, who takes away the sin of the
world!" John 1:29

Why did the Baptist call Jesus the *Lamb of God*?

It's possible he was thinking about a prophecy about the
Lord's suffering servant, who would be beaten on account of
our misdeeds and whose life would be a sin offering. It was
written that He would be tormented. The prophecy spoke
of Someone who was persecuted, who did not open His
mouth, just like a lamb led to the slaughter. A person could
hardly hear or read such a passage in Israel without thinking
about the sacrifices in the temple. They were commanded by
God. They were a reminder of how serious it was to violate
God's Commandments. If anyone rebelled against God and
broke His Law, they would certainly die, but God allowed
for a sin offering to be brought forward in place of the
person's death. The sin offering allowed people to acknowledge their sin and their need for forgiveness. It is written in
Hebrews that these sacrificial regulations were "a shadow of

the good things to come" (10:1). They were "external regulations applying until the time of the new order" (Hebrews 9:10 NIV). In these sacrifices was a "reminder of sins every year" (Hebrews 10:3).

John was saying that the time was now ready for the sacrifice that would once and for all atone for the sins of the world. Jesus would now accomplish what the old sacrifices could not by sacrificing Himself. The Baptist was the forerunner, proclaiming the great King's arrival. He could only baptize with water. His Baptism was a preparation, much like sacrificial service in the temple. But now the Messiah would come with God's own Spirit, and He would bring with Him the forgiveness John and his disciples were waiting for. He would baptize with a new Baptism, the Baptism in the Holy Spirit.

John also tells us that many of Jesus' disciples first learned to know Him by the Jordan River. They had been aroused by the Baptist's preaching and were among those who were instructed by him. They experienced what the Gospels later so emphatically pointed out: that the Baptist had come to prepare the way for Jesus. The Baptist was adamant. He preached the Law. However, since he constantly pointed to Christ, he became the forerunner for the Gospel. Law and Gospel belong together in the same way as the Baptist and Jesus. The Law prepares the way for the Gospel.

Oh, You, God's Lamb, who takes away the sins of the world, I come to You with everything I never get done by myself. For the sake of my pride and self-esteem, I would've liked to have been able to do it myself. It is so humiliating that You had to bear my burdens and die in my place. I wanted to come as a champion or as a good and faithful servant

who did everything You commanded, but now I see
that it doesn't work that way. Now I thank You
because You take responsibility for me and my lost
cause. Help me believe so firmly in You that I stay
as intimately close to You as You desire.

TUESDAY AFTER THE SUNDAY IN THE NEW YEAR
John 1:43–51

Come and see. John 1:46

We read here how Jesus called His disciples. He did not ask them what they believed or investigate how they lived. He never had to ask about these things. He knew the answers from the beginning, whether it was righteous men like Nathanael or God's problem children like the Samaritan woman. Neither faith nor deeds were of importance. Jesus had come to help. He came to the sick who needed a healer. That is why He always began by saying, "Follow Me." That meant the same thing as "Come and see." Who is Jesus? What does He desire, and what is He capable of? You can learn these things only from experience. There's no sense in sitting around wondering what is possible or probable. What can you compare it to? Someone like Jesus comes only once. He can't be compared to anything we have known before.

Phillip understood this. When Nathanael wondered if anything good could come from the notorious city of Nazareth, Phillip simply answered, "Come and see." There is no better answer even today, when people come with objections and theories that explain and excuse why they don't have time for Jesus.

The command to come and see pertains to all disciples and throughout life. There's always something new to discover. When Nathanael was impressed and surprised at Jesus' knowledge about him, Jesus said, "You will see greater things than these" (John 1:50). This statement remains true all through life. We will never learn everything. There is always something new to discover. There is only one thing we need to see (and it is necessary): we have to come to see, to constantly return to the Gospel and to Jesus Himself, to listen to the Word and speak with God in prayer. We will never cease being astonished over everything that is still to be discovered. And the biggest surprise is yet to come, when we can see Him as He is.

My Lord and Master, I thank You because You let me come and see with my own eyes. Here I come now, Lord. Open my eyes and my heart so I can see. There were so many who saw You and still missed seeing You. Give me an open heart that can receive You and eyes that can see You. Let me follow You so I see with my own eyes and hear all the voices and experience what happened and become one of them who walks with You.

WEDNESDAY AFTER THE SUNDAY IN THE NEW YEAR
John 3:22–4:2

"Therefore this joy of mine is now complete. He must increase, but I must decrease." John 3:29–30

We read about Baptism again in today's Bible reading. It was at the very beginning of Jesus' ministry. The Baptist had not yet been thrown into prison, and Jesus had not yet begun the sermon in Galilee that the other evangelists tell us so much about. He was still in the southern part of the country. During this time, His disciples were baptizing too. John emphasizes that Jesus Himself did not baptize. He had not yet instituted the Baptism the apostles would take out into the world. We don't know anything more about the baptisms described here. Presumably, they were a continuation of John's Baptism, the groundwork for what was to come.

In any case, there were already lots of people gathering around Jesus, even more than those around the Baptist. And, as is so often the case in spiritual movements, human jealousy came into play. There were those who were offended on the Baptist's behalf and looked to him for support. But they weren't successful. The Baptist let them know that this was the way it was supposed to be. John was not the Messiah; he was not the Bridegroom. The bride was a picture of God's people, God's chosen and beloved people. Only the Bridegroom, the Messiah Himself, had the right to the love of those people. The Bridegroom's friend and forerunner could stand aside and be glad that people now gathered around their rightful Messiah and Lord. So the Baptist said something that is true for every Christian life: It is as it ought to be. He shall increase, and I shall decrease.

This is how the Christian life should be. The Christian should decrease. In the beginning you may think you should grow, constantly feeling stronger, purer, wiser, and better, but the opposite often happens. You begin to distrust yourself and your own resources. You see how much weakness, cowardice, and selfishness still remains, but you receive a greater confidence in Jesus. You learn to trust all the more in Him, in His Word, in His faithfulness and help in the vicissitudes of life. Consequently, you become stronger, wiser in faith, and more persistent in affliction. That's because you begin to depend more and more on Christ and, therefore, possess more and more of Him. Faith and wisdom increase when you decrease and He increases.

I pray to You now about this, dear Lord Jesus. I pray for more and more of Your mercy. Take from me all that trusts in me if it prevents me from trusting in You alone. I am almost afraid to pray about this, Lord. I know that it hurts when You humiliate my pride and ruin my plans. But I know that it is a healthy and blessed pain because it prepares a place for You inside me and teaches me to be Your servant rather than my own master. So I pray that You fill my heart, my thoughts, my will, and all of my life so I may live in You, through You, and for You.

THURSDAY AFTER THE SUNDAY IN THE NEW YEAR
Matthew 28:18–20

Baptizing them in the name of the Father and of the Son and of the Holy Spirit. Matthew 28:19

Today we have taken a big step, from the beginning of Jesus' life all the way to the end of the book of Matthew. The reason we did this is to discuss Christian Baptism. We talked about John's baptizing. We heard about the Baptism of Jesus. But neither of these baptisms is a direct equivalent to the Baptism through which we ourselves entered God's Church.

Christian Baptism was instituted by Christ Himself. It was instituted by the Resurrected One, and it has great meaning. It wasn't until Christ suffered, died, and was resurrected for the propitiation of the world's sins that the time was ready for Baptism in the name of the Father and the Son and the Holy Spirit.

The Resurrected One commanded His apostles to go to the ends of the earth, to all nations, and promised to be with them until the end of the world. This was also a command to every generation for as long as this world remains. The Gospel is to be preached to everyone, and people should do as the disciples of Jesus did and be brought up in His Church. We become disciples by being baptized. Those who were baptized would also be reached by Jesus' own calling to follow Him. And just as His disciples were taken up into a living fellowship with Him and could take part in His life, so could all people throughout time have a vital, life-giving relationship with Jesus Christ.

This is also the significance of Christian Baptism. It's something far more than John's Baptism. John's Baptism was one of repentance; it was something people did. The

Christian Baptism is a Baptism of salvation; it's something God does. John's Baptism was an act of obedience, something people did to show that they listened to God's Word and were willing to repent and wait for salvation from God. The Christian Baptism is an act of election, a calling from God, through which we are taken out of the world and brought into a relationship with Christ.

Lord, I am beginning to understand that faith is far more than I can imagine. I thank You because You were there long before I had any idea about You. I thank You because You came to me. You laid Your hand on me and took me as Your disciple into Your kingdom, long before I could pray a prayer. I thank You because I cannot remember the first time I heard Your name mentioned. And I thank You even more because You did something to me that is far more than anything my intellect can understand. You, who laid Your hands upon the children and blessed them, have also touched me. I have received Your blessing. The world doesn't see it, but it is more than anything the world can give. Let this blessing stay with me, follow me, and surround me until my last day on earth and eternally ever after in Your kingdom.

FRIDAY AFTER THE SUNDAY IN THE NEW YEARS

Romans 6:3–11

Do you not know that all of us who have been baptized into Christ Jesus were baptized into His death? Romans 6:3

Today we read a part of Paul's letter to the Romans. It might have been taken a bit out of context, but it's an important part of what we're talking about now: Baptism. Here, Paul is mainly speaking about the implications of Christian Baptism and shows us a new and important side of it.

Paul tells us that we have been baptized into Christ's death. Maybe we recall that Jesus Himself spoke about a baptism He must go through—a baptism of agony and death. He was consecrated into this baptism through His Baptism in the Jordan.

Now Paul tells us that our Baptism is connected to this baptism. "We were buried therefore with Him by baptism into death" (Romans 6:4). We will understand more about what he means later. Here, it is made clear that everything that happened to Christ and through Christ when He died became ours when we were baptized. Christ died for us. He redeemed us from our sins. Now we are united with Him. What He did is now ours.

We really do unite with Him, Paul says. "We have been united with Him in a death like His" (Romans 6:5). We have been grafted like branches to the vine. We have become members of His body. We are incorporated as living stones by the Spirit's wonderful establishment.

That means we are united with Christ. We will grow together with Him all our lives. Just as He rose up to live a new life, we also rise up every morning and live with the Resurrected One. We live through Him and for Him. That is the meaning of Baptism.

My Lord and Savior, I thank You because it is not I who have chosen You, but You have chosen me and made me a Christian. I thank You because You have taken me, a shoot on a wild vine, and grafted me onto Your noble vine, the only vine that can bear fruit that never perishes. I thank You because it is Your life and power at work in me. For no one but You could ever soften up my hard wood and give life to my barren, rotten stem. It's more than I can ask for. Therefore, I heartily thank You because I know You wanted it this way. Your good will be done everywhere, always and also with me.

SATURDAY AFTER THE SUNDAY IN THE NEW YEAR
Titus 3:4–7

He saved us . . . by the washing of regeneration and renewal of the Holy Spirit. Titus 3:5

Was my Baptism as a child really a proper Baptism? There are those who contest that. They generally take for granted that our Baptism is similar to John's Baptism: an act of obedience performed in penitence and faith. But Christian Baptism is something quite different: It's something God does when He saves us and creates a new life within us. It's a great miracle that He does this, and the miracle is just as great for a little child as for a grown person. We make no contribution to the miracle. We can only put obstacles in its way. Whenever it happens, it's entirely God's work.

That's what Paul says in the text we read today. God didn't save us based on any good and meritorious works we might have done. He saved us solely through His mercy, and He did it through Baptism, the washing of regeneration, where He renews us in the Holy Spirit.

Now we might be able to understand why the Baptist said that Jesus would baptize with the Holy Spirit and fire. The words allude first and foremost to Pentecost, when the Holy Spirit, as tongues of fire, came to the apostles. At that time, it fulfilled the promise the Resurrected One had given them some days earlier: "John baptized with water, but you will be baptized with the Holy Spirit not many days from now" (Acts 1:5).

Through the Baptism of Spirit, the apostles became the Spirit's instruments. The Church became the Spirit's temple. Now they could preach with the power of the Spirit, and they could baptize. Earlier they had not baptized anyone with Christ's Baptism. But now they could baptize with the Baptism that means birth into a new life and renewal in the Holy Spirit. This is the life Jesus speaks about in the parable of the vine and the branches. It's the life that flows through His body, the congregation, where we are members. Therefore, Jesus could say that he who is least in the heavenly kingdom is greater than the Baptist, the greatest of the prophets. Through Christ, something entered the world that had never been there before. It's a gift, pure and simple. It can never be earned. Our reason, our willpower cannot help us receive this life. We can only receive it as children, whether we are children or adults.

Dear Lord Jesus, I praise You because You became our Savior through Your Baptism. I praise You because You have invited me to take part in Your salvation through my Baptism. Long before I was born, You bore my sins upon Your cross. And in Baptism You took me into Your death and Your new life. Now I need not die because I took part in Your death. Now I may live with You. I thank You for Your boundless mercy. Help me show my thankfulness in the way You desire and to those who need it most.

FIRST SUNDAY IN EPIPHANY
Luke 2:41–52

So I have looked upon You in the sanctuary, beholding Your power and glory. Psalm 63:2

Jesus prayed this prayer many times, ever since His child-hood. Already at the age of twelve, He spoke of the temple as the place where His Father lived. He also confirmed what the prophets had already said: the Lord is in His holy temple.

One can wonder how God can be a certain way in a particular place. He is everywhere, but there is something special about what is called His *revelation*. God operates in the world through visible and audible things. We Christians call them *means of grace*. We have them in God's Word and in His Sacraments. The fact that we can call our church God's house is because it is a consecrated and special place, where the Word is preached and the Sacraments are administered. It's also a meeting place, where God comes to meet us and where we meet Him face to face. It's a place consecrated for prayer and worship. Therefore, the tranquility therein is not just a nice custom but something God desires. Jesus has confirmed this. We see it in the way He regarded the temple as holy.

The means of grace are not the only ways God reveals Himself. The entire earth is full of His glory. The presence of God is in all created things, but He has a particular presence in the temple. The Bible is a witness to this. David tells of how he longs to see the glory of God and to behold His temple. He calls the temple of God the "place where [His] glory dwells" (Psalm 26:8). And we sing: "Holy this temple where our Lord is dwelling; This is none other than the gate of heaven. Ever your children, year by year rejoicing, Chant in your temple."[6] The atmosphere of worship—created by the vaulted ceilings where the architectural lines reach toward the heavens, stained glass windows that color the light, glowing candles with flickering flames, paraments at the altar, and the thrum of the organ's chords giving life to song and describing different moods—can hardly be expressed in words. But it all contributes to a feast in the abundance of God's house.

So I thank You, Lord, for the wonderful miracle that You live here among us on earth. The heaven's heavens cannot contain You. You hold all the worlds in Your hand. There is room for the whole universe there. And still You descended to us with all Your grace and all Your mercy. Give me, now, a heart that realizes this. Take away my indifference, open my eyes, and help me to receive. When I am critical and cold and unwilling, let Your glorious power overcome my selfishness and my laziness so I can rejoice in Your presence and help others understand how wonderful it is to be able to

---

6. *Lutheran Worship* 323:2, "Only-Begotten, Word of God Eternal."

stand before You, to know Your presence and be glad that You are who You are.

MONDAY AFTER THE FIRST SUNDAY IN EPIPHANY
John 2:13–25

He said to them, "It is written, 'My house shall be called a house of prayer' but you make it a den of robbers." Matthew 21:13

With these words, Jesus justified driving out the vendors from the temple and overturning the moneychangers' tables and the dove handlers' seats. Jesus seldom took such drastic actions. It caused resentment. The vendors and moneychangers were conducting lawful business. They sold sacrificial animals. They exchanged foreign coins for the Jewish shekels that were used to pay the temple tax. Yet Jesus drove them out. Mark tells us that He would not allow anything to be carried through the temple. He would not even allow people to carry their merchandise through the shortcut across the wide forecourts. And we hear His explanation for this: this was God's house, and it was supposed to be a house of prayer.

It was no accident that Jesus quoted the prophets. The Old Testament teaches us why God gave His people a temple. He is Lord of the world and heaven, and the highest heaven cannot contain him (see 1 Kings 8:27). For our sake, He created a meeting place to be built here on earth, a place where He promised to reveal Himself and present Himself to us. Therefore it is written: "Be silent, all flesh, before the LORD, for He has roused Himself from His holy dwelling" (Zechariah 2:13). And the psalmist said, "One thing have I asked of the LORD, that I will seek after: that I may dwell in the house of the LORD all the days of my life, to gaze upon the beauty of the LORD and to inquire in His temple" (Psalm 27:4). And, "O LORD, I love the habitation of Your house and the place where Your glory dwells" (Psalm 26:8).

This is what is meant by God living in His temple. He chose a place upon earth and said, Here I will come and reveal Myself to you. For this reason, it is a holy place, consecrated for meeting with God.

So we can also pray with the psalmist:

How lovely is Your dwelling place, O LORD of Hosts! My soul longs and yearns after the LORD's courts, my soul and my body rejoice to the living God. The sparrow has found a home and the swallow a nest for herself, where she may lay her young: Your altar, O LORD of Hosts, my King and my God. Blessed are those whose strength is in You, whose hearts are the highways to Zion. For a day in Your courts is better than thousands elsewhere. I would rather be a doorkeeper in the house of my God than dwell in the tents of wickedness. How precious is Your steadfast love, O God, the children of mankind take refuge in the shadow of Your wing, they feast on the abundance of Your house and You give them a drink from the river of Your delights (from Psalms 84, 36, and 26).

TUESDAY AFTER THE FIRST SUNDAY IN EPIPHANY

Luke 4:14–30

And as was His custom, He went to the synagogue on the Sabbath day, and He stood up to read. Luke 4:16

This is what we are told about Jesus when "He came to Nazareth, where He had been brought up" (Luke 4:16). It was His custom since He was a child to go to the synagogue on the Sabbath. Apparently, He kept this custom as an adult as well.

Sometimes people speak disparagingly about church customs, implying that if they are "only" customs, they are of no value. The mistake is not remedied by breaking with custom, however, but by filling it with content. The New Testament never speaks badly about the church's customs. On the contrary, it tells us that Jesus' devout parents faithfully observed good customs. They brought the child Jesus forward in the temple in order to "do for Him after the custom of the law" (Luke 2:27 KJV). And every year they journeyed the long way to Jerusalem for Passover, as was the custom for the festival. There is only one custom that is criticized, and it is "neglecting to meet together, as is the habit of some" (Hebrews 10:25). There are good and bad customs. Not attending worship is a bad custom.

As a child, Jesus went to the synagogue in Nazareth Sabbath after Sabbath. He went there as an adult as well. There "He stood up to read." The Divine Service Jesus experienced in the synagogue was the basis for the Swedish high mass without communion.[7] The Divine Service was rich with Jewish customs. Jesus and His apostles were, of course, Jews. During their Divine Service, the Law and the writings

---

7. Divine Service without Communion

of the prophets were read, the psalms were sung, their faith was confessed, and they prayed the usual prayers, like our collects and general church prayers. But there was no priest. The Old Testament priests served by sacrificing in the temple in Jerusalem. The synagogue's Divine Service was led by laymen. The synagogue's director was rather like a modern church's elder or trustee. His job was to find people to read the Scriptures. Sometimes, when there was someone capable of teaching, there would be some instruction, like a sermon. Reading the Scriptures required a lot of training in and of itself. The text was, of course, in Hebrew, which wasn't spoken in everyday life. It consisted only of consonants. It was to be read or sung in a ceremonious manner, with particular accents and tonal quality. We don't know how Jesus mastered that art. We do know that it must have been in part by attending the Divine Service regularly and diligently listening to others. It's also probable that He attended some sort of school.

It's not an accident that Jesus is an example and guide in loving and diligent attendance to the Divine Service.

Lord, You know how lazy I can be. You know how I resist going to church. There is a part of me that opposes everything You desire. Lord, You know this well. You were also a human. You also sat through the long Divine Service. Yet You heard Your Father's voice. You knew He was there, and You desired to be where He was. Give me that kind of mind and heart. When I am reluctant, let me catch a glimpse of You in order that I may know what I ought to do. And so I pray to You, Lord, that You will help our clergy instruct correctly so we may hear Your voice. Help us to listen to Your voice, and not the voices of those who speak.

WEDNESDAY AFTER THE FIRST SUNDAY IN EPIPHANY

Matthew 4:12–25

And immediately on the Sabbath He entered the synagogue and was teaching. Mark 1:21

Jesus called Peter, Andrew, James, and John. They left their nets, their boats, and old Zebedee. They knew something great and important was about to happen. But what?

"And immediately on the Sabbath He entered the synagogue. . ."

That's how Mark describes it. Jesus started teaching without delay, from the very beginning. This is why He said to them: "Follow Me" (Mark 1:17). They were invited to come along and listen. He had something of infinite importance to tell them. Today, we don't have to leave our homes and jobs to hear Jesus. You can find Him everywhere in our country. But even today He takes us to a place where He can teach us.

A lot has changed since Jesus' time on earth. The Sabbath is now observed on Sunday; the synagogue has become the church. But the fact that He teaches, that He is sent to us with a message for all of us, has not changed. He still says to us today: "Follow Me." If we want to have anything to do with Him, we have to listen to His teaching.

The Word says, "[Jesus] began to teach" (Mark 8:31). There is a special meaning to these words. The teaching was done in Aramaic, the language of the country that everyone spoke and understood. It was important that everyone was able to understand. The Holy Scriptures were always read in Hebrew. Jesus could also speak Hebrew. Ever since He was a child, He could recite large portions of Scripture by heart.

But since the Scriptures needed to be understood, they were interpreted into the common language. This is comparable to the situation today. Anyone who has read the Bible knows it can be hard to understand at times. That's why we have instruction during the church service. So that's why Jesus still today says to follow Him to the Divine Service where He teaches.

Lord, I pray that You would also take me along and teach me. You know how much I need it. There's so much I don't understand. But I want to think and believe only what You tell me. I trust in You. It's Your voice I want to hear. I want to stay close to You. I pray that You will let me hear things that can open up my eyes to see. I pray that You will take me where I can hear You teach. Awaken my heart so I can understand what You say. I want to know more. Help me so this happens.

THURSDAY AFTER THE FIRST SUNDAY IN EPIPHANY
Mark 1:14–22

And they were astonished at His teaching. Mark 1:22

They didn't think it was amazing that a carpenter from Nazareth stood up to teach. Lots of devout people felt at home with the Scriptures, and Jesus from Nazareth was one of them. Divine Service in the synagogue was a service for laymen. Here in Capernaum, Jarius was the leader, and the synagogue was crowded as usual. The men stood on the stone floor with the women up above them in the balcony. Up front were the carved wooden cabinets containing the scrolls of the Torah. The reader would step forward and take a scroll of parchment from the cabinets, unroll it and read—or chant, as we would say. It was like half singing, in East Asian melodies, rather like Gregorian songs.

Neither was it surprising that Jesus—like other laymen acquainted with the Scriptures— explained what He had just read with a few words of admonishment. But something different happened here. His proclamation had power and authority unlike that of the scribes. He didn't refer to any of the great rabbis. He didn't just repeat what others had said. He spoke directly on God's behalf and said: "I say to you." The unprecedented message was that God's kingdom was near. The time was ready for everything to be fulfilled. God's dominion was to be established. Therefore, there had to be repentance. The Baptist had already said it. But now there was something more: faith in the Gospel. The Baptist spoke about a wrathful judgment that was at hand, about the ax, which was put to the root of the tree. But now there was something different, something more: joyous news, God's invitation to those who labored and were burdened, to the abused and outcasts, for all who knew that they couldn't stand under the harsh scrutiny of the scribes. Here was something that glowed and shimmered with sheer joy!

I've felt this joy, Lord. Let it shine in my heart and warm me. I know that I don't deserve it. When You speak with power and authority, I know how I should be. And You know, Lord, that I am not like that. It's too great and too much. I wanted to *say: leave me, Lord, I am sinful. But You see, Lord, that I can't say that. Nothing would make me more unhappy than You turning Your back on me and leaving me alone. Therefore, I come to You with everything I cannot, am not, and am incapable of. I have only one hope and one way out: You, Lord. Speak Your powerful and authoritative words to my anxious and timid heart so I can believe in You with such a deep faith and joy that everything else becomes small in comparison and the impossible becomes possible. This I dare pray for because I know who You are.*

FRIDAY AFTER THE FIRST SUNDAY IN EPIPHANY
Mark 1:23–28

And immediately there was in their synagogue a man with an unclean spirit. Mark 1:23

Mark is telling us this story. Mark interpreted for Peter and followed him on his journeys. He tells us what he heard from Peter. Peter accompanied Jesus at that time. It was at a synagogue in his hometown of Capernaum. Jesus preached with power and authority. The Divine Service had just ended when a sharp cry cut through the crowd of people. It was a possessed man, one of the many people in Palestine suffering from mental illness. We don't often see people affected this way today, but it is common in other parts of the world.

This disease can make a person stiff as a board or give him convulsions. They might speak in strange voices or be strangely lucid and unpleasantly outspoken. At this time in history, people were convinced that there was an evil spirit at work here.

Now the possessed man began to cry, "What have you to do with us, Jesus of Nazareth? Have You come to destroy us? I know who You are—the Holy One of God" (Mark 1:24). Naturally, there was great commotion. "But Jesus rebuked him, saying, 'Be silent, and come out of him' " (Mark 1:25)! Then the evil spirit, shouting angrily, left him. At last, the man became himself again, speaking normally and in a calm voice. Then everyone began to ask in astonishment: What is this? He commands even the evil spirits, and they obey Him.

This happened in the synagogue during the church service. It was Jesus' peculiar words—words with power and authority—that had this strange effect. There are other spirits that possess us, and we know they can be very evil. They know very well who their worst enemy is—the wonderful Holy One of God. They are aware of His threat. They engage in the conflict, sometimes to the point where you can hear their choleric voices a long way away. But what happens then?

Lord, what happens then? You know how often we suffer defeat. The evil spirits refuse to yield. Were we too afraid? Too selfish? Did we not trust in You? Did we not dare to believe? Lord, I know that You possess power and authority. Let it come to me. Let it sweep through my heart and sweep everything away that prevents You from reigning therein. Lord, provide us with Your servants *today, who can speak Your Word with power and authority, the Word that really is Yours. The Word that makes evil shy away and makes all of us ashamed yet at the same time happy and joyous over Your intervention. The Word that puts us in our place and shows us how wonderful it is that You have the kingdom and the power.*

SATURDAY AFTER THE FIRST SUNDAY IN EPIPHANY
Mark 1:29–45

And immediately He left the synagogue and entered the house of Simon and Andrew, with James and John. Now Simon's mother-in-law lay ill with a fever. Mark 1:29–30a

When the church service was over, they returned home from the synagogue as they always did. There, the hardships of everyday life awaited them as they always do. Peter and the others had invited their new Master to be their guest, but now Peter's mother-in-law was feverishly sick, making it difficult and worrisome for Peter. It was hard to entertain guests in a cramped room and with a sick person there, but after seeing what happened in the synagogue, they thought it might be possible for the Master to deal with this matter also. "And immediately they told Him about her" (Mark 1:30). They probably didn't dare directly ask Him to heal her, but He understood. When He came into the house, He went immediately to her, "took her by the hand and lifted her up, and the fever left her, and she began to serve them" (Mark 1:31). And so, their anxiousness abated for the time being.

Last Sunday dealt with Christ and the temple, and we have returned to this subject again during the week. Tomorrow, a new week dealing with Christ and the home begins. There's a connection here, just like the time in Capernaum, and here we come across something very important right from the beginning. We have our own annoyances, our own small embarrassing difficulties waiting for us at home. They don't seem to have anything to do with the Church Year, but they do.

Thank You, Jesus, for allowing me to speak about these matters too. You know what I mean. You know everything so well, even the things that are hard to speak about. I can bring matters before You that I am embarrassed to tell others about. I come to You even with the small annoyances I grieve over and don't want anyone else to know about. I am glad that You know about them and that I can talk to You about them. You are the only one who can help me with them. You can take away what is really terrible: my guilt. So first I ask that You forgive me, and then I pray that You would help me with everything else. Guide me with the things I can't do anything about. Guide my heart so I do what I can in the proper manner, willingly and with a joyous heart. All to Your glory.

SECOND SUNDAY AFTER EPIPHANY

John 2:1–12

The wine ran out. John 2:3

At the very beginning of Christ's ministry, He and His disciples attended a wedding in the Galilean town of Cana. There, something disastrous happened to the host and hostess: They ran out of wine. Someone had miscalculated, or maybe they couldn't afford more. Now something was about to happen that we all dread: total shame. What would the guests think? What kind of rumors would be spread in the neighborhood?

We know how Jesus intervened. It was a great miracle, completely unbelievable for us. But let's remember that it's John who's telling the story. He was there. John lived for many years and died in Ephesus somewhere around the year 100 AD. His Gospel must have been written by then. A fragment of it found in the desert sands of Egypt has been dated to the beginning of the second century, if not earlier. By then this event was already well known among Christian congregations at a time when the last eyewitnesses still lived (or in any case, a large number of people, who knew them and heard the stories from them). We're presented with the same things that amazed the disciples in Cana: occurrences that went against everything we experience in everyday life, but are still factual. John himself drew the conclusion: This was Jesus' first miracle. He did it in the Galilean town of Cana and revealed His glory in this way, and His disciples believed in Him.

But let us ponder the reason behind Jesus' miracle: a small irritating mishap threatening a respectable Galilean family with great shame. This Sunday in the Church Year used to be called "Home Sunday" because it emphasizes Jesus' relationship to our home life, and now we immediately see what Jesus has to do in our homes. He is there—even during the trivial annoyances of everyday life. Christ descended into our everyday life when He became man. This is how He really shows us who He is. His glory is revealed to us not only on the Mount of transfiguration, but as a helper and a friend at the very center of every day's prosaic reality.

> *Lord, I would like to learn the art of holding Your hand and receiving Your help, at a time when the world seems to act as if You don't exist. Teach me to be like Your mother. Even she spoke to You about the wine that had run out. Remind me to speak to You about small annoyances and shameful things. I badly need the reminder she gave the servants: to do everything that You say. It's You I desire to listen to. Help me to do that and to remember the most important things of all when I need them the most.*

MONDAY AFTER THE SECOND SUNDAY AFTER EPIPHANY
John 4:1–19

A woman from Samaria came to draw water. John 4:7

It was at Jacob's well near Sychar, a town on the way from Jerusalem to Galilee. Jesus rested there. He was tired. It was about the sixth hour—twelve o'clock—and the sun burned its hottest. Then a woman from the village came carrying a heavy clay jar of the kind used for fetching water.

Jesus began to speak with her. He didn't ask if she was a Samaritan (self-respecting Jews did not associate with or speak to Samaritans). He began to speak in parables, as He often did. Parables like this one enabled people to understand things in ways they had never thought of before. He spoke about the water that quenches our thirst forever, water that becomes a spring flowing with eternal life inside us. This interested the woman and she wanted to have this water.

Then Jesus said for her to go and get her husband. It was perfectly natural that He would say that. We know, of course, that Jesus taught that man and wife are insolubly united. If the woman desired to receive this strange water of life, then it would be best if her husband received it also. But there was another intention behind Jesus' words. They played on the woman's conscience and moved her to speak about something she hadn't intended to. She tried to evade the subject a little by answering: "I have no husband" (John 4:17). Jesus confirmed this without a harsh word but very revealingly replied, "You are right in saying, 'I have no husband'; for you have had five husbands, and the one you now have is not your husband. What you have said is true" (John 4:17–18).

These words were enough for the woman to admit that Jesus was right. She possibly heard the same reproaches before from her conscience or her community. Although Jesus formulated the words more mildly and leniently, He said them in a way that cut to the heart. That's the way He is. When one comes close to Jesus, the idea of marriage becomes remarkably clear. It's God's desire that a man and a woman love each other and live their whole lives together. This isn't only to make themselves happy, but to bring happiness to each other. Their task in life is to help each other, make each other happy, and to benefit from each other. People have thousands of objections. Jesus says only: That's the way it is. He says it with all the authority of God's divinity.

We aren't given the opportunity to hear how this Samaritan woman put her life back together. The Gospels don't provide long lists of instructions for tricky situations such as these. It's not the instructions that solve the problems. Instead it's a new kind of love, a love first and foremost for Jesus. He doesn't come with a new moral code, He comes with mercy. And where mercy and rejoicing burst forth, there is always something new.

Lord, let Your mercy and Your joy fill us wretched people so we can, in all our confusion and all our difficulties, rejoice first and foremost that You are here among us. Help me come to You, Lord, when I don't know what to do. You, of course, do know. You've always known. You know even before anything happens. You knew it the day You baptized me. And yet, You still want me to belong to You. You laid Your hand upon me, and took me as Your disciple. So I pray, Lord: Thy will be done. Let it always be done in my life. Let it be obvious and convincing in my thoughts and allow it to have the power over my will, now and forever.

TUESDAY AFTER THE SECOND SUNDAY AFTER EPIPHANY

Luke 19:1–10

"Zacchaeus, hurry and come down, for I must stay at your house today." Luke 19:5

Zacchaeus wasn't prepared for this! He had gone to see Jesus because he was curious like everyone else. Maybe he had a particular reason. Rumor had it that Jesus was a friend of publicans and sinners, and Zacchaeus was a publican. Even by today's standards, he probably would be considered a despicable person. He collaborated with the occupational force and on their behalf extorted taxes from his own people. Zacchaeus had made his choice. He made a lot of money and was quite successful. He even became a foreman of the publicans. He didn't go to the synagogue. He was an outcast, but he had an expensive house and a huge income. And maybe he also had a miniscule longing for God at the bottom of his heart, something he probably didn't even want to confess himself.

And then this happened! Jesus stood under the tree Zacchaeus had climbed and looked directly at him. It was just as if He had gone out that morning only to meet Zacchaeus.

And that's what He did! He said the very same thing later that evening: "For the Son of Man came to seek and to save the lost (Luke 19:10). And so He chose this particular expensive and scorned home in Jericho.

And Zacchaeus? Jesus did not come for him with a moral lashing, but with mercy and rejoicing. And it did the trick. Zacchaeus stepped forward and said to Jesus: "Behold, Lord, the half of my goods I give to the poor. And if I have defrauded anyone anything, I restore it fourfold" (Luke 19:8).

It's not hard to imagine that from this day on, something new came into this fine home in Jericho. "Today salvation has come to this house," Jesus said in Luke 19:9. Before it was the fine carpets, beautiful clothes, good food, and all the money that gave the house its character. Now there was a different tone, a happier, safer, and warmer tone, and these are the things that make a home a nice place to be.

Lord, do I dare invite You to my home? I believe I do. You came to Zacchaeus because he was a son of Abraham. I have also been baptized by Your own hand. You decided it, not me. If You came then, I know You won't say no now. So I pray that You come with mercy and rejoicing. Let it fill my heart and my home. Come Lord, and fill everyday life and the silence and emptiness, conversation and laughter, work and business. Come, Lord Jesus.

WEDNESDAY AFTER THE SECOND SUNDAY AFTER EPIPHANY
Luke 5:27–39

And Levi made Him a great feast in his house, and there was a large company of tax collectors and others reclining at the table with them. Luke 5:29

"There was a feast in Capernaum." You may have heard this old expression. Few know where the expression comes from, but it is really worth knowing.

On this morning Levi, who was also called Matthew, sat as usual in his tollbooth and collected taxes. Here, as in Jericho, there was a well-traveled trade route where caravans from the East passed. So King Herod used this place to collect taxes. The publicans also took their share, lining their pockets whenever they got the chance. But Jesus came, this wonderful Jesus, who, although He was a great prophet, didn't turn up His nose at common sinners. Then something wonderful happened. Jesus went over to Levi, not to pay him, but to talk to him. He only said two words: "Follow Me." That was enough. Had a Pharisee said that, Levi would've expected a scolding and he would've been reluctant to follow. However, it was God's ambassador who stood there, the One everyone was talking about, and He really wanted Levi to become one of His disciples. A wretched publican, whom most had given up for lost to both man and God, was going to be a disciple of Jesus.

Levi got up and followed Him. That evening, Levi prepared a great feast in his home. His friends, the publicans and various other sinners, harlots and notorious types, came to this feast in Capernaum. There wasn't any bellowing and hollering at this feast, but an unmistakable joy mixed with amazed wonderment. Is it possible? Does God really care about people like us?

Yes, God really does. That's reason enough to feast every day.

If that's the way it is, Lord, then I must believe that I can be with You also. Thank You, for inviting me to Your feast. Thank You, for opening the door. Thank You, for having such wonderful guests. That's the way You want it. You invite the lame and crippled, blind and disabled, publicans and sinners. Help me never to turn up my nose at those

You have invited. Help me never to gaze with disdain upon Your goodness. Rather, help me rejoice in Your divinity so it fills my thoughts and reflects in all I say and do. This is, of course, the way You want it to be, and I thank You for that.

THURSDAY AFTER THE SECOND SUNDAY AFTER EPIPHANY
Luke 6:1–16

Do not be anxious about your life, what you will eat or what you will drink, nor about your body, what you will put on. Is not life more than food, and the body more than clothing?
Matthew 6:25

People were celebrating around Jesus. His enemies called Him a glutton and a drunkard. John the Baptist and his disciples had fasted. They were strict and lived a life of privation. But Jesus and His friends were not the same as John the Baptist. When someone criticized Jesus for this, He answered: Can the wedding guests fast as long as the bridegroom is with them? When God visits His people, when we have His Ambassador among us, there is a celebration.

This is what Jesus means when He tells us not be anxious. Naturally, it doesn't mean that we shouldn't think about or plan for tomorrow, but we needn't be anxious. We don't have to worry about what is going to happen. Unbelievers worry about tomorrow because it isn't easy living without God. The entire responsibility is their own and there is so much they have no control over.

But now God is among us. He's asking about us. We know the moment we take His outstretched hand that we are not alone. We can't tell God what to do. He decides that Himself. We are confident that He knows what He wants for us and that it's what is best. He was the One who gave us this life and body. He wanted us to live as His children. All other gifts pale in comparison to the gift of being His children. We know that God guides us one way or another. Jesus was able to celebrate with His disciples, but He could also send them out without money, shoes, or even a knapsack. When they returned, He asked them: Did you lack anything? And they answered, "nothing."

There are always problems at home: the household budget, health, and numerous other small or big conflicts. We can't avoid these problems, but we need not create problems. We can handle these problems the same way Mary handled the problem of the wine in Cana or the way Peter handled the problem with his sick mother-in-law when he didn't know if she would recover. They took the matters to Jesus. We should do likewise, no matter how small, common, or annoying the problem seems to be.

With this promise, I come to You now, Lord Jesus, and lay everything down before You. Take me into Your hands. You know what it's all about. You were also a man, in a poor home. They say that Your city had a bad reputation. It couldn't have been easy living there, with all the cursing, taunting, and fighting in the streets. You know all this, Lord—just as we know it. I thank You for the light

*that shined on Your mother; she did not have it
easy either. I thank You because You let us know
that Your own brothers once thought You were
crazy. There is nothing You don't understand.
That is why I dare to come to You with everything
and thank You: because I can.*

FRIDAY AFTER THE SECOND SUNDAY AFTER EPIPHANY
Luke 6:17–31

"Let the children come to Me; do not hinder them." Mark 10:14

This was a severe reprimand to the disciples. They thought children should wait until they were able to understand what the sermon was all about. That would be soon enough. But the parents wanted the right thing for their children.

Being a parent is one of the greatest gifts God can give. It's also one of the greatest tasks you could ever undertake. Having a child together allows parents to share in God's creative work. We couldn't live here on earth or be God's children eternally if the parents of countless generations before us had not labored with their own children and even given their lives for their children. Now it may be our turn to bring life into the world. We cannot take this task lightly.

God put us here in an immense generational context. Of course, not everyone is called to be a parent. Not everyone gets married and is gifted with children. But if you get the chance, you can't deny children their right to live. Is not life more than food and the body more than clothes? You can't exchange the life of one child as payment for the luxuries you want to provide another. Jesus says, "Let the children come to Me." It's awe-inspiring. The first condition for being able to be a child of God and share all the joy that is the meaning of life, now and in eternity, is that there are people on earth who are willing to take upon themselves the task of parenting.

"Let the children come to Me." Jesus doesn't share the view of those who say: Let the child grow up first so he can decide for himself. No, Jesus says. It is just these people who need the kingdom of God. It's for them. Who can bear to grow up in this evil world without clinging to God? People were never meant to struggle through life without God. We can see how hard it is all around us. We really do need Jesus to lay His hands upon us and bless us the way He does in Baptism. And then never let go of His hand.

Dear Lord, You must help us here because it's hard to see what Your will is. The world seems to be overpopulated. People say it's not right to bring children into this world. But Your country was also overpopulated, wasn't it? Still Your Father let You grow up in a large family. Wasn't there a reason for that? Can it possibly be wrong to give life to a child whom You love and want to be brought before You if that child is laid in Your arms and taught to live with You now, every day and into eternity? Lord, I must thank You because I have

received life and wasn't denied it. Of course, I
would never have learned to know You if I had not
seen the light of day on earth. Lord, help us all to
see clearly and do what is right in Your eyes.

SATURDAY AFTER THE SECOND SUNDAY AFTER EPIPHANY
Luke 6:32–49

"Lord, if You will, You can make me clean." Matthew 8:2

A leper approached Jesus. He wasn't supposed to do that. He had been quarantined because he was contagious. In the brutal manner of that time, he was expelled from society and shut out from all discourse with healthy people.

But he stood there. He didn't ask to be cured. He left the decision to Jesus. He only pointed out this fact: If You want to, You can.

This is faith. It was this kind of faith Jesus wanted to arouse when He spoke in the synagogues and visited homes. He wanted to open people's eyes. It was something they should see. There was something wonderful to discover, something that would be decisive in their lives. He didn't say it right out. He didn't command them to believe. It was an invitation, a possibility presented to them.

The leper understood this. Here we can see what characterizes faith. We understand from his words that didn't demand, threaten, or insist. He didn't mean: I know You can if You want to. You should be ashamed of Yourself if You don't make me clean. Instead he meant: I realize that I can demand nothing. I don't deserve it. But You, who are so wonderfully righteous and whose heart goes out for wretches like me, perhaps You will perform a miracle on me also.

And Jesus did perform a miracle. " 'I am willing,' He said. 'Be clean' " (Matthew 8:3 NIV). He could help where this kind of faith was found.

Tomorrow's reading is about this faith Jesus creates with His Word and with His actions.

Lord, if You want to, You can make me clean. Clean from all my guilt, clean from everything I am ashamed of, clean from all accusing memories. I know I don't deserve it, Lord. I am not able to promise that I won't ever again stain the white garment You gave me in Baptism. But You can make sin, red as blood, as white as snow. You are faithful and just, and You forgive our sins and cleanse us from all unrighteousness. My heart says there is a limit and You can't keep on forgiving. But You say that there is no limit to Your forgiveness. Therefore, I dare to come to You with the leprosy of my heart, and pray yet again: Make me clean. For Your name's sake, Lord.

Note: The number of weeks during Epiphany changes each year, depending on when Easter is. If Easter comes early, there are only two weeks in Epiphany. If Easter comes late, there can be up to six weeks in Epiphany. If you aren't sure how long Epiphany is this year, it is best to consult your calendar. This is very important because Candlemas Sunday is at the end of January or beginning of February. If it comes in February, it replaces the Sunday that would normally be celebrated. Usually it replaces Septuagesima or Sexagesima, but it could also replace one of the Sundays after Epiphany. There is a separate devotion for Candlemas Sunday at the end of this book. Normal reading of the devotions for each weekday should be resumed after Candlemas day. That is, if it is Wednesday, read the devotion for Wednesday.

THIRD SUNDAY
AFTER EPIPHANY
Matthew 8:1–13

"Lord, I am not worthy to have You come under my roof,
but only say the word, and my servant will be healed."
Matthew 8:8

Once again we encounter the faith Christ creates. He calls
it a strong faith Himself, the likes of which He hadn't found
in Israel. Who wouldn't like to hear these words coming from
the lips of Jesus?

So what does this strong faith look like?

It obviously doesn't have a lot of confidence in itself.
"Lord, I am not worthy to have You come under my roof."
The centurion meant what he said. Others spoke well of him,
even the Jews. They said, he's worthy of this act from You.
He loves our nation, and he is the one who built us our synagogue. But the centurion knew better. He was an officer, a
professional soldier with vast experience of living with brutal
mercenaries, forced to punish harshly and demand instanta-
neous obedience. Yet he sat and listened when the Law was
read. He knew what God expected. He wasn't arrogant.

And he believed in Jesus. "Only say the word." The
centurion understood what His Word was capable of. Maybe
he'd heard Jesus in Capernaum preaching in the synagogue he
had built himself. He realized that here was a compassion and
an authority that transcended all the normal rules of service
and retaliation.

And Jesus heard it. "Go; let it be done for you as you have
believed" (Matthew 8:13).

"As you have believed." With this kind of faith, the way
for help is wide open. This is why Jesus wants to arouse faith
in us. He doesn't speak much about faith, but there is an
appeal and an invitation to it in all He says. Once in a while

He blurts it out as He once did to Mary: "Did I not tell you that if you believed you would see the glory of God" (John 11:40)? But usually He lets the glory shine through in a subtle and almost secretive manner, in suggestions and parables, in His words and His deeds. Faith can't be forced on us. It doesn't mysteriously appear when we're threatened, frightened, humiliated, or when we feel someone has just talked circles around us. It can only grow as an inner conviction when we're faced with something we've had to discover for ourselves. And that's what Jesus wants to help us with.

Help me, too, Lord. Help me to believe firmly in You and not in myself. Many times I've wanted a faith that I think is strong. A faith that trusts in itself, that feels strong; a faith that doesn't wonder, isn't inquisitive, doesn't struggle to look for answers. You may take that faith away from me, Lord, as long as You teach me to always trust in You, only in You. Lord, I know that You can, and that You are capable because You are almighty. Therefore, I want nothing other than to do Your will because it is best. You see everything and know all. Everything is in Your hands. If You want to, You can. If You don't want to, then it's better that it doesn't happen. I want only one thing: You.

MONDAY AFTER THE THIRD SUNDAY AFTER EPIPHANY

Mark 5:21–34

"If I touch even His garments. . ." Mark 5:28

Once again we have an example of faith: This poor woman with her chronic bleeding. Mark describes her history of suffering vividly. She had gone from doctor to doctor and exhausted all her assets, but she only got worse. She had heard people talk about Jesus. It's possible that her confidence in Him grew as she listened to Him on a crowded beach or mountain slope.

What did she believe? Certainly that He came from God, that He was sent to help those people no one else wanted to help even if they could.

Now the woman had her chance. Jesus had just come back from the other side of the lake. Jairus, the synagogue director, had waited for Him on the beach and immediately took Him through the narrow alleys up to his house where his young daughter lay ill. Many people followed Him. As usual, it was pretty crowded; everyone wanted to hear and see. The woman waited for her moment. Then she pushed forward with desperate resolve and brushed His coat. Suddenly, she knew the instant it had happened—she was cured!

But Jesus also felt something. No one who needs His help can touch Him, even if it is only in thought or just for a moment, without His noticing it. For Him moments like those are the greatest moments in life.

Faith can also be like this: a timid question or a trembling hand that touches the Helper. It was the same type of faith held by the robber on the cross and the centurion and the leper and so many others. It's one small hope, one last chance in what appeared to be a hopeless situation. Faith doesn't comfortably rest in the fact that it can take things for granted. It isn't obvious that Jesus has to help. But faith realizes that He can help. Faith knows He is illogically merciful, so it dares to hope for a miracle—a miracle as great as when He forgives one more time, a miracle as great as healing lepers or raising the dead.

Lord, I'm on the path where You pass by. I'm forcing my way through the crowd, praying for one drop of Your power to emanate from You to me. Utter just one word, Lord. Utter it when I need it the most. Tell me if I'm on the wrong path. Block that way and do not let me go further. Give me the help I need most. You know my biggest problems. Only You can cure them. Only You can say that I can follow You anyway. I need to trust in You. Lord, have mercy on me.

TUESDAY AFTER THE THIRD SUNDAY AFTER EPIPHANY
Mark 5:35–43

"Do not fear, only believe." Mark 5:36

It isn't easy to "only" believe when you've just heard that your own beloved child has died!

Jairus was most certainly vigilant that night. He was desperate. His daughter was terminally ill, and her only hope was Jesus, who was on the other side of the lake. Jairus sent a messenger down to the harbor and, finally, at daybreak, there was good news. The boats were on their way home.

Jairus hurried to the wharf, and right in the middle of the crowd, he fell on his knees. Bowing his head to the gravel on the street, he pleaded tenderly and fervently for the Master to hurry home with him. He wanted Jesus to lay His hands upon the fever-stricken girl and heal her.

But on the way home, something devastating happened. Someone approached Jairus and said his daughter was dead. There was no reason for him to bother the Master anymore.

Of course, Jesus immediately knew what was happening and uttered these peculiar words: "Do not fear, only believe."

Unlike the woman with the discharge of blood, Jairus was among those who had many chances to hear Jesus and speak to Him. Maybe that's why he followed Him now, without question, without objection, and hoping against all odds.

Jesus blocked the road. Only Peter, James, and John went further with Him. These three were always allowed to follow Him. They went into the garden of the house belonging to the synagogue's director. Burial preparations were already underway. A dead person was to be buried before the sun went down. The mourners and musicians, who wanted to be a part of the ceremony and maybe make a little money at the same time, had already gathered and begun their wailing. But Jesus silenced them. There would be no weeping. The girl was not dead. She was sleeping.

They laughed scornfully. It must have sounded piercingly heartless to the grieving relatives, but there was a good reason for laughing. They knew the girl was dead. It was confirmed beyond any reasonable doubt. No one would take the risk of burying someone alive.

Jesus showed them out with an authority no one defied. Everything that happened after that is described in the Gospel of Mark with words that must have originated from Peter, an eyewitness, who stood by the door and observed what happened with astonishment.

Jesus took the dead girl's hand and said, *"Talitha cumi."* We still read these words in Aramaic. Peter could never forget them; neither could his audience. So the expression remained intact in the original language even when the story was translated into Greek and other languages.

Jairus's and Peter's confidence was justified. They had hardly thought that such a thing was possible. They hardly dared to pray for it. But they were confident that Jesus could help. They had no idea how it would happen, but they followed Him. Then they did what He said: They left everything up to Him. Maybe that's what He meant when He said, "Only believe."

Help me, Lord Jesus, to believe in this manner. You see that I think the same way as Peter and Jairus must have thought: Things like this aren't possible. But You let them see it with astonished eyes. You taught them to trust in You for everything. I pray for this kind of confidence in You. Only You can instill this in my heart. Help me to trust completely in You so I no longer demand anything or try to tell You what to do. I know that nothing is impossible for You. You are capable of everything. And You know what is best. Therefore, I pray that only Your will be done. I know that's the best for me. When Your will is done, I have nothing to fear. I thank You for that.

WEDNESDAY AFTER THE THIRD SUNDAY AFTER EPIPHANY

Mark 6:1–16

"What we have heard You did at Capernaum, do here in Your hometown as well." Luke 4:23

Luke tells us that the people in Nazareth had heard about Jesus' remarkable accomplishments. Now, they expected a lot from Him, their local hero. If He could really do all these amazing things, then He should do them in Nazareth before He did them anywhere else.

Here we see the essential nature of disbelief: It wants to prevail over God. It doesn't necessarily have to deny God's existence, but recognition of God's existence is not the same as believing. Faith is essentially the heart's true relationship to God. Love, reverence, obedience, and childlike trust are a part of faith. Self-centeredness and conceit are a part of disbelief. You put yourself in the center of existence. Everything else, including God, is considered as tools and possibilities, as assets or risks for yourself. If there is any significance to God at all, then He will help how, where, and when the individual deems best.

So the people of Nazareth knew exactly what kind of expectations they had for Jesus, Mary's Son. If He were a man of God as others maintained, He would be useful to them. But if He didn't legitimize Himself by being at their disposal, they would be finished with Him.

However, something remarkable happened. Mark explicitly says that, "He could do no mighty work there, except that He laid His hands on a few sick people and healed them. And He marveled because of their unbelief" (Mark 6:5). Mark says openly that Jesus could not help where He could not find faith. It doesn't mean that God in His almighty power isn't able to make an unrepentant and selfish man healthy. (As a matter of fact, all the workings in our bodies through which we recover from sickness, are God's work.) But it means that the Helper, whom God sent to us, did not come to help the body alone. He came to help the whole person, both body and soul. It's a matter of transforming us back into God's children and once again giving us a real relationship to God. This help isn't possible when the heart wants to do things its own way by defying or using God. Jesus wasn't just a doctor. He was the Savior. He was the cure for the disease that separates us from God.

So we stand again before this conundrum: He came to help us, but He can't help us if we don't believe. But we can't believe if He doesn't create faith in our hearts—and we can stop Him from doing that.

Lord, I believe I'm starting to feel it—both my helplessness and my responsibility. I know that I can't believe if You don't create faith in my heart. Therefore, I thank You because You have come to me. I am also thankful that I can see You and that I am able to get to know You. So now I ask You to open my heart. I know, of course, that I could let You stand out there and knock in vain. Let Your fire burn me if I attempt to lock the door against You. Give me no peace unless I have peace in You. You know there's something inside me that wants to avoid You. You know that I don't want that to take over. But I need Your help and I ask You for it now, my Lord, Jesus.

THURSDAY AFTER THE THIRD SUNDAY AFTER EPIPHANY
Mark 16:1–20

"Who do you say I am?" Matthew 16:15

This was the decisive question. Jesus had put it off until now. When He called His disciples, He required only one thing from them: "Follow Me." They were to follow, listen, and see for themselves. It's the same way for us. In the beginning, faith puts no demands on us. Faith is aroused in our hearts when we walk with Jesus.

The disciples had walked with their Master long enough. They were at the foot of Mt. Hermon, just outside the border of Caesarea Philippi, when Jesus took them aside. He began a conversation around an interesting topic that everyone could take part in and neutrally discuss without regard to common courtesies: "Who do people say the Son of Man is" (Matthew 16:13)?

There were many answers because "there was a division among the people over Him" (John 7:43), just like there is today. And religious debates can be interesting. The disciples also came with a lot of suggestions.

But then Jesus turned the question to the disciples: "Who do you say I am?"

Nobody needs to believe before it is possible for them to believe. But the day will come when it's possible for them, and then they have to confess the faith. You can't escape taking a stand indefinitely. An encounter with Jesus has consequences.

Peter dared to answer. He spoke these decisive words: "You are the Christ, the Son of the living God" (Matthew 16:16).

These words constituted a confession and a standpoint with consequences for the future. There were plenty of masters in Israel. You could follow one of them for a while and then go to another. But you no longer have any choice when you realize that Jesus is the Messiah, the Promised One, God's own Son, who in the world's fateful hour was sent for the world's salvation. Then there is only One to follow, trust, believe in, and serve. Our future and the fate of the world rest in Him alone.

Peter's answer caused Jesus to rejoice. He told the disciples that Peter's answer was the work of God. Peter didn't think of this on his own; God gave him this knowledge.

God also works in our hearts through Jesus when we hear His Word or see His actions and begin to understand what He wants. Faith is more than understanding circumstances or accepting a certain way of regarding God and Jesus. Faith is relating to God in a specific way. It's not just a matter of what we think, but what we desire and what we know. Faith says *yes* not only to a theory or teaching, but to a new life.

This was what Peter did in Caesarea Philippi, and Jesus rejoiced and said, "Blessed are you" (Matthew 16:17).

You rejoiced, Lord. Would You also rejoice if I believed? I want to make You happy, but it's You who must finally make it possible, Lord. Help me to do the little I can do. I want to hear and see You. I want to follow You and be a part of everything Your disciples were able to see. Help me to understand what I hear and to see with open eyes. I want to learn bit by bit as You let Your disciples learn. Let there be a creative power in my heart that is productive and allows me to believe. Lord, I believe. Help my unbelief.

FRIDAY AFTER
THE THIRD SUNDAY
AFTER EPIPHANY
Mark 7:1–23

"An evil and adulterous generation seeks for a sign, but no sign will be given to it except the sign of the prophet Jonah."
Matthew 12:39

This was the answer Jesus gave the Pharisees and Sadducees when they came to test Jesus, demanding to see a sign from heaven. He was supposed to prove that He came from God by doing something great before their eyes. If He did that they would believe in Him—maybe.

But Jesus didn't do any miracles for them. He didn't want their kind of faith because it wasn't really faith. Faith isn't a plan or circumstantial evidence to convince our selfish reason that we can count on God or that Jesus is worth betting on. To believe is to take hold of God's love and long to get away from everything that keeps us from having total fellowship with Him. To believe is to discover who God is and love Him for His own sake. This faith can never be ignited through miracles that frighten or impress. It can only be ignited by seeing a glimpse of God's love, by seeing how He looks for us and longs for us. This is why God descended to earth in Jesus Christ. That's why He walked on earth and sought out all the forsaken, lost, unfortunate, and despised people. Some were moved by this love. They gathered around Jesus. Others were only irritated. They couldn't share in God's love for sinners. At the same time, they were a little disturbed by all the excitement and remarkable deeds that no one could deny. Then they wanted to be on the safe side and asked for proof; but Jesus refused to give this proof. They wouldn't receive any sign except for the sign of Jonah. They would witness the Son of Man swallowed by death and resurrected to new life. But even this sign would be understood only by those who had come to Jesus with all their sins, loveless nature, and misfortunes to receive the forgiveness and help only He can give.

My Lord Jesus, You descended so we would know who God is. You have shown me that He is a Father who longs for His lost children. You tell me there is great rejoicing in the house of God when a wretched little man like me repents. You also let me know how far away I am. I'm not like You. I don't love my enemies. I don't pray for those who persecute me. Even when I try to pray for them, there is still bitterness in my heart. And still You say I can come to You. That is more fantastic than any sign or miracle. So I will come to You, Lord.

SATURDAY AFTER THE THIRD SUNDAY AFTER EPIPHANY
Mark 7:24–37

"My way is hidden from the LORD, and my right is disregarded by my God." Isaiah 40:27

That's how it can be perceived. That's what they said in Israel. We read it in the prophet Isaiah. We read the same thing in many other places in the Old Testament. We hear the psalmist cry:

Why do You hide Your face? Why do You forget our affliction and oppression? Psalm 44:24

O my God, I cry by day, but You do not answer, and by night, but I find no rest. Psalm 22:2

How long, O LORD? Will You forget me forever? Psalm 13:1

I have come into deep waters, and the flood sweeps over me. Psalm 69:2

Why should You be like a man confused, like a mighty warrior who cannot save? Jeremiah 14:9

Godless people aren't saying this. It comes from people who believe, who desire to walk with God, who need His help. It's not easy to live. There are so many unexplainable events in our world, and they hit us terribly hard.

But through all this we have Jesus. That means that something has come into the world that opens up completely new opportunities. This is what the text for the fourth Sunday in Epiphany is about.

Let us realize that we really can feel as if we're abandoned by God. We can feel defeated by a power that has nothing to do with God. This could be a storm or natural disaster. It could be war or people's malicious attitudes. It could be job loss, incurable disease, or the threat of death.

What does God do about all this? We find the answer in Jesus. It is He Himself who is the answer. He lived with all of this. He went through it Himself. Yet He conquered it, and He includes us in this victory. This is not so we can escape suffering but so we can say with the apostle: "No, in all these things we are more than conquerors through Him who loved us" (Romans 8:37).

Dear Lord and Master, You know how afraid I am to suffer. You know I want to evade everything that hurts, to escape sickness and pain, slander and criticism. I try to avoid difficult people and tedious obligations. Then I think about everyone who suffers. I think about how they could escape if the world were free from everything that causes so much pain and so many tears. If it was possible to take it all away, I know You would have done it long ago. But instead, You put Yourself in the middle of it all. Now You are here with us, in the midst of this evil world. Therefore, I pray to You that You help me to see all this as You see it. Teach me to endure suffering the same way You did. I don't want to pray for anything else except that You would always be with me, come what may.

FOURTH SUNDAY AFTER EPIPHANY
Matthew 8:23–27

Then He rose and rebuked the winds and the sea.
Matthew 8:26

That's what Matthew tells us Jesus did that stormy night on the Sea of Galilee. It was dangerous to sail. Today, the sea looks like a blue eye between the mountains, deeply nestled in the great crevice of the Jordan valley. During the oppressive heat of summer, you can see snow lying atop the summit of Mt. Hermon. And in a matter of minutes, the wind can sweep down from these cold heights against the glassy surface of the sea, turning the lake into a boiling pot. Crew members of small fishing boats must fight for their lives.

That was what happened that night while Jesus was sleeping in the boat. He must have been tired and used to sleeping in the oddest of places because they had to wake Him up. He calmed the storm. The disciples were amazed that He had such power. We are also amazed. What's even more remarkable is what the evangelist says: "He . . . rebuked the winds and the sea." He spoke to them as one speaks to annoying and disobedient servants. There seems to be something in nature that doesn't follow God's will. In the beginning, when God created the world, everything was very good. But after the fall, evil entered creation and harmony was disrupted. Again and again, things happen that are contrary to God's will. There is a struggle occurring and Jesus is in the middle of it. That's the reason He also fights against disease.

Now it's clear that Jesus' contribution in the world didn't consist of putting an end to all evil. Many of us wish He had done that. If that were the case, He would've annihilated the evil one Himself. Evil has penetrated creation in a mysterious manner and can't be separated from it. Therefore, Jesus says that flesh and blood cannot inherit the kingdom of God. The mortal must assume immortality. Even we carry some of this evil within us as a part of our own nature. Therefore, a new creation, a new heaven and new earth, is necessary. Everything must be born again. But since that day entails a judgment day for all, God is going to wait with that. Until then He fights to win back His children and save them. In the middle of this fight there is Jesus, our helper.

People are so incomprehensibly evil, Lord. There is so much happening here that bears more witness to evil powers than to the love of Your Father. Even

I have my old Adam. Who knows what evil it would do if it could. But You are here in the midst of this evil world. You were born in a manger. You grew up as a refugee. And despite this many were unthankful. They despised and slandered You. You were abused and tortured. They executed You like a common criminal. Yet in all this You won a great victory. I thank You because it is You who has the power and because You did not use it as we desired but as Your Father desired. Help me to trust in You at all times, most of all when life is the hardest.

MONDAY AFTER THE FOURTH SUNDAY AFTER EPIPHANY
Matthew 9:27–38

"And ought not this woman, a daughter of Abraham whom Satan bound for eighteen years, be loosed from this bond on the Sabbath day?" Luke 13:16

Jesus asked this of His opponents. It was the Sabbath and He was in the synagogue as usual. "There was a woman who had had a disabling spirit for eighteen years. She was bent over and could not fully straighten herself" (Luke 1:31). Jesus called her to Him, laid His hands upon her and healed her. The people rejoiced, but the director of the synagogue became indignant—no one was supposed to work on the

Sabbath day. But Jesus answered him with the question, "Does not each of you on the Sabbath untie his ox or his donkey from the manger and lead it away to water it?" (Luke 13:15)? Couldn't He then liberate this poor woman, who was one of them, from her eighteen-year bondage?

Satan had kept her bound, Jesus says. Her disease was one of many examples of the evil that disfigured God's good creation. Salvation is meant to restore everything that has been affected by the fall into sin. Salvation is not only for the soul. All of creation will be redeemed and again become what it was meant to be from the beginning. Therefore, Jesus cured the sick, fed the hungry, and raised the dead.

Jesus' work was limited in a way. He said it Himself: He was sent only to the lost sheep of the house of Israel, and even then He would withdraw when people flocked from everywhere and there was just too much to accomplish. His help was of a different kind. Humanity would receive a new start, and whole new possibilities would open up for the world. These selected miracles were only examples, only a small portion of His power at work. They were demonstrations of His work. There was something symbolic in them, as in so much of what Jesus did. When He chose twelve apostles, it was to show that they were the seed of a new Israel. When He rode into Jerusalem, He did it in a way that showed that He was the promised King but not an earthly ruler. In the same way, He performed a series of powerful acts that not only helped a few simple people and not only showed His mercy and consideration for the suffering, wretched individual, but also showed His power over evil. They revealed His mission on earth: to save this world from the destruction and suffering that are the consequences of rebellion against God. But this mission could not be fulfilled by His wandering around doing good things in Galilee. There was something else greater in store for Him.

Walking with You now, my Lord, and seeing all that You did, I begin to understand that this isn't just something that happened two thousand years ago. What You did was also meant for us. When You descended to earth, when You stepped into humanity, Your journey was for all ages and for all people. My intellect can't quite comprehend it, but my heart knows that You have drawn me and everyone else into it. And now I pray to You, Lord, to help me see and understand what You did—how You put an end to suffering, how You conquered evil, how You made it possible for those who follow You to appear victorious in the midst of what looks like defeat, how I can be without fear in the midst of this terrible life. Open my eyes that I may see. Open my heart that I may receive understanding. For Your name's sake.

TUESDAY AFTER THE FOURTH SUNDAY AFTER EPIPHANY
Matthew 10:1–15

"Heal the sick, raise the dead, cleanse lepers, cast out demons. You received without paying; give without pay."
Matthew 10:8

Jesus commanded this when He sent His apostles out to preach His Gospel, two by two, from village to village. It's amazing. Some people probably think this is an exaggeration or legendary embellishment. But we have the necessary documents to show that it isn't. We have one of Paul's letters where he says that "the signs of a true apostle" were performed by him for the Corinthians "with signs and wonders and mighty works" (2 Corinthians 12:12). It was a statement that could be verified by any one of the people receiving it. Paul knew he didn't exaggerate.

In other words, the apostles had received some of Jesus' own power. It was a part of their call. It was part of the Gospel. It wasn't only the apostles who had this power in the Early Church. Paul mentions it again and again as a commonly known fact that there were people who had the gift to perform miracles. The gift of faith healing existed then.

Again we see that the Gospel is for the soul and for the body. It's not just something "spiritual." When we pray, "Deliver us from evil," we mean sickness, war, racism, and all other forms of evil as well.

But why don't we see more of the power Jesus has over evil today? Why do the unbelievable things that obviously happened so often in the Early Church happen so rarely today? Jesus said that if we have faith the size of a mustard seed, we would be able to move mountains. But we can't do it. At least, we don't believe we can do it.

It's true, though, that we have to differentiate between two types of belief. One is saving faith. This is often a depleted, weak, and flickering faith that nevertheless completely trusts in Jesus and expects everything from Him. The second is miraculous faith. Paul considers this kind of faith a part of the gifts of the Spirit that only a few people possess. However, it's this weak faith that expects everything from Jesus that can receive the miraculous power of Christ and let it work. That's why Jesus calls it a great faith.

Lord, why can't we? We're ashamed, just like Your own disciples, who had to ask: Why can't we? Maybe Your answer to us is the same one You gave them: because of our unbelief. So teach us, dear Lord, to expect great things from You. Help us to attempt great things when You want us to attempt them. We need You, Your presence, and Your help, power, and guidance. Help us keep our lamps burning and not be asleep when the time comes for You to use us. Those times are for the good of man and to Your glory. So help us, Lord.

WEDNESDAY AFTER THE FOURTH SUNDAY AFTER EPIPHANY
Matthew 10:16–25

"Behold, I am sending you out as sheep in the midst of wolves." Matthew 10:16

This verse means that you will be defenseless and completely deserted. People will hate you and persecute you. They will drag you before the courts and charge you with crimes. Yet you have nothing to fear. Not one sparrow falls to the ground without your Father willing it. Even the hairs of your head are counted.

This is what's so strange about Jesus' authority over all evil on earth. He appears powerless. And He tells us that we should believe in Him and take His example. A disciple is not above his teacher. It's good enough if the servant meets the same fate as his master. Our Lord was brought before the courts and sentenced to death. They jeered and taunted Him saying: "He can't save Himself" (Matthew 27:42).

But that was precisely when He could help.

To understand how Christ conquered evil, we have to look at the cross and reconciliation. Evil is, first and foremost, guilt that separates us from God. So help must begin there. This is why Jesus said so surprisingly to the lame man, who had been let down through a hole in the roof, "Take heart, My son; your sins are forgiven" (Matthew 9:1). It may have seemed that this wasn't quite the kind of help the lame man needed most at that moment. He wanted his health restored. But forgiveness is where any real and lasting help must begin. We have to have the right kind of relationship with God. For this reason, the Gospel is first and foremost a message about the forgiveness of sins. It's God's message to us. Through His Ambassador, Jesus, He greets us by telling us everything is prepared, despite all we have done. It's also a promise that God will restore everything, sooner or later. It's also a call to us to help in the restoration with things that can be made better here on earth right now, like medical care, housing, food, justice, and freedom.

Lord, You know how I have been thinking that I would live in peace and tranquility if I became a Christian. It upsets me when people criticize me because I really want to do my best. When I only had to think about what was best for me, I was left alone. But that's just what You said would happen! Don't let me be bitter and indignant. Help me to think of it as something obvious. Of course, it

proves that You are right. Help me instead to be
so glad and free that people can understand how
good it is to be able to love and serve You.

THURSDAY AFTER THE FOURTH SUNDAY AFTER EPIPHANY
Matthew 10:26–42

"Are not two sparrows sold for a penny? And not one
of them will fall to the ground apart from your Father."
Matthew 10:29

There's so much that seems cruel and meaningless in the
world. Nature often frightens us with avalanches, hurricanes,
earthquakes, volcanic eruptions, viruses, and cancer. We
often speak of the environment in terms of "the blind power
of nature," but now Jesus says that nothing happens without
our heavenly Father's will, literally "apart from your Father."
That doesn't mean everything is an expression of God's good
and creative will. There is also an evil will at work. But it
means that nothing happens that God doesn't in some way
hold in His hand and include in His plans. He uses it eventually as a blessing for His children. We are more valuable than
many sparrows.

At the creation, God gave us dominion over nature, but
this was destroyed by the fall. Now we fight with thistles and
weeds, storms and floods, infection and disease. Our intelli-

gence can utilize the power of nature, but we can also abuse it. This causes destruction. This abuse of nature is our curse and we're guilty of it daily. But when we believe in Christ and, through the forgiveness of sins become children of God once again, the Savior holds His hand over us and the power of evil cannot do any real harm to us. We can be chastened, corrected, or tested, but there is a blessing in everything. "Why are you afraid?" Jesus asked His disciples in the boat (Matthew 8:36). There was nothing to be afraid of because He was with them. Darkness and storm, infection and disease, prison and death—none of this can threaten someone over whom Jesus holds His hand. Nothing can threaten us when He safely guides the boat through the winds of hell to the harbor of heaven. The tables are turned. In the boat on the Sea of Galilee, the Savior was resting, remarkably secure in the midst of the storm. Now we can finally lie down, tired, dejected and powerless, yet perfectly calm. The ship won't sink when Jesus is on board.

We may talk about disappointments. Sometimes our plans are ruined. For some, this appears to be a blind and meaningless twist of fate. Others bring reproachful charges against God or feel persecuted by mysterious powers. But we are not persecuted. It is Jesus who follows us, just as He followed Saul. His guiding and governing hand is in the confusion, a strong and good hand that knows what it wants.

Lord, I know I have nothing to fear; yet I am afraid. I want to steer my own boat. I have set the course and know where I want to go. And then there is a storm that I am responsible for. I know the risks and feel so small and frightened, all because of my unbelief. You took me aboard Your boat. When You baptized me, You took me aboard Your

Church's mighty ship. You set the course. I know
where we're sailing. All my days are recorded in
Your ship's log, Your Book of Life. Despite all my
concerns, I can't add a cubit to my life. And the
powers of evil can't really hurt me as long as I'm
with You. Therefore, I won't let go of Your hand,
and if I do, don't let me get into harm's way, but
always keep me close to You, Lord.

FRIDAY AFTER THE FOURTH SUNDAY AFTER EPIPHANY
Matthew 11:20–30

"Behold, this Child is appointed for the fall and rising of
many in Israel, and for a sign that is opposed." Luke 2:34

This is what Simeon said about the child, Jesus. These
words were confirmed when He began preaching the Gospel
and inviting others into God's kingdom. The crowds were
enormous. People came down from Jerusalem and up from
the coastal regions of Tyre and Sidon. Something like this had
never been experienced before. It was a religious revival.

But it was time to separate the wheat from the chaff.
Everyone saw the remarkable things happening, but there
were those who said it was with the help of Beelzebub, the
lord of the demons, that Jesus drove out the evil spirits. No
one could miss the power and authority in His speech. But
there were those who said, Who can stand hearing Him?
The evangelists distinctively bore witness to these things. The
people were divided over Him.

Jesus brooded over the matter and spoke about it. It was something God kept from the clever and wise but revealed for the little children. There was a kind of mentality that left people impervious. Jesus once described this with the picture of resentful and ornery children for whom nothing was good enough. Their friends said to them: "We played the flute for you, and you did not dance; we sang a dirge, and you did not mourn" (Matthew 11:17). They were resistant to both proposals. God's children also can be this way. God sends them a preacher of penance like the Baptist, an ascetic who lived in the desert and preached such that excitement went through the people. Then some people said he's mad. God sends them a merciful Messiah, who, in boundless compassion, gathers the lost and seeks out sinners. Then they say: "Look at Him! What a glutton and drunkard!" Their hearts seem to have an attitude that is never affected; as if they are saying, "Let God do what He wants. My answer is still no." This point of view can be a product of both intelligence and knowledge. It won't be won over by argument. It isn't even worth discussing.

But there is also an attitude that Jesus describes with a very difficult word to translate. It's been translated as "little children." The original meaning is to be simple, unaffected, not complicated or sophisticated, not duplicitous or dishonest in thought and deed. It describes a person who is open and prepared to be influenced even if it leads to a new Lord and a new purpose in life.

Am I like that, Lord? Help me to understand when I'm guilty of keeping a false account of what really happened. Help me to see if I doubt because it's just too uncomfortable to believe. Help me to see through all the arguments that are a result of my own laziness or cowardice. Help me to be like a child who says it like it is. Help me to be happy like a child who doesn't know enough to be afraid of things that are only foolish convention and empty etiquette. Help me to see You just as You are and dare to believe when You show me the truth.

SATURDAY AFTER THE FOURTH SUNDAY AFTER EPIPHANY
Matthew 12:1–14

But the Pharisees went out and conspired against Him, how to destroy Him. Matthew 12:14

That's the tragic consequence of not believing in Jesus. You're driven by an inner necessity to try to silence Him forever. So long as He's there, He's a disturbance. The Pharisees knew this all too well. If this Man was right, there would be a revolution in their lives. He couldn't be right. And since He seemed to have a particularly dangerous influence over some people, they were determined to do away with Him (naturally on good grounds and with lawful means)! They fought for order, justice, reason, and what was best for everyone.

Today, people try to destroy Jesus by explaining that He never existed. But even if someone is successful in blotting Him out of their reality and their pages of history, His Church remains. Even the Church can be such an annoyance that people try to destroy it. They attempt to do it through legislation and measures by the state. The persecution of Christianity has been more widespread in the last century than ever before.[8] However, the normal course of action is to wage a small private war of extermination in which individuals are shielded from everything that has to do with Jesus and His Church. If someone with a living faith is thrust into a secular environment, people respond by being superior or alienating. And so a person can unexpectedly become the object of degradation and ridicule because of an honest, faithful, and conscientious attempt to live as a Christian. This is the risk of believing. But this can also be a good sign. It shows that Jesus lives and that faith is a reality, and it also can be a sign that the persecutor's taking his last stand and he's not far away from the kingdom of God.

I thank You, Lord Jesus, because Your light lightens the darkness and because nothing dark in the world can have power over that light. I thank You because I can see Your light. And I pray to You for all those who have not seen it. You said that our light shall be a light for men so they see our good works and praise our Father in heaven. If You let this happen through me also, I bless You, Lord. If people become evil and scornful, help me rejoice in the fact that You haven't left them alone and haven't allowed them to be indifferent. Don't let my faults be obstacles for them. Give me Your joy so I can always meet cold with warmth, sourness with a sunny smile, and let them imagine the joy of Your existence.

---

8. Freedom of religion is not a guaranteed right in Sweden. Sweden has historically supported a Lutheran state church, but in the last century, many laws were passed in order to muzzle the church. Not the least of these laws was the mandatory ordination of women, which undermined the authority of Scripture in the Church of Sweden. This opened up a Pandora's Box of liberal theology.

Note: During the years when Easter comes late, there can be a fifth—and on some occasions even a sixth—week after Epiphany. There aren't any particular readings for those days in this book. The idea is that you should read some of the weeks at the end of Pentecost that would be omitted if Easter is late in the year. Consult a calendar to determine which of them you should read. It's best to start with the first of the devotions that are omitted for the year in question.

SEPTUAGESIMA
Matthew 20:1–16

And when those hired about the eleventh hour came, each of them received a denarius. Matthew 20:9

We talk about the point of Christ's parables because they have something specific to say. A parable is a poetic story. The basic material is often taken from real life, and parables are told in such a fashion that they portray something that actually happened in just that way. However, Jesus' parables almost always involve a twist, something unexpected. This is because His parables are about God's kingdom, God's actions, or the effects of Jesus sowing His Word.

When Jesus told the story of the employer who gave all his employees the same pay whether they worked one hour or twelve, He painted a picture of Himself. That is what Jesus does. He doesn't ration blessings. If you belong to Christ, He shares everything He has to give with you. This is true right here on earth. Here, He grants us the forgiveness of sins and the right to be God's children. If you believe in Christ, these gifts are yours without restriction. Christians may be strong or weak, but they have all been completely forgiven. They are all equally close to God's heart. This is also true of God's kingdom, the new world God will create. Everyone will have the same share in the heavenly kingdom's treasure, in God's boundless divinity, in the never-ending rejoicing, and the awesome privilege of living with God.

Strangely enough, this annoys many people. But maybe that's not so strange. By nature we are all Pharisees. That is, we tend to be legalistic self-righteous snobs. We know when we shine brightly, and we like to remember our shining moments. We think people ought to recognize us for these shining moments and are offended if they don't. We think it's unfair if others, who have done much less, are given preference over us. And since God is to be the final judge, we feel that He, if anyone, should judge us fairly, according to our merits and skillfulness.

But God doesn't do that. For our sakes, it's good that He doesn't do that. If He did, judgment wouldn't be in our favor at all.

Lord God, if You kept a record of sins, who could stand? I know that is true. If You examined my heart and tested me to see if I really loved or if my intentions were really pure and unselfish or if I really hadn't only thought of myself, I would not pass Your test. Yet You still love me. You still let me work in Your vineyard. I am still allowed to be Your servant and Your friend. Help me to remember how good You are to me so I am never jealous of Your goodness to others. Even if I am last in Your kingdom, it is much more than I deserve. In Jesus' name.

MONDAY AFTER SEPTUAGESIMA

Matthew 12:23–37

"I tell you, on the day of judgment people will give account for every careless word they speak." Matthew 12:36

Can that be fair? we ask ourselves. How often do we speak thoughtlessly using unnecessary, rash, slanderous, boastful, or half-true words? If we had thought a little more about them, we probably wouldn't have spoken them. If we knew that someone would take them seriously, we would have expressed ourselves more carefully. But we didn't think about what we said. It just came out.

That's exactly what's so revealing, Jesus says. "The good person out of his good treasure brings forth good, and the evil person out of his evil treasure brings forth evil" (Matthew 12:35). That's why we are judged by the words we speak spontaneously, uncontrollably, and thoughtlessly. They show what's inside of us. The tree is recognized by its fruits.

It's not only the words we speak, our actions can also be completely impulsive. They are often awful deeds. Sometimes we have violent and hasty reactions that we soon regret. And sometimes we stubbornly defend these unwarranted actions even as we wish they had never occurred. Or we react with spontaneous unwillingness. We have no desire to help someone else by contributing our time, money, or ourselves. It's as if we had a built-in opposition.

Actually, we do have a built-in opposition. The Bible calls it "the flesh," "the old Adam," "the old man," or "original sin."

This is why we need to be saved from our sin. This is why salvation is, first and foremost, forgiveness and reconciliation. Original sin cannot simply be removed. We can't eradicate it, not even through the most earnest repentance. God alone can cure this evil. This is why He gave us Christ.

Lord, You said Yourself that if the tree is good, then the fruit must be good. But my tree often bears awful fruit and, sometimes, no fruit at all. I can't force myself to bear good fruit. Only You can make it happen, Lord, only if Your power works within me, only if I can become a branch on Your vine. So I pray to You for that mysterious power that oozes out like sap from the vine. Allow it to fill my heart and soul. Let it work in me so I can finally bear the good fruit You speak about, good fruit that endures, that makes us rejoice, and that honors Your Father. If by grace You desire to perform a miracle on me, let it happen for Your name's sake.

TUESDAY AFTER SEPTUAGESIMA
Matthew 12:38–45

"And the last state of that person is worse than the first."
Matthew 12:45

Yesterday we read that Jesus is our Helper. How can anyone be sure of this? Is there any proof? People were asking for that proof even while He was alive. They came to Him wanting to see a sign from heaven, but He answered that they would not see any other sign than that of Jonah. Jonah had preached repentance with great authority. The Ninevites understood this sign and converted.

This was the only sign Jesus promised people would see: a sermon with power and authority that would touch their conscience. If people listened, they would know God and His salvation. They could be certain of that. If they didn't listen, nothing else could help them.

Yet God would give another sign. For just as Jonah was in the belly of the great fish for three days and three nights, so the Son of Man would be in the bosom of the earth for three days and three nights. If this great miracle, the death and resurrection of Jesus, didn't convince them, nothing else would.

Maybe that's why people try to solve their problem by themselves. Some try to remove evil from society and humanity or from their own hearts. Sometimes it looks as if they're successful on a personal level: they sober up, begin to work diligently, and get their marriage back on the right track. Maybe they are even able to change society for the better by helping to stop the hunger for profits or by passing good social legislation. Maybe everyone has the opportunity for higher education or free medical care or retirement benefits. The house is clean and in order.

Yet the house has one major flaw. Jesus says it's empty. There's a vacuum. God is missing. No one knows whom to serve. It's no longer easy to tell right from wrong. The whole system of norms is in chaos. Other spirits quickly fill vacuums like this, and they're not good spirits. Evil spirits come uninvited, and that's a much worse scenario.

That is why we need Christ.

And for this reason I ask You to come, Lord Jesus. Come to us all, even those who do not understand how much they need You. Fill our hearts so everyone can know how good it is that You are our Lord. I know so many who really want to do the right thing. They really want to make the world better, but they don't have You, so the evil spirits creep in another way and the world becomes even worse. Lord, help us show others what it means to believe in You.

WEDNESDAY
AFTER
SEPTUAGESIMA
Matthew 13:24-43

"An enemy has done this." Matthew 13:28

That's the answer Jesus gives to the question of evil in this world, the incomprehensible evil that decays the perfect world God created. "Master, did you not sow good seed in your field? How then does it have weeds" (Matthew 13:27)? By *weeds*, He means all the wars and cruelty, all injustice and oppression. Jesus says an enemy has done this. There is a power that does things against God's will. And so, many things happen contrary to God's will.

But what does God do about it? Most of the time we know what God should do. Just like the servants in the parable, He should demand that the weeds be exterminated, the sooner the better.

But the person who planted the seeds didn't want to do that. He was concerned about his small plants. It's easy enough to understand what Jesus means. If God exterminated all those who today cause others to fall and do what is unrighteous, He would end up sacrificing many who could still be saved otherwise. So He continues with what we may consider to be inadequate measures, but they are the only way to real help. He allows this world to continue to exist. He doesn't conquer evil by destroying the evildoers. He has another cure—forgiveness. He invites the lame and crippled, publicans and harlots into His kingdom. There would even be a place for Herod and Caiaphas, for Napoleon and Hitler, if they wanted to come.

Just as God is patient and waits, although men are defiant and do not want to wait, He asks His children to be patient. They have to live with the weeds. They might find themselves persecuted and possibly condemned to death. It's the price God pays to continue saving others. The harvest will come soon enough. Then God will separate the weeds from the chaff forever.

Lord, I ask You for a bit of Your patience. Teach me that no day can be meaningless as long as You are at work in this world. My blind eyes can't see how You can allow the weeds to grow and thrive the way they do. There's not enough room in my heart to hope and believe that it's worth continuing. But as long as You want to do it, I can only bow my head and pray that Your will be done and that I, too, can be a small instrument in Your service. Therefore, I ask for Your kingdom to come even into this evil world, where I don't believe it's possible. For Thine is the kingdom and the power and the glory forever and ever.

THURSDAY AFTER SEPTUAGESIMA
Matthew 13:44–58

"Then in his joy he goes and sells all that he has and buys that field." Matthew 13:44

Jesus often portrays common people in His parables. They aren't meant to be moral examples, but amidst human egoism, they usually illustrate something equivocal to God's kingdom.

That's the way it is with the man who dug in someone else's field and stumbled upon a treasure. Of course, He should have informed the owner, but he didn't. Instead, he cheated his way into buying the field. He isn't in any way meant to be a role model. However, in his joy, enthusiasm, and enchantment, he's a picture of something that is right. This is the way each and every one of us on our way to God's kingdom ought to be. The man in the parable knew he could be rich. A single thought possessed him: I can't let this slip through my fingers.

This is precisely the feeling a person should have when he has met Jesus. It's something unbelievable, a fantastic possibility, something far more than he ever thought possible. Maybe he doesn't understand it right away. Many think God benefits when they become Christian. The Church, in any case, should be glad they take their membership seriously. But it doesn't take long before such people discover that it isn't God who received a precious present when they gave Him their heart. The real problem is that there's something in such a person's heart that doesn't please God. If God really applied His law, none of us would belong in His kingdom. We can dig as much as we like in our heart's field and throw away all the stones until the shovel strikes solid rock. The sinful corruption at the bottom cannot be pried loose or carried away.

But suddenly the shovel scratches a chest full of hard cash where God's glory and His fatherly mercy shine forth, a gold mine, and every coin bears the exalted King's picture, the picture of Christ Jesus. Then I realize that this ransom is enough to pay for all of my sins. It's enough to guarantee me the right to be God's heir. It's impossible to assess the worth of this treasure. And I don't even need to buy the field it's buried in; the treasure is mine! I get it for nothing. No wonder I'm happy!

Even this joy is Your work, Lord. My own tired heart has so often taken it for granted. Is this why You showed me that it's completely preposterous that I should expect nothing but a closed door? That You have grounds to prosecute me for all my conceited words and for the weeds that grow in my heart's field? For my indifference and lack of interest in the salvation of others? For my unwillingness to obey without groaning? Yet You still give me reason to rejoice and be glad. You give me the precious pearl and an inexhaustible treasure. You carry my entire burden and You never tire of forgiving me. Lord, let Your joy fill my heart with a light of contagious joy for Your love for us. Give me joy that overflows and reaches out to others.

FRIDAY AFTER SEPTUAGESIMA
Matthew 14:22–36

And [they] implored Him that they might only touch the fringe of His garment. And as many as touched it were made well. Matthew 14:36

Just touching Jesus can be a source of incredible help. The woman who suffered an incurable discharge of blood trusted that she would be cured if she only touched His coat. The mothers brought their children to Jesus because they wanted Him to touch them. We see this power again in the story of Peter as he tried to walk on water: He took hold of Jesus' outstretched hand and was saved.

This isn't an illusion or magic. There's a superstitious belief in supernatural powers that people try to control like electricity. They're unpredictable, maybe even dangerous, but if we know how to handle them, maybe it's possible to get control of them. That's magic, the art of medicine men and witchdoctors. The Gospel is an entirely different matter. Certainly, Jesus possesses a power stronger than any human power that convinced the disciples He was God's own Son. Nothing is impossible for God. He is Lord over the world He created. Jesus also possesses this divine power.

No one is ever able to have this power under their control or choosing. It can help them, but only through faith. It doesn't need to be conjured up. God's power needs only an open heart. The heart is opened by God Himself and He takes it into His hands. The help Jesus gave is connected to the forgiveness of sins and a new relationship with God. He helps not only by restoring your health, but also by making you a child of God.

Then it's enough to touch Jesus. It's the truth we read last Sunday: Jesus gives a full day's wages. If someone believes in Him and gets to know Him, He gives those who follow Him everything. You don't need a certain amount of knowledge or faith, sanctification or strength of character. Forgiveness and a childlike faith are indivisible. If you have those things, you have it all.

It is to my great joy, Lord Jesus, that that's the way it is. You know how often I am like the sinking Peter. You invite me to come and I try to walk the path of faith. I try to do great things for You, but then I feel the wind blowing and see the stormy sea. I have a weak faith and begin to doubt. I ask You to reach out Your hand and touch me. I am calm when I am holding Your hand. Then I know that

there is always a way out. I am able to walk in the
dark without seeing or understanding because You
walk with me. Do with me what You will, but do
not let go of me!

SATURDAY AFTER SEPTUAGESIMA
Luke 7:36–50

"Your faith has saved you." Luke 7:50

We hear these words again and again in the Gospels. Jesus intentionally repeated them to stress something very important. What Jesus gives is received in faith and only in faith. But if we believe, we receive it without reservation.

Believing isn't just accepting an assertion. Naturally, to have faith also means to believe that Jesus is God's Son and that He comes to us from God bringing us salvation. But believing in Jesus means more; it means to trust in Him, to have confidence in Him, and to glorify Him. Those who believe will stay with Him and obey Him. Jesus could say, "Go, and from now on sin no more" (John 8:11) because He knew that those who believed in Him would do just that. The same thing is meant by the phrase "go in peace." That's not just a wish for peace and quiet. In the Bible, "peace" means God's wonderful order of things, a world where God's will is done. To have peace in the heart means to put your life in God's hands and let Him guide it.

That's faith, and that is what salvation, which we have through faith, contains. This will come up again and again during the coming weeks as we follow Jesus up to Jerusalem.

Lord, You know how much I doubt. You also know that I am being honest when I say there is nowhere else for me to go but to You. My faith is only a glowing spark, but it glows because You blow on it. I need Your help. I don't want to be without You. So I come to You for help. You said Yourself that You will not reject those who come to You. I would be delighted with having the last place in Your kingdom. I want only to see a glimpse of Your face and know that You won't abandon me.

SUNDAY OF SEXAGESIMA
Luke 8:4–15

"A sower went out to sow his seed . . . The seed is the word of God." Luke 8:5, 11

The parable of the sower gives us a realistic picture of what farming was like in the stony soil of the Galilean hill country. At the same time it's a parable about us. We're exactly like the Galilean soil. This parable tells what happens when Jesus sows His Word among us.

Some seed falls along the path, a winding path for donkeys that make their way down to the lake. Since the path cuts right through the field, where there is no fence or ditch, it's no wonder that a portion of the seed falls on the bare stones, where it is immediately trampled upon and plucked up by the birds. This often happens to God's Word. It ends up on the bare stones of a heart where anything is allowed in and all the world's impressions and experiences parade through endlessly. It's trampled on instead of planted. The devil's birds pluck it away before it has a chance to grow.

Some seed falls on stony ground. That would be the limestone under every field in the Palestinian mountains. In many places the limestone is exposed at the surface. The topsoil is thin around the edges of the field. In spring, the stones warm up and the fields are like a hotbed. The grain begins to grow there first. It looks promising, but when summer comes, the soil is too hot and everything dries up. This is a picture of the sort of person who easily becomes enthusiastic about Christ; but it doesn't last.

Some seed falls among the thorns. Thistles and thorns are the scourge of Palestinian farmers. They can grow as tall as men, growing together into an impassible snare of thorny brush. They get harder and sharper as they dry up. No one dares to try to harvest such a field. It will remain that way until it's burned. Jesus uses the picture of choking thorns to describe our hectic pace, the thousands of things we have to do. There are obligations and ambitions that haunt us in our daily lives, leisure and social activities that take up the rest of our days—and together all this chokes the life that, through the Holy Spirit, had begun to grow inside of us.

And finally, we have the fertile ground where the seed is planted, takes root, grows, and bears fruit. That's what ideally happens with the Word of God in our hearts, but we suspect that Jesus speaks here of His own experience. There's something about this parable that doesn't make sense. No one who understands farming would waste his seed like that, but Jesus does.

And what about the Word in my life? Is it going to waste or does it bear fruit?

You *sow* the good Word, Lord, even in my heart. I wonder how much of it has been trampled upon. I am ashamed to think how much I have let wither and die. And yet, Lord, You never tire of sowing again. Lord, I know it's You who makes it grow, so I ask that You hold Your protective hand on the seed. Chase away the enemy's birds and pull out the weeds. Let Your Word take root so it can bear fruit. Let it bear fruit that honors Your name and benefits my fellow man.

MONDAY AFTER SEXAGESIMA
Luke 8:16–39

"Take care then how you hear." Luke 8:18

Jesus sows His Word among us. We all hear it, but the results can be very different. Therefore, we should think about *how* we hear.

First of all, there are those who have ears that hear but still don't hear anything. They might not even want to hear. They prefer to do what Jesus' brothers did when they came to take care of Him because they thought He had gone mad. They stayed outside. They felt the power of His Word, although they were far away. There was an emotion, an intensity, a desire to hear more from their Brother that was very tangible. Therefore, they thought the best thing for them was to stay outside on the street and only send word that they wanted to meet with Jesus. But He wouldn't meet with them in this way. If you want anything to do with Jesus, you have to listen to His Word, really listen.

It's possible to hear the Word, see His deeds, and still react improperly. This is because people think about what it means for their own interests, economic or otherwise. The people in the land of Genesareth did that. There were small Greek towns and Roman colonies there, with theaters, baths, and contemporary culture. Their temple could be clearly seen on the other side of the sea, all the way to Tiberius and Capernaum. This was where Christ met the man who was possessed by evil spirits. He had been treated with the primitive and brutal methods of the Orient that were still used until the last century. They put him in shackles, but he broke the chains. Then, he lived in the mausoleums, wild and naked. He terrorized the whole area.

Jesus cured him. The evil spirits were forced to let go of him. The disciples obviously interpreted the strange episode with the pigs as an act of mercy. The evil spirits weren't forced to go down to hell. Jesus gave them a respite, but then the nature of evil showed itself. Evil is destructive. It has an innate desire to corrupt and destroy. It doesn't even know what is best for itself. It takes every opportunity given to it to be evil. This is what happened here. Unfortunately, the demon-possessed pigs, rushing to their own destruction, aren't an isolated incident. This also happens to us.

The people of the district couldn't help being impressed by what happened to the man. He sat there, at Jesus' feet, clothed and rational. They understood that they were dealing with a man of God, mighty in word and deed. It was precisely for this reason that they politely yet firmly asked Him to leave. They wanted to be left alone. There was no way for them to know what might happen if this power was unleashed among them.

And Jesus left them.

Lord, I have often been afraid of You. I've wondered if it was a good idea to let You decide. I admit that there are many things I would rather not talk about with You. That is why I ask that You don't let me become deceitful. If there is something I don't want to talk about with You, Lord, then speak to me about it. If I am afraid of what You will say, tell me that You both know and want what is best for me. Why should I be afraid of You? You have come to help me with everything. If I am afraid of losing something, let me see a glimpse of You. Then I'll be reminded that there is nothing worse than losing You. And everything You do and desire, everything You give or take can be nothing but a benefit and blessing for me. In Your name I pray.

TUESDAY AFTER SEXAGESIMA
Luke 9:46–62

"No one who puts his hand to the plow and looks back is fit for the kingdom of God." Luke 9:62

In a strange way, Jesus could be very strict. Today, we read about people who wanted to follow Him, but they wanted to wait a while. They had important things to do first. But when people said they wanted to attend to other matters first, Jesus unrelentingly answered, "Seek first the kingdom of God and His righteousness, and all these things will be added to you" (Matthew 6:33). This was the only way to do it.

Nothing else should come before the kingdom of God.

Maybe we recall Jesus' words about what was sown among the thistles. It isn't only obvious sins that can keep a person away from God, but also honorable duties, daily obligations, things we think can't be neglected.

The question is, what comes first? God created us to live with Him, through Him, for Him, and to Him. We can't do that without His Word. It's through His Word that God begins a relationship with us. The Word needs time. You can't hear it, read it, or learn it without devoting a certain amount of time to it. We have to take that time. We shouldn't let anything disturb us during that time. There are a great many distractions that try to do that. Jesus speaks about the concerns we have today that demand our attention and fill our day. They're already waiting for us at our bedside in the morning. They demand our interest and set the order of the day for us. They make us wonder how we will find time for everything. It's tempting to shorten our morning prayer or forget it altogether. It's so easy for us to say: I don't have time today. Now the thorns are beginning to grow over our heads. They will keep growing until one day we may no longer see heaven.

Lord, tell me every day that I need to seek Your kingdom first. I need to hear it so much. I know what is most important, and yet it is easy for me to let everything else get in the way. I know that Your Word is the bread of life and I can't live without it. Yet, I still try to, time after time. But I don't neglect my meals. I very seldom let anything get in the way of them. Lord, make me that concerned about my soul so it receives the bread of life it needs so much. Make it obvious to me that You come first and are more important than anything else in the world. I can live without most of what I have in this world, but I can't live without You.

WEDNESDAY AFTER SEXAGESIMA
Luke 10:23–42

"What is written in the Law? How do you read it?" Luke 10:26

The lawyer was trying to trick Jesus with the question: "What shall I do to inherit eternal life" (Luke 10:25)?

Jesus answered—like so many times before—by directing him to Scripture, where the key to eternal life is found. No one needs to be ignorant of this. We have God's Word. The question is how to read it.

We ought to know the truth about salvation better than the lawyer. Jesus told His disciples that many prophets and kings had wished to hear what the disciples were able to hear. We have received the complete Gospel. We know the truth. But how do we read it?

The thing is, we have to know what the Scriptures actually say. We hear so often that salvation is by grace, that we are given life although we don't deserve it, that it's not through our doing. In fact, we hear it so often that we are tempted to believe that all we have to do is sit with our arms crossed, occupied with the things of the world until someday, in some mysterious way, we experience some kind of revelation that makes us believers.

That's not how it usually happens. There is something that we can do and should do for our salvation. This is shown in the story of Mary and Martha, like so many other stories in the New Testament. One thing and one thing alone is most important, Jesus said to Martha. Mary understood this. She had chosen a good thing that couldn't be taken away from her. That good thing was described very clearly: She "sat at the Lord's feet and listened to His teaching" (Luke 10:39).

What we can and should do is receive the Word. God's Word is the means of grace. The Word creates something in our hearts: guilt for our sins and belief in the Savior. It creates a living faith that works through love. The Christian life is completely dependent on this. The Word can't be received just once and for all. It isn't merely a matter of knowledge and opinion. It's a creative power that perpetually renews our life. We need it as much as we need our daily bread.

We have to use God's Word. That means we should hear it, read it, remember it, and apply it. We do not earn points with God by using His Word. Instead, by using it, our hearts and lives are opened to the grace of God that can never be earned. It's a way we receive God's gifts.

Lord, thank You for this gift. Help me read Your Word in the right way, as if it were a letter to me from You. Help me read it as a greeting You have given me. Help me hear You speaking personally to me today. Help me realize that You've written it for my sake. I know of course, that You have sent Your Word out to all people in every era. So help me hear that You are speaking. Make Your Word come to life for me. You have sent Your Word to accomplish Your work. Let it work in me too.

THURSDAY AFTER SEXAGESIMA
Luke 11:37–54

"Woe to you lawyers! For you have taken away the key of knowledge." Luke 11:52

We learned this week to be careful about how we hear and read God's Word. Today's Bible reading is an example of hearing and reading the Scriptures the wrong way. It's meant to be a warning for us. The lawyers and Pharisees read Scripture diligently. They truly earned the name *scribe*, which means "versed in Scripture," but they had only a cursory understanding of it. They were careful to do what it said, but only in accordance with the superficial and immediate meaning of the text. They gave one tenth of their harvest of mint, cumin, and dill, even if the harvest was bad. They were meticulous about washing themselves and about the instructions for purification. They constructed minutely detailed applications of Moses' law and knew exactly what was allowed and what wasn't. These detailed rules were called the traditions of the elders. It wasn't easy to remember them all, even harder to actually follow them. And although it might have been possible for educated individuals like the scribes, it was next to impossible for the poor small farmers and day laborers. That didn't matter to the scribes. They would say that people who didn't know the law were cursed. They put burdens on people that were hard to bear and never lifted a finger to ease these burdens. In all their obedience to the law, the scribes had lost the love of God. They had lost the key to knowledge.

That key is the humility and honesty we need to receive God's Word in the right way. That is, first and foremost, to realize that we must submit to God's judgment, to realize our boundless need for forgiveness. We realize that despite all our efforts, we can never deserve God's love. We become what Jesus calls "poor in spirit" (Matthew 5:3). We begin to hunger and thirst for righteousness—the way we crave something we don't have.

Those who have lost the key of knowledge take it for granted that God's Word is to teach us how to better ourselves and be rewarded by God. They read God's Law as a set of instructions for becoming a better kind of person, a leader in both society and the kingdom of God. They see to it that the Law is complied with. They do like the Pharisees: They specify everything and are unbelievably meticulous with small details. Today it's more common to do things in a different way: We simplify everything, we construct common principles (for example, love and human kindness) to which we can attach a universal and "reasonable" application. In both cases, we avoid God's real demands. We are never confronted with the need for the real salvation that only Christ gives.

Lord Jesus, help me judge myself and not others. Let Your Word speak to me. Make me understand how far away I am from Your love and how much is needed before I love like You. When I have bad thoughts about someone and am disappointed in them, help me see that we are all the same. We are all brothers and sisters who need the very same forgiveness. None of us has earned it, but through You we all can receive it. It's not through my doing that I can see it. Help the others also, Lord. Let them see what You have allowed me to see. For Your name's sake.

FRIDAY AFTER SEXAGESIMA

Luke 12:13–34

"For where your treasure is, there will your heart be also."
Luke 12:34

There are those who prefer to apply God's Word to others. They say you can't just allow everything. The Church really ought to speak out against pornography, for example, and other tribulations. The pastor should naturally feel like I do in this marital conflict or inheritance dispute. God must agree with someone who's right.

A person like this came to Jesus. He had a disagreement with his brother over their inheritance. He was certain Jesus would help him. Certainly, God had something to say about this; God's Word deals with this sort of thing.

Instead, the man learned that Jesus wouldn't in any way be a judge or arbitrator in this controversy. God's Word is always about us. It speaks straight to our conscience. If we don't apply it to ourselves, we can't apply it to others. God isn't at our disposal. He isn't there to be our advocate or bailiff.

Then Jesus began to speak to the people who were standing there and who were probably a bit surprised. He told a story about a farmer who had several very successful harvests and planned a huge operational expansion, only to learn that he would be called to give an account for himself that very night.

Jesus was speaking to our anxiety about food, clothes, income, and health. Our heavenly Father knows that we need all this. He gave us life, and He will provide us with everything we need to live. But He doesn't demand of us that we create a situation where we and our families are absolutely secure and have water-tight guarantees for everything we'll ever need. He never meant for us to spend our lives devoted to collecting so many assets that we can feel completely independent. We don't know if we'll even be alive tomorrow. We have no control over the most important thing in life. Yet God promises to give us everything we truly need, if we first ask what He desires and want to live as His children.

The energetic and possibly successful endeavor to secure our existence in this world can pose a great danger. Jesus compares it to thistles and thorns in a field that grow up and cover the seed, block the sun, take away the light, drain the field of its nourishment, and choke the crops. Jesus offered advice to people in this situation, like the advice He gave to the rich young man: "If you would be perfect, go, sell what you possess and give to the poor, and you will have treasure in heaven; and come, follow Me" (Matthew 19:21). Others were able to keep what they owned, but He showed them that they were stewards without proprietorship. They were responsible to Him for their management.

But life like that can't be managed properly without listening to His Word humbly and faithfully.

Lord, I know very well that You can demand my soul from me this very minute. My life is in Your hands. When I go to work in the morning, there is no guarantee that I will return. Lord, help me be joyful and thankful in my heart for this. You decide about my life and You have a purpose for it. Let me realize this purpose every day. Don't let me waste time and energy on meaningless activities. Only You can fill my life with meaning. Make my life be a blessing and joy to You. Lord, lead me in such a way that there will be someone who thanks You for using me to honor Your name.

SATURDAY AFTER SEXAGESIMA

Luke 12:35–59

"I have a baptism to be baptized with, and how great is my distress until it is accomplished." Luke 12:50

We are nearing the end of Epiphany. We have followed Jesus around Galilee and heard Him teach. Now we are going to begin Lent. During this season, we will walk in the steps of Jesus on His journey to Jerusalem.

There's a lot of evidence to indicate that the decision Jesus made to go to Jerusalem was considered a fatal decision by His disciples. He had been there before, but the situation was different this time. His opposition was more ruthless. Everyone knew that His enemies were waiting for a reason to accuse Him. They planned to strike at the first chance. They were fanatical men of unrelenting principles and would not spare Him.

Therefore, it isn't strange at all that the disciples trembled on their way to Jerusalem. Jesus trembled too. This is obvious from what He says. Because He was true man, He was tempted in all the same ways we are. That means He knew fear. He was not indifferent to pain. He experienced these things the same way we do.

However, it wasn't only the thought of torture and death that caused Him pain. The ruthlessness, impenitence, and stubbornness of the people also caused Him pain. He came as a bearer of Good News, to call everyone to God's kingdom. As long as He cured, consoled, and helped people, crowds surrounded Him. But the crowds thinned out when He spoke about living as God's children, in forgiveness and atonement without demanding vindication, and about the joy of serving others. It was apparent that the people did not want to repent. He came to His own people, but they did not receive Him.

First He would be baptized. To be baptized meant to be submerged in water so all the old perished and something new would be born and emerge. Jesus used another picture for the same thing: A grain of wheat must fall to the earth and die in order to bear fruit.

Jesus would also die and pass away. Everything would be shattered. He would hear the enemies' triumphant taunts and heckling from the crowds. Their hatred would beat against Him like a black wave on His head. He would let this happen because of His faith in something preposterous, something that had never happened before. God would die. What would happen if God died?

It's on this journey that we now follow the Savior.

My Lord Jesus, I easily forget that although You truly are God, You also were true man. It's easy for me to imagine that everything was simple and obvious for You. I tend to think that You knew what would happen the whole time. Help me to understand that You, too, had to believe. You had to be led into the darkness by Your Father's hand, and, in the end, You had to let go of His hand. You were forsaken on the cross by Your Father because of my sins. You know what it means to feel anxiety and fear. Help me when I am afraid and hesitate when I'm confronted with opposition and risks. Help me when I think the world is so much more powerful and closer to me than You and Your kingdom. Let me experience Your suffering and Your victory. Let me share in everything You did for my sake.

QUINQUAGESIMA
Luke 18:31–43

They did not grasp what was said. Luke 18:34

It might be comforting for us to know that the disciples had such difficulty understanding. They had trouble comprehending what was most important: that the Son of man had to suffer and would be killed for our salvation. We, too, often find it difficult to understand this. We understand that God exists. We may even experience in a powerful way His love for all that is just and good. We know what He expects of us. So we draw the conclusion that we should live righteously if we want to have anything to do with Him. When we meet Christ and see how He embodies everything that is love and benevolence, we follow Him joyfully, thinking that is precisely what He wants us to do. We should do what He says and live as He lives. This must be the right way to God.

That's precisely what the disciples were thinking on their way to Jerusalem. They didn't understand what He meant when He said He would "give His life as a ransom for many" (Mark 10:45). Yet they knew they wanted to follow Him, come what may. And through following Him, they understood what they had been incapable of comprehending before. They were able to see what happened to Jesus. They experienced what we also witness as we celebrate Lent and Easter. They were able to see how unreliable their own intentions were. They intended to be faithful to death, but they abandoned Him and fled. They learned that they themselves had a debt they were incapable of paying and that their Master was able to bear that debt for them.

This is something we all realize if we follow Jesus. We need to really follow Him and really desire to learn from Him and to live as He lived. When we, without reservation, make kindness and love laws in our lives, then we begin to understand why our goodness and love are not the right way to God. That way ends before we reach the goal. An abyss separates us from God. Jesus alone is able bridge this gap. And we don't understand this until our eyes are opened and we are able to see both what we ourselves were not able to do and what He has done for our sake, in our place.

Lord Jesus, have mercy on me. Here I sit like the blind man at the gates of Jericho praying for Your help. Lord, let me see what I would never see or understand if You did not touch my eyes. Help me to see myself in the light coming from Your Father's throne. Help me to see You and all You have done in the clear light of Scripture so I understand what it means, why it was necessary, and what You have done. I pray that I may follow You and be a disciple, that I may hear and see what I need most day by day. Jesus, Son of David, have mercy on me.

MONDAY AFTER QUINQUAGESIMA
Mark 10:1–16

"Whoever does not receive the kingdom of God like a child shall not enter it." Mark 10:15

Today, we read Mark telling about the journey to Jerusalem. Jesus took the Pilgrim's road on the other side of the Jordan. That was the most common route. The shortest way to Jerusalem went through Samaria, but Jews were not welcome there, so they would go around Samaria, through Perea on the other side of the Jordan valley.

Again we detect a hostile mood. The Pharisees were trying to snare Jesus by asking Him about divorce. And Jesus gave the answer they hoped for: that Moses' law was not God's last word in the matter. It was just as easy for a Jew then to get a divorce as it is for someone today in our country. But Jesus said that even if you divorced according to the law, You still went against God's will. Jesus was not dictating civil law. The civil law permitted divorce "because of [their] hardness of heart" (Mark 10:5). But someone who wants to be God's child and live in peace with God follows God's good will and His Law. Man and wife become one in marriage. They are united by God. Marriage isn't just an agreement to stay together for the time being. It's a lifelong communion between one man and one woman that binds them to each other in an inseparable unity.

Matthew tells us how the disciples reacted. They said, "If such is the case of a man with his wife, it is better not to marry" (Matthew 19:10). We understand this very human reaction because we are often careless about marriage, as with so many other things.

Immediately after this, some mothers came and brought their children to Jesus—"even infants," Luke says (18:15). The disciples began to drive them away. They had just heard how hard it is to enter God's kingdom and started thinking about how much God demands. It took every ounce of their strength to be worthy of being with Him. It was just plain ridiculous, they reasoned, that children were brought to Him. What were they doing there?

And again the disciples were dumbfounded. Jesus seemed to imply that they should've known better. He took the children in His arms and put His hands upon them as a sign that

He received them into His kingdom. He said, "For to such belongs the kingdom of God. Truly, I say to you, whoever does not receive the kingdom of God like a child shall not enter it" (Luke 18:16–17).

God's kingdom is so strange. Sometimes, it appears as if it were unexplainably difficult to get into. And at the same time, we all need to be like little children, who are incapable of doing or understanding anything, if we want to be citizens of this kingdom. How does it all fit together?

To understand this, we have to follow Jesus to Jerusalem.

Lord Jesus, it's incredibly difficult for me to do what I know is right. When I hear You speak of God's will and purpose, I understand how life should be. I also see how we've changed it into something altogether different. I would've liked my life, at least, to be entirely the way You want it to be, but I realize how little I'm capable of doing. Through my Baptism, You took me in Your arms and blessed me when I was only a little helpless child. Now I feel like that again. Lord, is it possible that You want me to come like someone who is incapable of doing or understanding anything? Lord, You know everything and You are capable of anything. So I put my hope in You and only You.

TUESDAY AFTER QUINQUAGESIMA

Mark 10:17–31

"Then who can be saved?" Mark 10:26

This day has been called Shrove Tuesday since the Middle Ages. It was called that because the word *shrove* means a kind of cleansing. It is observed on the last day before the Lenten fast, which lasts from now until the evening before Easter Sunday. As such, it was the last day people could fill their bellies with meat, eggs, milk, and other foods that were forbidden during Lent. And that's just what they did. They would eat until they could eat nothing more. It's become a tradition that in some cultures is called Fat Tuesday.

Today, we Americans[9] have many more opportunities to eat until we're full than we've ever had before. We belong to the wealthy nations of the world. We should be thankful for this and not forget one thing.

Today, in our Bible reading, we read about the rich young man who came to Jesus. He had many possessions. That didn't stop him from being honest and kind. And he had a longing for God that was so strong he sought out Jesus. There was something inside of him that wouldn't give him any peace.

Jesus liked him. Mark 10:20 says He loved him when He saw him. That was precisely the reason Jesus told him as clearly as possible what was missing. He had to liberate himself from everything that tied him down—his good standing and wealth. In other words, good standing, security and standard of living can become the idols that keep us away from God. These verses are a severe reminder for us on Shrove Tuesday,

---

9. The original text says Swedes, but everything it says could be said about Americans as well.

and all the other days, that we're preoccupied with the good things in life, much more so than we should be and much more than so many other people in the world.

It wasn't strange, then, that the disciples asked, "Then who can be saved?" Jesus' answer shows what a difficult problem we face. It's impossible for us to be saved, to approach God, to be freed from everything that ties us down and keeps us outside of His kingdom. But everything is possible for God—even things that seem impossible, like managing things in such a way that even we can be saved.

Lord, dear heavenly Father, You say here just what I've thought and what I've feared. It's impossible. For us it's impossible to achieve salvation. I have to be a radically different person if I want to be a part of Your kingdom. I doubt that's even possible. I think about everything I own, everything I think I need, everything I would find so hard to leave behind. I realize how much I think about myself and how much I worry about my own interests and what is best for me. But for You, all things are possible. I am beginning to understand that it is precisely the impossible that You made possible when You let Your Son die, that whoever believes in Him would be saved. Help me see and believe. Work that miracle in me as only You can do. For the sake of Your dear Son.

WEDNESDAY AFTER QUINQUAGESIMA, ASH WEDNESDAY
Matthew 6:16–21

"When you fast . . . "Matthew 6:16

Today is Ash Wednesday. This day marked the beginning of the Lenten fast for the Early Church. Jesus fasted for forty days in the desert. In memory of that, Christians fasted for forty days. But since Christians didn't fast on Sundays, because it was the day of resurrection, and a day of great joy, they had to start on a Wednesday in order to fast for forty days before Easter. The evangelical church doesn't mandate a particular period of fasting. The practice has disappeared without a trace from many Christian lives.

Today we've read a portion of the Sermon on the Mount, which constitutes the ancient Gospel reading for Ash Wednesday. Actually, Jesus says something obvious: "When you fast . . ." Jesus Himself fasted. He spoke of prayer and fasting as a powerful resource in the fight against evil. But He didn't make a law of it. He definitely did not want anyone to use fasting to make himself look important. His opponents noticed that His disciples didn't fast like the Pharisees. Jesus answered that the wedding guests didn't fast while the bridegroom was among them. But He added, there will come a time when "the bridegroom is taken away from them, and then they will fast" (Matthew 9:15). In Acts, fasting is spoken of as if it wasn't even a question.

What does it mean to *fast*? It means to willingly abstain from something that in itself is both permissible and good. You abstain from it in order to free yourself to serve Christ. You show both yourself and your Lord that you can take this earthly thing or leave it. This is the right way for a Christian to live. We should use this world and its goods as if we didn't need them. There is a lot of good we should to rejoice over, but nothing should control us. We should not let ourselves be bound or captive to anything. Nothing should be allowed to be more important to us than the Lord Himself. By abstaining from certain things—at least for periods of time—we can give money and possibly time to serve Christ in a special way. It can be a good form of fasting to abstain from something and instead give the money to a special Lenten collection or to something else. To regularly give a portion of what you've earned is also a form of fasting. You abstain from something you otherwise could've purchased for yourself, and you do it for Christ's sake. Jesus tells us we should do it joyfully. We shouldn't make a big thing about it. It's a secret between you and your Lord that He alone knows.

Lord Jesus, You have to teach me about fasting Yourself. Show me what You want. Help me do it the right way and with joy in my heart. Help me rejoice when You give me this life's wonderful gifts, and help me to be twice as happy when You let me abstain from them so they will be of benefit and joy. Guide my will and rule over my heart so I can always do just what You want me to do, both when I receive and when I willingly choose to abstain from something. Your will be done, Lord, in everything.

THURSDAY AFTER QUINQUAGESIMA

Mark 10:32–45

"For even the Son of Man came not to be served but to serve, and to give His life as a ransom for many." Mark 10:45

Mark tells us that Jesus led the way, and they were filled with fear. They knew it was dangerous. Already from the heights on the other side of the Jordan, when there was still a two-day journey left, the houses on the summit of the Mount of Olives could be seen. Jerusalem, the city that murdered prophets, was just over that hill. It was clear that the final scene was approaching. What kind of resistance could they muster in the face of such powerful enemies? They would need a miracle. The disciples did not doubt that the Master would be victorious in the end, but what would it cost? They were only human, and they went to Jerusalem trembling.

Yet they followed Him. They had made up their minds. They would share all the dangers with Him, and then they would also share His victory.

The two brothers were thinking about this. These two were called Sons of Thunder because there was something of lightning and thunder in their character. They asked Jesus if He would promise them the two seats closest to Him in His kingdom. Jesus may have smiled a little despondently. They had so little understanding of what awaited them and what He expected from them. He asked if they could drink the cup He had to drink. They answered, "we can" without hesitation. They had, of course, made their decision—they would do what had to be done at any cost. Jesus answered them that it would be enough for them to follow Him one step at a time, in suffering, death, and martyrdom, but He could not promise them a place of glory. Then He called the Twelve together to teach them a small lesson they would never forget. Power and rank, authorities and officials are part of in the kingdoms of this world. It's entirely different in Christ's kingdom. Those who serve are the most important there. The Lord of the kingdom, the Son of Man, had Himself come to earth not to be served, but to serve. Now He would do that by giving His life for the salvation of many.

It was a bewildering speech, so incomprehensible that the disciples couldn't understand it until they saw it happen and it became a reality in suffering and death. The powerful secret of Christ lies in these words: to give His life for the salvation of many.

My Lord and Master, I know how important it is to serve. I have heard it so many times. Help it become knowledge that lives within me, something that's a part of my desire and being. If You give a mission to someone else and not to me, help me realize that it's entirely acceptable. If You give it to me, help me use it to serve others. Help me understand that everything people call power here is, in reality, toil, work, and responsibility, something we will have to account for. But help me know that it's also a joy and a treasure when I do it in service to You, even when I am a servant. Help me to be like You, You who do not come to be served but to serve.

FRIDAY AFTER QUINQUAGESIMA
Luke 13:1–9

"Sir, let it alone this year also." Luke 13:8

Only Luke wrote about the events we read about in today's Scripture reading. On the way to Jerusalem, people told Jesus about Pilate's recent outrageous action. He ordered an assault on some Galileans and mixed their blood with their sacrifices (Luke 13:1). Luke does not record why Pilate took this action. Those who reported the terrible news probably wanted to hear what Jesus had to say about it. Jesus bluntly replied that the same would happen to us all if we didn't repent. He reminded them of another tragic event. A tower had fallen in Jerusalem and took eighteen lives. The people wondered why things like that happened. Did the victims deserve to suffer for some reason? No more than anybody else, Jesus answered. If we don't repent, we will all perish.

To fall from God means to be separated from God. In the end, to be separated from God means ruin and destruction. This is true not only of the few who are such obvious and manifest sinners that everyone disapproves of their behavior. Falling away from God is to not love God more than everything else, to not have Him as the Lord of your heart.

Since the fall into sin, an unfortunate fate looms over humanity. That's what Jesus speaks about in the parable of the unfruitful fig tree. He was speaking about Himself and His people. He came from God. He was God's Messiah, a messenger bringing joy and forgiveness and calling men to God's kingdom. For three years, He had spread His message on earth. He could say, For three years, I've been here looking for fruit on the trees. But I haven't found any. The logical course of action would be to cut down the trees. That's exactly what the Baptist had said at God's command: the ax at the root of the tree. Every tree that doesn't bear fruit will be cut down and thrown in the fire.

But there is Someone who interceded for the wretched fig tree. Jesus is speaking about Himself here. He is like the gardener in the vineyard. He prayed that the owners of the vineyard would leave the vines alone one more year. During that time He would do His best, turn the soil around the tree, and fertilize it. Perhaps, in the end, it would bear fruit.

When Jesus went to Jerusalem, it was to make one last attempt. The people were given a respite. Jesus carried the burdens of His people and all of humanity in His heart. He saw the danger, and would do His best to avert it.

Lord, dear Father in heaven, how many times have You come, looking for fruit and not finding any? And yet You let me remain in Your vineyard. Lord Jesus Christ, I thank You for interceding. I know what would have happened if You hadn't taken me on Your shoulders. Help me seize the day today, tomorrow, and every other day as a day of grace and a gift from You. I know there is a good reason for it because You gave it to me. Help me to do and be whatever You wanted when You gave it to me.

SATURDAY AFTER QUINQUAGESIMA

John 12:20–33

"Unless a grain of wheat falls into the earth and dies,
it remains alone; but if it dies, it bears much fruit."
John 12:24

Today we again read a Bible text that allows us to peek through the door into Christ's heart. Like yesterday's text, it allows us to imagine what compelled Jesus to go to Jerusalem. The text describes something that happened after Jesus entered Jerusalem. When He had spoken to the people in the temple, it became all too clear that the people would forsake God's offer of forgiveness and throw away their last chance.

On one of those days, Jesus was given a message that there were some Greeks who wanted to meet Him. We aren't told why. Maybe it was some of the same curiosity and superficial sympathy that had drawn the crowds to Him in Galilee. Jesus knew how little this meant. So when He answered, He spoke of something completely different than what His admirers had expected. He spoke of the last way out, of God's secret plan, humanity's only possibility for justification. The Son of man, God's own Son, who was the only true God, would give His life for them.

Jesus openly said that His soul was in agony. He asked His Father to save Him from this hour (John 12:27). But He knew that was exactly why this moment was at hand: to carry out the ultimate plan of salvation, the most extreme demonstration of God's mercy. Now is the time for judgment of this world, He said. Now the prince of this world will be driven out. God can never compromise with evil. The eternal gap between Him and Satan can't be bridged. The destitute people on the wrong side of the gap still can be saved, but only if God's own Son gives His life for them. He is the grain of wheat that must fall to earth and die. If He didn't die, He would remain a single grain of wheat—the only Righteous One, the only One who remained faithful to God, and the only One who deserved a place in His kingdom. But when the grain of wheat dies, it bears much fruit. The prophet Isaiah foretold this: "Yet it was the will of the LORD to crush Him; He has put Him to grief; when His soul makes an offering for guilt, He shall see His offspring; He shall prolong His days; the will of the LORD shall prosper in His hand" (53:10).

My Lord and Savior, You didn't love Your life so much that You avoided death. You gave it so I would live. It was just as hard for You as it would've been for anyone to be tortured and die, and yet You did it. I know there was no alternative— otherwise Your Father would have spared You. We wouldn't have deserved anything else. But You took it upon Yourself for my sake. I can never thank You enough for that. Take my life and form it according to Your will, for Your service and for Your glory.

FIRST SUNDAY
IN LENT
Matthew 4:1–11

But one who in every respect has been tempted as we are,
yet without sin. Hebrews 4:15b

After Jesus was baptized in the Jordan, the Spirit led Him
out into the wilderness, Matthew says. The wilderness was
the rocky desert in Judah, where steep mountaintops rise
above the Jordan valley. Through deep ravines, You finally
reach the barren desert. Jesus withdrew to the desert where
John the Baptist had lived before making His appearance in
Israel. He wanted to be alone with God before He began the
work He had consecrated Himself to in Baptism.

This is where He met the tempter. Where did he come
from? People in Israel answered that he was once one of
God's angels, a being to whom God gave life, freedom, and
an independent will. He abused all of this to try to take God's
place. There's an allusion to this in Isaiah, chapter 14: "You
said in your heart, 'I will ascend to heaven; above the stars
of God I will set my throne on high; I will sit on the mount
of assembly in the far reaches of the north'" (14:13). Satan
wanted to be like God. He wanted to make his own decisions. He decided to do what God did not want: evil. He was
also successful in taking a part of creation with him in the
fall. He tricked the first people into trusting him more than
God. Ever since, there has been an unrelenting antagonism
between God and Satan, between light and darkness, between
love and selfishness.

The devil is a particular power with lifelike desires. He
thinks. He has a plan. He takes initiative. He fights to keep
his hold on us.

The decisive conflict came when Jesus came into the
world. Satan knew what this meant. He tried to take the

Christ Child's life. His plan was unsuccessful. Then he tried to win Jesus over to his side. God's Son was, of course, true man. He lived in the same relationship to God as the first humans. He lived in perfect confidence and childlike openness with God. Satan was successful once in destroying this relationship. Why shouldn't he be able to do the same thing again?

So he tried. It's imperative that we think about the temptations Jesus experienced as very real temptations. They were not imaginary. Christ was really tempted in everything just as we are. He could have done whatever He wanted. He could've secured all the advantages in life that usually entice us. That was, of course, what the temptation in the desert meant: He would not have to experience hunger or danger. He would be able to use His power to gain the respect of others. He would be able to create an empire with help from the resources the devil had at His disposal.

But Jesus said no. He was faithful to God. He was the first man ever to fully resist the tempter.

So You, too, had to struggle with temptation, Lord Jesus. Not just once in the desert, but Your whole life. And I once believed that Satan never existed! How could we be so blind, Lord? How could we blame Your Father for everything the evil one does? Lord, help me see the seriousness of it. Help me see how You fought and struggled against all the evil one's actions and his very nature. I thank You for Your victory and that I can be part of it. I submit myself to Your protection and thank You for allowing me to stand by Your side.

MONDAY AFTER THE FIRST SUNDAY IN LENT

Matthew 16:21–28

"Get behind Me, Satan!" Matthew 16:23

Luke tells us that after his unsuccessful attempt to tempt Jesus in the desert, the devil retreated from Jesus until a more opportune time.

One such opportune time occurred in Caesarea Philippi. Peter had just confessed that Jesus was the Messiah. Jesus rejoiced, and He praised and blessed Peter. Then He spoke about the Church that would be founded upon the confession Peter had just made. The relationship between Jesus and His disciples had never been better.

Then Jesus began to speak about His suffering. Peter was terrified. He took Jesus aside and began to rebuke Him zealously. What Peter said came from the best of intentions. He sincerely cared for his Lord. He thought God was on His side: "Far be it from You, Lord" (Matthew 16:22)!

Still Jesus said, "Get behind Me, Satan!" That sounds harsh, but it was the truth. The tempter had emerged again, the same one to whom Jesus once said in the desert, "Be gone, Satan" (Matthew 4:10)! He came with a temptation of the very same sort he tried to use in the desert. He begins with these kinds of temptations when he wants to separate us from God. They don't appear to be evil or something God had expressly forbidden. His proposals sound reasonable and well intentioned. If Jesus was God's Son, why would He then wander around in the desert hungry, starving like a beggar? If He had a good and merciful Father in heaven, then He shouldn't have to suffer and be killed.

This is one of the tempter's greatest opportunities: He appeals to what seems reasonable and right, but only in the short term as we see things. (He had already used this method to get the world to fall into sin the first time. It was, of course, a good tree that stood in the Garden of Eden. There wasn't any real reason for this good fruit to be forbidden.) But Jesus answered Peter, "You are not setting your mind on the things of God, but on the things of man" (Matthew 16:23). And to the tempter He said, "Man shall not live by bread alone, but by every word that comes from the mouth of God" (Matthew 4:4). The first and most important question is not what common sense says is most beneficial or appears more rational, profitable, or loving. The foremost question is what comes from the mouth of God: what God has said, His thoughts, His eternal will. Everything is encompassed in these things. A proper and successful life must always be formed after God's will—even when we think we know better.

Lord, how often do I think I know better? I feel sorry for myself and for others, and then I think that it isn't necessary to go the way You show us. It's so hard to crucify the old Adam in me. I might be willing to do it myself, but I feel that others shouldn't have to. I see how hard it can be for them to forgive, to demand justice, to obey all laws and decrees, to give their money and time. You know it's difficult for me to reproach and admonish them—but many times this isn't even Your desire. Help me to always live entirely after what You desire and do it so joyfully that others begin yearning to be with You and do Your will because nothing can be a wiser or better choice.

TUESDAY AFTER THE FIRST SUNDAY IN LENT
Matthew 17:1–13

"They did not recognize him, but did to him whatever they pleased." Matthew 17:12

That's what happened to the Baptist, Jesus says. It happens often to those who walk in the ways of the Lord. Jesus was absolutely convinced it would happen to Him too.

This is the reason the tempter is able to have power over us. This is how he attempted to get Jesus to at least modify His view of God's will. He placed Him high upon the temple wall. The height was dizzying. The people in the Kidron valley looked like small puppets from there. There Satan proposed that Jesus leap down amidst the throng of people and show His miraculous power in front of everybody. Wouldn't that open their eyes? Then they would follow Him wherever He led. Didn't He have God's word that He would succeed?

The Baptist had preached repentance, but it didn't help. The Church has done the same for two thousand years, and it still doesn't appear to have helped. It looks like other means are necessary to get people to listen. Shouldn't we show others that we can do something really impressive? That's a temptation that has pursued the Church throughout its history. Many times it's been tempting for the Church to get politically involved or intervene in society in an effort to make an impression, create good will, gain sympathy, and win support.

Jesus again answered from Scripture: "You shall not put the Lord your God to the test" (Matthew 4:7). God knows what He wants. He has His boundaries. There are things He keeps for Himself. His thoughts are far beyond ours and we can't change them. That's why Jesus abstained from doing a lot of the things His disciples and His adversaries thought He should do. His friends weren't allowed to fight when He surrendered to His enemies. He commanded Peter to put his sword away. He didn't step down from the cross. He didn't ask His Father for legions of angels that would have gladly hurried to His rescue. Even Christ's Church has to continue to preach repentance and faith, although the world says it should take the completely different position that it's better to get with the times and engage all resources in a cause they say is closer to the hearts of the people than the salvation of their souls.

Lord Jesus, teach me to see through the tempter's abuse of God's Word. Don't let him entice me into doing something You don't want. You could immediately counter with the right words from Your Father. Let those words speak to my heart when I need them most. Help me never test God. I know I do when I carelessly take risks and still hope that it will turn out all right. I know I do it when I am careless when I pray and imprudent with my life and still trust that You are merciful and faithful. Help me love You so Your will becomes my great joy, Your Word lives in my heart, and Your voice speaks powerfully and unquestionably to me, even in my hour of temptation.

WEDNESDAY
AFTER THE FIRST
SUNDAY IN LENT
Matthew 17:14–27

"Why could we not cast it out?" . . . "Because of your little faith." Matthew 17:19–20

The disciples were unsuccessful. They tried to exorcise a demon-possessed boy while Jesus was on the Mount of Transfiguration. It didn't work. The disappointed father turned to Jesus:

"If You can do anything, have compassion on us and help us."

And Jesus said to him, " 'If You can'! All things are possible for one who believes."

Immediately the father of the child cried out and said, "I believe; help my unbelief" (Mark 9:22–24)!

When Jesus had cured the boy, the crowds had dispersed, and He and the disciples were alone again, they shamefully asked why they weren't able to do the exorcism themselves. Jesus told them that the problem was their lack of faith. Then He said something that makes us all ashamed and feel that we've failed: If we had faith even the size of a mustard seed, we would be able to move mountains. Nothing would be impossible for us.

Jesus is speaking about miraculous faith here. We have already learned to distinguish it from saving faith. We have seen that miraculous faith is a gift of the Holy Spirit. But even if it isn't necessary for salvation, we still have to ask why we don't see more of it. Wouldn't Christ also call us a faithless and twisted generation? Isn't the reason it's impossible for us that we have more unbelief than faith?

We must remember, however, that we are not to test God. Testing God means going farther and expecting more from Him than what God wants to do. You can test God by taking dangerous liberties with the false expectation that everything will be fine. You can test God by expecting that He will intervene and come to your help when you follow your own plans and not His. To be certain of God's help, everything must be completely left in His hands. If you are a tool for His plans and do precisely what He wants you to do when He wants you to do it, then you can, with confidence, do great things for God and expect great things from Him.

Lord, I am now aware of my complete blindness. It's difficult for me to distinguish between my own plans and Yours. Sometimes I think I am doing Your will but I fail because of my lack of faith. At other times, I have left things You wanted me to do undone. Help me be attentive to Your Word and to always have the right understanding of it. Help me be alert to opportunities to speak and do Your will. Every morning, make me ready to act on the opportunities You give me that day. Help me be faithful in my daily work and obligations. I know that You gave these to me and You want to be served there, first and foremost. Give me a feeling of dedication for the little things in life, and if You want to entrust me with bigger things, give me both dedication and humility. For Your name's sake, Lord Jesus.

THURSDAY
AFTER THE FIRST
SUNDAY IN LENT
Matthew 18:1–14

"Woe to the world for temptations to sin!" Matthew 18:7

Jesus says that temptation must come. We have seen the reason. There is a tempter, a power that is an enemy of God, that upset the will of man.

Because of this, Jesus now says, Woe to the world! It's a question of an unfortunate result, something destructive and infinitely tragic. The word *temptation* means the same as *stumbling block* in Greek. For example, when Jesus said to Peter, "You are a hindrance to Me" (Matthew 16:23), it really meant a trap or snare or, more precisely, the part of the trap that causes it to spring and catch its victim at the critical moment. Temptation traps a person, beats him to the ground and destroys him.

The tempter does not come from God. The apostle James wrote, "Let no one say when he is tempted, 'I am being tempted by God,' for God cannot be tempted with evil, and He Himself tempts no one. But each person is tempted when he is lured and enticed by his own desire" (James 1:13–14). Here James means the sinful corruption inside us all. This doesn't come from God either. It's the tempter's dirty fingerprints, the mark he left on our very nature. It's an inborn selfishness that appears obvious and natural to us. That's why the tempter always finds our support in something that dwells inside of us. That's why it's so easy for him to recruit accomplices among us. Jesus' words are just that much more serious when He said, "Woe to the world for temptations to sin! For it is necessary that temptations come, but woe to the one by whom the temptation comes" (Matthew 18:7)! And, "Whoever causes one of these little ones who believe in Me to sin, it would be better for him to have a great millstone fastened around his neck and to be drowned in the depth of the sea" (Matthew 18:6). It's not our heavenly Father's will that a single one of us should be lost. Yet many are lost. Woe to the world for temptation's sake!

Lord, it isn't me, is it? I know that it very well could be. If You didn't hold Your protecting hand over me, I would be handed over to all the evil powers that confront me every day and that have a foothold in my heart. So I pray that You take charge there. You alone can keep the old Adam in me in chains. Whatever else happens, Lord, prevent me from being an evil power, an example of destruction, a reason for others to abandon You and accept what is evil. If something wants to destroy me, then put Your hand on it, and make me willing to leave it alone no matter how much I cherish it. You are my eternal hope. You know that, Lord.

FRIDAY AFTER THE FIRST SUNDAY IN LENT
Matthew 18:15–22

"Lead us not into temptation, but deliver us from evil."
Matthew 6:13

Many find the next-to-last petition of the Lord's Prayer very difficult. It sounds as if God deliberately leads us into temptation. This is not what it means. God tempts no one. How then should we understand this petition?

It should first be made clear that the Greek word for *temptation* also means *trial*. For instance, Jesus used this word at the Last Supper: He said, "You are those who have stayed with Me in My trials" (Luke 22:28). Many times, both interpretations of the word are meant: temptation and trial. The apostle James wrote, "Blessed is the man that endureth temptation: for when he is tried, he shall receive the crown of life, which the Lord hath promised to them that love Him" (James 1:12 KJV). Temptations give us an opportunity to show that we love God. They can also bring us closer to Christ.

Temptations are, at the same time, dangerous. In our frailty, we have a right to pray in an effort to escape trials. A prayer like this can bring us closer to God. In Gethsemane, Jesus encouraged the disciples to pray that they would escape temptation. The words have the same meaning when we pray: "Lead us not into temptation." We could also say, "Lead us in such a way that we are not tempted." But we know the whole time that temptations will come. We can't always avoid temptation, and so the petition, "but deliver us from evil," follows immediately. The word *evil* could also be translated *the evil one*, referring to the tempter and all the evil that comes from him.

Lord, lead us not into temptation. Rather, lead us in Your ways, by Your hand. Lead us past dangers. Help us to see them long before they come. Blind and thoughtless, we walk straight into danger. So please, keep us alert and restrain us. If we have to experience danger and temptation, hold us firmly

in Your hand so we won't let go but, instead, will
be protected and saved from all evil. Lead us not
into temptation, but deliver us from evil.

SATURDAY
AFTER THE FIRST
SUNDAY IN LENT
Isaiah 53:1–12

And the LORD has laid on Him the iniquity of us all.
Isaiah 53:6

Why did Jesus go to Jerusalem?

The disciples thought He was going to come to terms with
His opponents one way or another. But they didn't know
how it would happen. Today there are many who are just as
perplexed as the disciples were. That is because they didn't
understand the grasp evil has on us. Evil isn't merely a mistake
to be corrected with the right attitude. It's an integral part of
our own nature. Something inside us tries to get away from
God and neither can nor wants to humbly obey God's Law:
"All we like sheep have gone astray; we have turned—every
one—to his own way" (Isaiah 53:6). If repentance meant—as
many people believe—to better yourself and conquer your
mistakes, it would be a hopeless cause. The evil, which has no
association with God and can never enter into His kingdom,
is still inside us. Salvation cannot only mean that God turns a
blind eye to evil. If He opened heaven for us as we are, then
heaven would immediately become like earth is today: a place

where evil and good mingle; where God and Satan exist side by side; a world of conflict, suffering, pain, and tragedy. We cannot escape the consequences of evil.

What should God do? He doesn't want to lose His children. He can't pretend that evil doesn't exist. Evil and the evil one are just as real as God.

So God did something Paul called "the mystery of His will" (Ephesians 1:9). He allowed a glimpse of this mysterious will to be seen through the prophets. Isaiah showed it most clearly when he said, "And the LORD has laid on Him the iniquity of us all" (Isaiah 53:6). God took the unavoidable consequences of the fall upon Himself in Jesus Christ. He bore all of our infirmities. He was wounded for the sake of our transgressions. He was crushed for our iniquities. He became a sin offering.

That's why Jesus went to Jerusalem. This is the mysterious will of God that we now enter as we follow Him.

Dear Lord Jesus, You did it for me too. Here I stand guilty and ashamed. I'm so awful. I am beginning to understand it now. I would like so much to be Your servant in everything, pure of heart, filled with unselfish desire and enough love for everyone. But I also stand here in thankfulness and joy. Imagine that You did it for my sake! Even if no one else needed to be saved, You would still have died for my sake. I thank You, Lord, and pray that I will be able to do something for Your sake. Show me who I can serve and help as You have served me. Let me do it for Your sake and to the glory of Your name.

SECOND SUNDAY IN LENT

Matthew 15:21–28

"O woman, great is your faith!" Matthew 15:28

Again we hear Jesus speak about tremendous anxiety, and again, He speaks about someone who was not of His own people. The first time, it was a heathen centurion. Now, it's a Canaanite woman who also serves as an example of great faith.

This great faith puts all hope in Jesus. It believes that Jesus can and will help. The woman demonstrates this faith by looking for Him, following Him, begging Him for compassion and continuing to ask even when it seemed He didn't care about her. That's the way all genuine faith in Jesus works.

Strong believers in Christ don't have a lot of confidence in themselves. The woman was not too proud to hear that she had no right to ask or demand anything. She listened humbly as Jesus said He was sent for the children of Israel and referred to her people as dogs. The children of Israel were God's chosen people. They had received the promise and the Messiah came to them now. The Canaanite woman did not belong to His people. She accepted this, saying, "Yes, Lord" (Matthew 15:27). That's the way it always is with true faith. Faith knows that if He helps, it's undeserved grace.

There is another characteristic of true faith in this narrative: It sticks with Jesus, even if He doesn't seem to answer. At first, the woman received no answer, but she pursued Jesus with her shouting. Then He told her He was not sent to the heathens. Their time had not yet come. It would come, but while He still wandered the earth, He would go to the lost sheep of the house of Israel. He had only come there to rest before going to Jerusalem. Mark tells us that He went into a house and didn't want anyone to know it. Why? Even Jesus needed to be alone to pray. He also had a human nature with its physical limits. But when the woman agreed with Him about all this and still begged for a little crumb from the child's table, Jesus answered her prayer. Scripture shows that the apostles knew it was an exception, an important one that would teach something significant to them and us. The woman had great faith and the right kind of belief in Jesus.

Lord, have mercy on me! I thank You because I may shout this even when I don't hear an answer, even when I know I don't deserve it. I thank You because this is reason enough: I need You. I can't exist without You. I thank and praise You because Your mercy doesn't depend on the power of my prayer. I thank You because I don't need to find the right words. My knowledge and experience don't matter. The only thing I need is You. Therefore, I will not stop; instead I will pray over and over to You: Lord, Son of David, have mercy on me.

MONDAY AFTER THE SECOND SUNDAY IN LENT
John 5:1–18

"That nothing worse may happen to you." John 5:14

The miracle Jesus performed on the invalid in Bethesda is remarkable because the man didn't even know who Jesus was.

His faith isn't mentioned. But Jesus had the same power over nature as God. God can use this power to help even those who don't believe. He can change the course of disease and restore health to someone even when doctors have given up hope. He can save a person from danger even when it seems there is no chance. Some people speak about "unbelievable luck" without thinking about who helped them. There is no way for us to know how many times God has helped us escape danger, traffic accidents, infections, and acts of violence.

As God in the flesh, Jesus had the power to intervene in this way. He told this to the Jews immediately afterward: "My Father is working until now, and I am working" (John 5:17). The Jews were infuriated with this and wanted to kill Him because they—correctly—thought He had made "Himself equal with God" (John 5:18).

But if Christ can help, why doesn't He do it? In truth, He does it more often than we believe or notice, but He does not help all the time—far from it.

This is because Christ wants to give us real help. He wants to save us from real danger. That's the reason He said to the man He cured, "See, you are well! Sin no more, that nothing worse may happen to you" (John 5:14).

There is something worse, something much more serious than any disease or disaster that may threaten our physical lives. Being separated from God is the real disaster. This disaster can be impossible to help, eternal, and irreparable. God works to cure this disease. Yet He doesn't always help the way we think He should because our way may only lead us farther away from God. There is a divine pedagogy in His decision to help or wait with help. The whole time, He is helping us with something more important: finding Him. The only question is whether we will recognize His help. Without faith, it's impossible.

Lord, You are all powerful and capable of everything. This is my great comfort. It fills my heart with joy. Everything is in Your hands. You ignited the spark in my life, and You have decided when I will die. You see the whole future and know what's coming. I don't have to worry about what I can't comprehend or foresee. You have promised that I can make all my desires known to You. I can express my preferences and pray for what I want to happen. But, Lord, when I pray for something that's not sensible, mercifully grant me something better. I thank You because You're in control and because "Thine is the kingdom, and the power, and the glory forever and ever."

TUESDAY AFTER THE SECOND SUNDAY IN LENT
John 5:19–30

"For as the Father has life in Himself, so He has granted the Son also to have life in Himself." John 5:26

John explains things differently than the other evangelists. They graphically and concretely describe one event after another. When they record Jesus' words, they make it short and concise. These words were memorized by the disciples. Jesus taught using the same method as other Jewish rabbis and teachers. The disciples drummed their Master's words into their memories.

John explains things differently. He was "the [disciple] whom Jesus loved" (John 20:2). He was particularly close to his Teacher and understood His deepest ideas and thoughts. Later, John led the congregation in Ephesus until a very old age. He taught there and had his own apostles. We hear an echo of these teachings in his Gospel. He mentions things Jesus told the circle of His twelve disciples and things he heard in conversations with His opponents. This casts a different light on the works of Jesus. As a rule, John left out things the other evangelists recorded in their Gospels and wrote about a few other occurrences. He focused especially on these by emphasizing what Jesus said. This gives us insight into the thoughts of Jesus, His relationship to the Father, and profound ideas in His words and deeds that we don't get from the other Gospels.

When John reveals the thoughts of Jesus, he uses key words with particular meaning. We came across many of these words in today's Bible reading. We will start with life and death. Here, *life* means real life, a joyful and meaningful existence. In the beginning, God alone had life, and then God gave it to us also. *Death* means the opposite: a life destroyed, a life without God, a life that destroys itself and leads to suffering and unhappiness. This is life in our fallen world. Death has even struck those who "live" in the literal sense of the word. This is why Jesus could say, "Leave the dead to bury their own dead" (Luke 9:60). When He says the dead "shall hear the voice of the Son of God" (John 5:25 KJV), He means that those who live on the earth can come in contact with the Gospel. We should note that He makes a distinction between those living on earth and those "who are in the tombs" (John 5:28).

Those who believe, Jesus says, have gone from death to eternal life. Faith allows us to receive anew the real and eternal life that exists with God, and then we won't be judged.

Judgment, in John's Gospel, means to be separated from God forever. God doesn't want to judge us, so He has transferred all judgment to the Son. The Son did not come to judge the world but to give it life. He gave His own life so the world would live, but if someone refuses to receive this life, God can do nothing more for that person. There is something in the very nature of God that is in unrelenting opposition to evil. It is this unforgiving opposition, God's absolute repudiation of evil, that is called the wrath of God. Those who believe in the Son have eternal life. But he who does not obey the Son shall not be able to see life. God's wrath remains with him.

Lord, I ought to thank You for Your zeal and for Your wrath. If You weren't so inexorably steadfast and so relentlessly opposed to all evil, there would be no hope. Justice would collapse at its foundations and anything could happen. It's good You are like that. I know that, yet I tremble. I know that Your zeal and Your wrath could strike me too. Therefore, I thank You because You have given me the opportunity to cross from death to life and be certain that I never will be judged. I thank You because I, too, may believe in Your Son.

WEDNESDAY AFTER THE SECOND SUNDAY IN LENT

John 5:31–47

"The very works that I am doing, bear witness about Me . . . You search the Scriptures . . . and it is they that bear witness about Me." John 5:36, 39

How can we know that Jesus is so crucially significant for each and every one of us? The Gospel tells us again and again that there is no other name through which we can be saved. But how do we know that? Jesus speaks about this matter in today's text.

The Jews, who rejected Jesus, wanted to know how He could prove He was right. Jesus answered by pointing to three things.

He first pointed to John the Baptist. John was sent by God. He appeared as the greatest of all prophets at a time when it seemed all prophesying was dead. He proclaimed the coming of the Messiah, and the Messiah came.

Then Jesus pointed to the works the Father sent Him to accomplish. No one could deny that Jesus performed miracles. His antagonists tried to explain them away by saying it was black magic, witchcraft, or the devil's supernatural powers.

Finally, Jesus pointed to the Scriptures. For more than a thousand years, God had been preparing His people for what would happen. Even Moses had written about Him, the one who was to come. Now these promises were all being fulfilled.

None of this proof is conclusive. Spiritual and imperceptible situations can never be proven in an absolute and conclusive manner. But they can be convincing for the conscience. The conscience can be convinced even of what can't be seen. The heart can be convinced of the eternally valid truth although it can't be photographed or weighed.

Therefore, when it comes to Jesus, it's always a matter of the heart's determination. He could say to His opponents: "Yet you refuse to come to Me that you may have life. . . . How can you believe, when you receive glory from one another and do not seek the glory that comes from the only God?" (John 5:40, 44).

In the end, faith is always a question of admitting God is right. Do I or do I not want to?

My Lord and Master, You know I want to and at the same time I don't. Still, I dare to say that I want it to be. You are right. You are Truth. So now I say no to everything that says no to You in my life. I know my faith is subject to righteous judgment. You took it all upon Yourself and my condemnation became Your condemnation. Now I am sentenced to death, and to this sentence, I say yes. I shall be sentenced to death every day. My faith does not deserve to live. I want You to be my life because You came to me with the eternal life from Your Father.

THURSDAY AFTER THE SECOND SUNDAY IN LENT

John 7:1–24

"My teaching is not Mine, but His who sent Me. If anyone's will is to do God's will, he will know whether the teaching is from God or whether I am speaking on My own authority." John 7:16–17

We have seen that faith is a question of being convinced, not only by external circumstances that can be verified using common sense, but also by realities that become inescapable to the heart and conscience. Now we read that Jesus says the same thing.

There was discussion among the Jews. There were differing opinions about Jesus. His opponents were powerful, just like today. Those who knew Him and were drawn to Him were often afraid to show it, just like today. Some thought He was, at the very least, a good man they could learn something from. But His teaching was still offensive; He said He was God's Son, sent by God to save the world. What proof was there of this?

Here, Jesus shows us the way to wisdom. It doesn't come by discussing. There is something most people are not able to form an opinion about because it lies outside our everyday experiences. But we can widen our horizons. We can connect with something that we had no idea about before. This is why Jesus never began by questioning people about what they believed or thought. Instead He said, "Follow Me" (Mark 1:17) and "Come and see" (John 1:46). Here He says that anyone who wants to do God's will, will know whether the teaching is from God or whether He was speaking on His own authority. Something new has happened in the world. It's impossible to know what it's all about without trying.

And you can't try if you don't want to do God's will. Not God's will in general, but His will that sent Jesus. We're not familiar with God's will either. In Jesus, we encounter something new that God wants us to learn about and receive. You have to have confidence in Jesus and listen to Him. You have to consider it worthwhile enough to invest your time and effort into it. That's the way it was then, and that's the way it is today.

My Lord and Master, You are my teacher and guide. Teach me to believe as steadfastly as You want me to. Help me do what I have to do to understand. I know that I can't realize what truth is by pondering over it. I cannot understand Your mysteries by sitting with my arms crossed, just watching. Help me to pray and fight, act and obey, confess and take responsibility in Your service and for Your sake so I may see and experience what it means to follow You. Let me live in Your kingdom, walk on its paths, and breathe its air so I know that it is real and can declare that my eyes have seen Your salvation.

FRIDAY AFTER THE SECOND SUNDAY IN LENT
John 7:25–36

"I believe; help my unbelief." Mark 9:24

It can be difficult to believe.

If you think you can determine if Jesus is God's Son by using logic and known facts, then you will never know the truth. This mistake was made by many in the Jewish community. They believed they knew who the Messiah was. Some said no one would know where He came from; others said the Messiah would come from Bethlehem. They had heard Jesus was from Nazareth, so they rejected Him without knowing where He was born.

In truth, you can know Jesus only by following Him. You have to listen to Him to see who He is.

Even at that, it can be hard to believe because something inside us doesn't want to. A Christian has both a new man, who receives life from Christ, and an old Adam, who rejects Him. That is why, along with the father of the demon-possessed boy Jesus cured when He came down from the mount of Transfiguration, a Christian can say: "I believe! Help my unbelief."

We always have doubt. The old Adam may acknowledge the existence of God. But then the old Adam would try to exploit God and His Church for personal reasons: The Church and its office can be a good source of income; religion can be an effective tool for teaching servants and dependents to behave and stay in their place; politicians know that one single church can keep a whole nation together (which has led to religious persecution and war).

The old Adam constantly looks for new objections to the existence of God. He doesn't want to be bothered with obeying God unless he is absolutely sure that it somehow benefits him. Even then, he tries to restrict his service to a minimum and wants to be a part of something only because it's good for his reputation or results in influential friendships, a promotion, or a raise.

We shouldn't be alarmed or frightened that this doubt within us doesn't want to learn to believe. That doesn't prevent us from really believing in Christ. In fact, it can even help us come to greater understanding and more confident belief.

Lord Jesus, You help me with my unbelief. I know that You alone help me, even when I don't believe or love the way I ought to. Even so, I am still able to come to You, and You call it faith when I come to You weak and skeptical as I am. Lord, it can, of course, be the unbelief inside of me that drives me to You, and makes me hold on to You. So I come to You now and say: dear, Lord, I believe, help my unbelief!

SATURDAY AFTER THE SECOND SUNDAY IN LENT
John 7:37–52

"I will not let You go unless You bless me." Genesis 32:26

This is what Jacob said after he wrestled with the stranger by the ford of Jabbok. During the long struggle, Jacob realized he was wrestling with God Himself, so he refused to let Him go until he received a blessing. God gives this story to those who fight the fight for faith, which we all do in one way or another.

Scripture gives us many examples of this fight for faith. It can be newly awakened, as with the court ushers who were sent out to arrest Jesus but came back empty handed. They had to confess that they couldn't do it because of their conscience. It can be tentative and cautious, like Nicodemus who came to Jesus at night and asked that he not be judged without a trial. It can be hard pressed in many ways by doubt, anxiety, the darkness that accompanies emptiness, uneasiness in the heart, and nervousness. But faith seeks and struggles.

Faith seeks. It knows where help is, so it comes to Jesus. It prays and listens, not just one time out of fear before surgery or in joy over unexpected help. It seeks God because it can't be without God. It says with the psalmist, "O God, You are my God; earnestly I seek You; my soul thirsts for You; my flesh faints for You, as in a dry and weary land where there is no water" (Psalm 63:1). It seeks the Church to be near God. It can say as it is written in the psalm, "So I have looked upon You in the sanctuary, beholding Your power and glory. Because Your steadfast love is better than life, my lips will praise You" (Psalm 63:2–3).

Faith refuses to let go of Jesus. This is possibly the most distinguishing characteristic of struggling faith. It always hopes and prays. It always finds something to cling to. The centurion said, "Lord . . . only say the word and my servant will be healed" (Matthew 8:8). The Canaanite woman said, "Yes, Lord; yet even the dogs under the table eat the children's crumbs" (Mark 7:28). They, too, belong to the house and are in the Lord's custody. I, too, was redeemed by His own blood. He died for me. I, too, am baptized!

Fighting faith refuses to let go of Christ, and so it is

blessed. God allows it to fight so it can grow, be strengthened, and have a tighter grip on God and on His promises. Even when the Lord doesn't seem to answer, there is a blessing somewhere there. He teaches us to believe even if we do not see. He teaches us to trust not in our feelings, experiences, or even our own faith, but only in God's Word and promise. In the midst of all the distress and through all trials and tribulations, a struggling faith becomes a great faith.

Hear, O LORD! When I cry aloud, be gracious to me and answer me! You said to my heart, "Seek My face" (Psalm 27:8). LORD, I seek Your face. Hide not Your face from me. Do not turn away in anger from Your servant, You who have been my help. Do not cast me off or forsake me, O God of my salvation. Even if my father and my mother forsake me, You will take me in. I believe I shall look upon Your goodness in the land of the living! Wait for the LORD, be strong and let your heart take courage: Wait for the LORD (from Psalm 27).

Note: The Annunciation of St. Mary sometimes comes during the last half of Lent. There is a unique devotion for this Sunday in the back of this book. During the following weekdays, you should return to the devotions for the corresponding week in Lent.

THIRD SUNDAY
IN LENT
Luke 11:14–28

"And the enemy who sowed them is the devil."
Matthew 13:39

Talking about the devil shocks a lot of people, but Jesus speaks about him just as explicitly as He speaks about God. He calls him Satan (a Hebrew word which means enemy or opponent) or the devil (or *diabolos*, which is the Greek word for accuser). He also calls him the "the father of lies" (John 8:44).

Jesus says outright that Satan has a kingdom and compares Satan to a strong man who sits fully armed on his property guarding it, knowing it's protected. He calls him "the prince of this world" (John 12:31 KJV). The devil himself certainly doesn't want to be called this. Yet he told Jesus that this world with all its power and glory had been delivered to him and he can give it to whomever he wants. "And Jesus answered him, 'It is written, "You shall worship the Lord your God, and Him only shall you serve"'" (Luke 4:8). God is the world's rightful Lord. He alone has the right to demand our obedience and loyalty. The devil is a usurper, an assailant who forces his way in and takes possession of another's possessions. And He has created a position of power and a kingdom using these stolen goods.

But now, Jesus says, "one stronger than he attacks him and overcomes him, He takes away his armor in which he trusted and divides his spoil" (Luke 11:22).

This is what Christ has done—and continues to do— here in this world. "The reason the Son of God appeared was to destroy the works of the devil," John says in 1 John 3:8. The worst of all the devil's works was the destruction of the original relationship between God and mankind. He possesses a portion of human nature. He made his mark on our innermost desires so there is something in us that is just as incompatible with God as is Satan himself. That could have been his final victory, but Christ eliminated this victory when He took our lot, our guilt, and all the consequences of our fall upon Himself and died for us.

Lord Jesus, Help me always see all these things the way You have taught me to see them. Give me a healthy fear so I can understand the risks, see the dangers, and know what they mean. Grant me also the security that exists only in You because You are stronger than all the powers of darkness and more powerful than anything the devil can threaten me with. Keep me from being at ease around the evil powers that put You on the cross. What wouldn't they be able to do to me? Yet I am safe with You. Before You, they are powerless. When I am under Your protection and belong to You, they can do nothing. So I turn to You and lay my life in Your hands. You have redeemed, bought, and won me from the power of the devil.

MONDAY AFTER THE THIRD SUNDAY IN LENT
John 8:1–11

"Jesus of Nazareth . . . went about doing good and healing all who were oppressed by the devil, for God was with Him."
Acts 10:38

Why are people so shocked by talk about the devil? Is it more logical not to believe in an evil power that stands in opposition to God? Where, then, does evil come from? The fact is that many lose faith because they think God alone is in control of the world, so He alone is to blame for everything that happens. Therefore, if something happens that can't possibly be reconciled with their belief in an "all good and almighty God," they conclude that there is no God. In one sense, this is true. There is no such god, one that has no adversary and who alone is responsible for all that happens.

Today's Bible reading deals with the adulteress Jesus saved from being stoned. This is not a flattering picture of humanity. The Pharisees stood there with harsh and deceitful looks. They were looking forward to doubling their pleasure: making an example of the sinful woman and finding something to accuse Jesus of. The crowd stood with the stones for casting already in their hands. They were eager for blood. How do people get that way? Does this come from God? Did He create us this way? The Gospel answers with a definite no! The enemy has done this.

Knowledge of the prince of darkness is part of our Christian faith. The theme of our fight against evil powers is covered in the texts for the Sundays of Lent. Those who were baptized during the Easter vigil received a final and thorough preparation during these weeks. They would review the important articles of faith of the Christian life. They would also learn that they now had a fight to endure not "against flesh and blood, but against . . . the spiritual forces of evil in the heavenly places" (Ephesians 6:12). We need to be just as conscious of this theme as the ancient Christians were. We are confronted daily with powers that are opposed to every aspect of the will of God. We have to learn to recognize this and live so close to Christ that He alone has control of us.

Lord, I probably notice at times that the evil one is present, such as when I'm obsessed with prestige, covetousness, or when I desire to do things I know You don't want me to. However, I'm afraid that it's more often the case that I don't even recognize evil. So I pray to You, Lord, that You help me see more clearly, understand more, and make better distinctions. But most of all, I pray that You will always be so close to me that I will see everything that cannot be tolerated in Your presence as dirty and ugly. Let me see everything in Your light, even when I would rather not.

TUESDAY AFTER THE THIRD SUNDAY IN LENT
John 8:12–27

"I am the light of the world." John 8:12

In the preceding chapter, John told us that Jesus had come to Jerusalem during the Feast of Booths. It was celebrated in autumn, just after the Day of Atonement, Israel's annual day of penance. When the fasting and repentance were over, the people were filled with great joy as they celebrated the harvest festival's Feast of Booths by staying in tents to remind them of the trek through the desert during the exodus from Egypt. Every day, the high priest and all the people would march in a magnificent procession with water from Siloam up to the temple. Then one of the priests would pour it out of a gold vessel onto the altar as an offering while the people rejoiced and sang a verse from the prophet Isaiah: "with joy you will draw water from the wells of salvation" (Isaiah 12:3). It was in connection with this festival that Jesus spoke about streams of living water flowing from the souls of those who came to Him to drink. After this, the festival continued throughout the night in the women's courtyard. The offering chests were there and everyone who belonged to Israel's people had access to them. Huge candelabras were lit, the Levites played musical instruments from the steps to the inner courtyard, and the people held torches and danced. It was a popular and very exhilarating national festival. It could've been the morning after this festival that the adulteress was led to Jesus, as is told early in this chapter. Jesus was likely alluding to all the lights that lit up the darkness just hours before when He said, "I am the light of the world. Whoever follows Me will not walk in darkness, but will have the light of life" (John 8:12).

God is light, John says. Paul says He lives in light. This light was the life of man. But we live in darkness. Each of us has something inside of us that loves "the darkness rather than the light" (John 3:19). Now the true light, which enlightens everyone, has come into the world with Christ, John says in 3:19. Whoever follows this light, the light of life, will never walk in darkness. But if he doesn't follow the light, he will remain in darkness and die in sin. Everything Christ has to tell us about the light—life, joy, and peace—has this darkness surrounding it. It isn't something everyone has simply because there is a God, but it's something that saves us from darkness, from death, and from evil. Jesus tells us that we remain in darkness, "if you do not believe that I am he" (John 8:24). The original text simply says, "believe that I AM." This peculiar expression appears two more times in this chapter. The Jews wondered what Jesus really meant by these words, and when they finally understood, they wanted to stone Him. Jesus was alluding to God's very own name, the name He revealed to Moses in the burning bush when He commanded him to go to Israel's children in Egypt and say: "I AM has sent me to you" (Exodus 3:14).

This name expresses the idea that God is the only one who possesses life itself and is the only one who exists eternally. He is the beginning and origin of everything that exists. To be, to exist, to endure are qualities that belong to God and come as gifts from Him. We are servants He has "chosen, that you may know and believe Me and understand that I am He" (Isaiah 43:10).

Lord, I praise, thank, worship, and honor You because You are who You are, because You exist, because You are reality, He who is of eternity, the true life and the light that never goes out. I thank You because You haven't kept Your life for Yourself, but desired to give it to us also. I thank You because You are my origin, the basis of my existence, the meaning and purpose of my existence. I thank You because this is the first, the deepest, the truest, the last, and ultimate in existence: that YOU ARE (from Isaiah 43:10).

WEDNESDAY
AFTER THE THIRD
SUNDAY IN LENT
John 8:28–45

"Everyone who commits sin is a slave to sin." John 8:34

If God is the origin of everything, where does Satan come from?

We have already heard the Bible's answer—God created him. The Bible speaks about angels who sinned and "the angels who did not stay within their own position of authority, but left their proper dwelling" (Jude 1:6). At some point in the heavenly realm God created, there was a fall, a rebellion. It happened before our ancestors existed. Yet it occurred among the beings God had made.

Satan has been rebellious and defiant on every point in his opposition to God. He has been a "murderer from the beginning" (John 8:44). He desires to destroy, corrupt, and demolish the good God has done. "[He] has nothing to do with truth, because there is no truth in him" (John 8:44). Truth in the Bible doesn't just mean the sober reality of facts, but God's good intentions for creation. Evil, cruelty, and meanness can be facts, but they still conflict with God's truth. When the devil lies, it doesn't just mean he says things that aren't true, but that he invents and does things contrary to the good will of God. That's when "He speaks out of his own character" (John 8:44).

People often think they are free when they put themselves above God's commands and don't do what He wants. Actually, they only stop serving one power and begin serving another. Jesus tells us there is only one way to find true freedom: to remain in His Word, listening, receiving, and understanding. Then we perceive truth, and the truth sets us free, truly free.

My Lord and Savior, Son of God, You alone can make
me truly free. Create in me a heart that can experience Your freedom and rejoice like a child for
everything Your heavenly Father has given us,
everything that's pure, everything that is filled
with His joy, and the happiness in the righteous
life that exists only in Him. Allow me to feel that
His commandments are not a burden, that His will
is always a blessing, and that it is a joy, a treasure, and a source of perpetual happiness to live
as His child.

THURSDAY AFTER THE THIRD SUNDAY IN LENT
John 8:46–59

"Behold, I have given you authority to tread on serpents and
scorpions, and over all the power of the enemy, and nothing
shall hurt you." Luke 10:19

The seventy-two Jesus sent out came back. They were
completely overjoyed by their fantastic experiences. Even the
evil spirits had been humiliated. It was really true: a stronger
Man had come.

Then Jesus said something that can be understood only
if you know how well the Jews knew their Old Testament.
He alludes to one of Isaiah's prophecies about someone who

wants to be almighty like God. The story about the fall into sin tells us that the serpent tempted with this same temptation: "You will be like God" (Genesis 3:5). That prophecy goes on to say: "How you are fallen from heaven, O Day Star, son of Dawn! . . . But you are brought down to Sheol" (Isaiah 14:12, 15).

And now Jesus says some remarkable words: "I saw Satan fall like lightning from heaven" (Luke 10:18). Satan, who was created by God and wants to be like God and create his own kingdom, will be destroyed. He will lose his weapons. When Christ came into the world and His Gospel went out to the people, Satan's empire was finished. He seduced people into following his example to be like God, to write their own laws, and to take control of their lives. Christ offers something completely different to this self-assertive and presumptuous way of life. "Behold, I have given you authority to tread on serpents and scorpions," He says in Luke 10:19. You have to know the Old Testament very well to understand Him. Jesus was quoting a well-known psalm, which begins: "He who dwells in the shelter of the Most High will abide in the shadow of the Almighty" (Psalm 91:1). This is Jesus' way of life: not trying to be equal to God but to be under His protection. There's where you can receive the power He speaks about, to trample underfoot "all the power of the enemy" (Luke 10:19). Then we are promised: "And nothing shall hurt you" (Luke 10:19). While the desire to be self-sufficient causes us to be left alone in the midst of all the powers of darkness, the chance to sit in the shadow of the Almighty is a source of infinite security. When all is forgiven and we have laid our life in God's hand, Satan can no longer do any serious damage to us. He has no right to us. He has no power over us. He can tempt and torture, but he cannot snatch us out of God's hand.

My Lord Jesus, You who are the stronger one, You are able to open things that no one is able to shut. You forgive so that no one can ever judge. You are our hope, our strength, our help, and our security. Those who were devoted to You looked forward to Your coming. Abraham was able to see You and rejoiced. We have beheld what many kings and righteous men wanted to see, but never did in their day. Still they wanted to stone You because of who You were. That's how great blindness and the power of deceit are. They crucified You, and You let it happen so You could destroy the enemies' power. Praise be to You, O Jesus.

FRIDAY AFTER THE THIRD SUNDAY IN LENT
John 9:1–21

Jesus answered, "It was not that this man sinned, or his parents, but that the works of God might be displayed in him." John 9:3

Jesus said this about the sick man. The disciples had asked whether it was he or his parents who had sinned and caused him to be born blind. They reasoned like Jews normally did and like many people do today. If someone is miserable or even ill, it must be justified punishment. People think God is the cause of everything. God is supposed to make sure that order is upheld in the world, so He intervenes with suitable punishments for those who are obviously guilty. Otherwise there would be no justice.

There is, however, something not quite right with this line of thinking. This is why so many complain that God is unjust, unmerciful, and biased. They fail to take the devil into account. They have painted a false picture of the world for themselves and don't see the continuing fight between the Creator and the destroyer, between the Savior and man slayer. We can't fathom this enormous, universal struggle. We know only that it affects our entire existence. Evil is active even in nature, causing disease, deformities, and destruction.

We have already read that God can put an end to evil, but only on the final Day of Judgment. As long as He allows the world to continue, evil will continue. But God has the situation under control. He guides the course of the world to the great and final victory. Nothing happens that God doesn't include in His plans to, in some way, make things better for those who seek Him. Therefore, even in the midst of everything that is a result of evil, we can seek God's purpose.

This is what Jesus said about the man who was born blind. God let this happen to him so His works would be revealed. We read later how this man and many with him came to believe. It happens again and again with those who suffer from disease or are handicapped, prisoners of war and refugees, victims of accidents and economic ruin. It's to their advantage as well as a blessing for people who ask in the midst of their suffering, What do You want from me, Lord? Many have been able to see God's works revealed and found real meaning in their lives when they suffered from something that, on the surface, appeared to be meaningless.

Dear Father in heaven, Your ways are as far beyond ours as Your heaven is beyond this earth. I thank You that I don't have to comprehend everything.

*This world seems to me to be an entangled mess of
selfishness, folly, and incomprehensible injustice.
Yet I encounter You everywhere. I've been able to
do it in my own life. When I look for meaning in
my life, when I ask You for the opportunity to help
and serve, You are always there. I thank You that
I don't have to understand things that are too difficult for me and I don't have to fathom things that
I can't understand. I pray that I may take every
day from Your hand and that You will be with me
in all that I encounter. Help me see Your purpose.
Help me help someone else who also finds it hard
to see Your purpose.*

SATURDAY AFTER THE THIRD SUNDAY IN LENT
John 9:22–41

"The accuser of our brothers has been thrown down,
who accuses them day and night before our God."
Revelation 12:10

At the beginning of Job, we're told how the prosecutor—
Satan—comes before God and maintains that, if tested, Job
wouldn't make the grade. And the Book of Revelation tells
us that the devil, "the accuser of our brothers, ... accuses
them day and night before our God." This is a grave situation. When the liar becomes the prosecutor, he doesn't have

to lie. He can say dreadful things that are, in fact, true, and he can use God's own Law while doing so. Those he accuses have offended God. They are no longer God's children. Should God turn a blind eye and let them come into His kingdom, then the prosecutor would also come in with them because he is now a part of their nature.

This is the best weapon that a person of moral fiber can rely on: God's own Law and God's own nature are incompatible with all evil. Satan knows we belong to him. He has the right to possess us. He declares his rights before God because God cannot break His own Law.

But now Revelation speaks about a strange event: Satan was cast down. We heard Jesus speak about the same event when He said He saw him "fall like lightning from heaven" (Luke 10:18). Something happened, and the prosecutor can no longer state his case before God.

What happened was that God provided a way to save His children without violating His Law. Sin is incompatible with God. Evil can't be a part of God or His kingdom. It seemed that the only thing that could be done was to shut out evil. That would mean we would have to stand out in the darkness. When the people wouldn't repent, Jesus could have just returned to heaven and humanity would have gone further down the path they had chosen for themselves. Instead, Jesus went to Jerusalem to settle the score with evil. But it didn't happen the way the disciples expected it to happen. They expected Him to beat evil into submission. Instead, He offered His life as a ransom. He took upon Himself our transgressions. Evil and God would meet in a very different way when God's Son took all our guilt, all our crimes and failures, all our despicableness, vulgarity, and indifference, and made it His own—His own guilt, His responsibility.

When our evil encountered God's holiness, Jesus Christ bore all the consequences. That's when the prosecutor lost his power over us and his right to us. Now, when he steps before God, he meets the Redeemer and has to be quiet. His best weapon falls out of his hand. "If anyone does sin, we have an advocate with the Father, Jesus Christ the righteous. He is the propitiation for our sins, and not for ours only but also for the sins of the whole world" (1 John 2:1–2).

Who can ever thank You enough, Lord, for all You have done? If I didn't have You as my Lord and Savior, I would never dare approach God. I know just what the prosecutor can say. I have received so many wonderful gifts for so many years. Everything has been forgiven many times, yet I am still the antithesis of Your love. I know that You want only good for me. You take responsibility for all my guilt. You have taken my lost cause upon Yourself. I can only thank You, Lord, and pray that I can at some time and in some way show You how wonderful it is to believe and belong to You.

FOURTH SUNDAY IN LENT
John 6:1–15

"Where are we to buy bread, so that these people may eat?" John 6:5

This was a question Jesus asked His disciples. We should be thankful He asked it because it shows the real heart Jesus has for social situations, and He wants His disciples to share this interest. An enormous crowd of people had followed

Him. They were on the hillside. It was spring. The grass and flowers were blooming on the hills as they do during the Palestinian springs. But there was nothing to eat. A little boy had brought some bread and fish, but it wouldn't go very far.

This was the reason Jesus intervened and performed a great miracle. He used God's creative powers. He had refused to use them for His own benefit when He was hungry in the desert, but now He did it for the benefit of all these hungry people. Similarly, it's an equally tremendous miracle when God causes "grass to grow for the livestock and plants for man to cultivate, that he may bring forth food from the earth," as it says in Psalm 104:14. God performs this miracle annually before our eyes. We think of it as completely "natural," but it would never happen without the Creator's intervention.

Jesus fed five thousand hungry people. No wonder they were so enthusiastic. At last they found Someone who could solve their problems. They wanted to lead Him away triumphantly, with or without His consent, and make Him their leader.

But then He withdrew. This wasn't His task in the world. He didn't come to solve the world's problems by producing everything we might want to eat or to appease and satisfy all our desires. These solutions don't solve the real problems at all. The real problems are much more profound. They're part of an evil, egotistical, self-glorifying desire that causes new conflicts and sufferings no matter how many material things we acquire. As we know, problems and conflicts may increase with the acquisition of these things.

This doesn't give us the right to be at peace with ourselves as we sit with our arms crossed amidst suffering and injustice. Whatever can be corrected should be corrected. A Christian has social and political responsibility. Both righteousness and mercy need to be upheld as much and as often as possible on this earth. The Church has a particular responsibility to do even more than society does, especially through our welfare and social work.

But the Church cannot become what the people wanted Jesus to become: an executer of a worldly welfare program. You can't receive what Christ has to give as long as you are concerned with protecting your rights and getting the most out of this life. Social issues are important, but there are even more important issues. Neglecting them can have horrible consequences—often already in the here and now, but definitely in eternity. The way you resolve them determines everything else.

Lord Jesus, You put Your disciples to the test. You asked them where they could find bread for so many. Are You giving us this test also? I am afraid, Lord, that I haven't done very well on this test. There are an infinite number of people who need bread, and what we have to give them is insufficient. So often, the number of people in need is just an excuse to do nothing. Forgive us, Lord. Help us think about and do what we can to find enough bread for all to eat and be satisfied. You alone can help us here. Perform a miracle with us all. Make us instruments of Your will. Be our King the way You want to be so Your will guides our hearts, thoughts, work, laws, and society. Lord, perform a miracle with us, for Your name's sake.

MONDAY AFTER THE FOURTH SUNDAY IN LENT
John 6:24–47

"I am the bread of life." John 6:35

This was a controversy between Jesus and His Galilean countrymen. They wanted to use Him for their political purposes. They were nationalist freedom-fighting revolutionaries and wanted Jesus to lead them in their fight for freedom and food. Jesus touches on a sensitive subject when He tells them they sought Him out in order to eat and be satisfied and not because they saw His miracles. The miraculous feeding was a sign of something different and bigger: the fact that God's kingdom was at hand. It was time to repent and believe the Gospel. Jesus began to speak to them about this. They asked—like everyone who thinks God wants them to do something—what they should do. Jesus answered that they should believe, and this is the work of God. There was only one way to a new and better world: God had to create something new in their hearts. The best thing they could think of was something like the manna in the desert, something that would keep them from hunger. But Jesus told them that "the true bread from heaven" (John 6:32) gives us something more. It gives life to the world, life that will never end. It comes from the very source of life—God. And it guarantees that you will never again encounter real hunger, the hunger for meaning in meaninglessness, the hunger to live when threatened by death, the hunger for a new morning when you see darkness closing in forever.

It's this life that Jesus gives the world. He is the bread of life. This is why we believe in Him and come to Him.

This was just as offensive to the Galileans in Capernaum as it is for many today. He was their fellow countryman! He was human, just like them! But the disciples understood who He was. They understood the signs. They saw what was behind His ability to cure the sick, wake the dead, and give bread in the wilderness. They could say, as John would later write: "The life was made manifest, and we have seen it, and testify to it and proclaim to you the eternal life, which was with the Father and was made manifest to us—that which we have seen and heard we proclaim also to you, so that you too may have fellowship with us; and indeed our fellowship is with the Father and with His Son Jesus Christ" (1 John 1:2–3).

Lord of Life, You came to the world to give us Your life. You Yourself are the bread of life. I thank You for this life here on earth. I thank You for the tremendous miracle I can't comprehend: That You keep me alive day after day, my heart beats and my brain functions and wonders. I sit at a table and eat and drink. The food becomes one with my body; it's converted into a task, consciousness, thoughts, and prayers. I don't understand how it happens, but I know that it happens as long as You allow it. And You have also given me the bread of life. You come, Lord Jesus. I receive You and You become a part of me. Your life lives in me. I don't understand how that is, but I know that You are my life, and I have something that will never pass away. I thank You because You are the bread of life. You are the bread of life for me.

TUESDAY AFTER THE FOURTH SUNDAY IN LENT

John 6:48–71

The cup of blessing that we bless, is it not a participation in the blood of Christ? The bread that we break, is it not a participation in the body of Christ? 1 Corinthians 10:16

When Paul wrote these words, a quarter of a century had passed since the Jews quarreled with Jesus in Capernaum. Paul could now refer to uncontestable truths that all Christians were acquainted with, but when Jesus first spoke about these things in Capernaum, He aroused violent offense. John was possibly the first to understand his Master. That's why he was so eager to explain in his Gospel what Jesus meant.

John understood that the feeding of the five thousand in the wilderness alluded to the coming kingdom where Christ would nourish and give life to thousands upon thousands of people. He wouldn't just give them something comparable to manna in the desert. Jesus would give bread that afforded eternal life. He was this bread. "And the bread that I will give for the life of the world is My flesh" (John 6:51).

John understood that Jesus referred to two things when He said He would give His life so the world would live. He was talking about His death on the cross and about the Lord's Supper, which He would institute the evening before His death. This is why He didn't just speak about His body in Capernaum, but also His blood. He would give the invisible gifts in the bread and wine that were a part of Him and all He had to give. Paul would later call this a participation of Christ's blood and body (1 Corinthians 10:16).

The Jews in Capernaum misunderstood. They understood it as something that since has been called a "Capernaistic eating"—a purely literal consumption of a piece of flesh. But

Jesus says, "The flesh is no help at all" (John 6:63). By *flesh* He means the created and the material, not the bread of life. In a sense, it's still like bread and nourishment in that it's something we're in constant need of. We can't eat enough bread to satisfy us once and for all. We constantly need nourishment for the sustenance of life. In the same way, the life Christ gives is constantly needed. It can be compared to the blood that pulses through our veins and to bread that we eat.

And here Jesus offers more than a metaphor. He gives an outer sign, a Sacrament, a means of grace, through which we can receive Him and His life. There is an invisible gift in the bread we eat and in the wine we drink. The bread and the wine remain the same earthly substance as before, but under the visible exterior of the visible material, Christ hides the gifts that He alone can give.

> *Lord, they said this sermon was a tough one to take. They no longer wanted to follow You. But I say what Peter said: "Lord, to whom shall we go? You have the words of eternal life" (John 6:68). I thank You because You have so much more to give than I can imagine. I thank You because Your reality is much greater than my common sense can conceive. I gratefully receive everything You have to give. I praise You because You come to me so I can see Your gifts with my own eyes, receive You, and be one with You. You are the bread of life and have come to me so I can be with You and You with me. Praise be to You for Your unspeakable and incomprehensible gifts.*

Note: From now until the end of Lent, the readings for our devotions will come from the "The Passion of Our Lord Jesus Christ" taken from the four Gospels. They consist of six short books that are broken into chapters. For this section, I'll refer to them instead of Bible verses. It's important that you read these sections in order to understand the devotion. You can find them in the back of this devotional book. However, the Sunday devotions will still be based on the Gospel reading for that Sunday.

WEDNESDAY AFTER THE FOURTH SUNDAY IN LENT

The Passion of Our Lord Jesus Christ, book one, chapter one (see pages 810–811)

Now the Feast of Unleavened Bread drew near, which is called the Passover. Luke 22:1

The long journey to Jerusalem had ended. Jesus was resting with His friends in Bethany, near the top of the Mount of Olives. (On the day we now call Palm Sunday, He entered the city amidst celebrating crowds, but we'll come back to these events on Palm Sunday.) On the Monday and Tuesday of the week we call Holy Week, Jesus taught in the temple. In the evenings, He returned to Bethany, and early the next morning again walked down through the Kidron Valley and up to the temple. But the mood in Jerusalem changed over the course of the week. His adversaries decided He must die. They must have been disgusted over all the commotion around His triumphant entry and the attention He received. Yet they didn't dare lay a hand on Him, not even when He drove the crowds out of the temple. That might have caused an uproar, then the Romans might have gotten involved and no one knew where it would all end. Their country was occupied. The adversaries were forced to exercise caution.

They didn't want to lose the little freedom they still had. On top of the political considerations came the religious considerations. The leaders of the people could not tolerate a prophet who questioned all the control they had created with their regulations and minutely detailed law. Time after time they argued with Jesus in the temple in an attempt to expose Him as a heretic; they wanted Him to make a fool of Himself in front of everyone. Each time it backfired.

These conversations and events are given a lot of attention during Pentecost, so we'll pass on them for now. Instead, we'll look at Wednesday and Thursday of Holy Week. So much happens during these two days that we have to begin studying them now, long before Easter, so we have time with the most important events.

The Passover was near. The city was full of pilgrims. Pontius Pilate had come from his residence on the coast. And the Roman garrisons were reinforced. Passover was a huge folk festival, kind of like the Jewish equivalent to our Christmas season. It was a celebration of the exodus from Egypt, the night of liberation when the Lord God, with His mighty arm, led His people out of the land of slavery. Thousands of Passover lambs were sacrificed in the temple at this time. Every home was filled with the hum of songs in the evening.

The disciples also prepared for the Passover, but a threatening cloud hung over them that dampened their festive spirit. Their adversaries had sinister plans. The people were disappointed with this Prophet, who preached only repentance and not revolution. The Master Himself let them know that His time was near. He said the woman in Bethany anointed Him for His burial. What was about to happen?

You alone knew, Lord. You took the path that had been laid out and determined for You. We were the ones who caused it for You. Our fall, our sin, our selfishness forced You to take this path. It wasn't only Judas who betrayed You. Each of us betrayed You. We believed more in humanity than in You. We would rather have peace in the world than trust in You. But You took this path and made it Yours because we had gone astray. Praise be to You, O Jesus.

THURSDAY AFTER THE FOURTH SUNDAY IN LENT

The Passion of Our Lord Jesus Christ, book one, chapter two (see page 811)

"I have earnestly desired to eat this Passover with you before I suffer." Luke 22:15

The Lord lay at the table with His disciples. In ancient times, the Passover was eaten while standing with a walking stick in hand, a reminder of the hasty departure the night the patriarchs left Egypt. Now they lay at the table as was the contemporary custom. It was the year's biggest festival. Even the most down and out in Israel would lie at the table like a lord. It was a sign that they belonged to the people that the Lord Himself had chosen and saved from slavery.

The Passover lamb was on the table. It was eaten with salt, water, and bitter herbs to remind them of the bitter years in slavery. A brick-red paste made of dates and figs reminded them of their work as slaves at the brick ovens in Egypt.

This Passover was different. Two things had happened that the disciples didn't understand but never forgot. First, Jesus told them that this was the last meal He would eat with them. Then He said the table prayer over the wine and thanked God as He had done many times before, also for the last time. They wouldn't do it together again before everything was new in God's kingdom.

Could God's kingdom be so near? What was going to happen? He spoke to them again of His suffering. It was something they could not completely comprehend.

The Master took the prescribed unleavened bread. He thanked God again, praising Him for all of His blessings. Then He tore the tough thin bread into pieces and distributed it. He said it was His body, which was now given into death for their sake. They would do this in remembrance of Him.

In other words, He gave Himself to them. His body would be given, sacrificed, and torn apart like the bread in His hands, and it was done for them. Would He then also suffer for their sake? Wasn't His suffering for the sake of His enemies?

After the meal Jesus also took the last cup that was called the cup of blessing. He passed it to them and said, "This is My blood of the new testament, which is shed for many for the remission of sins" (Matthew 26:28 KJV).

This hour must have been filled with mystery for the disciples, but although they didn't understand everything, they did know that they were His. They were participating in everything His Father had sent Him to do on earth, so they knew they would inherit everything that was fulfilled through Him.

They all knew the old covenant, and they had even read about the new covenant in the prophets. Now it, too, was coming. This covenant would also be consecrated through sacrifice and it was Jesus Himself who would be sacrificed.

Again it was a complete mystery and at the same time a tremendous assurance. Whatever was going to happen, He was their Lord and they belonged to Him.

Lord, thank You for Your Communion. I thank You because I don't have to comprehend with my own reason what no one is able to comprehend or fathom. How can my inadequate human mind comprehend the infinity of Your being? How could I fathom Your secret? Yet a child can get to know You. My heart can worship, praise, and receive Your gifts although they're too great for me to understand. Therefore, I kneel at Your communion rail and pray for what You grant me. I pray for You, for Your life, and for a part in Your salvation and bliss. I thank You that I can receive so much more than I can fathom and that I can receive something I only partially understand. Praise be to Your name and blessed in eternity.

FRIDAY AFTER THE FOURTH SUNDAY IN LENT

The Passion of Our Lord Jesus Christ, book one, chapter three (see pages 812-813)

"If I do not wash you, you have no share with Me." John 13:8

John tells the story of Jesus washing the disciples' feet. He often skips what the other evangelists have already covered. Instead, he comments on it and helps us understand its deepest meaning. This is what he is doing now. He doesn't speak directly about the Lord's Supper, but he explains what Jesus meant by it. He reminds us of what Jesus did that evening: He washed the feet of His disciples. It's one of the humblest duties that could be imposed upon a slave. That's why Peter didn't want to let Him do it. Then Jesus said, "If I do not wash you, you have no share with Me." These words show that Jesus wasn't just giving them a lesson in humility and service, He was also giving them an explanation of what He meant when He broke the bread and passed the cup. He would also suffer and die for them. If He didn't purify them through His sacrifice, they wouldn't have any part in Him. It's possible that they believed they already had a part in Him. They had obeyed His calling. They had faithfully followed Him to this very evening. They could understand that He would have to suffer and die for those who hadn't repented. But them? They were His disciples, the faithful who understood and followed Him. Yet He made no distinction between them and other sinners when He spoke of His suffering. He said that His blood would be poured out for many for the forgiveness of sins. In Israel, *many* meant the great multitude of sinful people, the lost sheep of Israel's house.

Peter could hardly understand it, but he still had a deep and sincere faith in his Master, so he didn't object. On the contrary, when he heard that it was necessary for him to have a share in his Lord, he wanted to be washed even more.

That's what communion is. That's what faith is. We don't say: Do we really need it? Instead, we thankfully and joyfully receive it and look forward to more.

Lord, I want to do that also. If it's a matter of having a share in You, then nothing will stop me. There will be no boundaries. I won't question it. I will trust only in You. I pray that You will come with all You have to give. I know I need it too. I am ashamed that You should have to serve me, but I am also thankful that You do. I pray that You would teach me to serve You with joy and even more that You would give me the opportunity.

SATURDAY AFTER THE FOURTH SUNDAY IN LENT

The Passion of Our Lord Jesus Christ, book one, chapter four (see page 813)

"One of you will betray Me." John 13:21

How was it possible? One of those the Lord had chosen? One who had walked with Him and seen His divinity and power with his own eyes? If this could happen, then anything could happen to any one of them.

The disciples understood this. They didn't profess their innocence. They knew that if their Master said it, it was so. They were confronted with the unfathomable mystery of evil. No one could be sure of himself in this case. Everyone had to stand the test. They were willing to do it. They began taking turns asking: "Lord, is it I" (Matthew 26:22 KJV)?

This is the first question a disciple asks when he hears talk of betrayal, even in the inner circle. He asks his Master this question. He knows that only one thing is certain—the only one way to salvation is to hold on firmly to the Lord.

But Peter wanted to know more. He whispered to John, who was closest to Jesus at the table. Then Jesus did something even more profound. He broke a piece of the soft unleavened bread and folded it, as was the custom, and dipped it into a pot to pick up a piece of meat. Then He held it out to Judas. It was a sign of respect. The host would do this when he wanted to honor a guest. Judas must have understood the meaning of this. Jesus was offering him forgiveness, friendship, and fellowship. Everything would be as it was before. But Judas decided to go his own evil way. He took the bread, but he didn't take the outstretched hand. Judas looked away from Jesus and rejected His last offer of forgiveness and reconciliation. John says that Satan entered him in that moment. Judas forfeited his last opportunity for reconciliation. Jesus knew this, but didn't draw attention to it. He said only, "What you are going to do, do quickly" (John 13:27). He said it so naturally that the others thought He had just asked Judas to buy something for the festival or to give something to the poor from their little community purse.

So Judas left. The door opened for just a moment. "And it was night," John says (13:30). He is alluding to something more. Judas went out into the darkness, the outermost darkness that is eternally separated from God.

This can happen even to those who are very close to Jesus. They can turn down His last offer. They can harden their hearts to His final attempt to win back what is about to be lost.

This event teaches us what it means to receive Holy Communion in an unworthy manner. The Bible doesn't speak about worthy and unworthy communicants. None of us is worthy enough to receive Christ and His gifts, but we can receive them in an unworthy manner. That means to do what Judas did: to sit with Him at His Table with a firm conviction in your heart not to obey Him, to go your own way—at least on some particular point. That's when a person goes to Communion in unbelief and defiance or possibly in total indifference. To receive it in the right way means doing what the other disciples did. They wanted to follow Jesus. They trusted Him. There was a lot they didn't understand, but they knew the truth was in Him. They had their share of infidelities. They would fail in all their good intentions that same evening. But they knew He was right, and they could go to Him for help. Christ instituted His Supper for people like them.

Lord, You know everything. You know I love You. You know I have no one else to go to. Others may forgive or pass judgment on my faults. You alone can take away my guilt without making excuses for things that can't be excused. You alone can liberate me. Anything could happen with my own thoughts and desires. I know that, Lord. But when I have You, I have a rock that never falters and can't be budged. I build my hope on You and dare to believe that I will never be lost. You said it Yourself. Nothing can snatch Your children from Your hand. I lay my life, my future, and my eternity in Your hands.

FIFTH SUNDAY
IN LENT
Matthew 21:33–43

They perceived that He was speaking about them.
Matthew 21:45

They didn't understand it at first. They thought Jesus asked a judicial trick question, and compared to some this one was unusually easy to answer. Scribes were both theologians and lawyers. The Law of Moses was also their civil law, and they were accustomed to giving opinions in all sorts of legal cases. That was what they did here, with their usual explicitness: for landowners who did things like that, the process was short and sweet. But then Jesus said clearly enough for everyone to understand that the vineyard was Israel. They themselves were the landowners. And the rightful proprietor who was treated so badly was none other than God Himself.

It's easy and comfortable for us to let this parable deal with Pharisees and scribes. But Jesus' words are, in fact, about us. The disciples, like the Early Church, understood this. They remembered that Jesus said, "The kingdom of God will be taken away from you and given to a people producing its fruits" (Matthew 21:43). No one is secure here. The kingdom is given to those who bear its fruit.

It's easy for us to blame the Pharisees. We often forget that they were a part of the elite of their day, educated upholders of an ancient wisdom and distinguished culture. They were admired by both countrymen and foreigners for their high moral standards. They were pillars of society. But they were wrong: They rejected the Cornerstone.

The pillars of society of our times are progressive politicians and scientists, authors and editors, entrepreneurs and representatives, refined people of culture, responsible, hardworking, broad-minded individuals. The list of people with good judgment is long and covers most aspects of society. We are all inclined to trust these people and the culture, lifestyles, and values they represent.

But what about the Cornerstone?

Why were You rejected, Lord? Why didn't they accept You? Why don't we accept You? You gave us the vineyard. The ground under our feet is Yours. Everything that passes through our hands comes from You. You've planted a precious tree among us and made us into its branches so we could bear fruit. What kind of fruit do You get from us, Lord? We want to avoid that question. Is this why You are so often rejected? So these questions won't have to be asked? Don't allow them to be avoided, Lord. Let us know that You are speaking about us.

MONDAY AFTER THE FIFTH SUNDAY IN LENT

The Passion of Our Lord Jesus Christ, book one, chapter five (see pages 813–814)

"Now is the Son of Man glorified." John 13:31

What a strange choice of words! Judas had just gone out into the darkness. The point of no return had been crossed. Jesus knew what would happen and that it would happen soon. And just then He said that God's glory would soon be revealed in what would happen to the Son of Man!

Days later Jesus would explain it to two of the disciples on the road to Emmaus. The Messiah had to suffer in order to enter into His glory. Then the disciples began to understand what God had done. But at this point they were completely in the dark. The path Jesus would take, He would have to take by Himself. The work was His and no one else's. Everything depended on His completing His work, drinking His cup, and bearing His cross. No one would be able to follow Him down this road. He knew they would all fail. He told them that. They protested, honestly and sincerely, that they would go to prison and die with Him, but He knew they would leave Him. He alone would bear everything the others, even His most faithful followers, had neglected, disobeyed, and done wrong. He had prayed for them. Now He would die for them.

First, He had to make atonement for their guilt, redeem them from their sins, and sanctify them through His death.

They sang psalms 115–118, songs of praise that had been sung for decades during the Passover. These ancient songs took on their full meaning for the first time that evening as they are about Christ and His suffering, about the bondage of death and the anguish in the kingdom of the dead, about the kind of death that is highly respected in the Lord's eyes, about the cup of the Lord's Supper, the chalice of salvation, about the One who wouldn't perish but live and tell of the Lord's deeds, about the Cornerstone the builders rejected, and about the joy of salvation that fills the righteous, when the Lord's right hand does remarkable things.

So they went out and walked down the empty streets, out through the town gates, down through the moonlit Kidron valley, and up the Mount of Olive's steep hillside. Along the way, Jesus spoke to them about the future. He had once sent them out without money, backpack, or shoes, yet they lacked nothing. They had learned to trust in His Word. Now, they would begin a different and greater task. Now they could take both moneybag and backpack with them. Later, they would understand what He meant. They would still live in this old world in expectation of the new one. They would use whatever means needed to live in this world. Even swords would be needed, not to spread the Gospel, but to keep peace against robbers and insurgents. Even a disciple would have protection under the law and be able stand up for his rights in the face of violence and abuse. Paul did that in a couple of important instances. He knew that his Lord wanted it that way.

But on that night, they didn't understand any of this. Alone and misunderstood, the Messiah went to Gethsemane.

Lord and Teacher, my heart says I am willing to follow You to prison and to death if need be. But You have taught me that intentions like these are not the proper foundations to build upon. You laid the foundation when You alone took the path of suffering. You even made it possible for Your unsuccessful disciples to follow You into Your kingdom and share in Your glory. If the day comes when my conviction is also questioned, pray for me, Lord. Keep my faith in Your hands so it won't wither away. I thank You because in the end it doesn't depend on my bravery or success or that I fight the good fight. It depends only on You, the fight You have fought and everything You've fulfilled. Praise be to You because You were counted among criminals that I could be counted among the righteous in Your kingdom.

TUESDAY AFTER THE FIFTH SUNDAY IN LENT

The Passion of Our Lord Jesus Christ, book two (see pages 815–816)

And being in great agony He prayed more earnestly.
Luke 22:44

Gethsemane was nearby, the olive trees on the other side of the stone wall casting dark shadows on the stony ground in the moonlight. Behind the temple wall, on the other side of the valley, the city glowed with light from the windows where people celebrated the Passover in their homes. In the background, the towers of Antonia's fortress and Herod's palace rose toward the heavens in the night. Inside, in the cobblestone courtyard, the Roman guards waited. And somewhere in the dark of the night, Judas was on his way.

Jesus had taken three of His disciples with Him and gone aside. Then He left them and went to pray alone. Since He usually prayed aloud—they would hear what He said. It was an unusual prayer. He prayed to avoid what was about to happen, that the cup poured for Him would be taken away. He struggled with something so inhumanly difficult and unbearable that His body was hunched over the ground.

What was so hard? The fear of death and torture? He certainly knew what fear was; He was true man. But Jesus didn't lack courage. He had walked right through the crowd of raging men in Nazareth. He didn't have to die then. He didn't have to die now either. He didn't have to wait for the betrayer and guards to come. It was only a few minutes to the crest of the Mount of Olives. Over there, just on the other side of the hill, was where the vast Jewish wilderness began. It would've been easy for Him to escape to safety there. But

He stayed where He was. He prayed even more intently. It was something worse than death, this cup that He now took upon Himself.

Later the disciples would understand it. Peter, who fell asleep that night, would write many years later that Christ bore our sins in His body upon the tree of the cross. Paul would say that Christ was made sin for our sakes; He became a curse for our sake, subjected to God's righteous judgment.

What happened next is that Christ emptied the cup that contained the entire world's sin, the entire world's shame and disgrace, all its cruelty and evil, its dirtiness and vulgarity, from the greatest evil deed to the most deplorable pettiness of everyday life. Everything was squeezed together and was in this cup. He emptied it to the last drop. The entire contents became His. He bore it now in His body—He who loved His Father above everything and would always do His will, who had been tempted in every way but was never diverted from His course. Now, He would make all of this a part of Himself. That's what was so extremely hard, so terrible that He prayed to His Father to escape it if there was any possibility.

But there was no such possibility. Not if the world was to be saved. Not if the immense unhappiness that separated us from God would be bridged and everything would be good again.

You bore everything, my Savior. You bore what I was guilty of, all my sins, all I have done in the past and all I will do, all the things that surface in Your Father's presence and scream their accusations against me. When I see Your image on the cross, I know that You bore what I'm guilty of in Your tortured body. You bore everything that separates me from You. And then I know my sin can no longer separate me from You. I am ashamed and bow my

head, and then raise it anew, thanking You and
rejoicing because You took that cup, even for me.

WEDNESDAY AFTER THE FIFTH SUNDAY IN LENT

The Passion of Our Lord Jesus Christ, book three, chapter one (see pages 816–817)

"But this is Your hour, and the power of darkness."
Luke 22:53

The disciples fell asleep in Gethsemane. The Master had asked them to stay awake. Twice He woke them, but they didn't understand. They were tired. They had had a long day. They had slaughtered the Passover lamb, prepared the Passover meal, and listened to everything Jesus had said at the dinner that would be His last. It was too much for them. They slept.

By the third time Jesus woke them, the enemy was already there. Smoke billowed from the torches. The light from the flames reflected off Roman helmets as Judas led the soldiers. He approached the Master and kissed Him. It was a sign for the soldiers who were supposed to seize Him. Yet they hesitated. When Jesus came forward to meet them, they backed away, flinched, and stumbled to the ground. But then they conquered their fear before this strange Prophet. They regrouped and pushed forward to arrest Him.

Peter drew his sword and swung. He was rebuked. If anyone was going to fight for Jesus, there were more than twelve legions of angels ready to hurl themselves at anyone who dared to assault God's Son. But this wouldn't happen. The Scriptures had to be fulfilled. The powers of darkness ruled. The darkness that descended over the world after man had followed the tempter and became marked by his hand, was thicker now than ever. It closed in around God's own Son to annihilate Him. The disciples fled. There was nothing they could do. Their instincts of self-preservation took over. They hid among trees, climbed over the wall, and disappeared into the night.

Jesus said, "If you seek Me, let these men go" (John 18:8). Again there is a profound meaning in His words. Jesus was led away, bound and alone to bear all the consequences of all the evil He now took upon Himself. The others escaped. We belong to those who escaped.

Lord, how often have I done what Peter did? I strike out when You would heal. I sleep when I should be awake. Then I'm surprised by what I've done. I want to serve You. I don't want to let evil continue, yet I do everything wrong. I thank You because You make everything right, even the unrighteous things Your disciples do. Have mercy on us when we serve You so badly. Have mercy on those we fight against because we believe they are Your enemies. Help us to be vigilant, pray, and live so close to You that we know and understand what You want us to do even when times are hard. Don't let us be the reason Your name is abused. Rather, let Your glory shine forth even when we are inadequate. For Your name's sake and to Your glory.

THURSDAY AFTER THE FIFTH SUNDAY IN LENT

The Passion of Our Lord Jesus Christ, book three, chapter two (see page 816)

And Peter was following at a distance. Luke 22:54

He had calmed down, waited for the right moment, and made his decision. He was going to risk sneaking back into town. He followed the torch lights through the city gates and up through the narrow streets to the high priest's palace. There he stood at the gates. He wasn't sure what he should do. He didn't want to desert his Master, but now he was separated from Him. There was no one he could ask for advice.

Then a disciple who was acquainted with the high priest came along. In all likelihood this disciple was John. (When he tells about things he experienced, it's always anonymously; he never mentions himself.) He waved to Peter, and Peter pulled himself together. Now, all Peter had to do was keep quiet. He knew he was on dangerous ground.

It began to happen once he was in the doorway. Suspicious eyes appraised him, then the accusing question came. He was prepared to dismiss it. No, he had nothing to do with this man.

Peter tried to fit in with the crowd in the courtyard and stood with the others who were warming themselves by the fire. But they were suspicious and scrutinized him. The question was asked a second time. Peter dismissed it again. Then someone came forward who recognized him as the one who had drawn his sword in the garden. Now the bystanders approached. They all looked at him and formed a ring around him. Peter raised his hand and swore an oath that he never knew the man. And just then a cock crowed nearby.

Then, Luke tells us in verse 61, "the Lord turned."

Suddenly, He was there. He had stood in the darkness, possibly up on the balcony outside the second floor the whole time, tied up. He looked at Peter. He didn't have to do anything else. Everything was put in proper perspective again. It was no longer important to escape. Peter realized what he had done. He was exposed, caught in the gravest of degradation, and at the same time he was loved. There wasn't any malicious pleasure in the Master's glance, no triumph at the fact that He was right, only immense sorrow and love—despite everything.

Peter put his hand over his face and cried loudly. He ran out. No one stopped him. The danger was not so great as he had imagined. He slipped away, alone and abandoned—except He wasn't alone.

Lord, how many times have I followed You at a distance, afraid of people, anxious about what they might say and what I might answer? And the whole time You were with me. You see everything. Help me to always realize how close You are. Take all my fear. Help me to disregard their laughter and taunts. Help me to be glad that I am suspected of being Your disciple. Help me to show what a joy it is. You, who loved even Your unfortunate and cowardly disciples, help us love You back so that love conquers our cowardice and so we succeed with what we never could do when we merely followed You at a distance.

FRIDAY AFTER THE FIFTH SUNDAY IN LENT

The Passion of Our Lord Jesus Christ, book three, chapter three (see pages 818–819)

But He remained silent and made no answer. Mark 14:61

The council called a special meeting in the middle of the night because they had to act swiftly. The witnesses were present. The council members sat in a semicircle with the high priest in the middle. The prisoner was led in and stood before them. Then the trial began. The strange thing was that the accused made no attempt to defend Himself. Witnesses were called forward. Most of what they said was so obviously false or distorted that it wasn't a very good basis for sentencing. It would've been easy for the accused to prove His innocence against these preposterous accusations. He could've held His accusers liable for their obvious attempts to entrap an innocent man, but He was silent. Would He really accept the verdict for things He didn't do? Why? It was almost as if He wanted to be condemned to death.

The strange thing is that this judgment, the most unjustified verdict ever given on earth, was at the same time the most completely just verdict ever given. Jesus kept secret something that the high priests knew nothing about—He carried the sins of the whole world. He took the burden of guilt for the whole world upon Himself and made it His own. From where He stood, in front of His accusers, He was responsible for their sins also, for their envy and lust for power, their deceit and heartlessness. He took upon Himself all the trespasses of everyone in the past, in the present, and in the future. That sin warranted death. Without knowing it,

Caiaphas sentenced his own sin, and all our sin, to the punishment that since the beginning of time had been waiting to deal with the wickedness and the selfishness that said no to God's love: that death must die.

Hard pressed for proof, the high priest finally asked the question that He didn't really want to ask because it was so controversial. He asked Jesus if He was the Messiah, the long-expected Savior. And Jesus, who previously always let others answer, now did His judge the service of answering it plainly. In a fit of dramatic horror, the high priest tore his garments. He no longer needed any witnesses. This was blasphemy—provided it was not true. But "truth" was predetermined by the judge, so Jesus was declared guilty and sentenced to death. For the sake of order, they waited with the formal sentencing until dawn. They were, of course, the most eminent guardians of justice and knew how to observe the letter of the law, even as they sentenced God's own Son to death.

Your sentence was also my sentence. When they sentenced You to death, Lord, it was because You bore my guilt. You made atonement for my trespasses. You took the responsibility upon Yourself. You made my iniquity Your own and bore it in Your heart, where all of God's holiness and love dwell. That's where my guilt met God. And what happened is what happens when all wickedness and vulgarity is exposed and naked in the face of God. It has to be consumed and destroyed. It must perish. And You took all that upon Yourself. It happened to You and not to me. The yoke of chastisement was on Your shoulders so I would have peace. Praise be to You, O Jesus!

SATURDAY
AFTER THE FIFTH
SUNDAY IN LENT

*The Passion of Our Lord
Jesus Christ, book three,
chapter four (see pages
818–819)*

"See to it yourself." Matthew 27:4

Judas regretted what he did. His remorse was genuine. The catechism[10] provides us with three attributes of true repentance: that we acknowledge our sins in our heart, that we grieve over them, and that we desire to be liberated from them. All these things were true for poor Judas. He acknowledged what he did without trying to excuse or minimize his offense. He acknowledged it before the high priests. He wanted to give the money back. When the high priests wouldn't take it, he threw it at them. He wanted to get rid of everything that reminded him of his crime. He grieved over what he did so despairingly that he couldn't bear to live. No one could regret something more than that.

And yet, he was lost. Remorse alone simply can't save a man, no matter how deep and sincere it is. The desperation that arises in times of remorse can be defined in what the heartless high priests said to Judas: "See to it yourself." Someone who repents realizes what he has done. He is conscious of his guilt, but he cannot get rid of it.

The other disciples also had failed. Peter failed the most miserably. He, too, was weighted down by guilt that could hardly be heavier, but here was the difference. Judas went away and hanged himself. Peter went out and wept bitterly. The thing he desired most was to meet his Master again

10. Luther's Small Catechism

and ask for forgiveness. Therefore, Peter was still one of the disciples and found peace when Jesus sought him out and forgave everything.

Judas could have done this, too, but instead he went out into the darkness in despair. What was it that he lacked? It was faith. Judas had no hope. He expected nothing. He prayed for nothing.

Remorse alone isn't enough to reach out to Jesus. Faith also is needed. If a person is lost, it isn't because their sins are greater than anyone else's, it's because they aren't seeking help where help can be found. We understand better why Jesus said to Peter before the denial that He prayed for him that his faith would not fail. If only a person comes to Jesus in faith, everything will be all right. Even for a Judas.

Lord, pray also for me that my faith will not fail. Whatever happens, help me come to You. Let nothing shameful or dishonorable keep me away. Don't let me be slow or procrastinate before I dare to come to You with my failures and sins. I pray to You, Lord, for all those who have regrets but don't know they can go to You. I pray to You for everyone who thinks they have failed and done wrong, everyone who blames themselves for what they have done. Let them see what You offer them. Greet them the way You did Peter. Let them encounter the kind of people, events, thoughts, or words that can turn their thoughts and their hearts to You. Have mercy on us. Do not let any of us be lost in the darkness.

PALM SUNDAY
John 12:1–16

"She has anointed My body beforehand for burial." Mark 14:8

Today is the day Jesus entered Jerusalem to heralding crowds. We celebrated this event on the first Sunday in Advent. What an incomprehensible difference there is between that day and this! Then, we were disciples who greeted our Lord and welcomed Him with rejoicing. We followed Him to Jerusalem to begin Holy Week, the week when He was rejected, betrayed, insulted, and executed. So today, we will not sing hosanna. We begin this week in a mood of farewell and departure, gathered around the Master in Bethany.

Mary understood it well. In her love for the Master, she gave away the finest thing she could offer. In one sense, it was wasted, but there's a kind of wastefulness that God loves. It flows out of a heart that wants to do everything for Him. This love is better than all calculated wisdom that first and foremost considers the benefit. Judas was the voice of common sense. Certainly, his reason was driven by bad motives, but the argument he used is one many good Christians have used. But Jesus said Mary was right. There is a loving wastefulness, a joyful extravagance that gives its best to Jesus. We have a right to waste our time when it means listening to Jesus like Mary did when she sat at His feet and listened to His Word while there was so much to do around the house. We have the right to waste our gifts on Him. When the soldiers were dividing Jesus' clothes at Golgotha, they were astonished that this poor prophet had such an expensive garment that was woven in a single piece. Surely this was a gift from someone who wanted to give Him the best. Gifts like this can still be given today. It's completely all right to decorate our churches if we do it out of love for Jesus and a desire to glorify Him in a way that allows others to experience the heavenly joy of the Divine Service.

But we will always have the poor among us, Jesus said. So love for Him must, in the end, always be love for those who suffer here on earth. This world is also a place for a blessed wastefulness that gives without a calculating attitude or weighing the consequences and without always demanding guarantees that we will benefit from helping.

Jesus received Mary's gifts as a preparation for His burial. None of the others knew how soon it would be, but He left for Jerusalem knowing His time was at hand. When we follow Him today, we know more about the events to come than His apostles could have. It's not easy for us to rejoice with the crowds, but we understand Mary, who gave the best she had to Him who would give His life for her and for each of us.

Today, my Lord and Savior, You entered the city that murders prophets and stones messengers of God. We are all citizens of this city, we who so often want to silence Your voice so we can avoid hearing Your Word. We've always been willing to honor You because others did it. We hoped You would help us with our own plans and fulfill our desires. Now let us follow You instead to see how You fulfilled Your Father's will for our sake, doing what You alone could do. You've done everything for us. Help us do something for You.

HOLY WEEK
MONDAY

The Passion of our Lord
Jesus Christ, book four,
chapters one and two
(see pages 818–820)

(see pages 818–820)

"Everyone who is of the truth listens to My voice." John 18:37

Jesus was sentenced to death by the highest court in the Jewish nation. But because the land was occupied, the death sentence had to be confirmed by the occupying forces. So they marched off with the prisoner to Pontius Pilate. Like many other Roman officials, he was brutal and money hungry, but he possessed good judgment. He sensed the envy and intrigue behind the sentence. After a short conversation with the prisoner, it was clear to him that the man standing before him was a harmless preacher of a new doctrine. Besides that, He was a Galilean. So Pilate could skirt the issue by referring the case to King Herod, who just happened to be in Jerusalem to celebrate the Passover.

Pilate touched upon truth for a moment. This strange Prophet was a King in a kingdom that was not of this world. He had come to witness about the truth—the truth about the purpose of life, the truth about God and us. Pilate had the opportunity to learn about this truth, but he didn't want to know it. He shrugged his shoulders and asked, What is truth? It wasn't a sincere question. He didn't really want to know. His statement was simply a way of dodging the issues.

And Jesus was quiet. There's no sense in talking to a person who doesn't want to listen.

This was also true of Herod. He appeared eager to meet Jesus. He had heard of His remarkable deeds and wanted to see one of His miracles. But Herod wasn't open to the truth. He closed that door when John the Baptist was imprisoned.

Herod had summoned the Baptist. It is written that he enjoyed listening to him. But when he did, he became hesitant because he knew the Baptist was right. Herod had taken his brother's wife and this was against God's will. He could have repented if it wasn't so humiliating. So Herod put the matter off until that terrible day when he promised his daughter whatever she desired. The devious daughter went to her mother and received the horrific direction to ask for John the Baptist's head on a platter. Herod gave it to her. He silenced the only voice that told him the truth: God's voice beckoning him to repentance and forgiveness.

Herod didn't have anything against experiencing a great miracle. It's even possible that he was open to considering God again, but you can't eliminate repentance and still expect to be with God. Herod wanted to avoid repentance. So Jesus had nothing to say to him either. Since Herod had already heard God's truth, God was now silent.

Help me remember, Lord Jesus, that the day may come when You are silent. Help me always have room in my heart for the truth, even when it's humiliating, even when it hurts. Help me never use the excuse that there are different opinions, views, purposes, and religions. Our human errors can't destroy Your truth. You have come to us just so we would know the truth. Help us love and receive it. People speculate and wonder, but You know more than all the wisdom and thoughts of the prophets put together. Therefore, I ask You about the truth because You are truth itself.

HOLY WEEK
TUESDAY

*The Passion of Our Lord
Jesus Christ, book four, chapter three (see pages 822–823)*

"Away with this man, and release to us Barabbas."
Luke 23:18

Barabbas rather than Jesus! That was the voice of the people outside Pilate's palace. Those who shouted for him were no worse than we are. Barabbas was a national figure. There had been riots, probably a result of national and political events, that had ended in bloodshed. Now Barabbas, along with several others, was locked up. Matthew tells us that Barabbas was a notorious prisoner. Everyone knew who he was and the wicked crimes he had committed. Now they wanted him released. The high priests and the elders had an easy job. The people were tired of this Jesus, who didn't want to go from word to action. He only preached about the kingdom of God, repentance, and forgiveness. In His presence, everyone felt accused, so they preferred Barabbas, who only accused people he didn't like.

When Pilate stalled by trying to give Jesus one way out after another, the crowd revolted. They cried, shouted, and pressed forward, like crowds do when they get excited. Finally, Pilate gave in. Barabbas, the murderer who had been thrown into prison for inciting a riot, was set free and the innocent Jesus was sentenced and incarcerated.

This spectacle is deplorable and profoundly edifying at the same time. Once again, God had a deeper meaning in something that otherwise appeared meaningless and cruel. What happened here wasn't just the punishment of an innocent person while the guilty was set free. Something greater happened. Every guilty person was set free like Barabbas. Every guilty person was given an opportunity to go free, an opportunity to escape the just consequences of his or her guilt. Jesus suffered what the wicked Barabbas and the howling crowd, the cowardly Pilate and the scheming high priests, the self-righteous Pharisees and each of us should have suffered. We, who would rather hide from God and get rid of Jesus, instead receive Him as a brother who bears the whole burden of our enmity toward God, our selfishness, and our cruelty so we will never be separated from God again.

I was set free, while You, my Lord Jesus, were scourged and crucified. I deserved to be thrown into prison for my rebellion against God, for my misappropriations in the administration of His property because I so badly used the life I received from Him. I have often stood on the side of His enemies, and I still have a spirit of rejection and rebellion in my heart, but You died in my place. People screamed at You. They hated You. They were possessed with a desire to see Your blood. I have seen it also, and I know that it flowed for me. The sentence You suffered, Lord, was my sentence for all my evildoings. I know my guilt and I thank You, my Lord Jesus, that You bore it for me.

HOLY WEEK
WEDNESDAY

*The Passion of Our Lord
Jesus Christ, book four, chapter four (see pages 823–824)*

"Behold your King!" John 19:14

Jesus survived the beatings. Not just anyone could do that. Long leather straps with bits of lead and pottery tied to the ends were used in the beatings. This used to be called a horse whipping. The soldier who carried out the execution shouted to his colleagues. They liked to have a good time with prisoners before they took them back to their cell. They threw an old military cloak over Jesus' bloody shoulders. It was as red as a king's coat. They took a bundle of thorny twigs from a pile on the ground intended as kindling, formed a crown, and pressed it onto the prisoner's forehead. He was given a stick to be used as a scepter. Then, the guards knelt down and mockingly hailed the wretched King of the Jews.

These mercenaries acted as if they were representatives of a superior race. They spat on their powerless and unfortunate prisoner. They did the same thing we do so easily: They delighted in playing the bully. They delighted in it like children mobbing a schoolmate or co-workers who make fun of others.

There is a deeper meaning hidden in this repulsive spectacle, one that has offered perpetual inspiration to artists and caused common man to stand in awe and thankfulness. When we see this picture we, like Pilate, say: "So, You are a King!" The soldiers didn't know what they were doing. But they did what the heavenly hosts and thousands upon thousands of people on this earth do today, not in ridicule, but in all seriousness. They didn't know they were bowing to Him before whom "every knee should bow, in heaven and on earth and under the earth" (Philippians 2:10). They didn't know that He, at whom they spat, who bore the red military cloak, also bore their thoughtless cruelty as His guilt. He would take that guilt with Him to the cross so that both their cruelty and all the injustice in this world, great or small, would be forgiven.

Nor did Pilate realize the truth when he led the prisoner out and said, "Behold your King!" There He stood, as tortured and abused as a person can be on this earth, but without bitterness and hate—just a simple and immense desire to lead His tormenters to God. The people reacted the only way they could and not submit to and be conquered by this love. They yelled, "Away with Him" (John 19:15)! It was too much for them—just as it is for all of us. It's too much that in the midst of this evil world there is a love that will not let go of us. It's incomprehensible unless it dawns on us that we stand before the very essence of existence and that it is that love that gives our lives a purpose.

My Lord and my King, I, too, want to kneel before You. I know that I am one of those who brought You to the cross. I am also one of those for whom You died. I am one of the many included in Your love and for whom You will forgive everything. Because of my sin, I feel I should say to You, "Depart from me, Lord." But because of Your love, I dare say, "Stay with me, don't leave me, Lord." You came for me when You came to save the lost. I hail You, my King. Let me live under Your scepter, now and forever.

MAUNDY THURSDAY

The Passion of Our Lord Jesus Christ, book five, chapters one and two (see pages 825–827)

"He saved others; He cannot save Himself." Mark 15:31

Once again, the mockers expressed one of the most profound truths about Jesus. He saved others. Without thinking about it, they affirmed then and for all posterity that it really was true: Jesus "went around doing good and healing all who were under the power of the devil" (Acts 10:38). Now, because of this, they mocked Him. That's human egoism, which assumes that a person should use his resources, first and foremost, for his own benefit. It's natural to mock someone who doesn't. In truth, this was a part of the secret of Jesus' nature. He helped others but not Himself. He starved in the desert, but when His hearers were hungry, He worked a miracle to feed them. He used His power only to benefit others, never to make His life easier. His whole life was for our sake.

But the mockers were wrong on one point: Jesus did have the ability to help Himself. He could have climbed down from the cross, but He didn't because then we all would have been lost. He remained on the cross for our sake.

Even one of the robbers who was crucified next to Him mocked Him. He thought the way the world thought: If someone is powerful, then he should use that power to save himself. The other robber, however, began to understand. As he listened to Jesus pray for those who drove spikes through His hands, he began to understand that there was a possibility for help beyond all reason, beyond all common justice, and contrary to everything he expected and deserved. Maybe this

Messiah, who helped others but not Himself, would spare even this wretched wreck that left a wasted life behind him.

The robber dared to make his request, and he received a promise of salvation, just as quickly and unreservedly as Jesus ever made a promise: "Today you will be with Me in paradise" (Luke 23:43).

I thank You for Your Word, My Savior. Because of Your Word, I, too, dare to come even when I rightfully suffer as a result of my deeds and when my conscience accuses me and people wonder how someone like me can dare come to You. You hung helpless on the cross for me. You didn't use Your infinite power, and Your Father held back legions of angels that wanted to help You. For this reason, I now dare come to You. Lord, think about me as You reign in Your kingdom.

GOOD FRIDAY

The Passion of Our Lord Jesus Christ, book five, chapter three (see pages 827–828)

"My God, My God, why have You forsaken Me?" Mark 15:34

That cry must have burned itself into the disciples' memory. That's why it was recorded in the Bible in the original language Jesus used when the words left His lips. In fact, it was a direct quote from the beginning of Psalm 22.

A devout Jew would have memorized most of the psalms. As children, they learned to sing psalms in the synagogue. They used them every Sabbath and in daily devotions at home. In fact, they learned them so well that citing a single verse would call the whole psalm to mind. This is important to know when we read Jesus' cries from the cross. He truly was forsaken by God. He bore in His heart all the sin and evil that separates us from God. The darkness that covered the land was only a faint image of the ultimate darkness where evil belongs and will finally be locked up, forever separated from God. Jesus hung alone in this darkness. He experienced complete and absolute separation from God and all the good that He allows to embrace even those who deny and mock Him. None of us can really conceive what the Savior experienced at this time. As God, He could in a simple blink of an eye experience eternity. Yet here He was, separated from all the good, all the comfort, and the communion with God that we have even in our most difficult time of suffering.

Jesus was alone with evil and darkness. Yet His words were a prayer, not a cry of despair. He wasn't accusing God. He wasn't screaming out in disappointment because the help He had hoped for failed to appear. This is readily understood when we read Psalm 22. First and foremost, notice that the psalmist is a tortured man speaking in utmost distress, a distress that bears striking resemblance to what happened to Jesus. The psalmist was mocked. Men cursed him and said scornfully: "He trusts in the LORD; let Him deliver him; let Him rescue him, for he delights in Him" (Psalm 22:8)! He was despised among men and rejected by the people. He was surrounded by enemies. They pierced his hands and feet; they divided his clothes among themselves. His strength withered. His tongue clung to his jaw. Yet, in the midst of this distress, he confessed that God is God. "Yet You are holy, enthroned on the praises of Israel" (Psalm 22:3). Psalm 22 also says that

God will not despise the suffering of the afflicted, rather He will do something that all the ends of the earth will remember.

This isn't a cry from someone who has lost faith. It is a prayer that pours out from faith like a spring. At the same time, Jesus lets us know that He was truly forsaken by God and tasted the utmost extreme consequences of our fall from God. He shows us that He is still doing this in obedience to God's will and still has perfect faith in God. So this verse fits very well with the other words of Jesus from the cross. When He says, "It is finished," He means precisely the work that His Father gave Him to do (John 19:30). He did this when He kept the Law we break on every point and when He tasted the consequences of all our neglect and wrongdoing down to the last drop. And when He said, "Father, into Your hands I commit My spirit," (Luke 23:46) citing Psalm 31:5, He was also displaying the same obedience and faith. He was obedient to death, Paul says—"even death on a cross" (Philippians 2:8).

I know I will never be forsaken by God the Father because You are my Savior and my atonement— You, who hung forsaken on the cross at Golgotha for me. Even if I never finish what I ought to do and want to do in thankfulness and love for what You did for me, I can still know that You completed everything, even what I was supposed to do. You took upon Yourself all my guilt, all my trespasses, and everything I was responsible for. You took my sin upon Yourself when God saw it and it had to be consumed by the burning coals of His holy fire. I know I can never thank You enough for what You did out of love for me. Yet, I know You did it so I

*would receive it free of charge. Therefore, I stretch
my hands out to Your cross and take hold of it,
praying that I may rest under its blessed arms, now
and forever.*

EASTER EVE

*The Passion of Our Lord
Jesus Christ, book six (see
pages 829–830)*

For I delivered to you as of first importance what I also
received: that Christ died for our sins in accordance with the
Scriptures, that He was buried. 1 Corinthians 15:3–4

The fact that Christ both died and was buried are corner-
stones in the Christian faith. We confess this every Sunday
in the creed. The Gospels support Jesus' burial with details.
The disciples would always remember this terrible day when
darkness covered the land and an even deeper darkness covered their hearts. They didn't understand anything. There
was no glimpse of light in the darkness. They still loved their
Lord, but His life seemed to have ended with His enemy's
triumph. In Israel, crucifixion was the ultimate demonstration
of God's rejection. It meant that the crucified was cursed in
God's eyes.

As far as the disciples were concerned, there was nothing
to do but lavish vain love on a dead body. They successfully
arranged for it to be laid in a tomb and not cast among other
criminals in the city's dump. Some of Jesus' distinguished

friends dared to show their devotion. They found a new tomb for Him. They came with large amounts of spices, fit for a prince's burial. But they were just as powerless as we are at an open grave. They couldn't call Him back to life. They had no hope for the future. When the heavy stone was rolled into position and closed the grave, all they had hoped for was buried inside.

Yet this was the beginning of Jesus' victory. We confess in the creed that He "descended into hell." He didn't go as others, as a helpless prisoner through a gate that would never again open. He descended into hell as the overlord of the dead. He broke through the gates. A revolution occurred on this day that changed the balance of power forever. The earthquakes that shook Jerusalem were a sign of this. The curtain in the temple that had blocked the way into the Holy of Holies, to God Himself, where no one dared to go except for the high priest on the Day of Atonement, was torn from top to bottom. Now it was opened so we sinners could go straight to God's fatherly arms. Even the gates of death were opened.

Now, every knee, even those under the earth, will bow before Christ. Whoever believes in Christ need not fear death. Christ goes before him.

It's a great comfort for me, Lord Jesus, that Your body has also been in a grave. You allowed them to carry You away and lay You down, lifeless and cold. They closed Your grave and left You in the dark and cold. You went there, too, and You prevailed. The land on the other side You trampled with Your feet. Now I don't have to go down that path. I pray to You for the great comfort in life and

death that You alone can give me. Let me be with
You every day of my life until the Last Day, and
after that, forever in Your kingdom.

EASTER DAY
Mark 16:1–8

This is the day the LORD has made; let us rejoice and be glad in it. Psalm 118:24

This is the great day, the greatest God has created since the creation itself!

And it happened when it was impossible to imagine it. When the women went to the tomb in the morning, they thought of nothing but doing their last service for their deceased Lord. They had wrapped His body and buried Him in the tomb on Friday evening, but everything was done in haste so they could finish by sundown when the Sabbath began. Now they returned to the gravesite to complete their task. They bought spices Saturday evening when the shops opened after the Sabbath, and made their way to the tomb as dawn was breaking. They were worried about the stone in front of the grave—and rightly so. The tomb was sealed shut with something like a millstone that rolled on a track carved into the stony ground. To go into the tomb, they would have to push the heavy stone aside, and with a wedge secure it on the track. When they came out again, they would pull out the wedge and let the stone roll into place in front of the tomb.

This would seal the tomb shut as well as could be expected.

On this morning, when the women saw that the stone was rolled away and the tomb was empty, they thought someone had taken away Jesus' body. The strange man in white clothing only confused and frightened them even more when He spoke. When they got to the apostles, they were confronted with skepticism. No one could fathom what had happened. It was absurd to believe that Jesus had risen from the dead.

But it was true! The skeptical apostles were faced with this unavoidable fact. "The Lord has risen indeed" (Luke 24:34). God had intervened so wonderfully, so overwhelmingly, so far beyond everything that had happened earlier upon this earth that our entire life and our entire existence was fundamentally changed. A new era had begun. An entirely new opportunity was offered to mankind. God's wonderful plan concerning the cross and everything that had happened before this wonderful day was revealed. Now the disciples could finally understand the real meaning behind the words they had sung after eating the paschal lamb, words that seemed to have been ringing so peculiarly out of tune with reality: "This is the day that the Lord has made, let us be glad and rejoice in it!"

> *Lord,* we thank and praise You because we, too, can take part in this day of joy and rejoice in Your resurrection, rejoice that You are alive and are among us. We thank You because we can all be a part of this day. Fill us with joy and happiness that we may share it with everyone in the world. Let our hearts and temples resound with joy, singing: The Lord is risen! The Lord is risen indeed! Hallelujah!

MONDAY AFTER EASTER

Luke 24:13–35

"The Lord has risen indeed." Luke 24:34

The two disciples on their way to Emmaus were deeply distressed and disillusioned. Most likely, they were going back to their vocations, the everyday jobs they had before Jesus called them to be disciples. There was nothing else to do now that the Master was dead and everything was over. When the Stranger asked them what they were talking about, "they stood still, looking sad" (Luke 24:17). They said what all the disciples knew, that they had hoped Jesus was the one to redeem Israel. Now their hope was buried. Their Master, who "was a prophet mighty in deed and word before God and all the people" (Luke 24:19), had been shamefully handed to the Gentiles and executed like a common criminal. They couldn't understand how God could let this happen. They couldn't understand anything. They had nothing left to hope for.

Then the Stranger reproached them for their unbelief. He began explaining to them that it was just as it had to be. He "interpreted to them in all the Scriptures" (Luke 24:27)—all the books of the Old Testament—to show them that the Messiah had to suffer all these things in order to attain His glory. This is what He had to do to redeem Israel and the whole world. They listened and began to understand. But they still didn't recognize Him, not until He broke bread at the evening communion. Then He vanished from their sight.

In this story, Luke captures what makes Jesus come to life for doubting and distressed disciples throughout the ages. The Risen One comes and walks with us again. He does not come to us in public sentiment or vague feelings. Rather, He has specific means through which He works and in which He is present. He comes to us in the living Word, Scripture, which He Himself interprets for us, causing our hearts to burn when we hear His voice and see His image. He also comes to us in the Lord's Supper where He breaks bread and is recognized even today. For many, this is the final and decisive event, filling them with the secure certainty that He is living and present among us.

Lord, You know that I belong to these people who don't understand, who are slow at heart in believing in everything the prophets spoke. You know that I also easily despair and worry that Your enemies have been victorious. You know that even in the midst of my love for You, I can still doubt that You really are powerful and victorious. So I pray that You come to us in our congregation and walk with us as You did with Your depressed apostles on the road to Emmaus. I pray that we also can travel with You, day after day, that we may listen to Your voice and see how You bring the Scriptures to life and make our hearts burn. Come and be with us through Holy Communion. Let us recognize You again. I know that You live, Lord. Stay with us that we may feel Your presence.

TUESDAY AFTER

EASTER
John 20:1–10

He saw and believed. John 20:8

When John tells us of the events on Easter morning, it is clear that an eyewitness is speaking. Easter began for him when Mary Magdalene came back from the tomb, anxious and perplexed. She had gone there with the other women and obviously left them there. She didn't know what the other women saw or heard after she left. She could only report their first reaction: "They have taken the Lord out of the tomb, and we do not know where they have laid Him" (John 20:2).

Peter and John started off immediately. They ran, John says. It wasn't far. Golgotha and the tomb were just outside the city walls. John arrived first. He saw that it was just as the women had said. The stone had been rolled away and the grave was empty. He bent down to look in and saw the linen cloths lying there. But he didn't go in. It seems that from the very beginning he realized something incomprehensible had happened, perhaps a great miracle. He waited outside, possibly out of some kind of frightened respect.

Peter didn't do that. He wanted to unravel the mystery and find out what happened. He went straight into the tomb. The bandages in which Jesus had been wrapped were there. The cloth that covered His head was also there in its special place, but Jesus was gone.

Then John came in. "And he saw and believed," it is written in John 20:8.

What did John see? It's hard to understand when we read the English translations. The translations assume there was a cloth covering the dead man's head, just like we may put a cloth over the face of the dead in the coffin. But the text only speaks about "the face cloth, which had been on Jesus' head" (John 20:7). They usually wrapped the dead body in bandages, then left the face in full sight while wrapping the head. This cloth was now lying folded as before in its special place. The other cloths were also lying on the stone bed, untouched.

Then John understood. No one could have taken Jesus away. Something unheard of had happened here, something that assumes intervention from God. Jesus' body must have been transformed in some way. The outer wrapping, the bandages, remained, but the body they had covered was gone. John knew what had happened. Before anyone had even seen the Risen One, he understood that the Master lived. Not just as before, but in a new way, in a way no one had ever lived before.

Lord Jesus, it's good enough for me to know that You live. I pray that I will know what You want me to know, what I need to know in order to believe in You, love You, see Your power, and understand what You give us. I pray that You will let me know the power of Your resurrection, that You destroy my old Adam and revive true faith and real love in me, and that You allow me to live with You each and every day.

WEDNESDAY

AFTER EASTER

John 20:11–18

"My Father and your Father." John 20:17

Mary stood by herself crying outside the tomb. She had the same strange mixture of love and skepticism the others had. She would've done whatever she could have for her dead Master. She had no idea He was alive.

Then Jesus came and stood next to her. Mary turned and saw Him, but she had no idea who He was. Only when He said her name did she recognize His voice. Then, in her joy, she impulsively fell and grabbed His feet, but He didn't allow her to touch Him. Instead, He sent her with a message for the apostles. He chose them to take the message of His resurrection into the world, and be servants of the Word.

He called them "My brothers" (John 20:17). He hadn't said that before and it was not a coincidence that He did so now. They became His brothers when He carried their sins to the cross. Through His death, He created for them and for all sinners the way to be children of God. He now "had to be made like His brothers in every respect," as it says in Hebrews 2:17. Just as they had taken part in His death, they would also take part in His resurrection. He would even give them the life He now possessed. He was the first to have gone from death to life. The others would follow.

Lord, let me hear Your voice. Let me hear You call me by name. You did it already when I was baptized. You remind me of it when You say, "I have called you by name, you are Mine" (Isaiah 43:1). Teach me to recognize Your voice so I distinguish it from all the other voices in the world, the voice

of doubt, of temptation, of skepticism, and of fear.
Teach me to listen to what You say. It is Your
voice that allows me to know that You live. I don't
need anything else when I hear You. Let me also
hear it when I depart this world.

THURSDAY AFTER EASTER
Luke 24:1–12

He presented Himself alive to them after His suffering by
many proofs, appearing to them during forty days and
speaking about the kingdom of God. Acts 1:3

Luke says he "followed all things closely for some time
past" (Luke 1:3) and recorded the events "just as those who
from the beginning were eyewitnesses and ministers of the
word have delivered them to us" (Luke 1:2). So at the end
of his Gospel, Luke summarizes the events after the resurrection.

John's narration is far more detailed. He relied mostly on
his own memory and preserved many details we would not
otherwise know. For example, when Peter ran to the tomb,
Luke doesn't mention John, but that doesn't mean Peter
went alone. This is shown a little later in the story about the
journey to Emmaus, when Cleopas says, "some of those who
were with us went to the tomb" (Luke 24:24).

The events of Easter morning came as a complete surprise.
Confusion and commotion ruled as people ran back and forth,

to and from the tomb. Each of the witnesses had their own experiences in the course of events. Mary Magdalene had her story to tell. Peter and John saw things in their own way. The other women at the tomb clearly had not seen everything all at once. Some of them could tell about a young man in white clothes inside the grave. Others spoke about two men who stood before them in shining clothes. That's the way it always is when eyewitnesses recount surprising occurrences, where one thing happens after the other. No one person sees everything. Afterward, you have to try to reconstruct the sequence of events, but it is precisely the variations in the accounts of what happened that prove you are dealing with eyewitnesses. If all the accounts said the same thing, we might suspect the accounts to be doctored and collaborated.

As it is, we have the opportunity to experience the complete amazement, commotion, confusion, and doubt that the witnesses experienced on Easter morning. We also have the overwhelming joy when, "by many proofs," (Acts 1:3) it is shown to be true that Jesus rose from the dead. It was no longer a matter of speculation, nor was it a matter of the expectations the disciples had that inclined them to see visions and believe rumors. They were just as reluctant as we are to believe that someone could be resurrected from the grave. They were men of reality. And it was for this reason they were convinced by reality and could say, "This Jesus God raised up, and of that we all are witnesses" (Acts 2:32).

I thank, You, Lord Jesus, for Your disciple's doubts and because we've learned so much about them. When they first heard about Your resurrection, they thought it was hearsay, although You had told them it would be so. If they had such difficulty believing and could still be so completely convinced, there must also be hope for us with all our doubts. Your truth and Your reality are so much greater than everything that gets in the way of them. We think, wonder, speculate, and guess. But You are who You are and none of us can alter Your reality. Let us encounter, see, be conquered, and be convinced by it so we can be like Your first disciples and stand firm on Your confession until our death. In Your holy name I pray.

FRIDAY AFTER EASTER
Luke 24:36–49

"It is I Myself." Luke 24:39

After Luke tells us about the events on Easter morning, and of the two disciples on the road to Emmaus—the Gospel reading for the day after Easter—he continues with the events that occurred on the evening of Easter Day. Something very meaningful and important had happened prior to these events. Jesus had appeared to Peter. When the two apostles came back from Emmaus, they were met with great news: "The Lord has risen indeed, and has appeared to Simon" (Luke 24:34)! When Paul reminds us of the importance of the resurrection, he also says that Jesus "appeared to Cephas, then to the twelve" (1 Corinthians 15:5). But we don't know what happened when Jesus appeared to Peter, who had denied knowing Him.

The disciples, on the evening after the resurrection, were

gathered behind locked doors. They weren't going to risk persecution and imprisonment. Then Jesus suddenly appeared in their midst. Again, their first reaction was alarm and fear. Despite the fact that they had recently rejoiced over their Master being alive, the reality of it all was too much for them. They reacted the way we would if a relative we had just buried in the grave suddenly stood among us. They thought they were seeing a ghost, but Jesus asked them to make sure it was Jesus Himself. He was just as real as before. He had a body. He took the food they gave Him and ate it.

It was small details like these that gradually helped them understand what had happened. The Master was really alive. He was the same Jesus He'd always been, and yet He was completely transformed. He was no longer bound by time and space. He could come and go through locked doors as He pleased.

But that wasn't what He spoke to them about. It wasn't enough that they knew He lived. It was more important that they learn and understand that He had died for them. That's why Luke says, "He opened their minds to understand the Scriptures" (Luke 24:45). The Scriptures—our Old Testament—had already described and explained what they had witnessed: The Messiah would suffer and die, and on the third day rise again from the dead. The Scriptures also described what would follow: Repentance for the forgiveness of sins in the name of Jesus would be preached to all people.

We can also read the Old Testament as a testimony about Jesus. The best explanation of that testimony is in the life of Jesus. There you can see and understand what all of Israel's history pointed toward and the central core of everything God said through His prophets. We notice that after the resurrection, the disciples began to read the Scriptures with new understanding. As John says, "When therefore He was raised from the dead, His disciples remembered that He had said this, and they believed the Scripture" (John 2:22) and "His disciples did not understand these things at first, but when Jesus was glorified, then they remembered that these things had been written about Him and had been done to Him" (John 12:16).

Lord, I pray that You also open our minds today so we can understand the Scriptures. You hold the key to them. If we know You, we will understand them. And if we understand them, we will learn to know You better still. But You alone can do all this, You, our living Lord, when You come to us and interpret them for us. That's how You walk on earth today: in this living Word that You have sent to us. Let us meet You there, alive as You are. Let us also see Your image and recognize You among us. Tell us that it is You who is speaking and that You are present in Word and in Sacrament. Let us hear Your voice and know again that You are our living Lord.

SATURDAY AFTER EASTER
Matthew 28:1–20

He said to him, "If they do not hear Moses and the Prophets, neither will they be convinced if someone should rise from the dead." Luke 16:31

Matthew is the only evangelist who tells about the guard at the tomb. He is also the only one who suggests what happened when the stone was rolled away. It had already been rolled away when the first disciples arrived. Only the guard by the grave could have been there when it happened. In any case, frightened and confused, they went to the chief priests and reported what had happened.

You would think this would have opened the eyes of Christ's opponents. But they reacted as Jesus described in the parable about the rich man and Lazarus. The rich man turned to father Abraham with a request that he send Lazarus down to earth to warn his five brothers, who lived just as thanklessly and godlessly as he had lived. But Abraham said that the brothers had Moses and the prophets to listen to. The rich man knew only too well that his brothers were perfectly indifferent to everything the Scriptures said, so he replied: "No, father Abraham, but if someone goes to them from the dead, they will repent" (Luke 16:30). Then Abraham told him the bitter truth: "If they do not hear Moses and the Prophets, neither will they be convinced if someone should rise from the dead."

This might explain why Jesus revealed Himself only to His disciples and not to everyone. It wouldn't have done any good. There's nothing that can't be dismissed, when someone doesn't want to see the truth. If Christ has really risen from the dead, then there is only one correct, reasonable, and justifiable way to live, namely as His disciple, follower, and servant. The disciples were prepared to take the consequences, but one can also do the exact opposite. Some find it so unreasonable, unthinkable, and repugnant to admit that Jesus is right that nothing can convince them about His resurrection. That's how it was for the chief priests. Jesus couldn't be right. The resurrection was an illusion or, possibly, black magic. They needed to protect the people from this fraud, so they did what they had to do.

Naturally, some people believed the chief priests. Matthew says that the rumor was popular among the Jews in his time. Strangely enough, no one asked why the disciples would have stolen the dead body. What would they have gained by that? From the day they began to preach the resurrection as fact, their lives were filled with persecution and hardship. To be a Christian in Jerusalem meant being shut out and isolated. Christians lost the fellowship of their peers, which to us would be the same as losing our social benefits. Yet, they stood firm—even unto death and martyrdom—on their testimony. They knew that it was the truth.

I pray to You, Lord, for everyone who has trouble believing and everyone who refuses to believe. I know that it wasn't because of anything I did that You opened my heart to You and caused my eyes to see Your truth. I could just as well have belonged to those who choose to be blind and deaf. Therefore I pray to You, Lord, for us all. Help us to believe. Let us see things that will open our eyes. Let us encounter experiences, people, and ideas that will lead our imaginations and our feelings in the right direction without making us defiant. You have patience without limit. Therefore, I dare to pray to You to have even more patience. I also dare pray to You for those whom I think are helplessly far away. You can find ways to their hearts. Have mercy on us all.

FIRST SUNDAY AFTER EASTER

John 20:19–31

"As the Father has sent Me, even so I am sending you."
John 20:21

John first tells us what happened on Easter evening. He touches on what Luke writes about in more detail: Jesus had convinced them that it was really Him they saw and not a ghost or a vision. Then John tells of the new commission the apostles received. With the resurrection, a new era in world history began. The Gospel would be preached to all people. It was the apostles' task to go out with the message about what God did when He sent Christ into the world. There were other witnesses to the resurrection—the women at the tomb, for example—but they didn't receive the commission to preach the Gospel. The commission was for the apostles, and Jesus entrusted it to them. He gave them the Holy Spirit and full authority to forgive sins. They were now initiated as witnesses to the resurrection of Jesus, as Peter would later express it in Acts 2:32. The words Jesus spoke to the apostles on the evening of the first Easter are usually part of the Scriptures read during a pastor's ordination because the pastoral office is a continuation of the commission that the Resurrected One gave His apostles.

Then John tells us about Thomas, and we jump a week ahead to the Sunday we celebrate today. John says quite clearly that Thomas should have believed the news when he heard it from the others; he had no reason to doubt. Jesus' words are reproachful: "Have you believed because you have seen Me" (John 20:29)? Thomas should have been able to believe without sticking his hands in Jesus' wounded side. There is an exhortation in the words of Jesus: "Blessed are those who have not seen and yet have believed" (John 20:29). The exhortation is addressed to all those who, during the course of time, are reached by the message of the resurrection. Only a few could really be eyewitnesses, but their message would belong to everyone. Their eyewitness message was from God Himself concerning the essential thing He did for the world. The apostles realized their responsibility. They knew what they had to say. It resounded in all their preaching: "But God raised Him on the third day and made Him to appear, not to all the people but to us who had been chosen by God as witnesses, who ate and drank with Him after He rose from the dead. And He commanded us to preach to the people and to testify that He is the one appointed by God to be judge of the living and the dead. To Him all the prophets bear witness that everyone who believes in Him receives forgiveness of sins through His name" (Acts 10:40–43).

Lord, I thank You that I may believe without seeing. I thank You because You have let me see so much. How many times have You not met me in Your Word? I have been able to see Your image, and I have heard Your voice. You have come to me in my loneliness and my sorrow. You have forgiven my trespasses. And You have given me powers to do things I would never have otherwise dared or been able to do. My eyes have seen Your salvation, but more than all this is Your promise that I may believe without seeing. I don't need to know or experience or ask for proof. You allow me to trust in You alone. You guarantee that this is the truth. However poor I may be, I still have You. I couldn't ask for anything more.

MONDAY AFTER
THE FIRST SUNDAY
AFTER EASTER
John 21:1–14

And although there were so many, the net was not torn.
John 21:11

The last chapter of John's Gospel is a postscript that was written when the original book was finished. It may have been John who wrote this postscript, or it's possible that one of his disciples wrote it after his death. John himself says that there were many other things Jesus did that aren't written in his book. He understood that there was a profound purpose in everything Jesus said and did. In this Gospel, he (or one of his disciples) thought that at least some of the things that happened when Jesus revealed Himself to the disciples in Galilee should be recorded. We know Jesus did this because Matthew records it also.

John was the first to recognize Jesus when He stood on the beach at dawn. The disciples had worked hard fishing all night long and hadn't caught anything. But when they followed Jesus' advice, they got results. They got an unexpected and enormous catch. John understood the implication. Jesus had just turned them into fishers of men. Soon they would go out into the world with a mission that seemed hopeless. They received a reminder of what Jesus had told them on the last evening together: "You can't do it without Me." But if they followed Him, everything was possible.

John tells us there were 153 fish in the net. There seems to have been a reason for mentioning this particular number. One of the church fathers explained that contemporary zoologists believed there were 153 types of fish in existence. Jesus Himself had compared God's kingdom to a net that is lowered into the sea and gathers fish of every kind. It was the apostles' task to cast the net out into the sea of men. The enormous catch on this morning was an indication that the church's net would gather people from every tribe and nation. The fishermen's net would not be torn. Therefore, Christ's Church would accommodate every tribe and nation around the world. And just as the disciples hauled in the nets to the shore on that morning and brought the fish to their Lord, so shall they and their successors draw the Church's great nets onto the coast of eternity, where Christ stands waiting.

Later, on the beach, Jesus ate with His disciples, and again John gives us a glimpse of the timeless significance of what happened. The aging John knew that Jesus ate with him and the others in the same manner that He celebrated the Lord's Supper. And that's the way He always would be with His own, henceforth, until the day when the great net is hauled in and laid at His feet.

Lord, You live and are with us here today. So I don't need to ponder much over what happened two thousand years ago. I have Your resurrection fresh in my memory every day. That's why Your Church is alive. How would I have been able to meet You if You hadn't come here? What would the Lord's Supper be if You hadn't broken the bread and passed it to me to eat? How could my heart burn if You hadn't explained the Scriptures? I thank You because I was caught in the net You wove through Your love to draw us all to You. I praise You for Your resurrection that allows me to come to You.

TUESDAY AFTER THE FIRST SUNDAY AFTER EASTER

John 21:15–25

"Lord, You know everything; You know that I love You."
John 21:17

Peter denied his Master three times. And three times he was asked the question, "Do you love Me" (John 21:15–17)? On this occasion, Peter wasn't as sure of himself as he had been when he said he was ready to go to prison and even die for his Lord (Mark 14:31). When Jesus asked, "Do you love Me?" Peter avoided giving a direct answer. He didn't dare claim to love his Lord more than the others. But he did dare to say one thing: "You know that I love You." When Jesus repeated the question two more times, he became distressed and appealed to the Master, who knew everything. He must also know that Peter, the unstable Peter, who no longer dared to make big promises, could still honestly say that he loved his Lord.

That's how it is with true faith when it has been purified and tested by the Spirit. Those who "have decided for" or "given their heart to" Jesus, as people commonly say, believe strongly in the beginning that they're now on the safe side. They know what they want and to whom they belong. But Jesus teaches us to forget all prodigious thoughts about ourselves. He teaches us to distrust our own resolution and strength and to trust in Him alone. If everything else fails and falls short, He is still trustworthy. He is the One who has decided that we will go and "bear fruit."

This insight also allows us to truly love the Savior. If someone doesn't have a lot of confidence in himself, he at least knows he has Jesus' love. This is a better basis for discipleship and faithfulness than our own intentions. Peter, who denied his Lord in the chief priests' courtyard, would soon stand before the chief priests and the whole council and speak with a boldness that amazed everyone. Later, he would be crucified in the same manner as his Lord—although tradition claims that he didn't view himself worthy to die in the same manner as his Lord and therefore demanded to be crucified upside down. When John's Gospel was written, Peter had already "glorified God" in this way. That's what the text alludes to here.

"And after saying this, He said to him, 'Follow Me' " (John 21:19). That's the way it began when Jesus called Peter on the shores near Tiberias. Now Jesus said again, "Follow Me," but with a new meaning. Peter would follow his Lord, the living Lord, who would be with him every day on all of his journeys. This, too, was a consequence of the resurrection.

Lord, You know everything. You know all my weaknesses, how often I come up short. But You also know that I love You. It's my life's joy and my great comfort that I may follow You. I know that You are close to me. I know that I have You here, in Your Word, in Your Church, in Your Supper. I don't have to worry about all the others and what has become of them. I can leave that to You and follow You. That's how it was from the very beginning. That's what You did with the first disciples. That's what You do even today, and I thank You for that.

WEDNESDAY AFTER THE FIRST SUNDAY AFTER EASTER

1 Corinthians 15:1–20

But in fact Christ has been raised from the dead, the first-fruits of those who have fallen asleep. 1 Corinthians 15:20

The fifteenth chapter of First Corinthians, the most detailed account of the resurrection of the dead, was written approximately twenty years after the resurrection. Here we encounter the apostolic proclamation, based on the experiences of the apostles during the forty days when Jesus appeared to them and spoke about the kingdom of God, and about the whole priceless experience of life together with the Resurrected One in the Early Church.

Paul begins with a reminder of what he calls the main point of Christianity—that Jesus died, was buried, and rose again on the third day. He mentions the most important appearances very briefly: to Cephas (Peter) then to the Twelve (although on this occasion there were just eleven apostles and only ten were present). Then he mentions an appearance before more than five hundred brothers at once, possibly an appearance in Galilee that Matthew mentions but is not described anywhere else. He further mentions an appearance to James, the brother of Jesus, who once was not a believer but became one of the leaders of the Early Church. And finally he adds "all the apostles" (1 Corinthians 15:7) This is clearly a reference to the appearance one week after the resurrection that John speaks about.

All this Paul says that he "received" (15:3), a standard term for a fixed learning tradition, something was taught in elementary instruction. This might explain why he is so brief.

After this, Paul declares that the resurrection is beyond all doubt. There were people in Corinth who said there wasn't a resurrection. But Paul answers that because Christ has risen, there *is* a resurrection. Christ is the "firstfruits of those who have fallen asleep." And that He has risen is beyond all doubt.

Paul doesn't hesitate to list all the horrible consequences of a mistake on this point. If Christ hasn't risen, then Paul's witness is a false witness and he has borne false witness against God. Consequently, he and his fellow Christians are the most wretched of all creatures. And then all of humanity remains in its sin and has only one justifiable sentence to expect. Many hardly dare to think such thoughts. Paul can express them frankly, without beating around the bush. He knows that his message is the truth. He was once a doubter, denier, and persecutor. But now he can say as the other apostles said: "This Jesus God raised up, and of that we all are witnesses" (Acts 2:32). Or as Peter said before the council: "We cannot but speak of what we have seen and heard" (Acts 4:20).

My Lord Jesus, You are the firstfruits of those who fell asleep, the first God raised from the dead. You are the first flower on the tree of a new life. And you have made us shoots on that tree so we, too, will blossom like You. It was for our sake that You went from death to life. You didn't have to do it; You already had eternal life. You lived with Your Father in boundless joy. Yet You became man, suffered, and died to obtain a life that You could give to us. When I finally fall asleep in death, I will know that You are my Brother, who also died a physical death, and You shall lead me on the same path You took from death to life. I thank You because I, too, can be present in the multitude where You are the firstfruits among many.

THURSDAY AFTER THE FIRST SUNDAY AFTER EASTER

1 Corinthians 15:21–34

Christ the firstfruits. 1 Corinthians 15:23

"For as in Adam all die, so also in Christ shall all be made alive," Paul says in 1 Corinthians 15:22. Because we all belong to the family of Adam, those who have fallen away from God and ended up in the hands of death, we must all die. But now Christ has come as a new Adam, an Adam who didn't fall into sin but redeemed all the trespasses of Adam's family. He's the beginning of a new humanity. He possesses a new life, a life we can all have. Christ is the firstfruits. When He comes again in glory, we will be resurrected to the same life if, of course, we have responded to the opportunity offered when Christ comes to us with His Gospel of forgiveness.

Paul broadly outlines the whole course of the world here. We still live in a time of struggle. Christ is King, but all the powers of evil are against Him. These powers can still bring people to their destruction. They still torture those who belong to Christ. Paul says that he himself suffers death day after day. He's subjected to constant danger. In 1 Corinthians 15:32, Paul reminds us of something that happened to him in Ephesus. This might be what was recorded in Acts chapter 19, when the whole city rioted and dragged the Christians into the arena in a fury. But Christ will be victorious. He will deliver His kingdom back into God's hands. Creation will then be reestablished and God will again be everything for everyone. Evil will be forever isolated, powerless, constrained, and alone with its evilness.

When Paul speaks of this, it is clear that he realizes this will take a long time. At the beginning of his ministry he believed, along with all the other disciples, that Christ would return soon enough that they would see the day. In his earliest letter, First Thessalonians, Paul talks about what it will be like for us: "We who are alive, who are left until the coming of the Lord" (4:15). But in his later letters, he writes about being able to "depart and be with Christ" before the Savior returns (Philippians 1:23). The fact that Christ waited to return didn't create a crisis situation for faith. Everyone knew that the Master said, "concerning that day and hour no one knows" (Matthew 24:36). Paul has formulated the essence of our future hope in Christ in this way: "Whether we live or whether we die, we are the Lord's" (Romans 14:8).

Paul spoke in today's text about being "baptized on behalf of the dead" (1 Corinthians 15:29). This is an example of a Bible verse that may be hard to understand. Some have speculated that people in the Early Church could bring a dead person with them when a whole family was baptized. Just as people brought all their children to be baptized, they also brought dead relatives they thought would want to be present and commended to God's mercy. But all this is conjecture. When reading Bible verses like these, we should apply Luther's wise counsel to "take off their hat and pass on by." In any case, we can see how important Baptism was to them. They knew it was the gate to the world where we participate in the new life of the resurrection.

Lord Jesus Christ, You live and reign in Your kingdom. You have all power in heaven and on earth. You are the King of kings and the Lord of lords. Yet You reign only so everything can be laid at Your Father's feet. You use Your power only to help us and lead us back to Him so everything will be one in Him. Dear Lord, allow me to have this frame of *mind so I may have an immense longing to return to God, who is our origin and our Father, the source of all goodness, merciful Father and all-comforting God.*

FRIDAY AFTER THE FIRST SUNDAY AFTER EASTER
1 Corinthians 15:35–58

But someone will ask, "How are the dead raised? With what kind of body do they come?" 1 Corinthians 15:35

Sometimes we hear questions like this one, ironically posed. Is it naive to believe that our body will be raised from the grave? What would a body that was raised from the dead look like?

You fools! Paul answers. All bodies consist of some sort of substance and this is God's work. God is fantastic. He created the heavens, each in their own specific way. He created the organic substance that in its many different forms makes up all living creatures on earth. He creates every time He transforms a seed into a plant. With these same creative powers, He will again give us a new body in a completely new way, from a substance we can't even imagine. We know only about what is perishable, insignificant, and weak, possibly as an old broken-down and wasted human body, doomed to decompose and become earth again. That body will return in glory and immortality. Paul uses an expression here that refers directly to Christ after the resurrection, when He could no longer die, when He had clothed Himself in an image that Paul calls "a heavenly body" (1 Corinthians 15:40). The body we have now is the carrier of spiritual life, in the sense of a psychological life that has the capacity to think and be conscious of its own existence. In the same way, Paul says there is a spiritual body. Christ, the last Adam, became a life-giving spirit. This doesn't mean He was incorporeal. Instead, He possessed a new form of life that can create life and inspire us in a new way. Just as we were the image of the first Adam, so shall we also be like the second Adam, our resurrected Lord, He who is the beginning of a new creation and a whole new world.

The old creation is perishable. It had a beginning where it was created from nothing and one day it will return to nothing. But just as Christ was transformed in the tomb, so shall we also be transformed from perishable to imperishable, from mortal to immortal. God will create new heavens and a new earth. But into this new world, He will take something from the old world, namely His Son and all those who belong to Him. We, too, will enter the new creation. We, who once lived here, will live on as individuals and personalities, but we will be molded in a completely new image, about which we know nothing other than that we will be like Christ, the Resurrected One.

Thanks be to You, Lord God, who gives us victory through Jesus Christ! You, heavenly Father, can never be praised or thanked enough because You didn't reject the humanity that so poorly rewarded Your love. On the contrary, You deigned to save us, to bring us back to You. The fact that You gave this life to us and allowed us to live by Your side was far more than we could hope for or ask *for. And what do we have to say, now that You have sent Your own Son to save us from the fate we brought upon ourselves? Lord Christ, You gave Your life so we would live. You rose to give us life again. We thank You and praise You for Your incomprehensible mercy and for all the grace You showered on us, first in creation and then through Your salvation. Praise be to our Lord Jesus Christ, of whom, through whom, and to whom is everything. To You be glory in eternity.*

SATURDAY AFTER THE FIRST SUNDAY AFTER EASTER

John 10:1–10

The good Shepherd lays down His life for the sheep.
John 10:11

We are now in the forty days between Easter and Ascension, when Christ appeared to the disciples time and time again, instructing them about the kingdom of God (see John 21). Therefore, we devote these weeks to meditate about what the resurrection means for us and how the Resurrected One continues His work even today. The readings for this part of the Church Year deal with these topics. Most of them are taken from John's Gospel. John is the apostle who lived the longest and understood the words of Jesus in the light of a long life that was rich in experience.

Therefore he can teach us better than anyone else the meaning of Christ's resurrection.

First, the resurrection means that Christ continues His work. God sent Him out into the world to bless us, as Peter says in Acts 3:26. He is the Good Shepherd who continuously seeks what is lost. Traditionally, the second Sunday after Easter focuses on the Good Shepherd. The story of the good shepherd has possibly been more loved and utilized than any other of Jesus' parables. Sometimes, however, it is used in a very unbiblical setting. Many imagine the shepherd's life in much the same way as the perfumed aristocrats did in the idyllic poems of the 1700s, where the sheep are wonderfully combed and gentle, snuggling up to an appealing shepherd with soft white hands that have been miraculously protected from the sunlight and the rough stones of the desert.

The shepherd's life in Palestine was, in truth, very harsh. The sheep grazed in the wild and stony desert that lies just outside Jerusalem and Bethlehem. This area is still an area full of crags, broken gorges, and mountains descending down to the Jordan Valley. Small brooks and ravines become deep valleys where mountains steeply rise on both sides. During the winter, flash floods can suddenly fill the narrow canyons. During the long dry season, those same ravines are bone dry. A few small, malnourished bushes and clumps of grass grow along the ridges. The sheep graze there as they make their way along the low hills and cliffs. The shepherd sits in the shade under a ledge or stands on the precipices, following the sheep with his eyes. All of his sheep come back to him when he sounds out his call. Every shepherd has his own call, and the sheep know his voice. There have always been thieves and bands of robbers there, as well as wild animals. Jesus speaks about wolves that would come. David could say he fought both lions and bears. Shepherds had to be prepared to fight with them. A good shepherd would give his life for the sheep.

In sharp contrast to the good shepherds are the bad shepherds, who think only about stealing and slaughter. Bad and false shepherds can also be found in the church. Therefore Jesus gives us a picture of what a good shepherd is here. He will go in through the door that is Jesus Christ. He will be sent by Him, receive His commission, and be ordained by Christ Himself. He will come, as Jesus did, to seek out and save those who were lost. He will understand his responsibility to the sheep, love them, know them, call them by name, be prepared to work day and night for their sake, and even give his life in service. And the sheep will follow him. The congregation will not starve, but "will go in and out and find pasture" (John 10:9).

We pray to You, dear Lord, for good shepherds in Your Church. May those You call be certain of their call. Give them no peace if they try to escape, and let them taste the complete depths of Your peace when they say yes. Make them willing to suffer for Your sake. Interpret the Scriptures for them Yourself so their hearts burn. May they preach Your Word in such a way that we hear You and recognize Your voice. May everyone who believes hear Your voice so clearly that they follow in everything on Your path.

SECOND SUNDAY
AFTER EASTER
John 10:11–16

"I am the Good Shepherd." John 10:11

Jesus Himself teaches us what it means to be a good shepherd in the parable of the lost sheep. The good shepherd leaves the ninety-nine in the desert—behind the stone walls of their stall, of course. Then he goes out and searches for the lost one. It might be in scorching summer heat that lingers hot and heavy on the desert trails between the cliffs, long into the night. Or it might be during winter when the rain beats down on his face and causes his hands to freeze because it's so cold.

It's one of his sheep that is lost. It happens so easily with sheep. They all go their own way, as the prophet says. They venture far out on the precipices. They get stuck between stones or caught up in thorny bushes above the precipices. The shepherd hears their anxious bleating and makes his way along the ledges. Finally he reaches his sheep, and, laying it across his shoulders, he carries it home.

This is precisely what Jesus, our Good Shepherd, does. Each and every one of us wants to go our own way. We're preoccupied with our own affairs, worried about our livelihood, and we believe that we know best how to get by. We leave the flock and try to make our own way. Everything is fine for a while. Sheep don't comprehend the risks, sometimes not even when it's too late. What do sheep know about the wolves prowling about, looking for prey?

Then the Shepherd comes. Maybe we feel the touch of His hand. Maybe it's something harder than His hand—the staff—trying to get a good grip to pick us up. Both sheep and humans have only one thought in these situations: to get free. They don't want to be grabbed or lifted. They jerk and twist out of the Shepherd's grasp and slide even further down the slope. This is the Shepherd's greatest disappointment and the sorrow that weighs heaviest on His mind. "O Jerusalem, Jerusalem, the city that kills the prophets and stones those who are sent to it! How often would I have gathered your children together as a hen gathers her brood under her wings, and you would not" (Matthew 23:37)!

However, things can happen in another way, a way Peter describes: "For you were straying like sheep, but have now returned to the Shepherd and Overseer of your souls" (1 Peter 2:25).

Lord Jesus, You are the Shepherd and Overseer of our souls. Help us to always understand that You want what is best for us. Help us always remember what You took upon Yourself when You came to seek out those who were lost. You gave Your life for the sheep. You fought with the destroyer, the one who comes to steal, slaughter, and destroy. And You continue to look for us when we go astray. Help us understand what it means when Your hand touches us. Touch our hearts, so we are not afraid and do not try to escape. Let us experience how comforting and delightful it is to be lifted up in Your arms to be carried through all dangers.

MONDAY AFTER THE SECOND SUNDAY AFTER EASTER
John 10:17–29

Jesus answered them, "I told you, and you do not believe. The works that I do in My Father's name bear witness about Me." John 10:25

The Feast of Dedication (Hanukkah) was celebrated in December. It was an important national holiday to remind the people of the fight for freedom against King Antiochus IV two hundred years before (164 BC). Antiochus had tried to put an end to Judaism by forbidding circumcision and the Sabbath, destroying the scrolls where the Law was written, and transforming the temple into a house of idols. Judas Maccabee started an uprising that was successful against all odds. The temple was then purified and the Lord's altar restored. The people celebrated the memory of this victory. Solomon's colonnade, where Jesus walked, was on the east side of the temple facing the Mount of Olives and was protected from the bitter northwest winds blowing from the Syrian highlands. Here, once again, people gathered around Jesus and asked if He was the Messiah.

Jesus told them that if they wanted to see and understand, then His deeds as well as His words would be answer enough. But a very distinct line between us becomes apparent when this question is raised. There are those who instinctively say no to Jesus, just as there are those who are drawn to Him. Here Jesus characterizes those gathered around Him. They listen to His voice. When they hear God's Word, they understand who is speaking. They want to hear more. They don't tire of listening. They know that this Word is living and gives life.

Even more, He knows them. *To know* in the Bible doesn't mean simply to have knowledge about something. When it comes to God and us, *to know* means to have a real, deep, and inner mutual relationship, devoid of obstacles, reservations, or stipulations. To be a Christian consists, Paul says, in coming "to know God, or rather to be known by God" (Galatians 4:9). That's how the Good Shepherd recognizes His sheep and how they recognize Him. Therefore they follow Him. That's the third attribute. They won't each go their own way. They follow Him even if they have to go with Him alone, against the grain.

And finally: He gives them eternal life. They will never perish. Nothing can grab them out of His hand. The Lord has given His life so they will be able to live. He gave it freely of His own will. His death was not a tragedy, not a victory for violence and injustice. He had the strength to overpower His enemies, but He chose to give His life for them instead. Jesus also had "authority to take it up again" (John 10:18). This doesn't mean it was easy for Him to die. He bore the world's sin and was forsaken by God. None of us can fathom the depth of that suffering. But His life that His enemies thought they had extinguished was God's own life. "For as the Father has life in Himself, so He has granted the Son also to have life in Himself" (John 5:26). He gave this life in death as a propitiation for our sins. Therefore, His life—which conquered death—can be given to us sinners also. It's for this reason that no one can take believers out of His hand. There's no sin so great that it can't be forgiven when someone believes in Jesus.

> "*The* LORD is my shepherd; I shall not want. He makes me lie down in green pastures. He leads me beside still waters. He restores my soul. He leads me in paths of righteousness for His name's sake. Even

though I walk through the valley of the shadow of death, I will fear no evil, for You are with me; Your rod and Your staff, they comfort me. You prepare a table before me in the presence of my enemies; You anoint my head with oil; my cup overflows. Surely goodness and mercy shall follow me all the days of my life, and I shall dwell in the house of the LORD *forever" (Psalm 23:1–6).*

TUESDAY AFTER THE SECOND SUNDAY AFTER EASTER
John 10:30–42

"I and the Father are one." John 10:30

God is often spoken of as our Shepherd in the Old Testament: "The LORD is my shepherd" (Psalm 23:1). He, not we ourselves, made us His people and sheep in His flock. "You are My sheep, human sheep of My pasture, and I am your God, declares the LORD God"(Ezekiel 34:31).

It may seem confusing that Jesus also speaks about Himself as the Good Shepherd. Actually, this allows us a better understanding of who Jesus is. What the Father does, the Son does also. Everything the Father is, the Son is also. The Son and the Father are one. God is one. But the Trinity is a part of His nature. If God were a man, talk about the Trinity would be complete nonsense. None of us can at the same time be one person and three persons. But in God's boundless, unfathomable, and inexhaustible nature, there is an abundance and a profundity we can't understand. What we know about God's nature is only what God has let us know or perceive, and God has let us know about the Trinity. He, who eternally is the one and only God, appears to us as the Son and the Spirit. That's how He speaks, that's how He works, and that's how He enters into a relationship with us. Yet it's always the same one God who speaks and acts.

It was blasphemy to the Jews when Jesus said He was God's Son. For many people it appeared to be a fantasy or delusion. Here is the decisive difference of opinion among people. In this way God came into the world, came to meet us to show us who He really is. Here we can get to know the Father's heart. No one has ever seen God. But in Christ's face, God's glory is radiant. The Old Testament doesn't give us an inferior picture of God, but the picture isn't quite complete. The Scriptures needed to be carried out and fulfilled. That happened through Jesus Christ. There's the correct interpretation, the complete revelation. We have it in Christ. That's His mystery: "The Father is in Me and I am in the Father" (John 10:38).

Lord, You are the Lord of Israel. You led Your people as a shepherd leads his flock. You promise to seek out the lost, lead them back, and heal their wounds. I thank You because You've come to us as our Good Shepherd. I thank You because You revealed Your nature and mystery in this way. You've shown us who You are. You saw the crowds and You pitied them because they were in such a pitiful condition and dejected, like sheep without a shepherd. You sought out each and every one that had been led astray and lost. You ate with sinners. You became a friend to the despised and the lost. I praise You, *my Lord and my God, because You're like that. To You, merciful Father and all-comforting God, belong the kingdom and the power and glory, for-ever and ever.*

WEDNESDAY AFTER THE SECOND SUNDAY AFTER EASTER

John 11:1–16

"Our friend Lazarus has fallen asleep." John 11:11

We have already seen that John writes about only a few of Christ's miracles, but he comments on them in great detail. He takes into account small illuminating details and lets the words of Jesus Himself explain what has happened. In this way He has the opportunity to instruct us on the major points of the Gospel. In the eleventh chapter, He instructs us about the resurrection and eternal life.

He starts with Lazarus being sick. We are told that he was a brother of Mary and Martha, and the three of them were among the disciples who were particularly close to the Master. So the sisters sent word to the Master, who at the time was on the other side of the Jordan. When Jesus received their message, He said to the disciples, "Our friend Lazarus has fallen asleep, but I go to awaken him" (John 11:11). Since the disciples didn't know that Lazarus was dead, they misunderstood Jesus. He meant that Lazarus was already dead.

Jesus often referred to being dead as *sleeping*. He did this when Jairus's daughter was dead: "The girl is not dead but sleeping" (Matthew 9:24). We find again and again in the New Testament that the dead are referred to as "those who have fallen asleep" (1 Corinthians 15:6, 18).

Therefore, death is a kind of sleep. It's easy to misunderstand this expression because people often have an incorrect assumption about natural life and natural sleep. They think life is something we "own," something we have control over. Sleep is a pause, a period of rest in this life. We still own our lives during sleep and we will wake up. If death is called sleep, it must mean that we still possess our life. We possess immortality, and we will also wake up.

But life isn't something we possess. It's something we receive. It's a gift from the Creator. We are in His hand our entire lives, completely dependent upon Him. We live only as long as He continues His creative work and, second by second, gives us life.

That's what sleep is too. The biblical truth about sleep is found in the psalms: "I lay down and slept; I woke again, for the LORD sustained me" (Psalm 3:5). I'm in God's hands the entire time, completely dependent on Him, night and day, at work and while I sleep. If I wake to a new day, it's because God has sustained me.

When death is called *sleep*, it means that the dead are also in God's hands. The Creator has the same power over them that He has over those who are alive. The dead aren't "gone." Neither are they immortal. They can't count on a continued existence that is their own and have control over it the way they believed they controlled their lives in this world. They, too, are in God's hands, completely dependent upon Him.

O Lord, where shall I go from Your Spirit? Or where shall I flee from Your presence? If I ascend to heaven, You are there! If I make my bed in Sheol, You are there! If I say, "Surely the darkness shall cover me, and the light about me be night," even the darkness is not dark to You; the night is bright as the day, for darkness is as light with You. Search me, O God, and know my heart! Try me and know my thoughts! And see if there be any grievous way in me, and lead me in the way ever-lasting (from Psalm 139)!

THURSDAY AFTER THE SECOND SUNDAY AFTER EASTER
John 11:17–37

"I am the resurrection and the life." John 11:25

Bethany is on the other side of the Mount of Olives, the road to Jericho passes by there, approximately a mile and a half before the city gates. John had taken this road many times and knew it was a half-hour walk—or 15 stadia by Greek measurements. Because the village was so close, many friends came, as good custom demanded, to console the sisters and share in their sorrow. When Martha heard that Jesus also was coming, she went to meet Him. John records their conversation and, as always, he does it with a sense for the essentials.

As with other devout Jews, Martha believed in a resurrection on the Last Day when the Messiah would come and hold court, and then the dead would receive life again. There was something about this belief that Jesus had to set right. Many Christians make the same mistake when they believe that eternal life comes after death. The most important aspect is lost. The resurrection is connected to Jesus and His resurrection. "I am the resurrection and the life" (John 11:25). We will be resurrected after death because Christ has been resurrected. He is the firstfruits. The life He received through resurrection He can also give to others.

Jesus goes on to say that faith is needed to receive this new life. Those who believe in Him shall never die. They already are a part of Christ, and so they already have a part of this life now—"the eternal life, which was with the Father and was made manifest to us," as John later wrote in 1 John 1:2. He who possesses Christ really has something that can never die. He is a part of the One who is the resurrection and the life.

Martha, like the other disciples—understandably enough—couldn't comprehend Christ's resurrection. When Jesus asked: Do you believe? She answered a little evasively, saying that she believed He was the Messiah, God's Son. She at least dared to say that much, and it was a good answer. This is also a good answer for us to use when we have difficulty understanding what Jesus says and when we don't really know what we should believe. We do know one thing and we should confess this to Him and ourselves: He is the Messiah, the Son of the living God, our Savior, who knows the truth, shows us the way, and gives us life. When we hold onto Him and trust in Him in everything, He will help us see and understand everything we really need to know.

My Lord Jesus, You are the resurrection and the life. We have You to thank for the fact that there is

a resurrection—a resurrection we will experience.
Everything depends on You. Everything is in Your
hands. You sought me out. You gave me a part of
Your own life. You incorporated me, an unworthy
person, into Yourself and You won't forget those
who are members in Your body. So I know I will
never die. With You, death is only a sleep, a com-
forting rest before a joyous awakening to a new
day. I couldn't ask for anything more. I believe
that You are God's Son. I believe in Your promise,
and I thank You for it.

FRIDAY AFTER THE SECOND SUNDAY AFTER EASTER
John 11:38–57

"Did I not tell you that if you believed you would see the glory of God?" John 11:40

The story of Lazarus's resurrection from the dead is completely unbelievable. That a dead body that had already begun to decompose could live again is contrary to everything we know about nature. Martha, like all her friends, was appalled by the thought of opening the grave. But Jesus answered her: "Did I not tell you that if you believed you would see the glory of God?"

Why does the raising of Lazarus seem so unbelievable?

It's because we take into account only this world, matter, and the laws of nature—but not God. If God exists and if He is who He says and shows us that He is, then He is Lord over nature and not the other way around. He, who is the source of everything, can do whatever He wants with any little atom or electron. He made them, and He is constantly redesigning them. He can design them in any way He wants. The fact that He follows certain patterns, what we call laws of nature, restricts us but not Him.

He who believes will be able to see God's glory, Jesus said. God's glory means His nature, what makes Him God. If we believe, we have the opportunity to understand that God really is God and He has sovereign rule over everything. Then we can also begin to understand how He works both here in this world and after the resurrection when the world will be born again. Jesus gave us a glimpse of this when He raised Lazarus from the dead. It was something that could happen only if God the Creator, the Almighty, intervened. In this respect, it was a picture of the resurrection. But Lazarus wasn't "resurrected;" he was awakened to live this life just as he had before. The resurrection is different. It's a new creation that begins a new life and lets us see "what no eye has seen, nor ear heard, nor the heart of man imagined, what God has prepared for those who love Him" (1 Corinthians 2:9).

God, my God, my Creator, my Origin and my Savior—I, too, shall see Your glory! It's more than I can fathom, more than I dare ask for, more than my mortal eyes could ever endure. Yet You say it Yourself. You opened my eyes so I am able to see Your glory and take part in Your joy. You've allowed me to be one of those who would receive the unfathomable gift of living in Your presence and rejoicing in Your kingdom filled with Your glory. Lord, I know

everything is possible for You, even what seems
so preposterous and incomprehensible to me: That
even I should be one of them You chose to take
part in the life and the joy that is found in You.

SATURDAY AFTER THE SECOND SUNDAY AFTER EASTER

John 12:35–50

"While you have the light, believe in the light." John 12:36

Those who believe shall see God's glory. Those who believe shall not die but share in Christ and His resurrection. Those who believe receive the forgiveness of sins and will not be condemned. That's how important faith is.

But Jesus said to John that there are people who did not and could not believe in Him despite the many signs He'd given them. Jesus reminds us of what the prophet Isaiah wrote about people whose eyes God blinded and whose hearts He hardened. Does God still do this to some people?

God wants all mankind to be saved and come to the knowledge of the truth. It's one of the foundations of the Gospel. Yet not everyone is saved. One of the reasons for this puzzling mystery is revealed by Jesus in our verse today: "While you have the light, believe in the light."

We won't always have the light. God is the light, and He exists forever. But His light isn't always in our presence.

Sometimes it's as if it was extinguished. In every person's life, there is a duel between darkness and light. God comes with His light and reaches out to us. He's visiting us. We can follow this light, or we can be drawn deeper into the darkness. No one is left unchanged when dealing with God. Either we are drawn closer to Him or our hearts are hardened and we turn from to Him to avoid being drawn to Him. The Word can actually harden someone also. A person's heart can be hardened by encountering God time and time again. His light can blind them so they can no longer see or believe. That's why there is so much significance in the warning to be careful when we're sought and to believe in the Light while we have it.

Lord, have mercy on us. Let Your Spirit move our hearts so we understand that it's You who knocks on the door of our hearts. Lord, am I praying because of lack of wisdom? The more eagerly You knock, the more deaf those who don't want to open have to become. Is this why You wait? Do You leave them alone so they can continue to believe that You don't exist? Are You waiting for the right time? Lord, I pray that You have mercy on us and come in the hour You have chosen. Let the light shine where the heart's door is ajar. Have mercy on us all, Lord, and help us.

THIRD SUNDAY
AFTER EASTER
John 16:16–22

"A little while, and you will see Me no longer; and again a little while, and you will see Me." John 16:16

This sentence is repeated three times in this Sunday's Gospel. It was clearly something Jesus wanted to stress. We know He used the same teaching method as other teachers when He instructed in the Scriptures. They constantly repeated important things and let their disciples hear them over and over again so it would sink into their consciousness and stick in their memory.

What was so important about this lesson? What does Jesus mean?

First and foremost was what would happen the next day, when He would die. He would be separated from them for a little while, but He would rise up and they would see Him again. They would be very distressed, just like a woman who bears children, but the joy would be even greater. No one would be able to take that joy from them.

But Jesus alludes to something more here: the day He would leave them and return to His Father. Then they would no longer see Him as they would during the forty days after His resurrection. Yet even this separation would be for only a while; then the disciples would be able to see Him forever.

"A little while" is, in other words, the time until Jesus' second coming. It might seem strange to call it "a little while" since it's now been two thousand years. But it's a question of measuring time by God's own standard as it fits into His plans for the whole course of the world. It is a little time in comparison with the time that has passed since creation. It's an infinitely small amount of time in comparison with everything that awaits us in eternity. It will also be a little while for every individual—a few short years until we meet Jesus face-to-face as heirs to His kingdom.

It's a common and disastrous mistake to think that Jesus' return is a long time off, that we have plenty of time to fix all "that stuff about God" later. It's human and understandable to feel that times of difficulty and suffering last a long time. Time goes very slowly when we suffer. Yet the apostle Paul says that our affliction is momentary and weighs little. He can say this because he sees suffering in the big picture. "For this light momentary affliction is preparing for us an eternal weight of glory beyond all comparison" (2 Corinthians 4:17). That's the correct perspective. It shows us that it really is only a little while.

Lord, You know how a long time seems for us in our distress. You let Your devout followers speak about this and allowed their complaints to become a part of Your Word. You know how many of us could say, as Your servant Job did, "so I am allotted months of emptiness, and nights of misery are apportioned to me. When I lie down I say, 'When shall I arise?' But the night is long, and I am full of tossing till the dawn" (Job 7:3–4). You know, Lord, how long a lonely sleepless night can be. Therefore, we thank You that You have given us eyes to see the light of eternity now. You let us understand that suffering is but a moment in comparison to what lasts forever. You let us experience how the past becomes a blur, like a surreal dream, as our years fly by, as we fly away. We thank You because everything that happens in this temporal life has an end. Yet You remain the same and Your years have no end.

MONDAY AFTER THE THIRD SUNDAY AFTER EASTER

John 14:1–14

"You know the way." John 14:4

There is a lot that Christians don't know. There are things we don't have to know, so nothing is written in the Bible about it.

The Christian life is a journey. We constantly get to see more. We learn to better understand things. We are led deeper into the mystery of God. The Christian doesn't have to know everything from the beginning.

But there's one thing we have to know: the way that leads to God. It's impossible to get there if you don't know the way.

This is one of the things Jesus tried to impress upon His disciples in every way. As Jews, they learned that the Law was the way to God. If you lived in accordance with the Commandments, you were on the right path and would eventually end up at home with God. Jesus taught the disciples something different. He taught them He was the way—just as He was the truth and the life. No one can come to the Father, except through Him (John 14:6). The disciples learned to really understand this on the first Easter Sunday, through the cross and resurrection. Until then, they thought they would follow Him by fighting for His cause and, possibly, giving their lives. But there was a part of the way that Jesus had to go completely alone. Jesus, the only righteous person, took everyone else's guilt upon Himself. He alone could atone for the world's sin. And He alone could rise from the dead because death could not hold the only One who had been obedient until death. That's how the path to God unfolds.

No one can follow this path without Jesus. Proper teachings and honest intentions aren't enough. A new life is needed, a life that can be received only by being a member of Christ's body. It is only when we are united with Christ and belong to Him that we can move ahead on the path. Only when we are one with Him can we reach out to God.

That Christ is the Way also means that He is with us all along the way, at all crossroads, and in every new situation. We have a living Lord who is with us every day, and when we walk with Him we are, in a sense, already at our destination. He and the Father are one. We are with Him on our way to our Father's dwelling. At the same time, we're already home. We have returned as the prodigal son did, and we have been received with open arms and great joy.

Lord Jesus, I thank You because I have been able to see the Father by seeing You. Now I have seen His heart. Lord, this is enough for me, yet You want to give me even more! You want me to be where You are now—at home with God, amidst the overwhelming radiance that shines forth from Your Father's face, the radiance that forces the seraphim to cover their faces. You want me to live and see all the light and glory that my earthly eyes cannot endure to see. You want me to see it just as delightful, as unbelievably serene, and as joyous as it is. Then the blinding radiance will appear as a kind expression of satisfaction from a Father's eye. I will be warmed by His heart, but not burned. I will be able to see God and still live as a joyful child lives with his father. Praise be to Your name, Lord Jesus.

TUESDAY AFTER THE THIRD SUNDAY AFTER EASTER

John 14:15–24

"Lord, how is it that You will manifest Yourself to us, and not to the world?" John 14:22

We may want to ask the same question the disciples asked Jesus in this verse. If people had seen Jesus' resurrection with their own eyes, wouldn't they have believed?

We have already heard that this was not the case. The chief priests had knowledge of the resurrection through witnesses they had no reason to doubt, but they refused to believe. You can't believe in the resurrection if you don't believe in the Resurrected One Himself and His entire message. There is nothing to gain from hearing the facts if your heart refuses to accept the consequences.

That's what Jesus explained to His disciples when He answered their question. He said that a condition had to be met before He and His Father could reveal themselves—one must love Him and keep His Word. No matter how close Jesus gets to us, there's a barrier between us and Him if we don't love Him and keep His Word.

Keeping His Word is not the same as keeping His Commandments. It is not just a matter of doing the things He commands. The word *keep* means a lot more in the New Testament. It means to hold on to something, love it, respect it, let it penetrate, experience it, and regard it as so precious that you would rather lose anything else than lose it. And Christ's Word is more than commandments and regulations. He says His Word is spirit and life. Christ Himself is in the Word. When we listen to it, think about it, and let it sink into the essence of our souls, it's a power that gives life, gives new birth, heals our wounds, and carries us through all difficulties.

If someone receives the Word in this way, he also receives Jesus Himself. Then the Resurrected One is there with all He has to give. But if someone doesn't love Him and doesn't keep His Word, then no amount of knowledge concerning the resurrection can help. Instead, that person will try to get away from Him and hide from Him in an effort to avoid confrontation with Him.

We encounter Jesus in the Word. We encounter God in Jesus, and that's where our salvation is decided.

You promised us, Lord Jesus, that You would not leave us fatherless. You kept Your promise to Your disciples. You came to them and revealed Yourself to them. And I know that You come to me too. Lord, let me see as much of Your glory and be able to experience as much of Your presence as I need in order to serve You properly. I know I can't keep anything You give. Therefore, I pray for what best can benefit Your work. I pray for whatever I need to serve You and help others to experience the light Your resurrection has brought to our world.

WEDNESDAY AFTER THE THIRD SUNDAY AFTER EASTER

John 15:1–8

"Apart from Me you can do nothing." John 15:5

Many think that being a true Christian means having certain opinions about God, and following certain Christian principles. But in this reading, Jesus teaches something different.

You can be a Christian only by having such an intimate fellowship with Christ Himself that His life becomes yours. The branches on a tree live because the sap flows up through the trunk into the branches and throughout the tree. Only then can buds burst, leaves sprout, and blossoms bloom and bear fruit. But if the branches break or rot, so the flow of life from the trunk stops, then the foliage withers, the leaves fall, and there will be no fruit.

That's the way a Christian is. Paul says the exact same thing using a different analogy: We are members of Christ's body (1 Corinthians 12:27). An arm can live only as long as blood from the heart pulses through it. If you wrap a rope around it and tie it too hard, it becomes numb and cold, then gangrene can set in, and your life is endangered.

In the same way, we depend upon Christ for our life. This isn't only a question of attitude and behavioral patterns. It's a question of a living faith that creates an intimate fellowship, a constant relationship with Christ Himself so His life flows in us with forgiveness, with a power that heals our wounds, and with a warmth that constantly allows us to act, driven by His love.

Therefore, we need, first and foremost, to be integrated, engrafted, and incorporated in Christ. This happens to us in

Baptism. Maybe the connection has been terminated, but it can also be restored. That's what "to remain in Christ" means. It's very literally meant—just as the branches are connected to the tree and just as the individual members are integral to the body. To remain in Christ is to believe. Faith is something invisible, but many of the characteristics of faith are noticeable and visible. Prayer belongs to faith, as does constantly returning to His Word, listening to it, and taking it to heart. That's the way sap from the vine flows into the branches. The words of Jesus are spirit and life. They're the blood of life that flows from Christ's heart to all His members. Where this happens, one can say with Paul, "It is no longer I who live, but Christ who lives in me" (Galatians 2:20).

My Lord Jesus Christ, it seems too audacious to believe that You could live in me with Your love and be here on earth even today, here in me, a sinner. Every day I have to be forgiven again, and this is precisely why I need You. I know that it is You who comes to me to forgive everything. I could never be free from my guilt if You hadn't given me a part of Yourself. So You are here with me. Therefore, I dare to hope and pray that You will be with me with Your love, with Your victory, and with Your new resurrected life. Come, Lord, and work in me. Do what only You can do: the work that bears the kind of fruit that will glorify Your Father.

THURSDAY AFTER
THE THIRD SUNDAY
AFTER EASTER

John 15:9–17

"You did not choose Me, but I chose you." John 15:16

We often believe that the most important aspect in Christianity is to "decide for yourself." We see how many different lifestyles there are to choose. So if someone wants to become a Christian, it means he has "made a decision for Jesus" and consequently "chosen to follow Jesus."

But this isn't reality. Jesus says He is the One who has chosen us. Already before the foundations of the world were laid, before anybody was created, God chose us to be His children. Long before we were even born, Christ died so all our sins would be forgiven. Long before we could ever fathom what was happening, Jesus came and laid His hand on us in Baptism and chose us to be His disciples. And when we forgot Him, He was the one who sought us out and was close to us, long before we saw Him.

Because that's the way it is, we believe that He really wants to live inside of us. The results may not be immediately apparent. A branch doesn't bear fruit the day after it has been grafted to a tree. But if it attaches itself to the trunk that gives the rest of the tree life, it will grow stronger and be fruitful. Christ has decided that we should bear fruit like this.

The important thing is that we "abide with Him," that we receive what He has to give and stay close to Him every day. He says that to "abide in His love" (John 15:10) means, first and foremost, to receive His love and let it fill us. Then we can love for His sake, and that is what He wants. He said this not to put a burden on us and compel us to do our duty, sighing and puffing and worrying because we aren't prepared. He said this so His joy will live in us. This life, which flows from Him to us, is also full of joy, the great joy of living in a world whose innermost nature is mercifulness, forgiveness, and love. It's the joy of knowing that Christ has made it possible even for the greatest sinner and the most miserable wretch to be God's child. It's the joy of knowing there is nothing that can separate us from God when we trust in Jesus and stay with Him.

I take Your hand, my Lord and my Savior, and won't let go of it. Even if I become tired and have difficulty holding on to it, I know You won't let go of me. You came to look for me because You wanted me to be Your disciple. And when You say You chose me to go out into the world and bear fruit, fruit that lasts, then I can believe it. My only prayer is that Your will be done. May it be as You willed when You gave me this life. Blessed are You because this is Your undertaking and not mine.

FRIDAY AFTER THE THIRD SUNDAY AFTER EASTER
John 15:18–25

"If they persecuted Me, they will also persecute you."
John 15:20

Sometimes we hear about the persecution Christians before us had to endure. Sometimes we encounter persecution today. Maybe it's someone who taunts us or makes a derisive comment. Maybe it's something that indicates we're no longer considered to be useful or accepted because we've openly confessed our faith and shown that we want to serve Christ. We're usually upset over things like this. We consider persecution unthinkable in a civilized society.

It's important to know that persecution for Christ's sake was considered completely normal and common in the Early Church. It is the world's natural reaction to faith in Christ. "The world" in this case doesn't mean the world God created, but the one that has rebelled against God and is dominated by disgust for everything that has to do with Him or in any way recognizes His power and rule over creation. The world always smells danger when someone comes to faith in Christ. It's a reminder of something the world doesn't want to hear. The world wants to maintain at any cost the illusion that God is a myth and we have no reason to worry about His will. When a person today shows that God is a power to be reckoned with and a delightful Lord to serve, the reaction is just the same as it was for Jesus Himself. If we're a part of this world, we should be accepted by this world. But at the same time, when we are separated from this world by a Lord we would rather serve, the world responds with rejection and hate.

It might help us to understand that the world can hardly react in any other way. When the world reacts like this, it's a good sign. It indicates that the salt hasn't lost its saltiness. It proves that the Light still shines. And this is a prerequisite for allowing the world to see Jesus and discover how delightful it is to serve Him.

I pray to You, Lord, for all those who persecute Your friends and disciples. They must notice Your presence. They must have had an idea of Your power. Lord, let them see more of Your glory and help all

*those who suffer persecution. Help them to love
and to be filled with joy. Help them to find the
right words and act in the right way. Help us all
to show everyone that it is You we serve and that
it is good to serve You.*

SATURDAY AFTER
THE THIRD SUNDAY
AFTER EASTER
John 15:26–16:4

"But when the Helper comes, whom I will send to you from
the Father, the Spirit of truth, who proceeds from the Father,
He will bear witness about Me." John 15:26

As we approach Pentecost, we will hear more and more
about the Holy Spirit in the sermon texts. In the few verses
that constitute today's Bible reading, we're given the complete background of the Spirit's work.

Jesus promised the apostles that He would send them His
Spirit. They'd need it. They would encounter much persecution. The world that rejected both Jesus and His Father wants
nothing to do with the Gospel. Despite that, the Gospel will
be preached and there will always be people who will listen
to it.

This is the work of the Spirit. The disciples will witness
to the Gospel, but if they had only their own memories, their
own eloquence, and their individual organizational skills to rely
on, their efforts would have been hopeless. But Jesus would
send the Spirit, the Spirit of truth, and He would witness.

He told them so the last night they were together before His death. "I did not say these things to you from the beginning, because I was with you" (John 15:4). They didn't need the Spirit when they had the Master among them and could ask Him about everything and He spoke and acted on their behalf. But after His ascension, they needed the Holy Spirit.

Who is this Holy Spirit?

People often think that it's difficult to "visualize" the Spirit. They have difficulty getting a good grip on Him or getting a clear picture of Him. This isn't strange. It's much easier to imagine God the Creator because we have visual proof everywhere in creation. Everyone, even those who aren't Christian, can understand it. Forming a picture of Jesus isn't difficult either. He was, of course, a man like us. But the Spirit? Who can form a picture of the Spirit?

The answer is no one. First of all, the Spirit is invisible. He doesn't meet us in nature like our Creator. He hasn't taken the form of a man like Jesus. And when He comes to the world, it isn't to witness about Himself but to witness about Christ. His task is not to let us see Himself, but to turn our eyes to Jesus. Wherever and whenever we see the Resurrected One, the Holy Spirit is at work. However, we can also notice that the Spirit is present. We can have just as personal a relationship with Him as with the Father and the Son. We can experience things like that when we're reared by the Spirit.

Dear Lord and Master, You who promised to send us the good Spirit, send Him also to me. He is the Helper, the Comforter, and the Consoler. Let me recognize His voice in all my difficulties so I can be as calm and bold as is only possible in the Holy Spirit. He is the Spirit of Truth. Let Him show me the whole truth, the truth about myself, the truth

about You, and all You have done for us. Let Him
witness to us all so our hearts will be convinced,
our conscience convicted, and all our laziness and
selfishness overcome.

FOURTH SUNDAY AFTER EASTER
John 16:5–13

"When the Spirit of truth comes, He will guide you into all the truth." John 16:13

The task before the apostles was almost impossibly difficult. Eleven uneducated individuals of "the people" would go out to all people and preach the resurrection of Christ. They would go to the skeptical Greeks and the self-confident Romans, who despised the Jews and everything they stood for. They would preach the Gospel of this Jesus Christ that even they found hard to understand.

It isn't surprising that they felt helpless when faced with this task, but Jesus promised them a helper who would make it possible. He promised them the Holy Spirit, who would guide them to the truth. He would remind them of what Jesus had said. He would help them to use the right words to express it.

The Spirit of truth made the impossible possible. We can thank Him for the picture of Christ given to us through the evangelists, a picture that gives all the essentials we need to know. The Spirit led the apostles, and with them the Early Church, to the truth about everything God has done in

Christ. For this reason, there is something fundamental and of vital importance in the apostles' work. The Church is built on the foundation of the apostles and the prophets. This is why the Nicene Creed calls the Church not only holy and catholic (meaning the whole Church), but also apostolic.

Jesus summarizes the Spirit's work in three short points that we constantly encounter. He teaches us the truth about three things: sin, righteousness, and judgment. The Spirit convinces us of our sin, teaches us right from wrong, and alerts us to our most serious shortcoming, which is unbelief. The Spirit witnesses about true righteousness that comes from God, the righteousness Christ acquired for us and gives us after He completed His work and returned to the Father. And the Spirit also witnesses to the truth about the fate that Christ's death sealed for the prince of darkness and all the deeds of darkness, including the deeds we're guilty of in our own hearts—a judgment that is simultaneously a victory for forgiveness and mercy, so that we, who are in fact condemned, now stand in grace and limitless mercy instead.

The Spirit witnesses to all of this.

Dear Lord, let me hear this testimony so clearly that my heart comprehends it and so often that I always am conscious of it. Only Your righteous Spirit can make it a reality for me. It's so easy for me to regard sin the way the world regards it, and then I don't think it's that bad. It's easy for me to believe in my own righteousness as well because I start to also regard it the same way the world does. I begin to judge others, but not myself. Lord, let Your Holy Spirit show me the whole truth, the truth about my sin, my unbelief, my self-righteousness, and my lovelessness. Let Him show me Your righteousness and let Him pronounce the sentence that You

pronounce, the judgment over my entire old nature
that is completely in the bondage of sin. That
judgment is a merciful judgment, because it allows
us sinners to become Your friends, and children of
Your Father.

MONDAY AFTER THE FOURTH SUNDAY AFTER EASTER
John 17:1–8

"And this is eternal life, that they know You the only true
God, and Jesus Christ whom You have sent." John 17:3

Today, we begin reading from the chapter of John
that contains Jesus' High Priestly Prayer. Jesus prayed this
prayer during the Last Supper, right before He went to
Gethsemane.

Jesus usually prayed aloud, as was common at the time.
Here, John, who must have heard Him talk to His Father
many times, gives us insight into the way Jesus normally
prayed. The Master's prayer set the mood for the evening
and what was going to happen. The hour had come for His
suffering to begin. He prayed for His disciples in particular.
His intercession is called the High Priestly Prayer. Jesus is our
High Priest, who has offered up the sacrifice once and for all.
This ultimate sacrifice was now at hand, and He spoke about
it in His prayer.

But first He spoke about the work He had completed. He says He glorified the Father on earth by accomplishing this work. And just as He glorified the Father, the Father would now glorify Him.

To glorify doesn't mean the same thing here as it does in our common language. In our common language, the word means to praise something excessively, to almost overrate it. But here, *to glorify* means to make something a part of God's glory.

God's glory is God's very nature, the indescribable joy and happiness that fascinates us and at the same time blinds us. Jesus possessed this glory through His Father, but He descended to us in destitution, to reveal His Father's glory. "No one has ever seen God; the only God, who is at the Father's side, He has made Him known" (John 1:18). "And the Word became flesh and dwelt among us, and we have seen His glory, glory as of the only Son from the Father, full of grace and truth" (John 1:14). Jesus gives us these words as He received them from the Father. We can't receive them through our own understanding. These words contain something of God's glory, and they have to be received with our heart, with our entire being, and they have to be "kept." This means more than just understanding or obeying them. It means letting them become a part of ourself, treasuring them as more than our most valuable possession, and being willing to give up everything to keep them. To do this means to receive life itself, the eternal life that exists with God and now comes to earth in Christ. To know the only true God and know that He has sent Jesus Christ is eternal life.

My Lord and Savior, I thank You with all my heart because I have been able to see a glimpse of Your glory. I thank You because You made Your mark *on my forehead when I was baptized. I thank You because You have been with me even when I didn't want to follow You. I thank You because You gave me Your Father's Word and touched my heart so it would be opened to You. I thank You for the promise that I will see more of Your glory. I pray to You for those who can't see it. Bless them now, today, that they may also have a glimpse of Your glory so they will be drawn to You and will see You as You are.*

TUESDAY AFTER THE FOURTH SUNDAY AFTER EASTER

John 17:9–16

"They are in the world, . . . they are not of the world."
John 17:11, 16

To live in the world and still not be of the world is a big mystery for Christians. They have their place in the world, in society, in the workforce, in the family, in organizations, and among their friends, both Christians and non-Christians. Christians are needed there. Disciples are the salt of the earth and the light of the world.

Christians are not of the world. To be *of the world* means to be driven by particular ways of thinking, values, or patterns of behavior in a world that has fallen away from God, no longer depends on Him, and in countless ways is influenced and shaped by the "spirit that is now at work in the sons of disobedience" (Ephesians 2:2). We're influenced by the world's way of thinking every day. Lots of things are contrary to God's will, but obvious for the world: to first and foremost think of yourself, to live for this life only by attempting to get as much as possible out of it, to have evil thoughts about your enemies or those who've done you wrong, and see to it that they get what they deserve. To covet and the desire to be the center of attention, be in control and live the good life, are all self-evident motives for our actions. The whole world's values are affected by this view. And yet, Christians are supposed to live in, work in, and make contributions to this world while thinking in a completely different way with a completely different set of values. It isn't easy at all.

This is why Jesus prays that His disciples will be protected from evil. We need to pray this prayer every day. In fact, we do it every time we pray the Lord's Prayer. We pray that God leads us not into temptation, but delivers us from evil. Paul has given us the advice "to test everything; hold fast what is good" (1 Thessalonians 5:21). This doesn't mean we should try everything and experience for ourselves everything that's new, peculiar, or unexplored. It means we should be critical of everything, rejecting anything that doesn't meet the Christian standard and keeping only what turns out to be right when tested according to Christ's standard.

Dear Lord, help me use this standard properly. The standard is You Yourself. You are the truth that unveils everything false. Wherever You are in the world, selfishness and excuses are exposed. When I stand before something new and unknown, You are there, Lord, by my side with everything You

have said and everything You have taught me so
I can see clearly and judge properly—just as You
do in Your love. Let me follow You so I encounter
everything with You at my side.

WEDNESDAY AFTER THE FOURTH SUNDAY AFTER EASTER
John 17:17–26

"That they may all be one." John 17:21

Jesus also prays that His disciples would "become perfectly one" (John 17:23), just like He and His Father are one. He prays for everyone in the world who finds faith through the Gospel that is now sent out with His apostles.

He also tells us why it's so important that all His disciples are one—so the world may know that God sent Jesus and all His disciples are God's beloved children. Who can believe this if the disciples are at odds with one another and fight among themselves?

This prayer is a powerful exhortation to all Christians. It is a very serious reminder that the basis and condition for Christian unity are that we are all consecrated in the truth that Jesus has given us in His Word. Jesus came from His Father, and He was faithful to Him in everything. In the same way, He sends His apostles out into the world with the glory that God had given Him so they would be one. He let them see

God and led them to God so others would also be led to Him and they would all be one.

True ecumenism involves a unity with the Spirit among individuals who are "sanctified in truth" (John 17:19). It doesn't involve compromises with teachings and opinions that contain both truth and error. Neither can it involve organizing societies that are far from sanctified in the truth. Real unity in Christ cannot be organized. It is created by God when we become living members of His body. However, nothing should stop Christ's members from serving one another with the kind of unity and love Christ expects.

I pray to You, dear Lord, about this unity that is so difficult to achieve and seems to be so far away. I pray that You destroy everything that gets in the way of it. Eliminate all the apathy and distrust, all the error and false teaching, all the ideas and fabrications that have built walls between believers. I pray for the kind of replenishment and revival in Christianity that will lead us all closer to You, to be instruments of Your will so everyone can see Your truth, and everyone will gladly follow You in Your ways. Gather us around You, Lord. Let us come closer to You so we can also come closer to one another, not with ulterior motives and clever compromises, but by seeing Your truth more clearly, and loving You with all our heart.

THURSDAY AFTER THE FOURTH SUNDAY AFTER EASTER

Psalm 115:1–18

Why should the nations say, "Where is their God?" Psalm 115:2

We have finished reading Jesus' farewell address and will continue with the psalm He and the disciples sang right before they went to Gethsemane. We attempt to join in and sing it with Jesus. We, of course, read our Bibles to come closer to Jesus and take part in what is told there. We do this in a special way when we pray the psalms. We know that these words left the lips of Jesus countless times. Every Sabbath, every meal, every morning, and evening, He prayed using the words of the psalmist. There is so much in the psalms that point to Him. This is also true of the psalms He prayed on Maundy Thursday evening. We have just read the first one.

Here we learn something about how to pray. In general, people are too formal when they pray. They feel that God should be approached with respect. That feeling is correct, but some people draw the incorrect conclusion of believing that they can talk to God using only a very formal terminology and speaking about holy and sublime things. They try to pray in the same way as prayers are prayed in church. But the prayers in church have a very particular style. They are meant to be prayed together by everyone, in unison. Therefore, they are formulated generally enough so anyone can add their particular needs at different points during the prayer. They use a language fitting for the altar. Personal prayers don't have to be this way. Personal prayers can address those things that uniquely concern you or things you are personally thankful for. And you can use everyday language. And, what's most important, you can talk about anything.

The psalms can teach us a lot about such things. These prayers speak openly about doubt. The psalmist tells God that he can't understand why God does what He does. In bringing everything to Him in this way, the psalm writer begins to understand how God works and to see things in His light.

Many people today don't think they can mention their doubts about God's existence in prayers. But in the psalm we just read, this doubt is expressed. This often occurs in the psalms. Those who are devout in their beliefs complain about their distress. Heathens and adversaries rejoice. They say that the Lord, who rules in the heavens and does whatever He pleases, is an illusion, and it appears as if they are right. His troubled servant talks to Him about this in this psalm. This is something we should learn from him.

My dear Heavenly Father, You know that I am hesitant and filled with fear when I stand before You. How do I dare? You know me completely. And I think about the endless abyss between Your holy being and my human pettiness. Everything I received from You has been soiled and damaged. I am ashamed to show it, and yet You let me come before You. Because of Jesus, I can come to You as Your child. Although You know everything about me and have seen every sin, You let me come—with everything I am ashamed of, everything that hurts, everything that doesn't have to do with You. I now lay all of it at Your feet and pray for Your mercy. You have stretched Your atonement over me like a shield of grace over my entire wretched life. Praise be to You for Your incomprehensible and inexhaustible mercifulness, in Jesus' name.

FRIDAY AFTER THE FOURTH SUNDAY AFTER EASTER

Psalm 116:1–19

I will . . . call on the name of the LORD. Psalm 116:17

When you pray a psalm like 116 and consider the fact that the Lord Jesus prayed it just before His suffering began, then you can almost feel His suffering and victory too. You not only hear Him pray, you can look into His heart and comprehend the agony in the kingdom of the dead that took hold of Him. You see why He cried to His Father: "O, LORD, I pray, deliver My soul" (Psalm 116:4). You realize how His faith fought for our sake and achieved victory. You realize that we are included in His victory. You begin to ask in His own words: "What shall I render to the LORD for all His benefits to me?" (116:12) And the answer is the same: "I will lift up the cup of salvation and call on the name of the LORD" (116:13). I can, I dare, and I want to come to God with everything. I can, I dare, and I want to come to the Lord's Supper and drink of the cup of salvation.

This is what it means to pray in the name of Jesus and to end the prayer with the hopeful phrase "for Jesus' sake." Since Jesus has reconciled everything, even our inadequate prayers can be brought forward as an offering and gift to God. We can talk to Him about things we're not sure are right or wrong. Sin is also a part of our prayers. Sinners aren't as devoted, not as unselfish, not as filled with love for God and man as we ought to be, yet we dare to pray. Christ's reconciliation and His endless mercy encompass them, just as they encompass our entire lives. We can pray as children, perhaps a little foolishly and immaturely, always imperfectly, and still be encompassed by our Father's love and mercy.

It is good to praise You, Lord, and make music to Your name, O Most High; to declare Your steadfast love in the morning and Your faithfulness by night, to the music of the lute and the harp, to the melody of the lyre. For You, O Lord, have made me glad by Your work; at the works of Your hands I sing for joy. How great are Your works, O Lord! Your thoughts are very deep! The stupid man cannot know; the fool cannot understand this: but You, O Lord, are on high forever. Your throne is established from of old; You are from everlasting. O Lord, how long shall the wicked be jubilant? They pour out their arrogant words; all the evildoers boast. They crush Your people, O Lord, and afflict Your heritage. And they say, "The Lord does not see; the God of Jacob does not perceive." But blessed is the man whom You discipline, O Lord, and whom You teach out of Your law, for the Lord will not forsake His people; He will not abandon His heritage; If the Lord had not been my help, my soul would soon have lived in the land of silence. When I thought, "My foot slips," Your steadfast love, O Lord, held me up. But You, O Lord, have become my stronghold, and the rock of my refuge. (from Psalms 92–94).

SATURDAY AFTER
THE FOURTH
SUNDAY AFTER
EASTER

Psalm 118:1–18

All nations surrounded me; in the name of the LORD I cut them off! Psalm 118:10

When we pray a psalm like this one together with Jesus, we get an answer to a question that disturbs many people. There are, in many places in the Book of Psalms, prayers that ask God to punish and defeat Israel's enemies. These prayers were meant literally. Israel was threatened with ruin and extinction. They went to war with their enemies. They knew their enemies intended to "cut them off from being a nation; that the name of Israel may be no more in remembrance" (Psalm 83:4 KJV). And then faith in God would also be extinguished. Someone who desperately fights, not only for his own life but to save a nation that by itself recognizes the one true God, can pray to God for victory without abusing God's name for his own selfish purposes—as so often happens in war and human conflicts.

But now we pray these same psalms together with Jesus. He meant something totally different with these words. He isn't thinking about destroying His human enemies. On the contrary, He wanted to save them. That's why He died for them. But even He had enemies to fight in a battle for life or death—a battle for our souls, a battle for eternal life or eternal death for us all. Even Jesus could say that His enemies surrounded Him and did everything to render Him helpless. These enemies were all the powers of evil. Even He could say: In the name of the Lord, I cut them off. And that's how we think and feel when we pray the same prayer. Those who once were Israel's political enemies: Babylon, Assyria, Egypt, the Philistines, and the worshipers of Baal, were symbols in the New Testament of all the evil spiritual powers that fight against Christ and His Church. We pray for victory over them. It's our heartfelt desire that they will suffer defeat in our own lives and hearts as well.

When we speak about praying together with Jesus, we don't only mean that we pray as His disciples, gathered around our Master. There is something more profound in being able to pray with Jesus. We are members of His body. We are, as Paul says, one with Him. The blood from His heart flows through us. His love permeates and lives in everyone who belongs to Him. He is with us—yes, in us. Both He Himself and His apostles say this. We can share in His life. We may pray with Him in a way that gives us the opportunity to take part in His prayers. He prays with us and for us. We, along with our prayers, are included in His mercifulness, His new life, and in Himself.

My Lord Jesus, I want to thank You for this, but I'm almost hesitant to do it because the words are so insufficient and worn out. This is more than I can thank You for. You are here with us so we may be with You, despite the fact that we will never deserve it. We can participate in Your life and partake in Your prayers and go to God together with You, upheld by Your prayer. We thank You for Your presence among us, for this unspeakable, mysterious blessing that You are here with us and that we may be in You.

FIFTH SUNDAY
AFTER EASTER
John 16:23–33

"In that day you will ask in My name." John 16:26

What does it mean to ask in His name?

This expression occurs often in the Bible. We are supposed to pray in the name of Jesus, and Paul adds that whatever we do, we should do it in the name of Jesus. Our entire life should be a life in Jesus.

These are key words in Christianity. But until now we have hardly mentioned them. This has been intentional. It isn't really possible to understand what it means to be "in Jesus" before understanding what Jesus has done for us and what it means to belong to Him. The best explanation of the expression *in Jesus' name* is that it means "with faith in Jesus." But then we need to know what faith in Jesus implies. We have already seen that it isn't just a matter of opinions and knowledge; it's a matter of new life, a lifelong fellowship with Jesus. You can attempt to comprehend God or Christ using your powers of reason, but then you put yourself outside of them, making them into a sort of object to be observed for the sake of discussion. God becomes a topic of conversation.

No one can reach God in this way. He can't be observed from the outside. God has come to us in Christ. He has conquered the thing that made fellowship with Him impossible: our sin. Now He can come into our hearts and live with us. He doesn't just completely surround us, He penetrates our entire being. He has a mysterious presence here, a merciful love that radiates from us and flows through us so we become completely loved. This is what it means to believe. Luther says that faith is a cloud where Christ lives. And this cloud descends upon us, surrounds us, and fills our hearts.

Then we also learn to pray in a new way, in childlike confidence, with an inner desire for God's will to be realized, satisfied with what God wants to give, and fully confident that He listens to us and hears our prayers. This is what it means to pray in Jesus' name.

My Lord, heavenly Father, praise be to You for the blessed, childlike privileges You have given me. Praise be to Your name for allowing me to come to You as Your child. I don't deserve to lift up my eyes to You and even less to speak to You as a child does to his father. I thank You for Your great mercy because You wanted to come into our world and live among us and live in us, we who had death in our hearts. Now You are here, Lord, and we may be with You. Destroy everything in us that can't stand Your presence, everything that keeps it from filling us, so others can also understand what it means to meet You and live with Your love. We ask this in Jesus' name because You are our Lord Jesus Christ's Father, because You Yourself have come to us in our Lord Jesus Christ.

MONDAY AFTER THE FIFTH SUNDAY AFTER EASTER

Luke 11:1–13

"Lord, teach us to pray." Luke 11:1

Praying is an art—one that has to be taught. It can take time. You can't just give up after making a few unsuccessful attempts. You don't give up studying a language just because it's hard in the beginning. Learning to pray can be like learning a new language—the heart's language that speaks with God.

Jesus' own apostles knew they weren't good at praying. They had seen Jesus pray. Luke tells us that He stopped at a certain place to pray. He prayed often and long, sometimes the whole night through. When He finished, one of the apostles came to Him with a request: "Lord, teach us to pray."

What did Jesus teach them?

First He taught the Lord's Prayer, a rather short prayer. We can pray using other people's words. We don't have to use our own. Sometimes we're just too exhausted. Sometimes we lack the words. Then we can gladly pray using someone else's words. We've already seen that Jesus prayed using the psalms and we can pray these with Him as well. But we can also learn from Jesus to speak to God as our Father, with our own words, preferably simple and common words.

The other advice Jesus gave was that we should be persistent and not give up. We should compare ourselves with the man who, in the middle of the night needed to borrow some bread, and knocked on his neighbor's door. God isn't like the neighbor. He doesn't mind being inconvenienced, but it's a part of His fatherly way of rearing and teaching His children that He allows us to wait. Maybe He does it just so we learn to pray by being forced to think about what we pray for and being compelled to repeat what we have said in an effort to examine the contents. We have to be sure that what we pray for really comes from the heart. Then, we have God's promise that He opens the door for us and that He hears us. We might not get just what we prayed for, but it will always be a good gift and just what we need most. Jesus doesn't say that God gives us what we hoped for, but that He gives the Holy Spirit to those who pray to Him. He gives us the Holy Spirit when we pray persistently and faithfully and come to God with all our needs. The Spirit influences us and transforms us. Sometimes we stop praying about something because we understand that it wasn't God's will. Sometimes we discover that we've already received something that is better. Sometimes, as we pray, we see a completely different way of looking at what worried us. Or maybe God helps us in some other way—but He always helps us.

Dear Lord, teach us to pray. Give us such a longing for You that our hearts always pray, even when we don't pray with words. Let us live with prayer in such a way that we always know Your eyes are on us and that we can always lift our eyes to You in joy because You are here. But give us also the words to speak to You about everything, and the desire to do it in all of life's situations. You know how lazy we are. You know how easily our eyes and hearts want to look somewhere else. If we do this, show us that You are also there, that You understand everything, that You are a part of the things we thought were far from Your presence. Let us see that with joy. Teach us to realize how natural, secure, and wonderful it is that You are with us and that we live and exist in You and that we can talk to You about everything, even when we can't fold our hands or form our thoughts into words.

"Pray to Your Father who is in secret." Matthew 6:6

In today's Bible reading, we see again how Jesus instructs us in prayer. He says we shouldn't pray in an effort to be seen. Of course, this does not mean that we can't pray when others see us—in church, for instance. Jesus prayed often in the synagogue and in the temple or even out among the people. However, it means that we shouldn't pray in an effort to receive praise from others. This danger isn't so prevalent today. Lots of people are ashamed to show that they pray because it isn't considered proper behavior. Sometimes people don't even want to show that they pray in church. It's at times like these that we should think about another thing Jesus said—that we shouldn't be ashamed of Him in front of others.

But the warning remains: We shouldn't make a show of prayer. Prayer is never a merit. It's a privilege. We can pray whenever and wherever we want to, but we should do it where we can be alone. We have to have time for prayer. We know how important it is to eat at regular intervals. If you eat whenever you feel like it, you become careless with your eating habits and begin to suffer from bad health. In the same way, it's important to have particular times for prayer.

But the essential thing is that we pray to our Father in private. Prayer means entering an invisible world. We live in a reality the rest of the world doesn't see.

This is dumbfounding, but now we can, because of Jesus, speak as children to their Father. We don't have to be eloquent or verbose. The heathen think they will be heard for their many words, Jesus says (Matthew 6:5). We often think we have to choose our words carefully when we speak to God. That's why we sometimes are so bad at praying: We're embarrassed at our childlike and awkward words. But that's exactly how we should pray: in a natural, genuine, sincere way, full of childlike trust. No father or mother brushes off a two-year-old child who is trying to say something but can't express it properly. God is our Father who has mercy on us, His children. He understands us. He knows us. He knows what we need before we even pray to Him.

Jesus also teaches us the Lord's Prayer here, but with words that are, to an extent, different from the ones we read in Luke 11. This can teach us that the words are meant to be a help and guide, not a semantic formula that has to be strictly followed. It's more an example of what we have to pray about—first and foremost about God Himself: that His name should be hallowed (holy) among us, that His kingdom shall come, and His will shall be done.

"*To You*, O LORD, I lift up my soul. O my God, in You I trust; let me not be put to shame; let not my enemies exult over me. Indeed, none who wait for You shall be put to shame; they shall be ashamed who are wantonly treacherous. Make me to know Your ways, O LORD; teach me Your paths. Lead me in Your truth and teach me, for You are the God of my salvation; for You I wait all the day long. Remember Your mercy, O LORD, and Your steadfast love, for they have been from of old. Remember not the sins of my youth or my transgressions; according to Your steadfast love remember me, for the sake of Your goodness, O LORD" (Psalm 25:1–7)!

WEDNESDAY AFTER THE FIFTH SUNDAY AFTER EASTER

Colossians 3:1–11

Christ who is your life. Colossians 3:4

Tomorrow is Ascension Day, the end of the part of the Savior's life that began in Bethlehem. We can now look back and sum things up. This is what Paul has done in the text we just read.

Christ has died and risen. We also have died and have been resurrected with Christ. That's the essence of Baptism and faith. We are united with Christ. He took our sin upon Himself, and we have taken part in His death. Now we are a part of the new life after resurrection. This life is "hidden with Christ in God" (Colossians 3:3). It's a part of Christ's own life, and Christ is now hidden from the world. But He is still among us and lives in us. With God, in God's kingdom, this new life already exists in all its glory, as overwhelmingly tangible, alive, and real as it is. Someday—when the world is born again—it will appear, and then we will "appear with Him in glory" (Colossians 3:4).

We are part of a new kingdom and a new life, and this new life is decisive in how we live our lives on earth. "[Put to death] therefore your members which are upon the earth" (Colossians 3:5 KJV). This doesn't mean the members of your body. God has created those, and they belong to Him. But there is something in them that Paul calls "the law of sin that dwells in my members" (Romans 7:23). This belongs to the world. It's a consequence of the fall from grace. Paul accounts for these members, and we see immediately that it is not about our body, but about our evil and selfish will. We might have thought that all these selfish instincts were completely natural. We had our life in them, as Paul says. This is how the world lives: It's about putting ourselves first. You have to stand your ground. You only live once.

But now we are told that Christ is our life. In Christ's kingdom, the rule that applies is that He is all and in all. Now I no longer live, but Christ lives in me. This doesn't mean my old Adam has left me. On the contrary: I must destroy the members that belong to the world. This is something I have to do every day. I have stripped myself of my old Adam. I used to wear those clothes casually. But now I am clothed in a new garment, one that is modeled after Christ's standard. I wear this garment every day. The old garment is still there. I don't ever have to put it on. It's always there and is easy to put on. But if we're resurrected with Christ, we also want to live with Him. We may do it and can do it.

Lord, I wouldn't dare to believe it if You hadn't said it. I wouldn't dare try it if You hadn't called me to it. But now it's Your will and Your work. And You have let me see that nothing is impossible for You. You won the victory when everything seemed to be lost. You built Your Church and established Your dominion where people would never have been able to do it. And You continue Your work despite all our mistakes and infirmities. And now You have intervened in my life also, and did what never would have happened if it was up to me. I thank You, Lord, for this great and incomprehensible wonder, that You want to be my life and that I may live through You and with You. Help me to always live for You.

ASCENSION DAY
Acts 1:1–11

Then He led them out as far as Bethany, and lifting up His
hands He blessed them. While He blessed them, He parted
from them and was carried up into heaven. Luke 24:50–51

For forty days Jesus appeared to others and "He had given
commands through the Holy Spirit to the apostles whom He
had chosen" (Acts 1:2). Several times He disappeared from
their sight, but this time at Bethany He disappeared in such
a way that they knew they had seen Him for the last time.
He was "taken up." A cloud came and took Him out of their
sight.

This doesn't necessarily mean that God's kingdom is
somewhere above us in space, but that when God created the
heavens above us, He gave us a reminder of His kingdom's
immenseness and majesty, of the light and clarity there. It's
natural for us to look up when we lift our hearts to God. God
is "up there;" His throne is above us. All these are pictures,
but pictures that tell the truth, pictures that God has drawn in
His creation with His own hand. For this reason Christ also
chose, when He disappeared for the last time, to do it in such
a way that the disciples would understand He had returned to
His Father in heaven. It's not naive for us Christians to celebrate Christ's ascension. It is naive, however, to believe that
God's kingdom is "up there somewhere" and if we traveled
far enough into space, we should be able to get a glimpse of
God.

The Lord's ascension is a milestone in world history.
Christ sits at the Father's side and resumes full divine qualities. He is now the omnipresent Savior, who can intervene
anywhere with His saving presence. He leads His Church
on earth and has given His witnesses the power to witness
"in Jerusalem and in all Judea and Samaria, and to the end of

the earth" (Acts 1:8). It's because of what happened on that day on the Mount of Olives outside of Bethany that we now know our Savior Jesus Christ, can pray to Him, and belong to Him.

So I pledge allegiance to You, Lord, my heavenly King. You are enthroned above us all. You rule in Your kingdom. You are praised by all the heavenly hosts—and at the same time You also descended to us and walked among us to seek out those who are lost. I thank You for Your power and glory that is only a portion of Your immense love that You share with lavish kindness so we can rejoice and share with You the joy of living in Your Father's presence.

FRIDAY AFTER THE ASCENSION
Acts 1:12–26

All these with one accord were devoting themselves to prayer. Acts 1:14

After the ascension, the apostles returned to Jerusalem. They were quiet. They prayed. There was something they were waiting for. Jesus had just told them: "You will be baptized with the Holy Spirit not many days from now" (Acts 1:5). In this way they would be "clothed with power from on high" (Luke 24:49). Then their immense task would begin.

So, they were quiet during prayer, waiting for the Holy Spirit. It's these days we experience now, beginning today and ending at Pentecost. We, too, should live them in prayer and in anticipation of the Spirit.

The apostles gathered as usual in a hall on the top floor, probably the same place where the Lord's Supper was instituted. Other disciples were there too. Mary was there, as were other loyal women who had followed Jesus from Galilee. Jesus' brothers were there, the ones who came to Capernaum to take care of their brother because they were afraid He had lost His mind. Now they believed in Him. We know that Jesus had revealed Himself to James. He seems to have been the next oldest in the big family of brothers and sisters. We know also that this same James was later recognized as one of the founding fathers of the Early Church.

Now they prepared themselves for what was about to happen, first through prayer and then by choosing an apostle to replace Judas. There had to be twelve apostles. There was a message in that number. Israel had twelve tribes, and the apostles were the new Israel, God's people, who gathered around the Messiah.

They voted. It wasn't the apostles who made the choice, it was the entire Church. They knew what Jesus wanted: The new apostle had to be someone who had seen what He did, experienced His resurrection, and was a man. There was no question about that. It was also obvious that in the end it wasn't the people who made the choice, but Christ Himself. Christ's congregation prayed to their Lord and put the matter in His hands. He was the one who decided it.

Lord Jesus, You guide those who believe in You with their hearts and who are the leaders in Your Church. When we allow ourselves to be led, we pray to You for the kind of faith and confidence

*that allows us to be clay in Your hands so You
can form us just the way You want to. Send Your
Spirit to us. May He descend upon Your Church
today. Prepare our hearts, make us obedient and
insignificant, humble and open, and filled with the
desire that Your will be done and that Your love
form our lives also. Lord, clothe us with power
from on high, for Your name's sake.*

SATURDAY AFTER THE ASCENSION
Romans 8:1–11

To set the mind on the Spirit is life and peace. Romans 8:6

When we read these eleven verses from Romans, it's immediately apparent that they explain the very essence of Christianity: We "are in Christ Jesus" (Romans 8:1) and He is in us. This essence also describes life in the Spirit and through the Spirit, who is mentioned no less than nine times in these verses.

First we hear that salvation consists of the fact that we are in Christ Jesus. We used to live under the law of sin and death. Paul described this law in the preceding chapter. It lives in our members. It controls our old Adam. It neither can nor wants to be the humble servant of God's Law. It is sinful nature that makes it impossible to come to God through the Law, in other words, an intention to change your ways and become a new person. We must understand that the Law is weakened by the flesh. It can never change our old Adam. We are and remain sinners.

But what the Law could not achieve, God accomplished by sending Christ to us. He took our sins and the judgment they incurred upon Himself. God "condemned sin in the flesh" (Romans 8:3), but at the same time Christ set us "free . . . from the law of sin and death" (Romans 8:2), free from condemnation. Instead of the law of sin and death, there is now "the law of the Spirit of life" (Romans 8:2). We now live under this law.

Here Paul gives us a condensed version of what this law entails. We walk with the Spirit. We steer our senses to what belongs to the Spirit. We possess a sense of the Spirit. The Spirit lives in us. We have to die because the old Adam still lives in our body and can't inherit the kingdom of God. But at the same time, the Spirit lives in our bodies with His new life. Whoever has this life will be resurrected in the same way as Christ was resurrected. God will make our mortal bodies live through His Spirit that lives in us.

We will take a closer look into what this means during the week that remains until Pentecost, the season of the Spirit.

Send us Your Spirit, Lord Jesus. Let Him complete His work among us. No one can truly comprehend this. It's something new, something that doesn't exist on this earth, and something You send, Your promised gift from heaven. Give us this gift. Only the reality of it can teach us what Your Spirit is. So we pray for it in confidence, trusting in Your promise and Your power. Hear us for Your name's sake.

SIXTH SUNDAY AFTER EASTER

Romans 8:12–17

The Spirit Himself bears witness with our spirit that we are children of God. Romans 8:16

The Holy Spirit is the Spirit of childhood. This name indicates better than anything else the reason the Spirit has been sent into the world and what He accomplishes. The Spirit is also called the Helper, Comforter, and Consoler. The comfort and help He can give consists of teaching us that we can be God's children together with Christ and through Christ. Therefore, He witnesses about Christ and not about Himself. He paints Christ's picture for us. He helps us understand that Jesus died for us. He creates faith in our hearts, allowing us to be born again. This is something that might not be noticeable right away. We might just feel an immense helplessness instead. But in the midst of this helplessness grows a firm confidence in Christ, a confidence like that of the thief on the cross. He knew he didn't deserve it, but he couldn't help but hope and believe that Christ would have mercy on him.

If the Spirit has completed the work, then sooner or later He gives us childlike wisdom. He testifies through our spirit that we are God's children. This fills us with a great comfort, a boundless thankfulness, a lovely certainty that nothing can separate us from God's love because Christ is with us and has mercy on us. We can say Abba! Father! with childlike confidence.

There are people who think it's obvious that we are all God's children. They have never thought about how much separates us from God. But when the Spirit convinces us of our sin, it's possible that our own conscience, which is the Law's voice in our own heart, can pronounce such an irrevocable judgment on us for all our egoism and impurity that we no longer dare to believe we can be God's children. Only then can the Holy Spirit show us the truth, the great truth that Christ has died for sinners like us and that it's possible even for us to be God's beloved children. He alone, the Spirit of childhood, can convince us of this.

O You, God's Holy Spirit, You who are our helper on the way to God, our Teacher, Sentinel, and Comforter, speak to us in a way that we understand it is You speaking. Make the message from God so alive that we receive it both with fear and joy. Shed Your light in all the dark corners of our lives. Let it reveal everything that is in opposition to You. Show us our Lord Christ as He is. Give us Your nature. Teach us to love Your will. Lead us in Your truth. And when You see that we are God's children, testify to our spirit so we, too, can see it. Come to us, Holy Spirit, for Jesus' sake.

MONDAY AFTER THE SIXTH SUNDAY AFTER EASTER
Romans 8:18–27

We have the firstfruits of the Spirit. Romans 8:23

We live in a fallen world. The power that fights against God has broken into God's creation and gotten a foothold there. Therefore, creation has been corrupted. It's scarred with suffering, cruelty, ruin, and disintegration.

But in the midst of this world marked by death is the beginning of a new world where nothing more will be destroyed or broken; where nothing will perish. Christ is the firstfruits, the beginning of this new world. He gives the life and immortality of this new world to those who belong to Him through faith, and we receive the Holy Spirit as a gift from the firstfruits.

By *firstfruits* and *the gift of the firstfruits*, the Jews meant the first of the year's harvest, the firstfruits or grain that were usually brought as an offering to God. This offering was the very first harvest of the crop, a small, insignificant beginning, but it was proof that the new harvest was on the way. It was the symbol, the pledge, the proof of something that would come later.

We have received the Holy Spirit in this way. God's Spirit, who opened our eyes to see Christ, who led us into a relationship with Him, caused us to be born again and gave us a part in the life of the Resurrected One. He is the beginning of our new lives and someday He will completely transform us on the day of the resurrection. This life, salvation's new life, is still a secret. In hope we are saved, Paul says. We live in faith and not in a point of view. The Spirit is really there, but it goes wherever it wants to. No one can capture it, grasp it, or prove that it's there. It can rule over us, but we can never rule over it. It's not something we own or have at our disposal. But we can open ourselves to it and let it work in us. We can experience the Spirit's work and learn from it, but only to a certain degree. We want so badly to feel filled with the Spirit. We want the Spirit to help us in all our prayers so we can pray eloquently, inspiringly, and with a prophetic glow and avoid feeling the inferiority from which we so often suffer. But Paul says that the Spirit comes to help our weakness in a completely different manner. It's very possible that we can't find the words and don't know what we ought to pray about, "but the Spirit Himself intercedes for us with groanings too deep for words" (Romans 8:26).

There is great comfort in this. This new life is something that can exist inside us even when our intellect and understanding can't fathom it. Christ's life in us is not dependent on our logic, comprehension, or rational thinking. It's like the trust a child has for his mother. It's there without having to be formulated into words. It is reality, not a point of view or an idea.

Dear Holy Spirit, You want to encourage me even when I don't understand that I should pray for my own good. You want to take care of me, guide me, and give me God's fatherly help far more than I could ever imagine or wish for. So come to me and stay with me. Take care of my entire life, and do things to me that I don't understand myself. I pray for Your kind presence and give myself over to Your wise and merciful guidance, You who are God's pure Spirit, my helper and comforter.

TUESDAY AFTER THE SIXTH SUNDAY AFTER EASTER
Galatians 3:1–14

Having begun by the Spirit, are you now being perfected by the flesh? Galatians 3:3

Galatians has a lot to teach us about the Holy Spirit. Here we read that Paul is worried. In the beginning of the letter, he tells us what disturbs him is that the Galatians have fallen away and turned to a new gospel. He told them how he himself was guided to the correct Gospel, the only one there is. Now he's trying to convince the Galatians that they are on the wrong path.

What happened here? Everything began so well. The Galatians received the Gospel and believed. They received the Holy Spirit. It's worth noting that Paul considers this proof of a living Christianity. We read the same thing in his letter to the Romans: He who doesn't have Christ's Spirit, doesn't belong to Him (8:9).

But now it appears that those who began in the Spirit would end up in the flesh. This doesn't mean they reverted to their terrible habits. On the contrary: They were extremely particular about fulfilling God's Law. Traveling preachers had come to them and said they had to be circumcised to really obey the Law. This made an impression on them. They wanted, as Paul expresses it, to be "justified by observing the law" (Galatians 2:16).

This is the exact opposite of walking in the Spirit. Religion exists without the Spirit. That religion seems to be natural and correct to everyone. Before God opens our eyes with His Spirit, we have our conscience. The Law is written in our hearts. We conclude that we are God's children and that He loves us if we obey His Commandments. We believe that we are justified by works.

But this is completely wrong. "For all who rely on works of the law are under a curse" (Galatians 3:10). We can never put the Law behind us. We are all guilty according to the righteous Law of God. If God's Law is to be applied, then it will be applied without compromise—and that's not good for us.

Therefore, God has opened another door, through faith in Jesus Christ, our Atoner, who died for us. This doesn't mean that we can and may live however we want. To believe means that Christ has come to us with His Spirit. This Spirit is a powerful force who struggles constantly with the evil inside us, perpetually driving us to love and serve Christ. This is the right way—and it's the only possible way—to live as God's children.

I pray to You, God's righteous Spirit, that You come to me, dwell with me, remain with me, and preserve me with my Savior so I will never abandon Him by being indifferent and disobedient or by trusting in something else, not even my own obedience to Him or my love for His Commandments. Help me to always see what the only basis for my justification for being God's child is. Let nothing get in the way of the Savior and encroach upon my faith in Him alone. Lord, I want to listen in faith, and open my heart. Come in and complete Your work.

WEDNESDAY AFTER THE SIXTH SUNDAY AFTER EASTER
Galatians 3:15–29

For you are all one in Christ Jesus. Galatians 3:28

What good did the Law do anyway? Why was it given if it can't lead us to God? The common understanding—both among Jews and among modern people—is that we're at peace with God when we keep His Commandments.

That's right, Paul answers—if there really was a law that could impart life. He means a law that could unite us with God so His life would flow in us. But now it's just the opposite: The law is death. It ruthlessly exposes us as lawbreakers, helplessly separated from God. The law finds something wrong with everything we try to do because it lacks the most important thing: the love of God and the love of our neighbor. "The whole world is a prisoner of sin" (Galatians 3:22). No distinction is made. None of us is justified—none of us is righteous enough—when judged by the standards of the Law (which is the correct standard!). We can never honestly say: Lord I have done all that You commanded.

Therefore the Law forces us to Christ. We come to Him not in righteousness, but as exposed sinners, unsuccessful disciples, poor in the Spirit. And He meets us with the incomprehensible message that because of Christ we are blessed and that the heavenly kingdom belongs to us and we may be God's children.

It happens to everyone who believes, without exception. There are big differences among us, but all of us are one in Christ, united as members in His body. Paul points out some of the differences that are most noticeable: nationality, social class, and gender. These differences aren't eliminated, but all these different members now make up one body. They have all become one in Christ, and consequently these differences no longer divide us. All the members have the same merit. Those who received a pound are worth just as much as those who received ten. Each and every one of them serves with his gifts, in his place, and according to his Lord's will and command. However, all are members in service to one another. Here, the "unity of the Spirit through the bond of peace" (Ephesians 4:3) prevails. As Paul put it, "There is one body and one Spirit—just as you were called to the one hope that belongs to your call—one Lord, one faith, one baptism, one God and Father of all" (Ephesians 4:4–6).

My Lord and Savior, You who unite us all in You through faith, help me to be one with all those who believe in You with all my heart. When You unite us in Your Communion and give us a portion of You, You also make us one with one another. Help us to see every difference in Your light so they no longer separate us. Help me to rejoice in the gifts that others have received but I haven't. They are gifts from You. Help me to embrace with a warm heart and interest even the tasks that aren't mine because even these tasks come from You. Send Your pure Spirit also, who bears witness to You, to unite us all in the true faith, and in true love.

THURSDAY AFTER THE SIXTH SUNDAY AFTER EASTER
Galatians 4:1–11

So that we might receive adoption as sons. Galatians 4:5

Christ paid our ransom, just like someone who buys freedom for a slave. We were slaves to the powers of the world. Paul includes the powers and all the compulsions that control us when we are without God. We live under the pressures of convention and prestige, control and adversity, of the harsh economic reality and its unpredictable risks, bad times, unexpected sickness, and impending death that looms over us.

But there is an even more oppressive bondage, Paul teaches. It's bondage under the Law. It imprisons those who want to find God but go down the wrong path. The more seriously they take God's Law, the more hopeless it becomes for them. Our obligations never end. We always come up short.

But now Christ has bought our freedom from this bondage. We have received the right to be children of God. He has sent us His Spirit, who teaches us to cry Abba! Father! We have become known by God. The Bible uses this expression to distinguish something that our everyday language doesn't have a word for: the heart's invisible relationship with God. The great mystery is that Christ is with us and we are surrounded by His love, filled by His resurrected life, so we can rest in God and possess a part of the world, where God is everything for everyone, that will come.

What has upset Paul so deeply that we can almost feel him tremble when he writes to the Galatians? They've reverted to the bondage under the Law. They want to take the Law's path to God instead of trusting in Christ Jesus. The Galatians seem to have made the common mistake that those who are the most hard-nosed, who make salvation most difficult, who have the most conditions and demand the greatest performance must be God's true spokesmen. But they don't realize that these preachers of the Law have a completely different agenda than God has. They don't see their concealed egoism: They want to keep their followers away from other Christians so they can have their own clique to lead and dominate. In contrast, Paul reveals the truth: Christ has bought our freedom so we would be heirs. Christ alone is the foundation. And in Christ we are all one.

Come Holy Spirit, and instruct me in the true freedom that only You can teach. Liberate me from all false anxiety for the powers of this world, from the human point of view, and from the fear of being different from the world that doesn't know You. Liberate me also from all the false anxiety of people's demands and regulations in Your Church. Liberate my anxiety for all the threats in the Law when it says I cannot be God's child and may not come to Him before I'm righteous. Teach me to always come to my Savior and always speak like a child to my Father. Dear Lord, teach me to love You more than anything, to love You so Your Commandments are easy to follow. Help me so Your good will won't be something I have to do, but something I want to do because I am God's child.

FRIDAY AFTER
THE SIXTH SUNDAY
AFTER EASTER
Galatians 5:13–26

If we live by the Spirit, let us also walk by the Spirit.
Galatians 5:25

Here is another example of how no one can become a Christian without the Holy Spirit. Christ has made us free. We are no longer under the Law. Those who are under the Law and believe in it immediately ask: What now? Can we live however we want to? We only have to believe?

The answer, as we've already heard, is that this is impossible if you really believe in Christ because then you have received the Spirit, and the Spirit is a reality, a power, something that moves and works within us.

If you have freedom without having the Spirit, that's no good. Freedom can be and is abused. The flesh gets an opportunity, as Paul says here. The flesh, the old Adam, is always with us. Paul enumerates the acts of the flesh. We see that *the flesh* does not mean the body. Many of these acts are mainly mental or psychological in nature: strife, envy, anger, reluctance, jealousy, dissension, and rivalry. If we believe in Christ, there will always be a struggle between the Spirit and our old Adam. The old Adam reveals himself through his desires and suggestions, but it doesn't take command. It is crucified, Paul says. It doesn't mean that it's just shackled and can still protest and be in opposition yet unable to carry out its wishes. The word *crucified* means more. It reminds us of Christ's crucifixion. Our old Adam with all his works brought Christ to the cross, where its entire nature received judgment. I accept this judgment when I believe. I know what my old Adam stands for.

The old Adam is still able to get loose in an unguarded moment. It might surprise us. When it first happens, we take notice of what we have done. Even a true Christian needs to be constantly forgiven. But as long as we believe, it's the Spirit who's in control. The old Adam will be fettered and crucified over and over again. He can't get his way. The Spirit works in us, then the fruit of the Spirit comes too. The sap flows through the vine's branches and it bears fruit.

This is walking with the Spirit. Then, Paul says, we are no longer under the Law despite the sin that is still in us and despite the many mistakes we still make unknowingly, in haste, through lack of vigilance, and in other ways. We still live in perpetual forgiveness. We are God's children. Forever. This is the glorious freedom Christ has liberated us for.

Dear Holy Spirit, I thank You for fighting the good fight inside me against all that is in opposition to the Lord God. Help me to always see what this fight is about so I will always stand by Your side with all of my will and all of my heart. Help me crucify my flesh, even when it hurts. Let me know the joy and the power and the freedom that is in the heart when You let Your wind blow there. And if I only feel weakness, then fill this weakness with Your presence so I always know to whom I belong and can always comfort myself knowing that You pray for me and mean well, even when I myself don't know how I should pray. Come, dear Holy Spirit, for the sake of Jesus.

SATURDAY AFTER THE SIXTH SUNDAY AFTER EASTER, THE EVE OF PENTECOST
Galatians 6:1–18

The one who sows to the Spirit will from the Spirit reap eternal life. Galatians 6:8

"Whatever one sows, that will he also reap," Paul says in Galatians 6:7. There are two different seeds to sow, two kinds of fields to plow. They correspond to two basic outlooks on life.

One way is to sow in the fields of flesh. This can be done in an openly godless way by concentrating in this short life on getting as much as you can of sex, money, or enjoyment of food and drink. It can also be done by satisfying the desire to be someone or to be dominant and in control. But there is also a way of sowing in the flesh's field that appears respectable and even religious and Christian. This letter of Paul's points out this mistake. People want to be respected, both in their own eyes and in the eyes of others, for the things they do as Christians. The Law is a perfect tool for this type of action. They try to be more diligent than others, sacrifice more than others, and place themselves in an elite category. But that means dismissing Christ. "You are severed from Christ, you who would be justified by the law; you have fallen away from grace" (Galatians 5:4).

The other way is to sow in the Spirit's field. This means living in the Spirit and being driven by the Spirit. Paul gives us a long list of examples in this chapter of everything this entails. If someone catches someone else committing a sin, they don't think they are better than that person. They don't become indignant. They don't try to punish. They try to restore that person in a spirit of gentleness. They well know that they, too, can be tempted. The same thing could have happened to them if they hadn't been led to Christ without having deserved it. Therefore, we bear each other's burdens. We try to lighten their load and help, firm in the knowledge that people need mercy more than reproof. We know that everyone has their own burdens to bear. The burden I have, I can give to the Lord. He bears it and takes away my guilt. Whatever is left, I will bear patiently for His sake. In the Spirit, we can do good works without becoming weary. That's what is so hard to do: not give up, not lose courage and patience when it seems so unrewarding and useless to do what is good for everyone.

Dear Holy Spirit, on this eve of Pentecost, I pray to
You that You come to us. Come to our church
body and all our congregations. Come to all those
who will preach Your message tomorrow. Come to
all of us who gather to listen, and let us know You
are there. Come to me. Now I begin to understand
how much I need You. Let my entire life be a life
that You guide and control and fulfill. Come, Holy
Spirit, with all Your gifts, and give them to us. For
the sake of Jesus.

PENTECOST SUNDAY
John 14:23–31

"But the Helper, the Holy Spirit, whom the Father will send
in My name, He will teach you all things and bring to your
remembrance all that I have said to you." John 14:26

When Christians celebrate holidays, they are not just
memorial celebrations. Of course, we hear a message about
something that happened in the past, but at the same time we
are taking part in something that is happening in the here and
now. What once happened has a purpose throughout time.
It applies to all people. It's something that happens again and
again in our hearts and affects our lives.

That's the way it is at Pentecost today. It's the festival
of the Spirit. It doesn't just mean that we will hear how the
Spirit filled the apostles on the first Pentecost. We aren't just
celebrating the memory of that great day when the Church

was filled with power from heaven and received courage to stand before the world and bear witness to the resurrection. Pentecost is still a festive occasion when we fervently pray for the Holy Spirit and wait in faith for God to send Him out to His Church again.

Maybe you feel this isn't necessary. If it's true, as we have said again and again, that the Holy Spirit has been given to us in Baptism and through faith in Jesus Christ, and that He now lives in us, then we shouldn't have to pray for the Spirit to be poured out over us.

The Spirit is with us as a living, giving Lord, a river of life from God Himself that perpetually flows to us and fills us up again. That is why we constantly pray for the Spirit's renewal, for the Spirit's visitation, so He will come to us as our Helper, Consoler, Comforter, and Redeemer.

Dear heavenly Father, You have promised us the Spirit who renews us. You send Him out. You have mercy on Your people, and let Your Spirit fill them with power and joy. So let Him come to us also. Let Him purify us, and recreate us, filled with a healthy, living, newborn faith in You.

Dear Lord Jesus, we pray to You for the Helper that You promised, the Holy Spirit who can teach us all we need to learn and remind us of everything You have said, everything we forget so easily. Let Him paint Your picture for us and make Your voice vibrant and warm.

You, Dear Holy Spirit, You alone can make us born again and allow eternal life to bloom in this dead world. Give us a spring filled with the Spirit where everything is filled with life and grows and bears fruit—the fruit that only You can give.

Lord, You renew the earth's countenance every
year. You also can renew Your Church. Let it now
happen for the sake of Your holy name.

THE DAY AFTER PENTECOST
John 3:16–21

"That whoever believes in Him should not perish but have
eternal life." John 3:16

The Gospel reading for the day after Pentecost begins
with a verse that has been called "the little Bible." Many
can recite this verse, sometimes without even knowing what
it means. Certainly, they comprehend that God loves the
world, but they let it go at that. For them, the Gospel is the
common truth that God is good and there's nothing to worry
about; they will get to heaven in one way or another.

Now that we have followed Jesus from His birth to His
ascension, we understand how faulty this thinking is. The
deep and serious problem is how to unite the fallen world
and the evil in it with holy God. The fact that God loves us
doesn't matter. There's something in our nature that creates
an insurmountable wall of separation. It could be broken
down only by God giving His only Son, sacrificing Him, and
letting Him die for our sins. That is the only possible way
for us to be restored to God. It happens when we're united
through faith with the only begotten Son, who died for us.
Therefore, whoever believes in Christ will not perish, but
have eternal life.

Without Christ, we would be lost. Not believing means belonging to a world that must perish. It's not a matter of judgment that an angry God will pronounce on some of us in the future. It's judgment that is already impending on the world. The reason for this judgment is the fact that evil in its entirety pursues a course away from God. The world has said no to God, and persists in its no. John says it presented itself when the Light, Jesus, came into the world. People loved darkness more than Light (John 3:19). They don't want their deeds to be exposed. They prefer to live without God, apart from God. So, there is something inside us that cannot be united with God. Unbelief means allowing evil to control and decide. Faith means receiving the Light when it comes.

This Light has shined forth in the world since the first Pentecost. We live in the time of the Spirit and the Church. The Light has come to us too. Here, there is a possibility for salvation, and the Spirit is sent to help us to take advantage of this opportunity.

Come Holy Spirit, You who illuminate our hearts, and allow us to see the glory of Christ. Come to Your Church and help it witness with power and joy about God's love, that drove Him to give His only Son so we would be saved. Let the Gospel be preached with power and authority, as joyous as it is, so everyone's eyes will be opened and everyone's hearts will be filled with a longing for Your salvation. Let Your light shine in the darkness so we are drawn to the glory that shines forth from Christ's face. Holy Spirit, save us.

TUESDAY AFTER PENTECOST

Acts 2:1–21

Everyone who calls upon the name of the Lord shall be saved. Acts 2:21

Pentecost is commonly called the birth of the Church. This isn't quite correct. Christ had already founded His Church. He had chosen its leaders, the apostles, but there was one last decisive event that remained before the Church could begin to function. This decisive event happened on Pentecost.

Jesus told the apostles to stay in Jerusalem until they were clothed with power from on high. The Baptist had said that the Messiah would baptize with the Holy Spirit and fire. This is what happened. God, who "makes winds His messengers, flames of fire His servants," as it says in Psalm 104:4 (NIV), sent His Spirit with visible signs, the thunder of a violent storm and tongues of fire, and at the same time with radical invisible spiritual effects. The promise that the Holy Spirit would dwell among us to be our guide and source of strength was fulfilled.

There was another sign, a very peculiar event, that gives us a picture of Christ's Church. When the sound of the wind came, the people gathered. It's assumed that the apostles were in the temple. (The word *house* often means the temple.) In that case, there would be a number of pilgrims around the apostles, but people also may have gathered at the gates outside the temple where the disciples usually met. It was a huge festival, and the city was full of Jews who would have traveled to this place. Luke lists several of the countries they came from: Rome in the west to Persia in the east, from the beaches of the Black Sea in the north to the Sahara in the south. The sign that occurred was that the disciples began to speak in tongues, but it wasn't the same kind of tongues people then would have been accustomed to. The message was immediately understandable to those gathered, and strangely enough, everyone heard what the apostles said in their own native language. It was clear to the disciples what the sign meant. Christ's Church was for all the people of the world. The Spirit would bring the message to the whole world. Christ would be preached in every language on earth.

We pray to You, Holy Spirit, that You let Your wind blow over the world. May it destroy and eliminate everything that has decayed in Your Church and everything that is parched and dead in Christianity. Fill every heart with a faith that can conquer the world and with joy that warms the children of the world and with peace that the world cannot give. Make us all fortunate and happy witnesses who want everyone to see what You revealed for us. Send Your servants out to witness about You everywhere in the world where there are people who still don't know You and what You have to give us. Give us what only You can give: an open heart, joy, and peace in the Holy Spirit.

WEDNESDAY AFTER PENTECOST

Acts 2:22–41

"God has made Him both Lord and Christ, this Jesus whom you crucified." Acts 2:36

We have read the first missionary sermon known to have been given in God's Church on earth. It concerned the most important topic that should be preached: Jesus is God's Son and the Savior of the world.

Peter quoted the prophet Joel's words that "everyone who calls upon the name of the Lord shall be saved" (Acts 2:21). The Lord—that was God's name. But here Peter uses it to refer to Jesus. This was the most important news, a joyous mystery now proclaimed for the world. Jesus is Lord. God has given Him the name that is above all other names. This didn't belittle God in any way. On the contrary: God came to us in this way. He made Himself known to us. Peter repeats this again and again in his sermon. Everything that happened through Jesus, God did. His testimony came from God through miracles God performed. He died according to God's plan and God put an end to the agony of death. God resurrected Him again. He was exalted by God's right hand. He received the Spirit from God, which He gave to us. God made Him both Lord and Messiah. Everything is the work of God. This is how God came into the world. When we see Jesus we can say: Behold, here is our God!

Saying that Jesus is God isn't supposed to confuse things. It's supposed to make things clear and comprehensible for everyone. It's to show us who God really is. The Spirit does this when He glorifies Christ and allows us to understand that Jesus really is God's only begotten Son, the Lord.

I pray to You, dear Holy Spirit, that You would take me by the hand and lead me in the truth—the wonderful truth that only You can make alive. As long as I look at all this from the outside, as a mere observer, it is dead and strange to me, but when You let me see Jesus, then I realize that I see God. Everything becomes so simple and clear. I know that I possess what I can never understand. I exist in a situation that I cannot comprehend with my own powers of reason. I am carried by Christ's love that surpasses all knowledge. I have learned to know the Father, not like someone who's inquisitive, regarding Him from a distance, but like the prodigal son who finally comes home. Dear Holy Spirit, let me see Jesus so I can truly know God and be known by Him.

THURSDAY AFTER PENTECOST
Acts 2:42–3:15

And they devoted themselves to the apostles' teaching and the fellowship, to the breaking of bread and the prayers.
Acts 2:42

Here we have a description of the first congregation and, at the same time, a description of a living Church throughout time. There are characteristics of the Christian congregation that always exist and never change.

The first characteristic is the apostles' teaching. Then, it was oral. Today, we can read it in the New Testament. It is and remains fundamental. Christ gave the apostles the Spirit, which led them to the whole truth. Therefore, their authority was authentic. They spoke on Christ's behalf. Their words apply to the Church throughout time. A church that no longer follows the teachings of the apostles and refuses to follow their teaching is not a true Church of Christ.

The second characteristic is fellowship. Luke describes it: "all who believed were together and had all things in common" (Acts 2:44). All the time, every day, they were together in the temple. Their fellowship and harmony proved that they were one in Christ, both in everyday life and in the Divine Service. They lived together as one big family. Life was hard for many of the Christians in Jerusalem. To be a Christian meant to break the ties with your family. A Christian would lose all social protection, all help in times of sickness or in old age that only the family bond could provide. They would also, as a rule, lose their jobs. They were shut out of society. The few wealthy Christians liquidated everything, sold their estates, and helped others as long as their money lasted. In the final analysis, it was apparent that communal property wasn't the answer. The first congregation was so poor that Christians in other countries started a fund-raising activity, the first example of inter-church help we have. Paul tells us a lot about this in his letters.

The third is the Lord's Supper. While early Christians normally gathered for the Divine Service in the temple, they received the Lord's Supper in their homes. There, they "ate together with glad and sincere hearts, praising God" (Acts 2:46–47 NIV). The Lord's Supper will always be the center of a Christian's life in the living Church. Neglecting it is a warning sign that one's faith is about to be extinguished.

The fourth is prayer. It's called "the prayers," because first and foremost it meant regular, daily and frequent prayers. We hear that "Peter and John were going up to the temple at the time of prayer—at three in the afternoon" (Acts 3:1 NIV). They prayed in this way several times a day. Reading further in Acts, we learn that Peter, when he was in the city of Joppa, went up on the housetop about the sixth hour to pray. Christ's Church prays regularly, daily, and at specific times, not only when someone feels a particular need for it.

The Church and every Christian must examine himself regarding these four points, whenever the question is asked: What is most needed now?

> Lord, Holy Spirit, come to Your Church. You know it, Lord: A spiritless church is a mockery of God, a witness against His truth. But a Spirit-filled Church is a pillar of support for the truth, the source of life, and a refuge for all who are burdened and tired. Come to Your Church and fill it with the Spirit. Let the message You put in the apostles' mouths be heard with the same intensity today. Let everyone's heart burn with the same love You ignited in Your first witnesses so we can grow into a family that bears witness to Your power with our good works. Make our celebration of the Lord's Supper so full of joy and heavenly light that everybody knows that it is Christ who is among us. And let our prayer burn, clear and faithful, day after day, like the fire on the altar in the temple. Come Holy Spirit, from on high.

FRIDAY AFTER PENTECOST

Acts 4:1–22

And there is salvation in no one else. Acts 4:12

When we feel depressed by all the resistance there is to Christianity, it helps to read about the Early Church. From the very beginning, it was in conflict with the states and societies it emerged from. The apostles witnessed about Christ's resurrection, but this was just what the authorities wanted to put an end to. When the apostles did what Christ commanded, they were arrested. The Jewish state had the same view that many government authorities have today: that the Christian faith can be tolerated, but it can't be used as propaganda.

The apostles didn't hesitate about what they had to do. They had to obey God over man. They knew who Jesus was. They knew that He was the only possibility for salvation. It didn't concern only them. It concerned their countrymen, their enemies, and all of humanity. It would have been a crime to remain silent.

We are now at the end of the first half of the Church Year, the festive part of the Church Year, during which we see how God revealed Himself in Jesus Christ and sent us the Spirit. Now we have to take the consequences. For those who understand what God has done here, the consequences are inevitable. There is no salvation in any other name than Jesus. That concerns me. I must take all of this very seriously in my life, and let it form and determine my existence. But it concerns everyone else as well. Therefore, the Light should shine forth, visible for everyone. I can't keep it for myself. If I do that, I deny the fundamental truth that salvation is found in Jesus and in Him alone.

The season of Pentecost is said to be about the Christian life. This doesn't mean we should expect a long list of rules of conduct. Christianity doesn't consist of first speaking about what Christ has done and then what we should do. We really can't do anything without Christ. Speaking about the Christian way of life means also speaking about Christ and how He forms our lives, the Church, and the world. What happens in the Christian life is a continuation of what happened in Christ's life when He was a man, when He died, when He rose, and when He sent us His Spirit.

Lord Jesus, there is no other name under heaven than Yours by which we can be saved. I know that so well. Let this knowledge live in me. Fill my heart to the brim with the conviction that You are my salvation, that You are the Savior of the whole world. Let this conviction penetrate my thoughts, my feelings, desires, and entire being so I live, think, speak, and act as one who knows that everything depends on You, that You are the beginning and the end, our hope and salvation. I pray to You for the wonderful miracle that only You can perform on us, the miracle performed on the first disciples. Their judges were amazed by their candor, but that's because the disciples realized they were with You, Lord. Let that happen in my life also. Let others notice that I have been with You. For Your name's sake.

SATURDAY AFTER PENTECOST

Acts 4:23–37

"Enable Your servants to speak Your Word with great boldness." Acts 4:29 (NIV)

After their first night in prison, Peter and John returned to their own people and told them what the people's highest authorities, with all their power, had made clear to them: They would not be spared if they made a new attempt to defy society and its regulations.

And the people? When they heard this, Luke says, they cried to God: "Lord, consider their threats and enable Your servants to speak Your Word with great boldness" (Acts 4:29 NIV).

Let's put ourselves in their shoes.

Outside lies Jerusalem in the burning heat of summer, the city that murders prophets and stones God's messengers and that recently had executed Jesus. Now they were supposed to preach there. In this situation, you would really have to pray for boldness. It was blasphemy to the Jews that someone who had been crucified could be the Messiah. For the Greeks, it was ridiculous that God could die on the cross. For the Romans, the whole story wasn't worth more than a disdainful shrug of the shoulders, especially since it came from fanatic and obstinate Jews.

The apostles knew what to expect. The Master had said He was sending them as sheep among wolves, abandoned, to be abused and hated by all for His name's sake. An apostle could not expect anything more of his own destiny than what happened to his Master.

Now the test had come. Was it possible that they perceived it to be more difficult than it really was? Luke doesn't waste any words on feelings like this. He tells us that they prayed for boldness. Then he adds that they proclaimed God's Word with boldness.

We also need that kind of boldness. The world doesn't like the Gospel. The world tolerates common religiousness. Cautious Christians have, throughout time, attempted to adapt and avoid offending others. It's easy to regard belief in God and morality as the most important things. Jesus can be regarded as a shining example who revealed a loving God. But the most important thing is lost: faith in the Savior, who died and rose so we would inherit eternal life. Then the salt has lost its saltiness. What do you do with salt like that? It should be thrown away. The opposite of this is the joyous, childlike boldness that believes in Jesus. Jesus is right. Jesus loves me. He has saved me and led me to God. Should I be ashamed of Him? Shall I try to change His Word, simplify what He said, and retouch the picture of Him? Anything—but not that!

Lord, let us, Your poor servants, confess Your name in all boldness. We have been able to see Your truth. Don't ever allow us to be ashamed of it! We have encountered Your love. Let us not keep it for ourselves! You have given us Your light. Let us experience it joyfully so it shines for others! Don't allow us to make the blunder and commit the terrible sin of shielding it. You never meant us to be left alone. You have given us everything that is good, in lavish abundance and undeservedly. Make us so glad and joyful and proud of You that even the blindest perceive that Yours is the kingdom and the power and the glory, forever and ever. In Jesus' name.

TRINITY SUNDAY
Matthew 11:25–30

At that time Jesus declared, "I thank You, Father, Lord of heaven and earth, that You have hidden these things from the wise and understanding and revealed them to little children." Matthew 11:25

The Holy Trinity is a mystery: something mankind cannot visualize and only partially understand. The nature of God is incomprehensible. If we were able to fully understand God, we would probably think of Him as a product of our own imagination. The Holy Trinity is something no human speculation could have produced. People want to describe God and His nature as something comprehensible, logical, and consistent. However, God is something else than we think we want. He is a reality and has revealed Himself to us. He has showed us who He is piece by piece, to the limits of our understanding and needs. The inexhaustible depth of His nature caused the prophet to rejoice: "Oh, the depth of the riches and wisdom and knowledge of God! How unsearchable are His judgments and how inscrutable His ways!" (Romans 11:33).

We know the Holy Trinity because God has revealed Himself to us in that manner. He has not given us theoretical teachings, but has stepped forward and dealt with us as the Father, our Creator; as the Son, our Savior; and as the Holy Ghost, who works in the Church and in our hearts. Throughout the Bible we see the work of the Holy Trinity, sometimes so clear that we can say with certainty: "Here is the Son at work" or "This is the work of the Holy Spirit." It's the exception, rather than the rule, that He's called by all three names of the Trinity at the same time, such as during Baptism or in the apostolic blessing (2 Corinthians 13:14). However, many times we are confronted with the mystery that what the Father does, the Son and Holy Spirit do also.

All of Trinity Sunday's Scripture lessons examine the mystery of God's nature and how He has revealed Himself to us. The important thing is not to understand how He can be all three at once—Father, Son, and Holy Ghost—but rather to meet Him as He really is so you can believe in Him as your Father, your Savior, and your Helper, who leads you down the right path.

It doesn't matter if we address our prayers to our heavenly Father, to our Lord and Savior Jesus, or to our dear Holy Ghost. It doesn't matter if we choose to talk to God without directing our prayer to the Holy Trinity. What is important is that we are open for and willing to receive *all* of God's works, all the goodness and wealth lying in the nature of the Trinity.

Holy, triune God, how can I understand Your nature? How can I grasp the bottomless depth of Your mysteries? How can my mind understand something more vast than the universe and more mysterious than all the wonders of life? You are God and I am man. You are infinite, unfathomable, and incomprehensible. In Your boundless mercy, You have created me to be able to meet You and experience only a glimpse of Your incomprehensible nature. You come to me, and I welcome You as You are. I worship and thank You, my heavenly Father, my Savior, and loyal Helper, on my way to heavenly bliss. Blessed be Your name, the Holy Trinity, my Lord and my God.

MONDAY AFTER TRINITY SUNDAY

Acts 5:12–42

And we are witnesses to these things, and so is the Holy
Spirit, whom God has given to those who obey Him.
Acts 5:32

In the Bible reading today we once again are reminded
that the Holy Trinity is the reality behind which all our
knowledge of God exists.

The Jews were religious. Like many Christians, the Jews
believed in a just and merciful God, one who wanted His
people to live according to His Commandments. However,
the Jewish faith in God was hopelessly in conflict with actual
events occurring in Jerusalem. God had sent His Son to the
world. He was rejected and crucified, and resurrected by
God. God poured out His Spirit.

It was God who now witnessed. The apostles, ordinary
people, preached with a convincing intensity that the high
priests and Pharisees—the religious intellectuals of their
time—totally lacked (although they quoted Scripture constantly!). The apostles came with the new message that God
had fulfilled the promises He expressed through all the prophets: the promise of the Messiah and of the Holy Spirit. The
message was so obvious and certain to them that the prophets
defied society and openly declared that they were going to
do just what they were expressly forbidden to do: Obey God
over man!

The good news in this message was that the promises had
been fulfilled. The Son and Holy Spirit were now a reality.
The apostles spoke of something that had actually happened.
Their preaching made it possible to speak to and reach out
to God in a way no one ever could before. They preached
of events that Christians listen to and experience in Sunday

Scripture readings during the first half of the Church Year, which ended last Saturday. Those events were the cornerstone of a new life for them and for us. It is a life of faith in the Father, Son, and Holy Spirit. It is that life we hear about—and live—during the Trinity season.

> *Dear triune God,* thank You for what we can see and experience of Your abundant treasures. It's far more than any of us can understand, receive, or live up to. Yet You are so infinitely great, profound, and abundant! The day we see You face-to-face we will finally begin to understand. Even then You will constantly have something new to offer us, something that transcends everything that has been revealed. You remain the same, and however You meet us we always know it is You, our Creator, Savior, and Comforter. Blessed be Your name, the Father, Son, and Holy Spirit, the Holy Trinity!

TUESDAY AFTER TRINITY SUNDAY
Acts 6:1–15

Now in these days when the disciples were increasing in number, a complaint by the Hellenists arose against the Hebrews because their widows were being neglected in the daily distribution. Acts 6:1

It is helpful that stories such as this one are included in the Bible. We would like to believe that the first church had the ideal congregation, comprised solely of consecrated, pious constituents. There were always new faces at the services and at communion, which shows the church was growing. Surely the first church was vibrant, revealed by the love and care they showed one another and their eagerness to witness.

However, a vibrant congregation also consists of sinners unable to shed the mantle of the old Adam. True Christians try to hide the old Adam, but sometimes he surfaces. This happened in the first church as well. The congregation members complained and criticized, claiming that the daily distributions were unfair. These complaints still occur today, but something wonderful happened in the first church: they solved the problems without bitterness and without prestigious consideration.

We see how God's Church deals with similar difficulties. There was an established leadership with the apostles, who received their mandate from God. Instead of acting like dictators when they had a suggestion to make, they summoned the entire congregation and there was never any controversy over the decision. There was both an external order of things, the office of the apostles, and a spiritual unity; everyone was willing to let God put things right. They did not look for scapegoats and did not punish. The apostles had their share of guilt for not having completed their duties as they should have.

Everyone focused their efforts to establish a new office aside from the apostles. We usually call these seven apostles the first deacons, but we must remember that their duties were not limited to the duties of a deacon. They could preach and evangelize, as did Stephen and Philip. In any event, we have what distinguishes an office of the Church. These deacons were elected by the congregation and would act at the request and for the benefit of the congregation. However, this does not mean they received their call from man, but from God's Church—they would perform their duties as servants of Christ. That is why they came forth to the apostles, who consecrated them with prayer and laying on of hands—exactly as it occurs today.

The Church is Christ's Church, and He is at its head. Pastors and laity do not make decisions, Christ does. There is the external order, including elders and the decision-making process, but those who participate in the decision-making process do it on behalf of Christ and as His servants. That is one of the characteristics of a living congregation.

Dear Holy Spirit, visit us in our congregation. You know how much You are needed. Give us life in our Lord Jesus, so we are motivated by You and do Your will. Give us wisdom, so we always realize what is best for the church. Give us love, so we forget the wrongs and annoyances in life and focus on serving You. Give us Your strength, so we can use every opportunity to help those who have gone astray find their way back to Your Church. Consecrate us, so everyone can see that our church is Your Church, the congregation of the living God.

WEDNESDAY AFTER TRINITY SUNDAY

Acts 7:51–8:8

And falling to his knees he cried with a loud voice, "Lord, do not hold this sin against them." And when he had said this, he fell asleep. Acts 7:60

Jesus was right. He told His disciples He was sending them out like sheep to the wolves. The night before His crucifixion, He said, "the hour is coming when whoever kills you will think he is offering service to God" (John 16:2). This "hour" happened only a few months later. Even Paul would have appreciated it; he who sat at Gamaliel's feet, receiving the best religious instruction about God available; he who burned with desire to serve the Lord with all his heart and live impeccably after all His commandments and regulations.

How was it possible that God's people would be persecuted? Stephen explained this in his defense before the council. His speech spanned the history of Israel from the days of Abraham. He told how God's chosen witnesses were always misunderstood, always outcasts. Abraham was forced to leave his family and country, only to live for a promise he never saw fulfilled. Joseph was sold into slavery by his own brothers. Moses was rejected by the people he was chosen to deliver out of bondage. Jesus met the same destiny!

That is how God works in the world. His work can seem so unimportant, almost as if anyone could trample it into the ground, make a mockery of it, or end it. Those who serve Him and His work need to prepare to be trampled on without seeking revenge. God's "power is made perfect in weakness," as Paul explains (2 Corinthians 12:9). This is asserted from the witness at whose feet they laid their mantles before stoning Stephen.

It is just that weakness that the world cannot endure. It can't tolerate suffering injustice without revenge. However, Stephen understood whom he served. Just as Jesus committed His spirit into the hands of God, Stephen could say: Lord Jesus, take my soul. With Stephen's last words, we realize that Jesus gave the world something new with His Spirit. Compare Stephen's last words with that of another martyr, spoken before he was stoned in Jerusalem 800 years earlier: "And when [Zechariah] was dying, he said, "May the LORD see and avenge!" (2 Chronicles 24:22). Stephen prayed, "Lord, do not hold this sin against them."

Heavenly Father, Your faithful prophets had only Your Word and promises to follow. No one else cared. Mankind scorned them, but victory was Yours.

Dear Jesus, You declared that Your message would be scorned and Your messengers would be persecuted—but that they also would prevail. You allowed those who were expelled to spread the Gospel, and You allowed the blood of martyrs to become the seed of the Church.

Holy Spirit, You spoke through the prophets, laid Your wisdom on their tongues, yet You were contradicted and scorned. You've chosen that which was weak and witnessed through that which was nothing in the eyes of the world.

Teach us Lord, triune God, that Your weakness is stronger than all earthly power and that suffering in Your name is victory over the world.

THURSDAY AFTER
TRINITY SUNDAY
Acts 9:1–31

And immediately something like scales fell from his eyes,
and he regained his sight. Then he rose and was baptized.
Acts 9:18

Saul was converted to the Christian faith and believed in
the Holy Trinity. He had always believed in God, but refused
to believe that Jesus, the crucified, was God's Son. The idea
was absurd that God would have His Son killed. More than
that, it was impossible to believe that someone who was crucified, rejected, and exposed as a fraud could be resurrected
from the dead.

However, the resurrected Christ showed Himself to Saul,
who became blind and was knocked to the ground, physically
and spiritually. He neither ate nor drank and didn't know
which way to turn. He began to pray. We can only imagine
what he prayed for: perhaps that God's will be done and that
God might lead him down the right path at any cost.

At just that moment Ananias came along—that reluctant, wise, and careful man—whom the Lord was forced to
give a talking to in order to get him to go to this notorious
persecutor. Now the blindness fell like scales from Saul's
eyes, also in a spiritual sense. He could see what was not visible to him before: This Jesus was the Messiah, just as God
had promised, the One who "should suffer these things and
enter into His glory" (Luke 24:26). Saul had finally gotten
a glimpse of what he called in one of his letters "the glory
of God in the face of Jesus Christ" (2 Corinthians 4:6). He
saw that it was in accordance with the Scriptures. That is still
how we come to faith in Christ—not through speculation,
but by meeting Christ Himself, the resurrected, the One the
Scriptures bear witness to.

The Spirit also entered into Paul's life. That's the mission Ananias had received: to tell Paul that he would be filled with the Spirit. At that moment it was something new for Paul. Later he would live "in the Spirit" for many years and witness like no other how that life is.

That is how we find faith in the Trinity. Not through speculation, but by meeting God Himself, the true God that the Scriptures bear witness to and who comes to meet us as the Father, Son, and Holy Ghost.

Lord Jesus, You converted the persecutor Saul to the sanctified Paul, Your chosen servant. You showed him how much he must suffer for You. There are so many who speak only of how wonderful it is to believe in You. They offer pure joy and serenity when they come with Your invitation. Lord, teach us that we also have suffering to bear and that there is no glory in serving You in a worldly sense. It's only true life that exists with You, that which is the treasure in the field and the priceless pearl in the midst of all persecutions.

FRIDAY AFTER
TRINITY SUNDAY
Acts 10:1–23

What God has made clean, do not call common. Acts 10:15

Christ had come, the Holy Spirit had revealed Himself, and the Holy Trinity had manifested itself. The time of preparation was over, and something new had come. This led to many consequences for God's people. These consequences were hard to face at first, but the Holy Spirit did what Jesus had promised: He led the apostles to the truth.

Our reading today is a short episode in a long story. Peter experienced a strange vision and was commanded to do something a devout Jew would never consider. He was to eat meat that, according to the Law of Moses—the very Law God gave His people—was unclean and forbidden. Peter refused, but a voice told him that God had now declared it clean—the very same meat that was earlier forbidden to be touched! There were several sections of the Law of Moses that were no longer applicable. There were numerous stipulations that specifically applied to the people of Israel; for example, rules applying to burnt offerings and offerings of thanksgiving, the celebration of the Passover and Sabbath, the Day of Atonement, the wave offering of the sheaf, and the scapegoat. There were also regulations pertaining to what we call civil law, like the absolution of slaves, compensation for destroyed crops, betrothal, divorce, and much more. These regulations pertained to the people living under the covenant of the Old Testament. God had made a new covenant with a new Israel, the holy Christian, apostolic Church, and these old regulations no longer pertained in the same manner.

Then what is the point of the Old Testament?

The apostles have thoroughly instructed us on the answer

to this question. Principally, there is the promise of Christ, examples and prophecies of all that now had come. The examples are seen in Israel's institutions, temples, high priests, and offerings. We also see examples in what we call the moral laws, God's Commandments regarding love and justice, mercy, benevolence, and the purity of the heart. They all still apply, but no longer as the way to God or as a condition to be met in order to be called God's children. Jesus earned us that right through His death on the cross. It is given to those who believe in Him. God's Commandments still apply as guidance and as revelation of His will. It is the Holy Spirit who helps us understand them, love them, and willingly obey them, as good and thankful children should.

We read that the Holy Spirit told Peter there were men who came and asked for him. He added, "I have sent them." He could have said it was God our Father who sent them, or even that Jesus Christ had sent them. That is the secret of the Holy Trinity. There is only one God. He has *one* will and performs *one* task. Yet He meets us as the Father, Son, and Holy Ghost. Those who can heed the right call can sometimes sense, as Peter did, that now the Holy Spirit is talking.

Dear Holy Spirit, teach us all to understand everything You say, even what You have said in the days of Moses, David, and Solomon. You can teach us how to understand the true meaning. You can save us from the bondage of not having understood that Christ has made us free. You can preserve us from self-indulgence. You have said that all that is written is meant to instruct us. Help us listen to Your instructions and learn from everything You want to teach us.

SATURDAY AFTER TRINITY SUNDAY.

Acts 10:24–48

The gift of the Holy Spirit was poured out even on the Gentiles. Acts 10:45

"The ceremonial law" no longer applies to us in its original and literal sense for the Church of Christ. God had given Israel's twelve tribes rules and regulations that were to be obeyed until He saw fit to bring about a new order of things. That's how the Book of Hebrews summarizes the truth the Holy Spirit led the ancient Church to. The Bible reading today is one of the milestones on the way to the truth.

As long as the time of preparation lasted, God nurtured His people in the faith and loyalty of the one true God. The Jewish race was to be made conscious of its call and dare to live its own life, which is why there were laws regarding cleanliness and seclusion. These laws were necessary and life supportive. They preserved the truth and maintained faith in God. Now a new era had begun.

Peter was well aware of the basis for this new era. He depicts this with several strong statements, speaking of the good news and adding a quick synopsis of the life and works of Jesus. He doesn't forget to mention that, "To Him all the prophets bear witness" (Acts 10:43). The news was merely the consummation and fulfillment of all God's works in the past.

At precisely the moment when Peter breaks with the old traditions and laws, something happens that gives him and his Jewish brethren a reminder of Pentecost. The Holy Spirit fell on the Gentiles and they began speaking in tongues. Peter immediately understood what the Holy Spirit was saying. God had taken these Gentiles into His Church. They didn't have to be circumcised because they were baptized. They didn't have to be Jews to be Christian. Until now, all Christians had to have their religious foundation in the old Israel to reach the new. This was no longer necessary because the new path was through Baptism and faith.

Again, we see that the Holy Spirit has His given place beside the Father and the Son. The news consisted not simply of Christ's coming. Something equally important had happened. The Holy Spirit was evident. With Christ and the Holy Spirit a new era had begun, one where we could finally know and worship the one true God.

Lord, You have far more to give than we ever could receive. You have showered Your inexpressible riches on us so abundantly and generously that our minds and intellect could never begin to gather them in. Yet You allow our hearts to realize what our intellect cannot. We give thanks to You and open our hearts to receive all the inexpressible abundance and unfathomable beauty that showers over us when You appear in Your fullness and with the complete richness of Your nature. Praise be to You, the triune God, our Father, our Savior, our Helper.

FIRST SUNDAY
AFTER TRINITY
John 3:1–16

Unless one is born of water and the Spirit, he cannot enter the kingdom of God. John 3:5

The rabbis, the teachers in Israel like Nicodemus, were aware that one question was more important than all others: what must I do to attain eternal life? Jesus gives us the answer to this question in our reading.

For the Jews, as for many others, the question was obviously interpreted that there must be something *I do*. We take for granted that we only need to use the resources we already have to attain eternal life. For some of us, it's merely a theoretical problem. Can I believe this? Does the Christian faith hold up when put to an intellectual test? Maybe I can come up with something more probable or reasonable. For others, it's a question of morals. What choice should I make given all the possible choices available?

In both cases, we believe we already have the necessary resources to become a Christian, if we should make that choice.

Jesus says this is the big mistake. Something new is needed; something only God can give us. We must be reborn from above. Here Jesus uses a word that also means anew. Jesus explains to Nicodemus that rebirth is not being reborn from the womb, but that it is a new life seeing new light. It's something that comes from above, as an act of God. One is born "of water and the Spirit."

Nicodemus must have understood these words in the light of the prophets he knew so well. God was supposed to do a great miracle and intervene to save His people. He would pour water on the thirsty land, sprinkle pure water on His people, and put His Spirit in them (Isaiah 44:3, Ezekiel

36:25–27). John might not have realized that significance the night Nicodemus came to Jesus, but he understood it afterward. He had been a part of the fulfillment of God's promise to His people. It was clear to him that Jesus spoke of Baptism.

Consequently, the most essential thing to know about Baptism had been revealed: it is an act of God. God intervenes and gives us something that's absolutely necessary to come into His kingdom. Whatever we might receive through natural birth, it isn't enough for us to become Christians, God's children. Only the Holy Spirit can do that. Now the Holy Spirit comes with water. Water that cleanses and nourishes is a wonderful symbol, but through Baptism it becomes much more. It becomes the intermediary and bearer of the new thing to come, the Spirit, now here to perform His work.

We will learn more of that work in the coming week.

Lord, help me do what I must to attain eternal life. I'm beginning to understand that I have to start by recognizing what You want to give me and what You want me to do with my life. I thought I could choose my own path and come to You on my own merits. Now I realize that something else only You can do is necessary. Therefore, I thank You for being with me long before I realized who You were and for coming into my life before I understood Your power. I pray that Your work in me continues so I will have eternal life.

MONDAY AFTER FIRST SUNDAY AFTER TRINITY

Matthew 28:18–20

Baptizing them in the name of the Father and of the Son and of the Holy Spirit. Matthew 28:19

Today we read the next to the last verse from the Gospel of Matthew, the words that institute Baptism. We learned earlier about the Baptism of John and of Jesus' Baptism. However, neither of these baptisms compare with our own Baptism—when we were received into God's kingdom.

The resurrected Christ Himself ordained Christian Baptism, and this is of major importance. Christ had to suffer, die, and rise from the dead as atonement for the sins of the world before the time was right for Baptism in the name of the Father, Son, and Holy Spirit.

The Resurrected One commanded His apostles to go out into the world to all people, and He promised to be with them until the end of time. It was a command that applied as long as the earth would exist. The Gospel was to be preached to all people and they were to be made disciples of Christ and taken up into His Church. By baptizing people they were transformed into His disciples. Those who were baptized received the call of Jesus: "follow Me." Just as His disciples became a part of His own life and formed a fellowship with Him, so would all mankind through all time be able to connect with Jesus Christ Himself, as branches are connected to the tree.

This is the significance of Christian Baptism. John's Baptism was a baptism of improvement. It was an act of obedience, a way people proved they were moved by the Word of God and were now willing to better themselves and await God's salvation. The Christian Baptism is a Baptism for redemption. It's something God does. The Christian Baptism is a call from God through which we are removed from this world and connected to Christ.

Lord, I'm beginning to realize that Your power is much more than I can understand or comprehend. Thank You for being with me long before I realized You existed. Thank You for coming to me, putting Your hand on my shoulder, and taking me into Your kingdom as a disciple, long before I could say a prayer. I thank You because I can't remember when I first heard Your name. I thank You even more for influencing my life in a way that exceeds my ability to understand. You, who laid Your hands on the children and blessed them, have also touched me. I have received Your blessing, a blessing the world can't see but that gives me more than anything the world can give. May this blessing remain with me, follow me, and encompass me to my last day on earth and into eternity in Your kingdom.

TUESDAY AFTER FIRST SUNDAY AFTER TRINITY
Romans 6:3–11

Do you not know that all of us who have been baptized into

The portion of Romans we read today might appear to be a little out of context. Yet it's a very important part of the topic we are studying—Baptism. Paul here is speaking of the significance of Christian Baptism and showing us a new and essential aspect of it.

Paul says that we have been baptized into *Christ's death*. Jesus Himself spoke of a baptism He had to endure, one of anxiety and death, the initiation of which was His Baptism in the River Jordan. Paul is indicating that our Baptism is linked to *that* Baptism: "We were buried therefore with Him by baptism into death" (Romans 6:4). We will understand a little later what he really means. For now we must just understand that everything that happened to and through Christ in His death becomes ours when we are baptized. Christ died for our sake. He made atonement for our sins. What He has done becomes ours.

We are actually united with Christ, as Paul says: "We have been united with Him in a death like His" (Romans 6:5). We have been engrafted like branches on a grapevine. We have become members in His body. We are living building blocks in the Spirit's building. This means that we will be united with Christ, intertwined in Him, all our lives. As He led a new life, so shall we, every day, lead the new life with the Resurrected One. We will live through Him and for Him. This is the meaning of Baptism.

My Lord and Savior, thank You for choosing me, for it was not I who chose You. I thank You for having taken me, a bud on a wild tree, and engrafting me onto one of Your precious grapevines, a vine that bears fruit that never spoils. I thank You because it is Your life and Your power that works within me. If anyone can soften my barklike skin and give life to my dried up trunk, it is You. That's more than I can ask for. I thank You from the bottom of my heart that I have learned what You want to do for me. May Your will always and everywhere be done, even with me.

WEDNESDAY AFTER FIRST SUNDAY AFTER TRINITY

Titus 3:4–7

He saved us . . . by the washing of regeneration and renewal of the Holy Spirit. Titus 3:5

Was my Baptism as a child a valid Baptism? There are those who would contest it. They usually assume that our Baptism is in some way similar to John the Baptist's: an act of obedience we perform in repentance and in faith. The Christian Baptism is something different, something God does through which He saves us and gives us new life. It's a miracle that He does this, and the miracle is equally great whether it's done for a child or an adult. We can't contribute to the miracle; we only put obstacles in its way. It is exclusively the work of God.

This is what Paul is explaining in today's text. God doesn't save us because of the good works we do. He saves us solely through His mercy, which is revealed in Baptism when we are washed, born again, and renewed in the Holy Spirit.

Now we can understand why the Baptist said that Jesus would baptize with the Holy Spirit and fire. These words remind us of Pentecost, when the Holy Spirit descended as tongues of fire on the apostles. The promise that the Resurrected One gave a few days before was fulfilled; John baptized with water, but the disciples would be baptized in the Spirit.

Through Baptism in the Holy Spirit, the apostles became the Spirit's tools and the Church became the Spirit's temple. They could preach with the power of the Spirit, and they could baptize. In the past they hadn't baptized anyone in Christ. Now they could baptize with water that gave new life and regeneration in the Spirit. It's the life Jesus speaks of in the parable of the grapevine and the branches. It's the life that streams through His body, the Church, where we are the limbs. That's why Jesus could say that he who is least in heaven is greater than John, who was the greatest of all prophets. Through Christ something has come into the world that never existed before. It's purely a gift that can never be earned. There is nothing our intellect or will can do to help us achieve this new life in Christ.

Dear Lord Jesus, I glorify You because through Your Baptism You became a Savior. I glorify You because through my Baptism I become saved by You. Long before I was born, You carried my sins to Your cross. Through Baptism, You took me through Your death and into Your new life. As I have taken part in Your death, I no longer need to die. I can now live with You. I thank You for Your boundless mercy. Help me to show my gratitude, as You would want me to do, to those who most need it.

THURSDAY AFTER
FIRST SUNDAY
AFTER TRINITY

John 1:29–34

I came baptizing with water . . . this is He who baptizes
with the Holy Spirit. John 1:31–33

John baptized with water. It was a baptism of improvement, where people confessed their sins and prepared to receive God's coming Messiah. John said that this Messiah would baptize in the Holy Spirit.

Before His ascension into heaven, Jesus promised His disciples that they would soon be baptized in the Spirit, a promise that was fulfilled on Pentecost. Later, we read of three more incidents of spiritual Baptism, followed by signs from the Holy Spirit, such as speaking in tongues. On each occasion a new group of people were involved, and on each occasion God had a special purpose.

The first occasion concerned the Samaritans. They had been baptized, but "He [the Spirit] had not yet fallen on any of them" (Acts 8:16). Two apostles came to them and "laid their hands on them and they received the Holy Spirit" (Acts 8:17). In this way, God showed everyone that even the contemptuous Samaritans had a place in the new Israel.

The second occasion concerned the Gentiles in the city of Caesarea, where the devout centurion Cornelius had summoned Peter (Acts 10). Peter preached the Good News to the Gentiles here, and while he spoke "the Holy Spirit fell on all who heard the word" (Acts 10:44). This was taken as a sign from God—they could be baptized without having to be circumcised first.

The third occasion concerned a group of John's disciples in Ephesus (Acts 19). They had received John's Baptism but had no idea that the Holy Spirit had come. Paul then baptized them in Christ and "the Holy Spirit came on them, and they began speaking in tongues and prophesying" (Acts 19:6). After all these events, it was apparent that Christian Baptism was something other than John's Baptism and something that John's disciples needed.

On every occasion we see that groups of people were involved. It also involved affiliation to God's Church and a question of who was to be taken up or who was already there. The outpouring of the Holy Spirit was the answer from heaven. In the New Testament we never read of a Christian receiving Baptism from the Spirit in addition to his first Baptism. That's because the Christian Baptism is the true Baptism in the Spirit. Yesterday we read that it is a "washing of regeneration and renewal of the Holy Spirit, whom He poured out upon us richly through Jesus Christ our Savior" (Titus 3:5–6). Paul reminds us that everyone who is baptized is "made to drink of one spirit" (1 Corinthians 12:13).

The Spirit does not come to us as something we can take and own, but as a stream of life we must constantly receive. The Spirit does not fill us once and leave. We must constantly be refilled. Through Baptism we become a consecrated temple where the Spirit wants to live as long as we keep the doors open.

I pray, dear Holy Spirit, that I may be a willing vessel to receive Your love. Show me everything that's not suitable for Your temple. Show me everything You want to change. Give me the love and the power only You can give. If I forget You, please don't forget me. You remind me of the things my Savior said. You can teach me to believe in Him. Thank you for being my Admonisher, my Comforter, and my Helper.

What prevents me from being baptized? Acts 8:36.

Philip had been given a strange command. We usually refer to commands like this as God's "guidance." Anyone can be the recipient of similar guidance. Some people have been given the gift of the Spirit which allows them to be more susceptible to God's help.

Indeed, it was a strange command. Philip was told to travel a desert road, and that was all he knew. He obeyed the command, and it turned out that he certainly had heeded the Spirit's guidance. A traveler came along, a distinguished person riding in a chariot. Once again the Spirit's guidance came to Philip. He approached the stranger and found him reading the prophet Isaiah. (In those days people read aloud.) This became the beginning of a long discussion that allowed Philip the opportunity to talk about Jesus Christ. Christ was the one Isaiah spoke of, the lamb being led to slaughter. He was humiliated by men yet exalted by God and a Savior to all.

Philip and the traveler reached a place with water, and now we realize that Philip must have spoken about something else that was very essential. He must have explained the door to Jesus' kingdom. Something must happen to those who wish to belong to the Savior Jesus; they must be baptized.

Consequently the Ethiopian declared: "See, here is water! What prevents me from being baptized?" In older manuscripts and translations there is additional text here: Philip said to him, "'If you believe with all your heart, you may.' And [the Ethiopian] replied, 'I believe that Jesus Christ is the Son of God.'"

We see how obvious it was in the ancient church to baptize those who wished to be Christian. The Jews on Pentecost examined their conscience and wondered what they could do. The answer was: convert, and be baptized in the name of Christ Jesus. Whenever or wherever one received the Gospel, he was baptized. Thereafter he was taken up into God's people, into the new Israel, into God's Church. God Himself did this. That was what Jesus had commanded would happen to all mankind. They were to be made disciples through Baptism and keep all His Commandments.

Consequently, we are received into God's Church through Baptism. For every Christian the pertinent questions are: How could we drift so far away from the biblical view on Baptism? How can we best correct it?

I thank You, Lord, for my Baptism and for Your Baptism. You did this! I thank You that I was born in a Christian country and that I have been received into Your Church. Now I ask for guidance to become what You have created me for, to become a disciple who will follow You, listen to You, and agree with You, even when it is contrary to the world's views. I thank You for taking me to Your bosom and lifting me into the world where there is eternal forgiveness. Help me to live in that forgiveness, that I dare come to You every day with all my sins and leave them with You so I can live in Your presence, as a member of God's family, a happy child with his Father.

SATURDAY AFTER FIRST SUNDAY AFTER TRINITY

Luke 13:22–35

How often would I . . . and you would not! Luke 13:34

Will only a few be saved?

Jesus was asked that. The people had believed that maybe a few would be lost, but the vast majority would go to heaven. Now they were beginning to understand that this was not the case.

This truth is anything but obvious. Mankind has fallen from God. We all have something inside us that wants to keep God at bay because we're afraid of His judgment. In the New Testament the question is no longer if a person can be lost; of course he can. The question is how a person can be saved. The answer is: "For God so loved the world, that He gave His only Son, that whoever believes in Him should not perish but have eternal life" (John 3:16).

How many will be saved?

Jesus didn't answer this question. He encouraged those who asked to "enter through the narrow door" (Luke 13:24). He said many would try to enter and fail. He refers to the Last Day, when our lives are summarized and the final judgment is passed. Did we heed the call, come to the Savior, go through the door? The door is always open. Jesus invites: come to Me; follow Me. He's speaking on God's behalf, and He's serious. Tomorrow's Bible text is about this call. We will hear how the call was received, and how often things turn out in the way Jesus said in today's text: I wanted to, but you didn't. That's the seriousness of the choice we're in the middle of— God or the world. Everything depends on that choice. We heard Jesus say: Because you didn't want to, God will take away your city and country. God gave you your country so you would be His servants and witnesses. Choosing the world before God means finally losing everything, maybe losing things right now. We received life and all the good in it to live as God's children. To try to take the good in life and avoid God leads only to the loss of both.

Lord, giver of good gifts, You have given me the most marvelous of all gifts, the gift of existence, thought, and a will of my own. Help me use these gifts correctly. Help me to rejoice over them every morning upon waking, rejoice that I belong to the living, that I can see the heavens in all its color, sense every scent, and hear the wind blow. I thank You for the life I receive from You because You wanted me to be Your child and live like You, together with You, in Your bliss, a bliss that's never ending. Father, Your will be done, as with me.

SECOND SUNDAY AFTER TRINITY
Luke 14:16–24

A man once gave a great banquet. Luke 14:16

When we read this parable, it is easy to forget about the man planning the banquet. There's so much to ponder after learning about the reaction of the guests to the invitation.

We can't help but notice that people react in the very same way today.

This parable is descriptive and realistic. Preparing a banquet of this size took a long time. To be on the safe side, a preliminary invitation was sent out. When everything was prepared, the servants went out announcing to all the guests: Come, everything is ready! That is how God treated Israel. He spoke of what was to come. First John the Baptist, then Jesus, who also said: Come, everything is ready!

At this point the banquet guests began to make excuses. They apologized, but they couldn't come. Not just then anyway. One of them had bought property, another oxen (today tractors or cars), and another was recently married. They reacted exactly like we do: We have so many excuses. We don't have time for God. Not just now anyway.

Jesus says those excuses are unacceptable. The invitation goes to someone else. First it went to the people in the streets: the poor, blind, and maimed. We're reminded of the tax collectors and prostitutes, who came instead of the pious in Israel. Then the invitation went out along the paths and highways. We're reminded of the apostles, who were sent out to all nations. Now the invitation comes to us.

Let's not forget about this great banquet, a festival, the likes of which we have never seen. It's possible for us to find new meaning in life and to experience splendor and riches in company we could never acquire ourselves. This is a fantastic offer from an unbelievably generous donor who cannot keep all His happiness, all His riches, and all His essence to Himself. It can only be compared to the treasure in the field, or the precious pearl, as portrayed by Jesus in a couple of His parables.

Can we say no to all of this?

Dear heavenly Father, thank You for the great banquet and for inviting me. Thank You for wishing
to share the splendor of Your existence and allowing me to be a part of the never failing glory that
surrounds everything in Your presence. Forgive
my lack of faith, my apprehensive scheming, and
my petty skepticism about whether it will pay off.
Allow me to see a glimpse of You so I understand
that there is only one true meaning in life, just one
thing worth possessing and experiencing: being
with You. Thank You for offering this joy. Thank
You Lord, for allowing me to come.

MONDAY AFTER SECOND SUNDAY AFTER TRINITY
Luke 19:1–10

Zacchaeus, hurry and come down, for I must stay at your
house today. Luke 19:5

This was a development Zacchaeus hadn't imagined! He
came to see Jesus. He was curious, as were so many others.
Maybe he had a specific reason. Rumor had it that this Jesus
was a friend to tax collectors and sinners, and Zacchaeus was
a tax collector. He belonged to the kind of people who were
despised more than others, as is often the case today. He was
a collaborator, a Jew who cooperated with the occupational
government, aiding them by pressuring the Jews into paying

taxes. Zacchaeus made good money and had been promoted to chief tax collector. He owned a luxurious home and earned a handsome income. He was banned from the synagogue. Maybe he still had a yearning for God at the bottom of his heart.

Then it happened! Jesus stopped under the tree Zacchaeus had climbed for a better view, and looked at Zacchaeus as if it was His original and only intention to meet Zacchaeus that day. And it was His intention. Jesus said that very evening that the Son of Man had come to save those who were lost. He therefore chose this particular house of the rich and despised in Jericho.

What about Zacchaeus? He didn't get any sermons. Jesus offered compassion and joy. These attributes would take effect. Zacchaeus approached Jesus and said, "Lord, the half of my goods I give to the poor. And if I have defrauded anyone of anything, I restore it fourfold." From that day something new existed in that luxurious home in Jericho. Jesus said, "Today salvation has come to this house."

Until now, the beautiful rugs, the fantastic food, and all the other material riches set the tone. Now the tone had changed to something warmer, more secure, and more joyous. After all, it's things like these that make a home a nice place to be in.

Lord, may I ask You to be a guest in my home? I believe I can. You visited Zacchaeus because he was a son of Abraham. I am baptized by Your hand. You decided that, not me. If You came that time, I know You won't refuse now. Therefore, I ask that You come with Your mercy and happiness, and that You allow it to fill my heart and my home. Come, Lord, and fill the workday and the solitude, the conversations and laughter, our labor and pressures. Even emptiness when it comes. Come, Lord Jesus.

TUESDAY AFTER SECOND SUNDAY AFTER TRINITY

1 Thessalonians 1:1–10

He has chosen you. I Thessalonians 1:4

The rest of this week we will be reading 1 Thessalonians, which are Paul's oldest preserved letters. They were written around AD 51 to a young congregation in the city now known as Saloniki in northern Greece. At that time, the congregation was only a few months old, so Paul is writing to newly converted individuals. With these letters we can learn quite a bit about how it must have been to have received God's call and answered yes.

We tend to view God's call as a choice and a decision. The Thessalonians had "turned to God from idols to serve the living and true God" (1 Thessalonians 1:9). They had turned from the idols so many others worshiped, a decision that resulted in much unpleasantness and persecution. They had taken a step that attracted a lot of attention. They were spoken of in other congregations with pride and joy. At the same time their old friends and acquaintances mocked them. Accordingly, it wouldn't have been strange if they felt that they had taken a decisive step.

We also use the term "deciding for God." We're between God and the world and we make decisions, well aware of the consequences. There are things we have to reckon with, and things that, starting now, must be an obvious part of our lives. First and foremost is God's Word and prayer. We have become "determined Christians."

Now Paul tells us that there's another aspect to this that is far more important. Regardless of what we think, it is God who has chosen us. The fact that the Gospel came to Thessalonica, and that there were those who received it, meant they were among the chosen ones. That was shown by the Gospel coming to them not just in words. Many others heard the words and weren't influenced by them. Here the Word came "in power and in the Holy Spirit and with full conviction" (1 Thessalonians 1:5). That's exactly how it should come. We've heard the Word many times before without really paying any attention to it. Then one day it begins to speak to us, maybe on an occasion we will never forget, and we realize it's *me* God's talking to. What He's saying concerns me. It would be something pure and tremendous, something I really need, if I could really get to know God and become His child. I understand that I'm called into His kingdom. All this is dependent upon *God* reaching out to *me*.

Why me?

Because He loves me. There is no other answer. He loves everyone and reaches out to all. However, we can never explain or foresee how He does that. All we know is that when He reaches out to us, it's an important moment—full of possibilities we can't afford to waste.

Lord, I thank You for being able to hear Your Gospel.
Because it has reached my ears, I know You have
called me. You reached out for me at my Baptism,

*before I knew anything about You. I have no idea
how many times You've been with me since then.
Now I pray to remain with You. Whatever I feel
and whatever I experience or don't experience,
I know You're always the same and what You
expect because You've told me in Your Word. You
want me to come to the knowledge of Your truth
and be saved. Father, Your will be done.*

WEDNESDAY AFTER SECOND SUNDAY AFTER TRINITY

1 Thessalonians 2:1–13

When you received the word of God, which you heard from
us, you accepted it not as the word of men but as what it
really is. 1 Thessalonians 2:13

Life as a Christian begins with God's call. He chooses us.
He must be there before we can say yes. What happens if we
answer yes?

Paul depicts one of the most important lessons in this
chapter. We have "to walk in a manner worthy of God, who
calls you into His own kingdom and glory" (1 Thessalonians
2:12). We are chosen to live as God's children. That kind of
life can't be governed simply by a few rules and regulations.
We can't just stop doing some things and start doing other
things. It's a question of a whole new way of life; the kind
of life we lead when God is a part of everything. We live as

a child before his father. We can do this, despite the fact that we're sinners, because Jesus has given us that right. We can do this, despite the fact that we have no prior information or instruction regarding how we must act or behave in all possible incidences, because we have the Word and the Spirit.

When Jesus called the disciples, He said: "Follow Me." That meant: "Come with Me now, and I will teach you all you need to know." We learn in this same way today. We don't have to know everything from the beginning. Sometimes we're almost completely ignorant. But we can learn bit by bit on one condition: that we really listen. That's what Paul is talking about when he describes what happened in Thessalonica. What happened there was just as necessary then as it is now.

There are two things that determine if Christianity is living. The first is that God's Word be preached purely and clearly as Paul here described it, not in a flattering or patronizing way, by one who has no desire to be popular or appreciated but wants only to please God and say what God wants to be said. The second is that he who listens understands that this is not the word of men, but the Word of God. This condition has to be met if the Word will "work in you believers." If you go to church to only hear what the *pastor* says (and then compare it to what you believe), you're impeding the Word from doing its work. When God's Word is heard, we're standing in front of Him and the right question is: Lord, what do You want of me? That's why these two things are equally important: that the spoken word is the true Word of God, and that we receive it as such.

Dear Lord, help everyone who comes with Your Word
and Your message to us. Help them to see only
You when they ask what Your Word is trying to

*tell them, and only see us to ask what the Word
conveys. May we never be critical to Your Word,
yet all the more critical to words that don't come
from You. May we hear when You speak, and
may we notice the words of men. May we never
be critical simply because something doesn't agree
with our own views. Let us ask, instead, if it's
in conjunction with Your Word. May Your Holy
Spirit lead and inform us so we really know and
understand what You're saying.*

THURSDAY AFTER
SECOND SUNDAY
AFTER TRINITY
1 Thessalonians 2:14–3:13

And supply what is lacking in your faith.
1 Thessalonians 3:10

God's call is just the beginning. There's a lot more to
come. It's not impossible that everything can go wrong.

Paul knew this and was worried and concerned about his
Thessalonians. He had heard about the persecutions against
them. Twice he was ready to go to them, but obstacles confronted him both times—obstacles he knew were caused by
Satan, who wants to hinder the Gospel. Finally, Paul sent his
colleague, Timothy, and through him he had received good
news that the Thessalonians are "standing fast in the Lord"
(1 Thessalonians 3:8).

Paul feared that their labor would be in vain. You can sow the seed, it can grow and bloom, but if the drought comes and the harvest fails, there won't be any fruit. That's also the way it is when God calls us to His kingdom. We're reminded of Jesus' parable about the sower and what happened to his seeds. Everything looked promising but some didn't bear fruit.

Why does this happen? Largely because of the reason we read about yesterday. If we neglect God's Word and prayer, growth is stunted. Sometimes we might receive the Word with joy because the sermon was so captivating or touching, or maybe we experience a particular feeling in church; this is the time we realize we can no longer neglect our God in our soul. Now we want to experience that feeling again. However, that first joy was only a beginning that God gave us. Now we have to teach ourselves to love God in everyday life. We have to learn to receive the Word of God when there are no tremendous experiences or special atmospheres. If we search for the right atmosphere instead of God, we will not find it.

Paul mentions here another reason we give up—afflictions and persecutions. If we become Christians in order to live in an idyllic, glorious frame of mind, we will certainly be disappointed. When Paul speaks to the Thessalonians, he mentions the obvious, that their faith is inadequate. There is a danger in that. However, it can be remedied through instruction. Paul wanted most of all to come and instruct them. Thankfully there were others who could take his place. Paul himself isn't what's most crucial. The most important thing is that they remain steadfast in the Word and that the Word works within them.

We pray, good and faithful Lord, that You help us where we lack in our faith. We pray for the enlightenment and knowledge that can come only when

You speak and allow Your Word to live among us. We pray for the experience and maturity that comes when we faithfully do as You say and that we experience our own weaknesses and Your abundant loyalty. Above all, we pray for love, for You and for all people we meet so our hearts can comprehend what no words can explain and no amount of thought can understand, that being a portion of Your life and Spirit.

FRIDAY AFTER SECOND SUNDAY AFTER TRINITY

1 Thessalonians 4:1–18

For you know what instructions we gave you through the Lord Jesus. 1 Thessalonians 4:2

God's call does not consist of a number of commands. The invitation to God's kingdom isn't a list of entrance requirements. It merely says: Come, everything is ready. The King invites you to a banquet.

Consequently, Paul didn't come to Thessalonica with a list of new commandments. He came with Jesus Christ. He came with the offer of complete forgiveness, exemption from guilt, the right to be a child of God, a sibling to Jesus. However, he mentions that he had given them commandments they were well aware of—"instructions we gave you *through* the *Lord Jesus.*" That means the commands didn't come from Paul but from Jesus. They do not come as a condition, a payment, or an achievement that must be fulfilled for us to receive the right to be with God in His kingdom. They come as a consequence of the fact that we are already there. They're saying: You are a child of God, now live like one so your Father is pleased and so Jesus finds favor in you and not shame.

We then hear how Paul enumerates some of the things he spoke about to the Thessalonians on Jesus' behalf. First, God had not called them to uncleanness but to holiness. They were to have their own spouse, refrain from fornication, and refrain from extramarital relations. That was God's will. God's children know this and follow His will. They know they have no reason to boast or judge others because God looks into the heart, and Jesus said that adultery is also a product of the heart's desire. However, children of God do not consciously cheat and try to excuse the sin by saying that everyone else does it.

Furthermore, Paul speaks about doing the right thing, about not insulting or hurting anyone. As long as God allows us to live on this earth, we should attend to our duties properly, at work and in society. Paul especially mentions working with our hands. Finally, he mentions love. However, that subject was so obvious in their daily experiences that Paul didn't feel it necessary to expound upon. I wonder if he could've said that to us.

The chapter concludes with one of the particular questions that Paul sometimes addresses when the congregation needs guidance. This time the question concerns those who die before the return of Christ. This gives Paul the opportunity to speak of the second coming. However, we'll save that discussion until we approach the end of the Church Year.

Dear Lord Jesus, I know You made me a child of God. I could never deserve it, yet You allow me to be a child of God by taking responsibility for my sins. Therefore, I gladly serve You and want to be the person You want me to be. I pray for Your help in this, as with everything else. May I never disgrace Your name. I want to be called a Christian. I want to be one in such a way that others understand that the best thing that can happen to them is to meet You.

SATURDAY AFTER SECOND SUNDAY AFTER TRINITY

1 Thessalonians 5:12–28

He who calls you is faithful, He will surely do it.
1 Thessalonians 5:24

A Christian is called anew, every day. He's within God's magnetic field and under the influence of God's Word. God has sent out His invitation and He is constantly resending it so we won't forget why we're called—namely, to be God's child and have a part in His kingdom.

That call is integral to us. A Christian still retains the old Adam. Even a vibrant congregation consists of nothing but sinners who continue to bear the old nature of sin. That old nature requires constant attention to prevent new sins. We also see in the last chapter of Thessalonians how Paul admonishes his brethren to remain at peace and exercise patience with one another. He speaks of those who are idle, fainthearted, and weak. There are people like that among Christians as well. That's why Paul's letters are full of admonishments and, sometimes, reprimands and punishments.

As Christians, we live within the magnetic field of the Spirit and under the Word of God. Everything is incomplete. God is working with us. That's why both the Law and the Gospel are necessary. The Word must be preached to us and we must take it to heart. That's why Paul saw to it that every congregation had a leader. Here Paul exhorts the congregation's members to have respect for the called workers who taught them. Even that admonishment was obviously necessary.

If there are so many faults among those who heed God's call, can a church stand the test of time? What's going to happen to me if I constantly expect to be deceived by my own ego? Paul answers that "He who calls you is faithful." He will carry out His work and see to it that everything gets done. He can repair the flaws in your faith. He won't let you die before He has you safely in His hands. All we have to do is let Him work with us by taking His Word seriously.

Dear Lord, I thank You for calling me. You want me to be Your child and have made this possible. I pray that Your work touches me, and that You remove all obstacles in me that prevent Your work from reaching my heart and my life. Help me so I never extinguish Your light when it warns me, comforts me, and pushes me forward. Help me test everything with Your help so I can immediately see what emanates from You and keep only that which comes

from Your hand. Help me to always be joyous and
to be thankful to You for having received such an
undeserved abundance of riches and, first and last,
for being Your child.

THIRD SUNDAY
AFTER TRINITY
Luke 15:1–10

This man receives sinners and eats with them. Luke 15:2

The fact that Jesus was keeping company with sinners was shocking! Every pious person knows that God is holy and righteous and loves everyone who follows His will. That is the reason the Jews were very particular about the company they kept. However, publicans and sinners of all kinds came to this Jesus. We can just imagine how that would look today with all kinds of dubious characters collected in one spot, all the people who are a problem to society, swindlers, tax evaders, junkies, alcoholics . . . what would people think if all of these characters started filling up the pews and showing up for Communion? Would it be so strange if people began to grumble and say: *He receives sinners and eats with them? That can't be right!*

However, that was exactly the point. God doesn't accept and like all the wrong things that happen on earth, but He has mercy on us all—as we all do wrong—and allows us to come to Him and escape from all the wrong in the world for awhile. That's why God calls sinners and not the righteous.

God loves sinners, not because they sin, but because they are His children gone astray, in trouble, and threatened with irreparable misfortune if they can't find their way home. Just because the danger is so great, the joy will be that much greater in heaven when one of the lost finds the way back. God's angels know what it's like to abandon God and end up on the other side. They are a part of the tension in the events taking place on earth, so there is exultation and rejoicing when Jesus prevails and one of the lost ones returns.

However, the self-righteous, those who think they don't need improvement, don't make anyone happy, at least not anyone in heaven. Publicans and sinners understand that they can't be completely perfect all the time if what God says is true. One who really believes he's righteous also believes that God can't find any fault in him. He believes he will be accepted into heaven because he is who he is. This is what makes the self-righteous so hopeless.

Lord, is it possible that I could create happiness in heaven? I certainly know how much sorrow I have caused You with all my ungratefulness, unwilling- ness, tardiness, and cowardice. You have said, Lord Jesus, that You would be ashamed in the presence of heaven's angels if someone would deny You and not profess Your name in the presence of men. I have done just that so many times, in deed and through silence! Could there be joy in Your presence because I regret my actions and am ashamed, yet dare come to You because I have no one else to go to? I'm coming, Lord Jesus. I dare come to You because You call sinners and receive them. Praise be to You, Friend of publicans and sinners!

MONDAY AFTER THIRD SUNDAY AFTER TRINITY

Luke 15:11–32

There was a man who had two sons. Luke 15:11

We easily forget that the parable of the lost son is actually a parable of two sons; two different people, both of whom are created and loved by God. One was lost but returned. The other one stayed home yet was still lost.

The parable explains how one can become lost. The usual way is to demand your share so you can do with it as you please—be it your body, youth, health, money, or passion. Satisfying those desires will give you pleasure—for a while. Strangely enough, it's probably better the sooner it's over and you discover just how poor and miserable you really are. Maybe then you'll remember the Father you so thoughtlessly abandoned. In truth, the reason you remember Him is because you've always been in His thoughts. He has not forgotten you.

That's how the way home begins. You're regretful. You put yourself to shame. You've disgraced Him and caused Him great sorrow. Then you arrive, only to see that He's been waiting for you! You're greeted with joy. There's a feast and rejoicing in God's house. You can exchange your rags for the finest clothes. That's how Christ's righteousness is depicted, the righteousness He obtained that's enough for us to cover all our sins and allow them to disappear forever.

Then we have the other son. He was also lost, but in another way. He had always been at home, always behaved himself, and performed his duties well. Yet he had one fault that surfaced when his brother returned home: he had never loved his father or his brother. He was watching out for himself, waiting for the inheritance that was coming to him and what he could get his hands on now, which he felt wasn't much. This is the picture of the moralist who obeys God in an effort to stay out of trouble and is very conscious of the fact that he should be considered a man of higher rank in God's eyes. This is also a way of being lost, although it's a much more dangerous way and much harder to remedy.

Both sons were equally loved. They both made their father sad. However, one of them also made him happy. That's the way it is with us. We're all sinners. We've all made God sad. However, we can give Him and His angels the greatest of joy by repenting, confessing our sins, and asking for forgiveness. Then we will be welcomed into boundless happiness.

This is what the letter to the Romans is about, which we will begin with tomorrow.

Dear Father in heaven, You want to be our Father and love us, despite all the sorrow we cause You. We pray that You forgive us for loving Your gifts more than You and for so often receiving Your blessings without thanking You. We want to show our love for You. We thank You for giving us the chance to show that love by confessing that we are sorry that our love is so frail and that we haven't served You as we should. It's us You desire and not our gifts. May we always seek You and love You more than Your gifts.

TUESDAY AFTER THIRD SUNDAY AFTER TRINITY

Romans 1:1–23

For I am not ashamed of the gospel, for it is the power of God for salvation to everyone who believes, to the Jew first and also to the Greek. Romans 1:16

What is the Gospel?

Paul answers this question in his Letter to the Romans. He writes to the church in Rome sometime around AD 57, probably when he was in Corinth. As he is unknown to the recipients, he presents himself and the Gospel God has commanded him to preach everywhere among all Gentiles, even in Rome.

He says the Gospel is "the power of God for salvation." It's about God's Son, but it is more than just a doctrine. The Gospel is a force; God's intervention on earth, which leads to something we all need but cannot otherwise attain—righteousness from God. It was clear to the Jews, and to all religious people, that righteousness is something we must attain ourselves. Our conscience tells us that God knows what's right and that it's dangerous to go against God. The conclusion we form is obvious: To have the correct kind of relationship with God, we have to live the right kind of life because God loves all good people.

This is essentially correct. Paul emphasizes on several occasions that God rewards everyone according to his or her actions. Each person who does good will receive glory, honor, and peace. The only problem is that there is no good person, no one who has done everything God rightfully demands of us. All mankind is in debt to God. We all may know there is a God, simply because He's everywhere in creation. If people had nurtured that, and their conscience, as Paul talks about in the next chapter, they would've known God. However, they thought they were wise and didn't bother to thank and praise God. Their thoughts of God are a travesty. They really only believe in themselves.

It's in this world and among these people that God intervenes with His Gospel. The Gospel makes it possible for us to have a right relationship with God, despite everything else. The Gospel is God's power for salvation. In the Gospel, the righteousness we cannot achieve is manifested as a gift from heaven. You can only achieve righteousness in one way: through faith in Jesus Christ. The whole secret of redemption is behind those words.

We thank You, Lord, for Your Gospel. We thank You for acquainting us with it as children. We ask for help in understanding it and receiving it as a vibrant force and redeeming power that makes everything new. We pray for those who don't know Your Gospel and for those who misunderstand it. You once sent Your apostles to establish obedience in Your faith among all nations. Send even now Your faithful servants, men who have understood Your Gospel and feel its power and can preach it with the necessary authority and power, so we all understand that this is Your Word and not human reflection. Hallowed be Thy name. Thy kingdom come.

WEDNESDAY AFTER THIRD SUNDAY AFTER TRINITY

Romans 3:9–31

For all have sinned and fall short of the glory of God, and are justified by His grace as a gift, through the redemption that is in Christ Jesus. Romans 3:23–24

Here Paul summarizes what he said in previous chapters. He had a dispute with all those who consider themselves righteous. There isn't a righteous person on earth. There is not one man who can endure in the face of God. No one has loved God above all else and his neighbor as himself. Even if mankind hadn't committed all the sins mentioned in the psalm Paul quotes, the whole world is in debt to God. "For by works of the law no human being will be justified in His sight" (Romans 3:20). Through the Law comes the knowledge of sin. If we take that seriously, every mouth would be closed and no one would dare say they don't need forgiveness and redemption.

Then God speaks. Now there's room for the Gospel. In the Gospel something new is revealed: the righteousness that comes from God through Jesus Christ. God commissioned Him to be a means of reconciliation. There is redemption through Him. He bears all the evil in us. He carries the burden of our sins. He suffered the consequences of our desertion. He died on the cross, alone and abandoned. We all must suffer when confronted by God. Because of our sin, selfishness, and hostility toward God, He has suffered. That's how God showed His righteousness. He cannot be associated with evil. He will not be compromised by it. When He is confronted with it, it must be consumed. However, the consuming fire of His zeal wasn't aimed at us, but at the Son. God Himself took the responsibility for our wickedness. In this way He shows us that He is both righteous and wants us to be righteous, through faith in Jesus Christ. He makes no distinctions. We're all sinners. We all crucified Jesus. He died for us all. And all of us can receive complete forgiveness when we come to Him and believe in Him.

Lord and Savior, we come to You filled with shame and sorrow over the fact that You had to die to save us. We also come to You filled with gratitude and happiness over the fact that You wanted to do it for our sake. We stand before You with a debt we can never repay. Then You liberate us from that debt and allow us to stand side by side with You, liberated and joyous, as if we never broke one of God's Commandments, and as if there wasn't an ounce of selfishness or wickedness left in us. We thank You for having called us and allowed us to take part of Your Gospel and Your righteousness that we may be counted as Your own, Your called and holy ones. Praise be to You for Your love, Your cross, Your death, and Your kingdom!

THURSDAY AFTER THIRD SUNDAY AFTER TRINITY
Romans 4:13–25

For the law brings wrath. . . . That is why it depends on faith. Romans 4:15, 16

Sometimes we wonder why there's so much talk of the Jews in the Christian Church. If examined closer, we discover it is because we're so much alike—we're actually reading about our own spiritual heritage.

The Jews realized that it was out of undeserved mercy and compassion that God chose them above all others. He had given them His Law to uphold. If they did so, they would be made righteous in God's eyes and enjoy even more of His goodness. The fact that Abraham had been righteous before God through His obedience and deeds was obvious.

Many who call themselves Christian think in the same way. They know God calls them through sheer grace. However, once they're called, they focus on obedience. They've received the Law and it must be obeyed. They believe that if they do this, they are "real" Christians.

Paul says this way of thinking is wrong. Abraham was made righteous because he believed in God and trusted Him, not because of his own good works. His faith is an example of faith in Jesus, the kind of faith that allows us to receive righteousness from God. Abraham believed in a God who can give life to the dead and create life where there is none. Where there was no hope, he hoped anyway. This is exactly what we're expected to do. The Law produces wrathful judgment. The more serious we are in our wish to obey God in every way and be like Jesus—full of love, absolutely true to Himself and unselfish—the clearer it becomes that there is no plausible hope that people like us could ever be like Jesus. We can't create new life in our hearts. We can't bring forth love where there is none.

There is only hope. We must do as Abraham did and honor God by believing in His promises, not doubting them. All these promises are embodied in Jesus Christ. God tells us that He carried our sins. He came for our sin's sake. He rose again to make us righteous. God gave Him life, made Him

Lord, sent Him out once again, allowed Him to pass through time, and even come to us so He could give us the righteousness only He can give. And the promise is this: everyone who believes in Him shall not perish but have everlasting life.

I thank You, dear Lord Jesus, that belonging to You is not dependent on my half-completed, worthless deeds. My sincere intention is to be with You always and be like You. However, I'm constantly reminded of how much is lacking. Time and time again I must confess that I failed. You know that, Lord. You have seen and see all the shortcomings I can't see. I praise You for not looking at my shortcomings when I come to You. Instead, You let me exchange them for Your righteousness and those priceless clothes that can conceal all my misery and make me worthy of meeting Your Father with You. Thank You, my Lord Jesus.

FRIDAY AFTER THIRD SUNDAY AFTER TRINITY

Romans 5:1–11

Therefore, since we have been justified by faith, we have peace with God through our Lord Jesus Christ. Romans 5:1

The righteousness from God is none other than Christ Himself. We can never achieve this righteousness on our own. Paul says it is ascribed to us. We're included in it. We're a part of it. And that alters our whole situation.

We're now at peace with God because of Christ. God's peace is not a feeling. We do not experience it as an intense atmosphere of undisturbed harmony. *Peace* with God means *peace* with God. At one time we were in conflict with God. The holiness and devotion in His nature had to consume the unseemliness and selfishness in us. Christ made it possible for us to be united with Him. It didn't take place through us. It was for us ungodly creatures that Christ suffered death while we were still sinners. That's how God showed His love for us. Through Christ we can now come to God. Through Him we have obtained "this grace in which we stand" (Romans 5:2).

The foundation of grace is something that happened independent of us and outside of us. There are radical consequences for us when we believe. We are not only "saved by Him from the wrath of God" (Romans 5:9), in other words, from the fateful meeting between our impurity and God's purity, but we are also saved through the life of Christ, by being in constant connection with the living Christ. This is also a part of salvation. We literally belong to Christ, as members in His body. We're living with Him now. We can be proud and pleased with Him! We, who should be ashamed of ourselves, who didn't succeed, who stood there like failures—we can rejoice and be happy as winners on a football field. He won, and the victory is ours!

Praise be to You, Lord Jesus, that we can celebrate Your victory as our own and rejoice in it. You turned our defeat into victory. Despite the fact that we had every reason to be ashamed of ourselves,

You've allowed us to march with You in the trium-
phal procession and listen to the angels in heaven
rejoice and share this joy with You, where Your
Father's banquet hall will be full of those who
You've saved through Your tremendous victory.
We thank You and honor Your name, and we con-
sider ourselves blessed that we recognize the name
and use it as our own to call ourselves Christian.

SATURDAY AFTER THIRD SUNDAY AFTER TRINITY
Romans 5:12–21

Grace also might reign through righteousness leading to
eternal life through Jesus Christ our Lord. Romans 5:21

Through one man sin came into the world, and through
sin, death. Paul is not implying that Adam is the only sinner
held responsible before God; Eve also sinned. Paul earlier
declared that everyone is a sinner and responsible before God.
The fall has affected all of mankind. We inherited original sin,
which is a part of our nature. When the first humans deserted
God, when they began to trust in Satan and open themselves to
his spirit, Satan left a scar on human nature that will never heal.
This scar does not come from God and cannot be associated
with Him. We are therefore separated from God, deserted and

abandoned, just as the Bible describes sinners. It doesn't matter if we live one day or a hundred years—we have fallen victim to eternal death. The Bible doesn't mean only bodily death; it is also an existence apart from God, where we have lost the real meaning of life—life with God, the life we were created for—and end up in total emptiness, in the darkness outside.

All this has been changed through Christ. He is the new Adam, the head of a new mankind. Just as we all have inherited sin by nature and by being born into a world that has fallen away from God, so can we also become a part of Christ as limbs on His body and members of His Church, and be born again to a life that emanates from Him. Through Christ grace has come to His kingdom instead of death. Through Christ all is reconciled and can be forgiven. The evil in our nature no longer prevents us from being embraced by God. Our verdict makes us righteous and declares that we are a part of Christ through faith. Our debt is paid in full and our sin no longer matters.

Just as death completely and without exception reigns over all those who belong to Adam's family, grace so completely and unreservedly prevails over those who belong to Christ through faith in Him. Everything is forgiven. There is no condemnation. Nothing can separate us from God's love in Jesus Christ. Paul will explain for us exactly what this means.

Our merciful Father, we thank You for not abandoning us, although we turned away from You. You won us back. You let Your Son suffer for all the wrong we did. That's how vast Your love for us is. We thank You for that. We praise Your name. And we pray for the gift and the grace to do something day after day that shows how much we love You and that it's constantly a joy to do Your will.

FOURTH SUNDAY AFTER TRINITY

Matthew 7:1–5

Be merciful, even as your Father is merciful. Luke 6:36

This command is ridiculous! The Scriptures clearly state that no one can be like God. However, not only does Jesus say we should be as merciful as God is, but also that we should be perfect, as our Father is perfect. That's not possible!

This is exactly what we are supposed to realize and acknowledge. We are to acknowledge our sin as something serious, fatal, and overwhelming. That's our big problem, our affliction. We are created by God and for God, but we have wandered so far away that it's out of the question for us to be what we were created to be—an image of God.

As long as people assume that God doesn't expect much from them, they haven't understood that the real problem is our relationship with God. They assume that if we do good things, then God will be obligated to accept us. We deserve it. God can never demand more than we can deliver.

The truth is that God demands what is just. And what's just is His Spirit. It's boundless mercy, love, and purity. Each and every person who begins to understand who God is realizes that he cannot prevail before Him. There would be no deliverance or help to be found if God hadn't sent Christ into the world as our Savior and Redeemer.

To receive Christ and His righteousness—the gift of righteousness, as Paul put it—means that we enter a joyous world where the measurement is no longer justice, but faith. That's when you stop judging other sinners. If you don't live in this wonderful world, you see the speck in your brother's eye. You notice faults in others, and you might even want to correct them. However, you still haven't understood what loving

Christ is all about. You understand it when you're dealing with Jesus and want to be like Him and follow Him. That's when you see the log in your eye. You understand why Jesus uses such a drastic illustration. It's a question of my sin and my faults, my selfishness, my impurity, and my cowardice, as they appear when I stand before God. The log is the hopeless difference between God and me. It's the difference I speak of when I confess from my heart that I have not loved God above all things, nor my neighbor as myself.

Lord and Master, here I come, the hypocrite that I am, and ask You to take the log out of my eye, the obstacle that prevents me from seeing people as You see them. Only You, Lord, can make amends for my trespasses and fill the infinite depth separating me from God. I know You do it out of pure, boundless grace. May that grace penetrate me and fill me that I may see everyone as You see us and love us and have patience with us despite all our faults. Help me be just like You—a friend of sinners.

MONDAY AFTER
FOURTH SUNDAY
AFTER TRINITY
Romans 6:1–23

But thanks be to God, that you who were once slaves of sin have become obedient from the heart. Romans 6:17

Forgiveness that knows no boundaries, no demands, no laws; forgiveness out of sheer grace through faith without deserving it—this is the basic truth in the Gospel. People in Paul's day, as well as today, wonder: Does that mean we can sin as much as we want to? Can we live the lives we want to?

Paul answers energetically that how we live is extremely important. The way we live will show others if we've received the gift of forgiveness, the Gospel, Christ. If we've received the gift, it works within us. It can't stay inside of us without influencing us. We became a part of Christ's body through Baptism. If we believe in Him, we'll stay close to Him. We love Him. We gladly do as He says. Of course, we can fail. Of course, as disciples, we often find that we're ashamed of ourselves for not succeeding. Yet as long as we walk with Jesus, listen to Him, and don't want to be without Him, He will influence our lives.

We have become "obedient from the heart." When we lived without God and Christ, our bodies did service to impurity and iniquity. Now, as Paul says, we're members of Christ. He made contact with us and lives with us. You can be obedient out of fear—respect for "the dangerous one"—to escape bad conscience or punishment. However, it's completely different to be obedient from the heart. In the first instance, you're under the Law. You have principles, a concept of justice, morality. From these we judge others and ourselves. In the second instance, we have a Lord we love because He loves us, forgives us, saves us, and becomes our Friend.

In other words, sinning because everything is dependent on grace is proof that we don't have Jesus as our Savior. If we do have Him, we'll be as Paul said—made holy. It is not a condition, not a reward, but a consequence. We're allowed to follow Him even when things go bad, as the disciples experienced. Forgiveness remains the whole time. However, that doesn't mean we take sin lightly. On the contrary, we become obedient from the heart.

My Lord and Savior, I know it's only because of You that I'm a Christian, that I dare believe I can become a child of God, that I can pray and receive Communion. If You hadn't died for me, I would have no right to any of this. If You took Your hand away from me, I would once again be alone in darkness with everything that separates me from God. It is unbelievable that You care for me and count on me. Yet You say it Yourself and Your Word is the truth. How could I possibly throw all this away? How could I do anything but thank You, serve You, and follow You?

TUESDAY AFTER FOURTH SUNDAY AFTER TRINITY
Romans 7:7–25

For I have the desire to do what is right, but not the ability to carry it out. Romans 7:18

Our sinful nature is our great misfortune. It is this nature that makes it impossible for us to reach God in the way we consider most natural: by altering ourselves so we stop doing what's wrong and start doing God's will. Paul doesn't mean that we're incapable of doing *some* good things. Here we're talking about THE GOOD, the very nature of God, which allows us to be in accordance with Him, to be like Him in devotion and compassion. When we want it, struggle to achieve it, and wish to be it with all our hearts, we realize that we can't.

I find myself in a tragic state of split personality. Within is the urge and desire to do good. However, I find that I have another urge, one at odds with the Law I profess as correct. I find that "nothing good dwells in me" (Romans 7:18). Sin is a part of my personality. I can't liberate myself from it. It holds me prisoner, and I can't be what I want to be, namely, God's free, happy, and good child. It's this strange law inside me that is called "the flesh," which is the desire to do evil, to be selfish. It is that egotistical laziness that exists in my nature, what we usually simply call the fall.

No law can remedy this. Paul clarifies that when I take the Law seriously, it only gets worse. When I become meticulous and try to reveal sin in its innermost recesses and eradicate the desire to do evil, that's when the desire comes to life. When I live under the Law and believe that the condition to come to God is to succeed in exterminating all evil and become blameless and unpunishable in His presence, that's when sin begins to overflow. It seeps out all over. I notice that selfishness exists in everything I do, as does self-centeredness or pride or impurity. Finally, I end up in the misery Paul describes here. Oh, poor me! Who can save me from this doomed body?

For those who want to be made righteous through their own good works, in other words, by doing that which can reasonably be expected of them, this is a severe oration. They usually accuse Christianity of turning everything into sin. The truth is that when God is allowed to direct us, He shows us that on this earth, sin is everywhere. This is *exactly* why God provides another way to His house than the way of morality and excellence. This is the way Paul points to, when, while speaking of our powerlessness, he bursts out in joy: Thanks be to God through Jesus Christ, our Lord!

> *Yes, Lord,* thanks be to You for seeing hope in hope-lessness. I thank You for the wonderful thing You did when You sent Your Son, Jesus, and gave us the righteousness that exists only with You. May I be so happy about Your unfathomable gift that I become a good child in my heart. I thank You that You will someday completely liberate me from my old Adam and for having patience with me because he still exists. Thank You for allowing me to be Your child, through Jesus Christ, my Lord.

WEDNESDAY AFTER FOURTH SUNDAY AFTER TRINITY

Galatians 3:19–29

The law was our guardian until Christ came, in order that we might be justified by faith. Galatians 3:24

What is the purpose of the Law? Why was it given to us if it can't get us to God? The usual assumption is that God approves of us if we keep His Commandments. That's correct, Paul answers, if there was a law that "could give life" (Galatians 3:21). He means a law that could unite us with

God so His life flows in us. However, it is just the opposite: The Law is death. It reveals inexorably that we are criminals, hopelessly separated from God. Whatever we try to do, the Law exposes the wrong in it. The inadequacy lies in devotion to God and love to our neighbor. "But the Scripture imprisoned everything under sin" (Galatians 3:22). No distinction is made. Not one of us will be vindicated when the Law is put to the test (the correct test!). We can never truthfully say: "Lord, all You commanded, we have done."

On the other hand, the Law can lead us to Jesus. We don't come to Him as righteous individuals, but as exposed sinners, disciples who have failed, poor in spirit. Yet we are greeted with the unbelievable message that we are blessed and that the kingdom of heaven belongs to us. We are God's children for Christ's sake.

That applies to all believers—no exceptions. Although there are many differences among us, we are all one in Christ, united as members in His body. Paul enumerates several of the differences that are most prevalent, such as differences in nationality, social status, and gender. These differences are not invalidated. However, all the different members are now *one* body. They are all one in Christ. Their differences no longer divide them. All the members are equally important. The person who received one shilling is just as important as the one who received ten shillings. Each receives in accordance to his gift, in its place, and after his Lord's desire and command. However, all the members serve one another. What Paul describes here is the unity of the Spirit in the bond of peace. We are one body, one spirit, and have been called to live in one and the same hope, that which belongs to our call—"one Lord, one faith, one baptism, one God and Father of all" (Ephesians 4:5–6).

My Lord and Savior, You make us all one through faith. Help me to understand that I am one with all who believe in You. When You bring us into Your fellowship and allow us to be a part of You, we become one with one another. Help us to see all differences in Your light. Help me to be joyful over the gifts others have that I don't because they are gifts from You. Help me to be excited about the tasks that weren't given to me with a warm and interested heart. They are tasks You have given Your people. Send Your loving Spirit, He who bears witness to You, to make us all one in the true faith and true love.

THURSDAY AFTER FOURTH SUNDAY AFTER TRINITY
1 Corinthians 1:1–16

God is faithful, by whom you were called into the fellowship of His Son, Jesus Christ our Lord. 1 Corinthians 1:9

After having completed the first section of Romans, which we will return to, we now continue with the first Letter to the Corinthians. It was written in Ephesus a few years before the letter to the Romans, and is completely different in character. Paul doesn't provide a coherent account of salvation here. Instead, he speaks of several problems that have been bothering the Corinthians, allowing us to understand the difficulties of living as Christians in a heathen city.

What is one allowed to do, and what should one avoid? It was even more difficult to overcome whatever was unchristian within the congregation. If you believe that Christians are basically faultless, it will do you well to read Corinthians. Here we find samples of all the weaknesses and infirmities inherent in people.

Despite their actions, Paul didn't hesitate to call them Christian. They are called by God Himself, called to be together with His Son, called to the kingdom of forgiveness. They have heeded the call and arrived. They are "hallowed in Christ Jesus"—everything is forgiven through faith in Him. They have washed away their sins and had their debts paid. Now they have to live a life worthy of the call they received, as pure children in the house of God. That's why Paul immediately begins to admonish and reprimand them directly after reminding them of what they own in Christ.

The first thing he addresses is their internal dissension. Different factions and movements had evolved among them. As so often was the case, it's because each had their own teacher they admired, each one of them a good man but none of them the only bearer of the truth. There are those who faithfully follow Paul, but he forbids them to quote him if it means that they distance themselves from other apostles or their assistants. It's *Christ* who has died for them. They have been baptized in Him. His truth cannot be reduced to what one apostle received the mercy to put forward. We have to listen to the whole message in all its glory. What Paul stresses here is exactly what we confess every Sunday: that the Church of Christ is universal or catholic, which means "all-embracing," "all-encircling," "all-inclusive." In other words, it is much more than any single human being can express. We can possibly understand a portion of this glory; we can never be allowed to believe that that portion is the whole truth. Christ always has more to give.

Dear Lord and Savior, we pray we will see enough of Your truth so we will have the right faith in You, love You with all our hearts, and serve You wherever we are. We thank You for already having seen so much. May the most important message be written in our hearts so we never forget it. We thank You for everything You want to show us. We thank You for having encompassed everything in Your Word. May Your Spirit make the Word alive for us. May it make us so knowledgeable and experienced that we may never, in disbelief, reject that which is true and never, in gullibility, accept that which is wrong.

FRIDAY AFTER
FOURTH SUNDAY
AFTER TRINITY
1 Corinthians 1:17–31

The word of the cross . . . is the power of God.
1 Corinthians 1:18

Paul reminds us that we shouldn't divide ourselves into factions or movements, but instead listen to the complete apostolic message. There is only *one* Gospel and it is about Christ, about the cross and redemption through faith in the crucified Lord. Talk like this is foolishness to the world. For the moralists, it's offensive. They think it is obvious that you can *deserve* to come to God through good works. For rationalists, it's foolishness that God could become man in the first place, that He would die, and that Jesus would make atonement for our sins. Nothing coincides with their preconceived ideas of God. The fact that God could differ from our idea of Him has never been made clear to them.

However, it is now obvious that the talk about the cross is God's power of salvation for those who receive it in faith. It's something that affects us, something that shows it's a reality by intervening in our lives. We can't see God. However, we can encounter Him in such a way that there is no doubt who we're dealing with. That happens through the Gospel.

Paul realized that the work of God is more easily received and understood by those who are outcasts or belittled in the world. Paul appealed to the Corinthians' own experience. There weren't many powerful, distinguished, or wise of the world who were called. Instead, God chose those who were foolish, insignificant, and despised. Jesus often speaks of this: God has concealed the Gospel from those who think they're wise and revealed it to those who mean nothing in this world, the common and unsophisticated people, those who agree with God when He speaks to the heart.

It is good to give thanks to the Lord, to sing praises to Your name, O Most High; to declare Your steadfast love in the morning and Your faithfulness by night. For You, O Lord, have made me glad by Your work; at the works of Your hands I sing for joy. How great are Your works, O Lord! Your thoughts are very deep! The dull man cannot know, the ignorant cannot understand this. But You, O Lord, are on high forever. You have shown strength with Your arm, You have scattered the proud in the imagination of their hearts. You

have filled the hungry with good things, and the
rich You sent away empty. You have given light to
those who sit in darkness to guide our feet into the
way of peace. (From Psalm 92 and Luke 1.)

SATURDAY AFTER
FOURTH SUNDAY
AFTER TRINITY
1 Corinthians 2:1–16

But we impart a secret and hidden wisdom of God.
1 Corinthians 2:7

God's kingdom is one of forgiveness. It is where we
receive boundless forgiveness and forgive without reflecting
on our own perception of righteous justice. For the rest of
the world, this is inconceivable and foolish. When the world
is at its best, it professes "what's right is right." That's one of
the reasons many of those who are wise in the flesh, powerful
and respected, have a hard time accepting the Gospel. Just as
many common people do!

Paul speaks here of man as he is by nature. In the original
text it's called the "mentality" of man, and this word explains
men with a normal, human mentality. They possess the spiritual equipment that normal human beings have. They lack,
however, God's Spirit and all the knowledge and experience
the Spirit can give us.

People like this can be religious, but not Christian. They can know as much about God as they can imagine without the help of Christ and the Gospel. They may have met God in nature and in their conscience; they therefore believe in a moral order of things. They're convinced that morals exist and that we obtain human value by being moral individuals; in other words, we become righteous through works.

It's very tempting to interpret the Gospel in such a way as this. Paul felt that temptation when he preached in Corinth among all those savvy people. He decided to stick to what was of vital importance, however offensive that would seem, and "know nothing among you except Jesus Christ and Him crucified" (1 Corinthians 2:2). It's this speech that is the power and wisdom of God. That speech is truly wisdom, a true and accurate description of the world, and a deep and realistic look on life.

However, that wisdom is unattainable as long as we don't get a glimpse of God's secrets. It's not something we can be aware of, it's something "no eye has seen, nor ear heard, nor the heart of man imagined" (1 Corinthians 2:9). We often use those words to describe what will happen after the resurrection, when God makes everything new again. Here, however, Paul uses these words to describe something God has already revealed: the mystery of redemption, about Christ becoming man and dying for us and our becoming His members and receiving His righteousness. Paul says this is not human wisdom. He realizes that he and the other apostles can preach the Gospel because they have "the Spirit who is from God, that we might understand the things freely given us by God" (1 Corinthians 2:12). It's important for us today to reflect over what Paul says: the apostles preached the Gospel with words "taught by the Spirit" (1 Corinthians 2:13).

Beloved Holy Spirit, You who solely can teach us to see and comprehend God's wisdom, help us also to understand it. Instruct us, as only You can, by showing us who we are. Allow us to see the log in our own eye. Instruct us in the whole truth as to what separates us from God. Allow us to see the depth of God's plan of salvation, into the innermost parts of His fatherly heart that loved us so much that He gave His only Son so we could become His children. Give us the wisdom to understand God's secrets and become prisoners of His love.

FIFTH SUNDAY AFTER TRINITY
Luke 5:1–11

Depart from me, for I am a sinful man, O Lord. Luke 5:8

Peter stood face-to-face before Christ. He felt unworthy, or even more accurately, he realized he was unworthy. The edifying thing is that the early Christians could talk about it without being shaken in their faith. Both Peter and Paul, the princes of apostles, were unworthy. Paul was a persecutor and an enemy of Christ when he was called. Peter was a common man, a sinner like anyone else, who, despite his Lord's great love and trust in him, denied Him when he was put to the test. The first church understood that you don't have to be anyone special to be a Christian. The Church doesn't rest on our morals or intelligence. The Church is a church of sinners, but also a source of forgiveness, where one can get help and be cleansed. They used to compare it to a hospital, where Christ gathered all who were hopelessly sick and saved them from a certain death.

The situation is different when one is called to be a disciple. Peter was a common man, and he was called while he was working as everyone else. Jesus didn't ask him about his faith. He just asked Peter to follow Him. After that it was up to Peter to listen, learn, and see. Paul, on the other hand, had already heard and seen most of what could be learned from the Old Testament and the Law. However, he had never understood God's secret wisdom, what God's plan was, and how He intended to implement it. The crucial insight came to Paul when he understood that Jesus really was the Messiah, God's Son. At that time he had been a disciple of God's Word, but not of Jesus.

However God calls us, He calls us for this: to be with Jesus and learn from Him, to live with Jesus and receive what only He can give. We might not be able to receive everything right from the beginning. That's why we usually say that a disciple is someone who listens to God's Word and prays to come to the faith or remain in the faith. The main thing is to stay with Jesus and follow Him. He takes care of the rest. You might not understand and comprehend everything at once. You may not even understand the most important things. Peter could hardly have understood what Jesus meant when He said He would be a fisher of men. But Peter trusted in Jesus and followed Him. That's what a disciple does.

Lord Jesus, I thank You for calling sinners and not the righteous. This way I know that You're serious

*when You call me. I had every reason to do as
Peter did and ask You to depart from me because
I am who I am. You know, however, that I would
be heartbroken if You did. The sun would no
longer shine and life would lose its meaning. My
heart rejoices over the fact that You are a Friend
who receives sinners and allows them to stay with
You. You can use them and turn them into fishers
of men and allow them to be a blessing to others.
Dear Lord, may I also be a blessing through You.*

MONDAY AFTER FIFTH SUNDAY AFTER TRINITY
1 Corinthians 3:1–23

For God's temple is holy, and you are that temple.
1 Corinthians 3:17

This is what Paul announces to the Christians in Corinth.
He wasn't implying that they were model Christians. On the
contrary, there is no one Paul rebukes more in his letters for
their way of living than the people of Corinth. Despite this,
he states that they are a temple of God. When they were
baptized, they were incorporated into Christ. They became a
temple to the Spirit. They were consecrated, just as a church
is consecrated. A church like that, however, can be desecrated
and used for things other than God's house. This can happen
with Christians as well, for example, profanity, sacrilegious

activity, something shocking and reprehensible. "If anyone destroys God's temple, God will destroy him" (1 Corinthians 3:17).

That a Christian is sanctified in this way and dedicated to be a temple for the Spirit doesn't mean that the work is done. It's more like a field, Paul says, or a building that's being erected. Apostles, pastors, and parishioners are God's co-workers.

From the beginning a Christian can be a babe in Christ. Babies need milk. They can't handle solid food. That's also the way it can be with those who are babes in Christ. They don't understand the deepest wisdoms in the Gospel. For example, people who have become disciples and really want to be Christians may still not be in the right state of mind to understand the speech about righteousness from God. It's obvious to them that in order to be children of God, they have to stop sinning and be born again. It's also obvious to them that the improvement consists of being better and doing better. Their hearts want to follow Jesus. They haven't understood, however, that there is only one possible path to salvation, namely, to accept what Jesus has done for them, despite everything. They can understand it from a purely theological perspective, but they haven't understood it in their hearts. Giving them such milk to drink could mean allowing them to take in as much as they can understand. They do their best by improving themselves and living according to Jesus' admonitions. That's when they discover how inadequate they are and what Jesus really means. God is the one who works in the field and builds His Church.

Lord, I know no one can lay a different foundation than that which is laid. I know that what had to be done for me to be saved has already been done. Help me to build my life on that foundation. Help me to trust in the right way in what You've done so I don't want to try to do something better, then dare hope that You'll take care of me. Help me build onto the foundation with things that come from You so I'm formed by Your love, filled with Your goodness, warmed by Your mercy, and do the things You want me to do. Best of all, all the time I'll know that I'm Yours, not because of my conquests or improvements, but because You love me and gave Your life for me.

TUESDAY AFTER FIFTH SUNDAY AFTER TRINITY
1 Corinthians 4:1–21

When reviled, we bless; when persecuted, we endure; when slandered, we entreat. 1 Corinthians 4:12–13

The apostle is the trustworthy steward of God's secrets, and a steward is always loyal. Paul knows that loyalty is his first duty as well as his most sincere aspiration. He doesn't inquire about what other people say about him. He was obviously criticized and belittled in Corinth, although he didn't care. He knows who will be the final judge in his life, and he will remain faithful to Him. Paul knows he's a sinner. Even if he's not conscious of it, he needs forgiveness. That's exactly what he preaches: Christ died for us all so we could become

God's children through faith.

However, Paul says, God's kingdom does not consist of words. Christianity isn't what we call an ideology or outlook on life. It's not just a knowledge or conviction that things behave in a certain way. It's a force. It means that God intervenes and creates. Something new comes into the world and into our lives. This new thing is God's secret and the new life in forgiveness. The Law ended where Christ began. We are allowed to be God's children for Christ's sake and that fills us with joy every day. For the world and for all the Christians who continue to think like the world thinks—and there were plenty of those in Corinth—it's incomprehensible. For them it's foolishness to believe you can live without standing up for your rights and giving an eye for an eye when you're treated badly. Yet that's how Paul lived. He knows every Christian lives like that: never perfectly, yet in a way that shows something new has come. Paul can point out simple facts: He was reviled and blessed. He was slandered, and he spoke good words. He was persecuted, and he endured without giving an eye for an eye. He did as Jesus said: bear your cross every day and follow your Master.

As Christians we live in the kingdom of forgiveness, where retaliation and the common order of justice no longer apply. Living as followers of Jesus often means being strangers in the world, something people find absurd, provocative, unrealistic, or ridiculous. At the same time we bear witness to Christ and open the eyes of those who are "of the truth."

Dear Lord Jesus, help me to be a fool in the right way, a fool for Your sake, a humble and thankful fool in Christ. I know Your foolishness is superior to all the wisdom in the world. People mocked You when You were on the cross. They thought You

*were powerless. They thought they were right.
That's when You completed God's work with a
victory. Right there, God's wisdom paved the way
for a boundless blessing. While You suffered and
were downtrodden, You gave life and forgiveness to
the world. May I never be afraid of suffering that
leads to peace and reconciliation. May I be joyous and thankful and believe in Your power, even
when others think I'm throwing away what is right
and can't understand what's best for me. You are
what's right and what's best for me, and that's all
I need to know.*

WEDNESDAY AFTER FIFTH SUNDAY AFTER TRINITY

1 Corinthians 5:1–13

Cleanse out the old leaven that you may be a new lump.
1 Corinthians 5:7

Paul doesn't mince words when he rebukes the
Corinthians. We may be appalled by his outspokenness. If not
his words, then we might be appalled by all the sins and dis-
graceful things that existed among the Christians in Corinth.
Probably the strangest thing is that he still speaks to them as
Christians. That's the basis for his admonishments. You are
called. You are unleavened. That's because you are a part of
the Passover Lamb, Christ, who was offered for your sake.

See to it that you cleanse out the old leaven.

The first thing Paul discusses is fornication. He knows it separates man from Christ if man accepts it, excuses it, and begins explaining it as natural. Fornication in the Bible includes all sexual relations outside of marriage. Sexual relations exist to link one man and one woman into a new fellowship (one flesh) with mutual responsibility for each other and for the children God gives them. This outlook was as contrary to the antic heathen opinion as it is contrary to the secular opinion of today. If you perceive life as your lucky chance, where the main objective is get out of it as much enjoyment as possible, then sexual activity becomes one of the most important objectives.

The Gospel, however, states uncompromisingly that this type of behavior separates man from God. There is forgiveness for these sins just as well as for other sins. There is also forgiveness for the sinner who is fighting and has no victories to his name. Jesus' word about adultery of the heart makes us all sinners and puts an end to all self-satisfaction. What makes the judgment worse, however, is any attempt to compromise and make the sin innocent and acceptable.

Paul says the worst thing about the Corinthians is their arrogance and the fact that they haven't shown sorrow, despite events that should have shaken them up. There's a limit to how long a person can be treated as an erring Christian before he must be treated as one who has left the fellowship of Christ and His Church. Jesus Himself spoke of this; how one should talk to an erring brother: first alone, then with a witness, and then before the congregation. If he doesn't listen, you'll end up having the same relationship with him as you did with those who are outsiders. Besides this, there is another step Paul mentions a few times. In some cases, Paul and the congregation delivered men to Satan. That's equivalent to what later was called excommunication.

A person is excluded from the Church of Christ and from the fellowship of Christ, from His righteousness, forgiveness, and protection. That means being delivered into the darkness that he once left. Paul, however, still has hope and good intentions; the person is baptized and can be saved in the day of the Lord Jesus, just by being able to experience what it's like to be separated from Him and have his eyes opened, as did the prodigal son when he was sent to tend the pigs.

Lord Jesus, help us to love all sinners and hate all sin. May we never excuse that which can't be excused and never pretend that everything's all right when it's contrary to Your will. Help us to help others, and to be kind without deceiving people into believing everything is all right. Also, help us to act wisely and justly toward all those who are our brothers in the faith, but who are acting wrongly toward You and Your Church. Have mercy on us and all sinners, for the sake of Your infinite mercy.

THURSDAY AFTER FIFTH SUNDAY AFTER TRINITY

1 Corinthians 6:1–20

You were bought with a price. So glorify God in your body.
1 Corinthians 6:20

You are bought. Christ has paid the ransom with His own blood. You have received the gift. You have been baptized. You are now a member of the Body of Christ. You shall now live to God's glory. You will glorify God in your body. What's living in you is a temple to the Holy Spirit.

That's what Paul argues when he chastises. Once again we learn what the Gospel is about. It comes to us as a gift, but a gift that has radical consequences in every aspect of our life. We don't make ourselves pure, worthy, sincere, and loving. It begins with Jesus loving us, regardless how impure and unworthy we may be. That love takes hold of us. We come to faith in Him. We become His. Now that whole new life—the life we live with Him—begins in earnest.

When you get so much for nothing, the natural temptation is to think that everything will remain the same. That's what happened in Corinth, and they had plenty of arguments that sounded evangelical. In reference to fornication, they referred to something Paul had mentioned about food. He explained that all food was pure; there was just a small portion of creation we received so we could survive on earth. God's kingdom doesn't consist of food and drink. They used that argument to defend fornication. Sex was something natural, something that belonged to this world. A liberated Christian could also be liberated regarding sex. Paul, however, made it emphatically clear that this is a fateful mistake. The body is not meant for immorality. Sexuality isn't merely something physical. It affects the innermost part of our being. Neither immoral people nor adulterers can inherit the kingdom of God. Paul mentions both of these groups, so no one will believe that the Sixth Commandment applies only to those who are married. Let no one be fooled, Paul warns, because this is to be taken seriously.

We're not only talking about the Sixth Commandment, however. Paul hurries to point out several serious instances where evidence shows they weren't living the new life in Christ. He also points out sins that can be more or less accepted by decent, common, middle class individuals, such as the love of money, the right to your day in court, and so forth. Once again we see that the Gospel's world doesn't coincide with the world of common justice and law. Paul asks, why not rather suffer wrong? Why not let others do you harm? Do you really believe someone can harm you if you belong to Christ?

Lord Jesus, teach me to so completely trust in You that what You say becomes obvious to me and the way the world thinks loses its power over me. May I be so completely in Your grasp that I don't need to assert myself or be afraid that people will take something away from me that I really need. When I lose something, help me to speak with You about it. If I am unjustly treated, help me to choose You as my lawyer and advisor. May I see how rich and safe and well cared for I am, as long as I have You. I thank You, Lord. Help me to do this in all of life's circumstances.

FRIDAY AFTER
FIFTH SUNDAY
AFTER TRINITY
1 Corinthians 7:1–16

God has called you to peace. 1 Corinthians 7:15

He who believes in Christ is at peace with God. All is forgiven. The believer lives in a kingdom full of mercy and grace. God doesn't treat him according to what he deserves. God doesn't treat others according to what they deserve either. The believer doesn't have to stick to his guns and fight for his right.

This is one of God's great secrets and considered as foolishness to the world. The world assumes that a life like that can't work, that life is dependent on everyone asserting themselves. In other words, you have to do it yourself if you don't want to perish.

That law doesn't apply in Christ's kingdom.

Life functions there in a new and better way. In all aspects, it's obvious if a person is living in the new kingdom. It might take time for him to learn the new way of life, but if he remains close to Christ, he will learn it.

In 1 Corinthians, we see how Paul tries to explain to these new Christians, one step at a time, what this new life entails. He received several questions to answer. One of them was about sexuality in marriage. Some obviously maintained that there is no place for sex if you intend to live a radical life for Christ. Paul answered that he values celibacy highly—he lived in celibacy. He knew, however, that was because of a special gift of grace. He didn't demand it of anyone else. Abstinence must be the exception to the rule in a marriage, "except perhaps by agreement for a limited time" (1 Corinthians 7:5). Man and wife are one. One spouse cannot unilaterally decide something that affects them both. What Paul says must sound quite offensive to those who consider it a rule for unconverted and selfish people, who only think of themselves. Paul, however, is speaking to Christians who feel love and consideration for the other spouse is a natural thing. Here he points out one aspect of that love: you can't assume your spouse can live in a state of abstinence just because you can.

On the question of divorce Paul refers to Christ's words, which are very clear. A wife should not divorce herself from her husband. Neither should a husband disown his wife. What if one of the spouses doesn't follow the commandments of Christ, doesn't believe in Him, wants to get a divorce, and turns marriage into daily misery? Then they can get a divorce, Paul says. God doesn't force anyone to keep a non-believing spouse who only wants to be set free—not even if it's possible to convert another person.

There is, however, also the opposite extreme that Paul does not condone, namely, that you should always divorce yourself from an unbeliever. That idea was probably quite prevalent in the first church. They knew that the whole world outside of the church was saturated with wickedness. It was a contamination they had to avoid. How would things work out if one of the spouses were a heathen? Paul answers in the same way John expressed: He that is yours is stronger than that which is the world's. When both forces meet in a home, Christ defeats the power of evil. The newborn children are baptized and are no longer heathens. Also, the other spouse is consecrated, not in the sense of being saved, free from sin, driven by God's Spirit, but consecrated in the sense of the evil forces being at a disadvantage. A believer in Christ can confidently live with an unbeliever.

Dear Lord, teach us the great art of living off Your goodness so we might become good and radiate

warmth and kindness. Teach us that it is more
blessed to give than to receive, and that we don't
become rich by taking and hoarding but by giving
and spending. We get something for nothing every
moment in our lives. Teach us to give something
for nothing and be joyous and happy to do it.

SATURDAY AFTER FIFTH SUNDAY AFTER TRINITY
Matthew 5:1–19

Blessed are the poor in spirit, for theirs is the kingdom of heaven. Matthew 5:3

These words at the beginning of the Sermon on the Mount could also serve as its heading. The Sermon on the Mount is often misunderstood. It's part of "the solid food" you can't give to those who are children in Christ. The lessons from the Sermon on the Mount are not the starting point; they're the goal. The Sermon on the Mount speaks of how it will be in Christ's new kingdom, the kingdom of forgiveness. It speaks of the new righteousness that prevails where Christ has taken responsibility for everything and can forgive everything—where those who receive Christ's righteousness begin to live a new life, not after the old justice but after the new covenant of grace, forgiveness, and mercy.

First, Jesus talks about those who belong to the world's kingdom. They're weak in the spirit and regret their mistakes and lack of love. They're hungry and thirsty for righteousness. That's exactly why they can receive righteousness from God. The fact that they live in forgiveness allows them to forgive, be merciful, gentle, and peace loving. They can rejoice in the midst of persecution and slander. They are the salt and light in the world. They don't have to exert themselves to be that. It isn't demanded of them. That's just how they are when they're living in the kingdom of forgiveness.

This doesn't mean that Jesus has abolished the Law. Jesus didn't come to abolish but to complete. God doesn't alter His nature. Through time He is equally righteous. He remains in an eternal and unchangeable contrast to everything that's evil. He has carried out and fulfilled the Law. On the cross He could say: It is finished. He was obedient in every way all His life. The great miracle of redemption is that He has taken our disobedience upon Himself and granted us righteousness. We can be God's children despite the fact that we are sinners. However, we can only be righteous in the kingdom of forgiveness, when we live in fellowship with Jesus. Doing that influences every aspect of our lives, even in this world, even though we still possess our old Adam.

The Law has not been abolished. A Christian knows it's still valid. A disciple who revokes the least of God's Commandments and tells people they no longer need regard it will be counted as one of the least in heaven. The Commandments are still valid. However, they are no longer the *condition* to come to God. The question is no longer if we have kept His Commandments. The question is: Do we believe in Christ and go to Him? If we do, we will also follow Him, be like Him, and do God's will.

My Lord and Savior, there is so much I need to pray for. There is so much I feel I can't do and *don't understand. In the final analysis, however, there is one thing that is the answer to all my questions and the aid in all my difficulties—You. When You are with me, I can deal with everything else. With You, complicated things become simple and difficult things become easy; I can even succeed with the impossible. Therefore I pray: Remain with me, O Lord Jesus.*

SIXTH SUNDAY AFTER TRINITY
Matthew 5:20–26

Everyone who is angry with his brother will be liable to judgment. Matthew 5:22

Christ did not abolish the Law. On the contrary, He showed us that it applies, not only as rules for outward appearances, such as the laws of a country, but also inwardly, deep in the heart. That's what He teaches us in the Sermon on the Mount.

His first example is the Fifth Commandment: You shall not murder. Even civil law commands this. The laws in a society define what is meant by murder and manslaughter and what type of punishment is necessary. The danger here is that a person can believe he's fulfilled all the criteria for righteousness as long as he hasn't done anything punishable by the laws of society. Many believe that Christianity roughly means living a correct and decent life in accordance with existing laws and established customs. This is the mistake Jesus sets out to correct. Murder is not only killing and shedding blood. The desire to do it is just as bad. The same goes for the milder variations we can think of to get at people, like scolding them or subjecting them to psychological terror by teasing them, making fun of them or being impertinent. The punishment doesn't stop at what a court of law on earth can impose. The ultimate consequence is eternal separation from God.

A person can be completely righteous as far as civil laws and demands go, yet still be lost to God forever. The scribes and Pharisees were convinced they did all that was demanded of them. Many people within the Christian Church share the same conviction. Jesus says, however, that if we have no more righteousness than that, we will never enter the kingdom of heaven. If we live our lives after the laws of justice and revenge, we will be judged after those laws, and that puts us in a very poor position.

What, then, is the better righteousness? Jesus doesn't give us the answer here. In the Sermon on the Mount He speaks very little about it, but it is implied everywhere. There is no other path than the one that leads to the kingdom of forgiveness. We have to understand how bad it is, so we become poor in the spirit and start to hunger and thirst after righteousness. Then we can discover the precious pearl. We can understand why Jesus invites us to come to Him. We can receive His righteousness and begin to live with Him. That's when we can reconcile with a brother without demanding judgment against him. That's when we accept a speedy reconciliation without having to wait for the other party to confess to what he's done wrong and ask for forgiveness. We have been acquitted and escaped imprisonment, despite the fact that we were guilty of both rage and harsh words. The only gate available where you can escape imprisonment leads you to the kingdom of forgiveness. There we live a new life.

Lord, teach me continuously how much I've received for
nothing and how much I continue to receive without deserving it. May I remember this the moment
I have a bone to pick with someone. When I'm
angry and annoyed, help me remember all the reasons You have to be angry with me yet allow me
to live in a state of constant forgiveness. I couldn't
live without that. Let that penetrate me so it
becomes a part of my nature to do as You do, and
choose to suffer rather than repay evil with evil.

MONDAY AFTER SIXTH SUNDAY AFTER TRINITY
Matthew 5:27–48

You therefore must be perfect, as your heavenly Father is
perfect. Matthew 5:48

This verse is the summary of God's Law as Jesus interprets
it for us in the Sermon on the Mount. What we've heard
so many times before is confirmed: nothing can be attained
through the Law. No creature of creation is worthy to meet
God through the Law. What becomes clear through the Law
is the knowledge of sin. All Jesus says here shows us this. Even
those who outwardly never committed adultery or swore
falsely are in violation of the Law, for they have the desire
to sin in their hearts. Those who are known to be jovial and
friendly have nothing to be proud of. They're friendly when

it suits them and happy and pleasant when they're welcome and popular. "What's so strange about that? Don't the heathens behave the same way?"

The Sermon on the Mount does not provide us with the norms necessary to lead a good and upright life in this world. Instead, it shows us how far away we are from God, although we try to live an upright life by human standards.

One could make the same mistake as the scribes and believe we've attained this knowledge in order to shape up, start over, make stricter rules for our lives, and finally become the sort of person we should be. That's not the way to God, however. The whole New Testament tells us that. No one comes to the Father but through the Son. The only ones who can endure are those who become a part of Christ and in Him receive complete forgiveness.

What happens through Christ is that the right to be a child of God is no longer *conditional* on the Law. However, as an expression of what's right, the Law hasn't been abolished. It's a reflection of God's nature. That's how we live in God's kingdom. This is right, this and nothing else. God is perfect. We should be too.

We accept all of this and want to live like this if we belong to Christ. Just because everything is forgiven and we still are God's children, we still want to live as God's children and make our Father happy.

Therefore, we take seriously Jesus' admonishments about the purity of our hearts, about a faithful, lifelong marriage, about throwing away that which is tempting, however dear we consider it and however necessary it may seem. We are careful to be truthful in what we say. We begin to understand the glorious secret of not resisting an injustice but repaying evil with good. We start doing what we otherwise thought impossible: loving our enemies, praying for our persecutors, and being friends with those we don't want to be friends with.

Remember: This is a consequence, a fruit, a result of forgiveness, not a condition for it.

Lord Jesus, I realize I can never be right before You and can never have anything to plead for, except You. If I believe that everything can be as it used to be because You're so good and forgiving, I'm wrong. If I believe I have to be completely different because You're so strict, I'm wrong again. Only You can teach me Your truths and allow me to receive forgiveness so completely and for nothing that I rejoice and am willing to do anything. Help me, Lord. Give me a faith that is active in love. Glory be to Your name.

TUESDAY AFTER SIXTH SUNDAY AFTER TRINITY

1 Corinthians 7:17–40

And those who deal with the world as though they had no dealings with it. For the present form of this world is passing away. 1 Corinthians 7:31

The one who owns a portion of Christ's kingdom still lives in the world. He has, however, a new relationship with the world. Before, it was the world that brought meaning to his life. He didn't really count on anything else. The idea was to survive, seize his opportunities, and try to make a better life for himself. However, when he realizes what life's all about, these things are no longer of vital importance. There are many other important things that give content and meaning to life and, in the final analysis, are decisive in whether a person has "succeeded."

Therefore, Paul gives us the guiding principle that everyone should remain in the state in which he was called. A profession, a position in the community, a place in the family, normally implies God's calling. Here is a mission I've received from God. I'm in the company of people I can serve and help. I have the opportunity to create something good in certain situations. There are situations, however, that are so corrupt and evil that I have to free myself from them to be able to serve God. When I serve Christ, I begin to attach new values to other calls, such as professions and positions in society. All Christians are servants of Christ; they belong to Him.

Paul isn't speaking here about society and our place in it. He does that in his letter to the Romans (we'll come back to that later). Here he's expecting the second coming of Christ to happen soon enough that he and his contemporaries will experience it. That's obvious when we read his advice concerning marriage and everything else that touches our existence in the world. He emphasizes, however, that this is only advice. Some of his advice concerns relationships we have no comparison to today. Such relationships occurred where men and women, married or not, lived together in celibacy during times of prayer and fasting, as in a monastery. (These probably were the people Paul subsequently referred to with a word that, in our translation, freely—and incorrectly?—was expressed as "your unmarried daughter." Paul liked that, but emphasized that you didn't sin if you abandoned that kind of life.)

Later, Paul expected that he would die before Christ's

coming and that the Church would have to prepare itself for a longer period of waiting. That meant new attitudes regarding the work on earth, but it doesn't change our basic Christian outlook: we regard the world as something that is solely of temporary importance.

Lord Jesus, here I am in the middle of everyday life, surrounded by everything I need to sustain life and that causes me so much toil and so much joy. In the midst of it all, You're also there with Your kingdom and all the wonderful things only You can give. I thank You that in the middle of all this, You call me right where I am. Help me see everything as a means to serve You and the possibility to be of help, joy, and benefit to the people You allow me to interact with. Help me cultivate all this as a good trustee in Your service.

WEDNESDAY AFTER SIXTH SUNDAY AFTER TRINITY
1 Corinthians 8:1–13

Knowledge puffs up, but love builds up. 1 Corinthians 8:1

The Corinthians asked Paul a question about the meat used as offerings to idols. Only a portion of the meat was offered in the temple; the rest could be sold to a butcher, who then sold it to the public. Part of the meat could go to those who offered it, maybe an individual, an association, or an order, and any of these could have a banquet and invite a Christian. The Corinthians wanted to know if it was acceptable to eat this kind of meat.

Some were convinced that eating this meat was unthinkable. Idols were evil spirits, and whatever was offered to them was consecrated to serving evil. Therefore, they felt that eating the meat was the same as having fellowship with demons. However, others had more knowledge and regarded themselves as more enlightened. They knew idols didn't exist. They knew God created meat. Therefore, it was edible. We might see a parallel to this problem when we think about absolutism. For example, some people feel alcohol is something evil in any circumstance. It disturbs relationships with others.

Paul agrees with the "enlightened" that there is no other God but the one true God. There may be evil spirits, but they don't affect God's good gifts of creation. "For everything created by God is good, and nothing is to be rejected if it is received with thanksgiving" (1 Timothy 4:4). Knowing these facts, however, is not enough. One can know that God alone is God, yet have no part in the life that comes from Him. That knowledge is inflating. It makes people self-confident. *Life* in God—what Paul here calls love—builds up and creates faith and fellowship with God and man. The right kind of knowledge is very important. Even more important, however, is the devotion that comes through fellowship with Christ.

When applied to food and drink, neither determines our situation with God. A person who has hesitations and refrains won't be the better for it. A person who has no hesitations and exercises his Christian independence won't be the better for it either. The determining factor is whether we live in the love of Christ. Our first question then isn't what we have the right to do or what we should abstain from to remain pure. We care about others instead. We don't want to be a stumbling block for someone. By "stumbling block" the Bible doesn't mean—as we so often do—something annoying and upsetting, but something that is a cause of our brother's falling, something in our behavior he imitates without knowing what we know and without being protected as we are. What doesn't harm us harms him and can push him away from Christ. That's how the weak—a brother, whom Christ suffered and died for—gets lost through enlightenment. That can't be allowed to happen!

Lord, may I never be the cause of that! Never allow someone who seeks You to fall because of me. Liberate me in the right way, without despising those who have strange ideas and without using my liberty, if it can harm my brother. You have liberated me from debt and punishment. You have taken me into the kingdom of forgiveness. You don't measure by justice or by what I deserve. May I never take into account what I have the right to and demand to do what I feel like doing. The best is always what You wish. Your will be done.

THURSDAY AFTER SIXTH SUNDAY AFTER TRINITY
1 Corinthians 9:1–15

It was written for our sake. 1 Corinthians 9:10

Paul declares this in reference to the Old Testament. He knows it was given to Israel and he knows that God—through Moses and the prophets—spoke to the people of that time. But Paul also knew that God was thinking of all people in all time. God saw ahead to the time of fulfillment. His words were also aimed at Christ and His Church. Therefore, the Old Testament is also about us. The part of the Law that has to do with offerings and civil institutions doesn't concern us anymore. No one has stressed this more emphatically than Paul. At the same time, we are spiritual heirs, a new Israel, who, through Christ and the Holy Spirit, can understand all these examples and apply them to our lives.

In this case the question is if a servant of the Gospel has a right to wages for his efforts. Paul had been criticized and accused of making a pretty penny as an apostle. He replies that Jesus Himself decreed that those who preach the Gospel should make their living through the Gospel. Even in the kingdom of Christ there are rules and regulations regarding fairness and justice. Paul, however, makes an important addition: As far as he's concerned, he hasn't taken advantage of any such privilege. That's what a Christian oftentimes will say and do. When it comes to others, he can demand justice. At the same time, he can refrain from something he has every right to demand. The most important thing is never what I have a right to, but what I can give to and do for others.

Paul worked with his hands to make a living. He did it in his spare time, often long into the night. He was a tent-maker, and made primarily awnings that were put up in alleys and courtyards to create a little shade during hot summers. It wouldn't have been wrong if he chose to spare himself the trouble and toil that work entailed, especially since he received ingratitude for it, as in Corinth. Here he gives us an example, however, of how we can turn the other cheek and go the extra mile when living in the kingdom of Christ.

My Lord and Savior, You know how much there is inside of me that revolts against every injustice I encounter. I pray that I be given eyes to see the greatest injustice of all suffered by You, and to know You let it happen for my sake. You took it upon Yourself to carry my burden. You wandered from place to place with nowhere to rest Your head to help me when I was lost because I had wandered down my own path. Now You've called me to go with You. May I learn from You and be like You, so I can joyfully go the extra mile.

FRIDAY AFTER SIXTH SUNDAY AFTER TRINITY
1 Corinthians 9:15–27

I am still entrusted with a stewardship. 1 Corinthians 9:17

Paul asserted that he didn't take advantage of the right to be supported by the Church. He didn't think preaching the Gospel was anything strange. He was driven by an inner compulsion; he couldn't do otherwise.

He describes this inner compulsion for us. He wasn't the one who decided he would be an apostle. He didn't become one by his own initiative. It's the same way with him as with the other apostles, to whom Jesus said: You didn't choose Me; I chose you. Christ called Paul and made him His servant. Paul has become a slave who can no longer decide for himself. Yet Christ has turned this slave into a trustee. Things like that weren't unusual in ancient times. A proficient and knowledgeable slave could be entrusted with very responsible tasks. He could be made trustee of property or his master's business affairs. He was, however, a trustee in bondage. He owned nothing. Everything that passed through his hands belonged to his master. Everything was dependent on his being faithful to his Lord. That's how Paul experienced his position. He can do only what his dear Lord commands. "Woe to me if I do not preach the gospel!"

And what does Paul expect as payment? To do even more for his Lord! To be able to show Him, if possible, that he loves Him. Paul does that by not asking for compensation from the Church. There is only one thing he wants praise for: that he does all he can for mankind, and in that way tries to be like his Lord. He's willing to make adjustments, show consideration, live as others do, think as they do—as long as possible for a servant of Christ, who is always faithful to his Lord! Paul knows he's liberated and that there are any number of things he can choose to do or not to do. When it's time to make a choice, however, he always chooses to act and live in a way that allows him the greatest possibilities to reach out to others and gain their trust so he's able to help them and be useful to them. Someone might have said that by acting that way you're not really being yourself. Paul simply answers: I do as the athlete does in a race. He knows what to do. That's why he exercises self-control in all things. He is truly a free man, who can certainly be himself.

My Lord and Savior, I pray for devotion and faith that will set me free to experience my greatest joy: to be that which You called me for and to live for the tasks You've given me. When I am Yours,

I'm what You created me for. When I follow You, I find meaning in my life. When I try to find another meaning in life, and do things differently than You would, You who are the Lord of life, it will fail. I pray: Thy will be done, on earth and in my life, as it is in heaven where everything is as it should be.

SATURDAY AFTER SIXTH SUNDAY AFTER TRINITY
1 Corinthians 10:1–15

God is faithful. 1 Corinthians 10:13

When we say God is faithful, we mean that He keeps His word and promises. He is always the same. We can depend on Him. We can't tempt God. Tempting God means trying to prove He is different from what He claims. Is He really that meticulous? Is it really how He says it is in His Word?

Paul warns us about tempting God. He uses yet another example from the Old Testament, which was written for our instruction. From Israel we learn not to abuse God's mercy. The same thing happened to Israel that happened to the first church. God had mercifully chosen His people. He had delivered them and saved them. None of God's people, however, can be sure they've received a letter of indulgence that is valid under any and all circumstances.

Look at Israel! Everyone was baptized (even the infants!).

The clouds and the sea are examples for the washing in Baptism. They all drank the same supernatural drink from the same supernatural Rock, an example of Holy Communion. Despite this they didn't reach the Promised Land. Why? They thought they were safe when they got out of Egypt and could do as they pleased. They tempted God. They worshiped other gods. They desired evil. They committed adultery. They grumbled and complained. They acted in contradiction to God's word. We all know the outcome.

Paul says this is applicable to us. You can be confident even in ecclesiastical matters. You are baptized, you go to Communion, and you associate with other believers. Then you begin to tempt God. You start to wonder about the Commandments. You grumble over what God has said. You can't interpret it in that way in our time! You start to defend adulterous behavior. You begin to doubt. He who doubts, however, better keep watch so he doesn't fall. God will not be mocked. He is faithful and doesn't change.

God is also faithful and unchanging, however, even when it comes to His will to save us. If we let Him lead us and we love Him, we will be safe and secure. He will not allow us to be tempted beyond our strength. Whatever the temptation is, He will provide a way out. It's not always the broad and convenient way, where we can avoid discomfort and suffering. Whatever the way, however, we go together with Jesus.

Lord, only You can teach me the noble art of being secure without being confident. Give me the right kind of concern, the kind that fears coming away from You. Give me the right kind of confidence, the kind where I want to stay with You and experience joy in Your presence. Teach me to rejoice and be glad and open for all You've given me:

Baptism, Your Holy Communion, Your worship
services, and the honor to be called Christian and
be a part of Your Church. You are there in all
these gifts, Lord. If You weren't there, they would
be worth nothing. If I try to take them and make
them my own, they will be destroyed. When You
are there, however, I'm secure.

THE TRANSFIGURATION
Matthew 17:1–8

And when they lifted up their eyes, they saw no one but
Jesus only. Matthew 17:8

The observation of the Transfiguration of our Lord comes in the middle of the trinity season of the Church Year. The green color on the altar, signifying growth in the faith through daily repentance, is replaced by the white color, signifying Christ's heavenly glory. One could argue that this message is better suited to be heard during the festive part of the Church Year. It speaks of an event that represents one of the milestones in Jesus' life and His pilgrimages with the disciples.

There are good reasons, however, that this interruption is in the middle of a period when we otherwise speak of the Christian life. We need to be reminded that all of a Christian life is a life with Christ, in His presence, radiant with the light that comes from Christ, fulfilled by Christ Himself. There is no boundary between Christ, His light and glory, and our Christian lives. Nothing on this earth could be called Christian if Christ hadn't been here. All of heaven's glory exists wherever He is, even if it's concealed in an image of humility.

What happened on the Mount of Transfiguration? The disciples could see what they had a feeling they would see and what Peter eight days earlier confessed: that Jesus was the Son of God, and that all of God's glory and power existed in His body. What the disciples had seen only through the eyes of faith now became apparent with blinding clarity. They were afraid and confused. They saw two men. They knew who they were. They realized that heaven had come to earth and they would've liked it to stay. Peter made the awkward yet well-intended suggestion that they build three shelters. Suddenly it all ended in a bright cloud of light, where a voice said they were right: This was the Son of God. They should listen to Him. Then everything was gone. Only Jesus was left.

Only? Now they knew that's all that mattered. When they had Jesus, they had God. From now on they would follow Jesus, even down the mountain and to Jerusalem, the city that murdered the prophets.

All of this is a part of discipleship—ours too. We are allowed to see the glory of God that shines in the face of Christ. Many of us get the chance to be on the Mount of Transfiguration, but only for a little while. We all have to return to everyday life. We don't see the heavenly images and the blinding light. We have Jesus, however, and that's enough.

I thank You, Lord Jesus, for every glimpse of Your glory I'm allowed to see, and for all the joyous moments I've experienced in Your presence surrounded by Your light. You know I would gladly

live there with You and build myself a shelter.
However, because it's not Your will, I thank You
for sending me amid the heat and dust and anxiety
and struggle among men. You wander with me
all the way and I know that all Your glory is here
encompassing me, even when I see only clouds
and hard work and poor results. I thank You for
the grace to be able to lift up my eyes and see only
You, and know that where You are is where all
God's glory is. Amen.

MONDAY AFTER TRANSFIGURATION DAY

Revelation 1:1–20

To Him who loves us . . . to Him be glory. Revelation 1:5, 6

Power, glory, splendor, majesty—these are words in the Bible used to describe the nature of God. Behind these words is something that really can't be expressed in any language. God's glory is something we can only feel. There is a reflection of it in creation. However, if we get too close to His glory, like Isaiah, we bow down, cover our faces, and are afraid that this purity and this light will consume us.

Through Jesus, God comes to us in all His glory so we can see it and be surrounded by it without being consumed. This doesn't mean that God dimmed His glory and decreased the intensity of His holiness and light. The entire divine fullness lives in Christ's body, Paul says. When the disciples had a chance to see just a glimpse of that on the Mount of Transfiguration, they were frightened. John tells us the same thing in the beginning of Revelation.

The Book of Revelation was written during a time of persecution. John was on the island of Patmos, probably in exile. He tells us the story of how he met Jesus. John was overwhelmed by His glory and had a hard time finding words to describe it. Christ's glory radiated from Him like sparkling snow or like white wool that appears florescent when the sun shines through it. It glowed like molten steel when it pours out from the oven. There was a light that could only be compared to the brightest midday sun of summer, shining down from a clear blue sky. His eyes were like a flame of fire, and His voice was like the roaring of the Mediterranean surf after a storm, when it can be heard way up in the mountains. John could only compare the words to a sword, piercing, like lightning, overwhelming. He fell before His feet, he says, "as though dead."

Last Sunday we read how even Peter, upon meeting Christ and His supernatural power for the first time, fell down, overwhelmed, and said: Leave me Lord. I am a sinner. But Jesus said the same thing then and now: Fear not. Jesus gives us the reason why we need not fear, why we need not die, when met with God's glory. He died in our place. He lives and gives us life. He has the keys to death and the kingdom of the dead. There is no judgment and no death for those who belong to Him. John adds: He's the one who loves us. Therefore, He has saved us from our sins with His blood. He made us "a kingdom, priests to His God" (Revelation 1:6). This means He has made us citizens in God's kingdom and consecrated us so we can serve in the face of God.

Behind all this is the unbelievable, yet so simple, message that explains everything—Jesus loves you.

Your eyes are like a flame of fire, Lord. Your glance burns me and Your words can penetrate like spears; I can't protect myself from them. I know, however, that everything inside of me that burns from Your fire and stings from Your words belongs to the old Adam in me. You have allowed something new to come. You loved me and kindled my love for You. I was born into a new life, without blame or fear. Then the fire doesn't burn. It warms. Your Word is no longer a sword or a spear. It becomes medicine and life. You, the one who loves us and saves us from our sins, to You belongs the glory and kingdom in eternity's eternity.

TUESDAY AFTER TRANSFIGURATION DAY
Revelation 4:1–11

Holy, holy, holy, is the Lord God Almighty. Revelation 4:8

A door opened to heaven and John caught a glimpse of something no eye had ever seen. He had to use images and words he knew would not be able to give anyone an accurate description of what he saw. He was like a poet or painter, groping after peculiar symbols and words because what he wanted to express surpassed everything we experience in everyday life. The visions he saw we should not understand as something out of a manual, but as a work of art. They don't give us exact and coherent explanations regarding life in heaven and about the inevitable fate of the world, but instead visions and symbols, indications and metaphors that have to be understood with our imaginations and feelings as much as with our intellect. We have to accept them roughly in the same way we accept and understand a surrealistic painting or read modern prose.

When John, in his vision, catches a glimpse of heaven, he immediately realizes that everything revolves around God. God is the center and heart of everything that is occurring. God, however, doesn't reign in solitary majesty. He's surrounded by living beings and by a world as real as ours.

When John tries to describe his vision, there are two things he uses to help him in his description. There are two things on earth that in a special way reflect God's glory and the beauty of heaven and that help John immediately recognize some of the same beauty in God's world. The first are jewels, the most beautiful things in a barren land. They are the work of God, an expression of the Creator's joy over everything that's beautiful. The same beauty, though much more radiant and abundant, also exists in God's kingdom and in His nature, which is its source.

The second is the divine service. What is happening around God in heaven is very much like the worship service on earth, just as John so many times celebrated it. In the first church there was a throne—or maybe we would call it a seat of honor—behind the altar, where the bishop sat. Around him, in a semi-circle on each side, were the elders. John sees the same thing in heaven. They celebrate the worship service there, too, with songs of praise and thanksgiving, constantly, without interruption, day and night, in constant joy over this simple fact: God has created everything and He has given us the unfathomable gift of existing in His presence.

Lord, will You someday allow my eyes to see all this? I suspect that on that day I'll understand that all our thoughts about Your glory were only a vain attempt to understand what no man's mind or heart can embrace on earth. Despite that, You let our thoughts go to You and follow the tracks that Your unfathomable glory left here in our world. I praise You for those tracks, for all the beauty in Your creation, for all the joy in worshiping You, for everything that emanates from You. You, our Lord and God, are worthy of praise and glory and power, You who were and are and always will be.

WEDNESDAY AFTER TRANSFIGURATION DAY
Revelation 5:1–14

The Lion of the tribe of Judah, the Root of David, has conquered. Revelation 5:5

God is the Holy Trinity, before which all else is blemished and unclean. No sinful man can approach Him without trembling. The feeling of being little and helpless during a violent thunderstorm is a good picture of how a person who has fallen from God feels before Him. There's something in God's nature that we have no control over, but instead, must completely surrender to. John heard also in heaven how lightning and thunder emanated from God's throne. This is a picture of the power we can never ignore and never control. God is the All-powerful and the Unfathomable.

This is frightening for us. We want to know what God really means and thinks. What does He hold in store for us? John saw a scroll in His right hand. It was, however, sealed with seven seals, and no one could open it to see what was written on it. John was human; he cried grievously. He wanted so badly to know God's innermost intention.

It became clear that there was One—and only One—who was worthy of opening the scroll and revealing God's thoughts. It was the Lion of Judah, the one who resembled the Lamb who was slain. He took the scroll and the heavenly congregation sang a psalm, a *new* psalm. Through the Lamb, something new had happened, something that allowed the scroll to be opened and the innermost nature of God to be revealed. For the Lamb had been offered and, with His blood, ransomed men for God from every tribe and tongue and people and nation.

He *ransomed them* for God. They were gone, lost from God Himself. There was something about them that could never, not in eternity's eternity, unite them with the Lord God. If God took them to His breast, they must perish. Christ, however, *bought them* with His blood. He paid what it cost to fuse God with the sinner: death. The sacrificial Lamb was slain. God willed it! *This* is the essence of the nature of God.

You are worthy of taking the scroll, my Lord and Savior, and I praise You because it was You who broke the seal and You who are responsible for everything that happens to us. All fear is diverted. I no longer tremble at the fact that God's nature is unfathomable. I no longer have to understand *everything and grasp His ways. I know where they lead. I know that God is Your Father. He loved His lost children, so He let You buy us by paying the highest price that can be paid in heaven or on earth. To Him who sits on the throne and to You, O Lamb of God, who takes away the sins of the world, be praise and honor and glory, forever and ever.*

THURSDAY AFTER TRANSFIGURATION DAY
Ephesians 1:1–12

We who were the first to hope in Christ might be to the praise of His glory. Ephesians 1:12

Ephesians is one of Paul's letters written while he was in captivity, as are the letters to Philippi, Colosse, and Philemon, which probably were written while Paul was in prison in Rome around AD 62. An old, mature Christian who is waiting to die is speaking. The entire letter is a song of praise to Christ, filled with "the praise of His glorious grace, with which He has blessed us in the Beloved" (Ephesians 1:6). Therefore, we start the reading of this letter during the week after Transfiguration Day.

Paul starts by taking a look at the very beginning, the time before the creation. There's no way we can know anything about that time unless God reveals it to us. He's done this through Jesus Christ. It is revealed not simply with certain words or teachings, but through His whole life, death, resurrection, and His reign in the kingdom of forgiveness. He has made "known to us the mystery of His will" (Ephesians 1:9). He has allowed us to understand that He had already thought about us and decided how we were to be saved before the world existed. No matter how bad things got, He would make it possible for us to be His children by being redeemed through His Son who was offered for our sake. In Christ, all things would be accomplished. (Another way to translate that would be to say that Christ would be the head of all things.) As members of His body and subjects in His kingdom we would have "redemption through His blood, the forgiveness of our trespasses" (Ephesians 1:7).

We would have all this "according to the riches of His grace" (Ephesians 1:7). We have seen that God's glory is beyond words, overwhelming, and at the same time both the devastating and delightful side of His nature. This inexpressible side of God's nature can best be understood and interpreted when we let Christ be the interpretation. When we sinners, who all too well feel how unworthy we are and feel the vast distance between us and God's glory, still heed the call and dare come because we see that Christ has loved us and died for us, then we honor God. That's how we give praise to His glory. There is no better way to confess that God is God, and give Him the place fitting for the Lord of all worlds, than by coming to Christ and becoming a child of God through Him. That's when you've understood what God's glory really means. It's what Paul calls "the riches of His grace."

My dear Lord and Savior, our Redeemer, You who are the head of Your Church and have made us members of Your body, I praise You for being able to

*see You. When I see You, I can get a look at God's
secret thoughts and see what He determined before
the world was created. It would be hard for me to
believe if You hadn't already shown it to me. I
would have believed that I was the one who found
You and I would have wondered how I could comprehend You. Now I understand, however, that it
was You who thought of me before the beginning
of the world and died for me before I was born
and sought me out before I could comprehend it.
I praise Your name. Help me to believe and honor
Your merciful glory in my life!*

FRIDAY AFTER TRANSFIGURATION DAY
Ephesians 1:13–23

And He put all things under His feet and gave Him as head
over all things to the church, which is His body, the fullness
of Him who fills all in all. Ephesians 1:22–23

How do you become a Christian?

We often answer by listing everything we should do.
However, Paul points out that God has chosen us; He decided we should be His children. Therefore, we had the chance
to hear the Gospel and find faith. Then He gave us the Spirit
as a token or "down payment," "advance payment," as it also
can be translated.

After this happens, Christian life begins. God must also influence this on a daily basis. That's why Paul prays for the Ephesians that God, the Father of glory, will give them a spirit of wisdom and revelation in the *knowledge of Him*. We want to think that the most important thing is to gain knowledge of what's right and the strength to do it. The Bible, however, shows us another way. First, we need to have knowledge of God, love of God, respect for God. We need to get a look at His nature and His good will. Paul says here that He has to show us how wonderful the hope is that He's called us to, what a fantastic heritage we've received and what unbelievable power He possesses, even on us through faith. We don't learn that first and foremost by pulling ourselves together and practicing and showing others what we can do, but by once again looking at what God has done when He raised Christ from the dead and made Him Lord over everything and the head of His Church. In other words, it's by recognizing the glory of God and wanting to know more about the glory in His kingdom that we are sanctified. This has been called "egotistic redemption" and is considered by some to be a betrayal of our task here on earth. Christ, however, wants it that way. "Without Me you can do nothing."

Christ is the head of the Church. The Bible uses the same word (*ecclesiastes*) for "congregation" and "church." To be linguistically correct, we should translate "congregation" as a church in a city or town as in Ephesus, but use the word *church* when we speak of the entire Church of Christ. Here we mean the Church in the entire world, the beginning of God's kingdom on earth that someday will be made perfect, when God creates new heavens and a new earth. Christ is the Head of that Church and His life lives in all of its organs—as long as they're alive and not dead!—and His spirit works in all its means of grace.

Lord Jesus, everything is fulfilled in Your kingdom. God's glory is where You are. That's where everything is holy and pure, drenched in forgiveness and surrounded by mercy. You change our miserable church into Your holy Church. You transform miserable sinners to a holy people. Allow Your knowledge to penetrate me so I will see Your glory, understand what You give me, and become filled with joy over Your gifts and the power only You have. Praise be to Your glory.

SATURDAY AFTER TRANSFIGURATION DAY
Ephesians 2:1–10

For by grace you have been saved through faith. And this is not your own doing; it is the gift of God. Ephesians 2:8

We were dead, Paul says. By this he means, just as Jesus did, that we have strayed from the true life, a life in fellowship with God. We live, as Paul says in verse 2, "following the course of this world," in a way many people regard as completely natural. We have to hold our own and do what's right. We have to be able to strike back. We give an eye for an eye. What we do with what's ours, if it be our body or money, is nobody's business. That's what is meant in Ephesians 2:6–7 by following "the desires of body and mind." This is an illusion, however. We are under the influence of a power other than God's, "the spirit that is now at work in the sons of disobedience" (Ephesians 2:2).

If we're not children of God, we're spiritual sons of the enemy, the one who always wants the opposite of what God wants. That doesn't mean we always do his will. We are, after all, created by God. There are good urges, instincts, and an innate sense of justice in our nature. At the same time, however, the enemies of God have left their mark in the innermost parts of our character. That's why egoism comes so naturally. We don't have to learn to be envious. That's why Paul could say that we "were by nature children of wrath." Wrath is God's eternal and insurmountable antithesis to what's evil, making the encounter between God and evil something that must end in catastrophe for evil. For everything that's evil God's zeal is like a consuming fire.

God made us alive, we who were dead. He did it out of love, Paul says. He has given us a portion in Christ. He has raised us up with Him. This means that through God we are born again, and once again a light that we had lost shines in our lives. That life comes from Christ. Possessing that means possessing total forgiveness.

God has done all this purely out of mercy, without our deserving it or being able to make us deserving of it. It didn't happen through our works. No one has anything to brag about regarding their own redemption. This doesn't mean that good works don't exist. They're a part of the new life. We've been created to do them. They're in front of us, waiting. We should walk in them, which means doing them on our way through life. All this happens, however, in Christ Jesus. We were created in *Him* for these works. We receive them daily out of His hand. They're not a condition to be one of His children. They're a consequence of it.

Lord Jesus, how wonderfully secure it is to know that You have carved out the path of my future and placed all the works You expect of me along the way. Help me see them. Help me see that even what is little and dull and common and monotonous can be gifts from You, something great You've prepared just for me so I could do it to Your glory. Help me also see the unusual and unexpected and things I didn't believe I was supposed to do. May I never pass by a wretched human being You put in my way who needs my help. May I never take responsibility for something You wouldn't want me to do. Lead me only to the works God has prepared for me to do.

EIGHTH SUNDAY AFTER TRINITY
Matthew 7:15–21

Beware of false prophets. Matthew 7:15

Prophets were sent by God. Many believe that their sole task was to predict the future. However, they only did that occasionally as a part of something more important. They heard the voice of God and could tell His people what He was saying. God has a purpose in everything that happens, but that purpose can be hard to see if you're trying to live on your own and go your own way, as Israel so often did. God intervened then, and what He did to warn and revive His people, He let the prophets explain. Sometimes the prophets could speak of God's plans in the distant future. Those were the ones who came with the promise of the Messiah.

There were prophets even in the first church. The Church's foundation is built on the apostles and prophets, with Christ Himself as the cornerstone. Even the New Testament prophets interpreted God's intention by what happened. They gave instructions as to how God's Church should react in difficult situations they had never before experienced. They spoke words given to them by the Holy Spirit. Among the Spirit's gifts, Paul mentions the gift of prophesying as one of the most important. This gift could be given to men as well as women, but only a few received it.

Jesus warns that there are also false prophets. For all practical purposes they appear to be Christians. They appear to be God's spokesmen. In any event, they speak of God, and they can do it with great certainty. How can we know they are false prophets? The best proof, of course, is if they say something contrary to what Jesus said, either during His life or through His apostles. Even a false prophet, however, can sound pretty convincing. The crucial thing in Christianity is Jesus Himself, and faith in Him is always a piece of His own life. Christ is with His own people, and if He isn't there, they aren't Christians. If He's there with His Spirit, there will be *good fruit*. When we read more of Ephesians later on, we'll be hearing a lot about the fruit. Let's just remember for now that it does exist and that it has to be perceived so other Christians recognize it. The life of Christ in one person can always in some way recognize the life of Christ in another, if it really is a question of life from Christ.

Lord Jesus, You have commanded me to be careful of false prophets. You know what I need to be able to

*do that. I need Your help, Lord. I can only recog-
nize what doesn't come from You if You're with me.
Teach me to love You more and know You better
day by day so I immediately notice when another
spirit is speaking through people, be it through
their actions or their words. Teach me to examine
everything according to Your Word and through
Your Spirit, and to keep only that which is good.*

MONDAY AFTER
EIGHTH SUNDAY
AFTER TRINITY
Jeremiah 2:4–19

My people have . . . hewed out cisterns for themselves, broken cisterns that can hold no water. Jeremiah 2:13

God or the world? All mankind has to make that choice.
It applies to all people throughout all time. It applies to me.
It's no easy choice, especially if I live among those who have
chosen the world.

The best way to learn about this choice is to read Israel's
history. That's why we hear so much about what happened to
Israel in the Bible. God had chosen His people so He could
rear them in such a way that they would teach the rest of
mankind. Only Israel knew who God was, the God everyone
has an inkling of but can never really know until He reveals
Himself to us. Now, however, a strange thing happened.
While all other nations stuck to their false gods, Israel had an

unbelievable tendency to abandon the one, true God. Maybe it was because they were the only ones who knew Him but they wanted to be like everyone else.

Therefore, God sent His prophets, and they again made them choose between God and idols.

God not only speaks to Israel through the prophets; He also speaks to us. Therefore we'll be reading a few chapters from the prophet Jeremiah this week.

We immediately realize the similarity with our own situation. Jeremiah is living in a nation that has chosen the world and no longer cares about God. They pursue what they think is a realistic policy. They looked for support in Assyria. That didn't work out, so they tried Egypt. The leaders led the way, those whom Israel called "the ministers." The lawmakers, the officials, the judges, didn't want to have anything to do with God.

This is what we call secularization. Society no longer takes God into account. Laws are established and applied without regard for what is right in God's eyes. The entire government and civil service works as if this life is all we have to take into account and as if we can establish ourselves on this earth as best we see fit.

The worst thing is if the priests, those who should speak for the Lord in society, allow the spirit of the times to make an impression on them. Jeremiah speaks to them also. What God commanded him to say was that this way of life will not lead to happiness, not even happiness on this earth. Instead, it will lead to catastrophe. It's already noticeable. One misfortune and hardship after another has affected the country. What's more, "have you not brought this upon yourself by forsaking the LORD your God?" (Jeremiah 2:17)

As always, the Scriptures are a mirror where we can see our own reflection and examine ourselves, if we're willing to hear what God is saying.

Lord, I know I'm surrounded by a world that no longer cares about You. I see this repeatedly. At the same time I'm afraid I won't always notice it. Help me to love You so sincerely that I see everything in the light of Your countenance and can understand what You think and mean when You see it. Help me listen to Your voice and hear Your Word so faithfully and so often that nothing can drown Your voice in my heart. Let Your truth penetrate me so I always can notice what is fitting with it and what isn't. You are the well with the healing water. You want to lead me on the right path. I don't want to abandon You.

TUESDAY AFTER EIGHTH SUNDAY AFTER TRINITY
Jeremiah 2:26–37

My people say, "We are free." Jeremiah 2:31

This is the big illusion: that we can liberate ourselves from God. God surrounds us on all sides, as Psalm 139 says. He gives life to our body. Without Him our heart would stop beating and our consciousness would be extinguished. We would disappear into thin air. We live by Him, through Him, and for Him. We exist only because He wants to share His existence and life with us.

Yet people can feel relief when they stop thinking about God. That's because there's something inside us that doesn't come from God. Sin was invented the day one of God's angels opposed God and wanted to decide for himself. God always wants what's good, therefore Satan does the opposite. It was this innovation that he taught mankind when he led them to believe they could be like God and decide over good and evil. In reality they were obeying him instead. It's this spirit of disobedience, rebellion, and selfishness that characterizes the world in the way the Bible means when it speaks of "this world," the world without God.

It appears to be no problem to get along without God. The rich man we meet in the story of poor Lazarus probably thought he was doing just fine. He was envied by many at his death and was buried with honor. It's impossible, however, to summarize our life on earth. We'll see the final analysis in eternity, when God opens His account books. Oftentimes things turn out differently than we expected already on earth. Israel experienced that.

Strangely enough it happens that people do as Jeremiah said about the Jews: they start scolding God. They become indignant and say: Get up and help us! What's the use of God if He doesn't see to it that things like this don't happen? God answers: How dare you rebuke Me! You have fallen away from Me!

You can't be on your own, not caring about God, and still want Him as a kind of risk insurance. You can have God as Your Father and dear Lord, but not as the ultimate guarantee to be able to live Your life according to Your own plans without encountering any unpleasant surprises. We all live by Him and through Him. We should also live for Him and with Him. That's when life is as it should be.

Dear Lord, thank You for the great joy and happiness I find in knowing that You exist and have created us for Your sake, that we might get to know You and love You. I thank You for being the meaning of life and for being the reason I exist. I also pray that You, today and every day, help me to see how You surround me and carry me and give my body life. When I time and time again realize what doesn't emanate from You and is against Your will, help me immediately see what Your good will is so I know to whom I belong and what is the meaning of my life.

WEDNESDAY AFTER EIGHTH SUNDAY AFTER TRINITY
Jeremiah 5:1–13

O LORD, do not Your eyes look for truth? Jeremiah 5:3

It's considered trendy to search for the truth. Skeptics are often called seekers of the truth. Sometimes they're even considered quite superior to common believers. Jeremiah says here that *God* is searching for the truth. There's something God wants to know. He doesn't have to ask about the meaning of existence or the essence of the universe. The question is about us. He wants to know if there is truth in us.

We immediately realize that we're talking about something other than scientific truth. It's not merely a question of certain facts we can observe and register; it's also a question of the significance of all this. It's a question of mankind accepting that significance. That's why Jesus speaks about being of the truth. It's more than just recognizing the behavior of things.

When God looks for the truth in us, it's a question of whether we cheat in the presence of God. The prophet reproaches his people here because they stubbornly refuse to accept chastisement and convert. God smites them to wake them up, but they feel no pain, no sorrow, nothing that makes them reflect over their situation. Maybe they've become bitter, maybe they come with accusations against both God and man. But there's one thing that's unimaginable for them: that they question themselves and confess that maybe they've lived their whole lives after the wrong premise, when they wanted to live without God.

When it comes to the real truth, the educated have no preference before others, Jeremiah says. He believed that. He imagined that they must know better. They had also thrown away faith in God, however, because they considered it a tiresome yoke. No matter how much more knowledge you have than someone else, you can always have the same desire to decide about your own life and do what you feel like doing.

It's this desire that's decisive in so many individuals' outlook on God. The question of God's existence is not a question of truth for them. It's a practical question concerning the organization of their lives. That question has been decided for them a long time ago, maybe instinctively, partially subconsciously. The arguments are merely a defense for a lifestyle they have no intention of changing.

Among all the questions concerning God, there is one more important and more difficult than all the others: Do I *want* God to be right and will I not cheat in His presence in an effort to escape from Him?

Dear Lord, Help me to never cheat in Your presence—
and You are present everywhere. You know how
easy that is for me. I postpone what I should do. I
find something else to do when You give me something to do. I try to think of something else and
make excuses about having other duties to perform
when You chastise me for what I've neglected. I
blame my problems on not being able to understand when following Your Word doesn't suit me.
That's my old Adam. You know that, Lord. Help
me to always be honest and truthful so I love Your
truth and acknowledge You in everything.

THURSDAY AFTER
EIGHTH SUNDAY
AFTER TRINITY
Jeremiah 5:20–31

Do you not fear Me? declares the LORD; Do you not tremble
before Me? I placed the sand as the boundary for the sea.
Jeremiah 5:22

There are laws of nature, and there are moral laws. Both
types of laws originate from God. All people understand that
the laws of nature cannot be ignored. You know what's
going to happen if you jump off the fifth floor balcony. It's
just as precarious, however, to ignore moral law. In the animal kingdom the correct behavior is instinct, something that

works naturally with the laws of nature. We're not animals, however. God has created us as individuals with a will of our own and responsibility. That was the condition to be His children. It's exactly this privilege that can be abused. We can do something animals can't: choose evil.

If we choose evil, we are at conflict with life's innermost essence and purpose: God Himself. Life becomes unhinged. It's the same thing that happens when you ignore traffic regulations. It's possible that you can get where you're going a little faster, but it will be at the expense of others' safety and well-being, and the whole time catastrophe threatens.

The prophet says here that this is exactly what happens to a nation that abandons God. Naturally there are those who believe they've succeeded. They become rich and famous, fat and comfortable. Justice, however, is rocked at its foundation and ruthlessness spreads. The prophet points, as prophets often do, to social injustices as proof that something is out of order and over all of this hangs the threatening cloud of disaster.

In this prophesy a summary is finally made of all the appalling and horrible things that will happen to the nation. Then the fundamental damage is proclaimed: prophets prophesy falsely and priests rule at their direction. The prophets were the spiritual authorities and experts of their time. And the priests wanted to be with the times and followed what the prophets said. "My people love to have it so," says the Lord in Jeremiah 5:31. Behind all this there is vast public opinion that wants life to be lived differently than God wants it. That public opinion influences the prophets as well as the priests. But what will you do when the end comes? If you choose the world instead of God, you will share the fate of the world: to perish. Everyone who believes in the Son, however, will not perish.

Lord, have mercy on us. Have mercy on our nation.
The situation is the same for us as it was with
Your nation of Israel, foolish and unwise, having
eyes but not being able to see, having ears yet
not hearing. Send us Your Spirit to open our eyes
and ears. Put all Your fatherly love in every word
You speak, so everyone understands that it's You
speaking and that You mourn for us and are worried about us.

FRIDAY AFTER EIGHTH SUNDAY AFTER TRINITY
Jeremiah 6:10–17

Behold, the word of the LORD is to them an object of scorn.
Jeremiah 6:10

This is what Jeremiah declared about Israel a few years
before its destruction. It could just as well have been said
about us. Who could have thought, however, that it would
be possible that something *like that* would cause the destruction of a nation?

Jeremiah makes very clear what the fundamental problem
is among his fellow-countrymen: They abandoned God, the
source of the cleansing water. They don't want to hear God's
Word—they think it's ancient and unnecessary. They live
contrary to God's Commandments and aren't even ashamed
of it. "They did not know how to blush" (Jeremiah 6:15).

They have become so experienced in the ways of the world, so broad-minded, mature, and authoritative, that they no longer care about the ancient path, the path that leads to God and that has always been the same through time. If someone tries to get them to see the damage done to their nation in an effort to heal them, they just say everything's all right. Even when there is no peace.

Jeremiah was a prophet. That means he got a look at God's plans. He knew what was about to happen, and his mission was to proclaim the events. Affliction was knocking at the door. They were going to lose their land, be deported, everything they loved more than God was going to be taken from them. Only a prophet can make predictions like that. All of us, however, have received the prophetic word directed to us that allows us to see *how* God has reacted, *can* react, and *usually* reacts. God has left it to us to listen and draw our own conclusions. A person who has received the gift of prophesying can maybe hear what God is saying to us right now about something that's going to happen in our lifetime. In any event, there's something here we all can learn: If we abandon God, we abandon the power that shoulders everything. You deny yourself God's protection and have to try to make it on your own through a situation only God has the power over. It's a gift from God to be able to live in your country, go to your job, live in peace, and enjoy good health. God can continue to give these gifts even to those who never are thankful for them. He can just as easily, however, take them from us. Whatever He does, it's a step toward what is most important to Him: that despite everything He makes us realize He is our Father and doesn't want to lose us.

Lord, You were once merciful to Your people and forgave them for their misdeeds. You washed away their sins. Your outrage departed from You and You turned away from Your burning wrath. Turn Your face once again toward us, You our redeeming God, and stop being angry with us. Will Your wrath never end, plaguing us from generation to generation? Will You give us life so Your people can find joy in You once again? Lord, may we see Your mercy and receive Your salvation?

SATURDAY AFTER EIGHTH SUNDAY AFTER TRINITY
Matthew 6:19–23

So, if your eye is healthy, your whole body will be full of light. Matthew 6:22

Jesus says the eye is the light of the body. We seldom think of the eye this way. We generally think of the sun as the light, the source of light. The sun wraps its light around us, and that light must exist whether our eye can see it or not. However, what we call "light," in other words that which lights up and shines, what makes it possible to see far away and what allows colors to shimmer and change, exists only in the eye. All around us is nothing but darkness, where a kind of regular fluctuation in an electromagnetic field occurs. It's this kind of undulation that the eye can transform into light and color. It is only the eye, however, given to us by God, that receives this peculiar ability to perceive these undulations as light, or colors as colors, or the ability to see an object several feet, miles, or light years away.

The soul also has an eye. We all live in an energy field, emanating from God. It, too, is as undetectable as light waves. We have received the ability, however, to see it from above. The light in the darkness allows us to see things in their right colors through reflection, making it possible for us to see things and contexts that otherwise would be covered in darkness. It's this ability that separates us from animals. "The light in you" is something only we have.

If the spirit's eye is destroyed, all existence is covered with darkness. We can no longer understand the real significance of things and mankind. We grope in the dark and don't know where we're going. We spend time, interest, and energy on things that will be destroyed. We collect riches that have no enduring value. In the process we lose the real significance in life. "How great is the darkness!" Jesus proclaims in Matthew 6:23. He also says whoever follows Him will never wander in darkness, but will have eternal life.

Help me, Lord, to take care of my soul's eye. I received it so I could see You and Your light that You pour over our world. That's the light that makes everything so beautiful. It's You that gives meaning to everything. You created the colors so we could see them and find joy in them. You've allowed Your eternal light to shine through in the rays from the sun and drops of water, in the flowers and the evening clouds. You have also given us eyes to see eternity's clarity in Your Word. May that clarity shine through tomorrow so we all notice it. Bless those who witness about Your light and all of us who will come to receive it. Bless even those

who don't bother coming, that even they in some
way will see a little ray of it and notice that there's
a light that lights up the dark and will never be
extinguished.

NINTH SUNDAY
AFTER TRINITY
Luke 12:42–48

The faithful and wise manager, whom his master will set
over his household. Luke 12:42

We Christians are God's stewards. The New Testament
talks about stewards. They were more common then than they
are today. Many were slaves. They could be highly regarded
and could be trusted with important duties. They belonged to
their master, however, and didn't own anything.

That's exactly what we are. We often speak of *our* possessions. Even a Christian can talk about *my* life, *my* time, *my*
money, *my* car. He very well knows, or should know, that
he belongs to God and all that passes through his hands is
God's.

A Christian is a steward and not a tenant. A tenant pays
the agreed upon rent. After that, he has the right to keep
what he earns from the property. There are those who think
their relationship to God is something similar. They give God
a reasonable share of income, maybe they even tithe. After
that, they can do as they please with the rest. Even the rest,
however, belongs to God. We're merely here to manage it.

Even when we give something, for example in the offering, we have to say as David said when he came with generous gifts to the temple: "For all things come from You, and of Your own have we given You" (1 Chronicles 29:14).

It's easy for us to imagine the division of labor as something like this: God works through His Church. Giving to missionary work and other church activities is "giving to God's work." We'll take care of worldly problems ourselves. On the one hand it's true that God's will is primarily focused on our being saved from eternal damnation and the Church is His tool in doing that. On the other hand, God is also the Creator whose creation is kept in authority. Here He has incorporated us in His work, in production and management, in the home, in care of the sick, and in teaching. We're all stewards. We're taking care of God's property.

That doesn't mean we can't use it for our own sake. When people have understood that they're God's stewards, they sometimes have a guilty conscience as soon as they allow themselves the good things in life. It's God, however, who allows His children to indulge in the good things in life. When we're given something to take care of, God also gives the steward His share of these good gifts. The steward realizes, however, that he's accountable for everything to his master.

Here is the big difference between a worldly steward and a Christian. Both have to be faithful and sensible. Faithful, so they stick to their Master's orders, and sensible, so they can act in His stead when confronted with a new situation. We Christians have the great privilege of being with our Lord every day. In a sense, He's invisible, far away, sitting at the right hand of His Father, and we are like servants waiting for our master's return. At the same time, He's with us, present in His Word and Sacraments, like our best friend, to whom we can go to with our questions and troubles.

Dear Lord, make an invisible mark on everything that passes through my hands so I know it's Yours. Everything I have comes from You. The only reason I have it is because You've commissioned me to manage it. Everything I call my own, even my life and my body, are things You have entrusted to me. I belong to You, I'm in Your hands, and I thank You for that. Because of that there's meaning in my life, every new day, at work and at home, with my family and friends. Day after day I walk on Your ground, it belongs to You, and You want me to work with it and find joy in it. I thank You that everything is in Your hands.

MONDAY AFTER NINTH SUNDAY AFTER TRINITY
1 Corinthians 11:1–16

Nevertheless, in the Lord woman is not independent of man nor man of woman. 1 Corinthians 11:11

We now resume the reading of 1 Corinthians, and today we've come to one of the most difficult chapters in the New Testament. Scholars have not yet been able to come up with a convincing explanation of what Paul means when he says a woman who prays must have a veil on her head because of the angels. We would also hardly be able to understand his words about man being the head of a woman if we didn't have Ephesians, where he explains that the man should be the head of his spouse according to the example Christ gave us by being the head of His Church, that He loved and sacrificed Himself for her. It also says "the head of Christ is God." That means an intimate fellowship, not belittlement.

It's also difficult to understand what Paul means by man being the image and glory of God. It can't mean that man could in any way be closer to God and more precious in God's eyes. Paul himself taught that *all* of us lack the glory of God, that *all* of us can get it back in the same way (through faith), and that we will then *all* be one in Christ. On the other hand, maybe he's thinking of what he said in Ephesians: everyone who's called a father on earth has gotten his name from the Father in heaven. Something in God's nature is reflected in all true fatherhood. Even if man and woman are created differently, both of them are still created by God. They're created for each other and supplement each other. They do that even in church. Paul talks quite a bit about the woman's contribution to work in the Church in his letters. In this chapter he mentions that they could pray and prophesy. When people prayed in the home, the woman could lead the prayer. Also, if she had the gift of prophesy, she could speak with the Spirit's insight.

We see a difference here between the ancient church and Judaism. The Jewish nation was patriarchal, which they reasoned by referring to Genesis. Paul also refers to creation. Of course there are differences between man and woman. We have to see these differences, however, in the light of what happened through Christ. "In the Lord," in other words in Christ's kingdom, Christians must not think like the Jews did. Man and woman exist for each other. Each of them serves according to the gifts they've received, and we all are one in Christ. We are organs in the same body, serving one another. Therefore, there is no patriarchy in the New Testament. The fact that a woman could be gainfully employed and have a vocation went without saying.

Paul also brings up the question of outward appearances. How long should a man's hair be? What should be on your head during church services? There's a general rule in the New Testament for questions like these: one should act according to what's considered common decency. Given that rule, there will be different answers to the same question over time. What's considered offensive in one situation can be considered completely respectable in another. If Paul *only* recommends a certain kind of appearance in regard to this rule, then a Christian can react differently when outer appearances change. If, however, there's something deeper to what Paul says, his words are binding for all time. Since, in this case, he appeals to a feeling of decency (what's "proper") we mean, as Lutherans, that people today can act as custom allows. However, we might see women in other countries put a veil or handkerchief over their hair when they enter the church. There, Paul's words are regarded applicable through all time. If they are, we should certainly live after them. We Lutherans, however, see these as recommendations of the kind that can change over time, depending on custom and the good of mankind.

Forgive us Lord, for our abuse of Your Word. Forgive us when we don't want to understand and don't want to admit it. Forgive us when we introduce our thoughts and wishes in Your words. Make us childishly happy about having Your Word so we can receive it with open hearts. May all our ideas and all our manmade ways of thinking wither away so we can receive Your Word, simply and full of confidence, exactly the way You meant it.

TUESDAY AFTER NINTH SUNDAY AFTER TRINITY

1 Corinthians 12:1–13

To each is given the manifestation of the Spirit for the common good. 1 Corinthians 12:7

According to His will, the Spirit gives special gifts to every person. We're talking about all those in whom the Spirit has carried out His work so they have received the faith and can sincerely, from the heart, testify that Jesus is Lord, that He is God, our Savior and Redeemer.

All who believe in Christ are *one*. Believers are part of one body, although they are *different*. They are just as different as the organs of the human body. Each person has his or her own function. Therefore, each person receives a special gift, a spiritual gift, a *charisma* as the Greeks called it.

When we think of the charismatic gifts, we usually think of speaking in tongues or faith healing. Paul's list is much longer. We find several gifts here and even more in the twelfth chapter of Romans, including speaking in tongues and faith healing, which are probably the most noticeable ones. Paul takes great pains, however, to make it clear to us that there are a number of gifts. And it's the Holy Spirit Himself who decides which gifts He gives to each of us. He distributes them with the good of the congregation in mind. There are some gifts that are connected to the sermon, education, witnessing, and healing of the soul. Pastors, evangelists, and teachers have their gifts (and these are Christ's gifts to the congregation, as we hear in Ephesians). Others have the ability to comfort, admonish, and instruct. Everyone has to cultivate his gift and allow it to be useful. The fact that it's so hard to find Sunday School teachers, for example, must be because there are people who elect not to use their gifts.

Then there are gifts that give us the opportunity to serve our fellow Christians, where we can take care of people who need help, become youth counselors, or perform duties in the church, in committees or the church council, in the right way—as a service to Christ and through His power. Then there are also the remarkable and unusual gifts of being able to perform feats of strength and spectacular tests of faith that most of us aren't capable of.

The most important thing is that all of us serve with our gift. There is no blessing in trying to get a gift that someone else has because it appears impressive. It's always a blessing, however, when you use the gift the Spirit has given just to you.

Dear Holy Spirit, which gift have You given to me? Help me recognize it and receive it with joy. May I never neglect it, but be a good steward of God's mercy. I don't ask to be like others. I don't ask for something spectacular. I ask only to be able to serve where You want me to serve. For Christ's sake and to His glory.

WEDNESDAY AFTER NINTH SUNDAY AFTER TRINITY

1 Corinthians 12:14–30

God arranged the members in the body, each one of them, as He chose. 1 Corinthians 12:18

Equality does not mean similarity. Equality means equal merit, which has *nothing* to do with us being alike. God creates everyone to be His children. This is what equal merit is based on. There's a reason for existence and a mission for us on earth. That's exactly why He created us so differently. In difference lies the significance and value in life.

That's also the way it is in the Church. Everyone who belongs to Christ becomes members of His body. They belong together: man and woman, Jew and Greek, slave and master, as Paul writes. They're not *alike*, however. The hand and eye, foot and ear are not alike. If they were, the body would be a sorry sight. That's just how different we are. However, *just because* we're different we can't say: I don't need you. I don't feel any kinship with these people. Paul says when God put the body together from different parts, He did it so there would be harmony and not discord between the different organs. That's exactly the way it is with Christ's body.

It is God then who put the organs in the body and made them so different. In the same way God has given the different organs a different service in the Church. Paul makes a long list: Some should do this, others that. Everyone has a special gift. Everyone cannot do the same thing! They're not capable of that and it wouldn't benefit the congregation.

Once again we see the difference between Christ's kingdom and the world's. The world usually regards likeness as a prerequisite for human dignity. If we're not alike, we don't have the same merit. Therefore, we try to maintain the illusion that we're all alike. The mere thought that all jobs aren't intended for everyone is regarded as outrageous discrimination.

In the kingdom of Christ we speak of service, not rights. None of us have any other right to live and serve other than the right Christ gave us by dying in our place. We are all equally unworthy here because we are sinners, yet at the same time equally worthy because we are created by God and are members in Christ's body. The thing that makes us valuable, however, is also what makes us different. We are "the body of Christ and individually members of it" (1 Corinthians 12:27), each of us where God has placed us. An eye cannot be an ear. The merit it has is because it is an eye and nothing else.

Help me, dear Lord, to love and care for the task You have given me. Help me come to the place where You want me to be and find joy there because You brought me there. If I want something else, stop me. If I go my own way, forgive me. In Your mercy You can make right what I made wrong. If You want me to do something else than what I'm doing right now, show me what it is. If I can be a blessing and serve You where I am right now, let me do it. Take from me or give to me whatever You want to, as long as I serve You. For Jesus' sake.

THURSDAY AFTER NINTH SUNDAY AFTER TRINITY

1 Corinthians 12:31–13:13

[Love] does not insist on its own way. 1 Corinthians 13:5

What kind of love is Paul talking about? The fact that it's not regular earthly love, the kind we experience when we fall in love with another person, is immediately obvious. That form of love seeks out its own, sometimes to such an extent that it's painful for the person who is the object of it. You can't say that love doesn't perish. Our daily experience shows that.

Neither is Paul describing the kind of love many people believe is the main thing in Christianity: natural friendliness, a good heart, generosity, social responsibility, and consideration for the less fortunate. Paul says you can have a good portion of that kindness and still lack love. You can give away everything you own, and sacrifice yourself, your health, and your life, without having love.

Who has love? Do I have it? I can test myself by substituting the word "love" with "I" and reading this chapter once again. The result will be humiliating. Who dare says: *I* am not jealous, *I* don't insist on having my own way, *I* am not resentful, *I* do not rejoice in wrong, *I* bear all things, believe all things, and hope all things.

What then is Love? It certainly is the main thing in Christianity—it is *Christ Himself*. It's His life, the life that through faith lives in us also. The way love is described here is the way Jesus Christ is. It's also how the new life is that comes from Him, the life we live in the kingdom of forgiveness.

That's why it's so difficult to see this love in ourselves. A Christian is not only made up of a new man in Christ. We also still have our old Adam. We can't see the new man. It functions, but it can't be studied. Perhaps God did this so we wouldn't be tempted to admire it or base our wisdom on it. We can see the old Adam, however. It's important that we do because he requires constant supervision.

Despite this, love is there if you believe. The lifestyle Paul praises here, singing the song of love, is just what we are confronted with when the New Testament speaks of the new life in the kingdom of forgiveness. This simple, obvious love that forgives and serves is far superior to everything we usually admire and try to obtain as remarkable manifestations of faith: speaking in tongues, the gift of prophesy, and that miraculous faith that can move mountains. Things like that are temporary. They're popular for a while, then they perish. Right in the middle of this temporal state, in the middle of the life where we're in constant need of forgiveness, there's Christ with His love, working inside of those He forgives. That love will never perish.

Lord Jesus, I've asked You so many times to give me Your love. Now I understand that it's not something You can release to me. That love cannot be separated from You. It exists only where You are and where You are working. I pray to receive You, that You come to me, stay with me, and live with me. When You're with me, I'm not jealous and I don't hold a grudge because of injustice. Then I can endure anything, hope for everything, and bear everything. Then I'm not conceited over my success and not bitter and upset about resistance and defeat. All this can happen only when You fill my heart and control it. So come, Lord Jesus, and reign over me, for the sake of Your boundless mercy.

FRIDAY AFTER
NINTH SUNDAY
AFTER TRINITY
1 Corinthians 14:1–25

Pursue love, and earnestly desire the spiritual gifts,
especially that you may prophesy. 1 Corinthians 14:1

Of all the gifts we can receive, love is the greatest and
the most important. There is love where Christ is. Without
Christ, there is no genuine Christianity, faith is dead, everything is empty, and all efforts are in vain, just as all ecstasy and
all speaking in tongues is.

That's why Paul speaks of love right here, while he's
occupied with speaking about the *charismas*. Obviously there
was a tendency to overestimate the spiritual gifts in Corinth.
Paul emphatically points out the only thing that's really necessary, the thing that all Christians must possess: Christ and the
faith in Him that is at work in love.

Then the Spirit's gifts will fall into place. They're valuable.
There are many of them and they're all different. Each person
gets his or her own, and they're all necessary. They're given
in such a way as to be useful in the congregation. With *one*
exception, Paul says. That exception is speaking in tongues.
That gift is only useful and edifying to the one who possesses
it. In Paul's description, it isn't hard to understand that it's
the same gift the Spirit gives today. A person who speaks in
tongues speaks in spiritual ecstasy, secretive words. You can't
understand what he says if there's no one there to interpret.
One who possesses this gift can, if it's genuine, be greatly edified by it. It strengthens faith and love and enhances fellowship
with God. It is of lesser dignity, however, than the gifts that
are a benefit to others. Paul emphatically expresses this. He
would rather speak five understandable words in an effort to
instruct others than ten thousand words spoken in tongues.

Therefore, prophecy is superior to speaking in tongues. Even prophecy is inspired. The prophet was driven to speak the words God gave him. He wasn't a teacher in the congregation who taught at regular times. He spoke only when the Spirit touched him. Prophecy like this could be penetrating, revealing, so it seemed as though God saw right through them. It could be soothing, so it felt as though Christ Himself was there with forgiveness. (The spirit of prophecy can also exist in a normal sermon, when it is at its best.)

Prophesying, however, is temporal. The gift of prophecy will disappear, and speaking in tongues will end. Maybe sooner than we think; Paul isn't clear here. The things that small, common Christians possess, however—faith, hope, and love—will endure.

Dear Holy Spirit, we ask You for the fullness of Your gifts. May they pour down over us here in our church. Demolish and remove everything that hinders us from receiving everything You have to give us. Allow us to see how pitiful our cowardice and pettiness is, and show us Christ in all His glory. Make us small and poor in spirit, and let us live in Your mercy without being pompous. Make us rich in Your own way with the gifts You have in waiting for each of us so we will be useful, joyous, and edifying for Your Church.

SATURDAY AFTER NINTH SUNDAY AFTER TRINITY

1 Corinthians 14:26–40

The things I am writing to you are a command of the Lord.
1 Corinthians 14:37

Paul is giving instructions about the *church service*. Those who have spiritual gifts may use them, but order must be maintained. Too many people can't talk at once. Even an inspired prophet should be able to keep quiet, if he really has the spirit of God in him.

Paul then adds that, just as in all other Christian churches, the women should keep silent. It's not permissible for them to speak. (He uses the word *speak* that in the New Testament usually means "speak the word of God.") "In the church," as it's interpreted in the old translation, means "during the church service." Paul said just before that those who speak in tongues should "keep silence in church" if there's no one there to interpret. He should "speak to himself and to God," in other words, at home during his devotions, but not during the church service, "in church."

In this case the women should "be subordinate," Paul says. He uses the same word he used in Ephesians, which meant, "fall into order under God," so everything functions in the division of labor God wants.

What order is Paul referring to, however? He says that it's "shameful for a woman to speak in church." It could mean that he wants them to exercise common decency. If that's so, this instruction could of course be altered when it became clear that a woman could speak publicly on other occasions. The difficulty in that interpretation is that it wasn't considered shameful in the Hellenistic world for a woman to be like that. The fact that the Corinthians allowed it at their church services was probably an effort to accept the customs of that time. Above all, we're faced with the difficulty that Paul presents two reasons here. The first is that the Law *also* requires it. When Paul refers to the Law, he means God's Law that also applies in Christ's kingdom. Then the determining factor comes. Paul knows he will be contradicted. There are those who refer to the Spirit and say Paul is wrong. Paul answers that if someone really possesses the Spirit, they will realize that what he writes here is a commandment from God. Paul realizes he is bound by Christ's commandments in this case. Christ directed his apostles to keep all that He commanded. Those are the same words Paul uses here. He knows this is a commandment from Jesus, and he can't ignore it.

Why would Jesus command something like that? The fact that He Himself lived after that rule is clear: He chose only men to be His apostles. We know what Paul and Peter suggested as the reason for this: In marriage God has divided up the duties between man and woman. Despite the fact that they're "heirs with you of the grace of life" (1 Peter 3:7) and equal before God, they don't have the same functions. What applies in marriage also applies in the Church, Paul teaches us. In both cases God has created an entity from two independent individuals. In that entity man and woman also have different functions. The man is the head of the family and the shepherd who teaches God's servants.

In the ancient church the word *why* wasn't necessary in cases like these. If they knew that when God imposed something, no more discussion was needed. Out of faith in Jesus they unconditionally followed His Word. Therefore it was an undisputed rule in the Church that the "shepherds and teachers" who led the congregation after the apostles would be men.

Dear heavenly Father, You see how divided Your Church has become because of differing interpretations of Your Word. Forgive us for our trespasses. Penetrate each and every one of us with Your Word so we correctly understand it and do exactly what You want us to do.

Lord Jesus, You sent Your apostles with Your Word and gave them Your Spirit so they would lead us on the right path. Help us to correctly understand the message You've sent through them. Help us to love it and stick to it, exactly the way You want us to, so Your will and no one else's is done.

Dear Holy Spirit, open our eyes and hearts, so we see the truth, and humble us so we can receive it and allow it to reign over our wishes and intentions. Come to us and fill us all so Your Church can be united in the truth, do Your will, and glorify Your name among men.

TENTH SUNDAY AFTER TRINITY
Luke 19:41–47

Would that you, even you, had known on this day the things that make for peace! But now they are hidden from your eyes. Luke 19:42

Jesus saw the city. The group had reached the crest of Mount Olive where they could view the holy city. There lay the temple with its huge vestibules and rows of pillars. The golden pinnacles on the roof sparkled in the sunshine and the smoke from the burning altars rose to the sky. David and Solomon had prayed here. Jeremiah had prophesied here. For a thousand years this city was the center of God's work on earth.

Now, Jesus knew, it was over. He could see the Roman embankments and hear the roaring of the battering rams. He knew the temple would be destroyed, its defenders would fall to the sword or be nailed to a cross, and the survivors would be forced into exile. Why did this have to happen?

"Because you did not know the time of your visitation" (Luke 19:44). God is the living God. He interacts with us and every new generation. No one can live on their father's faith or count on their piety. We must be converted. The call reaches us. It's not enough that our ancestors said yes once upon a time. It's not enough that we once said yes a long time ago either. Jesus is entering here and now. His Church is the New Jerusalem. We are the new Israel. Do we understand where our peace comes from?

You can fall behind along the way, as the apostle says. You start living on last year's forgiveness and worn out experiences. Once upon a time we struggled to obtain a Christian conviction. We know what true and false teaching is. Are we alive? Do I understand *today* where my peace comes from? Am I listening when the Word chastises me for newly acquired bad habits or negligence? Do I speak of these things in my confession? Is God's mercy really new?

It is questions like these that we're confronted with this week. Christ is present with His people in His Church. Is He crying over us? Is He coming to a house of prayer or a den of thieves?

We thank You, dear Lord and Savior, that You come to us anyway. You cried over the city, yet You preached every day in the temple. Maybe You're crying over us too. We know You have reason to. Yet You preach to us Sunday after Sunday, and every day we can read Your Word and be showered with its treasures. If our eyes are blind to something You wish us to see, show it to us. Don't allow our hearts to be hardened or our eyes to be closed. Don't take Your hand from us. Save us, O Lamb of God, who takes away the sins of the world.

MONDAY AFTER TENTH SUNDAY AFTER TRINITY

Revelation 2:1–11

But I have this against you, that you have abandoned the love you had at first. Revelation 2:4

Christ's messages to the seven congregations in Asia Minor are important reading for all of us. We see here several examples of the dangers that threaten us as Christians when we feel our Christianity becomes old and routine. While Paul's letters are written to recently formed or young congregations, Jesus' messages address congregations that have existed for a lifetime.

The first letter is addressed to Ephesus, the same church Paul wrote to some thirty years earlier. The congregation was still growing. Their leader was none other than the apostle John. They're praised for their work and steadfastness. Although their burden was heavy, they never tired. They rejected false prophets and exposed heretics. There is one problem with them: "You have abandoned the love you had at first."

This abandonment is a serious problem. The abandoned love is Christ's love, the love that's inside of us when we belong to Him. If we don't have that, zealous behavior or sacrifice won't help. Yet that's exactly what happens to us all through the years of toil and difficulty. We persevere. We labor and do our duty. However, what about love?

How can we preserve it? Or get it back? John, in Ephesus, teaches: "In this is love, not that we loved God but that He loved us and sent His Son to be the propitiation for our sins" (1 John 4:10). Love comes from God. There is only one way to get it: to receive it. There's only one way to preserve it: to receive even more of it. The danger is that we start existing on leftovers, on old forgiveness, things we've already received. Mercy is in the freezer. That's not mercy any longer, however. We must receive Christ and His life anew constantly. We are organs in His body. Organs live and survive only as long as there's blood flowing through them from the body. We need Christ's blood, His atonement, His resurrected life constantly, like a river that constantly flows. That's the secret of living in daily grace and forgiveness. Then we'll experience love and acts of love.

Lord, when will I learn that I cannot own You as one owns a painting or a wedding ring? I own You only when You give. You are with me only when

You come with Your gifts out of Your unbelievable kindness. You come. You grant and give without interruption. It's only I who has such a hard time receiving it. Help me to come to You, constantly anew, just as I am, in the middle of daily life, with all my worries and vexations, with my old nature and all of my sins. Allow me to live in the miracle of forgiveness, in Your mercy that's always new, so I never wander from Your love.

TUESDAY AFTER TENTH SUNDAY AFTER TRINITY
Revelation 2:12–29

Only hold fast what you have until I come. Revelation 2:25

The churches in Pergamum and Thyatira have been faithful despite bloody persecution; therefore, they receive lots of praise. In Pergamum Satan built his throne—the enormous heathen temple that the Germans dug up about one hundred years ago and is now in East Berlin. It was dangerous to profess the name of Christ there. The church, however, persisted in doing that. Even the church in Thyatira has persevered and their latter works, unlike the Ephesians, exceed their first works.

Despite this, everything's not all right. Christ has something against His faithful servants. They're too easygoing and lenient with those who come with false prophecy and try to destroy the church. John mentions them only by their assumed name in the Old Testament (the Old Testament was written "for our instruction"!), but everyone knows what he means. We, too, can get an idea of what they were taught, especially because teachings like these were also opposed by Paul and Peter. It was false teachings of independence that brought mercy to immorality. It proclaimed that everything was pure and good for those who had the right knowledge. Therefore one could participate in eating meat that was sacrificed to idols without separating from the world. The boundary between heathen and Christian was erased. God was also found among heathens! A liberated view of sexual relations was also justified, the same kind that heathens practiced. Faith was, after all, something purely internal!

Christ's answer to all of this is a definite no. This is false teaching. It's not something one can give in to. It's no help that people who come with teachings like these call themselves Christian and want to be a part of the Church. They don't belong, and Christ wants nothing to do with them. It's possible that people like the woman Jezebel claimed to speak with prophetic authority, with insight that sees deeper and understands the Gospel better than anyone else had. They're still false prophets. They don't come with Christ's teachings; the teachings the apostles were faithful stewards of. It's probably just as an example of the deviation from the apostle's teachings that Jezebel is described as one who "calls herself a prophetess." That's just what Paul prohibited. He used exactly that expression when he, a generation before, wrote to Timothy in Ephesus a letter that undoubtedly was read in the churches and repeated what he said to the Corinthians: "I do not permit a woman to teach" (1 Timothy 2:12).

In contrast to this, Jesus comes with a warning: hold fast what you have until He comes. Everything in this world changes. There's only one thing that's eternal: the Gospel.

Heaven and earth will perish, but not the Word of Christ. It's the same warning we see in Jude: to "contend for the faith that was once for all delivered to the saints" (Jude 1:3).

My Lord and Savior, my heart is in agony when I hear how sternly You speak. Why is it so hard for us to see Your truth and allow it to unite us? Despite the fact that I'm a great sinner, I have a hard time saying that someone else is wrong. Because You're right in everything, it must be wrong when someone contradicts something You've said. Give us the faith to always realize that You are right and believe in You more than anything else. May we never lose Your truth when people change and form it to fit themselves. Help us see it and dare to stand by it, for Your sake only.

WEDNESDAY AFTER TENTH SUNDAY AFTER TRINITY
Revelation 3:1–13

I know that you have but little power, and yet you have kept My word. Revelation 3:8

You have the quality of being alive, yet you are dead, as Christ says in His message to Sardis. Dead here means, as it so often does when Jesus speaks, of spiritual death apart from

God. We can be like that even if we have the quality of being spiritually alive. A congregation can be lively, where all sorts of activity occurs, where contributions are very good, and still be dead. There's one thing missing: the life the Spirit arouses when He is allowed to lead us to and preserve us in a living faith in Christ. He had once led the Christians in Sardis there. Now, however, that life was dead or near death.

That life can be resurrected. A dead Christian can be compared with a person who's sleeping or to a numb limb. Once you've been incorporated into Christ's body, you're one of Christ's members. Whether you're dead or sleeping, you're still a member of Christ. That's why the expression "awake" is so often used when speaking about breathing new life into a dead Christian. We see it in Ephesians. "Awake, O sleeper, and arise from the dead, and Christ will shine on you" (Ephesians 5:14).

Wake up and stay awake! Christ says. How do we stay awake? We learn the answer in the message to Philadelphia: "I know that you have but little power, and yet you have kept My word and have not denied My name" (Revelation 3:8). You don't have to be strong, or a spectacular Christian, or one who is admired by everyone. There are weak Christians, simple, overlooked individuals no one seems to notice. They possess inner strength, however, that comes from obeying God's Word. They use it, receive it, and keep it, even when all others seem to be transformed by the world and act against Christ. Instead of denying Christ, they stick to what He said and taught. They see the world and what has happened through time in the light of the Word. Most of all, they live in that light, in constant awareness of their sins and their Lord's unfathomable mercy. Christ says about these people: Because you've stuck to My words about persever-ance, I will stick with you.

Lord, take care of me by giving me the perseverance
to hear Your Word. You know how badly I need
that perseverance. I tire so easily. I've heard Your
Word so many times before, I think I know all
about it—as if I ever could understand all Your
truths! I'm careless in the application and give up
when it becomes difficult. Give me the steadfastness to live after Your Word, so I hear the truth
speaking to me again, about my life right now, and
of Your mercy today.

THURSDAY AFTER
TENTH SUNDAY
AFTER TRINITY
Revelation 3:14–22

You are neither cold nor hot. Revelation 3:15

In Christ's eyes, a half-hearted Christian can be considered worse than not being a Christian at all. He spews these
words out of His mouth as if it were something that was
repulsive, distasteful, and sickening.

How does a half-hearted Christian behave? He feels prosperous and content. He has everything he needs. He doesn't
feel the need for revival or the need for self-sacrifice, no more
church or Communion. What we have here is a moderate
amount of religion. He isn't fanatic or excessive. He doesn't
like those who eagerly support more warmth and life in the
congregation. Everything is just fine as it is.

Jesus says that what you don't realize is that it's you who are miserable, pitiful, poor, blind, and naked! What you need is eye salve, the Spirit's ointment that allows you to discover what a sufficient dose of Christianity is: loving God above all else and your neighbor as yourself. He who sees this also sees his own poverty and nakedness. He starts looking for the "gold refined by fire" that exists only with Christ, that was purified in the fire of suffering when He took our sins with Him into death's melting pot. He can give us garments that are the righteousness of God. That's how strange it is in the kingdom of God—the poor become rich, the naked are clothed, and the frozen are warmed. There is nothing in between.

Each of the seven messages begins with a statement about Christ. (Some of the things that were said about Him in the first chapter of Revelation are repeated there.) They end with a promise to those who prevail. Christ acknowledges him, he'll be clothed in righteousness, all will be forgiven, and his name will be in the book of life. Christ has written His name on him; he belongs to Christ. He lives the new yet secret life, eats of the secret manna, and carries a secret stone with a name the world doesn't recognize. Some day he will also share Christ's glory in His kingdom and eat of the tree of life in God's paradise. Oh that we were there!

> *Lord,* how will I prevail? How will I prevail over the world? Faith in You is the victory that overcomes the world. I can't achieve that faith by myself. It's a gift from You. I pray for Your mercy to be able to receive the gift. Deliver me from my own self-satisfaction and complacency. May I never become half-hearted and satisfied and content with what I have. Give me the hunger and thirst that craves

You constantly and that You've promised to
quench. Then I'll know the victory is mine through
sharing Your victory, my Lord and Savior.

FRIDAY AFTER
TENTH SUNDAY
AFTER TRINITY
1 John 1:1–10

If we say we have not sinned, we make Him a liar, and His
word is not in us. 1 John 1:10

One of the main reasons we waste the opportunities God
gives us is because we assume there is nothing wrong with
us, just as the Christians in Laodicea assumed. They thought
they didn't need improvement. Maybe it's because we live
without God and never even consider testing ourselves by
the standards we receive in His Word. It's also possible, however, that there's room for the Word, the church service, and
prayer in our lives. We want to be Christians. We may have
a clear picture of when and how we became Christian. We
still belong to the kind of people, however, that John talks
about here; those who say they have no sin. John says that's
when we deceive ourselves. God's Word is not inside of us.
No matter how much we hear it and know about it, it isn't
living in us the way the Gospel should: like God's power of
salvation.

John says God is light. There is no darkness in Him. He's
a penetrating, revealing, overwhelming, bright, and pure

light. If we walk in that light, we won't be able to avoid seeing both the fact that we have sinned and that we have sin. Sin is deeply rooted in our nature.

John says this full of exuberant joy. He begins his letter with a surge of enthusiastic thanksgiving for what he's been a part of and what he can now share with others. He's writing because he wants his joy and the recipient's joy to be complete. He knows he has something fantastic, something unbelievably joyous and delightful to tell. He has seen God! The eternal, that which was from the beginning, the invisible, unreachable, inexpressible, that which was with God and was God, has come to us. He has seen it with his own eyes. He touched it with his hands. He knows it's there and that it's real. Life eternal that was with the Father has come to us. In this life there's forgiveness for everything. We can be cleansed from all unrighteousness. All we have to do is confess to it and come to Him, who is the life and the light.

> *Out of the depths I cry to You, O LORD! O LORD, hear my voice! Let Your ears be attentive to the voice of my pleas for mercy! If You, O LORD, should mark iniquities, O LORD, who could stand? But with You there is forgiveness, that You may be feared. I wait for the LORD, my soul waits, and in His word I hope; my soul waits for the Lord more than watchmen for the morning, more than watchmen for the morning. O Israel, hope in the LORD! For with the LORD there is steadfast love, and with Him is plentiful redemption. And He will redeem Israel from all his iniquities (Psalm 130).*

SATURDAY AFTER TENTH SUNDAY AFTER TRINITY

1 John 2:1–14

I am writing these things to you so that you may not sin.
1 John 2:1

John had just spoken about forgiveness of sins. Then he again summarized the message in the Gospel: Christ is our advocate, the expiation for our sins, the righteous one who shares His righteousness. However, John is not preaching this in order for us to think we can take sin lightly and assume that as long as we have Jesus, we don't need to worry about anything. On the contrary, the section of the Gospel that talks about the forgiveness of sins is preached to keep us from sinning. We're taken to Jesus and have the chance to get to know Him so we can live with Him. When we get to know Him, we show it by loving Him and doing His will. We keep His Commandments and keep His Word.

John uses the expressions he learned from Jesus that we often hear in the Fourth Gospel. Keeping the Word means loving it, sticking to it, living with it, and keeping it holy and precious. It's much more than receiving a few rules of conduct or instructions. It's about receiving the living Lord, whom you love, devote yourself to, and follow. You walk in the light, and it's clear in the way you value, think, and react. You can't hate your brother, hold a grudge, and think about revenge when you walk with Jesus. If you do, you've broken ties with Him and wander in darkness.

Walking with Jesus is walking in love. It's more than confessing to the commandment of love and realizing that it's the most important thing. John shows us the secret in the commandment of love. In a way it's an old commandment, something we've heard from childhood. At the same time it's something new. It's not something we know and recognize because we've heard it and agreed to it. It's new over and over again, and it applies to Jesus as well as us. Jesus is constantly showing us what love means. He shows us in real life situations. He gives us new duties, allows us to meet new people, have new difficulties and new problems, all so we once again have to learn how to love as He loved. Then the commandment becomes new to us. We understand better and more clearly what love is. We've started a process where "the darkness is passing away and the true light is already shining" (1 John 2:8). Daylight doesn't come all at once. Darkness lingers in our hearts also. Christ takes us step by step toward acts of love. We know it's the true light that shines when we stick by Him and let Him lead us.

True Christianity is not a principle that makes love the highest norm for our actions. True Christianity is living with Christ every day and allowing Him to teach us what love is.

My Lord Jesus, You have embraced me in Your love and allowed me to be with You in Your kingdom. I pray that You have mercy and patience with me, even though I'm a slow learner and make poor progress. Despite this, let me go to Your school and be instructed by You. Only You can teach me to love not only those who are far away, but even my brother whom I've seen, the people You've given me the opportunity to be with. May Your commandment always be new for my heart and mind and will, through Your guidance and Your permission for me to follow You and take everything from Your hand.

Luke 18:9–14

Some who trusted in themselves that they were righteous,
and treated others with contempt. Luke 18:9

Self-righteous people aren't uncommon. They're also not
alone in thinking they're the right kind of people. Usually
there's a group, maybe a race or nation, that agrees with
them. In fact, they're a devilish mutation of something good
that God created with the nature of man: a feeling of justice,
ambition, sense of duty, responsibility for the community,
the will to do what's right. The things they do are to a large
degree correct and proper. The things they condemn and
repudiate *are* often times harmful and shameful. Still there's
something askew with it all.

This self-righteousness can have a political dimension.
We feel that those who belong to our party or our ideology
are right. The others are selfish, ruthless, power-hungry, and,
at the very least, blind. Self-righteousness can be national.
Others don't have the same culture, the same willingness to
work, the same sense of law and order, the same fair social
system that we have.

Jesus tells us today, however, that self-righteousness can
be considered pious—and that's when it's especially bad. It
can be so deep-rooted in us that we don't see it even when
Jesus puts the Pharisee in the temple in front of us. We're
used to placing the Pharisees on the other side, among the vil-
lains and criminals in life. Of course we don't belong there.

What would a pious Pharisee look like today? He would
go to church, be respectable, conscientious, and generally
revered. He would be a proponent of law and order, pay
his taxes, respect traffic regulations, and be an exemplary
employee. He would admit that he's a sinner in general terms,

but he would be very aware of the fact that he wasn't the kind of sinner that all of these irresponsible, filthy, drug-addicts are, of which there are so many and that the police, who, according to his firm opinion, should be doing something about. He might also even thank God that he wasn't like certain people and their supporters in South Africa or Chile or some communist regime.

The picture can change. You see the best picture of yourself reflected in the mirror because we all have in us the old Adam, who is always inclined to find himself righteous and has very good reasons to find contempt in others. It's good for us to see that picture of ourselves. It can help us *sincerely* say as the publican did: God, be merciful to me, a sinner.

Lord, here I stand. I can only boast and confess that I have many times thought I was better than others. Lord, I know I should thank You for Your blessings. I know what could have become of me without Your mercy. It is with unbound joy that I may be a part of Your Church and Your kingdom, to be able to live like a Christian and not of the world. Help me to be thankful, joyous, and happy for all You've given me, without for a moment despising or looking down upon those who haven't received the same joy—not even when they despise or look down upon me. Make me one of Your thankful and happy children. God, be merciful to me, a sinner.

For all that is in the world—the desires of the flesh and the desires of the eyes and pride in possessions—is not from the Father but is from the world. 1 John 2:16

With the words, "the world," John is writing not about the world God created. God's creation is good; God's children find happiness in it. "The world" here means that which has fallen away and has turned away from God, the rebellious world. This fallen world is everywhere around the good world God created. John describes here what is in the world and is therefore evil. First, he mentions the carnal desires, literally "the lust of the flesh." The flesh is like the old Adam—evil, self-important, selfish. Everything man desires and wishes belongs to the kingdom of the world. It might be success or money, pleasure or fame. There's always something I want for myself, without God, simply because I want it, not because I receive it from God to use it as His steward.

Then John talks about the eye's desire, literally "the lust of the eye." That's a vivid description. You can almost see the eye dilating when it focuses on something it has to have. Inside of us there's the desire to have—an urge to possess, to be able to call it our *own*—that far surpasses what we really need and is useful. This desire is followed by its shadow: envy. It's a part of the old Adam's nature to envy what others have and to measure our own happiness not by what we own and can find joy in but what others have. When we have something that's our own, then the third thing John mentions comes naturally: vanity. We value ourselves by what we own, maybe materialistically by how much we make or how large our fortune is, or, in a more refined way, by everything beautiful and expensive we've collected.

That desire and that vanity are not of the Father but are of the world. If this is the love of my life, if this is what occupies my thoughts and what I long for; if this is what I am afraid of losing and am glad if I get more of it, then the Father is not in me. Some of this exists in all mankind because we're all of the flesh and the old Adam is with us wherever we go. The question is if we let him decide or take him to Christ and say: Be merciful to me, a sinner.

Lord, help me to be joyful for all Your wonderful gifts without becoming conceited. Help me to receive them with joy and give them back without regret when You ask for them. Help me be a good steward, realizing that everything is Yours and nothing is mine. Help me to be as happy about the prosperity of others as I am for my own. I thank You with all my heart for the good things You've given me. Bless my hands, so they don't clench themselves in an effort to keep these things but open to use them as blessings, and gladly let You take them when You want to give them to someone else.

TUESDAY AFTER ELEVENTH SUNDAY AFTER TRINITY

1 John 3:1–12

No one born of God makes a practice of sinning.
1 John 3:9

John recently said that if we say we have no sin, the truth is not in us. Here he says that if you're born of God, you won't sin and can't sin. How do we make sense of this?

John teaches the same thing Paul and the entire New Testament teach: even a Christian *has* sin. He still possesses the old Adam. He still possesses the flesh that neither can nor will yield to God's law. He's constantly at odds with the flesh. He can't deny it because it's a part of him and, therefore, is in constant need of forgiveness.

It's a different thing to *commit* sin deliberately without admitting that it's wrong. That's how the old Adam reacts. If he prevails, you can't be a Christian. A Christian is a new person, who is "born of God" besides possessing his old Adam. This new person, the man of Christ, can't sin. Christ has penetrated him and become a part of his life; he's guided by the Spirit. There are two forces in a Christian: the flesh and the Spirit, and those two are at odds with each other, as Paul says (Galatians 5:17).

If we allow the flesh to prevail, we extinguish the Spirit. Life dies in the branch that was engrafted in Christ. Then we're back to the world the devil dominates. He has rebelled against God since the beginning of time. He compels us to commit acts that go against God's will. The serious thing is that we can be the children of his spirit, as we could be the children of God's Spirit, and we must be one of these two.

If we're allowed to be God's children, it's because of God's love, John says. It's something that's undeserved, but genuine. For Christ's sake we're considered to be God's children and called God's children, and we really *are* also if we, through faith, become a part of Christ. We're still living with sin inside us here on earth. We're looking forward to the great transformation, however. It's not apparent yet what we'll become that day, but we do know we'll be like Him and look like He did after His resurrection. John then adds something very important: everyone who has hope will be cleansed as Christ is cleansed. We've become His members. We belong to Him. He lives inside of us. How could we do anything else?

That's the Gospel. By grace are we saved, through faith—not through good deeds, but for Christ's sake. He who is saved, however, serves his Lord with joy and wishes with all his heart that he could be like Him.

My dear Lord and Savior, once again I hear the tremendous truth about Your mercy, and once again I'm tempted to think that I've heard this so many times, I know it by now. Is that because I receive it with my head instead of my heart? Lord, touch my heart so Your Gospel becomes my heart's treasure and the driving force of my being. You promised to come to those who believe, to stay with us and live with us. Let that happen to me. Give me useful concern when I examine my deeds and actions so I come closer to You. Give me assurance when I look at You, so I know whom I believe in. Give me a joyous and kind willingness when I look upon my fellow men, so I can serve them with joy.

WEDNESDAY AFTER ELEVENTH SUNDAY AFTER TRINITY

1 John 3:13–24

But if anyone has the world's goods and sees his brother in need, yet closes his heart against him, how does God's love abide in him? 1 John 3:17

You can't open your heart to God if you close it to your neighbor. The rule in God's kingdom is to get for nothing and give for nothing. You can't receive something and just keep it for yourself. That stands for both forgiveness and the good things in the world. To close your heart to someone who is in need isn't only rejecting someone, it can also consist of blinding oneself to injustice and letting the world have its evil way, although you could've done something to create better conditions. John warns us about loving "in word or talk" (1 John 3:18). You can do that in pious conversation. You can also do it with resolutions and statements that aren't at all obligating and for the most part ineffective. John asks us to love "in deed and in truth" (1 John 3:18). Love consists of *action*. It takes form in exactly those deeds that God puts in front of us. At the same time it consists of *truth*: it's both realistic and sincere, both down to earth and warm. It's love for my neighbor, for the people I interact with and can do something for.

John tells us that when we live in that love, we know we're a part of the truth. That's a painful word for all those who are "awakened." That's the last thing an uneasy conscience can convince itself of: that I would be truly loving toward everyone else. On the contrary, any conscience that's alert to this point must let the old Adam come forth and decide *not* to love. Also, if we try to convince ourselves that we're right with God through self-sacrifice and self-denial, with big donations and lavish favors, we'll never find peace or feel we've done enough. As long, that is, as we listen to the reproaches of the law and our conscience.

John, however, is speaking here to people who know Christ, love Him, and believe in Him as our Savior and Redeemer. Therefore John can say that we know all this "by the Spirit He has given us" (1 John 3:24). He knows it's very possible that "our heart condemns us" (1 John 3:20). The Commandments are written in our hearts and no one can prevail when confronted by them. God, however, is bigger than our heart. He knows everything, even that which an uneasy conscience doesn't know. We find His thoughts in His plan for salvation, in His tremendous sacrifice when He gave His only Son for us. That's where we learned to know love.

When we believe this and live accordingly, then we know we have gone from death to life. The crucial thing won't be that we can say as the Pharisee said in the temple: I've done this, that, and the other thing . . . I've done it *all*. We can say as Peter said: Lord, You know everything, You know that I love You.

Lord, this is Your commandment, that we believe in Your Son and love one another, which we can do only with Your help. Send us Your wonderful Spirit to teach us to love and believe. We open our hearts and pray that You will let Your mercy shine on our dry land and let it grow there, together with everything that comes from You. Let us receive so we can give. Bless us so we can be a blessing. Give us Your love so we can love. Thy will be done on earth as it is in heaven, with us and through us.

THURSDAY AFTER ELEVENTH SUNDAY AFTER TRINITY

1 John 4:1–12

In this the love of God was made manifest among us, that God sent His only Son into the world, so that we might live through Him. 1 John 4:9

John says that God's love was made *manifest*. This is one of the things we humans would know nothing about if God hadn't let us see it. We know nothing about love, although many think they do. When they hear that God is love and that the commandment of love is the most important of all Commandments, then they think they know what Christianity is all about. They even correct their Christian friends and tell them how they should be: A Christian should be kind, and he shouldn't judge. He can't be so loveless that he can claim that others are wrong or that there actually are false teachings that could be dangerous. He must understand that all people are God's children, even if they don't show their Christianity outwardly by attending church or receiving Communion.

When you read John, the apostle of love, you notice that there must be something wrong with this. No one can speak more intensely and intimately about love than he can. At the same time, no one can warn more intensely or sincerely about false teachings and false prophets. Also, he doesn't digress from the objective when he points out false teaching. It's false if it doesn't clearly confess to what we call the dogma about Christ, the teaching that He is God's Son who came in the flesh, in other words, became man and that God sent Him as atonement for our sins. *In that way* God's love became manifest among us. That's what God's love is. It loves sinners like us, who are hopelessly separated from this divine love. To win us back, God offered His only Son. Each and every one of us who doesn't confess Jesus in that way is not of God. He shows us exactly the thing God's love wants to give us when He sacrificed the dearest thing He had. Anyone who denies this and teaches this denial to others is also dangerous for others. John doesn't hesitate to say that this is the spirit of the antichrist. This is a spiritual force that wants to destroy what Jesus came to accomplish. However "kind" one is, the denial of Christ is dangerous and fatal.

As clear and relentless as John is on this point, so is he equally clear when it comes to pointing out that God really *is* love, that He *wants* love, that everyone who knows Him and lives in His fellowship *possesses* love, and that love really is kindness, mercy, helpfulness, and a generosity that would give one's life for one's brethren. God's love is relentless rejection to lies and boundless generosity toward those who are lost.

Lord, it's so easy to be simply kind to others, so teach me about Your love. We are all sinners and need mercy. Help me to see that's exactly why we all need Your truth and salvation. It's so unmerciful to conceal it and pretend to think there are other paths than the one You paved. Help me maintain Your truth and do it out of love, only love. Not irritated, not condemning, not with reluctance toward anyone, but only because You love all of them and they all need You.

FRIDAY AFTER ELEVENTH SUNDAY AFTER TRINITY

1 John 4:13–5:3

We love because He first loved us. 1 John 4:19

All Christian love emanates from God's love. Without Christ, we wouldn't know what love is. Christ has not only shown us how to live in love, He instituted love itself into the world. He became one with us when He took our sins upon Himself. His love drowned our sins. As members of His body, He lets this love flow in us.

We have come to know this love, John says. It's not a theory or empty words. It works within us. If it doesn't, we deceive ourselves when we say we love God. Love is more than just a feeling. You can *feel* like you love God. That can be the same kind of self-deception you feel when you believe you have a good heart because you can suffer with people you see in the news or read about. If you really love, it becomes clear in the face of harsh and tangible reality where we meet people of flesh and blood with idiosyncrasies and problems, people who can be difficult and awkward, but actually suffer. John preaches that he who doesn't love his brother cannot love God.

If we test ourselves on this point, it'll happen time and time again that our conscience judges us. We're afraid of Judgment Day. This is proof that we aren't perfect in love. When we live in love and are driven by love, we no longer think of punishment. We don't think about what will become of us. Instead, we think about what we can do for others. Perfect love drives fear away. When we look ahead to Judgment Day, we do it with joy because we are like Him in this world. He has done everything. He has eternal life, and He's given us everything. We are His members. He's responsible for us, and we serve Him. We love because He first loved us. We keep His Commandments and consider it a joy, not a burden, to do as He wishes.

That's how the new man lives when he's become perfect in love. Still, the old Adam remains, causing resistance and struggle. However, He who abides in you is greater than that of the world. We know whom we belong to and are therefore in good spirits.

Lord, I think of all the many people I have encountered and precisely therefore have such a hard time to love. I've seen so much that has angered me, hurt me, and upset me. You, Lord, have also seen them. You know everything about them and still love them. They need You. Help me see when I can serve You by helping them. Help me to see them with Your eyes at that moment. Help me see the opportunity so I can take it. Help me see what You want done so I can do just that. Help me to see You so I am warmed by Your love and can give that love to others. For Your love's sake.

SATURDAY AFTER ELEVENTH SUNDAY AFTER TRINITY
1 John 5:4–21

This is He who came by water and blood—Jesus Christ; not by the water only but by the water and the blood. 1 John 5:6

John tells us in his gospel about an eyewitness, himself obviously, who stood under Jesus' cross when one of the soldiers pierced the side of the dead Savior. This witness saw blood and water come from the wound.

John saw a sign in this, something that had a deeper meaning. A stream of life came from the dead Savior on the cross that would reach the whole world. That stream would come with water in Baptism and blood in the Communion cup. It would carry with it Jesus' victory on the cross.

In his letter he writes about this sight. We can regard these words as a very useful reminder that Christ has come to us with water in Baptism. However, He has also come with blood. A Christian is not only baptized, but a guest at Communion. You can't take Communion once, as with Baptism, and then in belief go about your life. Communion is something to be taken regularly. Through Baptism we've been incorporated into Christ as members in His body. Now the stream of life from Him pulsates through us also. Through Communion this stream reaches us as the blood that cleanses us from all sin. In Communion we drink from the source of life and forgiveness. We are at the cross and the gates of heaven at the same time that open slightly and let us hear the never ending exultations surrounding the Lamb of God and catch a glimpse of His glory.

John explains that there are three witnesses: the Spirit, the water, and the blood. In those days we heard the Spirit's testimony in the apostles' and prophets' sermons and in the Old Testament scriptures. It's the same testimony we have in our Bible. The Spirit testifies there all the time. The Word becomes words *to* us, about us, and about the Savior who is *our* Savior. It becomes the property of our hearts. "Whoever believes in the Son of God has the testimony in himself" (1 John 5:10). And that's the only way to overcome the world.

Three witnesses. A Christian is thankful for all three. He doesn't say it's enough with only one or two of these witnesses. It's wonderful that we have the Spirit who speaks in the Word. That doesn't make Baptism any less precious. And it's only more wonderful that we also have Holy Communion.

Your steadfast love, O LORD, extends to the heavens, Your faithfulness to the clouds. Your righteousness is like the mountains of God; Your judgments are like the great deep; man and beast You save, O LORD. How precious is Your steadfast love, O God! The children of mankind take refuge in the shadow of Your wings. They feast on the abundance of Your house, and You give them drink from the river of Your delights. For with You is the fountain of life; in Your light do we see light. Oh, continue Your steadfast love to those who know You, and Your righteousness to the upright of heart! (From Psalm 36:5–10.)

TWELFTH SUNDAY AFTER TRINITY
Mark 7:31–37

Ephphatha! Mark 7:34

There are Aramaic words in a few places in the Gospels that have been preserved as Jesus uttered them, words that must have etched themselves into the minds of the apostles.

These words were so expressive and full of substance that they were repeated when the account was retold in Greek. It's not hard to imagine how Mark, who translated for Peter, used the word *Ephphatha* when he translated an account like this one about the man who was deaf and dumb. The word had a very special ring to it that was hard to express in Greek, just as he preserved the word *Abba,* in "Abba, Father" or *Amen* in "Amen I say to you" (which usually is translated as: Verily I say unto you).

What was it about this word *Ephphatha?*

They brought a man to Jesus, one who was deaf and almost dumb. Jesus did what they often did back then when they tried to cure diseases. He touched the ailing part of the body and wet it with saliva. This might have been His way of communicating with the deaf man and showing him that He wanted to help. After that, however, He didn't use a spell or incantation, as the witch doctors of that time did, but just one powerful word, a word with God's all-vanquishing power in it.

As with so many of God's words, it was a word that had a much deeper meaning than the everyday meaning. First of all it meant: Open, closed mouth. Move, lame tongue, and let the words you're holding back come forth. The underlying meaning, however, was: Open yourself to the power of God. May you, heart of man, receive this gift from God. The kingdom of God is near. You are being visited today. Open your heart and receive.

The disciples understood. Through the prophets they read that deaf ears would be made to hear at the time of salvation, when God is watching out for His people. They understood that this was a sign and testimony. They would open themselves and receive something that never before was offered to anyone on earth.

It's the same exhortation that then went out to all nations and once again applies to us: *Ephphatha!*

*I want to open my heart and my entire self for You like this, Lord Jesus. Only you can help me do that. Say Your powerful **Ephphatha** to my soul. Command my heart to open up even in its innermost hiding places to receive You and Your glory. Command my tongue to be untied so I can praise You and speak kind words to others, words that carry warmth and healing and blessings with them. Command my complete essence to open up so I can receive for nothing and give for nothing, richly and lavishly, as You would want me to do.*

MONDAY AFTER TWELFTH SUNDAY AFTER TRINITY

Luke 14:1–11

Is it lawful to heal on the Sabbath, or not? Luke 14:3

The little book *The Freedom of a Christian* is among Martin Luther's most famous works. In it he puts forth two theses:

1. A Christian is the most independent master over everything and subservient to no one.
2. A Christian is the most obliging of servants and subservient to everything.

Luther says this might appear to be a contradiction, but it is not. A Christian's soul is liberated through faith in Christ. He is liberated from all compulsion to try to deserve his salvation and from all demands that must first be fulfilled if he wants to be God's child. Therefore he's liberated from all matters of prestige and all attempts to assert himself. He is simply a pardoned sinner, a happy child of God for Jesus' sake.

That also means, however, that he is a joyous and obliging servant. He no longer has to fulfill the obligations of the Law to be God's child, but he does it gladly to serve his neighbor and do good for others in gratitude for everything good Christ has done for us. God's Commandments aren't there so we know how we can be saved. They exist so we can help our fellow man and be of joy and blessing to them.

It's this kind of liberation Jesus talks about in today's Scripture reading. For the Jews, the laws of the Sabbath were among many they obeyed, oftentimes reluctantly, so they wouldn't lose God's mercy. They fulfilled them for their own sake, to gain God's pleasure. Jesus shows what's wrong with this. The laws of Sabbath, like all other commandments, exist for our neighbor's sake. Therefore, helping your neighbor can never be an obstacle. God's children are liberated so they can serve each other.

When it then came to what place one had at the table and the exact order of preference that was so important at that time, "He told a parable." What Jesus said had a much more profound meaning. This parable is not to be understood as advisable rules for the person who wants to be honored. It has to do with the upside down order of things in God's kingdom. We are invited to the mighty king's wedding. We don't deserve it. If we come with expectations of where we should sit, be it among "the sincere seekers" or "those who did their best" or "those who at least aren't hypocrites," we'll be left standing with our shame. If we attend with the shame of not being able to offer anything, however, we will be led to one of the places of honor. He who is finally liberated from all prestige and the threat of the Law gladly serves in the most humble of tasks; and those are the finest.

O Lord, my heart is not lifted up; my eyes are not raised too high; I do not occupy myself with things too great and too marvelous for me. But I have calmed and quieted my soul, like a weaned child with its mother; like a weaned child is my soul within me. O Israel, hope in the Lord from this time forth and forevermore (Psalm 131).

TUESDAY AFTER TWELFTH SUNDAY AFTER TRINITY

Acts 15:1–21

But we believe that we will be saved through the grace of the Lord Jesus. Acts 15:11

What's written in this chapter happened around AD 50. Paul had returned from his first missionary trip in Antioch two or three years earlier. He had experienced exciting and fantastic adventures we can read about in the two previous chapters in Acts. Above all, he had experienced everywhere that the heathens were prepared to receive the Gospel. There were Christian congregations far in the highlands of Asia Minor. Also in Antioch, the Greek capital, the metropolitan of Syria, and the heart of the Mediterranean, congregations were growing continuously.

However, dissension began. It was started by some Christian Jews who came from Jerusalem. They found it alarming that the Greek Christians weren't circumcised and didn't follow the Law of Moses. They knew exactly what to say. "You must do that. Otherwise you won't be saved!"

After that, dissension was unavoidable. There are instances when the Gospel's purity is at stake; then there's no room for compromise. Here it was a matter of the very foundation for salvation. The Jews claimed that circumcision and the law were prerequisites. Paul knew that Jesus Christ was the only foundation, and that it was through faith in Him—faith *alone*—that we're saved.

It was a standoff. Their opinions were diametrically opposed. Both couldn't be right. Then something happened that would serve as a model for all the times ahead. They decided to summon all the best servants in the church regarding experience and piety, listen to the apostles and the faithful confessors in Jerusalem, those who were there from the beginning and remained steadfast during the times of persecution, and all this together they would present to God.

That's how the first synod was created. The obvious leaders were the apostles. The elders were at their side, and the priests, who were becoming the ministers, leaders, and teachers in the congregations.

At the meeting in Jerusalem, Paul was supported by Peter. He put his finger on the decisive matter, clearly and convincingly: We believe that we are saved through the grace of the Lord Jesus. Even James (Jesus' brother) agreed, although he lived as a law abiding Jew just as his ancestors had. Even he was completely convinced that the Law of Moses couldn't be imposed on the heathens as a condition for salvation.

That's how Christian liberation was established, and it's very clear what it entails: liberation from the Law as a condition for salvation, liberated to be God's child through faith in Jesus.

I thank You, dear Lord, that You've taught me where the right place is for Your Law. There was a time when it stood between us; it was in my way. When you showed me all my faults, it scared and threatened me and it meant that I couldn't stand before You as I am. Now You've paved the way and allow me to come for Your own sake. Your Law is behind me; I see it when I turn around to go out among my fellow men. I know Your Law is good and speaks with Your voice and comes from Your love and, therefore, I'll gladly listen to it when I make my decisions, do my work, and form my day. Thy will be done.

WEDNESDAY AFTER TWELFTH SUNDAY AFTER TRINITY

Acts 15:22–41

For though I am free from all, I have made myself a servant to all, that I might win more of them. 1 Corinthians 9:19

At the first synod meeting in Jerusalem, in AD 50, it was established that the Gentile Christians didn't have to follow the Law of Moses. They repudiated the proponents of the Law that had troubled people by saying that if you don't do this and that, you won't be saved. Salvation depends on Jesus and faith, not in the Law and good works.

If, however, you believe in Jesus, then you love Him

and are driven by your love for Him. Consequently, don't live for yourself but live with your neighbor's best interest in mind. We've seen that thought in Paul time and time again. He could fight like a lion for a Christian's liberty. He was also ready to refrain from liberty in an effort to avoid hurting someone. "To the Jews I became as a Jew, in order to win Jews. To those under the law I became as one under the law (though not being myself under the law) that I might win those under the law. . . . I have become all things to all people, that by all means I might save some" (1 Corinthians 9:20, 22).

We see the same point of view in the decision made in Jerusalem and that the Gentile Christians in Antioch, together with all the other congregations there, were informed of. They need not take upon themselves the burden of the Law of Moses. There were a few points, however, they should respect. They shouldn't eat food made from blood nor the kind of meat where blood remained in it (this concerned, among other things, all the meat butchered for the sacrifices in the temple and the major portion of meat sold in the market). This meat was an abomination for the Jews. They had their own way of butchering and ate only meat prepared in this way. Those who chose to live with them and enjoy the fellowship of a meal had to show consideration for this. Besides this, they had to restrain from fornication, which meant what were considered forbidden marriages. In the Law of Moses they were described in the same context as the rules regarding meat and food made from blood (Leviticus 17–18), and they would've caused quite a shock if these rules were ignored. (The fact that all forms of fornication were forbidden for a Christian was as obvious as was stealing or killing. It was a part of everything Jesus commanded, things all His disciples would learn and keep in accordance with Jesus' Great Commission.)

Here it was a question of showing consideration to "weak brethren," as Paul would've expressed it. Therefore, these special provisions regarding meat sacrificed to idols and blood food ceased to apply when one could no longer hurt someone by using his Christian liberty. Paul's letters clearly show this (1 Corinthians 8, Colossians 2, 1 Timothy 4). This doesn't mean that Paul violated the decision in Jerusalem. On the contrary, he understood it correctly, namely, as an expression of a Christian's liberation.

Lord, when You give us our freedom, we're really free. May we experience the freedom only You can give. Freedom from the fear that we'll miss something that will profit us. Freedom from the necessity to hold our own and be respected. The freedom to be generous, thankful, and helpful. The freedom to be what You called us to be: light and salt and contributors to others' joy.

THURSDAY AFTER TWELFTH SUNDAY AFTER TRINITY

Acts 16:1–22

Am I not free? . . . But if not of my own will, I am still entrusted with a stewardship. 1 Corinthians 9:1, 17

This is true liberation: you are a servant of Christ, making you wonderfully free. People usually think of freedom as being independent of all authority and rules they didn't make themselves. Real freedom is the freedom to be what we've been created to be: free from sin, free to serve, free to be God's happy children. Therefore we never hear in the New Testament that we can do as we please. "You were called to freedom, brothers. Only do not use your freedom as an opportunity for the flesh, but through love serve one another" (Galatians 5:13). A Christian "walks in the Spirit," driven by the spirit of Christ, as a ship sailing to its destination in fair wind. The sailor feels a sense of freedom and happiness as the wind fills his sails.

We notice how the apostles experienced their freedom in just this way, as they're carried forward by the Spirit. "The Holy Spirit and we have decided . . ." they wrote from the first synod meeting in Jerusalem. The Holy Spirit didn't allow Paul and Silas to go to the province in Asia or Bithynia. Instead, He led them to Europe. Because He directed them, they felt as if they were free, independent of random chance and the forces of the world.

In Lystra, Asia Minor, Paul met Timothy, who became one of his most faithful followers. He was half Greek and wasn't circumcised. He did this out of consideration for all the Jews, who would've had a hard time listening to someone who wasn't circumcised. It was in complete accordance with the rule about showing consideration to weak brethren. Paul, however, could also do just the opposite. In Galatians 2:3 he tells us about Titus, who followed him to the synod meeting in Jerusalem and who didn't have to be circumcised. There were of course a few false brethren who had infiltrated the congregation "to spy out our freedom that we have in Christ Jesus, so that they might bring us into slavery" (by saying you must be circumcised if you're to be saved). Paul says that time "we did not yield in submission even for a moment, so that the truth of the gospel might be preserved for you" (Galatians 2:4–5). When people make up false conditions for salvation, you can't give in. Then it's not a question of weak brethren but of spiritual tyrants. About them, Luther says, "we should stand up to them, in deed oppose them and fearlessly anger them, so that they can't with their sinful prejudice drag others with them in their error."

My Lord and Savior, I pray that You will give me the tremendous gift to be able to see clearly so I can distinguish between weak brethren and spiritual tyrants. Make me tender-hearted and gentle toward those who have a hard time holding their own and so easily lose sight of You. Make me steadfast and unyielding to everything and everyone who tries to hide Your Gospel and claim that there are other ways, other conditions, and other demands than those that come from You alone, our Lord and Savior.

FRIDAY AFTER TWELFTH SUNDAY AFTER TRINITY
Acts 16:23–40

About midnight Paul and Silas were praying and singing hymns to God. Acts 16:25

That's the way it is with Christian freedom. Paul and Silas couldn't be considered less free than they were. They sat chained in shackles, at the far end of a dark prison. There was dirt and excrement, humidity and insects. Despite this there were songs, hymns. And the other prisoners listened in the middle of the night.

The ones singing weren't better off than anyone else. They probably had it worse. They were imprisoned contrary to all law and justice. They were whipped time and time again. Their backs were covered with blood and bruises and their clothes stuck to the wounds. The shackles chafed their ankles and the insects crawled on their backs. Still, they sung their hymns.

We see that it wasn't an exaggeration when Paul, a decade earlier, wrote to the Philippians that he had learned to be content in all situations and that he was able to bear everything "through Him who strengthens me" (Philippians 4:13). He had shown that in Philippi.

A person can be free even when he's been imprisoned, insulted, and degraded. Luther says this freedom is spiritual and reigns among enemies and is powerful in the midst of distress. Even the cross and death are compelled to serve me and contribute to my salvation.

Paul and Silas had had it unusually good the previous days. Luke, who was most likely with them since he used words like "we" and "us," tells us how they met Lydia, who was evidently both rich and ambitious, one of the Greeks who frequented the synagogue and understood that the God of Israel was the only true God. She was baptized with her servants and invited the strangers to live in her house. Paul thankfully accepted and probably thanked God also, as he now thanked God in jail. "I can have abundance and endure scarcity," in both cases as a free man who isn't bound by either.

Then the unexpected events happened. Paul received proof that God meant him to be imprisoned; there were people who needed him even there. And the next day he was free.

Now he showed another side of his Christian freedom, however. He was a victim of injustice and ill-treatment. He would not let this injustice pass unnoticed. The judges deserved a warning. Paul referred to his position as a Roman citizen and gave them the scare they deserved. They had to apologize. It wasn't revenge but almost like a favor, a contribution to public law in the Roman Empire. Paul could both refrain from his rights and use them, all in the service of the Lord.

Lord, when I have You, I need nothing else on earth. May this be my heart's confession, something that's always inside of me and that works as a power and as security. What can harm me if You're holding my hand and leading me with Your advice? What do I have to be afraid of when You're with me? What must I cling to and try to hold on to when You free me from it? Lord, You are my light and salvation, my tomorrow and eternity. Praise be to Your name.

SATURDAY AFTER
TWELFTH SUNDAY
AFTER TRINITY
Romans 12:1–8

So we, though many, are one body in Christ, and
individually members one of another. Having gifts that
differ... Romans 12:5–6

We have different gifts, different talents, and different
purposes. Yet we all are one because we're members in
Christ's body. We are "individually members one of another"
as it is literally expressed in the original text. That means we
are members that serve one another.

Becoming a Christian means discovering this. I'm not an
isolated individual who has to take care of himself and live
his own life. I'm a member connected to other members. I'm
here to carry out something that other members need. The
eye, ear, and hand don't exist for their own sake. They exist
so the whole body can function. That's the way it is with us.
God has incorporated us into a family, a community, a congregation, and mankind *for the sake of others.*

In other words, God had a purpose when He put me
in the situation I'm in right now. It's not always easy to see
the purpose. Living like a Christian doesn't just mean living
respectably, honorably, and lovingly in accordance with how
the world sees it. When Paul admonishes others, he starts by
saying that the whole Christian life is something other than living by the standard of the world we live in. It's a question of a
transformation and an inward replenishment that consists of our
becoming one with Christ. Therefore Paul always begins by
telling us how it happens and what it means. *Then* we can talk
about how we live. He starts by saying we must offer our bodies, not only our hearts, as sacrifice to God. Our material lives,
everyday life with all of its down to earth realities, are spiritual

temple service we do in the face of God and at His command. The other people I have to deal with have received a different name. In the Bible they're called *my neighbors*, those God has placed closest to me, those I should love and serve first of all. Tomorrow, the scripture reading is about just that.

Lord, bless the Sunday we have in front of us. Bless all those You have chosen to serve Your Church. May they serve joyously so they can show us how wonderful it is to serve You. Bless all those You have given a gift to, that they use that gift to Your honor and to the benefit of the congregation. Bless those who let Your gifts go to waste, that they might realize what they're missing and how badly they're acting. Help us all to serve humbly and openly with the gift we've received, to the honor of Your name and to the joy and benefit of others.

THIRTEENTH SUNDAY AFTER TRINITY
Luke 10:23–37

And who is my neighbor? Luke 10:29

We receive the answer from Jesus Himself. Sometimes we want to excuse ourselves and ask who our neighbor is. We can't help everyone! There are so unbelievably many!

Destitution is so enormous. Maybe we try to excuse ourselves by saying that at least we have the correct opinions. We make an effort to protest against violence and oppression in the world. My *neighbor*, however, is someone I've interacted with, who's been close to me, someone to whom I can give a helping hand, and where I've so often committed the great sin of *passing him by*.

The priest and the Levite did that. God had placed a poor man at the roadside, exactly where they walked. They saw and quickly passed by. That sin is easy for all of us to commit. Especially when it's a question of those who are closest to us. It can be a question of our nearest and dearest, someone suffering from fatigue, who can't finish his work for the day and can't do what we feel he should accomplish. We pass him by, don't get involved, won't change our ways, don't want to take any more responsibility upon ourselves. It could be a young person who is about to fall into the hands of criminality. We sense the situation but do nothing about it, don't talk about it, don't come with any suggestions, don't have time. It could be families we see, living in close quarters in the slums. We see it, maybe every day, without asking ourselves how they're doing or if there's anything we can do to help. It could also be old, lonely, or forgotten individuals we pass by. Last but not least, all the hungry and homeless we see on television. They're far away yet still within reach. Fortunately, our church has a long, dependable arm in its relief organizations, as in its lay programs at home. There is always a hand that can reach out to someone in need. We, however, are the ones who offer help in that hand; otherwise it's empty and powerless.

Who is my neighbor? Someone I can reach with my service. *I* become his neighbor. Just like the Samaritan, of whom Jesus said: Go and do likewise.

Lord, You know how we make excuses and procrastinate when we have a difficult duty to perform. There are so many, and we don't have time for everything. There must be something in all this, however, that You give me the time and the opportunity to do. Don't allow me to neglect those duties. I know You have placed these duties on my roadside, just as the injured man was placed by the roadside in the desert of Judah to be helped there. Compel me to stop and not pass by. You are the compassionate Samaritan who saved us and paid our debt. Let us go with You on Your way and do what You want done.

MONDAY AFTER THIRTEENTH SUNDAY AFTER TRINITY
Romans 12:9–21

Love one another with brotherly affection. Romans 12:10

You shall love your neighbor as yourself. Everything we want someone to do for us, we should do for them. Everything we realize helps us so much: a helping hand, a kind word, a little attention, silent understanding in sorrow, and sincere participation in our joy. It's things like that we should do for our neighbor.

Love needs to be made concrete and apparent in this way. It's so easy for us to think that love is a general feeling of kindness. Love is not the same thing as decency. Love *must* hate what is evil. It *must* "hold fast to what is good" (Romans 12:9), even if no one else does. Love has its own image that sometimes doesn't fit in modern society at all. It can have a completely different view on abortion and divorce and how to spend your Sundays than other common, well-meaning people do, and it can do that without despising anyone. It prays for those who persecute and does favors for its enemies and is at peace with everyone, "if possible, so far as it depends on you" (Romans 12:18).

Above all, however, love is not a principle or theory or teaching. It's a way of behaving in a concrete situation. Paul gives us a long list of examples: you're appreciative toward people and take note of what they do, you aren't apathetic. Instead, you gladly help others. You're anxious to show hospitality and don't regard your home as private domain that you keep to yourself, but understand the happiness that exists in sharing the comfort of a home with others. You're happy when others are happy without feeling envious, but delighted that it's going so well for them. You can cry with those who cry and suffer with them, not with conventional phrases about your participation (that many mean nothing with), but as a friend who understands and experiences how others feel in a way that can be felt and experienced without words.

Love for your neighbor assumes there is a neighbor, a tangible human being. Love doesn't exist in general. It's always a question about living human beings. It's about the people we see around us.

Help me, Lord Jesus, to see not with cold eyes that see only indifferent people I want to avoid or dismiss as quickly as possible. Help me to see my neighbor whom You've put in front of me. Help me to be the kind of neighbor You want me to be for that person. Help us here in the congregation to sincerely love one another with our hearts so we can help one another, support one another, carry one another's burdens, and gladly do what we can. May we be joyful in hope, patient in suffering, and steadfast in prayer. For Your name's sake.

TUESDAY AFTER THIRTEENTH SUNDAY AFTER TRINITY
Romans 13:8–14

Love is the fulfilling of the law. Romans 13:10

Love is an important word, one that is often completely misunderstood. It doesn't mean that we need not care about any other commandments as long as we love (which usually means being friendly and well-meaning). It means least of all that everyone who has love is in fact a Christian who is promised eternal life.

The idea is that a person who has love will do what the Law requires, and by the word *love* is meant Christ Himself, who, with His Spirit, dwells in someone who believes. A living faith is always active in love. That's how the law will be fulfilled "in us, who walk not according to the flesh but according to the Spirit" as Paul expressed it earlier in this letter (8:4). If we have love, we're driven to do the right thing in new situations without having to have a written commandment. The old commandments, however, are not invalid. They all express what is needed to have God's love, and that's exactly how someone who has love acts.

If we were completely new, we would always act out of love and always do the right thing. Our old Adam, however, is always there acting as an obstacle, preventing us from seeing clearly and acting out of pure love. Therefore, we need the written law to open our eyes and lead us to Christ, to His forgiveness and His love.

"Owe no one anything, except to love each other," Paul says in Romans 13:8. When it comes to taxes and tariffs, bills and loans, you can pay what you owe so you have no debts. We can't do that when it's a question of love, however. It's never finished there. There's always something that remains to be done or given. Therefore, we're never finished with the fulfillment of the Law either. We must live in forgiveness. One who has much to forgive, however, also has much love to give, if he receives real forgiveness, because then he receives Christ Himself.

Lord, when You're with me, it's so obvious what I should do. When You look at me, I know how I should look upon others and all the things I should do among them. However, then I become preoccupied with everything around me and suddenly I'm alone, bored, annoyed, or occupied with amusing and interesting things I'm not accustomed to that are new to me and that I never heard You talk about. Help me to be able to talk to You then, and help me to not forget others in the middle of everything that's annoying and tempting. It's them You want me to see. Help me see them with Your eyes.

WEDNESDAY AFTER THIRTEENTH SUNDAY AFTER TRINITY

Romans 14:1–12

None of us lives to himself. Romans 14:7

Should I take care of my brother? Maybe we remember Cain's stubborn and negative answer. It's the old Adam's attitude to his fellow man. What do I have to do with him? He should take care of himself.

This is the complete opposite to what God wants. None of us lives for himself. None of us can renounce responsibility for someone else. We're all together. I must take care of my brother. I'll do it because Christ has taken care of me. If I'm a Christian, I live for Christ. I live through Him only because He cared for me, died for me, baptized me, dwells with me, and therefore I can be a child of God. I'm a member of His body, and members can't live alone. They live *through* the body and *for* the body. That's how I live for the Lord; in joy and thanksgiving over the fact that He is who He is.

I also live for the other members, however. If a member suffers, the other members suffer with it. You can't be indifferent to what happens with the members of Christ. That's why we have to take care of our brother.

In this chapter, Paul gives us an example of this. It's about the same kind of problem we see in 1 Corinthians. There were different opinions about several external things. Some were more careful and wanted to rigorously cut off anything that could be conceived as temptation. They refrained from freedom in an effort to avoid abusing it. They avoided wine. They avoided meat. They refused to work on certain days that could be considered holy. We probably would've called them decisive and strict. Paul calls them weak because he sees everything from a candid faith's view. The strong, as he considers himself, are those with such faith that they can use their freedom without abusing it.

In this case Paul calls upon us to neither judge nor scorn. A person who is convinced that all this is allowed should not look down upon someone who is in doubt, and someone who prefers to abstain should not judge someone who does otherwise. They belong together. They belong to the same Lord. Whatever they do, they do for His sake, some out of gratitude for His great gifts, others out of love that willingly sacrifices everything so they won't lose sight of Him. And they all will meet Him some day, when each of them will have to account for themselves.

Dear Lord Jesus, this must mean that You don't want me to control my brother. Is that only a form of selfishness? A way to uphold myself? Instead, You want me to take care of him when he really needs my help. I can do something for him so he can receive it as a gift from You. Help me to see so clearly and love so sincerely that I go about Your business and not my own. Teach me to see what You alone want to take care of, You who see if someone stands or falls, and help me to willingly and gladly take care of the things You've left for us to care of. Help me to never close my eyes and pass by when that moment arises. Your will be done.

THURSDAY AFTER THIRTEENTH SUNDAY AFTER TRINITY

Romans 14:13–23

Decide never to put a stumbling block or hindrance in the way of a brother. Romans 14:13

No one lives only for himself. We're dependent upon others, and our actions have consequences for them. Of course, a Christian is free, wonderfully free. Paul emphasizes this again and again. Everything God created is pure and we can receive it with joy. God's kingdom doesn't consist of food and drink, but of righteousness and peace and joy in the Holy Spirit!

Freedom, however, has distinct boundaries. I don't live only for myself. There are people all around me. There's my neighbor, and I should love him. What happens to *him* when I do what I do?

Then Paul comes to the important rule: I'm not to be a stumbling block or hindrance in the way of my brother. He uses two words for the same thing. The first one means a stone in the way someone can stumble on. The other one means the trap that causes one to swallow the bait. An offence or a stumbling block is therefore not something that annoys or angers someone. Jesus caused that kind of offence many times. Instead, it's something that can *harm* others, something that can draw them into danger or ruin. If I use my freedom concerning food or drink, clothes and pleasure, social life, movies, concerts, the theater, etc., I have to consider if some other person who is influenced by me can be drawn into something he can't handle. Then I destroy the work of God, Paul says. I destroy something for someone that Christ died for, and that cannot be allowed to happen. Then I should rather abstain from exercising my freedom.

Dear Holy Spirit, You have given me tremendous joy in the kingdom of God, joy over God's gifts, joy over being able to live as a happy child in God's presence, and to receive all the things He showers on us. May I never receive these gifts as if I were alone and had no one else to take into consideration. Help me so the things that bring me joy never bring sorrow or harm to someone else. Help me to share everything that's good, the joy as well as the gifts. Make my happiness for someone else, and fulfill all this with Your kindness and light so we're all strengthened in love and grow closer to each other and to You.

FRIDAY AFTER THIRTEENTH SUNDAY AFTER TRINITY
Romans 15:1–13

Let each of us please his neighbor for his good, to build him up. Romans 15:2

We don't live for ourselves; we live for others. In just that way our lives have meaning and content. In our nature there's a healthy need to be useful to others and to be validated by others. Our old Adam wants to fulfill this by dominating and deciding over others. Christ invites us to serve. Just by serving others we can experience that we mean something and that our lives have a purpose. We're really needed. Maybe we're actually shown gratitude; but that is not the most important thing. In this ungrateful world it's not unusual that an effort is hardly noticed until it's missed. It was an effort that was necessary, however, something meaningful and good. The effort we make isn't for our own sake so we'll be thanked and noticed. An effort is always for those who are availed by it.

Consequently, the service is done for someone else, for the people we interact with. God often widens that circle. First, He toiled with the people of Israel, but all the time He had other people, the heathen, in mind, as Paul reminds us. Christ also came for the heathen's sake. You can't keep the Gospel for yourself. It's obvious that every congregation must be a congregation that does missionary work to, first, those who are closest, all the unbelievers in our own surroundings. The responsibility stretches to all corners of the world, however. We can't excuse ourselves by saying we can't possibly help every one we don't know and will never see. It might be true that we can't go out as missionaries, unless, of course, we've received a call to do so, and try to stifle and hide from it as best we can. The Church is the Body of Christ, however. There are many members that don't have the same function, but still cooperate. Not everyone can be a missionary, but those who are do it for the whole body, and the entire body should be behind their work and support it. The members must literally receive their nourishment from the body. Missionary work can't be successful if the missionaries don't have room and board, and we're responsible for that. Our contributions to missionary work are our way of making an effort from the other side of the ocean. Only a small portion goes to their room and board. The major part goes to helping the young churches, chapels, schools, and hospitals; evangelism, education, and health care; and in that way a concrete, tangible aid for thousands of people; help for the body as well as the soul.

In other words, there's a love for your neighbor that is achieved through the congregation, through mission work, relief programs, and the lay ministry, even if the most important thing is that each of us should live for the benefit and edification of our neighbor.

I thank You, Lord, that I have this chance. I thank You for all the missionaries who work so far away, and for our ability to help support them. I thank You for their service because otherwise it would've been neglected, and we now reach all corners of the world to people we've never seen and help those we've never met. Bless all those who work out there and all those who are reached by their service. May it be a gift from You, where everyone realizes that it's Your love that drives all this forward. Thy kingdom come.

SATURDAY AFTER THIRTEENTH SUNDAY AFTER TRINITY
Romans 16:1–16

Help her in whatever she may need from you. Romans 16:2

This is what Paul commands regarding Phoebe, a deaconess in the service of the congregation in Cenchreae, a port in Corinth, who now had moved to Rome. She had helped many others as well as Paul. The congregation in Rome should receive her "in a way worthy of the saints" (Romans 16:2). This meant that the congregation should help her in all her needs.

Lay ministry and missionary work are very much alike. They're the serving hands of the congregation through which we reach and help other people we will never see or otherwise couldn't possibly help. Once again we see cooperation between the different organs in the body. That's why the *whole* congregation should acknowledge its responsibility. Lay ministers and deaconesses are tools for *our* work, so we should aid them in every aspect of *their* work where they need our help. That entails an economic responsibility. It could also mean a personal responsibility. In large congregations especially, there's so much to do that one deaconess doesn't have the time to do everything, like give attention to the elderly and shut-in members. The deaconess knows where they are, but she doesn't have the time for all of them. She needs a staff of assistants that can take the responsibility of visiting one or two of them, and we should "help her in whatever she may need."

After this command, Paul includes a long list of greetings. Maybe we feel it doesn't concern us. Let's imagine, however, that we replace those names with people in our congregation and that Paul is alive today. We then have quite a bit to think about. Would Paul have thanked Mr. and Mrs. Jones, who were his co-workers in Christ and maybe even risked their lives for him? Or give his regards to brother Evans, who was the first convert when revival swept over the congregation? Or the aging Mary, who worked so hard for us all? Or Smith and Hartford, men of note among the apostles, who have a good reputation in the synod? Or to all of those who join so faithfully in Bible studies and prayer? Or the other group who meets with Vicar Chaste? Or Lisa Andersen and Mabel Boyd, who labored so faithfully in Christ, and Anna Witt, who's done so much? Or the aging mother of the Byrds, who's been like a mother to her pastor? We see that the list is long. We have a feeling of how life in the congregation should pulsate and how there should be members who are ready, willing, and glad to help wherever they're needed. Is that the case? Am I one of them?

Lord, give us congregations like these. Allow something to happen in this congregation that makes us come alive so we all serve with the gifts we've received from You. Let us discover how much there is to be done, how much we are able to do, and how much fun it is to do it. Open our eyes so we see the needs of others and our own possibilities. Help us so we don't talk about what others can do, but ask instead what task You have for us to do. Give us faith in every detail and the willingness to do what no one else wants to do, and let everything come as the fruit of an intimate fellowship with You.

FOURTEENTH SUNDAY AFTER TRINITY

John 17:18–23

That they may all be one. John 17:21

Jesus prays that all His disciples shall be perfectly one, just as He and His Father are one. He prays for everyone in the whole world who will come to faith through the message He now sends with His disciples.

He also says why it's so important that all His disciples are as one: so the world will understand that Jesus was sent by God and all His disciples are children of God. Who could understand that if all the disciples were at odds with one another?

This prayer is also a powerful appeal to all Christians to be one. At the same time it's a serious reminder of the basis and condition for Christian unity. That being, the fact that all of us are consecrated in the truth, the truth Jesus gives us in His Word. With that Word He sent His disciples out into the world. Through that Word others would be converted. As far as Jesus was concerned, He came from His Father and was faithful to Him in every way. In the same way He commissioned His apostles. He says He's given them the glory that God had given Him so they can be one. He allowed them to see God and brought them to Him. In the same way others would also be brought to Him and become one.

Consequently, true ecumenism consists of spiritual unity between people who are consecrated in the truth. It can't be comprised of compromising teachings and opinions that contain both truths and mistakes. Neither can it be comprised of an attempt to organize different religious communities, each of which is far from consecrated in the truth. Real unity in Christ can't be organized. It's created by God when we become living members of His body. Then, nothing can be allowed to stop Christ's members from serving one another in the kind of unity and devotion He wants.

I pray, dear Lord, for the unity that is so difficult and seems so far away. I pray that You destroy all the obstacles, all the laziness and human doubt, all the mistakes and false teachings, all human opinions and fabrications, that have built walls between those who believe. I pray for such a replenishing and revival everywhere in Your Christianity, that we all come closer to You, become tools for Your will, see Your truth, and gladly follow You. Gather us around You, Lord, and let us come closer to You so we also can come closer to one another, not by clever calculating and shrewd compromises but by seeing Your truth clearly and by loving You with all our hearts.

MONDAY AFTER FOURTEENTH SUNDAY AFTER TRINITY

Ephesians 2:11–22

For He Himself is our peace, who has made us both one.
Ephesians 2:14

By grace are we saved and not of ourselves. A person who does not know what salvation is might draw the conclusion that deeds are of no importance. In reality, they play a very important part. They are the consequence, the result, and the fruit. Therefore, they're also a sign that something has happened. Jesus says we can expose false prophets with just the help of their bad fruit.

Faith carries with it radical consequences for one's whole life. Even concerning ingrained, at one time obvious, social relationships. Paul gives us an example here. Without admonishing or criticizing anyone, he makes a few comments that turn old prejudices upside down. He begins by speaking of the relationship between Jews and Greeks. They lived in two different worlds. If we try to get an idea of the differences and contrasts between them, we can imagine the relationship between black and white, communist and fascist, Israelis and Arabs, or other groups we usually refer to as in opposition to each other.

Now Paul explains to us that all those problems are overcome if we believe in Christ. He's torn down the wall that separates—the wall we've built between races, nations, and political parties. He has made us one, united us in one body, first by carrying all our sins in His body to the cross and suffering for them, then by turning everyone who believes in Him into a member in His body. In Him and only by believing in Him and joining Him do we have the chance to meet the Father. Consequently, Christ is our peace, both with God and between ourselves.

In other words, if you're a Christian, you can't persist in long-standing enmity and habitual distaste for certain types of people. Faith in Christ, if it's real, tears down barriers between races and nations. In countries with a strong racial antagonism, we usually find real fellowship among living Christians everywhere, despite all the prejudice.

When it comes to equality for everyone, we shouldn't stop with the unsatisfactory state of things in the world and repudiate it. That could lead to another kind of selfishness and prejudice. Our neighbors are those we interact with, and it should be clear to them that we belong to Christ and that we really can and want to be one with everyone that belongs to Him.

Lord Jesus, You know how much we want all boundaries and dividing lines to disappear so all people could live as brothers and sisters without acting unjustly. Help us to understand how we can make this happen. Give us the courage and unselfishness to accomplish this. You have torn down the wall that separates. You made it possible for all of us to become Your members and live new life. Make us one with You so we can be one with each other.

TUESDAY AFTER FOURTEENTH SUNDAY AFTER TRINITY
Ephesians 3:1–21

The Father, from whom every family in heaven and on earth is named. Ephesians 3:14–15

Those without faith generally imagine that God is some kind of heavenly enlargement of the things we value and fear here on earth. That's why He's called Father, for example.

It's just the opposite. The whole earth is full of His glory. There's a reflection of His essence in creation, the light from the heavens and the stability of the mountains. Therefore, I can call God my sun and my rock, my light and my fortress. The fact that I can call Him Father is because He created fatherhood on earth to reflect a part of His own disposition. A person who really is a father, as God would've wanted, reflects as a father a part of the very nature of God, just as a father has mercy on his children . . . just as a father carries his son . . . just as a father is the head of the family and cares for his own. Not to dominate and gain advantage for himself, but because he loves them. That's how God is, and He's included this in fatherhood on earth.

As the Father of all, God has, from the beginning of time, figured out how He can make it possible for everyone to be His children. Just when it looked like evil was going to prevail, God had a plan in waiting. He sent us Christ and opened a new door for us so we could, despite everything, come forth before God.

Paul describes all of this in this chapter. Then he kneels down before this God, the Father of mercy, and praises Him for His inexhaustible and unfathomable abundance that He's given us through Christ in the Church.

In the Church—it is worth taking note of that. The Church isn't an association of people that have the same religious interests. The Church is a work of God, a part of Christ. God's secret plan has been revealed so that even the heavenly spirits can see it, as well as the evil spirits, who had no idea what God planned to do. This happened "through the Church," and to the Father "be glory in the Church and in Christ Jesus throughout all generations, for ever and ever" (Ephesians 3:21). That praise ascends to the Father here on earth in His Church, throughout all generations, among all those who come to the faith, and it will continue to ascend in the kingdom of glory, in Christ Jesus, forever and ever.

Dear Father of mercy and ever-comforting God, we pray that You hear the prayer Your apostle is praying and allow it to be fulfilled in us also. Allow us to grow inwardly in power through Your Spirit. Let Christ live in our hearts. May we be firmly rooted and established in love so we also can understand something about Christ's love, the inexhaustible and unfathomable. In Your fatherly kindness, You also want us filled with Your fullness. You have given us life so we might receive a portion of all this. You can do so much more than we can pray for or imagine, and You want Your inexhaustible and unbelievable power to be at work inside us. Your kind, fatherly will be done. Praise be to Your fatherly name, forever and ever.

WEDNESDAY AFTER FOURTEENTH SUNDAY AFTER TRINITY
Ephesians 4:1–16

Rather, speaking the truth in love, we are to grow up in every way into Him who is the head, into Christ. Ephesians 4:15

Paul admonishes. As always, he begins by pointing out what we are and what we have. We are called. *Therefore,* we should live as if we're worthy of the call we've received. We are one. Therefore, we should take pains to be united.

Paul knows what threatens unity. We are one, but we're all different. We're supposed to be different. Grace was given to each of us according to the measure of Christ's gifts. All things are gifts from Christ, however. Gifts—important gifts!—are also all the servants of the Word. Paul enumerates them: First the apostles, who were appointed by Christ Himself. Then the prophets, those who received the gift of prophecy and spoke after being inspired by the Holy Spirit, when the Spirit gave them something to say. Then he mentions the evangelists, probably the same sort of assistants to the apostles we already learned of in Acts. Last, he speaks of those who are pastors and teachers, in other words, leaders in the congregation and preachers of the Word, the equivalent to our modern day pastors.

We receive all of these so Christ's body can be edified, so we all reach unity in the faith. That's where we meet the great danger to unity. From the beginning we were children in the faith, naïve in the knowledge of God's Son. It's not strange that we were led adrift by every flaw in the doctrine. New ideas arose, new fashions, new interpretations of Christianity, and there are plenty of false prophets. Jesus warned us about them and Paul met them. He knows what damage they can do. They are the worst enemy of unity. There's only one way to unity: that we become one in the knowledge of God's Son and grow up as members in Christ and mature in Christ's fullness. That can happen only when we're steadfast in the truth and accept the Gospel in its entirety, the Gospel the apostle knows he preaches and that is given to us in the Scriptures. Then we can "grow up in every way into Him who is the head, into Christ." Then differences and different tasks won't divide us but, instead, strengthen us in cooperation in the body of Christ, "from whom the whole body, joined and held together by every joint with which it is equipped, when each part is working properly, makes the body grow so that it builds itself up in love" (Ephesians 4:16).

Lord Jesus, we thank You for all the different gifts we have received. You've sprinkled Your fullness on us all, and You want us to serve You and one another, each with his own gift. Help us now so we don't hold on to what's ours and expect everyone to be like us. Help us to see Your entire kingdom and just be happy when we find more of it in others than we find in ourselves. Give us in Your Church, the gifts we need to grow. Give us good pastors and teachers who really can edify us with the Word that comes from You. Lead us to unity in the faith and the knowledge of You so we can grow in You, our head.

THURSDAY AFTER FOURTEENTH SUNDAY AFTER TRINITY
Ephesians 4:17–5:2

Therefore be imitators of God, as beloved children. And walk in love, as Christ loved us and gave Himself up for us. Ephesians 5:1–2

Once again Paul admonishes by pointing out what we already are and what we've already received. From that he draws the conclusion about what we should be and do. Good deeds are the consequence, not the condition.

Again we see that Christianity isn't the same thing as morals. It's not only a question of another bunch of rules that to a degree replace the rules we previously followed. Instead, it's a question of a new kind of life, something altogether different from a life without God. To not believe means you're "alienated from the life of God" (Ephesians 4:18). You're cut off from the source of life. When you come to faith in Christ, however, you're called to a new life. You do away with the old Adam. You can't do that once and for all so the old Adam is gone for good. It's a question of a vital process. A new life flows inside of us. We're replenished by the Spirit. We dress ourselves in the new man, the correct man, the one created in the image of God.

The Ephesians were in the middle of this transformation process, just like we are. They were just like most people were in ancient times when they lived without God, and just like people are once again becoming in the secular world of the west. They lived in a state of moral decay and promiscuity they felt was completely natural. They lied when it was the easiest way out. They stole when they ran no risk of getting caught. They could've spoken coarsely or indecently, nastily or spitefully. They scolded others when they were angry. Now, however, all of this was slowly becoming obsolete. When I walk with Jesus, when Jesus sees what I do and hears what I say, then everything is very different. Not because I'm afraid but because I love Him and because I don't want to grieve God's Holy Spirit. On top of that, I've seen my neighbor and realize that I live for his sake. Therefore I will work with my hands so I have "something to share with anyone in need" (Ephesians 4:28). My words are no longer a means to show off or be facetious or to upset others. They're a means to help others, be a blessing to others, a helping hand and joy for others and even "building up, as fits the occasion" (Ephesians 4:29).

I am in the kingdom of forgiveness. I no longer have to hold on to what's my own. Now I can walk in love, Christ's love, He who gave Himself as a gift to others.

Lord, You know there's a heathen inside of me who prefers to have nothing to do with You. Despite that, You've allowed me to come before You and see Your love for me. You've sacrificed Yourself. Now I want to sacrifice the heathen in me. He took Your life on the cross and now he shall be crucified. Now I will take off the old Adam, those dirty clothes I'm so ashamed of. I thank You that I can put on the new clothes You've given me, woven with Your righteousness. Help me to wear them as it befits those who are allowed in Your company.

FRIDAY AFTER FOURTEENTH SUNDAY AFTER TRINITY

Ephesians 5:3–21

[Submit] to one another out of reverence for Christ.
Ephesians 5:21

Paul continues to admonish. He knows that the Christians live in a world where it's considered natural to live in contradiction to God's will. He points out two forces that almost automatically take charge of people and begin to determine their wishes and values when they're not determined by God: sexuality and money. Both can be received as good gifts from God and be used joyfully and as a blessing. They can also be idols, however, from which we expect life's essential content and meaning. Then they have power over us. They become fornication and impurity, greed and the worship of mammon. We're constantly meeting people who defend and excuse such things, sometimes disguised as Christians. That's certain proof that you're dealing with false prophets. We can't let ourselves be fooled by their arguments, Paul says. These false prophets are disobedient, and the wrath of God awaits them.

Paul continues with a description of "the fruit of light"—everything good, righteous, and true. The driving force is a tremendous joy that the Spirit creates. There's playing and singing in the heart as well as during the church service, and in everyday life a new way of living emerges that Paul sums up: we submit to one another.

According to the world and to unbelievers, submission is considered repulsive. It's considered a violation of one's self and human dignity or a threat to live as one desires. A Christian has discovered that it is quite the opposite. When he submits, it means exactly what the word means in Greek and English: he is under an order, and he knows that order is *God's*. He finds a place in God's great work and begins to function as God wants him to. Freedom lies in this. He no longer has to assert himself and appear superior. He's no longer afraid he won't get what's coming to him. He realizes that life receives its meaning from God and that there are tasks waiting. He's sure he'll be a blessing because he's ready to serve where God puts him.

Knowing all this is the new life in God's kingdom. We've already seen it in the Sermon on the Mount and we continue to see it in the entire New Testament. It is life in the kingdom of forgiveness. It's *not* a law for people who haven't converted in the earthly community; it's impossible to transform it into civil law. It's something you can do only when you love Jesus and are driven by His Spirit. It's not something you demand of others, but something you are willing to do. Someone who doesn't live in Christ's kingdom can't understand it. When he hears that you have to submit for Christ's sake, his thoughts go in two directions and they're both wrong. Either he thinks: *What risks do I take if I live like this?* Or he thinks: *What do I have the right to demand (of others) if this is the right way to live?* A person who belongs to Christ, however, thinks: *I thank You, Lord, for Your good and blessed order, where there's also a place for me.*

I thank You, Lord Jesus, for showing me that this life is not a struggle for survival, as if I have to constantly keep an eye on the little I have or watch out for others. Instead, You give me the right and privilege to serve, and every day You give me new possibilities to bring joy to someone else. To wander down Your path and serve for Your sake is a greater fortune than all I could scrape together by toiling, struggling, and stressing if I took my life in my own hands. Instead, I put my life into Your hands, and I thank You for that.

SATURDAY AFTER FOURTEENTH SUNDAY AFTER TRINITY

Ephesians 6:10–23

Therefore take up the whole armor of God. Ephesians 6:13

Paul talks about a Christian's armor by calling it God's armor. All the things he enumerates are weapons that can be found only with God or come only from God.

We must fight against the evil spirits in the universe. This is the grim fact we read repeatedly in the New Testament. It's not only a question of flesh and blood, about people who are enemies of Christianity or indifferent. It's a question of the adversary of the soul, the Strong One, the one who's like a roaring lion looking for his prey. We are just frail individuals who are hardly capable of meeting a roaring lion. At least not unarmed.

Therefore we have to arm ourselves. The fact that we need spiritual weapons is obvious. Many believe, however, that they're weapons we manufacture ourselves. They hear what's mentioned: truth, righteousness, willingness, and faith, and immediately they think these must be Christian virtues that must be attained. The armor is weak, however, with many flaws. The attacker runs his spear through it, and wins the battle.

All of these weapons come from Jesus' armory. "The truth" is the great truth Jesus answers for us. If we've girded our loins with the truth, we can meet the evil one. "Righteousness" is Christ's righteousness. It is the breastplate that the attacker's spear can't pierce. It comes from the gospel of peace, from constant renewed forgiveness. And "the shield of faith" is made, thanks to Christ, so we can quench all the flaming darts from the evil one—even when he proves that we're no good, can't call ourselves Christian, and aren't worthy of going to Communion. It's the same thing with the helmet of salvation and the sword of the Spirit. They last, they can stand an attack, and they don't rust. Whatever happens to us, we will always have access to an inexhaustible supply of forgiveness, an impenetrable wall of mercy, and God's own fortress that can never be attacked.

Put on the armor of God!

I love You, O LORD, my strength. The LORD is my rock, and my fortress and my deliverer, my God, my rock, in whom I take refuge, my shield and the horn of my salvation, my stronghold. I call upon the LORD. . . . You have given me the shield of Your salvation, and Your right hand supported me, and Your gentleness made me great. You gave a wide place for my steps under me, and my feet did not slip. . . . You equipped me with strength for the battle. . . . The LORD lives, and blessed be my rock and exalted be the God of my salvation. (From Psalm 18.)

FIFTEENTH SUNDAY AFTER TRINITY

Matthew 6:24–34

You cannot serve God and money. Matthew 6:24

Jesus asserts that no one can serve two masters. That's hardly the case in our everyday experiences. We're free individuals in a free country, where even a common laborer has rights. In Palestine he was completely dependent on his employer's discretion, especially if he was a slave. If he served two masters, he could be sure that one of them would demand too much, and then it would be impossible to serve both.

It's the same thing with God and money, Jesus says. It's just not possible to split yourself between two masters. It's not worth trying, although many do.

Mammon is the Jewish word for money, earnings, profits, or savings. It's a word with a bad ring to it. To serve mammon meant that money was the most important thing in life and one would do anything to get it. Jesus figures that His audience doesn't *solely* serve mammon. The problem is that so many people want to serve God and mammon. Of course we want God's help, but it's great to have money too. Of course it's great to be able to put our trust in God, but it's even easier with money in the bank. And if it comes down to living without money or without God, the question is which choice we would make.

What should we do to avoid straddling both sides? A radical solution is to give away everything we own. Jesus could sometimes recommend that way (for example, to the rich young man in Matthew 20). Zacchaeus, however, gave away half of what he owned. We don't hear of Nicodemus and Joseph from Arimathea selling a part or all of their possessions. Paul says that thieves should start to work and receive an income so they can share with others who lack.

The decision is not *how much* mammon we're willing to give away because *everything* should be given into the hand of Christ. Once and for all we have to stop thinking that what we earn is ours and all we have to do is strike a bargain with God regarding His percentage. There are two ways to form your life. Either you take everything from the hand of God and manage it well, content and happy for what He gives, or you take it all and call it your own, the money as well as all the plans and everything you own and will come to own. We have to choose between these two life processes. You cannot try to combine them.

Dear Lord Jesus, You know how easily I worry despite Your promises. You know how easy it is for me to be joyful and secure when I have a little more money than I need. Help me to take everything from Your hand and be like Your faithful apostle, the one who was equally content in scarcity and abundance. Help me through all the ups and downs in life to be just as glad, just as secure and just as certain over the fact that You care for me and give me what I need.

And great was the fall of it. Matthew 7:27

This is Jesus' description of the house that was built on sand. This is also a description of a life that's built on a foundation other than His Word. Those who build houses like that often believe they're building on solid ground. They stick to stark reality. They know what counts in this world— money, money, and more money—so they lay a solid ground of real assets. Their lives rest on that ground. They definitely haven't built any castles in the sand.

Yet this house will fall, and the fall will be great. Some of these houses fall apart during the owner's lifetime. Some of the houses stand year after year and everything would've gone as planned, if it were only a question of economy. However, this passage is about a different kind of building, building a life, something we received from God and will someday give back. *That's* the building that helplessly falls apart if you *hear* but don't *do,* or do neither one.

The rain fell, as Jesus tells us. It can really rain in Palestine. Wide and muddy rivers stream down the mountainsides, dragging gravel and dirt and throwing itself like a foaming river at everything that comes in its way. At times like these it's not safe and snug to be sitting inside a house and listening to the rain patter on the roof. Instead, anxious questions come. Is the wall going to cave in? Will the roof fall down on us?

That is the kind of house we're living in. You can try to pretend that it isn't so. You've taken care of your money, but the years go by and you can't help noticing that there are cracks in the house. You try to fix it. It works for awhile with cosmetics, dying your hair, rejuvenating shots, and occupational therapy. Then, however, comes the tidal wave. Death makes its mark on the house. The poor soul crawls into a corner and refuses to believe that it's finally over. The end comes, however, and yet it's not really over. A naked, wretched soul wanders toward the final reckoning. Here he meets another river more powerful than any other. It's the river of eternity "whose streams make glad the city of God" (Psalm 46:4). Now another storm is raging, the breath from the four winds that breathes upon these slain, that they may live (Ezekiel 37:9). Everything that doesn't belong to Christ is swept away. However, everything that is born of the Spirit will rise up and sing and rejoice in the coming of the Lord. It turns out there's a dwelling-place that isn't made by hand, a building that comes from God. It rests on the Rock, Jesus, and not even the gates of hell are too much for it.

Lord, beloved heavenly Father, You've said You will lay a chosen cornerstone in Zion and whoever believes in it will never be disgraced. I know that cornerstone is the Savior Himself, He who was rejected by men but whom You turned into a rock and a fortress that will stand forever and ever. Now here I come and pray that my whole life and my deeds may be built on that Rock. May I always first seek Your kingdom and Your righteousness. I know now that I'll receive everything else if I build on the Rock.

Vanity of vanities! All is vanity! Ecclesiastes 1:2

That is the conclusion this wise preacher in Jerusalem reached. He describes for us how he searched for the meaning in life. The description is surprisingly modern. The preacher assumes he only has this short life to live; the promise of resurrection and eternal life hadn't been given yet. He knows nothing of Christ. He had, however, taken God and His Commandments into account. He's not an irresponsible person, not a selfish nihilist who doesn't care if he violates the rights of others. He wants others to enjoy the same good things he does. He wants to act like an intelligent and knowledgeable individual. At the same time he wants to get his share of happiness and profit in this short lifetime, which is the only thing he can be sure of. He could've been living today.

Now he describes for us his attempts at finding the purpose of life. He throws himself into his work, a productive and creative work. He builds houses, plants vineyards, builds pools, employs people, and accumulates a fortune. "So I became great and surpassed all who were before me in Jerusalem. Also my wisdom remained with me" (Ecclesiastes 2:9). The preacher was an intellectual human being, one who wanted to see how it all hung together. "I applied my heart to seek and to search out by wisdom all that is done under heaven" (Ecclesiastes 1:13).

Yes, the years go by, and with them all the questions, the emptiness, disappointment, and finally boredom. Work becomes so arduous that the routine wears off all the color and luster from daily duties. "What has a man from all the toil and striving of heart with which he toils beneath the sun? For all his days are full of sorrow, and his work is a vexation. Even in the night his heart does not rest" (Ecclesiastes 2:22–23). Otherwise, the preacher says, this is the best thing for people: they should be happy while they work. That's his portion. What happens if the joy in working disappears, however? If work becomes so stressful, so piled up, so arduous, so unrewarding or monotonous, that all the joy in it dies? If, one day, that natural happiness that could lead to a song or a hum at the machine or drawing board is gone? What's left? Then you begin to feel like the preacher: What's the point? It's striving after wind! Vanity of vanities!

Maybe it's best to try to enjoy life and make the most of all the joy and pleasure that are there. It's possible to do without having been considered depraved. The preacher tried this option. "I searched with my heart how to cheer my body with wine—my heart still guiding me with wisdom" (Ecclesiastes 2:3). "And whatever my eyes desired I did not keep from them. I kept my heart from no pleasure" (Ecclesiastes 2:10). There's a bottom to that cup too. Even that becomes monotonous after a while. Nothing new under the sun. Everything repeats itself constantly. What happens is what always has happened. Is there any significance in being born, toiling a lifetime, dying, and then being forgotten?

This is how the preacher witnesses about Christ in his own way. He says, just like Jesus said: What's the sense of gaining fortune on earth, and being worried? That being said, however, the preacher lacks something. Something only Christ can say.

I thank You, Lord Jesus, for the Word only You can say. Without You, life would be meaningless repetition, a circle, where nothing is new under the sun and all old mistakes and foolishness are constantly repeated. You, however, can make everything new. You allow us to be born again. You make us citizens in a new world. You give new meaning to the monotony of the workday grind and duty when You make them a favor for You and are with us when we work. I thank You, Lord, for being there.

WEDNESDAY AFTER FIFTEENTH SUNDAY AFTER TRINITY
Ecclesiastes 2:17–26

So I hated life. Ecclesiastes 2:17

It can be good to hear things like this in the Bible because being sick and tired of life is something that happens to us all. It's hard to function when you feel like that.

The preacher describes how we become tired of life. We read yesterday that work becomes monotonous and appears meaningless. Job satisfaction is gone. Pleasure isn't pleasurable anymore. The only thing that's left is pressure, worry, and obligation. All of this has become striving after wind, however.

I can try to find comfort in thinking about children, those who come after me. I toil for them. Then the question the preacher asked comes again: "And who knows whether he will be wise or a fool? Yet he will be master of all for which I toiled and used my wisdom under the sun. This too is vanity" (Ecclesiastes 2:19).

On top of the pain and boredom, there's also the fact that there is so much injustice and revolt. "Again I saw all the oppressions that are done under the sun. And behold, the tears of the oppressed, and they had no one to comfort them! On the side of their oppressors there was power, and there was no one to comfort them. And I thought the dead who are already dead more fortunate than the living who are still alive" (Ecclesiastes 4:1–2). What is it to die, however? "Who knows whether the spirit of man goes upward and the spirit of the beast goes down into earth?" (Ecclesiastes 3:21) Don't we all have to become dust again, disintegrate and disappear? What was the purpose of all this?

The preacher has seen it all. Even the loneliness that chills and isolates a person. "Woe to him who is alone when he falls!" (Ecclesiastes 4:10). And there's so little we can do about it, not even for ourselves and our faults. What's crooked can't be made straight again.

That's exactly the way it feels when a person gets old or tired or depressed or maybe is still young but has no goal or desire or maybe just pressured by his own inexorable clear sight that sees through all the humbug in everything.

All this is described in the Bible! It's there so we will know it's something God recognizes and cares about. Even those who are tired of life are included in God's mercy. Their needs and thoughts are inscribed in God's Book because they're written in God's heart.

There are a hundred reasons to be tired of life. There's just one reason, however—that's better and more important—to have the strength to get through life cheerfully. That reason is Jesus Christ. Just because there are so many reasons to despair, we've received this one tremendous reason to trust, despite everything and in the middle of everything that seems so hopeless.

I notice, Lord, that when I'm downhearted and tired of life, it's because I've tried to live without You. If life becomes meaningless, it's because I've tried to find a different meaning than the only right one, the one that comes from You. When I make my own plans and decide what I want to have, when I want to profit and be happy and receive appreciation for my own gains, then it seems meaningless. Or when I want things to go my way and result in what I expected. When I'm happy to do something for You at Your side, however, then there's always a purpose in every day and a purpose in every task that lies before me.

THURSDAY AFTER FIFTEENTH SUNDAY AFTER TRINITY

Deuteronomy 8:7–20

When you have eaten and are full and have built good houses and live in them, and . . . all that you have is multiplied, then your heart be lifted up, and you forget the LORD your God. Deuteronomy 8:12–14

It's a blessing that man was created to be able to eat and drink and enjoy the fruits of his labors. Even this comes from the hand of God, He who said: Who can eat and who can enjoy without Him?

That's what we heard the preacher say, and we have every reason to remember his words. We live in a welfare state and in a society that, compared to most others, is a society of unbelievable abundance. Our high standard of living is acknowledged everywhere, and that's exactly the reason many people believe we've become so secular and unchristian. "People have it too good," they say. "They don't need God anymore." It almost sounds like they mean we could use a little hardship.

That's not a Christian way of thinking. If we read the Bible, we realize that a high standard of living can be a gift from God. Among God's good deeds toward His people Israel—who are an example for Christianity—is also the fact that He led them into a land of milk and honey with fields and precious fruit trees, with ore in the mountains and everything necessary for a thriving economy and prosperity for everyone. Don't believe that the joy of all this only exists in the Old Testament. When Paul preaches about God, he could say that He made Himself known by giving us prosperous times and satisfying our hearts with food and gladness (Acts 14:17). We need not have a bad conscience when we receive gifts like these and build nice houses and live in them and when everything He gives us, food and gladness, grows and multiplies.

There is something else, however, that should be a matter of conscience for us. "Beware lest you say in your heart, 'My power and the might of my hand have gotten me this wealth'" (Deuteronomy 8:17). It's so easy to say that. Anyone can see we wouldn't have this prosperity without all the work, all the inventions, all our talent for organization, and all the craftsmanship necessary for production and the building of society. God says here, however: You shall remember the Lord your God, for it is He who gives you power to get wealth. It was God, through creation, who created man to rule over nature, the ingenuity, and all the other gifts we need to raise livestock and the necessary crops and to use our natural resources. We are stewards, and we can't take care of our resources correctly if we forget their purpose. That's what we do if we forget God.

You, our Father and Creator, have put all this in our hands. Help us to receive it with thankfulness and use it correctly. Show us that it comes from You and it's Yours: life itself and nourishment, home and family, work and friends, peace and tranquility. Help us to rejoice in our hearts for everything that is good. Everything that tastes good, everything that's good for us, everything that's enjoyable to listen to and enjoy, simply because it comes from You. Help us to share Your gifts with others. Show us how to do it if we can't figure it out ourselves. Make us good children who use Your wonderful gifts as You will it.

FRIDAY AFTER FIFTEENTH SUNDAY AFTER TRINITY
Hosea 2:1–15

And she did not know that it was I who gave her the grain, the wine, and the oil, and who lavished upon her silver and gold, which they used for Baal. Hosea 2:8

The prophet Hosea lived in the seventh century before Christ, at a time when clouds of misfortune hovered over Israel. They were bad times. There wasn't much left of earlier prosperity, and the situation in the world was as threatening as it could be. A true prophet, Hosea could interpret signs and say what God meant with what seemed to be meaningless events.

Hosea knew why times were bad: Israel was unfaithful to their God. The Lord had loved this nation as a man would love his bride. He showered her with gifts. The bride, however, had been an unfaithful wife. She accepted the gifts; she didn't understand who gave them to her or what His love was worth. Instead, she squandered them all on her lover.

This is what happens when we accept God's gifts but deny God. The children of Israel had done something that God had warned His people not to do: they had forgotten God when He gave them the good years. They thought to themselves, "My own power has given me this wealth. I don't need God."

The strange thing is this happens only when you acquire other gods. In Israel it was the Baals, the fertility deities, who played about the same roll as luck, chance, the state of the market and big profits—in business or betting—play for us. Not to mention all the other gods from which all those who don't have God expect everything that's good—the standard of living or sexuality, ideology or a political party, a career or leisure time.

The problem isn't God's gifts. His are good gifts and can be used for something good with a good conscience. The problem is in the heart of the recipient who wants to accept the gift but doesn't want anything to do with the Donor.

What should the Donor do then? The prophet tells us He'll take His gifts back, put an end to prosperity and, maybe, peace and freedom. He'll block the road to the future, where we thought we could walk toward ever increasing prosperity, ever increasing wages, ever more pleasure and happiness. People won't be able to understand why there suddenly has to be an end to perpetual progress. It just happens.

God has a good reason for it. He has drawn His beloved people from the path of disaster and led them into the wilderness again, and there He will "speak tenderly to her" (Hosea 2:14).

There's also another possibility. He can see that there's no use in trying anymore. He remains silent and allows us to go our own way—all the way to the bitter end. If this had not only been said about Israel but also about us, what would we have wanted?

You know us, Lord. We can't help but desire the third alternative: That we come back to You, thank You for Your gifts and use them as Your children. That we make an improvement and once again become Your people, who take their responsibility and take the gifts from Your hand and learn from You how to use them. If we don't do that, however, and instead are persistent in our ungratefulness and disobedience, please don't take Your hand away. Take instead the things that only destroy us. There's so much we can do without. We can't do without You, Lord, however. Take whatever You want to, just as long as You stay with us.

SATURDAY AFTER FIFTEENTH SUNDAY AFTER TRINITY

Amos 8:1–8

Shall not the land tremble on this account? Amos 8:8

What is something so shocking, so upsetting, that it can disturb the foundation of existence and cause the whole world to reel? It is what we call "social injustice," oppression, shameless exploitation of other people's needs, the heartless exploitation that creates income and fortunes at the expense of the poor.

Amos lived at the same time as Hosea. He, like Hosea, speaks to a nation that has abused God's gifts, and here he gives us a picture of yet another way to do something else with the Creator's good gifts than the Creator had intended.

We have seen that the gifts are good and that we can receive them and rejoice in them, when we do it as the good children of our heavenly Father. This also means that we know that the gifts are for *all* of God's children. Just in the same way it should be obvious that siblings share a candy bar, so also we should share God's gifts and not try to monopolize them.

However, that is exactly what happens. Amos describes it very dramatically. It's the Sabbath, God's day, but all we're thinking about is the profits we can rake in. If only the Sabbath were over! Times are tough, flour is expensive, and we've been shrewd and held on to the grain supply. Now it's time to sell at a premium. The method we use isn't that important. Who's going to complain about the exact amount if they run the risk of being without? And now labor is cheap; the poor will work for next to nothing.

The Bible paints the same picture in many different ways.

The oppressor can be the government, like it was in Egypt, where the children of Israel were taken as slaves under conditions that gradually became more inhumane (Exodus 5:6). Or as in the totalitarian state of the future, where no one can either buy or sell anything unless they accept the anti-Christian ideology (Revelation 13:17). The oppressors can be public officials who "turn aside the needy from justice and to rob the poor of My people in their right" or the lawmakers who "decree iniquitous decrees" (Isaiah 10:1–2). Or they can be employers who refuse to pay wages to the workers who mowed their fields (James 5:4). The conclusion is always the same, however. Those who do that accumulate the wrath of God upon them and will experience it.

We pray, righteous Father, for everyone on earth who speaks righteously and strives after justice. We pray for all statesmen and politicians, for everyone who has a possibility to allow justice to prevail in some way and can help so all men can share in Your gifts. We pray for ourselves, for eyes to see when something is wrong and hearts that react against it and the desire to dare to do what we can and should do.

To the Reader: Please observe: If Easter is early, the turn of the month between September and October is approaching. Therefore we point out a few things about the Sundays during the fall. Right up to the end of September, the Trinity Sundays follow each other chronologically. However, the Sunday closest to the end of September is observed as Saint Michael's Day and the Trinity Sunday that would've fallen on that Sunday will not apply. For Michael there is a special meditation at the end of this book, but during the rest of the following week you will have to read the passages that correspond to the week after Trinity that's in turn.

Thanksgiving Sunday is celebrated the second Sunday in October. For that day and the entire week there are special meditations at the end of this book. The same thing applies to the first Sunday in November that nowadays is called the Sunday after All Saints' Day. All Saints' Day is celebrated the previous Saturday. That day, too, has a special meditation at the end of this book.

These three Sundays—Michael, Thanksgiving and the Sunday after All Saints' Day—occur year after year at about the same time. That's why they can't be inserted among the other Sundays after Trinity in this book because occur at different times, depending on when Easter is celebrated.

SIXTEENTH SUNDAY AFTER TRINITY
Luke 7:11–17

I say to you, arise. Luke 7:14

Death is our enemy and keeps us in bondage. That's the realistic, Christian view of death. Death is not natural or something we can befriend. Deep in our nature there's a very real feeling that death for us is something frightening, something that shouldn't be allowed to happen. We weren't meant to die. Death is a sign that a catastrophe has happened, that life has become something it never should have become. It's both sound and correct to be afraid of death and experience it as an adversary, the destroyer, the foe.

The funeral procession that is coming through the city gates in Nain shows us how agonized we are by death, our foe. The sorrow here is as desperate it can be. There's a young man dead. Behind the bier is a widow who's lost everything, even her livelihood and security in the community. Since the funeral must take place the same day, she's had only a few hours before they shovel the dirt into the grave to ponder the most precious thing she had.

Then Jesus comes. What He does is what He always does when performing a miracle—preaches and gives us a lecture, a promise to all of us. He shows us that our enemy, death, has met his match. He shows us that there's a possibility, just one possibility, to escape the power of death. He says the same thing in deeds that He later says in words: He is the resurrection and the life, and that he who believes in Him will never see death. Exactly what He said here in Nain—"I say to you, arise"—He has the power to say to all of us at our graves. And He will.

Being a friend of death can mean resigning and surrendering, trying to accept the inevitable—we all have to die. Then we've renounced something that's the hallmark of mankind. You have to try to convince yourself that you're a fragment of matter that, in accordance with the laws of nature, will disintegrate and fall into pieces again. God, however, has put eternity into man's mind (Ecclesiastes 3:11), and therefore it's not so easy to wipe out the feeling that death is the destroyer. That's not the point either. We can't come to grips with death on our own. It becomes more and more important to become a friend of Jesus than a friend of death.

Without You, my Lord Jesus, death is just tremendous darkness and a huge mystery. No one can say what I'll meet on the other side. Some people say it's all over, but no one knows for sure, and no one can say when darkness overcomes me. I can try not to think about it, but it overwhelms me again. I see people who are younger than I go there. When is it my turn? You know when, Lord. Therefore I leave it all to You and only pray that You are also with me then. For the sake of Your faithfulness.

MONDAY AFTER SIXTEENTH SUNDAY AFTER TRINITY

Matthew 9:18–26

The girl is not dead but sleeping. Matthew 9:24

They sneered when Jesus said this. They knew the girl was dead. A deceased person had to be buried the same day, so it was very important that they were sure the person was dead. When Jesus talks of death, however, He sees it through the eyes of God. He speaks not only of the physical aspect of life, the part that's a function of the cells in our body. He speaks of the life that is related to God's own life. That life doesn't need any cells to function. It has to be in living communication with God, however. It comes from Him and is sustained by Him. If it's severed, it can die. That's why a person can be spiritually dead, yet still be healthy and well in this world. That's what Jesus is aiming at when He says: "Let the dead bury the dead."

In the same way a person can be spiritually alive despite lying dead on a bier. That's why dying in faith is called falling asleep. You're not dead; you're sleeping. You're in God's hands and will wake up when He says the powerful words: "I say to you, arise."

We've spoken before about the life we get from Christ, the new life that lives in us here on earth, although it is hidden and obscure, and in the resurrection takes on a new image so we become like Him, like Christ was after His resurrection.

This week we'll have the occasion to talk more closely about life, death, and resurrection. Death is the only sure thing that's going to happen in our future. Despite this, people have an apparent tendency to push away the thought of it.

It's something people don't eagerly talk about, and maybe don't even acknowledge. That's one of the signs of how unrealistic unbelief can be. Death and what happens afterward are a part of reality. It's true there's a lot we don't know about what happens to us after death. There is something we can know and that God wants us to know, however. That's what we're going to talk about this week.

Lord, it's important for me to know that You are with me now and that You are my Lord and Savior. You give me so much every day, and You have so much work for me to do, that I can't ask for more. Still, in Your kindness, You have spoken to me about things that no man can explore. You've given me the promise of a future that's far beyond anything I can understand. Therefore I open my heart and thank You for everything You want me to have. Preserve my heart in humbleness so I never ask for more and never try to search for the things You still hold secret. I know that someday I will see You face-to-face and know everything. Praise be to You for Your inexhaustible gifts.

TUESDAY AFTER SIXTEENTH SUNDAY AFTER TRINITY

Philippians 1:20–30

For to me to live is Christ, and to die is gain. Philippians 1:21

This is the Christian way to be liberated from the fear of death. When Christ is my life, even death is gain. That means I can depart and be with Christ—"for that is far better!"—as Paul says, and who can disagree with that? When our life on earth is at its best, it's just a premonition of the real life, at home, in my Father's house, with my Brother, Jesus.

However, we shouldn't believe that it's our duty and a demand to always be longing to be home in this way. Nothing is more natural and proper than a mother who wants to stay with her children, at least as long as they need her. Or that a person who's in the middle of a very responsible job prays to live on until someone else is ready to take over. No one has to have a bad conscience for feeling like that. Paul did it too. Of course he wished he could escape from all the persecution and toil. He said he would gladly depart to be with Christ. However, Paul didn't think about himself first. He knew that no one lives for himself or dies for himself. Christ gave him a mission here on earth, and he was still in the middle of it. He was needed here for the sake of others, and he was also certain that he would live on and that God would spare his life for a few more years. That's what happened, judging from the accounts of the Early Church. Paul was set free and traveled to Spain and Greece and wrote letters to Timothy and Titus during those years. He died as a martyr in Rome around AD 67.

Ultimately, it is not my business if I live or die. Christ is my Lord, and He's the one who decides. As long as He needs me here, I will live on. That's a great comfort to know. If He allows me to come home, He will be sad in one way or another over the fact that I maybe had to leave something undone. And if He lets me live, I can rejoice over every new day He gives to me, even if I become very old and maybe useless in the eyes of the world. As long as I can pray for others, I'm never useless.

Lord, I thank You that my time is in Your hands and that all of my days were written in Your book before they came about. I thank You that I can't add a cubit to the length of my life and don't have to worry about that. I thank You that You are my Lord and that I can be with You, regardless of whether I live or die. I thank You that my mortal day of death is my heavenly birthday, when I will come home and meet You and see You as You are.

Yes, thanks be to God who has given us the victory through our Lord Jesus Christ!

WEDNESDAY AFTER SIXTEENTH SUNDAY AFTER TRINITY

Philippians 2:1–18

He humbled Himself by becoming obedient to the point of death. Philippians 2:8

Life can be hard, so hard that you wonder how long you can stand it. When Paul enumerates all of the disgusting things he had to endure, they fill up almost a whole column in our Bible (2 Corinthians 11). And he says here that he expects his blood will finally be poured out in a sacrificial cup. Just as the priest in the temple in Jerusalem emptied his cup with red wine at the Lord's altar and let it run out over the stones, so does Paul expect that one day his blood will run out and be absorbed by the earth, as it did when he was beheaded a few years later. Yet he says that he's glad. Since he was called by the Lord Jesus, his life had been a sacrificial ministry, one huge offering of thanksgiving. Everything was laid on God's altar, the grief as well as the joy. He even had to bring forth the Philippians' faith as a sacrifice. The congregation at Philippi and all the other fruits he's seen in his work and in his suffering are things he received from God and lays down before God, full of joy over being able to serve Him.

Paul was able to live with all of his horrors and even be joyful in the middle of all his suffering because he learned to be as Jesus was. Christ was made destitute and poor and suffered for our sake, and He was obedient *unto death*; to the bitter end. Paul, therefore, says we also should be obedient and wish only that what happens to us is God's will. God directs our lives, not us. There are situations where death can appear to be liberating. A person can wish to die and can be tempted to take things into his own hands and end his own life. When you come to Christ with thoughts like that, however, they lose their power. If others take their lives, we should not judge them. "For each will have to bear his own load" (Galatians 6:5) and no one knows what goes on inside a desperate person. Personally we should follow this advice: "Cast your burden on the LORD, and He will sustain you" (Psalm 55:22).

You know my burden, Lord. You've already carried it. You carried my weaknesses, and took my suffering upon Yourself. My sin became Yours. You were tempted in everything and know how hard it can be. Therefore I come to You with everything, even things that no one understands. You, who were always obedient even unto death, help me take every day from Your hand, even the most difficult ones, right up until the last day comes.

THURSDAY AFTER SIXTEENTH SUNDAY AFTER TRINITY
Philippians 3:1–11

That I may know Him and the power of His resurrection.
Philippians 3:10

Who wouldn't want to experience this power? Just think—being able to *feel* the power of resurrection! Most of us probably think it must be a fantastic experience, being able to feel a heavenly, divine power fill our being. To be covered by a new life with all its feeling of triumph and joy. It's no wonder that Paul time and time again speaks about *joy!*

That's not exactly how it goes, however. When Paul talks about getting to know Christ and the power of His resurrection, he adds that he wants to "share His sufferings, becoming like Him in His death" (Philippians 3:10).

To overcome death and our fear of death is all a part of becoming one with Christ, uniting with Him and becoming one of His members. For us on earth this means that we must, in one way or another, be a part of His suffering. Christ was rejected and killed. Belonging to Him means participating in His disgrace, daring to fail and allowing people to jeer at us or scoff. What we feel is oftentimes just that participation in His suffering.

Paul enumerates all the things a pious Jew can do to form the basis for a secure feeling of having the correct attitude in life. Paul has learned to regard all of this as rubbish that can be thrown into the garbage can. He has one tremendous asset now: Christ, who died for him and has taken him into His service. That entails both suffering and joy. However, how it may *feel* has no real significance. The only thing that's necessary is Christ Himself.

Paul wants to share everything with Christ—"that by any means possible I may attain the resurrection from the dead" (Philippians 3:11). Reaching that is nothing we can regard as obvious. Eternal life with God is nothing we get merely by dying. Neither is it something we're sure to achieve because we, at some time, converted and came to the faith. It's something that is a result of Christ. It comes from Christ. We receive it if we're united with Christ. Everything is dependent on me belonging to Christ, in life and in death.

Paul understands all this. That's why he's careful in using exaggerations. There's only one thing that's really important to him: that he becomes incorporated in Christ, that he really is connected to Christ. That may come through victory and success or suffering and death. It still is joy, maybe not always emotionally, but still pure joy, what Paul calls *joy in the Lord*.

Lord, You see how my heart yearns for me to be able to reach the resurrection of the dead. I know it's all because You're there. As long as You're my Lord and Savior, I have a chance of sharing the power of Your resurrection. Therefore I grab onto the hem of Your mantle and won't let go. You know best, Lord, what forces and temptations and dangers await me along my way and want to take me away from You. Lord, put Yourself in their way and obstruct them. Be so close to me that nothing can come between us. Stay with me, Lord, and let me share Your life and Your death so I may share in Your resurrection. For Your name's sake.

FRIDAY AFTER SIXTEENTH SUNDAY AFTER TRINITY
Philippians 3:12–21

Jesus Christ, who will transform our lowly body to be like His glorious body. Philippians 3:21

This is the Christian's "hope of eternity." God has "put eternity in man's heart" (Ecclesiastes 3:11); therefore, every human being has received an existence that can't be destroyed. However, the big question to focus on is if the life we've received from God will be lived *with* Him or *without* Him. We've received the possibility to live *with* God through the forgiveness and reconciliation Christ has prepared for us. Paul clarifies that we have received citizenship in heaven. There's a goal "of the upward call of God in Christ Jesus" (Philippians 3:14). God waves the wages of victory in front of us. Still, we're struggling to reach the goal. We have to forget what lies behind us, all our failures, all the things we shamefully admit in our confession. We have to throw it off and leave it by the wayside. We don't have to drag it with us. We can forget it because God Himself forgets it and lowers it into the ocean of forgetfulness where everything is swallowed up by His inexhaustible forgiveness.

"Not that I have already obtained this or am already perfect," as we read in our passage today. I'm still living in an unbelieving world that doesn't want to serve Christ; a world that prefers to avoid every reminder of Him and His kingdom. Inside of myself, I carry the law of sin that lives in my members and prefer to be spared the constant chasing of the goal so I can take it easy and enjoy the good things in life that I know I have anyway. We know we have our citizenship in heaven. We know what the goal is. We await a Savior, the Lord Jesus Christ. He's the one who comes with the final, eternal, irrevocable salvation that consists of our being transformed so we become a part of a new creation. The old, lowly body is gone once and for all, the one that carries in it our inherited original sin and all our secretive resistance toward God. Instead, we'll be in the same image as the Resurrected, a new kind of reality Paul calls a "glorious body." Therefore, our Christian hope for eternity can be described with the words "Christ in you, the hope of glory" (Colossians 1:27). Christ lives in those who believe in Him. Because He lives in us, we know we will live in

Him. We will also partake in His new life, the life of the resurrected, the "glorious body." Our Christian hope is the hope of glory.

Lord, who would believe this without Your Word? If You hadn't risen from the dead? If You, our living Lord, hadn't come to us through Your call and allowed us to see a glimpse of Your glory? Help us to always see the goal in front of us and reach out to what lies ahead. May Your good Word be fulfilled in us so we hurry on our way without giving up and travel on without becoming tired. And if we tire, You'll carry us. Take us by the hand and lead us forward. You're loyal, and Your loyalty is our hope and our strength.

SATURDAY AFTER SIXTEENTH SUNDAY AFTER TRINITY
Philippians 4:1–23

I have learned the secret of facing plenty and hunger . . .
I can do all things through Him who strengthens me.
Philippians 4:12–13

A Christian is free. With these words in Philippians, Paul gives us the reason for a Christian's freedom. What does this mean?

Most often we think of freedom as being free *from* something—free from tedious duties and burdening obligations, free to do as we wish. Of course, there is an element of not being restrained in the word *freedom*. The important thing, however, is that a person is still free *to do* something, that he can and is allowed to do something that gives life a purpose and substance. And because God has a good reason for giving us life, real freedom always consists of the possibility to do what God created us for—that we fulfill our direction and be what God intended us to be when He created us.

Christians are free to live as God's children. Christians have the wonderful right to be able to talk to God and live in His presence like a happy child in the company of a kind father. However, because God created all of His children so differently and gave them different gifts, different talents, and different possibilities, freedom must also mean the *possibility* of using their gifts, developing their talents, and making use of the abilities they received from God. Christian freedom, therefore, has a social and political dimension: People should always have the possibility to receive the education and perform the work they're best suited for.

In the last chapter of Philippians Paul gives thanks for a gift he received, obviously a contribution to his missionary work. What he really wants isn't money, he explains, but that the gift will be used in a way that also benefits the Philippians—in other words, by spreading the Gospel and increasing the sphere of Christians who are of help and joy to each other. As far as he's concerned, he could've done without such gifts. He's learned how it is to be both full and hungry; he lived in both need and abundance. This is his freedom. When he can fulfill his mission by preaching about Christ, his life will always have meaning. He doesn't have to attach meaning to something else. He knows he can function in the place God wants him to be and fulfill the duty God wants him to perform. He is free because he's free to serve his Lord. He's independent of unessential matters simply because he's preoccupied with the essentials.

Lord Jesus, You've told us that we should seek God's kingdom and His righteousness and everything will be all right. Help us to be free from everything that's in our way, all the unnecessary worries, all the senseless hurrying, all our foolish beliefs that we have to do it ourselves and that it's because of us. Liberate us so we can do what we were created for, gladly, light-heartedly, and full of confidence. Give us a blessed Sabbath, when we can feel how happy we are to be given the chance to gather around You and hear You speak and find joy in one another. Hallowed be Thy name. Thy kingdom come.

SEVENTEENTH SUNDAY AFTER TRINITY
Luke 16:19–31

If they do not hear Moses and the Prophets, neither will they be convinced if someone should rise from the dead. Luke 16:31

God or the world? is the theme for this Sunday. Do they have to be in opposition? Do we have to choose?

First, we need to understand what is meant by "the world" in this context. It's not the world God created. That's good. The whole world is full of the glory of God. There's something good that comes from God in the sunshine and flowers, in job satisfaction and the joy of being a parent, in a healthy body and hearty laughter. You have a right to be happy about that. You don't honor God by belittling it.

However, the Bible often refers to something else with the words "the world." It's usually called *this* world, which means the *fallen* world, the world that has revolted against God and everything in this existence that doesn't want to obey God and hasn't become what He wanted. It's become some sort of oppositional world, a negation of God's good world. It's run by "this world's prince," who's also called the destroyer, the killer, or the adversary because his nature is to destroy, to disguise, to corrupt, torture, and kill.

The choice between God and the world may appear to be an easy one, but it is not. The destroyer, namely, has nothing against us enjoying the good gifts of God for the time being, just as long as we don't ask for God Himself. His job is to keep us away from God and see to it that we have nothing to do with the Savior and are not influenced by the Spirit. The fall has already occurred. We're already far away from God, and we've been that way ever since the tempter got hold of our human nature. If nothing else happens, he wins the game. Therefore it's enough to live like the rich man in our Scripture reading. It doesn't say he was a bad man. He did like most people did: he enjoyed life, he was interested in food and clothing, he was happy amongst his friends. He didn't *only* think about himself. Of course, he did forget the beggar Lazarus, but who could take care of all the needy people? He had a heart for his brothers.

Regardless, he forgot one thing: God. He didn't ask for Moses and the prophets—God's Word. He never paid any attention to the messages God sent him. He was lacking one thing, and it was the only essential thing.

Lord, my feet almost stumbled. My steps had slipped. I was envious of the arrogant when I saw the prosperity of the wicked. They are not in trouble as other men are; they are not stricken like other men. They increase in riches. All in vain have I kept my heart clean. For all the day long I have been stricken, and I am chastened every morning. Nevertheless I am continually with You. You hold my right hand. You guide me with Your counsel, and afterward You will receive me to glory. Whom have I in heaven but You? There is nothing upon earth that I desire besides You. (From Psalm 73.)

MONDAY AFTER SEVENTEENTH SUNDAY AFTER TRINITY
Luke 12:13–21

One's life does not consist in the abundance of his possessions. Luke 12:15

Although this should be obvious, it still needs to be said—especially in our day and age. Many people seem to believe that the proof of success, as individuals and as a nation, is a high standard of living, an ever-increasing gross national product. We're constantly getting new gadgets—newly invented items that we lived happily without twenty years ago, but now have become status symbols. Many people are quite unhappy if they can't afford everything everyone is talking about: bikes with twenty-one gears, DVD players, cell phones, and so on.

That's why the parable about the rich farmer still applies today. He was smart. He could show a constant increase in production. He considered expanding. His ideas were daring and maybe even modern: I'll tear everything down and build it up again.

There was really nothing wrong with that. Mankind should serve God in the great work, where He keeps the power of His creation. God wants life to be as good as it possibly can be for His children here on earth. Food and clothing, schools and hospitals are necessary. We all have a role in this tremendous work.

The problem with this rich man was that he took for granted that everything was a product of his own efforts. He was working for himself. He didn't talk to God about his work and his plans, and he spoke quite naturally about "*his* soul." He managed his own life. He laid a solid ground for his future and his happiness, all in accordance with his own plans and his own ability.

That's why God put him back in his place, suddenly and severely. "Fool! This night your soul is required of you" (Luke 12:20)—"your" soul, as he called it, as if he was the master over it.

James writes in his letter (4:13–16):

Come now, you who say, "Today or tomorrow we will go into such and such a town and spend a year there and trade and make a profit"—yet you do not know what tomorrow will bring. For you are a mist that appears for a little time and then vanishes. *Instead you ought to say, "If the Lord wills, we will live and do this or that." As it is, you boast in your arrogance. All such boasting is evil.*

You know best, Lord, how many times I receive Your gifts as a matter of course and count them as mine, although You put them in my hand. Help me take my life from Your hand every new day—my life and everything I have. Help me to remember that it's a loan, an entrusted possession I'm responsible for. I thank You for everything I have and everything I don't have, everything You give and everything You take away. I know my life depends on You alone and not on Your gifts. Therefore, I pray for only one thing: that whatever happens is in Your hands.

TUESDAY AFTER SEVENTEENTH SUNDAY AFTER TRINITY
Luke 16:1–8

There was a rich man who had a manager. Luke 16:1

We are all stewards. We own nothing ourselves. Everything that goes through our hands, our bodies, and our whole lives belongs to God. We aren't tenants leasing for a fair price, who can do what we want with the rest of our money, time, and natural abilities. We're stewards.

In other words, if you use your life, time, and possessions as if they were your own, you're embezzling. However, that's just what so many people do. They think it's the most natural thing in the world to live like that. That's proof of how far away they are from God. Then, one day, God confronts them. "What is this I hear about you? Turn in the account of your stewardship!" And in that situation we have something to learn from the unrighteous steward.

He was an impostor and a rascal, though clever, which is what Christ commended him for. In His parables Christ doesn't always portray exemplary behavior. Even the man who found a treasure in the field behaved dishonestly. However, common sinners like this one can, in the middle of his selfishness, give us a picture that illustrates something that should exist in a Christian's life.

Here it's a question of cleverness. The dishonest steward didn't do as many others would when confronted with God's Word. He didn't procrastinate. He didn't convince himself that everything was going to be all right. He knew what was in store, but he saw a way out—just one. And he grabbed it decisively.

All of God's stewards should react in the same way. The only difference being that their only chance is to confess everything and grasp the possibility of forgiveness and the new service offered them through what Christ has done for us.

If you read on in Luke, Jesus gives us yet another application for this parable: We can make friends with the unrighteous mammon. We can use money, which so often causes so much evil, for something good. We can manage it in such a way that people start to thank God. Everything we've been given to account for here on earth will vanish. What can be left, however, is fellowship and communion with those we could serve and make happy, and that will continue in God's kingdom.

Lord, am I also an embezzler who has used what is Yours as if it was mine to do with as I pleased? I know that everything is from You, through You, and for You. Even myself. From You I received my life and my body; through You I live today; and to You I will one day return to make an account. Help me then, Lord, that I may live every day with You and for You. Your will be done, even with me and through me.

WEDNESDAY AFTER SEVENTEENTH SUNDAY AFTER TRINITY
James 1:16–27

Let every person be quick to hear, slow to speak, slow to anger. James 1:19

We should be quick to listen, James says, to both God and man. First, we have to be at God's disposal so we can receive what He wants to give. Every perfect gift is from above, from the Father of lights. Gifts pour down to us in the sunshine and in our good health and in the new day. They become perfect in the Gospel, therefore we should receive with meekness "the implanted word, which is able to save your souls" (James 1:21). There we look into "the perfect law, the law of liberty" (James 1:25). James means the Law that is no longer compulsive. He knows, just as John, that God's Commandments aren't a burden when they're taken from the hand of Christ, not as a duty that has to be performed to achieve salvation but as something you have a chance to do as Christ's assistant, together with Him.

Second, we have to understand the meaning of being slow to speak. It doesn't mean that we should be quiet until we're absolutely sure what we can risk speaking without sinning. Instead it means we should open our hearts so we can both give and receive. You should be able to listen to others, not only sit and wait to say something yourself. You should also be able to give of yourself, and do it warm heartedly and with joy. Or as Paul put it: "Let no corrupting talk come out of your mouths, but only such as is good for building up, as fits the occasion, that it may give grace to those who hear" (Ephesians 4:29).

Lord, put a lock on my lips when necessary and unlock them when they can be of benefit and joy to someone. Put gentle words on my tongue and something kind to say when it's needed. Help me be slow to anger, and if I do become angry, help me to be slow to speak to others and quick to talk with You so I hear Your voice before I hear my own. And when I don't have time to think, guide my tongue anyway. Fill my heart every day with Your wonderful gifts, that I have a good supply of good words and right words I can use for every situation and every person.

James 2:14–26

For as the body apart from the spirit is dead, so also faith apart from works is dead. James 2:26

This "James, a servant of God and of the Lord Jesus Christ" (James 1:1) was—according to what we believe to be true from the ancient church—the apostle James, Jesus' own brother, the one who doubted while Jesus lived but was convinced when Jesus showed Himself after the resurrection. James became one of the leaders in the ancient church in Jerusalem until he, like so many others, was martyred.

In James's letter we can see what a pious and obedient Jew learned from Jesus. James thinks good deeds are very important, but he knows they have to be performed from the heart. He warns repeatedly against a Christianity that consists only of words or opinions—a warning we all need. Here in chapter 2, he especially warns us about a misinterpretation of the Gospel that some people can easily do, even among themselves. They hear the words "faith alone . . . through faith alone" and they think that deeds are not that important. James's answer to that is "Faith without works is dead." A living faith always includes good works. A body that doesn't move and function is dead. A faith that doesn't show itself through good deeds is just as dead. Or, as Paul expressed it: Everything is dependent on whether we have a faith that is active through love. There are extreme situations where a believer *can't* do any good works. That's the way it was for the thief on the cross and that's the way it can be for people who come to faith on their deathbed. That's when we see that faith alone can give us eternal bliss. It gives us a part of

Christ and then we have everything we need. The simple fact that faith is fellowship with Christ, which means you can't have it without wanting to do good works. A healthy tree bears good fruit.

This also applies to the words we use. Empty, thoughtless, selfish, and malicious words bear witness that there is no faith in the heart. Even pious words can have the same effect if they're not followed by deeds of love. The mouth expresses what the heart is full of. Even deeds, however, speak that language. You can't pick figs from thistles. The branch that is engrafted in Christ bears good fruit. If Christ lives in a heart, it's noticeable both in word and deed.

Dear Lord Jesus, help me to believe correctly so I can live correctly. Regarding my faith, help me so I see only You and not my works. If I see them, I dare not believe. Regarding my works, help me to see both You and everyone You want me to do something for. Help me to have an eye for You and see You everywhere among people. Then, it will be so much easier for me to do what You want. I can't do anything without You. So remain with me, O Lord Jesus.

FRIDAY AFTER SEVENTEENTH SUNDAY AFTER TRINITY

Acts 17:1–17

[I have had] far greater labors, far more imprisonments, with countless beatings. 2 Corinthians 11:23

Paul says he speaks "like a madman" (2 Corinthians 11:23) when he enumerates everything he's been through. He does this only to show that he has at least *one* advantage over his critics: none of them had suffered as much for his Master's sake as Paul had. He adds: the God and Father of the Lord Jesus knows he does not lie (2 Corinthinas 11:31).

This is confirmed in Acts. We can follow Paul from city to city and see what an apostle encounters. Because Luke included so many details, we can closely follow Paul's footsteps. Philippi is now a ghost town, but the square has been excavated and we can still walk on the cobblestones that Paul walked on and water still flows in that little stream where Lydia listened to the Gospel. A Roman highway went from Philippi to Thessalonica via Egnatia. You can still find these worn stone blocks with deep wheel tracks worn far below the surface. Amphipolis and Apollonia were on that road. Luke mentions them because they stayed over night there. They traveled three days and about thirty kilometers each day. Thessalonica was then, as it is now, a thriving merchant city with a large Jewish colony. Paul could speak in the synagogue there, but had to speak outdoors in Philippi because it was a Roman military outpost with few Jews and no synagogue. Thessalonica was an independent Greek city with its own authorities.

One wonders how Paul managed. In every new place he had to expect riots and persecution. Most of all one can wonder how Paul could regard himself as a free man at the same time. In fact, he gives us a vibrant picture of an essential side of Christian freedom, a side Luther often points out. Freedom becomes clear when you voluntarily and gladly discipline your old Adam and your body to be able to perform a duty that gives life purpose and happiness. As Paul put it: I give my body what it can tolerate and force it to be obedient so I won't be rejected when I preach to others.

I thank You, my Lord, for the freedom to throw aside whatever ties me down or restrains me. I thank You that I don't have to keep a lookout for all the possibilities to serve and need not grieve over lost money or profits I've missed. I thank You that I don't have to be afraid of what people say or their slander or diseases I have no control over. I thank You that every day is full of meaning and worth living when I have You. I thank You that nothing can separate me from Your love.

SATURDAY AFTER SEVENTEENTH SUNDAY AFTER TRINITY
Acts 17:18–34

What therefore you worship as unknown, this I proclaim to you. Acts 17:23

Paul had reached Athens, the city of wisdom, where sons of rich men gathered for casual instruction and where everyone was equally eager to follow the trend of cultural debate and political discussions. Paul had been shocked to see the massive religious ignorance, the primitive mythology, and the barbaric oriental cultures that thrived together with all this pride for learning. He spoke with the city's scholars and received a chance to speak at the Areopagus, the ancient court square, most probably not at a trial, but more like some type of informative gathering.

Paul begins his speech by generously acknowledging the positive thing behind all religions, however absurd they are. There is a genuine feeling for God. I can see that you're religious, men of Athens, he says. Paul had even seen an altar "to an unknown god" (archaeologists have, as a matter of fact, found an altar in Athens with this inscription). Then Paul says something that must have had everyone raising their eyebrows and cocking heads to listen: It's from this God, whom you worship without knowing, that I come with a message to you.

Then Paul clearly and in a condensed version develops the meaning behind what is usually called "the common revelation." Because all men are created by God in His image, all have a chance of sensing His nature and "feel after Him and find Him." It's in Him that we live and move and exist. This sense of God should already tell us that there must be something wrong with heathenism's primitive worship of objects. This knowledge of God will never be more than a feeling. That's why God has come to us, climbed down to be among us, and revealed Himself to us. He did this very decisively through Jesus Christ. In His presence, we all have to take a stand. God has proven that this is really the case by allowing Christ to rise from the dead. In this, Paul has said what the Gospel says to all religious seekers (those who sense that there must be a higher power, everyone who can't let go of the belief that there's a purpose in life). There's something to all of this that comes from God, and that is truth. Still, it is no more than worshiping an unknown god. From this God, however, there's a message, a greeting, a cluster of bright light. Make use of it!

Lord, Your testimonies are wonderful; therefore my soul keeps them. The unfolding of Your words gives light; it imparts understanding to the simple. Make Your face shine upon Your servant, and teach me Your statutes. You have appointed Your testimonies in righteousness, and in all faithfulness. I rise before dawn and cry for help; I hope in Your words. My eyes are awake before the watches of the night, that I may meditate upon Your promise. I have gone astray like a lost sheep; seek Your servant, for I do not forget Your commandments.
(From Psalm 119.)

EIGHTEENTH SUNDAY AFTER TRINITY
Matthew 22:34–46

Which is the greatest commandment in the law? . . .
What do you think about the Christ? Whose Son is He?
Matthew 22:36, 42

"Obedience through faith" is the topic for this Sunday. Faith and obedience belong to real Christianity, and real obedience comes through faith.

In our Scripture reading, we are confronted with two of the most important questions that can be asked. The first one is about God's will. What is the most important thing God expects from us, the thing we must remember above everything else? Everybody usually understands that this question is important. If you have any kind of faith in God, you're apt to understand that it is He who decides and not us, and it's not advisable to go against His will.

Jesus gave an answer that we all at one time probably learned was the synopsis of God's Law: We should love God above all else and our neighbor as ourselves. That answer could be accepted by every pious Jew. The ones who asked Jesus probably wanted to have something to accuse Him for, but they were completely satisfied with His answer. Mark tells us that the scribe said: Master, You are right. This is far superior to any kind of burnt offering or other sacrifice. When it came to the finest and most important thing in the law, there was no difference between Jesus and the Jews.

Then, however, Jesus counters with a question: "What do you think about the Christ? Whose Son is He?" This question is related to the first. It can reveal a very deep disparity concerning the way to God. For the Jews it was obvious that the way to God was the Law. Those who upheld the Law would prevail. Jesus, however, showed with all His preaching that those who take the Law seriously are as doomed and exposed. They are guilty through harsh words and unclean thoughts, through their carefully rationed friendliness and all their futile words. *That's* why the question of the Messiah is so important.

The scribe answered: He's David's son. That's exactly what many people would answer today. Jesus was a man, a

Jewish prophet from an old royal family, a wise teacher of the Law, a brilliant example, and one who taught us that love is what's most important. If that was all, Jesus would've sealed our fate. He would've shown us all how we should be and could've been, but aren't.

Happily He's something more. David called Him Lord, *my* Lord. He gives Him God's name, and rightly so. God not only gave us His Law with the most precious of all Commandments, He also gave us His Son, who is the fulfillment of the Law. He is the redemption for our sins, righteousness from God.

Joyous is he who has the right answer to both of these questions!

Lord, open my eyes so I can see the wonders of Your Law. Teach me to love Your Law because it's Your love that fills all Your Commandments. They're Your hand that guides me and shows me what I can do to please and help and be a blessing. Open my eyes so I see the path to Your kingdom, the way that is my Lord Jesus and no one else, not even Your precious Law. I can go to Your kingdom for Your beloved Son's sake, and I thank You for that.

MONDAY AFTER EIGHTEENTH SUNDAY AFTER TRINITY

Acts 18:1–17

For I have many in this city who are my people. Acts 18:10

Paul had arrived in Corinth and "was with you in weakness and in fear and much trembling" (1 Corinthians 2:3). Corinth was a new, rich, materialistic city with a population from every corner of the world, two harbors, and an immorality that was notorious. Among this money hungry population, Paul was careful not to ask for anyone's help. He worked in the evenings and preached during the day. There was plenty of work for a tentmaker and sail maker during the fall when the shipping trade had stopped and the harbors were full of ships that needed their sails repaired. For an assistant he had a refugee from Rome whose name was Aquila. There had been an uprising in the Jewish district and Caesar Claudius had sent all the Jews into exile. The reason for the uprising was a certain "Chrestus," recounts a Roman historian, and it's possible that it was the Gospel about Christ that was the cause. Aquila, and maybe even more important, his obviously very gifted and significant wife, Priscilla, became Paul's best friends and colleagues.

Work progressed. The director of the synagogue himself, Crispus, was baptized. There was also strong resistance among the Jews, however, and Paul had to relocate his work to a private home near the synagogue. The majority of the Christians came from the heathen in the slums. It appeared that even in this city God had many followers who were notorious for their corruption.

Then a new proconsul was appointed in the city—Gallio—a distinguished Roman who was the brother of the renowned philosopher Seneca (who dedicated two of his philosophical essays to him). This Gallio is noted historically for being an educated, honest man, maybe a little too softhearted for a pragmatic politician. It's possible the Jews wondered about his inexperience and cautiousness when they started the uprising, and accused Paul of teaching a belief in God that was contradictory to the law. The purpose was certainly that Gallio was to believe Christianity conflicted with Roman law. Gallio saw through the trick and declared that he wasn't appointed as a judge in disputes regarding Jewish law. Then he drove them out of the tribunal. The fact that he reluctantly got involved in other people's disputes was again proven when a fight broke out at the entrance to the synagogue. Apparently anti-Jewish Corinthians seized the custodian of the synagogue, Sosthenes, maybe the one who succeeded Crispus, and beat him, convinced they could get away with it.

But, just as God had many followers in godless Corinth, so also does His work go on right through all the bickering, all the fights, intrigues, and injustices that so often fill everyday life, even today and even for Christians.

I called on Your name, O Lord, from the depths of the pit; You heard my plea, do not close Your ear to my cry for help! You came near when I called on You; You said, "Do not fear!" You have taken up my cause, O Lord, You have redeemed my life. You have seen the wrong done to me, O Lord, judge my cause. You have seen all their vengeance, all their devices against me. You, O Lord, reign forever; Your throne endures to all generations. Restore us to You, O Lord, that we may be restored! Renew our days as of old! (From Lamentations 3 and 5.)

TUESDAY AFTER EIGHTEENTH SUNDAY AFTER TRINITY

Acts 18:18–28

He had been instructed in the way of the Lord. Acts 18:25

Sometimes the Gospel in the New Testament is simply called "the way." Sometimes it is called "The Lord's (Christ's) way." Antagonists could speak of "the way" as a sect (Acts 24:14). We see examples of that attitude today. Christianity is perceived as one conceivable point of view among many others in a pluralistic society. To believe in Christ, however, means confessing that He is *the way*. No one comes to God except through Him.

For the Jews *the Law* was "the way." To love the Law and live by the Law was, for them, the right way to God. They could be in complete agreement with the Christians about the goodness of God's Law and that love is the most integral element. The disagreement arose when the Christians declared that the Law doesn't lead to God. It is no way for us to live because we never can go that way all the way to the end. There will always be something that separates us from God. That separation can be bridged only by Christ, who alone complied with the Law and therefore is the fulfillment of the Law.

This is the reason for the violent resistance that the Gospel met among the Jews. The resistance had nothing to do with their godlessness. Paul says in Romans 10 that he can give his fellow countrymen—the ones who were knocked around with him—this testimony: that they have a zeal for God. He says, however, it is not enlightenment. "For, being ignorant of the righteousness of God, and seeking to establish their own, they did not submit to God's righteousness" (Romans

10:3). The law is their proud and distinguishing feature. They received it from God. They suffered for it. They can't understand that "Christ is the end of the law for righteousness to everyone who believes" (Romans 10:4).

Many may think that old disputes like these between Jews and Christians should now be forgotten. That's right, as far as some are concerned. Christians have persecuted the Jews much more unmercifully than the Jews have persecuted Christians. The problem remains, however, when we talk about *faith in the Law*. That faith is and will always be the Gospel's antithesis and worst enemy, and that faith is widespread within Christianity also. All too often it is noted as being a distinct and whole-hearted Christianity. It can also pose as a universally religious humanism. Christ is, however, no longer Lord and Savior when people build their trust in some kind of deed. Then we are no longer on the way He paved for us.

It is not good works Christ has liberated us from, Luther says, but the wrong view we have about them. Even Paul could do these extra deeds that pious Jews considered it their duty to do. He could bind himself to a promise, and shave his hair and bring forth sacrifices in Jerusalem on specific days. As Luther said, a man can go into a monastery just as long as he doesn't do it to earn eternal bliss but to serve his neighbor. Deeds belong to "the way," but the Way is Jesus and nothing else.

Lord Jesus, show us the way and make us willing to follow it. Show us that the only way to Your Father's house is the one You paved for us when You went up to Golgotha all alone and carried ours sins with You. Take us with You on that way and let us feel how good it is to follow You and be close to You, and show us how much there is to do there for Your sake.

WEDNESDAY AFTER EIGHTEENTH SUNDAY AFTER TRINITY

Acts 19:1–20

Many of those who were now believers came, confessing and divulging their practices. Acts 19:18

Ephesus, which is in ruins today, used to be the fourth largest city in the Roman Empire. There were already the beginnings of a church here under the leadership of the learned Apollos, who was instructed by the tentmaker Aquila, or probably even more so by his wife, Priscilla. In the ancient church, everyone realized their duty to bring others to the faith. Only men appeared in public as teachers, according to the commandment of God, but in private it was not only a right but a duty for a Christian—man or woman—to clearly show the way of God when someone found that another Christian lacked the necessary knowledge. This happened quite often. Many became disciples of Christ during His lifetime, then left Palestine. They weren't there at Easter or Pentecost. Maybe they were baptized by John in the Jordan River. Therefore, there may have been dedicated disciples who spoke of Jesus without having been baptized and without having heard the news of God fulfilling His promise of the outpouring of the Holy Spirit. Apollos was one of those disciples, along with the twelve men Paul met when he came to Ephesus. We see that they immediately were acknowledged as Christian brothers, but at the same time it was made clear to them what was lacking, and they were grateful to find that out. There was no talk of "you can believe in many different ways" or "there are many ways to God."

There was a revival in Ephesus and many came forth and

confessed what they had done. It's part of a true conversion to confess that one has lied, to make up for the damage one caused others, to ask one's enemies for forgiveness, or to return things that one came into the possession of in a wrong way or kept out of negligence.

Among the things that emerged from the people in Ephesus were the superstitions that existed among this modern and enlightened people. Witchcraft and magic, which entails trying to control and benefit from covert powers, have always existed as a degenerate side of religion. They can be conquered only by a vibrant faith. In Europe these practices and superstitions were prevalent until the national revivals of the 1800s. They continue even today, and show signs of increasing and returning in new and different forms (such as amulets and horoscopes and belief in lucky and unlucky days). This is a natural consequence of the disappearance of a living faith. When Christ becomes our Savior, we see that this kind of fear for unknown forces and all attempts to appease them is just a lack of faith and idol worship.

Lord, reveal for me everything I should confess to others. Help me to make amends for everything I can. Lord, is there anything I've hidden and tried to forget that stands between us? If there is anyone who is suffering or mourning for my sake, Lord, show me the way to make it right again. And if I can't, bless twofold whomever I've caused grief and injury to. You can turn evil into good and damage into profit. If this can happen through me, so be it, for Your name's sake.

THURSDAY AFTER EIGHTEENTH SUNDAY AFTER TRINITY

Acts 19:21–40

Great is Artemis of the Ephesians! Acts 19:28

That's what the masses cried during the huge uprising in Ephesus. Their goddess was called Artemis. (Ancient Bible translations called her Diana, a remnant of the Middle Ages habit of replacing Greek names with their Latin counterpart.) The Ephesian's Artemis was widely celebrated. It was a primitive statue, made partly of black stone, maybe a meteorite that actually had fallen from space. Her temple was one of the Seven Wonders of the World. Her festivals were celebrated with impressive splendor and pilgrims flocked to them from everywhere.

Paul remained in Ephesus longer than any other Greek city, and the Gospel achieved great success there. His opponents could say that Paul had persuaded and turned away a great many people. By doing that, he was in conflict with powerful economic interests. The silversmiths seemed to be the first to suspect that the Gospel could mean the end of ancient heathenism. That would also mean the end for one of their most important sources of income. Naturally, they said this only among themselves. Toward others they pretended to be concerned about the ancient patrimonial religion. That's usually what people do when the Gospel threatens their economic interests. Even in Christianity.

The result was a huge demonstration bordering on a riot, an example of mass hysteria, as Luke described it. People screamed in a deafening chorus (just as the people did outside of Pilate's palace on Good Friday), an old custom in the Orient that in our day and age has spread to the West. People were carried away and joined in and continued to scream, many of them without knowing what had happened. Paul wanted to go there and speak to the masses but was stopped by the disciples and by a few friends among the Asiarchs—elected political officials, who knew their fellow-countrymen and knew what was going to happen. A Jew—we don't know if he was a Christian—was brought forward and tried to speak but he was drowned out by the agitated crowd. Only when one of the city's own town clerks said a few wise and cautionary words did they calm down and start to go home.

That was the end of the long stay in Ephesus. Paul wrote 1 Corinthians in Ephesus and probably even Galatians. In the beginning of 2 Corinthians, which was written in Macedonia shortly after his departure from Ephesus, Paul tells how close he was to death during the riot. He might have been in trouble at some other time, since he (in 1 Corinthians 15:32) tells us that in Ephesus he "fought with beasts" (he probably meant people who acted like beasts). Luke left out many details like this. He didn't write Paul's biography but instead a portrayal of the Gospel's triumphal procession. We get a few glimpses of the suffering it cost and the joy it aroused. That's what makes Acts an edifying book.

My prayer is to You, O Lord. At an acceptable time, O God, in the abundance of Your steadfast love answer me. Rescue me from sinking in the mire. Let me be delivered from my enemies and from the deep waters. Answer me, O Lord, for Your steadfast love is good. According to Your abundant mercy, turn to me. Do not hide Your face from me, for I am in distress. Make haste to answer me. Draw near to me, redeem me. Set me free because of my enemies. You know my reproach. You know *my foes. But I am afflicted and in pain; let Your salvation, O God, set me on high! I will praise the name of God with a song; I will magnify Him with thanksgiving.* (From Psalm 69.)

FRIDAY AFTER EIGHTEENTH SUNDAY AFTER TRINITY

Acts 20:1–21

But going ahead to the ship, we set sail for Assos, intending to take Paul aboard there, for so he had arranged, intending himself to go by land. Acts 20:13

Why are details such as this included in the Bible? Is it edifying to hear about how Paul and his companions traveled?

We don't find many passages that go into such great detail as this one. Luke is telling about the trip to Jerusalem in such detail that we can almost follow the group from one day to the next. It's as if we're on a real trip with all its interruptions and variations. Luke brings us back down to earth. That's probably God's purpose: we shall know that all of this happened in the same world we live in and among individuals who had the same daily troubles we have.

If we read attentively, we can discover many remarkable things in everyday life. Why did Paul's friends set sail before he did? Probably because the ship was ready to sail and the crew didn't want to wait. There was cargo onboard and that, together with the wind, dictated the timetable. Paul, however, stayed in Troas. He wasn't ready yet. There was so much he had to take care of in the church. Despite the fact that he was up all night, he wasn't finished until sunrise. By then the ship had set sail and Paul let it go. He figured he could catch up with them at the next port, Assos, by land. It was 50 kilometers to Assos. After a sleepless night Paul headed out on the road, probably on foot, possibly with a donkey, and began a long day's journey. He knew how tough it would be, so he sent his friends by sea. He didn't conserve his strength in the service to his Master. He demanded more of himself than of others.

We notice one more thing when we read attentively. In the details, we see a picture of the Church developing; the Church that still stands today and that we belong to. We hear how the disciples gathered "on the first day of the week." It is Sunday, which is now beginning to be celebrated as the Christian day of worship instead of Saturday. They gathered to "break bread," in other words, to celebrate Communion. We hear that Paul called on "the elders" from Ephesus. They are presbyters, who had the task to lead and instruct the congregation, equivalent to our pastors day.

Consequently, what the Bible tells us isn't something that happened in a far distant, quasi-real existence. It's something that affects us very intimately, something that's happened in the world we live in and that has formed the Church we belong to.

Dear Father in heaven, You have allowed all this to happen to people on earth, among men of flesh and blood like me. You allowed it to happen for my sake, in order to give me a spiritual home and a *clear path to heaven. All the people I've read about today, those who were on their way to Jerusalem, You've taken them to Your Jerusalem in heaven. Now I wander on the same path. Maybe I'll see them sometime? Paul, Luke, and Timothy and Gaius and Tychicus, and others I know nothing about, only that they followed Your Son and that they're my brothers in faith and have gone before me on the same path. I thank You that I, too, can travel with them. Bless our journey and grant us a joyous homecoming in Jesus' name.*

SATURDAY AFTER EIGHTEENTH SUNDAY AFTER TRINITY

Acts 20:22–38

And now, behold, I am going to Jerusalem, constrained by the Spirit, not knowing what will happen to me there.
Acts 20:22

We can consider this passage Paul's farewell speech. Those who have read his letters and followed him on his journeys know that he paints an accurate self-portrait. That's the way he was: gladly willing to die as long as he could fulfill the mission he received from Christ in Damascus. He had willingly toiled and worked to fulfill that task. He had worked with his hands as a tentmaker so he wouldn't be a burden to anyone, but show that his Lord was right: It *is* far better to give than to receive. He worked even harder as an apostle and spiritual guide, admonished and comforted, warned and encouraged, day and night, personally and publicly. He knew he had proclaimed *all* of God's resolutions, *everything* important for salvation.

How could he do all this? We have the answer in his own words: He was "constrained by the Spirit." He was bound to the Lord who died for him and who revealed Himself to him despite the fact that Paul was His bitter enemy and persecutor. He couldn't and wouldn't do anything else but live for the One who died in his place. Accordingly, Paul is a role model, not only for all clergy through all of time but also for every Christian. He can teach us the innermost secret of Christian life: to be bound in the Spirit, bound to Christ, united with Him in an indissoluble band of blood, cleansed in His blood and incorporated in His body, filled with the new life that pours forth to us from His heart.

A person who is constrained by the Spirit in this way knows what the purpose of life is. He's on a journey to God's Jerusalem, to the city of God, and to continued service, infinitely better than the finest moments of service here on earth. In a way, he can say what Paul says, that he doesn't know what will meet him there, because what will become of us has not yet been revealed. There are things the human eye has not seen yet. The big difference, however, is that no dangers, no hostility, no distress can exist behind the gates of the new Jerusalem. For "God Himself will be with them as their God. He will wipe away every tear from their eyes, and death shall be no more, neither shall there be mourning, nor crying, nor pain anymore, for the former things have passed away" (Revelation 21:3–4).

I thank You, Lord, that tomorrow is again Your day
of resurrection, when we can gather around You,
our living Lord. Send us Your powerful words and
bind us in the Spirit, constrained by Your love.
Help all the servants of Your Word to watch over
one another and over the flock You've given them
to be stewards and shepherds for Your Church, the
one You saved with Your own blood. Give us a
pleasant Sunday, with a living church service and
living words from You, something You can say
Amen to. For Your name's sake.

NINETEENTH SUNDAY AFTER TRINITY
Mark 2:1–12

My son, your sins are forgiven. Mark 2:5

How strange! Do you think this sick man and the people
that carried him hoped to hear something else? Jesus saw their
faith. It was as apparent as it could be. They had elbowed
their way through the streets. The alley outside the house
was so crowded with people they couldn't come any closer,
so they climbed up onto one of the flat roofs near the house
and carried their friend from roof to roof until they were
right above the spot where Jesus was talking. There they tore

away the plaster on the roof, removed the twigs and branches between the beams and created a hole big enough to allow them to lower the man down on his mattress. All of this with the assurance that the Man down there, the Master and Prophet, would help their sick friend.

Now Jesus tells him to be of good cheer. However, He doesn't say: "Be healed" or "Get up and walk." Instead, He says, "Your sins are forgiven."

When Jesus surprises us, it's always worthwhile to listen carefully and reflect. If we don't understand Him, it's usually because we're looking at things from the wrong perspective. We assume that the biggest issues in life are suffering, sickness, poverty, or injustice, and we think Jesus has come to put everything right or show us how we can make everything right. Jesus, however, shows us that behind all these big issues is a deeper reason, more serious damage, something that has to be straightened out first. That damage is evil itself, the power that defies God and destroys His creation. That power has forced itself into our lives and we see it everywhere—in our own egoistic nature, in the oppression and injustice that happens to others, in race discrimination, in class struggle, and in war. About all of this we say as it says in this parable: An adversary did this, and it's *this* ever present evil that has to be conquered in one way or another so we can come to grips with its consequences.

How do we do that? The first step is the restoration of the right relationship to God through the forgiveness of sins. The second step is coming to grips with suffering (sickness, temptation, injustice, or whatever it might be) either through Christ taking it away or through Christ giving us the power to carry it and transform it into a testimony and a victory in faith.

We'll be talking more in depth about this during the coming week.

Lord Jesus, You, who have the power to forgive sins because You have carried all sin on Your back and made atonement for everything that went wrong, You can help us out of all our woe and torment that sometimes makes life so bitter. We pray that You lighten the yoke and relieve us from the burdens in the way You think is best. If it is Your will, let all that is evil disappear. Let good health come instead of torment, and strength instead of helplessness. However, if You would rather give us Your power in the midst of our powerlessness, and Your peace in the midst of sickness and death, we will praise You even then for Your tremendous gift and thank You with all our heart.

MONDAY AFTER NINETEENTH SUNDAY AFTER TRINITY
Luke 13:10–24

A daughter of Abraham whom Satan bound for eighteen years . . . Luke 13:16

That's how Jesus describes the poor woman, who was so deformed through some kind of disease that she was bent over, round-shouldered, unable to straighten up. We might be shocked that Jesus draws a parallel between bodily disease and evil spirits because disease has natural causes. We all know this fact.

However, here we meet the biblical view of nature and creation. In other words, this is the outlook Jesus teaches us, which is the right one when you look at things from an eternal point of view. Of course there are natural causes for diseases just like everything else! What that means is most things on earth happen in a certain succession we call cause and effect. What is behind this succession?

The Bible teaches us that creation, when it came from the hand of God, was good. "And God saw everything that He had made, and behold, it was very good" (Genesis 1:31). Into this good creation, however, the evil one has broken in and taken hold of us and our hearts. Our human nature has received its indelible impression that intrinsic individualism—and with it conceit, tardiness and harshness—is our tragic inheritance. Even the rest of creation, however, bears traces of wickedness. Jesus compares the world to a garden that an assailant has occupied. There he sits, the strong one, dependent on his weapons and exercising his brutal domination over everything he's seized and conquered. Therefore we see traces of him in nature also. There's something in creation that's become perverted and poisoned and no longer functions the way God wanted it to from the beginning. Something cruel and hard-hearted has been let in, something that causes pain and suffering, stench and decay. And this wickedness brings with it pain and torment. Therefore, Jesus also fights against sickness, just as He fights against death. It's an enemy, the work of the adversary. And since Jesus entered the world to wipe out all of Satan's evil doings, He then also cures the sick and raises people from the dead. Since the real damage is as extensive as it is, the necessary remedy has to come to grips with sin and blame so Satan has to let go of those who are condemned to death.

Therefore it's Christ's duty not only to cure, but to reconcile and forgive.

We pray, Lord Jesus, for all the poor souls who go bent and round-shouldered under the burden they bear. All those who have become bitter because of their sickness and misfortune. All those who ask: Why me? All those who believe they're forgotten and rejected because this has happened to them. Help them and us all to straighten up so we can see You and see that Your heaven of boundless forgiveness arches over us, that all evil exists because we live in a fallen world, that You have entered that world to help us, and that even if everything can't be perfect as long as we're here, at least nothing can separate us from You and no one can take Your heaven from us when we believe in You.

TUESDAY AFTER NINETEENTH SUNDAY AFTER TRINITY
Luke 10:15–20

I have given you authority to tread on serpents and scorpions, and over all the power of the enemy. Luke 10:19

Jesus speaks of what the enemy has at his disposal, what Satan can take into the field when he wants to destroy, make ugly, and torture. Jesus considers scorpions and snakes a part of this weaponry. This is the same fact we learned yesterday: There are things in nature that no longer function in accordance with God's will. Things happen that otherwise wouldn't have happened if the adversary hadn't caused it. That means even things like sicknesses, poisons, bacteria, and everything that damages in any way.

What does Jesus do? He fights against all of this. Earlier in this chapter, Luke said that He sent out 72 disciples to proclaim the Gospel and heal the sick. Now they return, full of enthusiasm. It happened! They even had power over the evil spirits.

Jesus says He saw Satan fall from heaven like a lightning bolt. We hear Him talk about this with John also. "Now is the judgment of this world; now will the ruler of this world be cast out" (John 12:31). Jesus is recalling a prophesy about Lucifer, who wanted to rise up, defy God, and make himself like the Most High; instead he is thrown out of heaven and into the kingdom of death (Isaiah 14). This is what happens to the prosecutor, Satan, when Christ, the Redeemer, takes the stolen treasure away from him. Now everything is forgiven and is given back to God. If you listen to the Gospel and receive forgiveness, if you act like Capernaum, that followed the path of disbelief and wanted to be its own god (it's the same thing throughout time!), then you will not be master over your destiny and future, you will not be taken into heaven. Instead, you will thrown into the kingdom of death.

So Satan is defeated. He has, however, as it says in Revelation 12:12, come down to earth in great wrath because he knows his time is short. The battles wages on here. Jesus says, however, that he can do us no harm. He doesn't have the power to take us from Jesus. He can't even touch us with his finger when Jesus intercedes with His power to do miracles. The apostles had this special protection. The viper on Malta (Acts 28:3) didn't harm Paul. Even the apostles had to die, however, most of them a cruel death at the hand of the enemy.

It's the same way with us also. We can experience Christ's victory in a very personal and tangible way. He can cure diseases that seemed incurable. He can allow old temptations to lose all of their power and leave our life forever. He can save us through manifested interventions and allow marvelous things to happen as an answer to our prayers. However, we still live in a fallen world and we sometimes feel it and become humble and obedient in suffering, as He Himself and His apostles did. The way He chooses is in His hand. In both cases it's a good way, a way where we walk with Him and that leads home to God.

You hold my right hand. You guide me with Your counsel, and afterward You will receive me to glory. Whom have I in heaven but You? And there is nothing upon earth that I desire besides You. My flesh and my heart may fail, but God is the strength of my heart and my portion forever. For me it is good to be near God. When my spirit is faint, You know my way. Teach me the way I should go, for to You I lift up my soul. Teach me to do Your will, for You are my God! Let Your good spirit lead me on a level path. (From Psalms 73, 142, and 143.)

WEDNESDAY AFTER NINETEENTH SUNDAY AFTER TRINITY
2 Corinthians 4:1–15

We have this treasure in jars of clay, to show that the surpassing power belongs to God and not to us.
2 Corinthians 4:7

We are the vessels, the "jars of clay." Sometimes *vessel* is used to describe the Bible, but that's incorrect. The vessel is our frail soul, a perishable body that bears "the law of sin that dwells in my members" (Romans 7:23). And the treasure is the Gospel, Christ, redemption. The tremendous miracle is that Christ can live in such a weak and inferior person and can perform such wonderful things with such frail tools.

Anyone could break the vessels. It's just a question of weak individuals, who, on top of everything else, are socially insignificant and lack esteem in cultural circles and political situations. Paul describes how this can feel: afflicted in every way, perplexed and persecuted, struck down and branded by defeat. Their opponents seem to have an irrefutable advantage, yet they'll never find the treasure. There's something here they don't see: "the light of the gospel of the glory of Christ, who is the image of God" (2 Corinthians 4:4). Something happens here they couldn't expect: the light that radiates in the face of Christ spreads its glow. There's life in the midst of what the world thinks is dead and defeated. Therefore, we are never left with no way out, never perplexed, never abandoned. Therefore, we also talk. The witnessing doesn't stop. Paul quotes Psalm 116 here, the one Jesus sang in Gethsemane the night before His death. This psalm talks about salvation from utter anguish in the kingdom of death, and from Jesus' lips, it meant a confession to God in the most disadvantageous of positions imaginable. That's how Paul also understood it. Because he believed in that Christ who was killed but still lives, he can continue to be so candid, no matter what kind of superior force is against him.

For us it's important to notice how Paul—the great warrior of the faith, the pardoned charismatic—talks so much about his human frailties. Sometimes we imagine that a Christian can solve all his problems so he can live in peace and joy, go from victory to victory, experience temptation withering away, old habits disappearing and sickness turning into good health. All this as an answer to prayer, and it's true and indeed does happen. The Bible bears witness to this, as does experience. The Bible and experience, however, bear witness to something else: many have to continue to fight the fight when it appears they're the underdogs. And now Paul can teach us that God can do great things even in what appears to be helplessly frail.

You have delivered my soul from death, my eyes from tears, my feet from stumbling. I walk before the Lord in the land of the living. I kept my faith, even when I said, "I am greatly afflicted." I said in my consternation, "Men are all a vain hope." What shall I render to the Lord for all His bounty to me? I will lift up the cup of salvation and call on the name of the Lord. I will pay my vows to the Lord in the presence of all His people. O Lord, I am Your servant. I will offer to You the sacrifice of thanksgiving. (From Psalm 116.)

2 Corinthians 11:23–33

If I must boast, I will boast of the things that show my weakness. 2 Corinthians 11:30

Paul praises himself like a "madman," as he describes. His character was defamed and he was outclassed. People say he wasn't a real apostle and possibly not completely sane; and people have said that to get at his gospel. That's why Paul answers with such passion. He wants to show us that he, if anyone, should have the right to be believed when he speaks as Christ's servant.

We can be glad over this outburst of human indignation. It's given us an understanding of how the life of an apostle is a picture we don't want to be without. We have to admire this irrevocable steadfastness with the willingness to do anything for his Master's sake. However, maybe it's even more valuable to get a good picture of the *weakness* that this "strong" Paul experienced. Here we get a profound and edifying picture of a true Christian. It's not quite the picture we have among Christians: that of the victor who has gone from darkness to wonderful light and now possesses an inward power to overcome all his weaknesses and a faith that can pray away all sickness and opposition.

It's true that this does exist. Maybe we'd have more of it if we asked for more. There is faith that can perform miracles. There is a faith-healing gift, just as there is the gift to perform feats of strength. Paul had these gifts to a great extent. In the next chapter he says, "the signs of a true apostle were performed among you with utmost patience, with signs and wonders and mighty works" (2 Corinthians 12:12). The

Corinthians saw it for themselves. Despite all of the gifts of mercy he possessed, he could still speak about his weaknesses.

Here it's not only a matter of the difficulties and obstacles that come from the outside world. There are plenty of those and Paul makes a long list of them. There are also obstacles and difficulties that come from within, however. Paul mentions how he becomes weak when others waver, and how he becomes aflame when others begin to fall. In another spot (1 Corinthians 7:9) he uses the same word—to become "aflame," "burn"—regarding sexual temptations. He knew the cost of constantly having to look into other people's defeats and offer them help. In Galatians 6:1 he gave advice that is probably based on his own experience: Look to yourself, lest you be too tempted. It's this weakness that Paul now says he *boasts* about, rather than his strengths. He shows that this isn't a question of human competence but about God's salvation.

Lord, help me see how wonderful Your salvation is. That I am saved although I live in a fallen world. Although I still have my old Adam in me, the one who tempts me and holds me back. Although I feel so helpless in the face of this world's resistance and scorn. Although I might get sick and die. Despite this I'm still in Your hands. Despite this all is forgiven. Despite this Your life works in me. And despite this You can, when Your mercy allows it, use even me for something good, something that glorifies Your name. Dear Lord, may all this happen according to Your will and in Your power.

FRIDAY AFTER NINETEENTH SUNDAY AFTER TRINITY

2 Corinthians 12:1–10

My grace is sufficient for you, for My power is made perfect in weakness. 2 Corinthians 12:9

That's the answer Paul received when he asked to have the thorn in his flesh removed. "The thorn" must have been a serious affliction, something he experienced as obstructive and humiliating, something that seemed like the angel of Satan hitting him in the face. People have guessed that it might've been a disease. We know Paul had problems with his eyesight. We're probably not supposed to know what it was, however. Instead each of us should think about our own afflictions. It could be a disease. It could be a flaw in our character. It could be someone who has become our tormentor. Or something else we perceive as a genuine obstacle and something humiliating in life—even for our Christian life.

Paul says he prayed three times to be liberated from this affliction. Three times. We assume that Paul usually experienced an answer to his prayers after one or two times. That can happen when you pray fervently and in faith. This time, however, Paul's prayers were answered in a different way. He found out that it wasn't God's will that he should be cured. He had to bear his affliction, and through bearing it he would glorify God. Just by being weak and still being able to live—entirely through Christ, entirely through mercy, entirely through faith in the liberation we're promised when Christ comes—would he bear witness to his Lord. He would show that life is worth living even when things go bad, even when we must sacrifice the dreams that are most dear to us, even when we have to do without things that others regard as necessary. When we have God, every day is abundance, a joy, and a possibility to do something good. That's what Paul would show us.

Some of us receive that mission in the same way. We live in a fallen world. Sin, temptation, disease, suffering, tears, and death can't be peeled away from creation. Wickedness has entrenched itself to such a degree that it can't be rooted out until everything becomes new again, when God creates a new heaven and earth. Right here and now we see how Christ prevails. The great victory is atonement that drenches our entire life in forgiveness. In the midst of our weakness, we're allowed to be God's children. Christ also shows His power by defeating His opponents: the Tempter, disease, and unrighteousness. Sometimes He does it through great miracles. (Although, like the time He was on earth, few got to meet Him through such miracles.) He didn't cure all the sick in Israel and raise all the dead. His miracles were a sign that God's kingdom was approaching and that a new time was about to begin; the time for forgiveness and the Gospel. Despite the fact that we still live in the old world with all its torment and agony, we live under His mercy, and the Lord says: "My grace is sufficient."

Lord, forgive me if I in my foolishness wished for extremely exalted revelations. As if they could make me a better Christian! Your power is made perfect in weakness. Help me to not be afraid of weakness when You want to make use of it. Allow my weakness to become a hand that reaches out for You, an emptiness You can fill, a longing that never stops hoping for You. And come in that way to me with all Your power, my dear Lord and Savior.

SATURDAY AFTER NINETEENTH SUNDAY AFTER TRINITY

Job 1:1–22

Does Job fear God for no reason? Job 1:9

That was the prosecutor's scoffing question. The story of Job begins in heaven, in God's invisible world, where "God's sons," all the living beings that the New Testament calls "all things . . . created, in heaven and on earth, visible and invisible, whether thrones or dominions or rulers or authorities" (Colossians 1:16), rejoice before the face of God and fill the heavens with exultation and songs of praise.

You can also hear the prosecutor's scoffing question here on earth. What do Christians actually give up? They seem to be doing well in every way. The pastors sit in their parsonages with a steady income. The parishioners seem to be well clothed and well fed. Judging by what they have to say, they've got everything they need. What's the big deal with believing in God?

So God gave Satan permission to test Job, and Job was subjected to all the terrible things, like war and natural catastrophes, that can happen to us poor human beings. It turned out, however, that he remained steadfast toward God. Even when he did it "for no reason."

The prosecutor wouldn't give up. We're told, as the story goes on, that Job was stricken with disease, repulsive disease. At first he remained steadfast. Then, however, he began to falter. His friends tried to comfort him, just as clumsily as we so often do. They tried to get him to admit that there must be a special sin in his life that was the cause of these misfortunes. If he only would repent and believe, everything would get better. Job refused. Not before he met God Himself did he retract or regret anything. He discovered that there is one thing in life that's enough to give it purpose: God Himself.

It happens all the time that certain individuals are chosen to answer the prosecutor's and the skeptic's sneering questions. They answer with their lives. They have to show that even if everything people consider necessary for a worthwhile life is taken away from them, they still have God, and that's enough. They can show it during a prolonged sickness that isn't cured despite many prayers. They can show it when they're struck by unexpected accidents or persecuted by misfortune that would make others bitter or paralyzed. Their misfortunes seem unexplainable, superhuman, meaningless, yet God's light shines on their way. Even in this way Christ can prevail over sickness, suffering, and death.

Lord, I understand that it can be a choice, a sign of trust from You, to be put to that test. Still, I dare not ask for it. I'm a weak person. I'm afraid of misfortune and suffering. I thank You for all the evil I've been spared. If misfortune comes, however, help me to take everything from Your hand, to take the bad days as I have taken the good days, and to thank You that You are with me even then and that no day can really be a bad day when it's a day with You.

TWENTIETH SUNDAY AFTER TRINITY

Matthew 19:1–9

What therefore God has joined together, let not man separate. Matthew 19:6

In this day and age, most people hold the opinion that how men and women handle their personal relationships is their own business. If they want to, they can marry. On the other hand, they could just as well live together or have a casual relationship.

This is clearly against God's will, as Jesus strongly emphasizes. Marriage is one of the laws of creation. It's not something we can make decisions about or regulations on as we see fit. "He who created them from the beginning made them male and female" (Matthew 19:4). He gave us something in our nature that attracts man and woman to each other, and he did that so "a man shall leave his father and his mother and hold fast to his wife" (Matthew 19:5). In other words, it's God's will that a man and a woman should find each other and unite in a lifelong, inseparable unit until death separates them. In a union like this, where the man and woman complement each other, support each other, and raise each other, lies one of life's greatest treasures, one of God's greatest gifts in this life.

Jesus was asked how Moses could allow divorce. Among the Jews, it was almost as easy to get a divorce as it is in our culture today. Jesus answers that that law was created "because of your hardness of heart" (Matthew 19:8). However, it wasn't what God meant when He established matrimony, and a person who wants to follow the will of God doesn't make use of a law that was created to suit hard and unrepentant hearts. From society's point of view, there can't be any sense in forcing two people to live together if they just make life miserable for each other. Among Christians, however, in the kingdom of God, it need not occur that we make life miserable for each other. There we live in forgiveness and can forgive each other.

However, what happens if only one of them is Christian? If one of them wants a divorce? Then the rule in the New Testament is this: In such a case, a Christian isn't bound, for God has called us to live in peace (1 Corinthians 7:15). Our church has, ever since the Reformation, taught us that there are two instances where a Christian is permitted to get a divorce—when one of them breaks their vows by committing adultery or when one of them abandons the other. Experience teaches us that there are other instances where a marriage, through people's sin, can become intolerable and irreconcilable. However, divorce is something a Christian can't count on as a possibility to be kept open. Of course a Christian knows that we can choose our life's companion, but it's God who unites us and gives us the great task of remaining one for better or worse. He knows that we will someday stand and answer before Him for how we completed that task.

Lord, I can't help but see how hopelessly far away from You and Your good will our nation has strayed and how much misery it's caused for our wretched souls and our homes and our children. Lord, give us what we need. You have given us good virtues in our hearts, the desire to bless and help and give joy, the need to have someone to love and someone to trust in every situation. Let these virtues work among us so they also make an impression on our customs and our society. However, most of all, Lord, we pray to You for the miracle that You

allow people to wake up and realize that we need
You so we can live properly and wisely and for the
joy and benefit of others.

MONDAY AFTER TWENTIETH SUNDAY AFTER TRINITY
Matthew 5:27–32

So they are no longer two but one flesh. Matthew 19:6

Once again we've read Jesus' stern words about indissoluble marriage. We have also received a useful warning about gradating sins, however, so we begin regarding divorce as something so disastrous that the divorced person can never get married again. In the Sermon on the Mount, Jesus teaches us another gradation of sins. The worst is in the heart, and we're all guilty of that. A person who is angry at his brother incurs the judgment of God. A person who looks lustfully at a woman has already committed adultery. There's forgiveness for these sins, however, when you take them to Jesus. There's no such thing as a sin so great that it isn't included in Jesus' atonement. We are God's children, forgiven sinners, who want to make our Father happy. Even as a married couple.

However, why does God take lifelong marriage so seriously? We find the answer in Jesus' words: "They are no longer two but one." There is a profound purpose in the fact that in creation, God "made them male and female" with different natures and as a complement to each other. According to God's will, a man and a woman can grow together both in body and soul in a way that otherwise isn't possible for two individuals. That's why God has given us something in our nature that attracts a man and a woman to each other. The fact that we can fall in love is a gift from God, but it has to be handled according to God's will. The natural avenue to a marriage is through falling in love deeply and seriously.

Love is more than falling in love, however. Falling in love can be very powerful and overcome many obstacles. As long as it lasts all one can see is the good points of the one he loves. However, that's not a tenable basis for marriage. Falling in love seeks its own objectives. It expects happiness by owning the object of its love. It naturally expects that happiness exists when you own each other. Then the problems come, however. The romance cools down. That's when true love shows what it's worth. You see a lasting marriage isn't only built on infatuation but on love. God's intention isn't that you should be happy by getting something for nothing, by and through another person. God's intention is that you experience happiness by making somebody else happy. Marriage contains the greatest mission in life: to be useful, a blessing, to be supportive and helpful to someone else, with whom God Himself united you to be able to fulfill just that mission. The idea is that we two, who now are one, should grow together in a devotion to each other that doesn't seek its own objectives, but instead finds its happiness in being able to give and to share troubles, obligations, responsibilities, and decisions.

Lord, have mercy on us, Your poor mankind that takes such poor care of Your wonderful gifts. You know *best, Lord, how often the greatest possibilities You give us to happiness turn into great misery and none of us are blameless. Forgive us and help us to have the right view of You, Your intentions, and Your possibilities. Help all those who have experienced misfortune, all those who are disappointed, bitter, and unhappy, or looking for happiness without understanding the foundation it requires. You have the power to make everything new. Help us all to open up ourselves for that.*

TUESDAY AFTER TWENTIETH SUNDAY AFTER TRINITY

Ephesians 5:21–6:9

As Christ loved the church and gave Himself up for her.
Ephesians 5:25

Paul repeats over and over that it's all because of Christ. Without Christ, no one can live the new life, where he who serves is first and where we gladly accept the order of things that others revolt against but that we adore because they are God's.

Paul has three examples of such order. In all three examples he emphasizes that it's a question of obedience "in the Lord," in other words, in Christ's kingdom. In all three examples he emphasizes that the one who is the "subject" is himself a servant of Christ and has the same duty to serve for Christ's sake.

Children should obey their parents. They're not the parent's property, however, not toys for parents to play with, tease, or order around as they please.

It's the same thing at work, the second example. Someone has to be the boss and give orders, and others have to do as they're told. The boss, however, has a superior in heaven. He'll have to answer before Him for everything he has said and done as a boss. A Christian knows who he's subject to, whether he is a foreman or a subordinate. Therefore, he's liberated when he takes orders and is a responsible servant even when it's he that makes the orders.

In other words, this is all about being "in Christ," the innermost meaning of which can never be expressed in civil law. That is even more important in the context of the third example Paul mentions here: marriage. Many grave injustices have been brought about, as well as a lot of suffering, because in times past civil law ordered the wife to do what the New Testament says a Christian wife can voluntarily do out of love for Christ. Because of this the woman was declared a minor and at the mercy of her husband, even if he least of all loved her as "Christ loved the church and gave Himself up for her" (Ephesians 5:25). Christian matrimony is a parallel to the relationship between Christ and His Church. In both instances it's a question of one entity, an intimate unification that God established. In both cases you can say: Two have become one. And just as Christ is the Head of the Church, His own body, so the husband is his wife's head. That doesn't mean leadership as the world defines it. It means he has a call to treat his wife as Christ treats us. He is one with his wife, he is willing to accept her weaknesses and faults as his own, he doesn't blame her when something goes wrong. He doesn't put the responsibility for the home and the children on her.

He takes her burdens and carries them as his own. He never gets tired of forgiving and doesn't say: enough is enough. And the wife, on the other hand, loves her husband and is willing to share everything with him. And if they have different opinions at times, despite the fact that they both spoke out as Christians, she'll let him decide if they have to make a decision. She does that for Christ's sake because she knows God has shown that solution to that situation so there won't be friction and bitterness.

Lord Jesus Christ, help us all to see and appreciate the strange and wonderful order of things in Your kingdom, where everyone You give a task to and everyone You choose to be leaders are mere servants, and where those who serve are the most prominent and distinguished. Help us to take everything from Your hand, no matter what You give us to do or what You put before us. You Yourself came not to be served, but to serve. Help us follow You on that path and be happy every day that we have a chance to walk on it.

WEDNESDAY AFTER TWENTIETH SUNDAY AFTER TRINITY

Luke 6:17–31

Let the children come to Me, do not hinder them. Mark 10:14

That was a word to the disciples—a rather sharp reprimand. They thought the children could wait. When they finally began to understand what it was all about, it was almost too late. This time the parents wanted the right thing. However, that's not always the case.

Being a parent is among the greatest gifts and greatest tasks one can get. Having a child together means we take part in God's work of creation. We could never live here on earth and could never have become God's children with an eternity in front of us if parents through uncountable generations before us hadn't had so much patience with their children and maybe even died for their sake. Now it's our turn to make life go on. We can't arbitrarily avoid that task. God has put us here in the grand picture of the generations. Of course, everyone isn't called to become a parent. Everyone doesn't get married and not everyone can have children. Where the possibility exists, however, you can't deny the children the right to life just because you want to live more conveniently or so only one or two children could have it so much better economically. Isn't life more than food and the body more than clothes? You can't offer one child's life as payment for all the good but unnecessary things you want to lavish on another child. Jesus says "let the children come to Me." That's peculiar: the first condition for someone to be able to be a child of God and share all the joy that is the purpose of a human life, now and in eternity, is that there are people here on earth who are willing to take upon themselves the task of becoming a parent to a child.

"Let the children come to Me." Jesus doesn't share the view that says: Let them grow up first, and then they can decide for themselves. No, Jesus says. They are exactly the ones who need God's kingdom. It's there for them. Who can bear growing up in this evil world without clinging to God? The idea was never that mankind could be capable of existing without God. When we look around us, we also see how difficult it is. We really need to let Jesus lay His hand on us and bless us, as He does in Baptism, and then not take it away.

Dear Lord, You've got to help us here. It's hard to see what Your will is. The world is over-crowded. They say it's not right to bring children into the world. However, can it ever be wrong to give life to a child whom You love and who is brought to You? If we put him in Your arms and want to teach him to live with You now, every day, and in eternity? Lord, I have to thank You that I myself have been given life and haven't been refused it. I would've never gotten to know You if I hadn't seen the light of day on this earth. Lord, help us all to see clearly and do what is right.

THURSDAY AFTER TWENTIETH SUNDAY AFTER TRINITY

1 Peter 3:1–12

Have unity of mind, sympathy, brotherly love, a tender heart, and a humble mind. I Peter 3:8

In other words, it's "one word for everyone." First of all it's about those closest to us and our homes. The apostle has just comforted and admonished wives who wrestle with one of the gravest problems that can exist in a marriage: those who are married to men who don't believe. He comforted them with the fact that they can win them over to Christ without saying a word, through the way they live. He knows the power that lies in love can serve and be subordinate, not out of weakness but for Christ's sake. Then he also gives husbands a reminder that they should honor their wives. Otherwise their prayers will be hindered. A sulky and self-centered husband who loses touch with his wife also risks losing touch with God.

Consequently, it's at home that love first and foremost exists and is nurtured. Of all the things faith can achieve to make the world a better place to live in, this is the first and most important. It's a common mistake to believe that a raise in salary and more vacation is what counts most in one's well-being and happiness in everyday life. It's much more important to have a home and a job where you're surrounded by kind and helpful people, where you're welcome and where you can do a good job and be appreciated.

First and foremost it's about our homes. That's where devotion should begin, as the old saying goes: Charity begins at home. It's easy to honor the commandment of love in theory. It's easy to have warm feelings for suffering individuals you've never seen. It's more difficult when it concerns people you have to live with on a daily basis. Since we all have our faults, you can't help but notice them most clearly in those who are closest to you. For all of us, it's easier to be friendly, courteous, and indulgent with people we meet more or less accidentally than with those we have to live with. It is rather revealing how much friendlier you can sound on the telephone than you did immediately before when you talked with one of the people closest to you.

What did the apostle say to us all? "Have unity of mind, sympathy, brotherly love, a tender heart, and a humble mind."

Help me, dear Lord, with just that. You know how much I need Your help. You told me that he who doesn't love his brother, whom he's seen, can't love You, whom he hasn't seen. You want me first of all to love those closest to me. If my unjust heart has difficulty doing it with sympathy, then help me to at least do it in word and deed. Help me to also do it to those who least deserve it. Maybe they need it most of all just then. I really don't deserve Your love, and yet You do love me. Thank You, Lord. What would otherwise become of me?

1 Peter 2:1–10

You yourselves like living stones are being built up as a
spiritual house, to be a holy priesthood, to offer spiritual
sacrifices acceptable to God through Jesus Christ. 1 Peter 2:5

Again we hear the apostle admonish his fellow Christians
to live as God's witnesses in the world. He calls us "out of
darkness into His marvelous light" (1 Peter 2:9). We are a
new people, His people, and "a royal priesthood" (1 Peter
2:9).

This is what we usually call "the universal priesthood."
What is meant by *priesthood?* It's obvious that we immediately
think of our priests and mean that the universal priesthood
must mean that we're all priests, at least in principle. That's
not at all the meaning, however.

Our word *priest* comes—as we have seen—from the
New Testament word *presbyter* (which is usually translated as
"elder"). Presbyters were the pastors and teachers. They were
supposed to "Pay careful attention to yourselves and to all
the flock, in which the Holy Spirit has made you overseers,
to care for the church of God" (Acts 20:28). It was never a
question of all Christians becoming presbyters.

What then is a priesthood? With this word we mean something altogether different, for which, in the New Testament,
completely different terminologies are used. It refers to sacrificial priests like those who were employed in the temple in
Jerusalem. They were "appointed to act on behalf of men in
relation to God, to offer gifts and sacrifices for sins" (Hebrews
5:1). They prayed for the people and brought forth sacrifices
of redemption that would give the people forgiveness. They

were the representatives of the people before God. The presbyters were God's ambassadors to the people. They had no sacrificial duty, but, instead, a duty to preach. They weren't supposed to come to God from the people with sacrifices, but, instead, from God to the people with the Word and the Sacraments. That difference was obvious in the early Church because they used completely different words and terminologies in both cases.

Now, when Peter says that we are a holy priesthood, he means we *all* have a task similar to the one the sacrificial priests had in the temple. The sacrificial priests were a prototype of Christ. He is the great High Priest, who brought forth a redeeming sacrifice, valid through all time. Now there is no need for any more redeeming sacrifices. There are, however, "spiritual sacrifices acceptable to God through Jesus Christ." Those sacrifices are prayer and thanksgiving. The sacrifices of our lives and our deeds are also a part of what we are to bring "as a living sacrifice, holy and acceptable to God" (Romans 12:1), which is our spiritual worship. Before only the high priest could enter the Holy of Holies. Now we all can. We all are God's holy sacrificial priests, who, for Jesus' sake, can go all the way to God Himself. This is the significance of our universal priesthood.

Lord, You who have consecrated me as Your holy sacrificial priest, help me to take my position seriously. You consecrated me for that already through Baptism, when You made me one with Christ, my High Priest, and let me go in His name all the way to Your heavenly altar. Help me, Lord, to faithfully carry forth the sacrifice of prayer, to keep the holy fire burning, and never allow Your praise to cease. And help me to sacrifice myself, my old Adam *and my sins, my talents and my possibilities every new day during my whole life on Your altar as a complete sacrifice, completely delivered into Your hands. For Jesus' sake.*

SATURDAY AFTER TWENTIETH SUNDAY AFTER TRINITY

1 Peter 2:11–25

Be subject for the Lord's sake to every human institution.
1 Peter 2:13

This portion of Peter's first letter leads us into next Sunday's subject. Here, Peter speaks of a Christian as a citizen in society. He offers a fundamental rule for life in society: You should be subject to its laws for Christ's sake because you believe in Christ and love Him.

You should be subordinate. In the old translation, it says "be subject to," but that's a poor translation. It has a touch of obsequiousness for those in power. A Christian is free, and when he obeys the law, he does it as a free man, of his own free will, out of love for Christ. The word Peter uses here is the same one that otherwise is translated as "being subordinate." We have seen what it means to be subordinate to *God's* order. To accept the order of things not because you're forced to but because you know who you're serving: God Himself.

However, are the state's laws really God's? No, not always. Maybe they're so contrary to God's laws they have to be defied. Christians in the Roman Empire found that out pretty fast. They refused to acknowledge Caesar as God and sacrifice to him, and they suffered as traitors. There are other laws that don't actually force you to disobey God but allow for the potential of the abuse of power. There are laws that absolutely should be changed and that are changed when people start to listen to Christ. Slavery was abolished, for example, when Christianity prevailed in ancient times. (When Peter says "servants" in 1 Peter 2:18, he means slaves.)

Despite all this, the judicial system is still relatively fair, and it is God's will that we should be subordinate to it. Even in a faulty judicial system there are some things that come from God. We'll talk more about this as we go on.

Let's just remind ourselves of where we started. We view society as Christians. We know Christ suffered for our sins. He "bore our sins in His body on the tree." When we now should "live to righteousness" that doesn't mean that we should live to crush and punish all unrighteousness on earth, but that we should "follow in His footsteps" (1 Peter 2:21–25).

You know, Lord, that I gladly want to serve You in every way. Even here in the world, in all that's trivial and secular. Even when it concerns taxes and politics and voting. Now I hear that I, for Your sake, should be a loyal and law-abiding citizen here in our society. But what do I do about the things I don't like? The things I want to change? And the things You don't approve of, Lord? Give me the understanding to comprehend and the eyes to see what is Your will and how it should be done. Help me to think like You and do what You want in all things.

TWENTY-FIRST SUNDAY AFTER TRINITY
Matthew 22:15–22

Therefore render to Caesar the things that are Caesar's, and
to God the things that are God's. Matthew 22:21

There are things that belong to Caesar. It's not that
the world is divided between him and God. Instead, God
has two ways of governing. We have already seen that the
authorities—the state and government authorities—receive
their mandate from God. They should see to it that justice
prevails. That's what Caesar did. The Romans maintained
peace and order around the Mediterranean Sea. In Palestine,
the people had tangible experience of this. They finally lived
protected from attacks from the desert tribes and at peace
with the Persians.

However, Caesar charged taxes which are seldom popular. Besides that, Caesar's taxes were a constant reminder
that they had lost their independence. Rome was a super
power that occupied Israel, and it wasn't hard to see that
many Roman officials, like Pontius Pilate, were unscrupulous
extortionists. No wonder the embers of revolution smoldered
among the people!

Jesus, however, did not revolt. He was a revolutionary,
of course, if we consider the total upheaval He caused in the
lives of people, in the way they managed their money in
general, treated their employees, or performed their work.
When the people wanted Him to be their leader against the
Romans, He refused. That cost Him His popularity in Galilee
and finally took Him to Golgotha. He Himself said to Pilate
that His followers would've fought for Him, if He had come
to start a revolution. He didn't want that, however, and He
knew that Pilate wouldn't have had any power over Him at

all if he hadn't obtained it from God. When it was a matter of taxes and tariffs, law and order, Caesar would have his way. That is a part of God's way to rule the world.

Yet God has another way of ruling—through His Word. He establishes His empire in our hearts, and the question is whether we want to give God what belongs to Him: ourselves. We were, once upon a time, created in His image. Just as Caesar put his picture on a coin, God left His impression on us so we would be His property, His servants, His children. We are lost coins, but we were found again, where Jesus walks. Do we want to give ourselves to God? Completely? Without reservations? With everything we own? Do we want to be a part of the real revolution? The one where the old Adam is dethroned and God has power?

Lord, what comfort and security it is to know that You can do so much good, even through people who don't believe in You. How wonderful is Your creation! You have left Your mark everywhere in nature. You have left Your impression on people, also, so they love Your justice and defend Your Law without knowing whom they serve. How much more willing wouldn't we be to serve You, we who can feel You and know who You are! Lord, Thy will be done, out in the world and in our own lives.

MONDAY AFTER TWENTY-FIRST SUNDAY AFTER TRINITY

Romans 13:1–7

For he is God's servant for your good. Romans 13:4

Paul writes to the Christians in the capital of the world, Rome. They literally have the power of Caesar, up there in the palace on the Palatine, hanging over them. Now they have faith and have Christ over them. He's their Lord and King. How does this all factor?

What Paul gives as an explanation has often been perverted and abused. Someone who's out to get power can hardly understand it. Either he takes it as a defense for his abuse of power or he becomes embittered because he perceives it as a demand to slavish submission to the oppressors. Both of these are wrong.

First, we have to understand what Paul is saying. "Authorities," as they were called then, mean government institutions—the state, society, municipality, those who govern, the public, the IRS, the courts. To be "subject to" means to be subordinate to something that, in the final analysis, goes back to God's will.

It's specifically a result of God's will that there is a judicial system and government institutions. These things belong to God's order of creation. God has put instincts and urges in the nature of man that make humans strive after order and justice, pass laws, and establish court systems. If individuals take the law into their own hands, there will be chaos and complete lawlessness, which always affects the small and weak the most. When an orderly society comes into existence, it's because there are powers at work that come from God. God wanted a judicial system to exist. That's why we should be loyal to the judicial system and not sabotage it or exempt ourselves from obeying tax laws, customs law, speed limits, and the like. Not even if you think the laws should be changed and the government resign.

Now, however, Paul addresses these words not only to us who are "subjects" but also to government institutions. They talk about what the state's and government institution's duties are: to maintain justice, prevent violence and injustice, and support and promote all that is good. In those days there wasn't much of what we call social care. It's obvious, however, that just the concern for the defenseless, disadvantaged and neglected is included in the task the state has received from God. In western Christian societies, this task has become one of the state's most important.

What if the state and their laws are unfair, however? The Bible has something to say even about this that we will look at later.

Lord, give me eyes to see everything that comes from You, even the things that seem so temporal. The world is Yours and all that is in it. You are active all around me, in everything You've created. You compel people to do Your will without them even knowing it. You make a place for Your justice and Your mercy in the middle of our selfishness. Teach me to see all the good things You do in our society, and to be thankful for all those through whom You do it.

TUESDAY AFTER TWENTY-FIRST SUNDAY AFTER TRINITY

Matthew 12:15–21

He will proclaim justice to the Gentiles. Matthew 12:18

What justice is it that Jesus proclaims?

People ask: Whose side is He really on? Who does He agree with—the oppressed or the oppressors?

Naturally, Jesus is on the side of the oppressed. Matthew saw that He was just like the prophet had said He would be: one who wouldn't break a bruised reed or quench a smoldering wick. He pitied the masses because they were so badly treated and dejected. He invited the working class and the oppressed into His presence. He knew how hard it was for a rich man to get to heaven.

Nevertheless, it's impossible to have the sole right to Jesus in politics. You can't confine Him to a particular political agenda. He's the Savior of *all* people. His criticism is aimed at all of us. We all need His forgiveness. Those who are lost and dejected are found in every political party and in every social class. What did Jesus say about the wealthy man Zacchaeus? "He also is a son of Abraham. For the Son of Man came to seek and to save the lost" (Luke 19:9–10).

How then does He carry justice forward to victory? Not with usual political means. Christ doesn't use propaganda, He doesn't challenge people to debate, He doesn't send His disciples to demonstrate and shout slogans. "Nor will anyone hear His voice in the streets" (Matthew 12:19). One can win victories for justice in that way, but victories are relative, temporary, and constantly threatened by our unbelievably imaginative selfishness that can throw its weight around and win the game in every administration and every political system.

For Christ, it's a matter of achieving the victory over evil itself and over our own old Adam. The decisive battle took place on Good Friday. Christ was silent, and the masses screamed in the streets. Christ Himself became the bruised reed and smoldering wick that His opponents—the priests, the politicians, and the people—thought they could crush and extinguish. Then justice achieved the victory—first and foremost our lost right to be God's children was restored, but also God's righteous Law wasn't revoked by Christ's death but fulfilled—and that victory for justice echoes in every heart that Christ has the power over. Now a new constitution exists: Our Lord is one and we are all brothers. See to the best in others; you live to serve.

That victory will not be complete until Christ returns. Until then the battle rages, even the political battle that has to be fought in this world and will be fought according to God's Law, which demands both truth and justice. Until then, His mercy, which with infinite tenderness takes upon itself everything that is destroyed and dejected in every camp and class and party, also prevails.

Lord, whose side am I on? Help me always to be at Your side, where You stand—under Your protection, shielded by Your atonement, enveloped by Your forgiveness, pervaded by Your love. As Your willing servant, may I always be prepared to stand up for Your justice and make room for Your love. May I always be willing to help those who are forgotten, left out, and badly treated. May I always be ready to stand up against injustices and abuse, even those caused by pure thoughtlessness and habit. Lord, lead Your justice to victory, in my heart and in my deeds, in our people and in the whole world.

WEDNESDAY AFTER TWENTY-FIRST SUNDAY AFTER TRINITY

Amos 5:6–15

Establish justice! Amos 5:15

What do you do if those in power abuse their power?

That certainly happens. The judicial system comes from God, as we have learned. Those who govern have God's mandate to see to it that justice prevails. Therefore, you should be subordinate to the system and the laws that exist in a country. However, what if the laws, as well as the administration of justice, are improperly used as a means for injustice and oppression? What do you do then?

The Bible has a lot to say about this dilemma. The prophet's wrathful judgments were often directed exactly to those in power who abuse their power. Just listen to Amos in chapter 5!

He accuses the government, the lawmakers, civil servants, and the courts for "turning justice to wormwood," a bitter and repulsive drink that the people were forced to drink. They "cast down righteousness to the ground." They "trample upon the poor and take from him exactions of wheat." They "take a bribe and turn aside the needy in the gate" (in other words, in court; the city gate was the usual place for court trials). If someone comes forward and defends what is right, they hate him and "abhor him who speaks the truth." Consequently, social critics, who attacked deeply rooted social evils and injustices, could be regarded as enemies of society, dangerous to be seen with.

All of this the prophet now proclaims on God's behalf. He tells us what God's going to do: All of this will come to a disastrous end. Things like this don't go unpunished.

The rich who have built houses of hewn stone and planted vineyards around them will have no happiness in the riches they've gotten through extortion. They will become poor and oppressed unless they make an improvement and let justice prevail, just like the mandate God gave them commanded them to do. It doesn't help that they claim to have God on their side and it doesn't mean that the God of the rulers has to agree with them. They said like so many after them said, in war and in politics: God is with us; we're the ones who support God and His Church.

Accordingly, here we see what has to be done when those in power don't fulfill their duties: They must be urged to do it. Their acts of cruelty must be criticized. We often speak of criticism as one of the Church's duties in society. It's right that the Church should speak out and take on the plight of those who are treated badly. The "Church," however, too easily becomes the wastepaper basket, where we discard all of the troublesome cases we would rather avoid. We have to remember that this is a responsibility God has placed on all of us. It's everyone's duty to constantly remind those in power of their responsibility: Let justice prevail!

> *Lord, give us all that courage, although we would like to avoid it. We know that we don't have to get out of what we don't get into, so we stay out of the way. We want so much to live in peace. And You have told us that we shouldn't get involved if it's none of our business. Therefore, we ask You to burn our consciences with Your fire when it comes to things You want us to get involved in. We ask for eyes to see, courage to speak, and wisdom to act when Your time comes.*

Isaiah 1:13–27

Correct oppression! Isaiah 1:17

Once again we have the prophetic criticism of an unjust society. Amos had turned against Samaria and the Northern Kingdom. Isaiah lived a generation later and prophesied to Judah and Jerusalem. He experienced how punishment overtook Samaria, how their palaces went up in smoke, and how their kingdom was taken into captivity. He saw how his own country was pillaged and had no doubt as to the reason why. The same thing happened there as it did in Samaria. "Your princes are rebels and companions of thieves. Everyone loves a bribe and runs after gifts. They do not bring justice to the fatherless, and the widow's cause does not come to them" (Isaiah 1:23).

There are two things that are especially worth noting. First, Isaiah says that "your princes are rebels." They have rebelled against the judicial system they were supposed to uphold. They are corrupt through and through and don't abide by the laws they were supposed to uphold. Consequently, they "resist what God has appointed," as Paul put it in Romans 13:2. Therefore, they must also surrender themselves to the sentence that disobedience entails. And God will see to it that someone executes that sentence when the appointed judges don't do it.

The other thing worth noting is that the religious custom flourished in the middle of all this. Huge crowds gathered in the temple for the big days of festival. There was no end to the sacrificing. However, God says: Evil in conjunction with the gathering at festivals (let us translate: beautiful, sometimes very well-attended church services and first-rate ceremonial statistics) is something He cannot endure (see Isaiah 1:11–15).

And now, the prophet says God is going to intervene. Judgment will fall on the oppressors. The goal of God's actions is that justice shall be upheld so the country gets "judges as at the first, and your counselors as at the beginning" (Isaiah 1:26).

You can't read things like this without thinking about what a good thing democracy is. Isaiah could demand that someone would show the oppressor a better way. However, he didn't have the possibility of changing things, like we have in a country where everyone has the right to vote. In a democracy, we all have a portion of the power and thereby also a portion of the responsibility. This means we all have our share of the responsibility God has given those in power: to uphold justice and show the oppressor a better way.

We thank You, Lord, that we live in a country where we share responsibility. We thank You that our government acts in such a way that they have the people's trust. Bless our politicians and help them to act correctly and wisely and mercifully. Help us so we never wish that they patronize only our group and our interests. Help us all see to the best of everyone as You would've wanted.

When they saw the tribune and the soldiers, they stopped beating Paul. Acts 21:32

Half of Paul's letters in the Bible would never have been written without that Roman battalion with an alert commander at Fort Antonia, from where you could oversee the temple square, where the Romans always had troops ready and waiting. That's what saved Paul's life.

He had come up to Jerusalem and with four others had spent a week in the temple and fulfilled a promise. His opponents from Asia Minor saw him inside the temple. Once again they managed to work up the crowd. Paul was dragged out to the forecourt where they planned on getting it over with quickly. However, those alert guards in the tower of Antonia had reported the riot and the governor immediately marched out with his legions. Paul was saved at the last minute.

"They stopped beating. . . ." With those words you can describe the first great blessing of the judicial system. It puts a limit on violence to individuals, on assault and battery, theft and looting. It gives people the prospect of living unmolested, in peace and in safety. This is the first and fundamental duty the authorities have received from God. Therefore, we should respect the legal system and not try to take the law into our own hands. Since no legal system is perfect, you have to take the good with the bad, try to better and change what can be made better, but not put yourself above the legal system. The fact that there is a functional state is something that took decades of toil and sacrifice. That's a basic value we should be thankful for and be careful of; something that is not as self-evident as we westerners sometimes think. We have, rightfully so, gotten used to demanding a lot from society. We are critical of all its shortcomings and failures. However, the failures shouldn't blind us to the fact that the mere existence of a society that functions is a great gift from God we should thank Him for.

So we thank You, Lord, that today we go to our job and live in our homes without fear and without having to arm ourselves for protection from assault, as our ancestors had to. We thank You for government institutions and courts, for unions and wage negotiations, for everything that makes us show consideration for one another and try to reach a mutual agreement on. We thank You that we can openly criticize and say what is wrong and can take part in making it better. Help us to use all of this correctly, for the betterment of others and not only ourselves. And help us not to forget You, just because we can live safely.

SATURDAY AFTER TWENTY-FIRST SUNDAY AFTER TRINITY

Acts 22:22–23:5

Is it lawful for you to flog a man who is a Roman citizen and uncondemned? Acts 22:25

Paul had spoken to the people from the barrack stairs and had told them why he served Christ. He was confronted with yet another fit of rage. The governor thought it would be safest to take him into the guardhouse.

A short time before, Paul had had a chance to experience the good side of the Roman legal system; now he met the unpleasant side. The governor, who still was suspicious that he had a troublemaker before him, ordered that Paul be interrogated under torture to get the truth out of him.

What does Paul do now? He demands his legal rights. Just as he fulfilled his obligation to the Roman state, now he demanded that the state fulfill its obligation to him. And it turned out, in this case, that the legal system worked.

The next day Paul was faced with the same problem again. He was slapped in the face in the presence of the court. Paul answered just as one of the prophets could've answered: "You whitewashed wall! Are you sitting to judge me according to the law, and yet contrary to the law you order me to be struck!" (Acts 23:3). When he was informed that it was the high priest himself who stood before him, Paul apologized that he had used such harsh words. Essentially, however, he didn't take it back. He was willing to show respect for the office and the governmental institutions because they were his superiors. That didn't mean, however, that he allowed them to violate the law without being challenged.

But what if they do it anyway? What if protesting doesn't help? What if those in power pass laws of violence, as the prophet said? Could Paul have revolted?

He wouldn't have, just as Jesus Himself wouldn't have. That's a consequence of the new life in God's kingdom. Someone who is God's free and fortunate child no longer has to assert his rights, least of all with violence. He takes the suffering upon himself and knows that it's being a good enough disciple if the same thing happens to him that happened to his Master.

But now, this is about those who live in faith, in fellowship with Christ. Life on earth, within the state, among those who don't believe, is regulated by justice and not by boundless forgiveness. There we have to confront injustice with righteousness, not with blessing and voluntary suffering. If the legal system becomes so corrupt that it serves injustice and not justice, it has to be replaced with something better. It becomes a political agreement, oftentimes, but not always, through peaceful means. No one can, in advance, determine which means are right and which are wrong. You have to be in the midst of reality, as it is in a specific country and specific age, to be able to act as a conscientious person in the face of God.

Lord, we call upon Your mercy. You see all injustice and hear the lamentations of the oppressed. You know how people distort justice and pass laws as a means to oppress instead of protect. Lord, You can awaken the people to stand up against everything that is unjust. You can give the weak strength and allow the powerless to succeed. You can overthrow those in power from their thrones and destroy their evil plans. You alone know what's best. Let everyone who has a sense for justice see this and do it. Thy will be done.

TWENTY-SECOND SUNDAY AFTER TRINITY

Matthew 22:1–14

And those servants went out into the roads and gathered all whom they found, both bad and good. So the wedding hall was filled with guests. Matthew 22:10

Here we have a description of a church for the people, like ours. Its foundation lies in a commandment from God. He has sent out His servants with the Word and Baptism. They were to invite people to the great king's marriage, and that's what they did to everyone they ran in to. The wedding reception room was full of people.

By the wedding reception room we don't mean the heavenly one, where we're guests at the table in God's kingdom. Instead it means the courtyard here on earth, the visible Church. It's just like Jesus says. Many are called. Both good and bad. God wants *all* men to be saved. Today we can be a guest at the Table and taste the heavenly gifts, in the Word, in absolution, at Communion.

However, despite the fact that many are called, only a few are chosen. That doesn't mean that God, from the beginning, decided there would be those who will be lost. God is serious with His call. At the same time, however, He knows what's going to happen. He knows that what He does in many cases is in vain. He acts like a kind father on earth. Even if common sense says it's hopeless with an incorrigible child, the kind father can't help doing everything for the child. So God does everything, even for those who trample on His love.

God also knows when His love will reach out and win a person over. He leads and protects that person so nothing can tear him away from His love. That person is called "chosen." We hear Jesus say that there are *few* that are chosen (Matthew

22:14). Immediately we want to ask: "Lord, are there only a few who will be saved?" We know His answer, however: *Fight* to come through the narrow door. See to it that you're not standing outside.

Now, what about the man who didn't have a wedding garment? This is a parable, not an allegory. (In other words, we can't decipher all the details.) We don't have to bother with the question whether it was reasonable to punish a poor man for his clothes' sake. Here, it's a question of a garment he got for free. It's a question of being clothed in the "new man," the garment that comes from faith in Jesus. Those old, soiled, every day clothes, that's the old Adam. You can't get into God's kingdom wearing those. Through Baptism you are clothed in Christ and His righteousness. That garment can't be dirtied or destroyed. Then you can come again and appear in Church. "Preserve us, therefore, gracious Lord God!"

Lord, is it I who doesn't have the wedding garment on? Who goes to Your Church and to the Communion table, but doesn't belong there? I come and sit down; do I regard it as an obvious right? You look at me, Lord. What do You see? Are rags all that's left of Your ceremonial dress? Is my old Adam seen through all the holes? Lord, have mercy on me. If I'm a lost son, let me come home and once again receive those precious clothes. Allow me to be one of them who washed his clothes and made them white in the Lamb's blood.

MONDAY AFTER TWENTY-SECOND SUNDAY AFTER TRINITY

1 Corinthians 11:17–34

Let a person examine himself, then, and so eat of the bread and drink of the cup. 1 Corinthians 11:28

We are invited to the mighty King's wedding, that great festival of joy in heaven. We've received the invitation and replied with a yes. So the King invites us to a feast, here and now, while we're on our way. He's setting His Communion table.

It's a premonition, an anticipation, a little feast before the great feast. "For as often as you eat this bread and drink the cup, you proclaim the Lord's death until He comes" (1 Corinthians 11:26). We can already sing the song of victory about the death of the Lord, the one that echoes before God's and the Lamb's throne: "For You were slain, and by Your blood You ransomed people for God from every tribe and language and people and nation" (Revelation 5:9). When we sing it, we know He will come, and we profess it before the world every time we take Communion.

Consequently, Communion is God's meal; it is the Lord's body that we offend if we eat and drink in a shameful manner. Paul had just said (in chapter 10): The cup of blessing which we drink is a participation in the blood of Christ. The bread which we break is a participation of the body of Christ. That's what was forgotten in Corinth. They came to this meal as if it was an ordinary one, and they came with all of the old Adam's bad habits. They built factions and groups; they didn't want to wait and show respect. They still had their social prejudices and restrictions. They showed kindness only to their own. That is the kind of thing that makes you go to

Communion in a shameful way and that results in your eating and drinking judgment upon yourself.

Therefore, Paul says, you have to examine yourself. What does the King see when He comes to look at His guests? Have I come without my wedding garment? Examine yourself, Paul says in verse 28. To help us with that there's a confession before every Communion. The result of an honest examination of ourselves can have only one outcome: "I haven't loved God above all else and my neighbor as myself. Maybe I discover very tangible things I should've done differently or not have done at all." When we try to judge ourselves, we hear God's judgment.

And what are we supposed to do?

We should examine ourselves and then eat of the bread and drink of the cup, Paul says. Not coming is just as bad as coming without examining yourself. Self-examination is supposed to lead us to Christ, to the well of forgiveness, to the words of absolution that are proclaimed to us in church. The right wedding garment is with Christ. Only there.

Dear Lord Jesus, You who are our soul's shepherd and caretaker, we ask You for the Spirit of truth who can show us all our faults and make us honest so we don't conceal the things You want to bring out into the light or defend the things You condemn. Allow us to judge ourselves so we won't be judged but, instead, be allowed to hear the delightful words of forgiveness from Your lips. And if we should be careless and cheat, so chastise us in mercy, just as You chastised Your thoughtless and beloved children in Corinth so we know we're warned and wake up and don't become lost with the rest of the world. Give us the right kind of

*hunger for You so we come to Your Communion to
proclaim Your death and join in Your victory.*

TUESDAY AFTER
TWENTY-SECOND
SUNDAY AFTER
TRINITY
Hebrews 4:9–16

[God's word discerns] the thoughts and intentions of the
heart. Hebrews 4:12

There is a "Sabbath rest for the people of God" (Hebrews
4:9), a secure and delightful Sunday morning at home with
God Himself, when the air is full of church bells ringing,
shouts of thanksgiving, and all of existence breathing joy
over the fact that everything is as it should be—healthy and
indestructible.

This is yet another picture of the joy at the great King's
feast. We can speak only in images about that day, but each
of them has something to say. When the author of Hebrews
talks about the rest that lies ahead, he connects the picture to
Israel's wandering through the desert and their entry into the
Promised Land. He reminds us that God's people betrayed
their Lord that time and fell into disbelief; that's why they
couldn't reach His restful state. The same thing can happen to
us. We could be on our way. We have been delivered from
the land of bondage by the Lord's hand. We have come to

the faith and received the forgiveness of sins. Still, we can be left behind along the way and be lost.

You have to examine and judge yourself, as we read yesterday. And here we have a chance to learn how to examine ourselves. It's not only an examination of our conscience, where you feel that something's wrong. Of course it's true you should take that seriously and immediately talk to God about it. There is a lot we're hardly conscious of, however. We're all influenced by the world around us, and people do, obviously and with no qualms, lots of things that are evil and incompatible with God and His kingdom. That's why we must examine ourselves through the Word of God. We must appoint a judge over our heart's intentions and thoughts. Reading the Bible means allowing God to hold an inquiry with you, for you have to receive the Word, not as the word of man, but as God's Word, which it really is and not constantly question the passages that don't suit our usual train of thought. The Word from God penetrates, cuts through our smoke screens, and allows us to see the innermost parts of our hearts as stripped as they are before God.

Just as important, however, is to remember what comes afterward and go forth to the throne of grace, where we can receive both mercy and grace as help at the right time, help both with our sins and help to live.

Lord, we open our hearts for Your Word. May it come to us in all its power. Allow it to penetrate all the obstacles our tardiness creates, and tear down all the walls behind which our old Adam hides with his deeds. Allow us to hear just the words we need to hear, even if they come as a sword's blow or a spear's head. We know You are in this Word, Lord Jesus. When we open our hearts, then You open

the gates to heaven and to Your throne of grace,
You who have been tempted in all things and never
tire of forgiving.

WEDNESDAY AFTER TWENTY-SECOND SUNDAY AFTER TRINITY
Hebrews 9:24–10:7

For Christ has entered, not into holy places made with
hands, which are copies of the true things, but into heaven
itself, now to appear in the presence of God on our behalf.
Hebrews 9:24

The temple in Jerusalem was the pride of all Jews. It was
one of the world's most well-known structures. Its foundation was like a mountain, erected with huge boulders that
amazed all visitors. It had countless courtyards. The porticos
were fascinating in the blazing, hot sunshine; the roofs were
crowned with thousands of golden pinnacles. In the middle
of all this splendor towered the Holy of Holies, completely
covered with gold. There the Lord resided with His holy
presence, His invisible majesty, and His glory that was both
enchanting and frightening. No mortal human being except
for the high priest, the anointed one, could enter through the
veil. Just once a year, the high priest went behind the veil
to make a sacrifice for the people's unintentional sins, while
the masses crowded outside and with reverent fear saw the
heavy veils move when the path to God was opened for a
moment.

All of this happened according to God's will. All the sacrifices that time and time again were carried out in the innermost courtyard were constant reminders of the essence of sin and the seriousness of guilt. Because of sin we were separated from God. We deserved to die. The people confessed that as they brought their sacrifice. They prayed for purification and forgiveness. That purification, however, could never be complete; it had to be constantly repeated.

In all of this there now was a God-given example. It was a shadow that appeared, a long shadow that announced the rising of the sun. When Christ came, it was to finally, once and for all, fulfill the things that sacrifices promised and depicted. He would sacrifice Himself. He had received a human body so that He, through His body, would carry our sins upon the tree. He was the great High Priest who entered into God's presence, into heaven itself, with God's own sacrifice, brought forth by God's Son, for eternal atonement for all trespasses on this earth.

Hebrews talks about all of this. The Old Testament talks about Christ. We receive new insights in the work of Christ. For instance, we learn that Christ comes the second time "not to deal with sin" (Hebrews 9:28), for He did away with sin once and for all when He died. Atonement and forgiveness is there, more than enough for all time. It's just a matter of receiving it. We shouldn't wait until He comes the second time, however.

Dear Father in heaven, I know I will die someday and then be judged. I know I that have only this life and then accountability awaits me, irrevocably and inevitably. You, however, have allowed Your Son to come here to us. He died just once and suffered for all our sins, finally and indelibly. He has

won an eternal redemption and forgiveness that
has no boundaries. And He will come again, just
once more, to judge—finally and indelibly. And
now You say there will be no judgment for those
who believe. He will save those who wait for Him.
May I be among them, for Jesus' sake.

THURSDAY AFTER TWENTY-SECOND SUNDAY AFTER TRINITY

Hebrews 10:19–25

Let us draw near with a true heart in full assurance of faith.
Hebrews 10:22

We may go forth, all the way into the Holy of Holies, to God Himself. What only the high priest could do in Israel, each and every one of us can do in the new Israel. Christ has consecrated a new and living way. He Himself is that way. The fact that the veil in the temple was torn apart on Good Friday is a picture of what happened on Golgotha. When Christ's body was given into death, when His hands were pierced, when His side was cut open and His heart broken, then the veil that obstructed the way to God was torn apart. Fault was gone, that eternal contrast between God's love and our sin was overcome.

Therefore, we should not hesitate but go forth all the way to God. We should do it with clean hearts that dare speak about everything, even our most secret and humiliating sins. We should approach "in full assurance of faith," assured that we can come for Christ's sake. We can do it because we come "with our hearts sprinkled clean" (Hebrews 10:22) with the drops of Christ's blood that quiets the accusations of a bad conscience, even when it shows us that we still have our old Adam. We are "washed with pure water" (Hebrews 10:22). We are baptized as a sign that Jesus Himself has chosen us and paid for all our sins.

Now we shall "hold fast the confession of our hope" (Hebrews 10:23) and not for a second allow ourselves to be impressed over the deluge of disbelief that streams over our society and seems to be all the more prevalent where there's power and influence. Instead, we should "stir up one another to love and good works" (Hebrews 10:24). Oddly enough it's a duty that Christians of our time aren't always conscious of. It's not considered proper to get involved in other people's religions. What if it concerns their salvation, however? Or what if it concerns the Gospel's good reputation and its possibilities to convert? Of course it's not a question of nagging and being critical. A person can be both loving and discreet and still show which way is Jesus', often better with their example than with some statement or contribution to a discussion. And lastly: Let us not abandon the fellowship in our congregation and fail to come to worship services. Already at that time there were those who made a habit of that. That is and remains a betrayal not only to the congregation but to Him who is the head, Christ.

Lord, I ask You for three things. First, that I always dare and always want to go straight to God, the way You have opened for me. Even with all my faults and all my worries. With everything that is dear to me and everything I have to be thankful for. Then I ask You that I will always dare and always want to take responsibility for everything You tell me in Your Word and that You have instilled in my heart. Help me to not be silent and agree, not even among friends and fellow Christians, when I see that they haven't listened to You. And finally, I ask You to always be among those who gather in Your name, in Your house, and at Your Holy Communion. For Jesus' sake.

FRIDAY AFTER TWENTY-SECOND SUNDAY AFTER TRINITY
Hebrews 10:26–39

For if we go on sinning deliberately after receiving the knowledge of the truth, there no longer remains a sacrifice for sins. Hebrews 10:26

This is an essential and serious truth. You have to understand it correctly. It isn't a question of being "overtaken in a trespass" (Galatians 6:1) or "opposing him to his face," something that happened to Peter himself (Galatians 2:11). There's forgiveness for things like that. "If someone sins, we have someone who intercedes for us before the Father, Jesus Christ." In this case it's a question of a very particular sin. It's described earlier in Hebrews (6:4 and following) in this way: that one apostatizes and once again crucifies God's Son on his own account and holds Him in contempt. This happens despite the fact that he has received the light and tasted the heavenly gift and received the Holy Spirit and learned to recognize the powers of times to come. In other words: he has been at the very heart of the most holy. He has received a piece of Christ, he knows from experience who Christ is and he has tasted all the good things Christ has to give. *Nevertheless* he falls away once again and goes over to his enemies, blasphemes His name, and scoffs at His gifts. It was just like what the Pharisees almost did, when they saw Jesus' good deeds with their own eyes, but said that it was Satan's work. Then Jesus warned them about the sin against the Holy Spirit, the sin that cannot be forgiven. That sin consists of trampling on forgiveness with your feet, blaspheming it, and forever throwing it away.

The ancient Christian Church saw examples of that. People fell away, became fierce adversaries, and murdered Christians. Not because they didn't know what Christianity was. Not because of any misunderstandings. Not because of disappointments caused by bad Christians. Instead, it was just because they knew what true fellowship with Christ really means. They had rejected Christ Himself, His love, His forgiveness, life with Him, and deliberately chose something else, something opposite, something that was a denial of Jesus and His love. One has to call attention to this terrible fact: It's impossible to get them back. As the writer of Hebrews quotes in 10:38, "'My righteous one shall live by faith, and if he shrinks back, My soul has no pleasure in him.'" They are beyond recall.

When the text speaks of sinning "deliberately," we have to remember that all sins, when we see them ourselves and acknowledge them, appear to have been committed deliberately. There was always a voice inside of us that said yes and desired whatever happened. In that sense, all sins are intentional, even if they partially are caused by ignorance and hastiness. When it comes to receiving forgiveness, there's no difference between intentional and unintentional sins. "If we confess our sins, He is faithful and just to forgive our sins" (1 John 1:9); they may have been intentional or unintentional.

Will the Lord spurn forever and never again be favorable? Has God forgotten to be gracious? Has He in anger shut up His compassion? Your way, O God, is holy. What god is great like our God? You are the God who works wonders. In the day of my trouble I seek the Lord; in the night my hand is stretched out without wearying. Heal me, O Lord, and I will be healed; save me and I will be saved; for You are my praise. (From Psalm 77 and Jeremiah 17.)

SATURDAY AFTER TWENTY-SECOND SUNDAY AFTER TRINITY

Hebrews 12:1–11

Let us run with endurance the race that is set before us.
Hebrews 12:1

The Letter to the Hebrews says the same thing Paul says to the Philippians and the Corinthians: We're participating in a contest. The race has begun. The race track lies before us. Now we have to hurry to reach the goal.

The Letter to the Hebrews makes a small, expressive addition. We have spectators around, a whole cloud of witnesses. The sprinters on the track can only imagine all the faces in the bleachers, but they hear their cheering. The noise from the crowd carries them and helps them to do their very best.

Likewise, we also have a cloud of witnesses that we have a glimpse of above us. The author of Hebrews described them in the previous chapter about the heroes of faith, those who could persevere because it was as if they could see the invisible one in front of them. They shout to us to persevere. They know that victory waits. They are witnesses that can confirm that God is faithful, that promises are kept, that the goal is there, that no one regrets when they finally get there.

You don't win any contests without training and self-discipline. There are things that only prevent and impair, and those things you should refrain from, willingly and consistently, well aware that you won't be missing anything but, instead, be in better shape that way.

However, the Letter to the Hebrews adds, there is also the sort of privations and training that *God* imposes on us. We wouldn't have done it ourselves. God knows what's best for us. This is called God's fatherly discipline. This word, *discipline,* that the Bible uses here also means "guidance of children," "bringing up." In other words, it can be an expression of God's love and His kind consideration for us if He takes something from us that we're fond of or block a path we want to follow. When we fail at our job, when we're criticized and run into unpleasant things, when sickness comes when we least expect it, or we have financial problems to wrestle with, it's always wise to fold our hands and ask: Lord, is there something You want to teach me with this? It's possible we will see that we have here new proof of God's love. Seldom right away because "for the moment all discipline seems painful rather than pleasant" (Hebrews 12:11). Afterward, however, when we can see everything in the right perspective, it's possible that grief's knotty and crooked tree bears the kind of fruit no one could have ever picked somewhere else.

Lord, who dares ask for Your chastisement? You know we all fear Your hand of discipline. Who can love something that hurts? However, if You, Father, in Your goodness, see that it's for the best and can do us good, then let it come. Be close to us in that moment, however, so we can sense that we are under Your fatherly hand even then.

TWENTY-THIRD SUNDAY AFTER TRINITY
Matthew 18:23–35

Judgment is without mercy to one who has shown no mercy.
James 2:13

Is *that* the way it is in God's kingdom? Like a king who wished to settle accounts with his servants?

Jesus says that's the way it is. Of course, settling the accounts isn't the most important thing. God's kingdom is forgiveness—boundless forgiveness that erases an unappeasable debt. For that to happen, however, the debt has to come out in the open. The guilty party has to be aware of it. *I* have to be aware of it, for Jesus is talking here about me.

I owe ten thousand talents. That's several million, more than any person could pay. How could I owe so much? By increasing my debt day after day. I should've lived in perfect love toward my heavenly Father and toward my brothers and sisters on earth. These were the most important things of all, the finest commandments—and I haven't kept them. Not for one single day.

At one time, maybe I thought I could pay in full, if I only had the time. However, I finally realized it was hopeless, and then only one thing remained: Jesus. That undeserved, unreasonable, all-encompassing forgiveness. That God remits my astronomical debt and sets me free.

That's the way it is in the kingdom of heaven, Jesus says. He has one addition, however. The fortunate one, who no longer has any debts, runs into an acquaintance who owes him a small amount of money and now he acts in a worldly way. Now, it's a matter of watching out for his monetary claims. Using all legal means available, that's exactly what he does.

And then, once again, a demand is made on him. He's stands there with his enormous debt, and payment is demanded. Without mercy.

You see, it's mercy itself that man has separated himself from. God has, in His boundless mercy, made forgiveness possible by paying all our debts and giving His only Son. That inexhaustible forgiveness exists with Him. With Him, we can partake of it without limits. However, it exists only with Him. If we possess Him, we have forgiveness. Forgiveness without Jesus doesn't exist.

If we live with Jesus, we can't take our fellow servant by the neck and make him pay for what he's done. Loving Jesus means forgiving. Not wanting to forgive means not loving Jesus, not being with Him, and not possessing His forgiveness. It's either Jesus and forgiveness, or neither of them.

My Lord and Savior, You've forgiven me everything, and You never tire of forgiving again and again. Now You want me to forgive from the heart. You know that I want to. However, You also know how hard it can be for me to forgive from the heart. Lord, help me to not say something to get revenge or make people pay for what they've done. Help me also to not think about things like this and not feel the desire to do them. And if I do, then let me immediately go even with this sin to You. Lord, forgive us our trespasses as we forgive those who trespass against us.

MONDAY AFTER TWENTY-THIRD SUNDAY AFTER TRINITY
Luke 17:1–10

I do not say to you seven times, but seventy times seven.
Matthew 18:22

Is seven times enough? Peter asks. He knew how hard it could be to forgive. Most of us think it's enough to forgive two or three times. Then it's certainly time to call it quits!

Jesus says, however: Stop counting, Peter. You can never forgive so many times that it will be enough. Or, as Jesus says in today's reading: If he turns to you seven times and says, "I repent," you must forgive him.

That's the way it is in the kingdom of forgiveness. Christ forgives us seven times a day and more. He never tires of forgiving. He doesn't say: That's enough. And when we live in that forgiveness, we act in the same way.

We can't hide behind Jesus' words "if he repents." We shouldn't wait for our brother to confess that he did something wrong and come to ask for forgiveness. We should even forgive someone who continues to do wrong. We should love him and pray for him and do good things for him, if we get the chance. In God's kingdom, it's no longer a question of justice or payment for services rendered. Before God we never have any merits, only debts. Even if we did everything we were commanded to do—and who's done that?—we are just an insignificant servant who has done no more than his simple duty.

To forgive doesn't exclude "to reprimand." Or, as it's written in Matthew 18:15, to "go and tell him his fault, between you and him alone." Or, as it says in the next verse, "take one or two brothers along." Not to punish and demand what's coming to you, but to do as the shepherd did, who went out to look for the sheep that had strayed, because "it is not the will of My Father who is in heaven that one of these little ones should perish" (Matthew 18:14).

Dear Lord Jesus, my kind Master and Savior, You know how afraid I am to be abused and offended by relinquishing my rights. And yet it's very safe and secure to be in the shadow of Your wings; to be able to live in Your kingdom, without debt, and

be happy; to have been saved from solitude, where
everyone only thinks about themselves and has
to succeed and assert oneself to keep from going
under. Now I'm in Your hands, Lord. And I know
You'll change it to my advantage and blessing,
what for the world and my old Adam is only injury
and misfortune. May I follow Your good will, and
may I be a tool for it.

TUESDAY AFTER TWENTY-THIRD SUNDAY AFTER TRINITY
1 Peter 3:8–17

But even if you should suffer for righteousness' sake, you
will be blessed. 1 Peter 3:14

"Blessed are those who are persecuted because of righteousness, for theirs is the kingdom of heaven. Blessed are you when people insult you, persecute you and falsely say all kinds of evil against you because of Me" (Matthew 5:10–11).

We remember that Jesus said these words in the Sermon on the Mount. We know it's the truth because He said it. However, it's so easy for us to move that truth somewhere far away where everything is illusory. Jesus can say it. On the blessed mountain you can say that, when it's spring in Galilee and Jesus is among us. . . .

It's another thing altogether in our suburban life, wherever that is. When people really abuse and persecute me. When they hurl abuse at me in the stairway or in the machine shop. When maybe I'm threatened with violence. Or when the media lie but everyone believes them. And all of this just because I want to take Christ seriously. It's disturbing for them to see someone who dares to be different. Maybe that reminds them of something they thought was finished for good. It irritates them. They want to put an end to it.

At times like this it's not easy to say: "Still, I'm blessed." It doesn't feel right at all, and we shouldn't think it has to *feel* blessed if we're going to be Christian. Paul teaches us that even a Christian can be "afflicted at every turn—fighting without and fear within" (2 Corinthians 7:5). No, blessedness is knowing that God's kingdom belongs to us. We belong to Christ, the rejected and abused one. We have received blessedness as our inheritance and have come into a world where everything is forgiven and where forgiveness is offered boundlessly. You don't have to fight for existence alone, don't have to stand your ground by returning evil with evil and abuse with abuse. On the contrary: we have received and daily receive so many blessings that there's enough left over to bless others.

And this is not just words. Here, in Peter's first letter, we find ourselves in the middle of persecutions, where the authors as well as the recipients of the letter know what's going on. It was tough and it was going to get tougher. We should think about the worst persecution of Christians in our day and age to be able to understand what went on then. Yet we hear how firmly and calmly they spoke. They had Jesus' word to stick to. They took the word seriously and knew it could stand the test.

Dear Lord Jesus, help me to always see what a privilege, what a favor, and how gracious it is to be able to do good, to not have to be dragged into the great misfortune of the world and try to repay evil with evil. That's the curse: to not be able to forgive, believing that we'll be destroyed if we don't fight back; to have to maintain Your own honor and try to refute all liars instead of loving them and waiting for that great day when we can also do something good for them. Help us, guide us, and strengthen us so we can conquer evil with good. And even if we can't conquer it, may we never be conquered by it.

WEDNESDAY AFTER TWENTY-THIRD SUNDAY AFTER TRINITY

1 Peter 3:18–4:6

The Gospel was preached even to those who are dead.
1 Peter 4:6

There are mysterious passages in the Bible. Some are explained by other passages that are explicit and clear. Some, however, remain alone and mysterious. They give us a hint of something, but we're not really sure what. We would gladly like to ask more questions, but we won't get any answers.

This is one of those passages. It's something that's only

mentioned in passing, an example Peter uses to illustrate his main point. What he wants to say is even Christ, our role model, has suffered. Through that suffering, He won the victory and returned from the dead. And what's more: He won life for us. So, we should not be afraid of suffering. On the contrary, we should arm ourselves with the thought that if we suffer with Christ, we have shown that we no longer want anything to do with sin.

In this message, Peter weaves in a small reminder that Christ's blessed suffering led Him to the fact that "He went and proclaimed to the spirits in prison" (1 Peter 3:18) and that "the gospel was preached even to those who are dead" (1 Peter 4:6). We're probably not wrong if we tell ourselves that this must have something to do with Christ being "descended into hell" as stated in the Apostle's Creed. Consequently, we have an indication that His victory and His atonement were also intended for those who lived before Christ. He died even for them. We dare hope that God, who wants all men to be saved, keeps the possibility open even for those who, in their lifetime, never got to hear the Gospel. It's not more than an indication, however, and we can't try to get more out of these insinuations than the Bible actually says. If God has only given us an indication, there's a reason for it. In this case maybe there are two things He wants to teach us. Partly that He has all of those who haven't heard the Gospel in His heart, and partly that we or someone else can't be safe by saying it's possible to be converted after death. Our duty and responsibility is clear. Our instructions are clear. Here and now, in this life, is where we receive the possibility of salvation. Here it's a matter of believing and receiving. And here it's a matter of letting the message go forth by evangelizing and through mission work. For *today* is the day of salvation! That's what we have to hold on to. We'll have to leave the rest with God.

Dear Savior, now we leave all those who are dead and whom we know nothing about in Your hands. We thank You that we know that You love them, that You have died for them, that You want all of them to come to You, and that You do all You can to help them, much more than we could pray for or believe. We thank You that all this is upon Your heart and that we don't have to worry about it. Instead, give us the right things to worry about concerning our souls and the right kind of concern about others and their salvation. Help us to thankfully leave alone whatever we can't do anything about and thankfully and faithfully devote ourselves to the things you've given us responsibility for.

THURSDAY AFTER TWENTY-THIRD SUNDAY AFTER TRINITY

1 Peter 4:7–19

Therefore let those who suffer according to God's will entrust their souls to a faithful Creator while doing good.
1 Peter 4:19

Can it be God's will that someone should suffer?

The answer is yes. And the strange thing is that it's God's will that His beloved children should take suffering upon themselves. God isn't the cause of suffering. It's the work of the adversary. It's caused by people who do his will instead of God's. God could put a stop to suffering, but only by getting rid of everyone who causes it. He doesn't want to do that. That would entail passing judgment. That judgment won't come before God has exhausted all His possibilities of saving more of His lost children, freeing them from the grasp of wickedness and leading them into the kingdom of forgiveness.

So God takes His time. He's patient. He gives the world yet another period of grace, and people abuse it by doing even more evil. That's the price that has to be paid for mercy and grace. Suffering affects evil and good, the unrepentant as well as the repentant. Many become bitter and hard-hearted. When it affects God's children, however, God wants them to understand the connection. They should be willing to suffer so forgiveness will constantly be available to the world. They've received the chance to come into the kingdom of forgiveness. Now they have to help others have the same chance. That's why I should be willing to suffer, to humble myself under God's powerful hand, forgive and do what is good. "Do not repay evil for evil or reviling for reviling; but on the contrary, bless" (1 Peter 3:9). "For it is better to suffer for doing good, if that should be God's will, than for doing evil" (1 Peter 3:17).

Lord Jesus, You have suffered for us. When You were reviled, You didn't revile. When You suffered, You didn't threaten. You prayed for Your executioners and died for Your tormentors. You suffered rather than judged, and You still refuse to judge our evil world. Instead, You keep the door open to the kingdom of forgiveness and let Your call go out.

*Lord, then it's an honor and a privilege to suffer
for You that Your blessing can reach out into the
world . . . that You give us that chance . . . that we
can be a part of something so tremendous! When
You walk ahead of us, Lord, we willingly follow.*

FRIDAY AFTER TWENTY-THIRD SUNDAY AFTER TRINITY
1 Peter 5:1–14

Casting all your anxieties on Him, because He cares for you.
1 Peter 5:7

We can cast *all* our anxieties on the Lord. Just as we can
make all our wishes known to Him. That's part of what's so
wonderful with God's kingdom. There's One who cares for
us, who knows us in every detail, who follows us day after
day, who knows and understands.

Now, however, it's a special kind of anxiety that Peter
thinks about here. It's the suffering someone accepts when
they follow their Lord Jesus on the path of forgiveness, when
they refrain from avenging themselves, when they rather suffer wrong than bring the church into disrepute (1 Corinthians
6:7). Peter calls acting in this way to "humble yourselves,
therefore, under the mighty hand of God" (1 Peter 5:6). That
means acting like Christ, He who didn't threaten when He
suffered but, instead, presented His cause to Him who judges
righteously.

If we do this, it might just happen that we pile up burning coals on his head. It might just happen that we conquer evil with good. It's also possible that we will suffer, that we'll be made fun of and despised, that some of us will lose our rights or our good name and reputation. And that's when it becomes clear that faith really is genuine. It's not a program for happiness in the world, not a kind of therapy that will give us peace of mind and psychological balance. Faith gives, as we see in the big chapter about faith in Hebrews 11—"conviction of things not seen." Genuine faith is that which cannot see and yet believes. God Himself is at stake here. It's Him I love, not just His good gifts. I can live without the gifts, but not without Him. "For Thine is the kingdom, and the power, and the glory, for ever and ever. Amen."

Dear heavenly Father, You who have taken us to be Your beloved children, help us to walk in Your love, to live in Your presence in the light of Your love and warmth, like good children in the presence of their dear Father.

Dear Lord Jesus, You who have forgiven us everything and loved us despite everything, allow us to be like You and forgive and love for Your sake, as a token and a testimony to Your love.

Dear Holy Spirit, may we never grieve You. You have come to us to live inside of us. Drive out everything that doesn't want to obey you. All bitterness and violence and anger, all desire to slander and judge, all that's evil and wicked. Make us kind-hearted, full of mercy, showing tenderness to everyone.

SATURDAY AFTER TWENTY-THIRD SUNDAY AFTER TRINITY

2 Chronicles 19:4–11

And [Jehoshaphat] said to the judges, "Consider what you do, for you judge not for man but for the LORD. He is with you in giving judgment." 2 Chronicles 19:6

"Boundless forgiveness" has been our topic this week. Maybe it's the right time to be reminded, however, that God wants justice to prevail in this evil world. We've talked about how the judicial system is a part of God's way of fighting evil, and today we read a piece out of Israel's history that says something worth thinking about concerning this.

King Jehoshaphat reigned in Judah for 25 years (875–850 BC) and has received a good posthumous reputation. He instructed the people in the Law of the Lord and created order in the government and judicial system. His rules of justice, that Paul of course was aware of, gives us a good picture of the New Testament's teachings about the state and governmental institutions.

The judge judges on God's behalf, just as all people in power rule on God's behalf. This doesn't mean that every sentencing, every law, and every statute corresponds with God's will. If that were the case, judges wouldn't have to be admonished, as they were in this case. Of course people in power can act unjustly! They will know, however, that "He is with you in giving judgment," or when they pass laws or when they appoint officials or when they appropriate funds.

It's a responsibility to have power. Superficial individuals think it's a privilege. They take it for granted that if you have power, you can in one way or another use it for your own purposes. All power, however, exists for the sake of others. It's a mandate from God that we defend justice and watch over the common good. We act on God's behalf. We can abuse this authority. Whoever does that won't go unpunished.

Israel was a religious state. Moses' Law was also civil law. Therefore, in the supreme court in Jerusalem, priests also sat in the jury. Even there, however, they could distinguish between "the Lord's matter" and "the king's matter." There were laws and cases that were in the hands of the civil government, but they also were a part of God's commission. Even there the people in power would be God's servants for the benefit of man.

Even the heathen authorities have their mandate from God, Paul says. Even the heathens have the Law of God written in their hearts. People knew that also in Old Testament times. In Proverbs God's wisdom says: "By Me kings reign, and rulers decree what is just; by Me princes rule, and nobles, all who govern justly" (Proverbs 8:15–16).

Lord, if I ever get the chance to decide something and am part of a decision that affects others, help me to remember that You are present and that I am acting through Your mandate. Help me realize that I can be Your servant for the benefit of others and that You have given me the responsibility for their welfare. And when others govern over me, help me to think not only whether they're benefiting me and my interests, they have others to think about too. Govern their hearts and minds so they really do what's best. And when they do their best, help me to be thankful for it.

TWENTY-FOURTH SUNDAY AFTER TRINITY

Matthew 24:15–28

Then there will be great tribulation, such as has not been from the beginning of the world until now, no, and never will be. Matthew 24:21

Today we celebrate a Sunday that often is forgotten about among the other celebrated days. This Sunday is about something that isn't discussed very often. It's namely about the final things, about what will happen during the last days on earth when the time approaches for the return of Christ and the final judgment. This is something we generally don't expect to experience. However, it is something a Christian should know about because it is Jesus' will. He talked to His apostles about these things. They're a part of the Gospel. Not the essence of it. Not the most important part that we time and time again come back to. But still as something we *also* should know about and reflect over. Therefore, this week we will be reading what the Bible has to say about the last times.

Even the prophets talked about it. In this situation, Jesus quotes the prophet Daniel, and consequently shows us that we have, in his book, a message from God about the future. The first thing we can learn from this message is that the world isn't on its way toward its own kingdom of happiness but toward huge catastrophes. We've already heard the reason why several times. Our world is fallen. Wickedness is so deeply rooted that it can't be healed or operated on. On the contrary, it grows. It takes human intelligence, the ability to be inventive, and the talent for organization into its service. The result is disintegration, disorder, and an onset of all the evil powers against the Church and everything that has to do with Christ. During this final disaster it's impossible to resist. All the forces that normally restrain evil—the legal system, the government, society, the family—are disintegrating. The only thing left to do is to flee. The Church becomes a catacomb. Its final testimony to the world will be martyrdom.

The Bible speaks about all of this in images that aren't easy to understand. They allude to things that lie ahead, beyond everything we know about. Still, sometimes there's a resemblance to things that already happen now so we can learn something from them. However, what is really meant by the work of destruction or the great disaster or the vultures probably won't be apparent until that day has come. The Bible is God's Word to all people and all times, even the final time.

Lord, here I stand before Your veil, and You lift it a tiny bit and let me glimpse into the unknown, that which will come. I thank You for Your confidence. Help me to use it as You want. May I never try to lift the veil more than You would've done. Make me thankful and tranquil, even when my questions remain unanswered, and give me eyes to see what's useful for me to see, even if it's something completely different from what I wanted to see.

2 Thessalonians 2:1–12

The coming of the lawless one is by the activity of Satan with all power and false signs and wonders. 2 Thessalonians 2:9

Paul had said to the Thessalonians that the day of the Lord comes "like a thief in the night" (1 Thessalonians 5:2). In other words, it was a question of being prepared. His advice had consequences Paul never intended. Some had, as the apostle says in the following text, started to live carelessly. They neglected their work because they were convinced that the world would soon end. This gives Paul a reason to give them a serious warning to be calm and work so they can earn their daily bread and not be dependent on anyone else. "If anyone is not willing to work, let him not eat" (2 Thessalonians 3:10). Then Paul also mentions why he himself isn't expecting Christ's immediate return: something has to happen first. Here Paul mentions things he learned directly from Jesus. First, a great falling away has to occur. Furthermore, there will come a time of lawlessness and anarchy, when all existence will be in disorder. During that time a great seducer of the people will come forth, a false messiah of sorts, and many will believe in him and follow him. The end of world history will be the great showdown between him and Christ.

"You know what is restraining him now so that he may be revealed in his time," Paul says in 2:6. We may wish we knew as much as the Thessalonians about this point. However, we have to rely on presumptions. Paul likely thought about the Roman Empire, the prevailing legal system. The legal system is from God. It exists to keep violence and injustice in check.

When it finally helplessly falls apart, it's a sign that the world is ending. That's when the lawless one establishes his empire. He does what is called "miracles of the Antichrist." He implements reforms and wins impressive victories, but they only benefit injustice and deceit. It's possible that from the outside it looks like a magnificent empire where everything is subject to the supreme state. However, it will be a demonic state, whose nature is deceit, violence and injustice. That's the ultimate consequence of the fact that man "refused to love the truth and so be saved" (2 Thessalonians 2:10). God takes His hand away. He lets the powers of delusion loose and they can complete their work. That time is at hand.

Lord, You say that the secret of lawlessness is already active. Help us to recognize it, in everything it does to destroy and prevent Your good labor. Also inside of us. Help us so we don't get discouraged if it grows and seems to spread. That just means that You've come closer. Help us in such a way that our love doesn't become colder if lawlessness increases. Help us to hold on to everything that is good and just, now, in the small sense, and then later in the final test, if it comes while we're alive. Lord, make us steadfast to the end. For Your name's sake.

TUESDAY AFTER TWENTY-FOURTH SUNDAY AFTER TRINITY

Revelation 8:1–13

The lamb opened the seventh seal. Revelation 8:1

The last seal was broken and it became completely quiet in heaven. A silence of breathless anticipation before the final act in the great drama. What was going to happen now?

When we read Revelation, we're constantly reminded with its visions, images, that are revealed to us. The veils are lifted, colors, images, clouds of incense are observed for a moment. The roaring of water, the noise of uncountable voices, thunder and rumbling, and the sound of trumpets flows towards us. Then the scene changes again.

It's impossible to say what all these pictures mean. They can't be arranged into a logical system and then interpreted into an account depicting everyday life. Much of it probably won't be comprehensible before the time of fulfillment. However, if we look at these pictures, they'll begin to talk to us. Although a lot of it is difficult to express, it fills us with a strong and vivid premonition of what's going to happen.

When we read the eighth chapter in Revelation, our thoughts go time and time again to the disastrous threat that has hung over our generation since we discovered we could use atomic energy to destroy and terrorize one another. The images close in on us: hail and fire that burns up a third of the world's forests, the burning mountain that falls into the ocean so fishermen die and their boats perish, the poisonous star that fell on the land and makes the water dangerous to drink. A disaster like this that would take a large portion of the human life on earth can happen at any time. We know that. And if it comes, maybe the intention is that we should know that the seventh seal has been broken and the end is near.

What do we think about, however, when we read about incense, the prayers, and the fire from the altar? The image of prayers from the holy ones, rising like clouds of incense up to God, carried in the hand of an angel, mixed with heaven's own wonderful scent, would cause everyone to pray with joy. But why are the same censors filled with fire from the altar and why is this fire thrown down to earth? In both cases it's the same fire, God's fire—the fire of love and holiness. It lights faith's prayers, it lifts them and receives them, and fills them with heaven's own scent of incense. For faithlessness, however, it becomes a fire that falls from heaven, burning and hot, like rain over Sodom and Gomorrah. The *same* fire . . .

You, God, are our refuge and strength, a very present help in trouble. Therefore, we will not fear although the earth should change, although the mountains shake in the heart of the sea, although its waters roar and foam, although the mountains tremble with its tumult. There is a river whose streams make glad the city of God, the holy habitation of the most high. She shall not be moved. God will help her right early. The Lord of hosts is with us even then. You are our refuge, even when everything is shattered. (From Psalm 46.)

WEDNESDAY AFTER TWENTY-FOURTH SUNDAY AFTER TRINITY

Revelation 11:15–12:6

[You shall destroy] the destroyers of the earth. Revelation 11:18

The seventh angel blew his trumpet. It's time for God to settle up. It's taken a long time. It looked like He didn't care about evil spreading everywhere. Many have wanted to ask as did the "souls of those who had been slain for the word of God and for the witness they had borne . . . 'O Sovereign Lord, holy and true, how long before You will judge and avenge our blood . . . ?'" (Revelation 6:9–10). The martyrs were told that the time wasn't right, however. It was still the time of sacrifice. There were still those who must die so mercy and forgiveness could be available and someone who was lost could be saved.

However, now everything has been done that could've been done. Now it's time for the great reckoning.

Then John has a flashback. As so often, his visions sweep forward and backward through time, like a movie camera filming the story of salvation. We see in one little glimpse what happened when Jesus came. John sees a pregnant woman. She's going to give birth to a boy, and that birth causes her great agony. The woman is the Church, God's congregation, the chosen people. It's the same people, the same woman, in the vision's imagery, in the old and new covenants. God's Israel is Christ's mother. He was born there. The dragon was ready to devour the baby, but he couldn't. Christ performed His duty and was taken up to God. The woman, however, God's Israel that now is the Church, is left on the earth and has to flee into the wilderness, down into the catacombs, to go underground, or however we want to express it. For now all of the dragon's rage is turned toward her. Up to the end, he's the destroyer, someone who destroys and annihilates all the good God has done. From the destroyer has come everything that makes creation ugly and evil, everything that breaks it down and destroys it. However, now the end time has come for the destructive powers, just when it appears that they would be victorious.

Lord, why do the nations conspire and the peoples plot in vain? The kings of the earth and the rulers take counsel together against the Lord and His anointed, saying: Let us burst their bonds asunder and cast their cords from us. But You who sit in heaven laugh, You talk to them in Your wrath and terrify them with Your fury when You set Your king, Your Son, Your only begotten, and give Him the ends of the earth as His possessions. He who can break them with a rod of iron. Blessed are all who take refuge in Him. (Paraphrased from Psalm 2.)

THURSDAY AFTER TWENTY-FOURTH SUNDAY AFTER TRINITY
Revelation 12:7–17

The accuser of our brothers has been thrown down.
Revelation 12:10

The great dragon, the ancient serpent, was thrown down. Until now he was a prosecutor before God's throne, just as it is told to us in the Book of Job. However, when Christ came and the dragon could not stop it, that's when his power was lost. Jesus atoned for the sins of the world and twisted the most effective weapons out of the prosecutor's hand. After that there was no place for him in heaven. He has nothing to say about God's judgment. If he tries to say that everyone has sinned and that they all deserve death, according to God's holy law, then God can point to His Son. Satan is conquered, by virtue of the Lamb's blood that cleanses from all sin.

"But woe to you, O earth and sea, for the devil has come down to you in great wrath, because he knows that his time is short!" (Revelation 12:12). He reacts as a desperate dictator who can see defeat before his eyes. He casts everything he has in the battle and stops at nothing. Therefore, the outbursts of evil will become worse and more brutal the closer we come to the end of the world.

Satan's wrath is directed first and foremost at the woman, God's Church. The last great persecution rages. There is only one thing to do here, as Jesus said: flee. The Church in the final days will be a catacomb church, an underground church. God will keep possibilities, places of refuge, secret meeting places, and hidden forms for church services available. *How*? We don't know. We can imagine it when we see what has already happened. This is the way it is with the hardships of the final days; it's like a dress rehearsal. Evil rises up in new waves, each time higher and more threatening. The destruction is worse after each wave, the violent rulers more ruthless, the concentration of power more effective, war even more devastating. And the characteristics of the Antichrist appear more frightening in the godless and blasphemously arrogant leading figures.

Does anyone think this sounds frightening, depressing,

and hopeless? Can you remember how well John's strange visions correspond to the picture of the future that Jesus Himself has given us? The last days are days of great hardship. The great showdown with the strong one won't be a make-believe war but a dead serious and real one. Those who have understood why all this must happen, however, hear the hymn of victory the whole time, resounding through everything. Now salvation and the power and the kingdom have become our God's and the empire His anointed ones. And He prays His Lord's Prayer with a new understanding of the infinite depth in those ancient, worn out concluding words: For Thine is the kingdom and the power and the glory for ever and ever. Amen.

Yes, Lord, I know the kingdom is ours and it will endure. All of evil's victories only prove that You are right. Human dreams of happiness go to pieces. Our own attempts to create heaven on earth show their emptiness. Your kingdom prevails, however. For Yours is the power. Even the power to carry Your salvation to fulfillment right through the great destruction and in the middle of all the ruins of this world that the destroyer laid in ruins. And Yours is the glory, that great happiness in real life that is songs of praise and joy and pure goodness. The kind that will last forever.

FRIDAY AFTER TWENTY-FOURTH SUNDAY AFTER TRINITY

Revelation 13:1–18

No one can buy or sell unless he has the mark, that is, the name of the beast. Revelation 13:17

A horrible picture is painted here. Maybe what's most horrible is that we might have seen something like it in reality. No previous century has produced anything that comes closer to the kingdom of the beast.

It's obviously a question of what we would call a totalitarian state, a state with unlimited power and with totalitarian demands on its subjects, not only over their daily lives, their right to buy and sell, but also their ideology, their opinions and desires, all the way into their most secretive thoughts. And this state no longer has anything to do with the authority that comes from God. It's a demonic state. Just as Satan can put himself in Christ's place, so can he also take the state ordained by God into his service and make it his tool. In fact, he's *always* trying to do this through selfishness, corruption, oppression, and torture. There's an ongoing struggle between God and Satan even in social and political arenas. Through good virtues that God has instilled in the nature of man, he wages an ongoing struggle for justice and mercy, even with the help of non-Christians. During the last days, however, it'll be different. Then, the evil one will be totally mobilized. The restraint that stood in the way (2 Thessalonians 2:6) will be removed. The beast will gain power, whatever that means. We don't know. All we can say is: Those who live will see.

In that moment all human resistance is doomed to fail. Who can fight against the beast? Those who try, even the Christians, will be conquered and lose the battle over society and its institutions. Evil reigns there now. All that's left is steadfastness, faith of the heart, the confessions of the mouth, and, finally, martyrdom. Human kindness isn't enough here. Everyone gives up and surrenders, if their name isn't written in the Lamb's book. Only those who are faithful to Christ, those who live in Christ's atonement, have the chance to preserve their inner freedom and stand against it without surrendering and accepting. But it won't be easy for them either. "Here is a call for the endurance and faith of the saints" (Revelation 14:12).

What is meant by the beast's number? Those who live will see. We don't know that now. You can fiddle and mess around with numbers and get just about anything you want. It's been said that you can arrive at the number 666 by summing up the numerical value of the Greek letters for Caesar Nero, but to reach that number, you have to assume that John used Hebrew letters, left out the vowels, and spelled it wrong. Here, as in all the other numerical information in Revelation, we have to hold our imagination in check. We can only guess that this is something that, in due time, will be of benefit and comfort and guidance to those who live then. Maybe it'll be us!

Lord, I pray every day that Your kingdom will come. Help me to pray for it with all my heart even if I realize what it can entail. Help me to see how Your kingdom is approaching, just as it becomes dark in the fall and winter throughout the world. Help me to hear Your voice even if the storm rages and the ocean roars. Help me to see that even the great dragon is only a forerunner, a sign that time is short and summer is near. Thy kingdom come.

Revelation 15:1–8

In the path of Your judgments, O LORD, we wait for You.
Isaiah 26:8

How can God allow it? How can so much suffering occur?

This question has been asked throughout time. The prophets wonder and complain. They cry to God that He should intervene and put evil in its place. "If favor is shown to the wicked, he does not learn righteousness; in the land of uprightness he deals corruptly, and does not see the majesty of the LORD" (Isaiah 26:10). "Why do You make me see iniquity, and why do You idly look at wrong? Destruction and violence are before me; strife and contention arise. So the law is paralyzed, and justice never goes forth" (Habakkuk 1:3–4).

God has His own ways, however. The Bible describes them to us. Time and time again we've been confronted with the great milestones on God's highway: first, atonement, then the preaching of the Gospel, then righteousness for everyone who believes, and *then* judgment. Of course, God has allowed His judgment to be spread out over the world even during what's called His time of patience. Then, they come together with the Gospel and forgiveness. That's why what Isaiah said could happen: God could come down the path of judgment, and even that could lead to salvation.

It's different during the last days, when the world is governed by the spirit of the beast. Then, all possibilities of mercy are exhausted. Those who wanted to receive mercy have received it. Now, when God's judgments fall upon the earth, there is no longer any salvation with them. Those who are affected didn't "repent of their murders or their sorceries or their immorality or their thefts" (Revelation 9:21). What happens now is the last great judgment over ultimate, incurable evil. It's obvious for those who have eyes to see: Thy judgments have been revealed. Great and wonderful are Thy deeds. Just and true are Thy ways.

If you understand what that means, when God actually judges and once and for all comes to grips with evil, then you are less eager in your questioning of why God waits and how He can allow so much pain. Instead, you start being grateful that the world has received yet another period of grace and that there's still time for improvement and forgiveness. It sounds so strange: That evil can still occur is proof that mercy is still available.

But how bad is it then, to use even a few of the remaining days of mercy to do even more evil!

Let Your steadfast love come to me, O Lord, Your salvation according to Your promise. For my hope is in Your ordinances. Godless men utterly deride me, but I do not turn away from Your law. When I think of Your ordinances from of old, I take comfort, O Lord. I know, O Lord, that Your judgments are right, and that in faithfulness You have afflicted me. Righteous You are, O Lord, and right are Your judgments. You have appointed Your testimonies in righteousness and in all faithfulness. O Lord, in Your justice preserve my life. (From Psalm 119.)

SUNDAY OF
END TIME SAINTS
TRIUMPHANT
Matthew 25:1–13

As the bridegroom was delayed, they all became drowsy
and slept. Matthew 25:5

The people in this parable all had gone out to meet the
bridegroom. They had not refused the wedding invitation.
They wanted to be a part of it and had prepared themselves.

Then, however, there was a delay. Jesus is telling us that
we should expect this. Jesus can be delayed. Years go by, and
everything is as it should be. Christian life becomes drab and
we become accustomed to it. Nothing special happens.

Then "they *all* became drowsy and slept," it says. We
have to expect that. Everyone gets tired. You can't be excited
the whole time. We all have to sleep. We all have times when
all our attention is focused on something else or when all our
attention goes numb and no longer functions.

Then the bridegroom comes, and that's when the big
difference becomes clear. Half of those who were waiting
had oil in their lamps and half didn't. It didn't help that they
asked their neighbors if they could borrow some. What this
parable is trying to tell us is that there's something one of us
cannot give to another. Not with our best intentions. There's
something no one can share. Not with his best friend or his
own beloved child. And this thing that is so very personal is
also necessary and decisive.

What, then, is this secret oil that's so indispensably
necessary? It is faith, the faith that unites us with Christ and
lets Him live inside of us. Where that faith exists is where
you're ready to meet Him when He comes. Through that
faith you constantly live in the forgiveness of sins. Even
when you can't think about Jesus. Even when you sleep.

Even if you lie unconscious and near death.

What can you do to get the oil? The answer: Use God's words and pray, diligently go to your Savior's Communion, watch over your heart so you don't extinguish the Spirit and don't close the door to the Savior. You can do that by conscious disobedience or by simply breaking off the relationship, by neglecting to pray and no longer listening to His Word. And if you break off the relationship, it can't be repaired when the bridegroom has come and shut the door.

Consequently, this parable contains both a warning and comfort. See to it that Christ keeps you in the faith. Then you're ready, even if He comes in the middle of the night or on a day when none of us expect it.

Lord Jesus, increase our faith, strengthen our faith, preserve our faith. Keep us ever watchful and vigilant, like servants who wait for their master so they can open immediately. And when we have to think about something else, when we have to sleep, when we become old or senile or unconscious, don't forget us. We thank You that You don't abandon us. We thank You for that fellowship in faith that makes us Yours, every day and every minute, when we're awake and when we're sleeping, even when our consciousness is extinguished. Be close to us, O Lord Jesus, day and night, in life and in death.

MONDAY BEFORE LAST SUNDAY OF END OF TIME

1 Thessalonians 5:1–10

But you are not in darkness, brothers, for that day to surprise you like a thief. 1 Thessalonians 5:4

How can you be prepared? Always? Even when you're busy with something else and can neither pray nor be vigilant?

Paul gives us the same answer we got from Jesus yesterday. He does it with the illustration of night and day.

Those who don't believe live in darkness. They sleep or get drunk. All of this of course is meant in a spiritual sense. They don't see where they're going and don't notice what's about to happen. They say: Don't worry about it! All that stuff about the Last Day is all in your imagination, something the clergy has invented just to scare us. Besides, they say, there's a professor that says it's an old Jewish superstition, and that Jesus never could've said something like that!

And while they're talking, the day comes. And that means a catastrophe for that part of the world they were so certain to be able to keep and for the world of illusions they live in.

But that's not the way it is, Paul says. You don't belong to the night or darkness. You are all sons of the light and of the day.

All? Who is "all"? All of you who believe in the Lord Jesus, Paul would've answered. All of you who have received forgiveness and now live with the Lord. One who belongs to the day doesn't have to worry about light. It's everywhere. He's surrounded by it. It pours down from heaven and fills his world. Of course, he can go into the closet or down to the basement and shut himself in. Then it'll be dark. However, as long as he stays in the light of day, it's everywhere and surrounds him on all sides.

That's how it is when you have faith. You're surrounded by forgiveness. It saturates your whole existence. It pours down from heaven every moment and everywhere. You don't have to light a candle or take a flashlight along when the sun is out. That's how God's children live in the light.

However, they can also go down into the basement. Maybe to hide. Maybe to avoid talking to their Father right now. Maybe to do something they don't want their Father to see. Then it's dark. Then we say: "Awake, O sleeper, and arise from the dead, and Christ will shine on you" (Ephesians 5:14). Those who follow Christ "will not walk in darkness, but will have the light of life" (John 8:12).

Lord, in Your presence there is fullness of joy, in Your right hand are pleasures evermore. For the Lord God is a sun and shield. He bestows favor and honor. No good thing does the Lord withhold from those who walk uprightly. O Lord of hosts, blessed is the man who trusts in You. Blessed are the people who know the festal shout, who walk, O Lord, in the light of Your countenance, who exult in Your name and extol Your righteousness. Therefore I will sing of Your steadfast love, O Lord, forever. For Your steadfast love was established forever, Your faithfulness as firm as the heavens. (From Psalms 16, 84, and 89.)

TUESDAY BEFORE
LAST SUNDAY
OF END OF TIME

2 Peter 3:8–18

The Lord is not slow to fulfill His promise as some count slowness. 2 Peter 3:9

Christ will come again. We have His word on that. But what's taking Him so long?

That's been the burning question for Christians through-out time, especially in times of persecution and religious revival when we've been very close to our Master. The more we experience the nearness of God's kingdom and the more we have "tasted the powers of the age to come" (Hebrews 6:5), the more natural it seems that the kingdom should break through and come in all its glory. What's holding it back? Peter answers: God's patience. God doesn't want anyone to perish. There still must be some poor human being on whom Christ can make an impact. Only God knows how many. As long as there's something to salvage, He'll delay, and the time for the arrival of His kingdom depends on His measure of time, not ours. Two thousand years for Him is like two days to us, and that's not a long delay. Maybe He'll wait one or two more days like that. No one knows, except for the Father Himself.

However, Christ *is* coming! There's a limit for our world. God's creation isn't eternal. It exists by a command of God and will, with roaring haste, perish and dissolve in the fire on the day He sees fit. In the beginning of the previous century, many people scoffed at the thought that this stable, compact, and indestructible material could dissolve. Now we know that the closest equivalent to an atom is a planetary system, where infinitely small packages of waves or power particles or whatever you want to call them travel in a void, and in that material God has contained such unbelievable amounts of energy, that when we start to untie a little of a millionths millionth, we have the power to burn up most of the face of the earth. What can't happen if the Creator unties all the bands that hold creation together?

For unbelievers, all this just means a catastrophe. In reality, it's something that gives all of life a purpose. That day is "the great day," "the Day of the Lord." What unbelievers call the end of the world means, in fact, that we—finally!—will receive "new heavens and a new earth in which righteousness dwells" (2 Peter 3:13), that creation—finally!—will be good again and the world a paradise, as it was meant from the beginning. Oh, if we were only there!

Lord, we know Your day will come, and You let us look forward to it yearningly, like we look forward to spring. Lord, can we hurry it along? You say that we can. Now You complete Your great work. You allow the Gospel to go out to all people. You gather in Your harvest. You allow us to be with You in that task. Can we hurry it along? We're open for that, Lord. May it happen to all of us. Make us ready and willing, and help us to fulfill our part of that which remains to be done. Thy kingdom come!

WEDNESDAY BEFORE LAST SUNDAY OF END OF TIME

Matthew 24:1–14

And because lawlessness will be increased, the love of many will grow cold. Matthew 24:12

The disciples had asked for signs of Christ's coming and the end of time. That wasn't so strange. They understood from all that Jesus had taught them that God's kingdom would come and that must mean new heavens and a new earth. This era is coming to an end. We're living in a world that's getting old. But when will the end come? Can we sense it in advance?

Jesus answers by giving a glimpse of the future that differs substantially from what people in general prefer to imagine. They usually want to believe in progress. The thought of it becoming better here on earth gives purpose to our work. It can motivate denying ourselves things and sacrificing. However, this is an illusion. Of course technology makes advancements. But increased technology is a power that is good and bad. How it's used depends on if it's controlled by good or selfish intentions, and good intentions aren't something that will increase on our planet. We are in the middle of the final struggle between God and Satan. We've already heard it: Satan has lost his best weapon. He can no longer stand in the presence of God as our prosecutor. Now he wages the last bitter battle for the world he took with himself into the fall. He's mobilizing all of his resources. Therefore, it will be as we can learn from both Revelation and from experience: wars will be bloodier, persecution harder, renunciation more open, the catastrophes worse. The future is not characterized by peace and prosperity in mankind that is imbued with the Gospel. Instead, it's characterized by the force of all evil.

It looks as if love would become extinct in the world. This will be the great time of apostasy.

And right in the middle of all this, the false prophets and those who claim to be the Savior and a God-sent liberator appear. They claim to come with the correct interpretation of the Gospel. They attract many people. But don't believe them, Jesus says. Don't follow them.

These things that will happen during the last days are important to us now. From time to time, things happen that remind us of the great disasters of the last days, and each time they resemble more strikingly the last great rebellion against God. The devastations are worse, the cruelties greater, the blasphemies more coarse. Therefore, Jesus' words have application for every such disaster. They show what kinds of forces are involved. They reveal what's at stake. It's possible that evil will retreat once more. Revival with a new spiritual life can evolve. However, it can also be a question of the last great test. And throughout time Jesus' words apply: He who endures to the end shall be saved.

Praise be to You, O Lord, that I never have to despair. I have seen so much indescribable evil. Despite the fact that so much has become better in the world, it seems like we haven't. I thank You that I don't have to believe in others and progress and every-thing else that I've seen go to pieces. I thank You that in the end it won't be wickedness and torture and persecution and lies that prevail, but You and Your kingdom. Help me to faithfully and coura-geously do what has to be done for others in this evil world, and then always be glad and in good spirits because every day for us is a day closer to Your great day.

THURSDAY BEFORE LAST SUNDAY OF END OF TIME

Matthew 24:29–36

Heaven and earth will pass away, but My words will not
pass away. Matthew 24:35

Whom do we believe the most? Christ or professor U,
president V, editor W, Mrs. X, alderman Y, and candidate
Z? It's not unbelievable that all of them, if asked, would say
the opposite of what Jesus says here. They would be sure that
heaven and earth would endure at least a couple of billion
years, but that Jesus' Word would perish and become more and
more antique and finally be impossible to apply in a modern
society.

That this world will perish and Christ will come again
is something as incomprehensible and unverifiable as the
resurrection must have been for the disciples while they still
walked with their Master. They didn't quite understand what
He meant. But He was right. And it wasn't strange that they
trusted His Word when He said to them that He would come
back and that something would happen that was just as fantastic and radical with the whole world and with themselves that
happened to Him when He rose from the dead.

Maybe it's comforting for many disciples today to know
that it was so difficult for the apostles to understand that the
talk about the resurrection really concerned a tangible reality,
something they themselves would be a witness to. Their difficulty in understanding didn't stop them from being sincere
disciples. It didn't impede their fellowship with their Master.
And, at last, they witnessed what they had such a hard time
imagining.

Things like that can happen among disciples today also.
Some people have difficulties understanding all this about

the end of the world and the return of Christ. But they stick to Christ and follow Him. They count on doing that until they die, and they rely on His promise of resurrection and a new life. Disciples like this are true disciples. Faith in Christ's return isn't the first thing we have to believe in order to follow Him. That's usually something we learn through the years. We believe His Word, just as we've learned to trust our Lord Jesus in everything else.

However, what if the end comes in a completely different way? If those lunatics drop their nuclear bombs and put an end to the whole human race? And Christ does not come? Jesus has an answer even to these questions: "This generation will not pass away until all these things take place" (Mark 13:30). An atomic war is a possibility. Maybe that'll be one of the great disasters during the final days of the world. The human race, however, won't become extinct but will live to meet the Son of Man. And on that day everyone will see that He was right about this too.

Lord, who can help but be afraid when catastrophes threaten? When clouds of misfortune hover over us? When the light is turned off and the walls cave in? When there's no more food and our neighbors flee? When our very existence seems to falter in its foundations? Help us remember what You have said. Help us to lift up our heads and be on the lookout and wait. Then we will know that You are near, that summer is coming, lovely summer, when everything is fine.

Matthew 24:37–51

What I say to you I say to all: Stay awake. Mark 13:37

No one knows when Christ is coming. We're not sup-posed to know. We're not even supposed to be able to figure it out. If someone comes with calculations like that, don't listen to him. As sure as it is *that* the Lord is coming, equally sure is it that no one knows *when* He's coming. That's why Jesus says: "Therefore, stay awake, for you do not know on what day your Lord is coming" (Matthew 24:42).

There's spiritual power in that thought: My Lord Jesus might come today. If someone has experienced the brink of death, perhaps under the threat of an incurable disease, then he knows the urgency of the moment. Even in a life of faith, there was seriousness in the soul-searching, a concentration on the essentials, a responsibility for how we spend our time, a loving care for those closest to us, that, put all together, were very useful. And more than one of us thought: *That's* the way you should always live.

Yes, that's the way a Christian should always live. And that's how you learn to live if you follow your Savior's instructions to watch, which means to wait for Him every day. To not take for granted that you can count on having the whole week and the whole year and the whole life at your disposal. It's so easy for all of us to say: My Lord isn't coming that quickly. When you start to think like that, you start procrastinating with important things that should be done, even things that are important for the soul. To make amends with someone you're no longer friendly with. To see if you really act correctly in a certain situation. To settle a debt. All of these are things that you'd obviously attend to if you knew you had six weeks to live.

It's dangerous to think: He'll be delayed. Jesus expressly warns us about this. It happens so easily and it can have fatal consequences. To know your Master's will and not do it is always dangerous. And most often it doesn't start with downright disobedience but with postponement. We notice how serious Jesus is when He talks to His apostles about this. And He adds: "What I say to you I say to all: Stay awake."

Lord, I hear You speaking to me, and I know I need that. It's so easy for me to think that time isn't so short and I have many years left. Lord, help me to think every night that You can come during the hours of the night. May I fall asleep every evening, certain that I am Yours. Help me to start every new day prepared to stand before You, if You should call me to Your throne of glory. And help me to do my daily chores and provide for the future, as faithfully and perseveringly as You want me to, just because I know that every hour can be accounted for and every moment lived in Your presence. Make me a faithful and wise steward who does everything at the right time, as You've commanded, and who every moment is ready to open myself for You and receive You with joy. For Your name's sake, Lord Jesus.

SATURDAY BEFORE LAST SUNDAY OF END OF TIME

Matthew 25:14–30

You have been faithful over a little. Matthew 25:21

A Christian is a steward. He's been entrusted with specific tasks: to live in this world as God's child, to have Jesus as his brother, to use all of God's good gifts to the joy and blessing of both himself and others.

The gifts can vary, but they can always grow and yield something. They can always be an avenue to even more good. And when Christ comes back to hold us accountable, we'll be tested as to what each and every one of us has done with his talent.

In other words, will it be judgment according to deeds? Will it be a question of how much we've accomplished? What have we been good for? How kind and sacrificing we've been. Isn't all of this dependent on mercy?

Everything is dependent on mercy; the Gospel is very clear on this point. But that mercy shouldn't make us idle. Christ's love forces us. A good tree bears good fruit. So our deeds are a testimony of our faith and our fellowship with Christ of the saving fellowship with the Savior. That's why time and time again the New Testament tells us that each of us must come forth before Christ's tribunal to receive an account of our good works from this life on earth. But still, salvation is dependent on mercy. No amount of good deeds is enough. We all need forgiveness. Everyone can receive it through faith in Jesus. However, if we believe, with just and living faith, then we'll be able to invest our talent so it grows. Not so that we'll deserve salvation; we already have that. But because we love the Lord.

There are those who think only about getting by. They

know they will have to account for themselves and they're scared about that. Jesus says it will go badly for them. They're like the third servant who buried his talent. He was so afraid of doing something wrong that he preferred to do nothing at all. The most important thing for him was to be blameless, not to serve and give of himself, with all the risks that can entail. That's the moralist's way of living, but not a Christian way.

Consequently, there'll be a reckoning. That's why we celebrate the Last Sunday of End of Time. But it's important that we celebrate this day correctly. What's crucial isn't that we haven't done anything wrong or, in any event, no greater sins. The important thing is that we love the Lord Christ and live in faith in Him.

Lord Jesus, help us to have the right Last Sunday of End of Time tomorrow. Put us in the presence of Your face and all-seeing eyes. Let us feel in the depth of our hearts that we could never have passed the test if You hadn't died for us. May we feel such thankfulness and joy that we become glad and willing servants, faithful in everything, even in the smallest thing You give us to do. Bless your entire Church with a deep feeling of what's lacking, sincere regret for all that's been neglected, and cheerful eagerness to serve You, if You give us yet another period of grace and yet another Church Year.

LAST SUNDAY BEFORE END OF TIME
Matthew 25:31–46

He will separate people from one another as a shepherd separates the sheep from the goats. Matthew 25:32

That's how it goes. The shepherd doesn't have to wonder if it's a sheep that is in front of him or not. It's not a fine line between a sheep and a goat. The difference is obvious. All you've got to do is separate them.

What is it that makes this fundamental difference, a difference that becomes decisive in judgment, without any hesitation and without need for witnesses or interrogation?

These people have met Jesus before, He says. They've shown what they think of Him. They've made up their minds. But how? How did they meet Him?

In the least of these, Jesus says. As they treated them, they treated Jesus. But who are these "least of . . . My brothers" mentioned in Matthew 25:40? Jesus asked that question Himself once and answered it. "Who are My brothers?" And stretching out His hand toward His disciples, He said, "Here are My mother and My brothers" (Matthew 12:49). It was those who heard His call and followed Him and did His Father's will. *Those* were His brothers.

Jesus is pretty restrained with that word, but He uses it in important situations. When He appeared for the women on Easter Sunday He said to them: "Go to My brothers." It's by being a part of the resurrection's new life that we become His brothers. God has predestined us to be conformed to the image of the Son, Paul says, so that Christ becomes "the first-born among many brothers" (Romans 8:29). It's easy for us to forget the remarkable thing about this, that we are Christ's brothers and heirs. In Hebrews it says that Christ is not ashamed to call them brothers (2:11), when we belong to them "who are sanctified" and consequently have the same Father that He has.

Since Christ lives inside of His own, we meet Him every time we meet a disciple, even if it's one of the least of them. Someone who takes in a disciple, takes in Jesus Himself, "And whoever gives to one of these little ones even a cup of cold water because he is a disciple, truly, I say to you, he shall not lose his reward" (Matthew 10:42). In the same way it's awfully serious if you "cause one of these little ones to sin" (Luke 17:2).

Consequently, we misunderstand the Gospel of The Last Sunday before End of Time if we think that the decisive judgment will be based on whether we've been "good" by being charitable or by working for social justice. What's decisive is your attitude toward Christ. And that shows when you meet His distressed and persecuted disciples. *Naturally,* however, Jesus expects us to help *everyone,* whether they're disciples or opponents, friends or persecutors, with the same love He showed.

Lord Jesus, we pray to You for the kind of love that's enough for everyone. We know You don't want us to ask who we have in front of us. Show us all the good we can do to those You put in our way. Help us to meet them so they meet a little of Your love and get a glimpse of You. Lord, You want us to do this for Your sake. Thank You that the idea isn't that we should be able to see the good works in ourselves or remember them. But dear Lord, let us have the surprise on Your great Day that we were a source a joy to someone anyway. Not for our sake, Lord, but for the sake of those who needed that joy.

Revelation 18:1–10

Fallen, fallen is Babylon the great! Revelation 18:2

The end is near.

Revelation, with mysterious and suggestive visions, describes how order in the world falters during the final days. It looks as though evil has been victorious. The State, which was supposed to uphold the law, becomes a totalitarian state. There is one misfortune after another. The Church becomes a persecuted minority that exists covertly. Everything is in the hands of a world power that is an enemy of God, symbolized by the beast, the great prostitute, and the evil city of Babylon.

Then, however, a mighty voice resounds from heaven: "Fallen, fallen is Babylon the great." God has intervened and "mighty is the Lord God who has judged her" (Revelation 18:8). The evil city collapses, her smoke rises up, and all her admirers see it from a distance with terror and anxiety, similar to what you see when a mushroom cloud rises over a city hit by a nuclear bomb.

What is the great city of Babylon? It got its name from Babel that once upon a time was the city of oppression and captivity, a proud city that laid claim to controlling the whole world and didn't have to fear either God or man. Already among the Jews, Babel was a symbol for an earthly kingdom, for the devil and all his power, for everything that was against God. For the ancient Church, Rome was the new Babel, since the blood of martyrs was shed there more than any other place. John and all of his contemporaries had heard about this. Refugees had told them how Peter was crucified and Paul was beheaded and how their brothers and sisters—among whom the Christians in Asia Minor had relatives and old friends—had been torn to bits by wild animals in the amphitheater and been burned liked living torches during the nightly parties in Nero's gardens. It wasn't strange that Rome was seen as a new Babel. At the same time, however, the great Babylon was something more. It's the timeless symbol for all the arrogant, self-important, wealthy, and inconsiderate world powers that are hostile toward God, that deny Him and put themselves in His place. That's why it says (in the last verse of this chapter) that all martyrs, from all nations and throughout all time, have shed their blood in that city.

Now it's over, however. Suddenly the end is here. During all of the previous miseries, the evil one has strengthened his grasp on people. Now, however, it turns out that in some way it has weakened itself and undermined its own power. It can't create, can't restore, only exploit. And it destroys whatever it exploits. When the time is right, God's judgment will fall, and then everything is over.

And at the same time everything will be new. Now it's God's time to create and renew and make everything right.

Lord, You Yourself have said that here it's a matter of faith. When it looks like all those who deny You have all the power. When those who mock are triumphant and sneer and seem to be dead sure. When faith in You seems to be trampled on or is extinguished in the ice cold environment of doubt. When the whole world seems to be in agreement that You were wrong or that You don't even exist. Lord, I know that there's only one thing I have to adhere to: You alone. Your voice that I can hear.

Your Word that lives in my heart. Your Communion
where I meet You. Everything the world doesn't
see. All that can't be proven but can still convince
my heart. Lord, I believe. Help my unbelief.

TUESDAY AFTER LAST SUNDAY BEFORE END OF TIME
Revelation 19:5–16

The marriage of the Lamb has come. Revelation 19:7

The heavenly kingdom is just like when a king arranged a wedding for his son, Jesus says. He sent out the invitations. Some people declined. There are more important things in life than this thing about God. Things they preferred. That's how it's always been and that's how it'll always be right up to the end. With only one exception: that the world's no to this huge wedding invitation has never been so conclusive, so presumptuous and so scornful as in the final days when it's time for the marriage of the Lamb.

However, "Blessed are those who are invited to the marriage supper of the Lamb" (Revelation 19:9). When John received the command to write these words, they meant more than when Jesus let the first invitation be sent out. "The invited" now means those who have said yes. Those who have understood what bliss it is to have received such an invitation. Those who have been watchful. Those whose names are already written in the guestbook in heaven, the Book of Life.

John received a reminder of how fantastic it is to be invited to the wedding. He fell down before the angel of heaven that he talked to. It was a being from another world, so exalted and pure, that an insignificant sinner like John felt himself standing in the presence of something heavenly and divine. However, John was commanded to stand up. He was in the presence of a fellow servant. He was a member of the same brotherhood. He was invited to the marriage feast of the Lamb.

Then the King comes with all His angels. The images whirl by, all the things that allow John to imagine who it is that's going out to administer justice on earth. His cloak is dipped in blood, like the cloak He wore among the soldiers and on the steps to Pilate, the red cloak that became soaked in blood from His lashed back. It's the Redeemer who is going, the One who died for us all. Everything's been done that could be done so no one would be lost. He is the Word that was from the beginning and that came to the world to give the world life (John 1:1–4). Now the word goes out from His mouth, "living and active, sharper than any two-edged sword" (Hebrews 4:12). It has gone forth like that before, like a judge over the intentions of the heart and mind. Some people allowed their hearts to be judged at that time. Others refused. Now it goes forth for the last time. Now the iron scepter is stretched over the earth. "Scepter" is the same word as "rod" as in "Your rod and Your staff, they comfort me" (Psalm 23:4). The shepherd's rod, iron clad at the end, is there to keep the wild beasts at bay. It was good to find refuge under that scepter. Now it's serving its final purpose as the great divider. Joyous, then, is the one who can say: "The Lord is my Shepherd, I shall not want" (Psalm 23:1).

Lord, my heart trembles when I think about this and realize how serious it is when You pass judgment. How foolish I've been when I sometimes have wished You would come and intervene. Now I understand why You're waiting. Wait as long as You can. You didn't come to pass judgment on the world, but to save the world. And when You finally must judge, I know that You have done everything You could so no one has to serve the sentence. You alone know when the time is right. Thank You that even that is in Your hands and You carry it in Your heart.

WEDNESDAY AFTER LAST SUNDAY BEFORE END OF TIME
Revelation 20:11–21:8

Behold, I am making all things new. Revelation 21:5

It is Christ, the King on His glorious throne, who says this. Now the time has come when everything can be new again, when death no longer exists, when no one complains, not a tear is shed, and there's no more pain.

This means that the time is over for the old world, for heaven and earth. Just as they were created from nothing, they disappear again into nothing.

However, all the creatures that were once created in the image of God and shared a part of His life still exist. They stand there, great and small, before the throne. And there the unavoidable separation is carried out, which is a prerequisite for a new world without torment: everything that causes suffering must be taken away. The first concern is death and the kingdom of death, the evil prince and his whole gang. But that also happens with some of them who should've been God's. That is the great tragedy. They've made the choice themselves. They didn't want to come when the invitation was sent out. They didn't get a part of the eternal life that came into the world. They're not in the Book of Life. And their deeds testify to that. They didn't love God. They are spared being part of what for them probably appeared to be the most unbearable thing of all: an eternity with God. Their world will be a world where God is gone forever. That it had to be like that is the great misfortune. We wonder how anyone can be happy again. We can only guess that God bears this sorrow alone and that He hides it in His heart. In the new world there will be no sorrow and no lamentation.

Everything is new. A new heaven and a new earth, and here we can hardly say any more. Where everything is new, then there is nothing to compare it with. All we know is that it'll be a real world, as real as the one we live in now, and that it's in some way united with God's heavenly world. The gap that sin and Satan created between God's world and mankind's world is gone. "God Himself will be with them" (Revelation 21:3) as He was in paradise. The new world comes "down out of heaven from God" (Revelation 21:2) and becomes one with the world, where seraphim and cherubim rejoice before the face of God. We can't describe that; we can only imagine it.

Lord, You who are unfathomable, You who are inconceivable in mercy and holiness, You see how our
hearts are in agony and writhe in pain over the
thought that someone could be lost. Someone
we love. Someone we think deserves only good.
Someone we would give everything for, maybe
even our own lives, if it could help them. Lord, we
suspect that You suffer much more, as much as
perfect love can suffer. Therefore we'll stop asking.
We lay even that sorrow on Your heart. We have
only one prayer: Lord, save us, Lord, have mercy
on us. For Jesus' sake.

THURSDAY AFTER
LAST SUNDAY
BEFORE
END OF TIME
Revelation 21:9–27

The holy city of Jerusalem came down out of heaven from
God. Revelation 21:10

John could see it and tried to describe it. We see, however, that it surpassed his ability. He uses all the words for
crystals and precious stones that he knows. He takes examples
from all the most beautiful among all the precious materials
he's seen on earth. He's amazed over the enormous sizes.
He notices that the Holy of Holies in the destroyed temple
of Jerusalem, whose length and breath and height were the

same proportions, in some way was a copy of the heavenly Jerusalem. He barely manages to give us a clear picture of all this splendor. Who can imagine a city that is as high as it is long? And what was it with the streams and trees John saw later? We have to stop asking. All we have left is a vision of something shining, crystal clear and at the same time brilliantly colorful, unfathomable and fascinating.

Here, however, there's a little feature we should notice. "They will bring into it the glory and honor of the nations" (Revelation 21:26). God had already promised that through the prophets, and this must in some way allude to the best and most precious that exists here, in the creation we live in now. It still is God's good creation. There is something here that bears witness to God's glory, something that bears His kindness inside itself. It can be color or shape, melody or rhythm. It can be the ring in a kind voice or the warmth of a mother's caress. In some way this will be preserved and be taken into God's New Jerusalem. In the new world we'll see sights that we were overcome by in this world already, or listen to sounds, hear a bird sing, and smell scents that are already a song of praise to God. It'll be different and yet still possible to recognize. We can only have a vague idea of all this, however, and reality will show how pale and paltry our ideas were, even the happiest ones.

Lord, here we are in silent worship. So much beauty and fascination, so much joy and fellowship You've already given us. If we only had received this life and nothing more, that would be reason enough to thank You continuously. Now You say to us, however, that all of this is just a premonition, a little reflection of the glory to come. We bow our heads for Your majesty and worship You in Your glory, not because You wish to give us a portion of it, but because You alone are holy, You alone are powerful, You alone are exalted and adored in Your glory. Praise be to You, Father, Son, and Holy Ghost, for ever and ever.

FRIDAY AFTER
LAST SUNDAY
BEFORE
END OF TIME
Revelation 22:1–15

Blessed is the one who keeps the words of the prophecy of this book. Revelation 22:7

Those words are in the Bible's last chapter. That's probably not a coincidence. Although from the beginning they obviously refer to Revelation, they can be said about the entire book, for the entire Scripture contains the prophetic Word, the message from God. And blessed is he who keeps the Word.

It's Jesus who says this. The Resurrected One said the same thing to John that He said to His disciples in Galilee. Blessed are those who hear God's Word and keep it. These words are wise and true. They are a greeting from God, from the Father who longs after His children. They are the invitation to His house, where the great feast of joy has been prepared. They're the call to the delightful world where there shall no more be anything accursed. Everywhere here on earth we meet the judgment that must pervade over all evil, everything that breaks down and stains God's wonderful creation. Since we ourselves are a part of that which is broken down and stained, that judgment pervades over us also. But now it can be revoked. Now the gates have been opened to a world where everything is whole and pure again and will remain that way forever. Now, as the saying goes: Come, for now everything is ready.

John says he once again fell on his knees before the angel that spoke to him. Once again, however, he was prevented from doing that, and this time the angel's words are directed at us. He says he is only a servant, even unto those "who [keep] the words of the prophecy in this book." Availing ourselves to the prophetic word means that we now are already servants, heirs, citizens in the world where the seraphim worship and where praise bustles around God's throne in never-ceasing joy. Today already. Already while I'm still here amidst temptations and anxieties, as a sinner who needs forgiveness every day. And still I am one of God's blessed, one of those who are His and who someday will see His face and eat of the tree of life and enter into that peculiar and wonderful city through its gates.

You, our Lord and God, are worthy of receiving praise and honor and power, You who were and are and shall come. Who shall not fear You, Lord? Who would not honor and love You? You alone are holy. You alone are the source of all goodness, the source of all forgiveness. You are righteous in Your judgment, infinite in Your mercy, incomprehensible in Your wisdom. To You belongs praise and wisdom and thanksgiving and honor and power and strength for ever and ever.

SATURDAY AFTER LAST SUNDAY BEFORE END OF TIME

Revelation 22:16–21

"Surely I am coming soon." Amen. Come, Lord Jesus!
Revelation 22:20

The Spirit and the bridegroom say: "Come." It's this call, this yearning, this hope that resounds throughout all genuine Christianity. It's the Spirit who compels us to say it. It's the bridegroom of the Church that says it. And whoever hears it can say: "Come." Every one of us who hears the peal in the call is infected with the same yearning and joins in: Come, Lord Jesus.

Living as a Christian is living with this yearning. It's not only believing in something that's always existed and will always remain the same, for example, that there is a God, that there are eternal laws regarding justice and love, that there's another world that's waiting for us when we die. No, Christianity means living in a fantastic drama. It's something that's happening right now. God is in the middle of saving and re-establishing the creation that has been subjected to a catastrophe. I am in the middle of this, God's fantastic achievement. I have heard the invitation. I've met the Master who was on His way and called me and said He must visit me in my house. I've been thirsty and have been able to drink from the well with the water of life.

And now I'm here with the Book that no man can add anything to or subtract anything from. I've heard the news. I know where I'm going. Every new day receives its purpose and content from the future I will meet: the great meeting with the Lord Jesus.

And the remarkable thing is that even if He waits, He

will come sometime anyway. He comes every day. He comes invisibly, and yet I can hear His voice. He comes secretly, and yet I notice that He's there. He comes every morning with a new day of mercy. And He'll come on the great day with an eternity of mercy. And He who can testify to that says: yes, I'm coming soon.

Come, Lord Jesus! I praise You, who came to me long before I knew You. I thank You for leaning over me and taking me in Your arms and baptizing me. I thank You for coming to me day after day, for looking for me and following me. I thank You that You're the one who's coming and that every day that lies ahead of me is Yours. Even my day of death. I thank You for the great day when You come again, when You come in all Your glory, You who are the same yesterday, today, and forever, my Savior and my King. *Amen. Come, Lord Jesus!*

THE NATIVITY
OF ST. JOHN
THE BAPTIST
Luke 1:57–80

Because of the tender mercy of our God. Luke 1:78

Midsummer Day is John the Baptist's birthday. That's what determines the day's Scripture reading, although we've also tried to include something about God's revelation in nature. In Sweden, midsummer is the time when things bloom and smell, grow and flourish. We're in the middle of the wonder of creation. Maybe that's why we think the first Epistle text for this day sounds strange when it refers to the grass that dries up and the flower that withers. That text is chosen, of course, because it includes a prophecy about John the Baptist. It was chosen a long time ago, by the Christians down by the beaches of the Mediterranean Sea. There, it also fits the time of year. In June in Palestine everything that is green withers and the hills are all brown. Even we, who live in the middle of the Nordic summer, may need to be reminded that the flower withers and that we are grass that dries up, but that the Lord's glory is revealed in the Word and that even we are created to see it.

For this is what midsummer reminds us: that God has revealed Himself not only in nature but through His Word, by sending His spokesmen, His prophets, and finally, His Son. John is one of the most peculiar and striking examples of how God reveals Himself. He was sent in a time when prophecies were thought to be dead. No one had heard from a prophet for several hundred years. His appearance is a result of a long series of strange interventions by God. Against all odds, Zechariah and Elizabeth have a son. Against every custom, Elizabeth wants to name him John. To everyone's surprise, the mute Zechariah writes the same name on a tablet they give him. Contrary to what is normal, the preacher's son goes out into the dessert, and when they least expect it, he emerges with the message for Israel that the great day is at hand. God has taken care of His people and now He's sending the Messiah. The kingdom of God is at hand.

When confronted with this, we must remember that this whole revelation has happened "because of the tender mercy of our God." All the abundant wealth and beauty we see in nature and life at its best is nothing, and at last would be just a temporary ray of sunshine over those who "sit in darkness and in the shadow of death" (Luke 1:79), if God hadn't in His mercy let "the sunrise . . . visit us from on high" (Luke 1:78) and given us knowledge of redemption so our sins can be forgiven.

Praise be to You, our Lord God, for You have taken care of Your people and prepared us for redemption. You wanted to give us the possibility to serve You without fear and do service before You in holiness and righteousness, we who had every reason to be afraid because all our righteousness is like a stained garment. We praise You for the sun and the seas, for the flowers and the bird's song, and for everything that gives us a glimpse of the paradise that our sin has shut us out from. We thank You that much more for Your merciful love that opens paradise for us again and that You send us the knowledge of Your redemption so our sins can be forgiven.

ST. MICHAEL
AND ALL ANGELS
Matthew 18:1–10

I tell you that in heaven their angels always see the face of My Father. Matthew 18:10

In the old days on Holy Michael's Day, people celebrated the archangel Michael. The reading is about him. The Gospel was chosen with the thought that Jesus speaks of angels. However, since it also is about children, Michael's Day has more and more taken on the character of a Sunday for the children.

Let's first look at the angels. Jesus, as well as the whole Bible, tells us that there's an invisible, heavenly world, a creation of a different sort from the heaven and earth we can see with our eyes. There God has surrounded Himself with myriads of beings who praise and serve Him: angels and archangels, princes, mighty ones, and whatever else they're called. Jesus tells us that the heavenly angels rejoice over a single sinner who repents. He says God could have sent twelve legions of angels to His rescue if he had wanted to conquer the wicked instead of dying for them.

These heavenly beings serve God as soon as He commands them. Since they belong to the world, that for us is the invisible world, we don't notice them. It's only when they serve God's revelation that they appear in a visible form, for example in the great milestones in the history of Revelation: Jesus' birth, His struggle in Gethsemane, His resurrection and journey to heaven. Once in a while they're sent as God's messengers to a specific individual, and it's been suggested that we humans, or at least some of us in certain instances, have our own guardian angels who watch over us.

That obviously applies to children, a group that includes the insignificant, the poor, the neglected, the despised. Their angels always see God's face, Jesus says. That shows how God watches over these who are the least. That allows us to imagine what a terrible sin it is to be seductive and destroy their faith. When Jesus points to a child as an answer to the disciples' question about who is the greatest in the kingdom of heaven, it's because a child in ancient times didn't have any rights or claims and least of all could be the object of any kind of leading position. That's what we all must become to get into the kingdom of heaven: Those without the claim of having deserved it. Only those who are (or become) small like that can come into the kingdom of heaven and God watches over them as over His darling children and His reasons for rejoicing.

We pray, our kind Lord and Savior, for all our small ones. We thank You for carrying them in Your heart. We pray that You protect them from everything that can take them away from You. Let us become the kind of people who never doubt the sincerity of our faith. Help us to show what deep security and joy it is to believe in You. Let our entire being emanate the joy and goodness that exists where You are. And when we can't do anything for them, then let Your guardian angel follow them. We ask this in Your blessed name.

THANKSGIVING DAY

Luke 17:11–19

Where are the nine? Luke 17:17

Of the ten lepers there was only one who made the effort to give thanks when Jesus healed them. The others showed gross ingratitude. Many show their ingratitude just by giving thanks in this way, only when they feel they have something special to give thanks for.

That someone who denies that God exists doesn't thank Him for His gifts is understandable. But there's an infinite number of those who count on God's existence, who receive most of His gifts without saying thank You. They do it day after day. Everything we receive regularly we so easily regard as something we have a right to, something we naturally should have. To live and be able to go to work, to have our near and dear ones around us, to have food on the table and heat in our homes so easily become things we take for granted. That's why it's such a useful reminder to thank God for food. Just that, however, is something many feel is so unnecessary, an old custom we can put away.

This is the attitude of dead faith. God has become something in the background. Almost everything goes on by itself. Only when things get difficult, when the children are missing, or your heart starts acting up, or the company starts to lay people off, or the rain pours down during the harvest season—*then* God should come to the rescue. If He does it right and like we asked, then we have a reason to give thanks.

The problem is that we don't know who God is. We've reduced Him to an aid in distress, a reserve we have in an emergency. We don't see Him just when He's the closest to us: in every event of everyday life, in everything we see around us, in everything that grows and blooms, everything that lives and moves, in our own body and all its cells and tissues. We don't realize how He says "let there be" in each and every new moment and how dependent we are on His words of creation. And least of all can we imagine how, in the middle of creation, there's an ongoing struggle between the Creator and the destroyer, where only God's constant help and mercy can save us from destruction.

Knowing God is having a well of thanksgiving that never runs dry.

Bless the Lord, O my soul, and all that is within me, bless His holy name! Bless the Lord, O my soul, and forget not all His benefits, who forgives all your iniquities, who heals all your diseases, who redeems your life from the pit, who crowns you with steadfast love and mercy, who satisfies you with good as long as you live, so that your youth is renewed like the eagle's. The Lord has established His throne in the heavens, and His kingdom rules over all. Bless the Lord, all His hosts, His ministers who do His will! Bless the Lord, all His works, in all places of His dominion. Bless the Lord, O my soul! (From Psalm 103.)

MONDAY AFTER THANKSGIVING DAY

2 Corinthians 1:1–11

For as we share abundantly in Christ's sufferings, so through Christ we share abundantly in comfort too.
2 Corinthians 1:5

Paul usually begins his letters by thanking God. In this letter he thanks "the Father of mercies and God of all comfort" (2 Corinthians 1:3)—what a wonderful name for God!—because He "comforts us in all our affliction" (2 Corinthians 1:4) so we, in turn, can comfort others in all the affliction that falls upon them. He says he has experienced the worst kind of affliction, so much so that he, who so many times before had seen the face of death, now was about to give life up. He says he needed that. He really had to trust solely and exclusively on the God who raises people from the dead. He was obviously saved from mortal danger at the last minute. He doesn't tell us what happened. Paul knows that even if he had been killed, God would still be the Father of all mercies and God of all comfort, worthy of praise and blessings forever.

For Paul, danger and affliction weren't small exceptions he was saved from so he could return to a peaceful and pleasant existence. "We were so utterly burdened beyond our strength that awe despaired of life itself. Indeed, we felt that we had received the sentence of death" (2 Corinthians 1:8–9). Yet Paul can give thanks. It's Christ's sufferings that overcome, and with them comes comfort. That comfort is enough for others also. Here comes a good, healing, redeeming power into the world, in the middle of afflictions.

What is meant by Christ's sufferings? Not just sufferings that we endure *for Christ's sake* (persecution, for example) but everything we suffer *through faith in Christ* (sickness, for example). We are His members. Therefore, we experience the hate that was directed at Him. That'll be plenty for the disciple if the same thing happens to him that happened to his Master. But we must also share in the sufferings that torment all men. Perhaps sickness, perhaps starvation, perhaps war. But we also share them with Christ. He is with us, He lives inside of us, He is present in the midst of affliction, just like He was with the robber on Golgotha. Christ's sufferings can seem to be overflowing, Paul says. However, then comfort comes that is also overflowing. That comfort is the assurance that I'm not alone, that He'll help me through this and I can receive it in such a way that I'll come closer to Him and allow His life to flow in me and, consequently, flow out in the world. As a matter of fact, your suffering can be a blessing in the world. Paul experienced it, and that's why he can say that when he's hit with affliction, it is for the comfort and salvation of others. And that's why he can also give thanks in the midst of affliction.

Blessed be the God and Father of our Lord Jesus Christ, the Father of mercies and God of all comfort! Blessed are You because You also share in suffering. I thank You for all the difficult days in my life that brought me closer to You. I thank You for the darkness, where I learned to believe without seeing. I thank You for those who carried their suffering through Your power and showed me that life is always worth living when we have You. Blessed are You, always and for everything, through Jesus Christ, our Lord.

TUESDAY AFTER THANKSGIVING DAY

2 Corinthians 3:1–18

The letter kills, but the Spirit gives life. 2 Corinthians 3:6

Of all the things Paul has said, these words may be the most often quoted. In some way it coincides with what people think is right. However, what they think doesn't at all coincide with what Paul says here.

As these words are normally translated, they say—as we all know—that you don't have to take seriously what the Bible literally says. Then you'll just become a slave of the written word and run the risk of acting in diametric opposition to the Spirit of Christ. Instead, you should allow yourself to be led by the Spirit and follow your heart's feeling for what is just and correct. Then you'll be a living person who honors a more spiritual Christianity.

From the context it's obvious that Paul doesn't say or mean anything like that. When he speaks of the letter, he means the Law, *God's* Law, the Law that was carved into stone tablets. God's Law plays an important part in the world. It is the dispensation of death, the dispensation of condemnation. For the Law sentences us all to death. The Law can't make us alive. It can't bring us to God. Still, it comes from God. Even the dispensation of condemnation has its glory. But since no one has been able to keep God's Law—"the letter"—God has established the "ministry of righteousness," "from the ministry of the Spirit" (2 Corinthians 3:8–9) when He gives us life by bringing us to Christ. To be able to do this, the Spirit also needs help from the Law and the letter now. The Spirit is going to convince us of our sin. We have to take the Law seriously for that to happen. If we start to fiddle and tamper with the Law by giving it a more "spiritual" interpretation, then we lose its point. It doesn't kill anymore, and we find ourselves in the false Christianity the Bible warns us about so often. We think everything is fine. When God's Commandments become difficult, we give them a spiritual interpretation. When the world takes offense at Jesus' words, we can always adjust them a little to avoid the worst.

That slavery under the Law the Bible warns about is making the Law the way to salvation so it becomes the focus of our faith. Then we still have the same veil over our hearts that prevented the Jews from seeing the real meaning of the Scriptures. That veil can remain hanging, even if we don't ask for the letter of the Law but, instead, make a spiritual interpretation of it. We live under the Law anyway (but under a watered down and harmless law). Here it's important that we allow the Spirit to convert us to Christ. And for that the letter of the Law is also necessary.

Dear Holy Spirit, I praise You and thank You for Your wonderful freedom, which only You can give. I thank You that I don't have to fiddle with Your Commandments to be able to feel free. I thank You that You have made me free from all guilt and that I don't have to deserve my happiness and bliss. I thank You that You have made me free to serve. You have taken me to my Savior. You have allowed me to see what He has done for me. You have filled my heart with joy and thanksgiving. Now, help me to look at Him and live so closely to Him that a ray of His glory can also fall on me and be reflected in my joy and my service, to the glory and honor of my Lord Jesus.

WEDNESDAY AFTER THANKSGIVING DAY

2 Corinthians 4:16–5:10

Though our outer nature is wasting away, our inner nature is being renewed day by day. 2 Corinthians 4:16

What do I *really* have to thank God for?

That's what a lot of people wonder when it's time to thank God: I have an ugly nose, no one says that I'm charming, I've always been unlucky in almost everything. In all my life I've never been happy with my work, and now I'm getting old. I notice that I get short of breath on the stairs and I can't read the fine print like I could before. . . .

What's strange is that another person could experience the same things and thank God the whole time, sincerely thankful, happy and satisfied with life. Where the discontented see only difficulties, the thankful always find something to be happy about.

Like this thing about getting old! No one likes to get old. Paul describes it dramatically. It's like living in a condemned building. You've been given notice to move out and already the first preparations are made for demolition. One thing after the other is turned off and doesn't work anymore.

Still, we're in good spirits, Paul says. We know where we're moving to. We know God has other living arrangements for us. We're moving *home*, home to the Lord Christ. God is doing something fantastic to us. Not only did He give us life and allow us to live on this earth all these years, He has something even better prepared for us. He's going to provide a new existence for us with a new body, one like Christ received at His resurrection. He's already begun. He's allowed us to come to faith in Christ and ignited a new life in us. So far, it's still invisible, something internal. But it's there. As proof and as an inkling of what's to come, we've received the Spirit, He who witnesses with our spirit that we're the children of God.

The move itself can be unpleasant. Who wants to die? Paul says he would prefer to live until Christ comes. Then he could go right into the new life. Dying means being deprived of the body we live in and becoming naked, destitute, deserted. And yet, this grief is just like every kind of grief. It's as light as a feather, if you see it in the correct context and know what comes later. What can you say besides thank You?

I say thank You and thank You again, dear Lord, that I have come into Your world and live there. That You surround me on all sides and fulfill every day. That You wanted me to recognize Your name and be Your child. Not only that You've given me this life with everything that's good, but also a life in Your glory, where one day contains more joy and delight than a thousand years on earth. I thank You, Father of mercies and God of all comfort, You who are the well of inexhaustible joy and the giver of all good gifts, through Jesus Christ, our Lord.

2 Corinthians 5:14–6:2

In Christ God was reconciling the world to Himself.
2 Corinthians 5:19

That's theology.

You sometimes get that response when you bring up reconciliation. "Common people don't understand things like that." In a way it's true. Jesus and the apostles have told us that there are huge, infinitely important contexts that none of us can see or understand unless God's Spirit works on us. This reality and this context is what people so often call—a little disparagingly and negatively—theology. They mean it's something only pastors care about. Maybe that is true sometimes and, if so, that's really bad because here it's a question of something that is necessary for us all if we want to be right with God.

Even someone who seriously wants to be a Christian and therefore listens to God's Word can initially have a hard time understanding verses in the New Testament like the one we've read today. However, if they've been at it awhile and have the contexts explained to them, they notice that there is content as well as logic. The words become understandable and meaningful. The entire New Testament talks about this, that God was in Christ, that He Himself came down to us, that He made atonement for us by taking upon Himself the consequences of our fall and our wickedness. Christ was literally "made to be sin for us," when He made our sin His own. And now we can "in Him become the righteousness of God" (2 Corinthians 5:21). When we, through faith, become His and become a part of Him, and receive a portion of the righteousness that otherwise is only His. In that way something new comes. The old—guilt and the bondage of sin—now belong to the past. The new man, a new creation, lives inside of us.

The one who claims that this is theology can at best know Christ "after the flesh" as Paul put it; in other words, in a purely human way, without understanding what God meant and wanted. However, it's just that way of seeing that we have to conquer.

Now, two important things come from reconciliation, Paul says. First, that there's an office of reconciliation. God wants this to be preached. He's sent out His messengers to speak on Christ's behalf. And they should preach just this theology: Be reconciled to God!

Furthermore: Christ's love forces us to. Thankfulness and devotion to Him who died for us and reconciled us with God become the driving forces in our lives. He died for me. Consequently I have died. My sin was also there on Golgotha. My old Adam with all its godlessness received its death sentence there. But He took that sentence upon Himself. Now I can live with Him and for Him. Now every day is a day of salvation and a time of pleasure, when His mercy surrounds me and carries me once again, and when He has duties for me once again that I can do in His service.

You have multiplied, O Lord my God, Your wondrous deeds and Your thoughts toward us; none can compare with You! Were I to proclaim and tell of them, they would be more than can be numbered. Burnt offering and sin offering You have not required. Then I said, "Lo, I come; I delight to do Your will, Your law is within my heart." So then I know that You, O Lord, will not withhold Your mercy from me, let Your steadfast love and Your faithfulness ever preserve me! As for me, I am poor and needy; but the Lord takes thought for me. You are my help and my deliverer; do not tarry, O my God! (From Psalm 40.)

FRIDAY AFTER THANKSGIVING DAY
2 Corinthians 9:1–15

Thanks be to God for His inexpressible gift!
2 Corinthians 9:15

True thankfulness is when someone can always give thanks. A strange kind of thankfulness in the eyes of the world! Here, it's not a question of receiving, but, instead, giving. The whole chapter is really the kind of begging letter churches and charitable organizations usually send out that we're so tired of getting.

Here we have the first example of a big relief action between churches. The ancient church in Jerusalem was in need. Many were unemployed and rejected from their families when they became Christian. Those who had possessions sold them and lived on that money as long as they could. But that was no long term solution.

Now they were collecting money among the Gentile Christians. Paul was the driving force. In the previous chapter, he talks about the fund-raising in Macedonia (for instance in Thessalonica and Philippi). He does it with great joy. Although the congregations there lived in great poverty, they *insistently* asked for the *favor* of participating. And they gave voluntarily and way beyond their means. And best of all: "They gave according to their means, as I can testify, and beyond their means, of their own accord . . . and this, not as we expected, but they gave themselves first to the Lord and then by the will of God to us" (2 Corinthians 8:3–5). They were truly committed with their hearts and souls for Christ's sake.

Now Paul organizes the fundraiser in Corinth. He sends Titus and two other brothers there, who were chosen by the congregations as auditors to see to it that everything was handled correctly.

Paul didn't dictate what each individual should give. He left that to Christ. Each one should give according to his own mind. God loves a cheerful giver. Instead, Paul describes what a gift like this means when it's given willingly and from the heart. It not only alleviates distress, it also generates thanksgiving to God. It creates fellowship between the giver and receiver. It arouses the desire in others to give for Christ's sake. It results in people honoring and praising God because there are others who "obediently acknowledged the gospel of Christ." In other words, the gift becomes a sermon, a proclamation of Christ's love and of the happiness of being His.

I thank You, my Lord and Savior, for the great mercy and favor of being one of those You use when You want to help and please others. Help me to always serve You with joy. When I have to force my old, obstinate self, let me even do that with joy, as a tribute of thankfulness to You and as a sacrifice for everything You've done for me. Help me to sow abundantly, as You sow, without questioning if a portion is lost. Allow me to be lavish, like You,

and give of what I have, in a way You can bless.
Everything to the honor of Your name and for the
sake of Your love.

SATURDAY AFTER THANKSGIVING DAY
Psalm 103:1–13

Bless the LORD, O my soul; and forget not all His benefits.
Psalm 103:2

"Has God been good to me? I certainly haven't noticed
that!"

That reaction isn't unusual when people are encouraged
to thank God. They think they've had enough problems:
accidents, sickness, problems with the car, lousy weather, difficulties within the family. And I'm supposed to thank God
on top of all that!

Behind that reaction there's a view of existence that
may be obvious but is false nonetheless. It's the unconverted
person's way of regarding God. Maybe God exists. In that
case He's very kind. We've heard so often that He is Love.
He should also show that then, particularly when it's needed
most: in other words, when I'm in trouble. I can handle most
things by myself and don't need God's help. I can handle my
job, make my own plans, have my own interests, and plan
my own life. Then an unforeseen obstacle turns up. There
are things I can't control. The weather, for example, or business cycles or the normal function of cells that guarantee that

I won't get cancer or a heart attack. God should watch over that. But, according to many, He's not good at that at all.

Behind this whole way of thinking is a perception of God and the world that is common, but false. It's the egocentric individual's view of the world. Here I am. I exist and what's most important for me is *my* life. It's *mine* and I decide over it. Then, of course, there are many things and forces around me that I have to take into consideration and that may be of use to me. God, for example.

If you have that view of God, it's not strange if you become dissatisfied with Him. For God has a completely different plan for my life and He is carrying out that plan. When He allowed me to be born—among uncountable other reasoning beings, men and angels, in this world and the heavenly world—it was because He wished to share the most fantastic of all gifts and possibilities: the gift of life. He wanted to share His happiness with us, the happiness of being a conscious being with a will, prepared to experience the joy of being a living, thinking being. And to be able to experience that joy in God's fellowship, in a world of harmony and beauty.

We know how the unforeseen obstacle arose, the great insurrection that disturbed the harmony in the work of creation. God could have destroyed His fallen creation. Instead, He's done His utmost to save and re-establish it. And His plan for every little human being is just this: to win that person back.

Consequently, God doesn't exist to help us in problematic situations or with the plans we have for what we call *our* lives. We've received our lives to be able to be His children and share His joy. He's made that possible for all of us through His great deed in Christ. And He's the boundlessly loving One who is constantly making new attempts and finding new ways to reach us through His good work and bring us home to Him.

We truly have a reason to remember all His benefits: He forgives us all our iniquities, redeems our lives from the pit, and crowns us with steadfast love and mercy.

Praise the Lord, O my soul! I will praise the Lord as long as I live. I will sing praises to my God as long as I have being. Our God is a God of salvation, and to God, the Lord, belongs escape from death. Praise is due to You, O God, in Zion. O You who hear prayer! To You shall all flesh come. When our transgressions prevail over us, You forgive them. Blessed is he whom You choose and bring near, to dwell in Your courts!

(From Psalms 146, 68, and 65.)

ALL SAINTS' DAY
Matthew 5:1–12

Blessed are the poor in spirit, for theirs is the kingdom of heaven. Matthew 5:3

All Saints' Day has become the day when we talk about heaven, think about the dead, and decorate their graves. It has become roughly what is called "all souls day" in southern Europe, which is the day after All Saints' Day. The combination has its risks. It has probably contributed to the misunderstanding that all dead people are saints and that you will certainly go to heaven when you die.

All Saints' Day is about the saints. Even we evangelicals

talk about saints. As a matter of fact, all Christians can be called "holy." That's what they're called in the New Testament. That means they've been taken away from this world, cleansed in Christ's blood, and united with Christ Himself. However, there are those among God's holy ones who have been so affected by the fellowship with Christ that they become a living testimony that He truly is the living Savior. They help the rest of us to believe. They become irrefutable proof that God lives. We call those people saints.

We often times imagine people like these must be very impressive, strong, and successful in every way. Jesus describes what they are really like in the Beatitudes. He gives us a picture of the new life that follows from faith in Christ. These blessed ones don't *feel* blessed. They are poor in the spirit and feel that they are lacking in everything. That's why they are hungry and thirsty for righteousness. Actually it says: for *the* righteousness, the only true righteousness is that which Jesus possesses and which won't be fulfilled until we become like Him in the resurrection. They mourn, both for themselves and others. They're abused, persecuted, and lied about because they don't live like other people. However, they're gentle. They don't demand their rights. They don't put themselves on a pedestal. They establish peace by suffering rather than fighting. They're merciful because they know how much forgiveness they need every day. And they're pure in their hearts, sincere, without trying to find blame or make excuses.

And what does Jesus promise them? Everything that came with Him and will be victorious and apparent when the world is born again. They will be comforted when God dries their tears. They will possess the new earth that God will create. They will be satisfied when they become the dinner guests in God's kingdom. They will be counted among God's children and will see Him face-to-face. In other words: they belong to God's kingdom.

Dear Lord Jesus, we ask You to give us saints. You see how much we need people to strengthen us in our faith and show us how to live. But help us, Lord, so we don't want saints to be different from how You want them. Help us to let go of all our longing for things that impress and strengthen in a worldly manner. And make us willing to follow the path of Your true saints so we renounce what is grand and gets a response and, instead, dare to be small and powerless in Your way so Your power can fill us. Honor be to Your name and help to our fellow human beings.

SUNDAY AFTER ALL SAINTS' DAY
Luke 12:4–7

I will warn you whom to fear. Luke 12:5

Who isn't afraid of dying?

It's human to be afraid. Atheists sometimes try to convince themselves and others that we have absolutely no reason to be afraid of the fact that we someday will cease to exist. Not existing is something absolutely no one should feel any unease about. It's nothing to be afraid of.

Yet we can't get away from the fact that death scares us. As a matter of fact, it's something of a hallmark, something that shows that man isn't only an intelligent animal. We are created by God, and God has instilled eternity in the hearts of mankind. There's something inside of us that says that life is the right thing, the natural thing, the purpose of it all. We certainly don't have to be ashamed of flinching in the face of death.

But—here's another "but"—it's what Jesus speaks of in today's text. Jesus tells us there is something we really should fear. It's not only dying. God has given us a life no one can take away from us. If we belong to those whom Jesus calls here His friends, those who believe in Him and have received the gift only He can give, then no one can take away life from us. You can slay the body. It's going to die anyway. But he who believes shall live.

What we really should fear is falling away from God. You can lose your soul, lose the connection to forgiveness, and the well of life in Jesus Christ. And if you die in that condition, separated from God, you will remain separated from Him. You can truly be lost, helplessly and forever. There's a state that Jesus, like the Jews of His time, called *Gehenna*. The Bible speaks of it in pictures that can be interpreted differently. However, one thing is perfectly clear: Jesus tells us that it is the greatest of all imaginable misfortunes to end up in that state. It's something we really should fear.

The Sunday after All Saints' Day has been translated to "our eternal hope." That hope isn't that we have an immortal soul and therefore will find ourselves in a more joyous state when we die. We have another hope, and this week is about that hope.

Lord, teach me the right way to both fear and not fear. To love You so deeply that I'm afraid of everything that could separate me from You. To not be afraid of death, which is only the gate to home for believers. To be able to be glad if I someday find out that I soon will be home.

MONDAY AFTER SUNDAY AFTER ALL SAINTS' DAY

Luke 20:27–40

For they cannot die anymore, because they are equal to angels and are sons of God, being sons of the resurrection.
Luke 20:36

That's what eternal life is about. It's a completely new existence that's all together different from life here on earth.

But "how" is it?

Jesus gives us a hint. It's a life like the "angels" and "sons of God." In order to understand those words, we must look a little closer at them and the world—the invisible world.

There's an invisible world. In the Bible it can be called "heaven" or "the heavens." That's where God's throne is. There God is surrounded by all the beings He's given life and existence to so they could be joyful about living. We get a glimpse of them in the New Testament: "dominions or rulers or authorities" (Colossians 1:16). Sometimes they're called "sons of God."

The heavenly world is created by God. Only God Himself is eternal—the eternal Father, the Son, who is "the firstborn of all creation" (Colossians 1:15), and the Spirit who from eternity emanates from the Father and the Son and therefore already at creation "hovering over the face of the waters," as it says in the creation account (Genesis 1:2).

The heavenly world was created *before* the visible world. God laid the foundation for the world and stipulated its proportions "when the morning stars sang together and all the sons of God shouted for joy" (Job 38:7). In other words, they were witnesses to the creation of the universe, these joyous spirits that God had already created (even "the morning stars" are mentioned here as spirits like this).

Now, however, God has also created a visible heaven that we see arching over us. It's a part of our universe, which the Greeks called "cosmos." The Jews didn't have a comparable name and instead used to say "heaven and earth." However, they could also indicate that there was a visible heaven. They used to speak of the firmament. "And God called the firmament heaven" (Genesis 1:8 KJV), as it says in the creation account. In other words, God gave the visible heaven something that would give us an idea of what the invisible one is. He put His majesty in heaven (Hebrews 1:1–3) so it allows us to get a glimpse of the invisible heaven's majesty and brilliance, its brightness and glory. But of course it isn't the invisible heaven where Christ now stands before God for our sake.

It's that heaven that even we some day will go into in Christ's hands.

Lord, the heavens are telling the glory of God, and the firmament proclaims His handiwork. O Lord my God, You are very great! You are clothed with honor and majesty, covered with light as with a garment; You stretched out the heavens like a tent. The Lord is high above all nations, and His glory above the heavens! Who is like the Lord our God, who is seated on high, who looks far down upon the heavens and the earth?
(From Psalms 19, 104, and 113.)

TUESDAY AFTER
SUNDAY AFTER
ALL SAINTS' DAY
Isaiah 14:12–17

I will make myself like the Most High. Isaiah 14:14

In these words devout Israelites found the answer to the question of how evil originated. We've already talked about this place, Babylon, the wicked city that "made the world like a desert and . . . did not let his prisoners go home" (Isaiah 14:17). However, like so much else in the Old Testament, Babylon has a double meaning. It embodies all the power that's hostile to God in the world: It's a symbol for the kingdom of Satan. Here we can see what its innermost spirit is.

Even the devil is created by God. Even he at one time belonged to the spirits that rejoiced in the presence of God. He revolted, however. He wanted to climb up and sit next to God, establish his own throne and become like the Most High. He wanted to decide all by himself. He wanted to show that he no longer had to obey anyone. And since all good things are subject to God, only evil remained for someone who wanted to be different.

Even the New Testament talks about "angels that did not keep their own position, but left their proper dwelling," "angels that sinned" (Jude 6, 2 Peter 2:4). They no longer wanted to be in God's world. They followed Satan, and all this happened *before* the creation of the world. The serpent, the evil one, meets us already in paradise. And his temptation is just that demonic thought that possessed him: You can be like God! You can declare what is right and wrong, allowed and prohibited!

Accordingly, the invisible world has met with a disaster, a great catastrophe that forever will divide it into two kingdoms. The instigator managed to remain in God's heaven for a long time. He came as the Prosecutor. He had the option to quote God's own Law. However, we have already heard that he was brought down. Christ has taken from him every possibility of referring to God's righteousness in an effort to condemn us. There is no longer a place for him and his angels in heaven. However, in the visible world, the cosmos we are now part of, he is still at work, he who is called "the destroyer of mankind," he who never sets his prisoners free and whose rightful name is "The Destroyer." Consequently, the powers of evil are a reality. You can follow him, "the prince of the power of the air, the spirit that is now at work in the sons of disobedience" (Ephesians 2:2). But you can also be saved from him. "The Lord will rescue me from every evil and save me for His heavenly kingdom. To Him be the glory for ever and ever. Amen" (2 Timothy 4:18).

Lord, so all evil comes from not wanting what You want. Not thinking like You, not loving like You, not being like You. And I know I'm guilty of all that. I know how often I think the thoughts the foe wants me to. And You've forgiven me everything! You've lowered it all into the bottomless ocean of atonement and mercy! We, who were supposed to descend into the kingdom of death, You've allowed to be taken up into heaven. We praise You. And we thank You that we can also praise You in Your heavenly world, in the immense happiness that only exists where everything is Yours and filled with Your glorious light and joy.

Colossians 1:13–23

For in Him all the fullness of God was pleased to dwell . . .
whether on earth or in heaven. Colossians 1:19, 20

How should we come back? How was God supposed
to get us back? When the catastrophe had occurred and
the kingdom of Satan was established, when mankind was
dragged along in the fall and wickedness forced its way into
creation everywhere?

In the first ten verses of the first chapter in Colossians,
Paul made a sweep over the complete course of the world
and answered all those questions. Everything happened
through Christ. At one time everything was created through
Him, and *for* Him. That means that Christ was already there
in the creation, and as firstborn, the possibility for salvation
would remain open, no matter what happened. And when
the catastrophe had occurred and creation was blemished and
destroyed, Christ stepped into it. He, who belonged to the
invisible world, which was still pure and unspoiled, He took
upon Himself the image of something that belonged to the
visible world, which had fallen away. He came "in the likeness of sinful flesh and for sin" (Romans 8:3). However, in
this earthly body God allowed all fullness to dwell. Godhead's
complete fullness came into our world. It took upon itself
everything that was evil and unjust and suffered all of the
consequences. So God could "reconcile to Himself all things,"
Paul emphasizes that it occurred "on earth or in heaven"
(Colossians 1:20). Reconciliation included the entire cosmos.
This means that everything that before, through its wicked
nature, was helplessly separated from God, now can be purified from guilt and be reunited with God. However, that can

only happen through Christ. God has "reconciled [us] in His body of flesh by His death" (Colossians 1:22). It happened in Christ, we find it in Him. He stood up and became "the beginning, the firstborn from the dead" (Colossians 1:18), the Head of His Church, the King in the new kingdom. And now God has "transferred us to the kingdom of His beloved Son" (Colossians 1:13), the kingdom where everything is reconciled.

This doesn't mean that now we're ready to go into God's heaven and unite with the invisible world. The marks from the grasp of evil are still there. With us we carry the only desire, temptations, and therefore also suffering, sickness and death. Not before God intervenes with a new creation and transforms everything that was old, can we be a part of His world. And this will happen first in the resurrection.

Lord, I long. I long to finally be free from everything I hate because it's evil in Your eyes, and that I nevertheless drag along with me. From everything that makes work heavy and the day gray. From everything that hinders me from living in Your presence and to be able to talk to You and rejoice in Your kindness. Forgive me for my ingratitude. I know it's far more that I could imagine or request that I, with all my sin and all my burdens, still can be Your child, free from guilt now already and certain of being spared the burden the day You call me home. Your mercy is enough for me. I can't ask for more. And yet You will give me much, much more, You who are incomprehensible, ever kind, ever merciful.

THURSDAY AFTER
SUNDAY AFTER
ALL SAINTS' DAY
Colossians 2:6–15

In Him the whole fullness of deity dwells bodily.
Colossians 2:9

Twice in today's Bible reading it talks about "principalities and powers." It's correct that it's about forces in the spiritual world. We can't believe that they're far away in another world. What Paul says, namely, is that they're all around us.

He warns us about a philosophy that wanted to make the Gospel more accepted by adapting it to the generally accepted view of the world and what people thought they knew about the forces of nature (which the Romans called "the elements"). That was a mixture of knowledge that was thought to be able to control these forces and an indefinable fear that sensed something unpredictable, superior, possibly hostile behind the forces of nature. The modern man is, when all is said and done, very much like people in Paul's day and age.

Now Paul tells us that all this fear is false and unnecessary. Certainly there are unknown forces and they're not to be played with. The fact that people have a superstitious fear for all kinds of things, or that they talk about "fate," is the last remnant of a completely correct knowledge about the existence of an invisible world and that we can be helplessly left in the hands of the unknown. However, now Christ is the Head of all of the world's spiritual forces. The good ones are in His service. He has conquered the evil ones. Evil's triumph and its real asset was that we were a part of it. There was an indictment, established in God's Law that was proof of it. However, that was what was nailed to the cross.

Accordingly, there's forgiveness and salvation in Christ.

In Him all of God's fullness lives "bodily"—in other words, in His body. However, in this body He has also borne all our sins. They have been reconciled with Him; now we have forgiveness. We've been incorporated in His body, become a part of it at Baptism. Paul calls Baptism the circumcision in Christ. Just as the Jew was taken up into God's nation after six days, so shall we now walk in Him, openly and securely, well aware that all kinds of forces and principalities and powers, whatever they may be, cannot separate us from God's love in Christ, our Savior.

Therefore I lift my eyes, my Lord Jesus, and look up to You. When I see You, I know that I have the whole heavenly world in front of me. At one time it was so far away from me and so unreal. But now You've come to me and I know that Your heavenly world is also my world, that I also belong there and that I will some day see it, as real and as near as my world is to me today. And I can already imagine how it is, filled with joyous spirits, of life and motion, of song and worship. It's gotten so close to me since I got to know You. I want to thank You for that also.

FRIDAY AFTER
SUNDAY AFTER
ALL SAINTS' DAY
Revelation 7:9–17

Therefore are they before the throne of God, and serve Him day and night in His temple. Revelation 7:15

What is eternal life like?

We can only guess about eternal life. We hear accounts from those who have seen the veil drawn aside. They describe their visions for us and we at least get an idea of life in the face of God.

It's namely a life in the presence of God, in uninterrupted fellowship with God. God's glory shines through the entire existence. Christ is among His own. Heaven isn't a place where we live by ourselves with our own things, and now and again get a glimpse of the Most High and visit Him once in awhile. No, everything is about God. Just because of that everything is filled with joy we can't understand now. It's God's personal joy, that great original joy over being alive and existing in a world that's pure goodness, power and beauty.

At some time life with God can be described as a rest, as wonderful relaxation after the battle here, where we always run the risk of getting off the path and being lost. However, rest shouldn't be misconstrued with idleness. Everything we know about God's kingdom speaks about life and commotion, something like a billowy liturgy with constant changes, always new contents and constantly new efforts, something that never gets old, never wears down, never becomes routine.

Maybe we begin to sense why a "good" person, someone who's always done his best but never really cared about God, wouldn't have been able to live in heaven. To become one with God in this way and live in constant worship is something that our fallen human nature feels is absurd and impossible. We have to be born again, reunited with Christ and created anew in the resurrection. Therefore, the distinctive feature for those who stand before God's throne and serve Him day and night is also that "they have washed their robes and made them white in the blood of the Lamb" (Revelation 7:14). They have been won over by "Him who loves us and has freed us from our sins by His blood and made us a kingdom, priests to His God and Father" (Revelation 1:5–6). That's why they now can serve Him in His temple and experience it as complete joy.

I will extol You, my God and King, and bless Your name for ever and ever. Great is the Lord and greatly to be praised, and His greatness is unsearchable. On the glorious splendor of Your majesty, and on Your wondrous works, I will meditate. All Your works shall give thanks to You, O Lord, and all Your saints shall bless You. They shall speak of the glory of Your kingdom, and tell of Your power. Your kingdom is an everlasting kingdom, and Your dominion endures throughout all generations.

Praise the Lord from the heavens; praise Him in the heights! Praise Him, all His angels; praise Him, all His hosts! For His name alone is exalted, His majesty is above earth and heaven. (From Psalms 145 and 148.)

1 Thessalonians 4:13–18

For the Lord Himself will descend from heaven.
1 Thessalonians 4:16

How are the dead going to be resurrected?

We can ask and we can ponder. There's no point, however. The only thing we know about these things is what the Bible tells us. And in the Bible the whole interest revolves around one thing: Christ is coming, Christ will judge, Christ will be victorious, Christ redeems. About the other things, the things that concern the resurrection and the new existence we'll experience, we get only a hint.

The Thessalonians, who hadn't been Christian for a year yet and had only been instructed by Paul during the short time he was in town, believed that Christ's second coming was so near that they all would experience it. That's why they were so dismayed when one of their own died. What's going to happen to them?

Paul explains that they don't need to mourn. Even their dead will meet the Lord on resurrection day. Obviously he figures that most of them, as well as he himself, will live to see that day. (As we've seen, he later understood that maybe it wasn't God's will.)

Then Paul tells about the great day when Christ Himself will come. "A cry of command" resounds, a word with power, a command that penetrates everything. God's trumpet and an archangel's voice resounds, something that can be compared only with God's all powerful words of creation, something all-encompassing, all-penetrating, overwhelming.

How could Paul know that? He says it himself: he had Jesus' word on it. The evangelists tell us about how much

Jesus, during the last week in Jerusalem, talked with them about things like that.

That Christ "descended" means that the invisible world, that which, literally speaking, is up there, on high, now comes to us, visible, in all its power and glory. That means the end of the old creation. Space and time are no longer what they were. Those who have lived in the past are again present. The entire population of the world is gathered in front of the Judge.

Those who died in the Lord rise to a new life. The old one is forever past, and they bear the image of a new world. Those who are still alive (those of us who are still living, maybe we should rightfully say—who knows?) will be transformed so we're like Him. Just as Christ once went into the invisible world when He was taken away by a sparkling cloud and disappeared from the disciples' sight, so shall we the same way go into the light. However, now it will be to see Him as He is and "always be with the Lord" (1 Thessalonians 4:17).

Teach us, dear Lord Jesus, not to mourn when we don't need to, and to mourn in the right way when we have a reason to. Death is not our great misfortune; it is life without You. To die in You is to live with You. Help us to live faithfully so we have no anxiety for our souls when we die. Help us to live so faithfully and die so openly that everyone understands that they don't have to mourn as if we had no hope. And help us to be conscientious about other people's souls while they're alive and relieve us from powerless concern for them when they're dead.

CHRISTMAS EVE
Isaiah 9:2–7

For to us a child is born, to us a son is given; and the
government shall be upon His shoulder. Isaiah 9:6

This would be the sign, of something tremendous: The
Messiah was born, God had intervened and tremendous joy
awaited the whole world—a joy that caused all the angels in
heaven to sing.

It was a peculiar sign! A newborn child, swaddled in
clothes, and lying in a manger. A homeless baby, born in a
stable. This was God's gift to humanity, with whom He was
well pleased.

A Son to us was given. God gave us His own Son. He
was born as a defenseless human child on a cold winter night
in one of the caves where Bethlehem's farmers kept their
animals.

"And the government will be upon His shoulder." How
was this possible?

One of the great church fathers, Heironymus, gave the
answer in a childish but charming story. "Often, when I
look to Bethlehem," he wrote, "my heart converses with the
child Jesus. I say: 'Lord Jesus, You are freezing. You shiver.
It is so hard and uncomfortable where You sleep—so that
I may be blessed. How will I ever be able to repay?' Then
I think I hear the Child answering: 'I don't want anything,
dear Heironymus. Just wait. Difficult times await Me, in
Gethsemane and on the holy cross.' Then I continue to speak:
'Dear Christ Child, I have to give You something. I'll give
You all my money.' The Child answers: 'The heavens and
earth are Mine. I don't need your money. Give it to the poor,
and then I will receive it as if it was given to Me.' Then I
continue: 'Dear Christ Child, I will gladly do that, but I still

have to give something to You. Otherwise, my sorrow will kill me.' Then the Child says: 'Dear Heironymus, since you are so generous, I will tell you what you can give to Me. Give Me your sins. Give Me your bad conscience and your perdition.' I answer: 'What will You do with them?' Christ answers me: 'I will take them upon My shoulders. They will be My glory and My kingdom. Isaiah prophesied that I would bear your sins, and take them away.' Then I begin to cry and say: 'Child, dear Christ Child, You move my heart to tears. I thought You wanted to have something of mine that was good, and You only want to have the evil within me. Take away what is mine! Give me what is Yours so I will be free from sin, and certain of eternal life!' "

This is the kind of government that rests upon the Christ Child's shoulders: a kingdom of forgiveness, with a King who dies for His people, and a God who forgives His children's transgression.

Dear Jesus Child, I want to kneel by Your crib. I know I can never thank You enough. I know I can't give You anything that would sufficiently thank You for what You've done. But since You want to have everything that's evil in me, I will give You everything: my life and my heart, my past and my sins, my future and my eternity. I wouldn't dare to come to You if You hadn't come to me. But now You are here, and I know that it's for my sake. Therefore, I kneel here and thank You, Jesus child, Prince of peace, You who are called Wonderful Counselor and Mighty God.

CHRISTMAS DAY

Luke 2:1–20

"Glory to God in the highest, and on earth peace among those with whom He is pleased!" Luke 2:14

The song the angels sang on the night of Jesus' birth contains the whole Christmas Gospel. Every word in it is filled to the brim with the Gospel. This is why the song is repeated in the Divine Service.

Glory be to God—that's not a very good translation. The word *glory* stands for something that can hardly be expressed in our language. It's God's glory, His unspeakable being that excites us and at the same time makes us tremble. It's something that fills us with joy and attracts us to Him; at the same time it makes us want to cover our faces. It's a light that our earthly eyes cannot endure, a light none of us can reach. When Isaiah was allowed to see a glimpse of it, he said: "Woe is me! For I am lost; for I am a man of unclean lips" (Isaiah 6:5).

We should really be prevented from ever experiencing this light, but a wonderful miracle occurred. God descended to earth—not in God's splendor, but in the shape of a newborn human child. And now, all heaven's angels sing, amazingly, overwhelmingly, and joyously about this wonder. "Glory be to God," they say. To Him be the power and the glory that fills the heavens with songs of praise. But now that power and glory descends in order to give peace to the earth.

Peace is another word so abundantly filled with meaning that it's hard to translate. It means both peace and tranquility. It means harmony, a delightful and secure situation, the wonderful order of things God incorporated in creation, but was lost. Now it will be restored. All will be well again. Forgiveness, renewal, and all the wonderful powers of divine mercy will descend upon us—upon men on whom His favor rests. That's what it says. We can translate it: people with whom He is pleased. What's important is that God's wonderful grace, His fatherly love, His desire to save, His untiring mercy, now embrace us completely—especially the downtrodden: the outcasts, the unfortunate, those who are badly treated. It was no accident that only the shepherds received the message. They belonged to the lower classes of society. They were only allowed to take the work no one else would take. That's why they kept watch all night, while Bethlehem's residents slept soundly.

To You, Lord, be the glory. I know it. You alone are holy. You alone are good and just. I know that Your holiness would destroy me, if I could force myself into Your world. Even Your love burns me. Everything about You is good. But I'm not the kind of person who can meet You and live in Your presence. And yet now You come, Lord, with all Your glory, so strangely hidden and in such a way that You meet me as a brother and a friend. What incomprehensible love You must have, Lord, when You can do so much to have fellowship with those who are the complete opposite of You. You have come to us, down among us, so far down that no one could be farther down or farther away. Blessed are You for Your goodness and for Your boundless mercy toward us.

THE DAY AFTER CHRISTMAS (BOXING DAY)[11]

Matthew 23:34–39

"Do you think that I have come to give peace on earth?
No, I tell you, but rather division." Luke 12:51

There is something wonderful about the day after Christmas, yet many people don't see how this day fits into the Christmas season. Christmas is a celebration of peace. Jesus is the Prince of peace. Then, in the middle of the Christmas celebration, we talk about Stephen and the martyrs!

As a matter of fact, there is a very good reason to celebrate St. Stephen's Day today. Stephen was the first martyr. The first Christians knew what martyrdom meant. It was a birthday, not a memorial day. On this day, a person was born into his real life at home with his Lord. When the Early Church chose a day to celebrate the memory of St. Stephen's death, they chose the day nearest Jesus' birthday. The first martyr received a prominent place in the Church Year. The place next to that was given to John, the disciple whom Jesus loved. In the following days, they celebrated the children in Bethlehem whose lives were sacrificed so Jesus would live, and then Abel, the first righteous person to be killed upon our earth. You can still find these days mentioned in the traditional Christian calendar.

The first disciples knew from their own experience that believing in Christ would cause unrest and bring suffering and death. Yet He is the Prince of peace. How often had they heard the words, Go in peace? "My peace I give to you," Jesus said to the Eleven in John 14:27. But He added

---

11. Boxing Day is traditionally the first weekday after Christmas. It is a legal holiday in many European countries, and is celebrated by the giving of Christmas boxes to postmen and other service workers.

that He did not give them what the world gives. By *peace* the world means not to be disturbed, to live a comfortable life, and avoid conflict and trouble. Christ's *peace* means peace of mind, peace with God, peace with others by forgiving instead of disputing and defending ourselves. Being at peace with God means being in contention with all the powers that oppose God. Jesus was born into the world to bring us back to God. That requires a battle of life or death against all the powers that want to keep us away from God. These powers can have a devastating hold on our own free will. They make their move as soon as God is near, and that's exactly what happened when Jesus was born into the world. It wasn't only the shepherds and the Wise Men who made their move. It was also Herod and his soldiers. That's the way it's always been. The Gospel will be contradicted, vehemently contradicted and opposed, and that's the way it always will be until the day when contradiction is no longer possible: the day when the King sits upon His glorious throne and says for the last time, "Blessed is He who comes in the name of the Lord" (Luke 13:35)!

Dear Lord Jesus, help me never to be afraid of the dissension that must come because there is so much here in the world that isn't compatible with Your goodness and peace. Never allow me to even attempt to be at peace with what is evil and unjust, the things You came to conquer. Instead, give me Your peace amid all dissension so I can see all Your opponents as You see them—with Your love and Your heartfelt desire to help them. You want to gather us all as a hen gathers her chicks under her wings (Luke 13:34). Forgive me for all the times I didn't want to. Now I want it, Lord, even if it must cause dissension, even if I must share in

Your disgrace. Let Your peace, which surpasses all
understanding, keep my heart and mind in You.

NEW YEAR'S DAY
Luke 2:22–40

And at the end of eight days, when He was circumcised, He
was called Jesus, the name given by the angel before He was
conceived in the womb. Luke 2:21

In the Jewish tradition, boys were circumcised and named
a week after they were born. This was the day Jesus received
His name, which means "God saves," and which, as the
angel said, was to be given Him because He would "save His
people from their sins" (Matthew 1:21).

This is not just a name. It contains a portion of what it
signifies. Just as God's nature lived in Jesus' body, a part of
the Savior and His salvation lives in the name. Therefore,
the name can give us both comfort and anxiety. For some
people, it heals the heart's wounds. In other hearts, it awakens
anxiety and wrath. It is whispered by dying lips with endless
thankfulness and tenderness. Other lips blaspheme and curse
it. It's the most loved and the most despised of all names. The
same is true for discussion about the cross. For some people
it is foolishness and offensive, but for those who believe, it is
God's power to save.

We encounter this name again on the first day of the new
year. We can begin the new year in Jesus' name. His name
is inscribed on every one of these days. First and foremost,
on the Sundays. In the Bible, Sunday is called "the Lord's
day." It is Jesus' day, the day He rose from the dead. Each

and every new Sunday, the bells ring to celebrate His victory and to call us to Him. God has set aside from work and business, from toil and obligations, one seventh of our life so we can gather in the name of Jesus. The apostle James speaks about "the honorable name by which you were called" in his Epistle (James 2:7). It was spoken over us when we were baptized. It is spoken over us every time we attend a church service. It is inscribed on every new week during this new year. Therefore, we want to receive these Sundays as a good gift from God and take part in them.

The same is true for weekdays. Before each and every one of them, the name Jesus is inscribed. "Whatever you do, in word or deed, do everything in the name of the Lord Jesus," the apostle says in Colossians 3:17. This is foundational for a Christian life. In Jesus' name, we begin our day with prayer and devotion. In Jesus' name, we go to the table, thankful for His gifts, remembering that He is our invisible guest. In Jesus' name, we go to sleep in the evening. And what we do in our work, we do from the heart, so we serve the Lord Jesus and not men. Then we are faithful in what seems to be insignificant. Then we can forgive grave injustice. We can bear immense grief because we do not bear it alone, but in the name of Jesus, with a silent and steadfast friend by our side.

So I pray to You, Lord Jesus, that Your blessed name remains inscribed over everything I encounter. I do not know what waits for me, but I know You will be with me no matter what happens. I thank You because Your name is inscribed over every new day, over days of work and of celebration, over days of grief and of sickness, over days of temptation and success, and over the day of my death. Be near me, Lord Jesus; then I will have all I need.

THIRTEENTH DAY OF CHRISTMAS, EPIPHANY

Matthew 2:1–12

In Him will the Gentiles hope. Romans 15:12

What nation did these people belong to, these Wise Men from the lands in the east? We don't know. That there were three of them, that they were kings, and that one of them was black is all subsequent and legendary embellishment. But, as is so often the case, there is some truth to the legend. The Wise Men represent a longing for God that exists in all people. All over the world, people offer sacrifices and pray to God, they have worship services, they know that God is our Lord and has dominion over us. Throughout time, there have been those who, with great earnestness, have sought God and asked themselves how they can achieve the right kind of relationship with Him.

This was one of the reasons people in ancient times studied the sky. They hoped to be able to interpret God's will by studying the paths of the planets. We have been able to preserve amazingly exact calculations of the movements of these heavenly bodies that were made for exactly this purpose. We know that at just about the time of Jesus' birth, something very uncommon and remarkable occurred among the constellations, something that could have been interpreted as a sign that a leader was born, a leader that would usher in a new era for the world. We see here a glimpse of the truth even in astronomy, that otherwise would've been a search for God in an entirely erroneous way.

It isn't only we who seek God, but God who seeks us.

The Wise Men embody not only the hearts of men longing for God. They were able to recognize a sign in the heavens and they followed it. It turned out that God led them the right way. He guided them to Bethlehem. They were able to meet the God who stepped out of the unknown and descended to earth and became man in order to make Himself known to us. Consequently, this story tells us that God, who created all people and awakened their longing for Him, also has intervened in this world with a salvation that is for all people, that answers all questions and guides all our longing to the final goal.

To be a Christian means to be a servant of God and a steward when it comes to bringing the message from God to all people. At the time in question, the Wise Men journeyed very far and spared no pains to find Jesus. Now it's the Christian Church's calling to make the long journey and spare no effort to reach out to all people with the message of what happened in Bethlehem. The Gospel is for the whole world. We can't receive it without wanting to pass it on. The Light should shine and not be hidden!

Lord Jesus, I thank You for Your Gospel. You know that I don't want to be without it. The world would be dark and meaningless if I didn't have it. Don't allow me ever to forget those who haven't heard it. I thank You for the opportunity to help others receive the gift. I ask You to bless all those who don't have Your Gospel so they may hear it. I pray for all Your ministers, all who work in Your name for those who don't know You. Fill us all with such joy that no one can escape noticing that we reflect You, the Light of the world and the source of all good.

CANDLEMAS DAY
Luke 2:22–32

"For my eyes have seen Your salvation." Luke 2:30

Their days of purification were over, Luke tells us. According to the law of Moses, a woman should stay away from the temple for forty days after childbirth. Then she should come to the temple with an offering. If it was her first child and the child was a boy, the offering would be a lamb. If she was poor—and Joseph and Mary were—two doves would be enough. The offering reminded them that Israel belonged to God. For this reason, every first-born child that was a boy was consecrated to the Lord. That's what the law of Moses stipulated. And it was also written that if in the future the son asked, What does this mean? the parent should answer that this custom was "like a sign on your hand and a symbol on your forehead that the LORD brought us out of Egypt with His mighty hand" (Exodus 13:16 NIV). The Lord has a particular right to the people He delivered from bondage.

The forty days had passed. (This is the reason that Candlemas Day is celebrated at this time of year.) So when Joseph and Mary, with their two doves and with the baby Jesus in their arms, went through the vestibules, they met Simeon, who was "righteous and devout, waiting for the consolation of Israel" and who, in his old age, lived wholly for the church services, the study of Scriptures, and in the hope of the Messiah (Luke 2:25). This pious old man took the baby Jesus in his arms and thanked God with the words that have become one of Christianity's most-used evening prayers—still used whenever we pray the Compline.[12]

---

12. *Compline* is an evening service that grew out of the monastic orders of the Middle Ages. It is still used to this day and is included in many different hymnals.

He spoke about seeing God's salvation. The words talk about the great mystery of Christianity. We have been able to see what others have only imagined. Something that by nature is spiritual, invisible, unfathomable, and incomprehensible stepped into our world in such a way that every child can see it. In every other instance, the declaration that "no one has ever seen God" is true. But the disciples could say: "That which was from the beginning, which we have heard, which we have seen with our eyes, which we have looked at and our hands have touched—this we proclaim concerning the Word of life" (1 John 1:1). We saw the glory of the Father in His only-begotten Son. The same joy is in those words as in old Simeon's. After Simeon had taken the child Jesus to his heart, he could die peacefully. Life was not meaningless, and neither was death.

My eyes also have seen Your salvation, Lord Jesus. I ask You to forgive me because I so often passed by indifferently and there were so many other things that filled my life. Now I pray that I may see You as You wanted to be seen when You became one of us. Help me to see not only what everyone's eyes could see, but also what Your apostles saw, those who understood and loved You. Lord, I thank You particularly that You came as "a Light to lighten the Gentiles" (Luke 2:32 KJV). We are also Gentiles. Your salvation could be seen by all nations. We also have been able to see it. Help us really see it, and help others to see it.

THE
ANNUNCIATION OF
OUR LORD
Luke 1:26–38

"How will this be?" Luke 1:34

It's a fantastic miracle we celebrate and worship today: the incarnation of God. It's a miracle that God became man, that a child was born through supernatural conception, that the fullness of the Godhead lived in this little child's body. It's the greatest miracle that has ever occurred on earth.

It means that the invisible God became a visible man, that God's Son was born of a woman. A human child was God's child. Mary's first-born was God's only-begotten Son.

This is beyond comprehension. Experience says it's impossible. Mary herself was startled. Even today there are many who prefer to say, as King Ahaz, "I will not put the LORD to the test" (Isaiah 7:12). I do not desire such a miracle. I do not demand that anyone believes it. I don't ask myself if I believe it. It has no bearing on my Christian faith.

But King Ahaz received the grievous answer: Is it not enough that you put man's patience to test? Do you want to test God's patience? You do not test God by believing His Word, receiving His miracles, and praising Him for them. It is, however, to challenge God and to test His patience when you do not wish to believe His promise and do not receive His miracle, which He in His mercy has done for our sake.

But how is this supposed to happen? That's what Mary asked, and we could ask the same. It seems altogether impossible. It was over and above everything she knew and far beyond anything that had ever happened on earth before. The answer was, through the Holy Spirit and the power from on high. God's Holy Spirit is God Himself. The power from on high is His outstretched hand that creates something from nothing, that renews and transforms, that ignites or extinguishes life. It's a power that brings into existence what otherwise didn't exist and obliterates what does exist, that prevails over all of nature's laws with the right of Him who made those laws and over every living thing with the Creator's omnipotence.

Nothing is impossible when this God intervenes with His power. Therefore, Mary bowed her head: "Behold, I am the servant of the Lord, let it be to me according to Your word" (Luke 1:38). That's how faith speaks when God does miracles. It speaks like the psalmist: "For You are great and do wondrous things; You alone are God" (Psalm 86:10).

So the Lord's angel said, "The child to be born will be called holy—the Son of God" (Luke 1:35). For this reason, the Word has become flesh. For this reason, God's invisible being, His eternal power and divine glory, came to us in human form. For this reason, the child who was to be born would be called God's Son. Since then, everyone who understood this has spoken and confessed the same thing. They know who was born of the virgin Mary: "You are the Christ, the Son of the living God" (Matthew 16:16).

Lord Jesus, Son of God, You who have become our brother, I praise You for the miracle of coming to us and dwelling among us. For You it was a monumental sacrifice; for us it is a boundless treasure. You were impoverished and took upon Yourself the image of a servant. You made us rich and carried God's light into our darkness. You became man. You were cold and hungry. You were persecuted and murdered. Then You made us God's children. You gave us back joy and life. We praise You because You descended into darkness to let the light ascend into eternity.

THE PASSION OF OUR LORD JESUS CHRIST DRAWN FROM THE FOUR GOSPELS (ESV)13

Book One — Chapter 1

Now the Feast of Unleavened Bread drew near, which is called the Passover.

When Jesus had finished all these sayings, He said to His disciples, "You know that after two days the Passover is coming, and the Son of Man will be delivered up to be crucified." Then the chief priests and the elders of the people gathered in the palace of the high priest, whose name was Caiaphas, and plotted together in order to arrest Jesus by stealth and kill Him. But they said, "Not during the feast, lest there be an uproar among the people."

Then Satan entered into Judas, called Iscariot, who was of the number of the Twelve. Then he went to the chief priests and said, "What will you give me if I deliver Him over to you?" They were glad, and agreed to give him money. They paid him thirty pieces of silver. So he consented and sought an opportunity to betray Him to them in the absence of a crowd.

Then came the day of Unleavened Bread, on which the Passover lamb had to be sacrificed. So Jesus sent Peter and John, saying, "Go and prepare the Passover for us, that we may eat it." They said to Him, "Where will you have us prepare it?" He said to them, "Behold, when you have entered the city, a man carrying a jar of water will meet you. Follow

---

13. This last section of the book is the Bo Giertz's own compilation and translation of the Passion of Christ as laid out in the four Gospels. It is based on the English Standard Version of the Bible.

him into the house that he enters, and tell the master of the house, 'The Teacher says to you: My time is at hand; where is the guest room, where I may eat the Passover with my disciples?' And he will show you a large upper room furnished; prepare it there." And the disciples set out and went to the city and found it just as He had told them, and they prepared the Passover.

Book One — Chapter 2

When it was evening, He reclined at table with the Twelve, and the apostles with Him. And Jesus knew that His hour had come to depart out of this world to the Father, having loved His own who were in the world, He loved them to the end.

Now He said to them, "I have earnestly desired to eat this Passover with you before I suffer. For I tell you I will not eat it until it is fulfilled in the kingdom of God." And He took a cup, and when He had given thanks He said, "Take this, and divide it among yourselves. For I tell you that from now on I will not drink of the fruit of the vine until the kingdom of God comes."

As they were eating, Jesus took bread, and after blessing it, broke it and gave it to the disciples, and said, "Take, eat; this is My body, which is given for you. Do this in remembrance of Me."

In the same way also He took the cup, after supper, and when He had given thanks, He gave it to them, saying, "Drink of it, all of you. For this cup is the new covenant in my blood, which is poured out for many for the forgiveness of sins. Do this, as often as you drink it, in remembrance of Me." And they all drank of it.

A dispute also arose among them as to which of them was to be regarded as the greatest. Jesus, knowing that the Father had given all things into His hands, and that He had come from God and was going back to God, rose from supper. He laid aside His outer garments, and taking a towel, tied it around His waist. Then He poured water into a basin and began to wash the disciples' feet and to wipe them with the towel that was wrapped around Him. He came to Simon Peter, who said to Him, "Lord, do You wash my feet?" Jesus answered him, "What I am doing you do not understand now, but afterward you will understand." Peter said to Him, "You shall never wash my feet." Jesus answered him, "If I do not wash you, you have no share with Me." Simon Peter said to Him, "Lord, not my feet only but also my hands and my head!" Jesus said to him, "The one who has bathed does not need to wash, except for his feet, but is completely clean. And you are clean, but not every one of you." For He knew who was to betray Him; that was why He said, "Not all of you are clean."

When He had washed their feet and put on His outer garments and resumed His place, He said to them, "Do you understand what I have done to you? You call me Teacher and Lord, and you are right, for so I am. If I then, your Lord and Teacher, have washed your feet, you also ought to wash one another's feet. For I have given you an example, that you also should do just as I have done to you. And He said to them, "The kings of the Gentiles exercise lordship over them, and those in authority over them are called benefactors. But not so with you. Rather, let the greatest among you become as the youngest, and the leader as one who serves. For who is the greater, one who reclines at table or one who serves? Is it not the one who reclines at table? But I am among you as the one who serves. Truly, truly, I say to you, a servant is not greater than his master, nor is a messenger greater than the one who sent him. If you know these things, blessed are you if you do them.

Book One — Chapter 4

As they were eating, Jesus was troubled in His Spirit and He testified, "Truly, I say to you, one of you will betray Me. The Son of man goes as it is written of Him, but woe to that man by whom the Son of man is betrayed! It would have been better for that man if he had not been born." The disciples looked at one another, uncertain of whom He spoke. One of His disciples, whom Jesus loved, was reclining at table close to Jesus, so Simon Peter motioned to him to ask Jesus of whom He was speaking. So that disciple, leaning back against Jesus, said to Him, "Lord, who is it?" Jesus answered, "It is he to whom I will give this morsel of bread when I have dipped it." So when He had dipped the morsel, He gave it to Judas, the son of Simon Iscariot. Judas, who would betray Him, answered, "Is it I, Rabbi?" He said to him, "You have said so." Then after he had taken the morsel, Satan entered into him. Jesus said to him, "What you are going to do, do quickly." Now no one at the table knew why He said this to him. Some thought that, because Judas had the moneybag, Jesus was telling him, "Buy what we need for the feast," or that he should give something to the poor. So, after receiving the morsel of bread, he immediately went out. And it was night.

Book One — Chapter 5

When Judas had gone out, Jesus said, "Now is the Son of man glorified, and God is glorified in Him. If God is glorified in Him, God will also glorify Him in Himself, and glorify Him at once. Little children, yet a little while I am with you. You will seek Me, and just as I said to the Jews, so now I also say to you, 'Where I am going you cannot come.' A new commandment I give to you, that you love one another: Just as I have loved you, you also are to love one another. By this all people will know that you are My disciples, if you have love for one another."

Simon Peter said to Him, "Lord, where are you going?" Jesus answered him, "Where I am going you cannot follow me now, but you will follow afterward." Peter said to Him, "Lord, why can I not follow you now? I will lay down my life for you." Jesus answered, "Will you lay down your life for Me? Truly, truly, I say to you, the rooster will not crow till you have denied me three times." And when they had sung a hymn, they went out to the Mount of Olives. Then Jesus said to them, "You will all fall away because of Me this night. For it is written, 'I will strike the shepherd, and the sheep of the flock will be scattered.' But after I am raised up, I will go before you to Galilee." "Simon, Simon, behold, Satan demanded to have you, that he might sift you like wheat, but I have prayed for you that your faith may not fail. And when you have turned again, strengthen your brothers." Peter said to Him, "Even if I must die with you, I will not deny you!" And all the disciples said the same. And He said to them, "When I sent you out with no moneybag or knapsack or sandals, did you lack anything?" They said, "Nothing." He said to them, "But now let the one who has a moneybag take it, and likewise a knapsack. And let the one who has no sword sell his cloak and buy one. For I tell you that this Scripture must be fulfilled in Me: 'And He was numbered with the transgressors.' For what is written about Me has its fulfillment." And they said, "Look, Lord, here are two swords." And He said to them, "It is enough."

THE PASSION OF OUR LORD JESUS CHRIST DRAWN FROM THE FOUR GOSPELS ^(ESV)

Book Two

Then Jesus went out with His disciples across the Kidron Valley, where there was a garden, which He and His disciples entered. Now Judas, who betrayed Him, also knew the place, for Jesus often met there with His disciples. And they went to a place called Gethsemane. And He said to His disciples, "Sit here while I pray." And He took with Him Peter and James and John, and began to be greatly distressed and troubled. And He said to them, "My soul is very sorrowful, even to death. Remain here and watch." And going a little farther, about a stone's throw away, He fell on the ground and prayed that, if it were possible, the hour might pass from Him. And He said, "Abba, Father, all things are possible for You. Remove this cup from Me. Yet not what I will, but what You will." And He came and found them sleeping, and He said to Peter, "Simon, are you asleep? Could you not watch one hour? Watch and pray that you may not enter into temptation. The spirit indeed is willing, but the flesh is weak." Again, for the second time, He went away and prayed, "My Father, if this cannot pass unless I drink it, Your will be done." And again He came and found them sleeping, for their eyes were very heavy, and they did not know what to answer Him. So, leaving them again, He went away and prayed for the third time, saying the same words again. And there appeared to Him an angel from heaven, strengthening Him. And being in agony, He prayed more earnestly; and His sweat became like great drops of blood falling down to the ground. And when He rose from prayer, He came to the disciples and found them sleeping for sorrow. Then He said to them, "Are you still sleeping and taking your rest? It is enough; the hour has come. The Son of man is betrayed into the hands of sinners. Rise, let us be going; see, My betrayer is at hand."

THE PASSION OF OUR LORD JESUS CHRIST DRAWN FROM THE FOUR GOSPELS ^(ESV)

Book Three — Chapter 1

While He was still speaking, Judas came, one of the Twelve. And Judas, having procured a band of soldiers and some officers from the chief priests and the Pharisees, went there with lanterns, swords, torches, and weapons. Now the betrayer had given them a sign, saying, "The one I will kiss is the man. Seize Him and lead Him away under guard." Then Jesus, knowing all that would happen to Him, came forward and said to them, "Whom do you seek?" They answered Him, "Jesus of Nazareth." Jesus said to them, "I am He." Judas, who betrayed Him, was standing with them. When Jesus said to them, "I am He," they drew back and fell to the ground. So He asked them again, "Whom do you seek?" And they said, "Jesus of Nazareth." Jesus answered, "I told you that I am He. So, if you seek me, let these men go." This was to fulfill the word that He had spoken: "Of those whom you gave me I have lost not one." And when Judas came, he went up to Him at once and said, "Rabbi!" And he kissed Him, but Jesus said to him, "Judas, would you betray the Son of man with a kiss?" And they laid hands on Him and seized Him. And when those who were around Him saw what would follow, they said, "Lord, shall we strike with the sword?" Then Simon Peter, having a sword, drew it and struck the high priest's servant and cut off his right ear. (The servant's name was Malchus.) Then Jesus said to him, "Put your sword back into its place. For all who take the sword will perish by the sword. Do you think that I cannot appeal to My Father and He will at once send Me more than twelve legions of angels? But how then should the Scriptures be fulfilled that it must be so? Shall I not drink the cup that the Father has given Me?" And He touched his ear and healed him. Then Jesus said to the chief priests and officers of the temple and elders, who had come out against Him, "Have you come out as against a robber, with swords and clubs? When I was with you day after day in the temple, you did not lay hands on Me. But this is your hour and the power of darkness. But all this has taken place that the Scriptures of the prophets might be fulfilled." Then all the disciples left Him and fled. And a young man followed Him, with nothing but a linen cloth about his body. And they seized him, but he left the linen cloth and ran away naked.

So the band of soldiers and their captain and the officers of the Jews arrested Jesus and bound Him. First they led Him to Annas, for he was the father-in-law of Caiaphas, who was high priest that year. But Annas sent Him bound to Caiaphas. It was Caiaphas who had advised the Jews that it would be expedient that one man should die for the people. And they led Jesus to the high priest. And all the chief priests and the elders and the scribes came together.

Simon Peter followed Jesus, and so did another disciple. Since that disciple was known to the high priest, he entered with Jesus into the court of the high priest, but Peter stood outside at the door. So the other disciple, who was known to the high priest, went out and spoke to the servant girl who kept watch at the door, and brought Peter in. The servant girl at the door said to Peter, "You also are not one of this man's disciples, are you?" He said, "I am not." Now the servants and officers had made a charcoal fire, because it was cold, and they were standing and warming themselves. Peter also was with them, standing and warming himself. So they said to him, "You also are not one of his disciples, are you?" He denied it and said, "I am not." One of the servants of the high priest, a relative of the man whose ear Peter had cut off, asked, "Did I not see you in the garden with Him?" And some bystanders came up and said to Peter, "Certainly you, too, are one of them, for your accent betrays you." Then he began to invoke a curse on himself and to swear, "I do not know the man." And immediately the rooster crowed.

And the Lord turned and looked at Peter. And Peter remembered the saying of the Lord, how He had said to him, "Before the rooster crows today, you will deny Me three times." And he went out and wept bitterly.

Jesus stood before the high priest, who questioned Him about His disciples and His teaching. Jesus answered him, "I have spoken openly to the world. I have always taught in synagogues and in the temple, where all Jews come together. I have said nothing in secret. Why do you ask Me? Ask those who have heard Me what I said to them; they know what I said." When He had said these things, one of the officers standing by struck Jesus with his hand, saying, "Is that how You answer the high priest?" Jesus answered him, "If what I said is wrong, bear witness about the wrong; but if what I said is right, why do you strike Me?" Now the chief priests and the whole council were seeking testimony against Jesus to put Him to death, but they found none. For many bore false witness against Him, but their testimony did not agree. And some stood up and bore false witness against Him, saying, "We heard Him say, 'I will destroy this temple that is made with hands, and in three days I will build another, not made with hands.'" Yet even about this their testimony did not agree. And the high priest stood up in the midst and asked Jesus, "Have You no answer to make? What is it that these men testify against You?" But He remained silent and made no answer. Again the high priest asked Him, "Are You the Christ, the Son of God?" And Jesus said, "I am, and you will see the Son of man seated at the right hand of Power, and coming with the clouds of heaven."

Then the high priest tore his robes and said, "He has uttered blasphemy. What further witnesses do we need? You have now heard His blasphemy. What is your judgment?" They answered, "He deserves death." Then they spit in His face and struck Him. And some slapped Him, saying, "Prophesy to us, You Christ! Who is it that struck You?" And the guards received Him with blows.

When morning came, all the chief priests and the elders of the people took counsel against Jesus to put Him to death.

Then when Judas, His betrayer, saw that Jesus was condemned, he changed his mind and brought back the thirty pieces of silver to the chief priests and the elders, saying, "I have sinned by betraying innocent blood." They said, "What is that to us? See to it yourself." And throwing down the pieces of silver into the temple, he departed, and he went and hanged himself. But the chief priests, taking the pieces of silver, said, "It is not lawful to put them into the treasury, since it is blood money." So they took counsel and bought with them the potter's field as a burial place for strangers. Therefore that field has been called the Field of Blood to this day. Then was fulfilled what had been spoken by the prophet Jeremiah, saying, "And they took the thirty pieces of silver, the price of Him on whom a price had been set by some of the sons of Israel, and they gave them for the potter's field, as the Lord directed me."

THE PASSION OF OUR LORD JESUS CHRIST DRAWN FROM THE FOUR GOSPELS (ESV)

Book Four — Chapter 1

Then the chief priests held a consultation with the elders and scribes and the whole council. And they bound Jesus and led Him away and delivered Him over to Pilate. They themselves did not enter the governor's headquarters, so that they would not be defiled, but could eat the Passover. So Pilate went outside to them and said, "What accusation do you bring against this man?" They answered him, "If this Man were not doing evil, we would not have delivered Him over to you." Pilate said to them, "Take Him yourselves and judge Him by your own law." The Jews said to him, "It is not lawful for us to put anyone to death." This was to fulfill the word that Jesus had spoken to show by what kind of death He was going to die. And they began to accuse Him, saying, "We found this man misleading our nation and forbidding us to give tribute to Caesar, and saying that He Himself is Christ, a king."

But when He was accused by the chief priests and elders, He gave no answer. Then Pilate said to Him, "Do you not hear how many things they testify against You?" But He gave him no answer, not even to a single charge, so that the governor was greatly amazed. So Pilate entered his headquarters again and called Jesus and said to Him, "Are You the King of the Jews?" Jesus answered, "Do you say this of your own accord, or did others say it to you about Me?" Pilate answered, "Am I a Jew? Your own nation and the chief priests have delivered You over to me. What have You done?" Jesus answered, "My kingdom is not of this world. If My kingdom were of this world, My servants would have been fighting, that I might not be delivered over to the Jews. But My kingdom is not from the world." Then Pilate said to Him, "So You are a king?" Jesus answered, "You say that I am a king. For this purpose I was born and for this purpose I have come into the world—to bear witness to the truth. Everyone who is of the truth listens to My voice." Pilate said to Him, "What is truth?"

After he had said this, he went back outside to the Jews and told them, "I find no guilt in Him."

When Pilate said to the chief priests and the crowds, "I find no guilt in this man," they were urgent, saying, "He stirs up the people, teaching throughout all Judea, from Galilee even to this place."

When Pilate heard this, he asked whether the man was a Galilean. And when he learned that he belonged to Herod's jurisdiction, he sent Him over to Herod, who was himself in Jerusalem at that time. When Herod saw Jesus, he was very glad, for he had long desired to see Him, because he had heard about Him, and he was hoping to see some sign done by Him. So he questioned Him at some length, but He made no answer. The chief priests and the scribes stood by, vehemently accusing Him. And Herod with his soldiers treated Him with contempt and mocked Him. Then, arraying Him in splendid clothing, he sent Him back to Pilate. And Herod and Pilate became friends with each other that very day, for before this they had been at enmity with each other.

Pilate then called together the chief priests and the rulers and the people, and said to them, "You brought me this Man as one who was misleading the people. And after examining Him before you, behold, I did not find this Man guilty of any of your charges against Him. Neither did Herod, for he sent Him back to us. Look, nothing deserving death has been done by Him. I will therefore punish and release Him."

Now at the feast the governor was accustomed to release for the crowd any one prisoner whom they wanted. Among the rebels in prison, who had committed murder in the insurrection, there was a man called Barabbas. And the crowd came up and began to ask Pilate to do as he usually did for them. And he answered them, saying, "Do you want me to release for you the King of the Jews?" For he perceived that it was out of envy that the chief priests had delivered Him up. Besides, while he was sitting on the judgment seat, his wife sent word to him, "Have nothing to do with that righteous Man, for I have suffered much because of Him today in a dream." Now the chief priests and the elders persuaded the crowd to ask for Barabbas and destroy Jesus. The governor again said to them, "Which of the two do you want me to release for you?" And they said, "Barabbas." Pilate addressed them once more, desiring to release Jesus. Pilate said to them, "Then what shall I do with Jesus who is called Christ?" They all said, "Let Him be crucified!" A third time he said to them, "Why, what evil has He done? I have found in Him no guilt deserving death. I will therefore punish and release Him." But they were urgent, demanding with loud cries that He should be crucified. And their voices prevailed. So Pilate decided that their demand should be granted. He released the man who had been thrown into prison for insurrection and murder, for whom they asked, but he delivered Jesus over to their will.

Book Four — Chapter 4

Then the soldiers of the governor took Jesus into the governor's headquarters, and they gathered the whole battalion before Him. And they stripped Him and put a scarlet robe on Him, and twisting together a crown of thorns, they put it on His head and put a reed in His right hand. And kneeling before Him, they mocked Him, saying, "Hail, King of the Jews!" And they spit on Him and took the reed and struck Him on the head.

Pilate went out again and said to them, "See, I am bringing Him out to you that you may know that I find no guilt in Him." So Jesus came out, wearing the crown of thorns and the purple robe. Pilate said to them, "Behold the Man!" When the chief priests and the officers saw Him, they cried out, "Crucify Him, crucify Him!" Pilate said to them, "Take Him yourselves and crucify Him, for I find no guilt in Him." The Jews answered him, "We have a law, and according to that law He ought to die because He has made Himself the Son of God." When Pilate heard this statement, he was even more afraid. He entered his headquarters again and said to Jesus, "Where are You from?" But Jesus gave him no answer. So Pilate said to Him, "You will not speak to me? Do You not know that I have authority to release You and authority to crucify You?" Jesus answered him, "You would have no authority over Me at all unless it had been given you from above. Therefore he who delivered Me over to you has the greater sin."

From then on Pilate sought to release Him, but the Jews cried out, "If you release this man, you are not Caesar's friend. Everyone who makes himself a king opposes Caesar." So when Pilate heard these words, he brought Jesus out and sat down on the judgment seat at a place called The Stone Pavement, and, in Aramaic, Gabbatha. Now it was the day of Preparation of the Passover. It was about the sixth hour. He said to the Jews, "Behold your King!" They cried out, "Away with Him, away with Him, crucify Him!" Pilate said to them, "Shall I crucify your King?" The chief priests answered, "We have no king but Caesar."

So when Pilate saw that he was gaining nothing, but rather that a riot was beginning, he took water and washed his hands before the crowd, saying, "I am innocent of this Man's blood; see to it yourselves." And all the people answered, "His blood be on us and on our children!" So he delivered Him over to them to be crucified.

THE PASSION OF OUR LORD JESUS CHRIST DRAWN FROM THE FOUR GOSPELS (ESV)

Book Five — Chapter 1

Pilate turned Jesus over to the chief priests, the Sanhedrin, and the people in order to do their will. The soldiers stripped Him of the purple cloak and put His own clothes on Him. And they led Him out to crucify Him. He went out, bearing His own cross, But they compelled a passerby, Simon of Cyrene, the father of Alexander and Rufus, who was coming in from the country, to carry the cross behind Jesus. And there followed Him a great multitude of the people and of women who were mourning and lamenting for Him. But turning to them Jesus said, "Daughters of Jerusalem, do not weep for me, but weep for yourselves and for your children. For behold, the days are coming when they will say, 'Blessed are the barren and the wombs that never bore and the breasts that never nursed!' Then they will begin to say to the mountains, 'Fall on us,' and to the hills, 'Cover us.' For if they do these things when the wood is green, what will happen when it is dry?"

Two others, who were criminals, were led away to be put to death with Him. And when they came to a place called Golgotha (which means Place of a Skull), they offered Him wine to drink, mixed with gall, but when He tasted it, He would not drink it.

There they crucified Him, and with Him two others, one on either side, and Jesus between them. And it was the third hour when they crucified Him. And Jesus said, "Father, forgive them for they know not what they do." Pilate also wrote an inscription and put it on the cross. And the inscription of the charge read, "Jesus of Nazareth, the King of the Jews." Many of the Jews read this inscription, for the place where Jesus was crucified was near the city, and it was written in Aramaic, in Latin, and in Greek. So the chief priests of the Jews said to Pilate, "Do not write, 'The King of the Jews,' but rather, 'This Man said, I am King of the Jews.'" Pilate answered, "What I have written, I have written."

When the soldiers had crucified Jesus, they took His garments and divided them into four parts, one part for each soldier; also His tunic. But the tunic was seamless, woven in one piece from top to bottom, so they said to one another, "Let us not tear it, but cast lots for it to see whose it shall be." This was to fulfill the Scripture which says,

"They divided My garments among them,
and for My clothing they cast lots."

So the soldiers did these things, but standing by the cross of Jesus were His mother and His mother's sister, Mary, the wife of Clopas, and Mary Magdalene. When Jesus saw His mother and the disciple whom He loved standing nearby, He said to his mother, "Woman, behold, your son!" Then He said to the disciple, "Behold, your mother!" And from that hour the disciple took her to his own home.

And the people stood by, watching, and those who passed by derided Him, wagging their heads and saying, "You who would destroy the temple and rebuild it in three days, save Yourself! If You are the Son of God, come down from the cross." So also the chief priests, with the scribes and elders, mocked Him, saying, "He saved others; He cannot save Himself. He is the King of Israel; let Him come down now from the cross, and we will believe in Him. He trusts in God; let God deliver Him now, if He desires Him. For He said, 'I am the Son of God.'" The soldiers also mocked Him, coming up and offering Him sour wine and saying, "If you are the King of the Jews, save Yourself!" One of the criminals who were hanged railed at Him, saying, "Are You not the Christ? Save Yourself and us!" But the other rebuked him, saying, "Do you not fear God, since you are under the same sentence of condemnation? And we indeed justly, for we are receiving the due reward of our deeds; but this Man has done nothing wrong." And he said, "Jesus, remember me when You come into Your kingdom." And He said to him, "Truly, I say to you, today you will be with Me in Paradise."

Book Five — Chapter 3

It was now about the sixth hour, and there was darkness over the whole land until the ninth hour, while the sun's light failed. And about the ninth hour, Jesus cried out with a loud voice, saying, "Eli, Eli, lema sabachthani?" that is, "My God, my God, why have You forsaken Me?" And some of the bystanders, hearing it, said, "This Man is calling Elijah."

After this, Jesus, knowing that all was now finished, said (to fulfill the Scripture), "I thirst." A jar full of sour wine stood there, and someone ran and filled a sponge with sour wine, put it on a reed and gave it to Him to drink. But another said, "Wait, let us see whether Elijah will come to take Him down."

When Jesus had received the sour wine, He said, "It is finished." Then Jesus, calling out with a loud voice, said,

"Father, into Your hands I commit My spirit!" and He bowed His head and gave up His spirit.

And behold, the curtain of the temple was torn in two, from top to bottom. And the earth shook, and the rocks were split. The tombs also were opened. And many bodies of the saints who had fallen asleep were raised, and coming out of the tombs after His resurrection they went into the holy city and appeared to many.

When the centurion and those who were with him keeping watch over Jesus saw the earthquake and what took place, they were filled with awe and said, "Truly this was an innocent man and the Son of God!" There were also many women there, among whom were Mary Magdalene and Mary the mother of James and John, the sons of Zebedee, looking on from a distance, who had followed Jesus from Galilee, ministering to Him. And all the crowds that had assembled for this spectacle, when they saw what had taken place, returned home beating their breasts.

Since it was the day of Preparation, and so that the bodies would not remain on the cross on the Sabbath (for that Sabbath was a high day), the Jews asked Pilate that their legs might be broken and that they might be taken away. So the soldiers came and broke the legs of the first, and of the other who had been crucified with Him. But when they came to Jesus and saw that He was already dead, they did not break His legs. But one of the soldiers pierced His side with a spear, and at once there came out blood and water. He who saw it has borne witness—his testimony is true, and he knows that he is telling the truth—that you also may believe. For these things took place that the Scripture might be fulfilled: "Not one of His bones will be broken." And again another Scripture says, "They will look on Him whom they have pierced."

THE PASSION OF OUR LORD JESUS CHRIST DRAWN FROM THE FOUR GOSPELS ^(ESV)

Book Six

And when evening had come, since it was the Day of Preparation, that is, the day before the Sabbath, there came a rich man from Arimathea, named Joseph. He was looking for the kingdom of God, and was also a disciple of Jesus, but secretly, for fear of the Jews. He was also a respected member of the council, a good and righteous man, who had not consented to their decision or action. Now he took courage and went to Pilate and asked for the body of Jesus. Pilate was surprised to hear that He should have already died. And summoning the centurion, He asked him whether He was already dead. And when he learned from the centurion that He was dead, he granted the corpse to Joseph. And Joseph bought a linen shroud, and taking Him down, Nicodemus, who earlier had come to Jesus by night, came bringing a mixture of myrrh and aloes, about seventy-five pounds in weight. So they took the body of Jesus and bound it in linen cloths with the spices, as is the burial custom of the Jews. Now in the place where He was crucified there was a garden, and in the garden Joseph had a grave that had been cut in the rock and in which no one had been laid. So because of the Jewish Day of Preparation, since the tomb was close at hand, they laid Jesus there. And he rolled a great stone to the entrance of the tomb and went away. Mary Magdalene and Mary the mother of Joseph, who had come with Him from Galilee, followed and saw the tomb and how His body was laid. Then they returned and prepared spices and ointments. On the Sabbath they rested according to the commandment.

The next day, that is, after the Day of Preparation, the chief priests and the Pharisees gathered before Pilate and said, "Sir, we remember how that impostor said while He was still alive, 'After three days I will rise.' Therefore order the tomb to be made secure until the third day, lest His disciples go and steal Him away and tell the people, 'He has risen from the dead,' and the last fraud will be worse than the first." Pilate said to them, "You have a guard of soldiers. Go, make it as secure as you can." So they went and made the tomb secure by sealing the stone and setting a guard.